Sam

The Disciple-Making Minister

Other books by David Kirkwood

Christ's Incredible Cross

Forgive Me for Waiting so Long to Tell You This

God's Tests

Modern Myths About Satan and Spiritual Warfare

Your Best Year Yet

The Great Gospel Deception

'THE'
DISCIPLE-
MAKING
MINISTER

Biblical Principles for Fruitfulness and Multiplication

DAVID S. KIRKWOOD

ETHNOS PRESS
Pittsburgh, Pennsylvania

The Disciple-Making Minister
Biblical Principles for Fruitfulness and Multiplication
First Printing: March 2005

All Scripture quotations in this book, except those noted otherwise, are from the New American Standard Bible, © 1960, 1962, 1963, 1971, 1972, 1973, 1975, and 1977 by The Lockman Foundation, and are used by permission.

Cover Design: Charity Kirkwood
Printed in the United States of America
International Standard Book Number: 978-0-9629625-8-5

To the many dedicated Christian leaders around the world whose God-given passion is to reach their villages, cities, and nation with the gospel of Jesus Christ.

"And when the Chief Shepherd appears, you will receive the unfading crown of glory" (1 Peter 5:4).

Acknowledgements

My special thanks to three generations of very special women: my wife, Becky, for her proofreading and encouragement, my mother, English major LaVerne Kirkwood, for finding every split infinitive, and my daughter, Charity, for her cover design and text lay-out. It certainly is not good for a man to be alone.

Contents

Introduction

Over the past twenty-five years, I've had the privilege of traveling to over forty nations of the world to speak to tens of thousands of ministers at three- to five-day conferences. Those conferences have been attended by dedicated Christian leaders from many different denominations and streams within the body of Christ. Every trip has confirmed that three- to five-day conferences are simply not sufficient to meet the needs that exist. So much more needs to be done to equip Christian leaders, and this book is an effort to fill the gap a little bit more.

I've also had the privilege of experiencing twenty-or-so years of pastoring churches. Although I was "successful" by some measurements, much of the time I found myself struggling because I lacked understanding of some very foundational principles of biblical ministry. I consequently have a deep concern for the millions of sincere ministers who are missing what I missed and who need to be better equipped for the task set before them. Some of the principles of which I lacked understanding are so significant that once they are understood, they set the course of ministry for the rest of a minister's life. They become the standard by which every aspect of ministry is measured. Those principles are found in the initial chapters and should not be overlooked by any reader, as all later chapters are practically useless without their foundation.

This book has particular application to pastors, as they are certainly the most common Christian leaders, but everything I've written also applies to evangelists, teachers, missionaries, church planters, prophets, Sunday-school workers, and so on. There isn't anyone in the body of Christ who couldn't benefit from reading this book, because every member of the body of Christ has been graced with a God-given function.

I've written primarily to ministers who live outside of North America, Western Europe and Australia/New Zealand. This is not to say, however, that what I've written has no application to ministers in those parts of the world. Indeed, I think what I've written could help them considerably, but they already have plenty of teachers. In any case, depending on your knowledge, experience and nation of ministry, you will find certain chapters more helpful than others. Many Chinese, Cuban, and Vietnamese house church pastors, for example, will find the chapter on house churches to contain very little that they don't already know. Yet pastors who are unfamiliar with the house church model should find that chapter extremely helpful.

It is highly unlikely that every reader will agree with everything I've written on every topic in the book. Five years ago, I wouldn't have agreed with some of what I've written in this book! So don't let minor disagreements stop you from learning as much as you can from every chapter.

As Jesus taught us, no one puts new wine into old wineskins, otherwise the stiff and inflexible old wineskins burst. It is only new wineskins that are flexible enough to withstand the pressure of fermenting new wine. Although some of what I've written might be considered to be new wine, it is actually wine that is quite old—at least as old as the New Testament. So any bursting of old wineskins is not the fault of the wine poured from the pages that follow! Jesus rejoiced that God reveals His truth to babes and hides it from "the wise and intelligent" (Matt. 11:25). Likewise, God gives grace to the humble, but He resists the proud (see Jas. 4:6). Thank God for the multitudes of humble Christian leaders all over the world. May God bless them as they read.

David Kirkwood

ONE

Setting the Right Goal

To be successful in God's eyes, it is essential that a minister understand the goal that God has set before him. If he doesn't understand his goal, he has no way of gauging if he has succeeded or failed in reaching it.[1] He may think he has succeeded when he has actually failed. And that is a great tragedy. He is like a first-place runner who jubilantly sprints across the finish line of an 800-meter race, basking in his victory as he raises his hands before the shouting crowds, not realizing that he was actually competing in a 1600-meter race. Misunderstanding his goal has guaranteed his failure. Thinking he has won has assured his loss. In his case the saying is certainly true: "The first shall be last."

Most ministers have some kind of specific goal that they often refer to as their "vision." It is what they uniquely strive to accomplish, based on their specific calling and gifting. Everyone's gifting and calling is unique, whether it be to pastor a church in a certain city, evangelize a certain region, or teach certain truths. But the God-given goal to which I'm referring is *general* and applies to *every minister*. It is the *big* vision. It should be the driving general vision behind every unique vision. But too often, it is not. Not only do many ministers have specific visions that do not harmonize with God's general vision, some have specific visions that actually work *against* God's general vision. I certainly did at one time, even though I was pastoring a growing church.

What is the general goal or vision that God has given *every* minister? We begin to find the answer in Matthew 28:18-20, a passage so familiar to us that we often miss what it is saying. Let's consider it verse by verse:

[1] Throughout this book, I refer to ministers using the masculine pronoun *he*, purely for the sake of consistency and because the majority of vocational ministers, such as pastors, are men. I am convinced from Scripture, however, that God calls women to vocational ministry, and I know quite a few with very effective ministries. That is the topic of the chapter entitled, *Women in Ministry*.

1

And Jesus came up and spoke to them, saying, "All authority has been given to Me in heaven and on earth"
(Matt. 28:18).

Jesus wanted His disciples to understand that His Father had granted
Him *supreme* authority. Of course, the Father's intention was (and is) that
Jesus be *obeyed*, as is the case any time the Father gives someone authority.
But Jesus is unique in that His Father gave Him *all* authority in heaven
and on earth, not just a limited authority, as He at times gives to others.
Jesus is Lord.

This being so, any person who doesn't relate to Jesus as Lord is not relating to Him rightly. Jesus, more than anything else, is *Lord*. That is why
He is referred to as "Lord" over 600 times in the New Testament. (He is
only mentioned as Savior 15 times.) That is why Paul wrote, "For to this
end Christ died and lived again, that He might be *Lord* both of the dead
and of the living" (Rom. 14:9, emphasis added). Jesus died and came back
to life for the purpose of reigning as Lord over people.

✗ True Saving Faith

When modern evangelists and pastors invite the unsaved to "accept Jesus as Savior," (a phrase and concept never found in Scripture), it usually
reveals a fundamental flaw in their understanding of the gospel. When
the Philippian jailer, for example, asked Paul what he must do to be saved,
Paul did not respond, "Accept Jesus as your Savior." Rather he said, "Believe in the *Lord* Jesus Christ, and you shall be saved" (Acts 16:31, emphasis
added). People are saved when they believe *in* the Lord Jesus Christ. Mind
you, they are not saved just because they believe a doctrine *about* salvation
or Jesus, but when they believe in a *person*—the *Lord* Jesus Christ. That is
saving faith. Too many think because they believe that Jesus' death was a
sufficient sacrifice for their sins, or salvation is by faith, or a hundred other
things about Jesus or salvation, that they have saving faith. But they don't.
The devil believes all those things about Jesus and salvation. Saving faith
consists of faith *in* Jesus. And who is He? He is *Lord*.

Obviously, if I believe that Jesus is Lord, I will act like he is Lord, submitting to Him from my heart. If I don't submit to him, I don't believe
in Him. If someone says, "I believe there is a deadly poisonous snake in
my boot," and then calmly puts his boot on, he obviously doesn't really
believe what he says he believes. People who say they believe in Jesus but
haven't repented of their sins and submitted to Him in their hearts don't
really believe in Jesus. They may believe in an imaginary Jesus, but not the
Lord Jesus, the one who has all authority in heaven and on earth.

All of this is to say that when a minister's understanding of the most
fundamental message of Christianity is flawed, he is in trouble from the
start. There is no way he can succeed by God's appraisal, as he misrep-

resents the most foundational message God wants the world to hear. He may be a pastor of a growing church, but he is failing miserably at fulfilling God's general vision for his ministry.

The Big Vision

Let's go back to Matthew 28:18-19. After declaring His supreme lordship, Jesus then gave a commandment:

> Go therefore and make disciples of all the nations, baptizing them in the name of the Father and the Son and the Holy Spirit, teaching them to observe all that I commanded you" (Matt. 28:19-20a).

Notice that Jesus used the word "therefore." He said, "Go *therefore* and make disciples…" That is to say, "*Because* of what I just said…*because* I have all authority…*because* I am Lord…people should *of course* obey Me… and so I am commanding *you* (and you should obey Me) to go and make disciples, teaching those disciples to *obey* all My commandments."

And that, simply put, is the general goal, God's great vision for all of our ministries: *Our responsibility is to make disciples who obey all of Christ's commandments.*

That is why Paul said that the grace of God had been given to him as an apostle to "bring about the *obedience of faith* among all the Gentiles" (Rom. 1:5, emphasis added). The *goal* was obedience; the *means* to obedience was faith. People who have genuine faith in the Lord Jesus obey His commandments.

That is why Peter preached on the day of Pentecost, "Therefore let all the house of Israel know for certain that God has made Him [Jesus] both Lord and Christ—this Jesus whom you crucified" (Acts 2:36). Peter wanted Christ's crucifiers to know that God had made Jesus *Lord* and *Christ*. They had killed the one whom God wanted them to obey! Under great conviction, they asked, "What shall we do?" and Peter responded first of all, "Repent"! That is, turn from disobedience to obedience. Make Jesus Lord. Next Peter told them to be baptized as Christ commanded. Peter was making disciples—obedient followers of Christ—and he was starting the right way with the right message.

This being so, every minister should be able to evaluate his success. All of us should ask ourselves, "Is my ministry leading people to become obedient to all of Christ's commandments?" If it is, we're succeeding. If it isn't, we're failing.

The evangelist who only persuades people to "accept Jesus," without telling them to repent of their sins, is failing. The pastor who is trying to build a big congregation by keeping everyone happy and organizing many social activities is failing. The teacher who only teaches the latest charismatic "wind of doctrine" is failing. The apostle who plants churches that consist of people who say they believe in Jesus, but who don't obey Him, is failing. The prophet who prophesies only to tell people what blessings will soon be coming their way is failing.

My Failure

Some years ago, when I was pastoring a growing church, the Holy Spirit asked me a question that opened my eyes to see how far short I was falling in fulfilling God's general vision. The Holy Spirit asked me the following question as I was reading about the future judgment of the sheep and the goats described in Matthew 25:31-46: *"If everyone in your church congregation died today and stood at the judgment of the sheep and the goats, how many would be sheep and how many would be goats?"* Or, more specifically, *"In the last year, how many of the people in your congregation have provided food for hungry brothers and sisters in Christ, water for thirsty Christians, shelter for homeless or traveling followers of Christ, clothing for naked Christians, or visited sick or imprisoned believers?"* I realized that very few had done any of those things or anything similar to those things, even though they came to church, sang songs of worship, listened to my sermons and gave money in the offerings. Thus, they were goats by Christ's criteria, and I was at least partly to blame, because I wasn't teaching them how important it was to God that we meet the pressing needs of our brothers and sisters in Christ. I wasn't teaching them to obey all that Christ commanded. In fact, I realized that I was neglecting what was extremely important to God—the second greatest commandment, to love our neighbor as ourselves—not to mention the new commandment Jesus gave us to love one another as He loved us.

Beyond that, I eventually realized that I was actually teaching what worked against God's general goal of making disciples as I taught a modest version of the very popular "prosperity gospel" to my congregation. Although it is Jesus' will that His people not lay up treasures on earth (see Matt. 6:19-24), and that they be content with what they have even if it is only food and covering (see Heb. 13:5; 1 Tim. 6:7-8), I was teaching my wealthy American congregation that God wanted them to have even more possessions. I was teaching people *not* to obey Jesus in one respect (just like hundreds of thousands of other pastors around the world).

Once I realized what I was doing, I repented and asked my congregation to forgive me. I started to try to make disciples, teaching them to obey all that Christ commanded. I did so with fear and trepidation, suspecting that some in my congregation really didn't want to obey all of Christ's commandments, preferring a Christianity of convenience that required no sacrifice on their part. And I was right. By all indications, quite a few didn't care about suffering believers around the world. They didn't care about spreading the gospel to those who had never heard it. Rather, they primarily cared about getting more for themselves. When it came to holiness, they avoided only the most scandalous sins, sins that were condemned even by unregenerate people, and they lived lives comparable to average conservative Americans. But they really didn't love the Lord, because they didn't want to keep Jesus' commandments, the very thing He said would prove our love for Him (see John 14:21).

What I feared proved to be true—some professing Christians were really goats in sheep's clothing. When I called them to deny themselves and take up their crosses, some became angry. To them, church was primarily a social experience along with some good music, just what the world enjoys in clubs and bars. They would tolerate some preaching as long as it affirmed their salvation and God's love for them. But they didn't want to hear about what God required of them. They didn't want anyone questioning their salvation. They were unwilling to adjust their lives to conform to God's will if it cost them anything. Sure, they were willing to part with some of their money, as long as they could be convinced that God would give them more in return, and as long as they directly benefited from what they gave, such as when their money improved their church facilities.

A Time for Self-Examination

This would be a good time for every minister reading this book to ask himself or herself the same question the Holy Spirit asked of me: *"If the people I minister to died right now and stood at the judgment of the sheep and the goats, how many would be sheep and how many would be goats?"* When ministers assure people of their congregations who act like goats that they are saved, they are telling them the exact opposite of what God wants them to be told. *That minister is working against Christ.* He is taking sides against what Jesus wants such people to be told according to what He said in Matthew 25:31-46. The entire point of what Jesus said there was to warn the goats. He doesn't want them to think they are going to heaven.

Jesus said that all men would know we are His disciples by our love for one another (see John 13:35). Surely He must have been speaking of a love that exceeds the love that non-Christians show each other, otherwise His disciples could not be distinguished from nonbelievers. The kind of love of which Jesus spoke is a self-sacrificing love, when we love each other as He loved us, laying down our lives for each other (see John 13:34; 1 John 3:16-20). John also wrote that we know we have passed out of death to life, that is, been born again, when we love each other (1 John 3:14). Do people who grumble, speak against, and hate ministers who teach Christ's commandments display the love that marks them as being born again? No, they are goats, on the road to hell.

Disciples of All Nations

Before we move on, let's look once more at Matthew 28:19-20, the Great and General Commission that Jesus gave to His disciples, to see if we can glean any other truths from it.

Go therefore and make disciples of all the nations, baptizing them in the name of the Father and the Son and
the Holy Spirit, teaching them to observe all that I commanded you" (Matt. 28:19-20a).

Note that Jesus wants disciples made in all the *nations,* or more correctly stated according to the original Greek, all the *ethnic groups* of the world.
If Jesus commanded it, I am led to believe that it must be possible to do
so. We *can* make disciples of Jesus in every ethnic group of the world. The
task was not given just to the original eleven disciples, but to every single
disciple after them, because Jesus told the eleven to teach their disciples
to observe *all* He had commanded *them.* Thus, the original eleven taught
their disciples to obey Christ's commandment to make disciples of all the
nations, and this would then be a self-perpetuating commandment for
every subsequent disciple. *Every disciple of Jesus is supposed to be involved in
some way in the discipling of the nations.*

This explains in part why the "Great Commission" has not yet been fulfilled. Even though there are millions of professing Christians, the number
of actual disciples who are committed to obey Jesus is much less. The large
majority of professing Christians do not care about disciples being made
in every ethnic group because they simply aren't committed to obeying
Christ's commandments. When the subject is brought up, they will often
use excuses such as, "That's not my ministry," and, "I just don't feel led in
that direction." Many pastors make such statements, as do all goats who
pick and choose which commandments of Christ are worthy to fit their
agenda.

If every professing Christian truly believed in the Lord Jesus Christ,
before long everyone in the world would hear the gospel. The collective
commitment of Christ's disciples would make it happen. They would stop
wasting all their time and money on temporal and worldly things, and use
them to accomplish what their Lord commanded them to do. Yet when
godly pastors announce that a missionary is going to be speaking at an
upcoming church service, he can often expect that attendance will drop.
Many of the goats will stay home or go elsewhere. They aren't interested
in obeying the last commandment of the Lord Jesus Christ. Sheep, on the
other hand, always become excited at the prospect of being involved in
making disciples of all the nations.

One last point in regard to Matthew 28:18-20: Jesus also told His disciples to baptize their disciples, and the apostles faithfully obeyed this
commandment. They immediately baptized those who repented and believed in the Lord Jesus. Baptism, of course, represents a believers' identification with Christ's death, burial and resurrection. New believers have
died and been raised as new creations in Christ. This truth Jesus wanted
dramatized in the baptism of every new believer, imprinting upon his

mind that he is now a new person with a new nature. He is one spirit with Christ, and is now empowered to obey God by Christ who lives within him. He was dead in his sins, but now has been washed clean and made alive by the Holy Spirit. He is more than "just forgiven." Rather, he has been *radically transformed*. Thus, God is indicating once again that true believers are different people who act much differently than they did when they were spiritually dead. This is certainly also implied by Jesus' closing words, "Lo, I am with you always, even to the end of the age" (Matt. 28:20). Would it not be reasonable to think that Christ's continual presence with people would affect their behavior?

Jesus Defines Discipleship

We've established that Jesus' overriding goal for us is that we make *disciples*, that is, people who have repented of their sins and who are learning and obeying His commandments. Jesus further defined what a disciple is in John 8:32:

> If you abide in My word, then you are truly disciples of Mine; and you shall know the truth, and the truth shall make your free.

True disciples, according to Jesus, are those who are abiding, or making their home, in His word. As they learn His truth from His Word, they are progressively "set free," and the later context indicates that Jesus was speaking about being set free from sin (see John 8:34-36). So once again we see that by Jesus' definition, disciples are learning and obeying His commandments.

Jesus later said,

> By this is My Father glorified, that you bear much fruit, and *so prove to be My disciples*" (John 15:8, emphasis added).

Thus, by Jesus' definition, disciples are glorifying God by bearing fruit. Those who bear no fruit are not proved to be His disciples.

Jesus more specifically defined that identifying fruit of His true disciples in Luke 14:25-33. Let's begin by reading just verse 25:

> Now great multitudes were going along with Him; and He turned and said to them…

Was Jesus satisfied because great multitudes were "going along" with Him? Had he attained His goal now that He had succeeded in gaining a large congregation?

No, Jesus was not satisfied that great multitudes were hanging around Him, listening to His sermons, watching His miracles, and sometimes eating His food. Jesus is looking for people who love God with all their heart, mind, soul and strength. He wants people who obey His commandments.

He wants *disciples*. Thus He said to those multitudes who were going along with Him:

> If anyone comes to Me, and does not hate his own father and mother and wife and children and brothers and sisters, yes, and even his own life, he cannot be my disciple (Luke 14:26).

There can be no mistake about it: Jesus laid down a requirement for a person to be His disciple. But must His disciples actually hate those people whom they would naturally love the most? That seems unlikely since we're commanded in Scripture to honor our parents and love our spouses and children.

Jesus must have been speaking in hyperbole, that is, exaggeration for emphasis. At bare minimum, however, He meant nothing less than this: If we are to be His disciples, we must love Him supremely, much more than the people we naturally love the most. Jesus' expectation is certainly reasonable since He is God whom we should love with all our heart, mind, soul and strength.

Don't forget—the job of ministers is to make disciples, which means they are to produce the kind of people who love Jesus supremely, who love Him much, much more than they love even their spouses, children and parents. It would be good for every minister reading this to ask himself, *"How am I succeeding at producing people like that?"*

How do we know if someone loves Jesus? Jesus told us in John 14:21: "If you love Me, you will keep My commandments." So it would certainly be reasonable to conclude that people who love Jesus more than their spouses, children and parents are also people who keep His commandments. *Disciples of Jesus obey His commandments.*

A Second Requirement

Jesus continued speaking to the multitudes that day who were going along with Him by saying,

> Whoever does not carry his own cross and come after Me cannot be My disciple (Luke 14:27).

This is the second requirement Jesus laid down to be His disciple. What did He mean? Are disciples required to literally carry large beams of wood with them? No, Jesus was again using hyperbole.

Most, if not all, of the people in Jesus' Jewish audience would have witnessed condemned criminals dying on crosses. The Romans crucified criminals along major thoroughfares outside the city gates to maximize crucifixion's effect as a deterrent to crime.

For this reason, I suspect that the phrase, "Carry your cross" was a common expression back in Jesus' day. Every person who was crucified had heard a Roman soldier say, "Take up your cross and follow me." Those were words the condemned dreaded, as they knew it marked the beginning of hours and days of gruesome agony. So such a phrase could have easily become a common expression that meant, "Accept the inevitable hardship that is coming your way."

I imagine fathers saying to their sons, "Son, I know you hate to dig out the latrine. It's a smelly, dirty job. But it's your responsibility once a month, so *take up your cross*. Go dig out the latrine." I imagine wives saying to their husbands, "My dear, I know how you hate to pay taxes to the Romans. But today our taxes are due, and the Tax Collector is coming up our road right now. *So take up your cross*. Go pay the man."

Taking up one's cross is synonymous with self-denial, and Jesus used it in that sense in Matthew 16:24: "If anyone wishes to come after Me, let him deny himself, and take up his cross, and follow Me." It could be paraphrased, "If anyone wishes to come after Me, let him put aside his own agenda, embrace the inevitable hardship that is coming as a consequence of his decision, and follow Me."

So, true disciples are willing to suffer for the sake of following Jesus. They've already counted the cost before they began, and knowing that hardship is inevitable, launched out with determination to finish the race. This interpretation is supported by what Jesus said next about counting the cost of following Him. Two illustrations made His point:

> For which one of you, when he wants to build a tower, does not first sit down and calculate the cost, to see if he has enough to complete it? Otherwise, when he has laid a foundation, and is not able to finish, all who observe it begin to ridicule him, saying, "This man began to build and was not able to finish." Or what king, when he sets out to meet another king in battle, will not first sit down and take counsel whether he is strong enough with ten thousand men to encounter the one coming against him with twenty thousand? Or else, while the other is still far away, he sends a delegation and asks terms of peace (Luke 14:28-32).

Jesus' point could not be clearer: "If you want to be My disciple, count the cost in advance, lest you quit when the going gets rough. True disciples accept the hardship that comes as a result of following Me."

A Third Requirement

Jesus listed one more requirement of discipleship that day:

> So therefore, no one of you can be My disciple who does not give up all His own possessions (Luke 14:33).

9

Again, it would seem logical to conclude that Jesus was using hyperbole. We don't need to give up all of our possessions in the sense that we are left without shelter, clothing and food. We must, however, certainly give up all of our possessions in the sense of turning their ownership over to God, and to the degree that we are no longer serving mammon, but serving God *with* our mammon. The result could certainly mean giving up many unnecessary possessions and living a simple life of godly stewardship and sharing, as did the early Christians we read about in the book of Acts. Being Christ's disciple means obeying His commandments, and He commanded His followers to not lay up treasures on earth, but to lay them up in heaven.

In summary, according to Jesus, if I am to be His disciple, I must bear fruit. I must love Him supremely, much more than even my own family members. I must be willing to face the inevitable hardships that will arise as a result of my decision to follow Him. And I must do what He says with my income and possessions. (And many of His commandments have something to say in this regard, so I must not fool myself, as so many do, saying, "If the Lord told me to do something with all my possessions, I would do whatever He said.")

And these are the kinds of committed followers of Christ that we as ministers are supposed to be making! That is our God-ordained goal! We are called to be disciple-making ministers!

That is a foundational truth that many ministers around the world are completely missing. If they evaluate their ministries, as I did, they will have to conclude, as I did, that they are falling far short of God's desire and expectation. When I considered the level of commitment to Christ demonstrated by the people of my congregation, I had little doubt that there were many who could not be classified as true disciples.

Pastors, take a look at your congregation. How many of your people does Jesus consider to be His disciples according to His criteria in Luke 14:26-33? Evangelists, is the message you preach producing people who are committing themselves to obey all of Christ's commandments?

Now is the time to evaluate our ministries, before we stand before Jesus at the final evaluation. If I'm falling short of His goal, I'd rather discover it now than then. Wouldn't you?

A Final Sobering Thought

Clearly, Jesus wants people to become His disciples, as revealed by His Words to the multitudes recorded in Luke 14:26-33. How important is it to become His disciple? What if one chooses not to become His disciple? Jesus answered these questions at the close of His discourse in Luke 14:

> Therefore, salt is good; but if even salt has become tasteless, with what will it be seasoned? It is useless either for

> the soil or for the manure pile; it is thrown out. He who
> has ears to hear, let him hear (Luke 14:34-35).

Notice that this is not an unrelated statement. It begins with the word *therefore*.

Salt is supposed to be salty. That is what makes it salt. If it looses its flavor, it is useless for anything and "thrown out."

What does this have to do with being a disciple? Just as salt is expected to be salty, so Jesus expects people to be His disciples. Since He is God, our only reasonable obligation is to love Him supremely and take up our crosses. If we don't become His disciples, we reject His very reason for our existence. *We are good for nothing and destined to be "thrown out."* That doesn't sound like heaven, does it?

At another time, Jesus said to His *disciples* (see Matt. 5:1):

> You are the salt of the earth; but if the salt has become
> tasteless, how will it be made salty again? It is good for
> nothing anymore, except to be thrown out and trampled
> under foot by men (Matt. 5:13).

These are sobering warnings indeed. First, only those who are salty (an obvious metaphor for "committed obedience") are of any use to God. The rest are "good for nothing…except to be thrown out and trampled." Second, it must be possible for one who is "salty" to become "unsalty," otherwise Jesus would not have seen any need to warn His disciples. How these truths contradict what so many teach today, saying that one can be a heaven-bound believer in Christ but not be a disciple of Christ, or that it is not possible to forfeit one's salvation status. We'll consider those erroneous ideas in more detail in later chapters.

TWO

Beginning Rightly

Biblically speaking, a disciple is a sincere believer in the Lord Jesus Christ, one who is abiding in His Word and consequently being set free from sin. A disciple is one who is learning to obey all of Christ's commandments, and one who loves Jesus more than his own family, his own comfort, and his possessions, and he manifests that love by his lifestyle. Jesus' true disciples love one another and demonstrate that love in practical ways. They are bearing fruit.[2] These are the kinds of people Jesus wants.

Obviously those who are not His disciples cannot make disciples for Him. Thus we must first be certain that we ourselves are His disciples before we attempt to make any disciples for Him. Many ministers, when weighed against the biblical definition of what a disciple is, fall short. There is no hope that such ministers can make disciples, and they in fact, won't even try. They are not committed enough themselves to Jesus Christ to endure the difficulties that come with making true disciples.

From this point on, I'm going to assume that ministers who continue reading are disciples of the Lord Jesus Christ themselves, fully committed to obeying His commandments. If you are not, there is no sense in your reading any further until you make the necessary commitment to become a true disciple. Don't wait any longer! Fall on your knees and repent! By His marvelous grace, God will forgive you and make you a new creation in Christ!

Redefining Discipleship

Although Jesus made it quite clear what a disciple is, many have replaced His definition with one of their own. For example, to some the word *disciple* is a vague term that applies to anyone who professes to be

---

[2] This definition is derived from what we've already read in Matthew 28:18-20, John 8:31-32; 13:25, 15:8 and Luke 14:25-33.

13

a Christian. To them, the word *disciple* has been stripped of all its biblical meaning.

Others consider *discipleship* to be an optional second step of commitment for heaven-bound believers. They believe that one may be a heaven-bound believer in Jesus but not be a disciple of Jesus! Because it is so difficult to simply ignore Jesus' demanding requirements for discipleship that are recorded in Scripture, it is taught that there are two levels of Christians—the believers, who believe in Jesus, and the disciples, who believe in and are committed to Jesus. Along these lines, it is often said that there are many believers but few disciples, but that both are going to heaven.

This doctrine effectively neutralizes Christ's commandment to make disciples, which in turn neutralizes the making of disciples. If becoming a disciple means self-denying commitment and even hardship, and if becoming a disciple is optional, the large majority of people will elect not to become disciples, especially if they think they will be welcomed into heaven as non-disciples.

So here are some *very* important questions that we must ask: Does Scripture teach that one can be a heaven-bound believer but not be a disciple of Jesus Christ? Is discipleship an optional step for believers? Are there two levels of Christians, the uncommitted believers and the committed disciples?

The answer to all of these questions is *No.* Nowhere does the New Testament teach that there are two categories of Christians, the believers and the disciples. If one reads the book of Acts, one will read repeated references to *the disciples*, and they are obviously not references to a higher-class of more committed believers. *Everyone* who believed in Jesus was a disciple.[3] In fact, "the *disciples* were first called *Christians* in Antioch" (Acts 11:26, emphasis added).

It is interesting to note that the Greek word translated *disciple* (mathetes) is found 261 times in the New Testament, whereas the Greek word translated *believer* (pistos) is only found nine times (as it is translated *believer* in the *New American Standard* version). The Greek word translated *Christian* (Christianos) is found only three times. Those facts alone are enough to convince an honest inquirer that those in the early church who believed in Jesus were all considered to be His disciples.

Jesus' Commentary

Jesus certainly didn't think that becoming a disciple was a secondary, optional step for believers. His three requirements for discipleship that we read in Luke 14 were not addressed to believers as an invitation to a

---

[3] *Disciples* are mentioned in Acts 6:1, 2, 7; 9:1, 10, 19, 25, 26, 36, 38; 11:26, 29; 13:52; 14:20, 21, 22, 28; 15:10; 16:1; 18:23, 27; 19:1, 9, 30; 20:1, 30; 21:4, 16. *Believers* are mentioned only in Acts 5:14; 10:45 and 16:1. In Acts 14:21, for example, Luke wrote, "And after they [Paul and Barnabas] had preached the gospel to that city and had made many disciples…" Thus Paul and Barnabas made disciples by preaching the gospel, and people became immediate disciples at their conversion, not at some later optional time.

higher level of commitment. Rather, His words were addressed to everyone among the multitudes. Discipleship is the *first* step in a relationship with God. Moreover, we read in John 8:

> As He [Jesus] spoke these things, *many came to believe in Him*. Jesus therefore was saying *to those Jews who had believed* Him, "If you abide in My word, then you are truly *disciples* of Mine; and you shall know the truth, and the truth shall make your free" (John 8:31-32).

No one can intelligently argue against the undeniable fact that Jesus was talking to newly-professing believers about being His disciples. Jesus did *not* say to those newly-professing believers, "Sometime in the future you may want to consider taking the next step, a step of commitment, to become My disciples." No, Jesus spoke to those new believers as if He expected them to be disciples already, as if the words *believer* and *disciple* were synonymous terms. He told those newly-professing believers that the way they could prove they were His disciples was by abiding in His word, which would result in their being set free from sin (see 8:34-36).

Jesus knew that just people's *profession* of faith was no guarantee that they really did believe. He also knew that those who truly believed He was the Son of God would act like it—they would immediately become His disciples—yearning to obey and please Him. Such believers/disciples would naturally abide in His Word, making it their home. And as they discovered His will by learning His commandments, they would be progressively set free from sin.

That is why Jesus immediately challenged those new believers to test themselves. His statement, "If you are *truly* My disciples" indicates He believed there was a possibility that they were not *true* disciples, but only *professing* disciples. They could be fooling themselves. Only if they passed Jesus' test could they be certain they were His true disciples. (And it seems from reading the rest of the dialogue in John 8:37-59 that Jesus certainly had good reason to doubt their sincerity.)[4]

Our key scripture, Matthew 28:18-20, itself dispels the theory that disciples are a higher class of committed believers. Jesus commanded in His Great Commission that *disciples* be baptized. Of course, the record of the book of Acts indicates that the apostles didn't wait until new believers took a "second step of radical commitment to Christ" before they baptized them. Rather, the apostles baptized all new believers almost immediately after their conversion. They believed that all true believers were disciples.

In this regard, those who believe that disciples are the uniquely com-

---

[4] This passage of Scripture also exposes the mistaken modern practice of assuring new converts of their salvation. Jesus did not assure these newly-professing converts that they were surely saved because they had prayed a short prayer to accept Him or verbalized faith in Him. Rather, He challenged them to consider if their profession was genuine. We should follow His example.

mitted believers are not consistent with their own theology. Most of them baptize anyone who professes to believe in Jesus, not waiting for them to reach the committed level of "discipleship." Yet if they really believe what they preach, they should only baptize those who reach the discipleship level, which would be very few among their ranks.

Perhaps one final blow to this diabolical doctrine will suffice. If disciples are different than believers, why is it that John wrote that love for the brethren is the identifying mark of true born-again *believers* (see 1 John 3:14), and Jesus said that love for the brethren is the identifying mark of His true *disciples* (John 13:35)?

The Origin of this False Doctrine

If the idea of two separate classes of Christians, the believers and the disciples, is not found in Scripture, how is such a doctrine defended? The answer is that this doctrine is solely supported by another false doctrine about salvation. That doctrine alleges that the demanding requirements for discipleship are not compatible with the fact that salvation is by grace. Based on that logic, the conclusion is drawn that the requirements for discipleship cannot be requirements for salvation. Thus, being a disciple must be an optional step of commitment for heaven-bound believers who are saved by grace.

The fatal flaw with this theory is that there are scores of scriptures that oppose it. What, for example, could be more clear than what Jesus said near the close of His Sermon on the Mount, after He had enumerated numerous commandments?

> Not everyone who says to Me, "Lord, Lord," will enter
> the kingdom of heaven; but he who does the will of My
> Father who is in heaven" (Matt. 7:21).

Clearly, Jesus linked obedience with salvation, here and in many other statements. So how can we reconcile the numerous scriptures like this with the Bible's affirmation that salvation is by grace? It is quite simple. God, by His amazing grace, is temporarily offering everyone an opportunity to repent, believe, and be born again, empowered to live obediently by the Holy Spirit. So salvation is by grace. Without God's grace, no one could be saved, because all have sinned. Sinners cannot possibly merit salvation. So they need God's grace to be saved.

God's grace is revealed in so many ways in regard to our salvation. It is revealed in Jesus' dying on the cross, God's calling us though the gospel, His drawing us to Christ, His convicting us of our sin, His granting us an opportunity to repent, His regenerating us and filling us with His Holy Spirit, His breaking the power of sin over our lives, His empowering us to live in holiness, His discipline of us when we sin, and so on. None of these blessings have we earned. We are saved by grace from start to finish.

According to Scripture, however, salvation is not only "by grace," but "through faith": "For *by grace* you have been saved *through faith*" (Eph. 2:8a, emphasis added). Both components are necessary, and they are obviously not incompatible. If people are to be saved, both grace and faith are necessary. God extends His grace, and we respond by faith. Genuine faith, of course, results in obedience to God's commandments. As James wrote in the second chapter of his epistle, faith without works is dead, useless, and cannot save (see Jas. 2:14-26).[5]

The fact is, God's grace has never offered anyone a license to sin. Rather, God's grace offers people a temporary opportunity to repent and be born again. After death, there is no more opportunity to repent and be born again, and thus God's grace is no longer available. His saving grace must therefore be temporary.

A Woman Whom Jesus Saved by Grace Through Faith

A perfect picture of salvation offered by grace through faith is found in the story of Jesus' encounter with the woman caught in the act of adultery. Jesus said to her, "Neither do I condemn you [*that* is grace, because she deserved to be condemned]; go your way; *from now on sin no more*" (John 8:11, emphasis added). When she deserved to die, Jesus let her go free. He sent her away, however, with a warning: *From now on sin no more.* This is exactly what Jesus is saying to every sinner in the world—"I'm not condemning you now. You deserve to die and be condemned forever in hell, but I'm showing you grace. My grace, however, is only temporary, so repent. Stop sinning now, before My grace ends and you find yourself standing before My judgment seat as a guilty sinner."

Let us imagine that adulterous woman repented as Jesus instructed her. If she did, she was saved by *grace* through *faith*. She was saved *by grace* because she could never have been saved without God's grace, being a sinner. She could never rightly say that she earned her salvation by her works. And she was saved *through faith* because she *believed* in Jesus and thus believed what He said to her, heeding His warning, and turned from her sin before it was too late. Anyone who has genuine faith in Jesus will repent, because Jesus warned that unless people repent, they will perish (see Luke 13:3). Jesus also solemnly declared that only those who do the will of the Father will enter heaven (Matt. 7:21). If one believes in Jesus, one will believe and heed His warnings.

But let us imagine that the adulterous woman didn't repent of her sin. She kept on sinning and then died and stood at Jesus' judgment seat. Imagine her saying to Jesus, "Oh Jesus! It is *so good* to see You! I remember how You didn't condemn me for my sin when I was brought before You

---

[5] Moreover, contrary to those who maintain that we are saved by faith even if we have no works, James says that we cannot be saved by a faith that is alone: "You see that a man is justified by works, and not by faith alone." True faith is never alone; it is always accompanied by works.

on the earth. Surely You are still just as gracious. You didn't condemn me then, so surely You won't condemn me now!"

What do you think? Would Jesus welcome her into heaven? The answer is obvious. Paul warned, "Do not be deceived; neither fornicators…not adulterers…shall inherit the kingdom of God" (1 Cor. 6:9-10).

All of this is to say that Jesus' requirements for discipleship are nothing more than a requirement for genuine faith in Him, *what amounts to saving faith*. And everyone who has saving faith has been saved by grace *through* faith. There are no biblical grounds for the claim that, because salvation is by grace, Jesus' requirements for discipleship are incompatible with His requirements for salvation. Discipleship is not an optional step for heaven-bound believers; rather, *discipleship is the evidence of genuine saving faith.*[6]

This being so, *to be successful in God's eyes, a minister should begin rightly the process of disciple-making by preaching the true gospel, calling people to an obedient faith.* When ministers promote the false doctrine that discipleship is an optional step of commitment for heaven-bound believers, they are working against Christ's commandment to make disciples and are proclaiming a false grace and false gospel. Only Christ's true disciples possess saving faith and are going to heaven, just as Jesus promised: "Not everyone who says to Me, 'Lord, Lord,' will enter the kingdom of heaven; but he who does the will of My Father who is in heaven" (Matt. 7:21).

The New False Gospel

Because of a false concept of God's grace in salvation, the modern gospel has often been stripped of essential biblical elements that are considered incompatible with a message of grace. A false gospel, however, only produces false Christians, which is why such a large percentage of modern new "converts" will not be found even attending church within a few weeks after they "accepted Christ." Moreover, many who do attend church are very often indistinguishable from the unregenerate population, possessing the same values and practicing the same sins as their conservative neighbors. This is because they don't really believe in the Lord Jesus Christ and haven't actually been born again.

One of those essential elements now removed from the modern gospel is the call to repentance. Many ministers feel that if they tell people to stop sinning (as Jesus did to the woman caught in the act of adultery), it will be tantamount to telling them that salvation is not of grace, but works. But this can't be true, because John the Baptist, Jesus, Peter and Paul all pro-

---

[6] It is also helpful to keep in mind that the reason Paul often affirmed that salvation is by grace and not works is because he was constantly fighting the true legalists of his day. Paul was not trying to correct people who taught that holiness is essential for heaven, because he himself believed and often affirmed that fact. Rather, he wrote to correct Jews who, having no concept of God's grace in salvation, did not see any reason for Jesus to have died. Many did not believe that Gentiles could ever be saved because they had no concept of God's grace making salvation possible. Some thought that circumcision, physical lineage, or keeping the Law (which they did not do anyway) earned one's salvation, thus nullifying God's grace and the need for Christ to have died.

claimed that repentance is an absolute necessity for salvation. If preaching repentance somehow negates God's grace in salvation, then John the Baptist, Jesus, Peter and Paul all negated God's grace in salvation. They, however, understood that God's grace offers people a temporary opportunity to repent, not an opportunity to continue sinning.

For example, when John the Baptist proclaimed what Luke refers to as "the gospel," his central message was repentance (see Luke 3:1-18). Those who didn't repent would go to hell (see Matt. 3:10-12; Luke 3:17).

Jesus preached repentance from the start of His ministry (see Matt. 4:17). He warned people that unless they repented, they would perish (see Luke 13:3, 5).

When Jesus sent out His twelve disciples to preach in various cities, "They went out and preached that men should *repent*" (Mark 6:12, emphasis added).

After His resurrection, Jesus told the twelve to take the message of repentance to the whole world, because it was the key that opened the door to forgiveness:

> And He said to them, "Thus it is written, that the Christ should suffer and rise again from the dead the third day; and that *repentance for forgiveness of sins* should be proclaimed in His name to all the nations, beginning from Jerusalem" (Luke 24:46-47, emphasis added).

The apostles obeyed Jesus' instructions. When Peter was preaching on the day of Pentecost, his convicted listeners, after realizing the truth about the Man whom they had recently crucified, asked Peter what they should do. His response was that they, first of all, should repent (see Acts 2:38).

Peter's second public sermon at Solomon's portico contained the identical message. Sins would not be wiped away without repentance:[7]

> *Repent* therefore and return, that your sins may be wiped away (Acts 3:19a, emphasis added).

When Paul testified before King Agrippa, he declared that his gospel had always contained the message of repentance:

> Consequently, King Agrippa, I did not prove disobedient to the heavenly vision, but kept declaring both to those of Damascus first, and also at Jerusalem and then throughout all the region of Judea, and even to the Gentiles, *that they should repent and turn to God*, performing deeds appropriate to repentance (Acts 26:19-20, emphasis added).

[7] Likewise, when God revealed to Peter that Gentiles could be saved simply by believing in Jesus, Peter declared to Cornelius' household, "I most certainly understand now that God is not one to show partiality, but in every nation the man who fears Him and *does what it right*, is welcome to Him" (Acts 10:34b-35, emphasis added). Peter also declared in Acts 5:32 that God gave the Holy Spirit "to those who obey Him." All true Christians are indwelt by the Holy Spirit (see Rom. 8:9; Gal. 4:6).

In Athens, Paul warned his audience that everyone must stand in judgment before Christ, and those who have not repented will be unprepared for that great day:

> Therefore having overlooked the times of ignorance, God is now declaring to men that *all everywhere should repent,* because He has fixed a day in which He will judge the world in righteousness through a Man whom He has appointed, having furnished proof to all men by raising Him from the dead (Acts 17:30-31, emphasis added).

In his farewell sermon to the Ephesian elders, Paul listed repentance along with faith as an essential part of his message:

> I did not shrink from...solemnly testifying to both Jews and Greeks of *repentance* toward God and faith in our Lord Jesus Christ (Acts 20:20a, 21, emphasis added).

This list of scriptural proofs should be enough to convince anyone that unless the necessity of repentance is proclaimed, the true gospel has not been preached. A relationship with God begins with repentance. There is no forgiveness of sins without it.

Repentance Redefined

Even in the light of so many scriptural proofs that salvation depends on repentance, some ministers still find a way to nullify its necessity by twisting its clear meaning to make it compatible with their faulty conception of God's grace. By their new definition, repentance is no more than a change of mind about who Jesus is, and one that, amazingly, may not necessarily affect a person's behavior.

So what did the New Testament preachers expect when they called people to repent? Were they calling people to only change their minds about who Jesus is, or were they calling people to change their behavior?

Paul believed that true repentance required a change of behavior. We have already read his testimony regarding decades of ministry, as he declared before King Agrippa,

> Consequently, King Agrippa, I did not prove disobedient to the heavenly vision, but kept declaring both to those of Damascus first, and also at Jerusalem and then throughout all the region of Judea, and even to the Gentiles, that they should repent and turn to God, *performing deeds appropriate to repentance* (Acts 26:19-20, emphasis added).

John the Baptist also believed that repentance was more than just a change of mind about certain theological facts. When his convicted audience responded to his call for repentance by asking what they should do, he enumerated specific changes of behavior (see Luke 3:3, 10-14). He also derided the Pharisees and Sadducees for only going through the motions of repentance, and warned them of hell's fires if they didn't truly repent:

> You brood of vipers, who warned you to flee from the wrath to come? Therefore *bring forth fruit in keeping with repentance.*...the axe is already laid at the root of the trees; *every tree therefore that does not bear good fruit is cut down and thrown into the fire* (Matt. 3:7-10, emphasis added).

Jesus preached the same message of repentance as John (see Matt. 3:2; 4:17). He once stated that Nineveh repented at Jonah's preaching (see Luke 11:32). Anyone who has ever read the book of Jonah knows that the people of Nineveh did more than change their minds. They also changed their actions, turning from sin. Jesus called it *repentance.*

Biblical repentance is a willful change of behavior in response to authentic faith born in the heart. When a minister preaches the gospel without mentioning the need for a genuine change of behavior that authenticates repentance, he is actually working against Christ's desire for disciples. Moreover, he deceives his audience into believing that they can be saved without repenting, thus potentially insuring their damnation if they believe him. He is working against God and for Satan, whether he realizes it or not.

If a minister is going to make disciples as Jesus commanded, he must begin the process rightly. When he doesn't preach the true gospel that calls people to repentance and an obedient faith, he is destined to failure, even though he may be a great success in the eyes of people. He may have a large congregation, but he is building with wood, hay and straw, and when his works go through the future fire the quality of his work will be tested. They will be consumed (see 1 Cor. 3:12-15).

Jesus' Calls to Commitment

Not only did Jesus call the unsaved to turn from sin, He also called them to commit themselves to follow and obey immediately. He never offered salvation on lesser terms, as is often done today. He never invited people to "accept" Him, promising them forgiveness, and then later suggested that they might want to commit themselves to obey Him. No, Jesus demanded that the very first step be a step of whole-hearted commitment.

Sadly, Jesus' calls to costly commitment are often simply ignored by professing Christians. Or, if they are acknowledged, are explained away as being calls to a deeper relationship that are supposedly addressed, not to the unsaved, but to those who have already received God's saving grace. Yet so many of these "believers" who claim that Jesus' calls to costly commitment are addressed to them rather than the unsaved *do not heed His calls as they interpret them.* In their minds, they have the option not to respond in obedience, and they never do.

Let's consider one of Jesus' invitations to salvation that is often interpreted to be a call to a deeper walk, supposedly addressed to those who are already saved:

> And He [Jesus] summoned the multitude with His disciples, and said to them, "If anyone wishes to come after Me, let him deny himself, and take up his cross, and follow Me. For whoever wishes to save his life shall lose it; but whoever loses his life for My sake and the gospel's shall save it. For what does it profit a man to gain the whole world, and forfeit his soul? For what shall a man give in exchange for his soul? For whoever is ashamed of Me and My words in this adulterous and sinful generation, the Son of Man will also be ashamed of him when He comes in the glory of His Father with the holy angels" (Mark 8:34-38).

Is this an invitation to salvation addressed to unbelievers or an invitation to a more committed relationship addressed to believers? As we read honestly, the answer becomes obvious.

First, notice that the crowd Jesus was speaking to consisted of "the multitude *with* His disciples" (v. 34, emphasis added). Clearly then, the "multitude" did not consist of His disciples. They, in fact, were "summoned" by Him to hear what He was about to say. Jesus wanted everyone, followers and seekers, to understand the truth He was about to teach. Notice also that He then began by saying, "If *anyone*" (v. 34, emphasis added). His words apply to anyone and everyone.

As we continue reading, it becomes even clearer whom Jesus was addressing. Specifically, His words were directed at every person who desired to (1) "come after" Him, (2) "save his life," (3) not "forfeit his soul," and (4) be among those whom He will not be ashamed of when He "comes in the glory of His Father with the holy angels." All four of these expressions indicate Jesus was describing people who desired to be saved. Are we to think that there is a heaven-bound person who does not want to "come after" Jesus and "save his life"? Are we to think that there are true believers who will "forfeit their souls," who are ashamed of Jesus and His words, and of whom Jesus will be ashamed when He returns? *Obviously*, Jesus was talking about gaining eternal salvation in this passage of Scripture.

Notice that each of the last four sentences in this five-sentence passage all begin with the word "For." Thus each sentence helps to explain and expand upon the previous sentence. No sentence within this passage should be interpreted without considering how the others illuminate it. Let's consider Jesus' words sentence by sentence with that in mind.

Sentence #1

> If anyone wishes to come after Me, let him deny him-
> self, and take up his cross, and follow Me (Mark 8:34).

Again, note that Jesus' words were addressed to anyone who wished to come after Him, anyone who wanted to become His *follower*. This is the only relationship Jesus initially offers—to be His follower.

Many desire to be His friend without being His follower, but such an option does not exist. Jesus didn't consider anyone His friends unless they obeyed Him. He once said, "You are My friends, if you do what I command you" (John 15:14).

Many would like to be His brother without being His follower, but, again, Jesus didn't extend that option. He considered no one His brother unless he was obedient: "Whoever does the will of My Father who is in heaven, *he* is My brother" (Matt. 12:50, emphasis added).

Many wish to join Jesus in heaven without being His follower, but Jesus conveyed the impossibility of such a thing. Only those who obey are heaven-bound: "Not everyone who says to Me, 'Lord, Lord,' will enter the kingdom of heaven; but he who does the will of My Father who is in heaven" (Matt. 7:21).

In the sentence under consideration, Jesus informed those who wanted to follow Him that they couldn't follow Him unless they denied themselves. They must be willing to put their desires aside, making them subordinate to His will. *Self-denial and submission are the essence of following Jesus.* That is what it means to "take up your cross."

Sentence #2

Jesus' second sentence makes the meaning of His first sentence even more clear:

> For whoever wishes to save his life shall lose it; but who-
> ever loses his life for My sake and the gospel's shall save
> it (Mark 8:35).

Again, notice this sentence begins with "For," relating it with the first sentence, adding clarification. Here Jesus contrasts two people, the same two people who were implied in the first sentence—the one who *would* deny himself and take up his cross to follow Him and the one who *would not*. Now they are contrasted as one who would lose his life for Christ and the gospel's sake and one who would not. If we look for the relationship between the two, we must conclude that the one in the first sentence who would *not* deny himself corresponds to the one in the second sentence who wishes to save his life but will lose it. And the one in the first sentence who *was* willing to deny himself corresponds to the one in the second sentences who loses his life but ultimately saves it.

Jesus was not speaking about one losing or saving his physical life. Later sentences in this passage indicate that Jesus had eternal losses and gains in mind. A similar expression by Jesus recorded in John 12:25 says, "He who loves his life loses it; and he who hates his life in this world shall keep it to *life eternal*" (emphasis added).

The person in the first sentence who would not deny himself was the same person in the second sentence who wished to save his life. Thus we can reasonably conclude that "saving one's life" means "saving one's own agenda for his life." This becomes even clearer when we consider the contrasted man who "loses his life for Christ and the gospel's sake." He is the one who denies himself, takes up his cross, and gives up his own agenda, now living for the purpose of furthering Christ's agenda and the spread of the gospel. He is the one who will ultimately "save his life." The person who seeks to please Christ rather than himself will ultimately find himself happy in God's Kingdom, while the one who continues to please himself will ultimately find himself miserable in hell, there losing all freedom to follow his own agenda.

Sentences #3 & 4

Now the third and fourth sentences:

> For what does it profit a man to gain the whole world, and forfeit his soul? For what shall a man give in exchange for his soul? (Mark 8:36-37).

In these the person is highlighted who will not deny himself. He is also the one who wishes to save his life but ultimately loses it. Now he is spoken of as one who pursues what the world has to offer and who ultimately "forfeits his soul." Jesus exposes the folly of such a person by comparing the worth of the whole world with that of one's soul. Of course, there is no comparison. A person might theoretically acquire all the world has to offer, but, if the ultimate consequence of his life is that he spends eternity in hell, he has made the gravest of errors.

From these third and fourth sentences we also gain insight into what pulls people away from denying themselves to become Christ's followers. It is their desire for self-gratification, offered by the world. Motivated by love of self, those who refuse to follow Christ seek sinful pleasures, which Christ's true followers shun out of love and obedience to Him. Those who are trying to gain all that the world has to offer pursue wealth, power and prestige, while Christ's true followers seek first His kingdom and His righteousness. Any wealth, power or prestige that is gained by them is considered a stewardship from God to be used unselfishly for His glory.

Sentence #5

Finally, we arrive at the fifth sentence in the passage. Notice again how it is joined to the others by the beginning word, *for*:

> For whoever is ashamed of Me and My words in this adulterous and sinful generation, the Son of Man will also be ashamed of him when He comes in the glory of His Father with the holy angels (Mark 8:38).

This again is the person who would not deny himself, but who wished to follow his own agenda, pursuing what the world had to offer, and who thus ultimately lost his life and forfeited his soul. Now he is characterized as one who is ashamed of Christ and His words. His shame, of course, stems from his unbelief. If he had truly believed that Jesus was God's Son, he certainly would not have been ashamed of Him or His words. But he is a member of an "adulterous and sinful generation," and Jesus will be ashamed of him when He returns. Clearly, Jesus was not describing a saved person.

What is the conclusion to all of this? The entire passage cannot rightfully be considered to be a call to a more committed life addressed to those who are already on the way to heaven. It is obviously a revealing of the way of salvation by means of comparing those who are truly saved and those who are unsaved. The truly saved believe in the Lord Jesus Christ and thus deny themselves for Him, while the unsaved demonstrate no such obedient faith.

Another Call to Commitment

There are many we could consider, but let us look at one other call to commitment by the Lord Jesus that is nothing less than a call to salvation:

> Come to Me, all who are weary and heavy-laden, and I will give you rest. Take My yoke upon you and learn from Me, for I am gentle and humble in heart, and you will find rest for your souls. For My yoke is easy and My burden is light (Matt. 11:28-30).

Evangelists often use this passage of Scripture in their evangelistic invitations, and rightly so. These words are clearly an invitation to salvation. Here Jesus is offering rest to those who are "weary and heavy-laden." He is not offering *physical* rest for those who are *physically* burdened, but *rest for their souls*, as He says. Unsaved people are weighted down with guilt, fear and sin, and when they become weary of it, they then become good candidates for salvation.

If such people want to receive the rest that Jesus is offering, they must do two things according to Him. They must (1) come to Him and (2), they must take His yoke upon them.

False grace teachers often twist the obvious meaning of the expression "taking Jesus' yoke." Some actually claim that Jesus was speaking of a yoke that must be around His own neck, which is why He called it "My yoke." And Jesus must have been speaking of a *double-yoke* they say, one half of which is around His neck and the other half of which is empty, waiting for us to take on our necks. We should understand, however, that Jesus is promising to do all the pulling of the plow because He said that His yoke is easy and His burden is light. Thus our only job, according to such teachers, is to make sure we stay yoked to Jesus by faith, allowing Him to do all the work for our salvation, while we just enjoy the benefits offered through His grace! That interpretation, obviously, is quite forced.

No, when Jesus said that weary people should take His yoke, He meant that they should submit to Him, making Him their master, allowing Him to direct their lives. That is why Jesus said we should take His yoke and then learn of Him. Unsaved people are like wild oxen, going their own way and ruling their own lives. When they take Jesus' yoke, they give up control to Him. And the reason Jesus' yoke is easy and His burden is light is because He empowers us by His indwelling Spirit to obey Him.

Thus we see again that Jesus called people to salvation, in this case symbolized as a rest for the weary, by calling people to submit to Him and make Him their Lord.

In Summary

All of this is to say that a truly successful minister is one who obeys Jesus' commandment to make disciples, and who knows that repentance, commitment and discipleship are not options for heaven-bound believers. Rather, they are the only authentic expression of saving faith. Therefore, the successful minister preaches a biblical gospel to the unsaved. He calls the unsaved to repent and follow Jesus, and he does not assure the uncommitted of their salvation.

THREE

Continuing Properly

For many years and in many ways, I unknowingly followed practices that worked against the goal that God wanted me to pursue, the goal of making disciples. But gradually, the Holy Spirit graciously opened my eyes to my errors. One thing I've learned is this: I should question everything I've been taught and believed in light of God's Word. Our traditions, more than anything else, blind us to what God has said. Worse, we are very proud of our traditions, certain that we stand among an elite group who has a greater grasp of truth than other Christians. As one teacher sarcastically said, "There are 32,000 denominations in the world today. Aren't you fortunate to be a member of the one that is right?"

As a result of our pride, God resists us, because He resists the proud. If we want to make any progress and be fully ready to stand before Jesus, we must humble ourselves. To those, God gives grace.

The Role of the Pastor Considered

The minister's goal of making disciples should shape everything he does in ministry. He should continually be asking himself, "How does what I'm doing contribute to the process of making disciples who will obey all of Jesus' commandments?" That simple test question, if asked honestly, would eliminate much that is done under the banner of Christian activity.

Let us consider the ministry of the pastor/elder/overseer,[8] a person whose ministry assignment focuses him on a specific local church. If that

---

[8] It seems quite clear that a pastor (the Greek noun is *poimain*, meaning *shepherd*) is equivalent to an elder (the Greek noun *presbuteros*), and is also equivalent to an overseer (the Greek noun *episkopos*, translated *bishop* in the KJV). Paul, for example, instructed the Ephesian *elders (presbuteros)*, whom he said the Holy Spirit had made *overseers (episkopos)*, to *shepherd* (the Greek verb *poimaino*) the flock of God (see Acts 20:28). He also used the terms *elders (presbuteros)* and *overseers (episkopos)* synonymously in Titus 1:5-7. Peter, too, exhorted the elders *(presbuteros)* to shepherd *(poimaino)* the flock (see 1 Pet. 5:1-2). The idea that a bishop (the KJV translation of *episkopos*) is a higher office than pastor or elder, and is one who oversees numerous churches is a human invention.

27

person is going to make disciples who obey all of Jesus' commandments, what should be one of his primary responsibilities? *Teaching* naturally comes to mind. Jesus said that disciples are made by the means of teaching (see Matt. 28:19-20). A requirement for one to be an elder/pastor/overseer is that he be "able to teach" (1 Tim. 3:2). Those who "work hard at preaching and teaching" should "be considered worthy of double honor" (1 Tim. 5:17).

Therefore, a pastor should evaluate every sermon by asking himself this question, "How does this sermon help accomplish the task of making disciples?"

Is a pastor's teaching responsibility fulfilled, however, solely by means of his Sunday or midweek sermons? If he thinks so, he overlooks the fact that Scripture indicates his teaching responsibility is *primarily* fulfilled by the life he lives and the example he sets. The teaching example of his daily life is simply supplemented by his public teaching ministry. That is why the requirements for elders/pastors/overseers have much more to do with a person's character and lifestyle than his verbal communication skills. Of fifteen requirements listed for overseers in 1 Timothy 3:1-7, fourteen are related to character and only one to teaching ability. Of the eighteen requirements listed for elders in Titus 1:5-9, seventeen are related to character and only one to teaching ability. Paul first reminded Timothy, "In speech, conduct, love, faith and purity, show yourself an *example* of those who believe" (1 Tim. 4:12, emphasis added). He *then* said, "Until I come, give attention to the public reading of Scripture, to exhortation and teaching" (1 Tim. 4:13). Thus the example of Timothy's character was mentioned before his public teaching ministry, underscoring its greater importance.

Peter similarly wrote:

> I exhort the elders among you, as your fellow elder and witness of the sufferings of Christ, and a partaker also of the glory that is to be revealed: shepherd the flock of God among you, exercising oversight not under compulsion, but voluntarily, according to the will of God; and not for sordid gain, but with eagerness; nor yet as lording it over those allotted to your charge, *but proving to be examples to the flock* (1 Pet. 5:1-3, emphasis added).

Who inspires us to deny ourselves and obey Christ? Is it those whose sermons we admire or those whose lives we admire? Uncommitted, soft-style pastors inspire no one to take up his cross. If such pastors do preach an occasional message of commitment to Christ, they must preach in vague generalities, otherwise their listeners would question their sincerity. *Most of the great Christian leaders of the past are not remembered for their sermons, but for their sacrifices.* Their example inspires us long after they are gone.

If a pastor is not setting an example of obedience as a true disciple of Jesus Christ, he is wasting his time delivering any sermons. Pastor, your example speaks ten times louder than your sermons. Are you inspiring people to deny themselves and follow Christ by denying yourself and following Christ?

But how can a pastor, by means of the example of his lifestyle, teach people who primarily know him as a Sunday-morning orator? The closest they actually get to seeing him live his life is a five-second handshake as they dutifully exit the church building. *Perhaps there is something not quite right about the modern pastoral model.*

The Weekly Sunday Morning Sermon

A pastor makes another wrong assumption if he thinks that his teaching responsibility is primarily one of delivering *weekly public lectures*. Jesus' teaching ministry consisted not only of public sermons (and for the most part, it seems they were fairly short), but also of private conversations that were initiated by His inquisitive disciples. Moreover, such conversations were not limited to one half-hour of one day of the week at a church building, but occurred along seashores, in homes, and walking along dusty roads, as Jesus lived His life in full view of His disciples. That same teaching model was followed by the apostles. After Pentecost, the twelve taught "in the temple and from *house to house*" (Acts 5:42, emphasis added). They had daily interaction with the community of believers. Paul also taught "publicly and from *house to house*" (Acts 20:20, emphasis added).

At this point, if you are a pastor, you may be comparing your teaching ministry to that of Jesus and the first apostles. Perhaps you are even beginning to wonder if what you have been doing is what God intends for you to do. Or are you just doing more of what hundreds of years of church traditions have taught you to do? If you *are* wondering, that is good. That is *very* good. That is the first step in the right direction.

Maybe you've thought even further. Perhaps you said to yourself, "Where could I ever find the time that such a ministry would require, teaching people from house to house, or involving them in my daily life so that I primarily influence them by my example?" Now that is a *wonderful* question, because it could lead you to keep wondering if there is something even more wrong with the modern concept of the pastor's role.

Perhaps you even thought to yourself, "I'm not sure I would want to live my life so closely with people in my church. I was taught in Bible school that a pastor should never get too close to his congregation. He must keep some distance in order to maintain their professional respect. He can't be close friends with them."

Such a thought reveals that something is indeed *very* wrong with the way things are so often done in the modern church. Jesus was so close with the twelve that one of them felt quite comfortable leaning his head on His breast at a common meal (see John 13:23-25). They literally lived together for several years. So much for keeping a professional distance from one's disciples in order to successfully minister to them!

A Comparison of Methods, Ancient and Modern

If the goal is to obey Jesus and make disciples, wouldn't we be wise to follow His methods for making disciples? They worked quite well for Him. They also worked quite well for the apostles who followed Him.

And how well are modern methods working to make disciples who obey all of Christ's commandments? When studies of American Christians, for example, repeatedly show that there is virtually no difference in the lifestyles of most professing Christians when compared to non-Christians, maybe its time to ask some questions and re-examine Scripture.

Here is a revealing question to ask ourselves: How did the early church succeed so well at making disciples without any church buildings, professionally-trained clergy, Bible schools and seminaries, hymnals and overhead projectors, wireless microphones and tape duplicators, Sunday school curriculums and youth ministries, worship teams and choirs, computers and copy machines, Christian radio and TV stations, hundreds of thousands of Christian book titles and even personally-owned Bibles? *They didn't need any of those things to make disciples, and neither did Jesus.* And because none of those things were essential then, *none are essential now.* They *could* be helpful, but none are essential. In fact, *many of those things can and actually do hinder us from making disciples.* Let me give you two examples.

Let's first consider the modern essential of having only Bible school- or seminary-trained pastors lead churches. *Such was an unheard of concept to Paul.* In some cities, after he planted churches, he departed for a few weeks or months, and then returned to appoint elders to oversee them (see, for example, Acts 13:14-14:23). That means those churches, absent from Paul's presence, had no formal eldership for some weeks or months, and that most elders were fairly young believers when they were appointed. They had nothing close to a two- or three-year formal education that prepared them for their job.

Thus, *the Bible teaches that pastors/elders/overseers do not need two or three years of formal education to be effective in their ministry.* No one can intelligently argue against that fact. Yet the modern requirement continually sends a message to every believer: "If you want to be a leader in the church, you need years of formal education."[9] This slows the process of

---

[9] The modern emphasis on professionally-trained clergy is in many ways a symptom of a larger disease, that of equating the gaining of knowledge with spiritual growth. We think that the person who knows more is more spiritually mature, whereas he may be less so, puffed up with pride from all he has learned. Paul did write, "knowledge makes arrogant" (1 Cor. 8:1). And surely the person who listens to daily boring lectures for two or three years is prepared to give weekly boring lectures!

creating leaders, thus slowing the making of disciples, thus slowing the expansion of the church. I wonder how well the American companies Avon and Amway would have saturated their targeted markets if they required every salesperson to move his or her family to another city to receive three years of formal training before he or she could be released to sell soap or perfume?

"But pastoring is such a difficult and complex task!" some say. "The Bible says we shouldn't put a new convert in the position of an overseer" (see 1 Tim. 3:6).

First, it comes down to the definition of a new convert, and clearly Paul's concept was different than ours, because he assigned people to the office of elder/pastor/overseer who had only been believers for a few months.

Second, one reason modern pastoring is so difficult and complex is because our entire system of church structure and ministry is so far removed from the biblical model. We've made it so complex that indeed, only a few super-human people can survive its demands!

"But God forbid that a church might be overseen by someone without a Bible school or seminary education!" others say. "That untrained overseer might lead his flock into false teaching!"

That apparently wasn't Paul's concern. The fact is that today we have Bible-school and seminary-trained clergy who don't believe in the virgin birth, who approve of homosexuality, who teach that God wants everyone to drive a luxury automobile, who claim that God predestines some people to be damned, or who say without flinching that one can gain heaven without obedience to Christ. The modern Bible school and seminary have often served to *further* false doctrine, and the professional clergy have served to further it more.

Church "commoners" are afraid to challenge them, because the professionals have been to seminary and can pull out more "proof texts." Moreover, those clergy have defined and divided their churches from the rest of the body of Christ by their peculiar doctrines, to the point of even advertising those differences by the very names they place on signs in front of their church buildings, sending a message to the world: "We are not like those other Christians." To add further injury, they label anyone who disagrees with their unchallengeable and divisive doctrines as "divisive." The Inquisition is still very much alive and well, led by men with diplomas. *Is this the example Jesus wants set by those who are supposed to be making disciples who are known to the world by their love for one another?*

Christians now choose churches based upon particular doctrines, and having the right theology has become the most important thing rather than having the right lifestyle, all because a biblical model has been abandoned.

A Biblical Alternative

Am I advocating taking three-month old believers and giving them oversight over churches (the very thing that Paul did)? Yes, but only if those believers meet the biblical requirements for elders/overseers, and *only if they are given oversight of churches that follow a biblical model.* That is, those churches must first of all be newly-planted gatherings that are submitted to a mature founding minister, such as an apostle, who can provide some oversight.[10] That way, newly-appointed elders are not entirely on their own.

Second, the congregations must be small enough to meet in homes, as did the early churches.[11] That makes churches much more manageable. That is probably why one of the requirements for elders/overseers is that they successfully manage their own households (see 1 Tim. 3:4-5). Managing a small "household of faith" is not much more challenging than managing a family.

Third, the congregation must consist of people who have responded in repentance to a *biblical* gospel, and who are thus genuine disciples of the Lord Jesus Christ. That eliminates all of the challenges that arise from trying to pastor sheep who are actually goats.

And fourth, the pastors/elders/overseers must follow their biblical role rather than a cultural role. That is, they must not hold a central, all-important, spotlight position as they do in most modern churches.[12] Rather, they must be single parts of the entire body, humble servants who teach by example and precept, and whose goal is to make disciples, not by being Sunday-morning orators, but by following Jesus' methods.

When that pattern is followed, then *some* three-month-old believers can oversee churches.

Church Buildings

What about church buildings? They are another modern "essential" that the early church did quite well without. Do they help in the process of disciple-making?

---

[10] In Paul's first letter to Timothy and his letter to Titus he mentions leaving them behind to appoint elders/overseers in the churches. So Timothy and Titus would have provided oversight to those elders/overseers for some time. They would have probably periodically met with the elders/overseers to disciple them, as Paul wrote, "The things which you have heard from me in the presence of many witnesses, these entrust to faithful men, who will be able to teach others also" (2 Tim. 2:2).

[11] See Acts 2:2, 46; 5:42; 8:3; 12:12; 16:40: 20:20; Rom. 16:5: 1 Cor. 16:19; Col. 4:15; Philem. 1:2; 2 John 1:10

[12] It is notable that Paul's letters to the churches are addressed to *everyone* in the various churches, and not to the elders or overseers. In only two of his letters to the churches does Paul even *mention* elders/pastors/overseers. In one instance they are included in the salutation, added as if he didn't want them to think that they were excluded recipients (see Phil. 1:1). In another instance Paul mentions pastors among a list of ministers who equip the saints (see Eph. 4:11-12). It is also especially notable how Paul makes no mention of the role of elders as he gives certain instructions that we would think would involve elders, such as administrating the Lord's Supper, and the resolution of conflicts between Christians. All of this points to the fact that elders/pastors did not hold the central, all-important role that they hold in most modern churches.

When I was a pastor, I often felt more like a realtor, banker, general contractor, and a professional fundraiser. I've dreamed of buildings, searched for buildings, remodeled old buildings, rented buildings, built new buildings and repaired them when God sent rain through their cracks. Buildings consume lots of time and energy. The reason I did so much that revolved around buildings is because I was certain, like most pastors, that there was no way to succeed without a building, a place for the church to gather.

Buildings also consume money, lots of it. (In the United States, some congregations spend tens of millions of dollars on their church buildings.) After my dreams of having buildings were fulfilled, I often dreamed of the day when the mortgages on my buildings would be paid off, so we could use all that money for ministry. It once occurred to me, as I was teaching my congregation about good stewardship and getting out of debt, that I had put the whole of us in debt together! (I was certainly teaching by example.)

Most church buildings are used for a couple of hours once or twice a week. What other organization in the entire world builds buildings that will be used so little? (Answer: only cults and false religions.)

That money-sucking hole causes a lot of problems. A pastor with a building always needs a flow of money, and that affects what he does. He is tempted to cater to the wealthy (who often give without any sacrifice), compromise any teaching that might offend some, and twist Scripture to make it serve his end. His sermons gravitate to subjects that don't hinder the money flow and encourage its increase. Because of that, Christians sometimes begin to think that the most important aspects of being believers are (1) paying tithes (which, incidentally, Jesus said is a minor commandment) and (2) attending church (where the tithes are collected each Sunday). This is hardly the picture of disciple making. Yet many pastors dream of having congregations where everyone would just do those two things. If a pastor had a congregation where just half of the people would do those two things, he could write books and sell his secrets to millions of other pastors!

The facts reveal this: *There is no record of any congregation buying or constructing a building in the book of Acts.* For the most part, believers met regularly in homes.[13] There were never any collections for building funds. There are no instructions in the epistles for church building construction. Additionally, no one thought of building a church building until Christianity was 300 years old, when the church married the world under Constantine's edict. Three-hundred years! Think of how long that is! And the church flourished and multiplied exponentially, even during times of intense persecution, all without buildings. Such phenomena have been re-

---

[13] See Acts 2:2, 46; 5:42; 8:3; 12:12; 16:40: 20:20; Rom. 16:5: 1 Cor. 16:19; Col. 4:15; Philem. 1:2; 2 John 1:10

peated many times in the centuries that followed. It has happened in China rather recently. There are probably more than a million house churches in China.

Eleven O'Clock Sunday *is* the Most Segregated Hour

Modern church facilities that copy the American model are expected to have, at a minimum, enough divided space to provide separate rooms for separate ministries to all age groups. In the early church, however, special segregated ministries for men, women, and all age groups of children were unheard of. The church was unified in every sense, not fragmented in every sense. The family unit was kept together, and parental spiritual responsibility was reinforced by church structure, rather than eroded by it as it has under modern church structure.

Does a church building contribute to the making of disciples or hinder it? Historically, disciple making throughout the centuries has succeeded better without them, and for many good reasons.

Meeting in houses, as did the early church for the first three centuries, where a joy-filled meal, teachings, songs, and spiritual gifts were shared for probably three to five hours, provided an environment for genuine spiritual growth for believers. Members of Christ's body felt like participators, as they sat facing each other, rather than how modern church attendees feel—like spectators in a theater, seated to look at the backs of each other's heads while trying not to miss the show on the stage. The casual atmosphere of a common meal led to transparency, authentic caring relationships and true fellowship, of no comparison to modern "fellowship," which too often is little more than a shallow shaking of hands with complete strangers in the next pew when the pastor gives the cue.

Teachings were more like question and answer sessions and open discussions among equals, rather than lectures given by those who wore odd clothing, spoke in theatrical voices, and stood high above the polite (and often bored) audience. Pastors didn't "prepare a weekly sermon." Anyone (certainly including the elders/pastors/overseers) might receive a teaching that the Holy Spirit gave.

When a house became cramped, the elder(s) wouldn't think of obtaining a bigger building. Rather, everyone knew that they had to split into two house meetings, and it was just a matter of finding the mind of the Spirit regarding where the new meeting should be held and who should provide the oversight. Fortunately, they didn't have to collect resumes' of strangers and church-growth theorists in order to scrutinize their philosophical or doctrinal slant; there were already aspiring overseers right among them, who had on-the-job training and already knew the members of their future little flock. That new house church had the opportunity to reach out evangelistically in a new area, and demonstrate to unbelievers what Christians were—people who loved one another. They could invite unbelievers to their meetings as easy as inviting them over for a meal.

The Blessed Pastor

No house church pastor/elder/overseer suffered ministerial "burnout" because of being overwhelmed with pastoral responsibilities, something that is widespread in the modern church. (One study reported that 1,800 pastors are leaving the ministry per month in the U.S.) He had only a small flock to look after, and if that flock supplied his financial needs so that the ministry was his vocation, he actually had time to pray, meditate, preach the gospel to unbelievers, assist the poor, visit and pray for the sick, and spend quality time equipping new disciples to do all those things right along with him. Church administration was simple.

He worked in unison with the other elders/pastors/overseers in his region. There was no striving to have "the biggest church in town" or compete with his fellow pastors to have the "best youth ministry" or the "most exciting kids' church program." People didn't go to church meetings to judge how good the worship team performed or how entertaining the pastor was. They had been born again and loved Jesus and His people. They loved to eat together and share whatever gifts God had given them. Their goal was to obey Jesus and be ready to stand at His judgment seat.

To be sure, there were problems in house churches, and those are addressed in the epistles. But so many of the problems that inevitably plague modern churches and hinder disciple making were unheard of in the early church, simply because their model of the local church was so different than what evolved after the third century and since the dark ages. Again, allow this fact to sink in: *There were no church buildings until the beginning of the fourth century. If you had lived during the first three centuries, how would your ministry have been different than it is now?*

In summary, the more closely we follow biblical patterns, the more effective we will be in accomplishing God's goal of making disciples. The greatest hindrances to disciple making in churches today stem from unbiblical structures and practices.

FOUR

House Churches

When people first hear of house churches, they often mistakenly imagine that the only difference between house churches and institutional churches is their size and their relative abilities to provide "ministry." People sometimes conclude that the house church cannot offer the quality of ministry provided by churches with buildings. But if one defines "ministry" as that which contributes to the making of disciples, helping them become like Christ and equipping them for service, then institutional churches have no advantage, and as I pointed out in the previous chapter, they may well be disadvantaged. Certainly house churches cannot provide the *quantity* of multi-faceted *activities* of institutional churches, but they can excel at providing *true* ministry.

Some people reject house churches as being true churches, simply because they lack an actual church building. Had those folks lived at any time during the first three hundred years of the church, they would have rejected every single church in the world as being a real church. The fact is that Jesus declared, "For where two or three have gathered together in My name, there I am in their midst" (Matt. 18:20). Jesus said nothing about *where* believers must gather. And even if there are only two believers, He promised to be present if they gather in His name. What Christ's disciples often do in restaurants, sharing a meal and exchanging truth, teaching and admonishing one another, is actually closer to the New Testament model of church gatherings than what often happens in many church buildings on Sunday mornings.

In the previous chapter, I enumerated some of the advantages that house churches have over institutional churches. I'd like to begin this chapter enumerating a few more reasons why the house church model is a very valid biblical alternative that can be quite effective in accomplishing the goal of making disciples. First, however, let me state at the outset that my purpose is not to attack institutional churches or their pastors. There are multitudes of godly and sincere pastors of institutional churches who are doing everything they can within their structures to please the Lord. I minister to thousands of institutional pastors every year, and I love and appreciate them very much. They are among the finest people in the world. And it is because I know how incredibly difficult their jobs are that I want to present an alternative that will help them suffer fewer casualties and be more effective and happy at the same time. The house church model is one that is biblical and that potentially lends itself to the effective making of disciples and expansion of God's kingdom. I have little doubt that the large majority of institutional pastors would be much happier, more effective and more fulfilled if they ministered in a house church setting.

I was an institutional pastor for more than twenty years and did my best then with what I knew. But it was after spending several months visiting many churches on Sunday mornings that I had my first glimpse of what it is like to attend church as a mere "layperson." It was an eye-opener, and I began to understand why so many people are so unenthusiastic about attending church. Like almost everyone except the pastor, I would sit there politely waiting for the service to be over. When it was, at least then I could interact with others as a participant rather than as a bored spectator. That experience was one of several catalysts that started me thinking about a better alternative, and I began my research on the house church model. I was amazed to discover that millions of house churches exist all over the world, and I concluded that house churches have some definite advantages over institutional churches.

Many of the pastors who read this book are not overseeing house churches, but institutional churches. I know that much of what I've written might be initially difficult for them to accept as it may seem so radical at first. But I ask that they give themselves some time to contemplate what I have to say, and I don't expect them to embrace everything overnight. It is for pastors I have written, motivated by love for them and their churches.

The Only Kind of Church in the Bible

First, and foremost, institutional churches that meet in special buildings are unknown to the New Testament, whereas house churches were clearly the norm in the early church:

> And when he realized this, he went to the *house* of Mary, the mother of John who was also called Mark, where many were gathered together and were praying (Acts 12:12, emphasis added).

> ...how I did not shrink from declaring to you anything that was profitable, and teaching you *publicly* [but not in

church buildings, obviously] and from *house to house*… (Acts 20:20, emphasis added)

Greet Prisca and Aquila….Also greet *the church that is in their house* (Rom. 16:3-5, emphasis added; see also Romans 16:14-15 for mention of two other probable house churches in Rome).

The churches of Asia greet you. Aquila and Prisca greet you heartily in the Lord, with *the church that is in their house* (1 Cor. 16:19, emphasis added).

Greet the brethren who are in Laodicea and also Nympha *and the church that is in her house* (Col. 4:15, emphasis added).

And to Apphia our sister, and to Archippus our fellow soldier, and to *the church in your house*… (Philem. 1:2, emphasis added).

It has been argued that the only reason the early church didn't build church buildings is because the church was still in her infancy. But that infancy lasted through quite a few *decades* of recorded New Testament history (and more than two centuries after it). So if the building of church buildings is a sign of the church's maturity, the church of the apostles of which we read in the book of Acts didn't *ever* mature.

I suggest that the reason none of the apostles ever built a church building is because such a thing, at bare minimum, would have been considered outside of God's will, since Jesus left no such example or instruction. He made disciples *without special buildings*, and He told His disciples to make disciples. They would have not seen any need for special buildings. It is just that simple. When Jesus told His disciples to go into all the world and make disciples, His disciples did not think to themselves, "What Jesus wants us to do is to build buildings and give sermons to people there once a week."

Additionally, building special buildings may even have been considered a direct violation of Christ's commandment not to lay up treasures on the earth, wasting money on something that was entirely unnecessary, and robbing God's kingdom of resources that could be used for transformational ministry.

Biblical Stewardship

This leads to the second advantage that house churches have over institutional churches: The house church model promotes godly stewardship of its members' resources, which is certainly an extremely important aspect of discipleship.[14] No money is wasted on church buildings, owning,

[14] See "Jesus on Money" under *Biblical Topics* on the home page of www.shepherdserve.org.

renting, repairing, expanding, remodeling, heating or cooling them. Consequently, what would have been wasted on buildings can be used to feed and clothe the poor, spread the gospel, and make disciples, *just as it did in the book of Acts*. Think of the good that could have been done for God's kingdom if the billions of dollars spent on church buildings had been used for spreading the gospel and serving the poor! It is almost unimaginable.

Moreover, house churches that consist of no more than twenty people could actually be overseen by "tent-making" (that is, "non-paid") elders/pastors/overseers, a real possibility when there are a number of mature believers in a house church. Such churches would require virtually no money at all to operate.

Of course, the Bible seems to indicate that elders/pastors/overseers *should* be paid in proportion to their labor, so those who devote their full time to ministry should make their full living from it (see 1 Tim. 5:17-18). Ten wage earners in a house church who tithe can support one pastor at their average standard of living. Five tithers in a house church can free up a pastor to devote half his workweek to his ministry.

Following the house church model, money that would be used on buildings is freed to support pastors, and so institutional pastors should not think that the proliferation of house churches threatens their job security. Rather, it could mean that many other men and women could realize the desire God has placed in their hearts to serve Him in vocational ministry.[15] That in turn, would help accomplish the goal of making disciples. Moreover, a house church with twenty wage earners could potentially give one half of its income to mission outreach and the poor.[16]

If an institutional church transitioned to a network of house churches, the people who might lose their paying jobs would be church administrative and program support staff and perhaps some staff members with specialty ministries (for example, child and youth ministers in larger churches) who would be unwilling to trade ministries that have little biblical basis for ministries that do. House churches don't need child and youth ministers because parents are given that responsibility in the Bible, and people in house churches generally strive to follow the Bible rather than the norms of cultural Christianity. Christian youth who don't have Christian parents can be incorporated into house churches and discipled just as they are incorporated into institutional churches. Does anyone wonder why there are no "youth pastors" or "children's pastors" mentioned in the New Testament? Such ministries didn't exist for the first 1900 years

[15] Although it may sound radical, the only real reason that church buildings are needed is because of the lack of leaders who would oversee smaller house churches, which is the result of poor discipleship of potential leaders within institutional churches. Could it be that pastors of large institutional churches are actually guilty of robbing God-called pastors within their congregations of their rightful ministries? Yes.

[16] This one-to-ten or -twenty ratio should not be considered pastoral overkill in light of Jesus' biblical model of discipling twelve men and Moses' delegated judges over ten people (see Ex. 18:25). Most institutional pastors oversee many more people than they can effectively disciple on their own.

of Christianity. Why are they suddenly essential now, and primarily in wealthy western countries?[17]

Finally, in poorer nations in particular, pastors often find it impossible to rent or own church buildings without being subsidized by Western Christians. The undesirable consequences of this dependency are manifold. The fact is, however, that for 300 years the problem didn't exist in Christianity. If you are pastor in a developing nation whose congregation can't afford your own church building, you don't need to flatter some visiting American in hopes of striking gold. God has already solved your problem. You really don't need a church building to make disciples successfully. Follow the biblical model.

The End of Fragmented Families

Another advantage that house churches have is this: they excel at discipling children and teens. One of the great falsehoods perpetrated by institutional churches today (especially large ones in United States) is that they provide wonderful ministries to children and youth. Yet they hide the fact that the large majority of the children who experience years of fun attending their exciting children and youth ministries never return to church again upon "leaving the nest." (Ask any youth pastor for the statistics—he should know them.)

Additionally, churches that have youth pastors and children's pastors continually promote the falsehood to parents that they are either incapable or not responsible for their children's spiritual training. Again, "We'll take care of your children's spiritual training. We're the trained professionals."

The system as it stands breeds failure, because it creates a cycle of ever-increasing compromise. It begins with parents who are looking for churches that their kids enjoy. If teenager Johnny says on the ride home that he had fun in church, the parents are thrilled, because they equate Johnny's enjoying church with Johnny's being interesting in spiritual things. They are often dead wrong.

Success-driven senior pastors want their churches to grow, and so youth and children's pastors often leave staff meetings feeling pressure to create "relevant" programs that kids think are fun. ("Relevant" is always secondary to "fun," and "relevant" doesn't necessarily mean, "Lead kids to repent, believe, and obey Jesus' commandments.") If the kids can be sold the program, naïve' parents will return (with their money), and the church will grow.

The success of youth groups in particular is measured by attendance numbers. Youth pastors find themselves doing whatever it takes to pack

---

[17] We might also question why there are no "senior pastors," "associate pastors" or "assistant pastors" mentioned in Scripture. Again, these titles that seem so essential in the modern church because of *its* structure were unnecessary in the early church because of *its* structure. House churches of twenty people don't need senior, associate and assistant pastors.

them in, and that too often means compromising genuine spirituality. Pity the poor youth pastor who hears reports that parents are murmuring to the senior pastor that their kids are complaining about his boring or condemning messages.

But what a blessing youth pastors could be in the body of Christ if they became house church leaders. They normally already have great relational skills and possess young zeal and no lack of energy. Many of them are only youth pastors because that is the required first step for them to gradually acquire the super-human skills required to survive being senior pastors. Most are more than capable of pastoring a house church. What they've been doing in their youth group could well be closer to the biblical model of a church than what has been going on in the main sanctuary of the church! The same could be said of children's pastors, who might be miles ahead of most senior pastors in being able to serve in house churches where everyone, including children, sits in one small circle, all participating and even enjoying some food together.

Children and teens are *naturally* better discipled in house churches, as they experience true Christian community and have opportunities to participate, ask questions, and relate to people of other ages, all as part of a Christian family. In institutional churches they are continually exposed to a big show and "fun" learning, experience very little if any true community, are often made very aware of pervasive hypocrisy, and just as in school, only learn to relate to their peers.

But in a gathering of all ages, what about babies who cry or little children who become restless?

They should always be enjoyed, and practical steps can be taken to handle them when they pose problems. They can, for example, be taken to another room to be entertained, or given crayons and paper to color on the floor. In the community of a house church, the babies and children are not problems who are dropped off at the nursery staffed by a stranger. They are loved by everyone in their extended family. A baby who starts to cry in an institutional church is often a disturbance to the formality of the service and an embarrassment to the parents who may feel the disapproving stares of strangers. A baby who starts to cry in a house church is surrounded by his family, and no one minds the reminder that a little gift from God is in their midst, a person they've all held in their arms.

Parents whose children are uncontrolled can be gently taught by other parents what they need to know. Again, believers have genuine, caring relationships. They aren't gossiping about one another as is so often the case in an institutional church. They know and love each other.

Happy Pastors

Having pastored churches for two decades, having spoken to tens of thousands of pastors around the world, and having many pastors as personal friends, I think I can say that I know something about the demands of pastoring a modern church. Like every pastor of an institutional church, I have experienced the "dark side" of the ministry. It can be *very* dark at times. In fact, "brutal" might be a better word to describe it.

The expectations that most pastors encounter naturally create incredible stresses that sometimes even ruin their relationships within their own families. Pastors are discouraged for many reasons. They must be politicians, judges, employers, psychologists, activity directors, building contractors, marriage counselors, public speakers, managers, mind readers and administrators. They often find themselves in fierce competition with other pastors to gain a larger slice of the body of Christ. They have little time for personal spiritual disciplines. Many feel trapped in their vocation and are underpaid. Their congregations are their customers and their employers. Sometimes those employers and customers can make life very difficult.

By comparison, the house church pastor has it easy. First, if he leads an exemplary life of a true disciple and teaches uncompromised obedience to Jesus' commandments, few goats will have an interest in being part of his group. In fact, just meeting in houses is probably enough to keep many goats away. So he'll mostly have sheep to pastor.

Second, he can love and disciple all his sheep on a personal basis, because he only has twelve to twenty adults to oversee. He can enjoy real closeness with them, as he is like the father of a family. He can give them the time they deserve. I remember when I was an institutional pastor, I often felt alone. I couldn't get close with anyone within my congregation, lest others resent me for not including them in my close circle of friends or become jealous of those within that circle. I longed for genuine closeness with other believers, but wouldn't risk the potential price of gaining true friends.

In the close-knit family of a house church, the members naturally help keep the pastor accountable, as he is their close friend, not an actor on a stage.

The house church pastor can spend time developing leaders of future house churches, so when the time comes to multiply, leaders are ready. He doesn't have to watch his most promising future leaders take their gifts from the church to a Bible school in another place.

He may well have time to develop other ministry outside his local congregation. Perhaps he could minister in prisons, personal care homes or be involved in one-on-one evangelism to refugees or businesspeople. Depending on his experience, he could conceivably devote some of his time to planting other house churches, or mentoring younger house church pastors who have been raised up under his ministry.

He feels no pressure to be a Sunday-morning performer. He never needs to prepare a three-point sermon on a Saturday night, wondering how he can possibly satisfy so many people who are at so many different levels of spiritual growth.[18] He can delight in watching the Holy Spirit use everyone at the gatherings and encourage them to use their gifts. He can be absent from meetings and everything works well even without him.

He has no building to distract him and no employees to manage.

He has no reason to compete with other local pastors.

There is no "church board" that exists to make his life miserable and through which political infighting becomes common.

In short, he can be what he is called to be by God, and not what is imposed on him by cultural Christianity. He is not the lead actor, the president of a company, or the center of the hub. He is a disciple maker, an equipper of the saints.

Happy Sheep

Everything about true, biblical house churches is what true believers desire and enjoy.

All true believers long for genuine relationships with other believers, because God's love has been shed abroad in their hearts. Such relationships are part and parcel of house churches. It is what the Bible refers to as *fellowship*, genuine sharing of one's life with other brothers and sisters. House churches create an environment where believers can do what believers are supposed to do, which is found in the many New Testament "one another" passages. In the house church setting, believers can exhort, encourage, edify, comfort, teach, serve and pray for one another. They can provoke each other to love and good works, confess their sins to each other, bear one another's burdens, and admonish one another with psalms, hymns and spiritual songs. They can weep with those who weep and rejoice with those who rejoice. Such things don't occur very often during the Sunday morning meetings of institutional churches where believers sit and watch. As one house church member told me, "When someone is sick within our body, I don't take a meal to a stranger's house because I signed up for the 'meal ministry.' I naturally take a meal to someone I know and love."

True believers enjoy interaction and involvement with each other. Passively sitting and listening to irrelevant or redundant sermons year after year insults their intelligence and spirituality. Rather, they prefer having an opportunity to share the personal insights they gain concerning God and His Word, and house churches provide that opportunity. Following a biblical model rather than a cultural one, each person "has a psalm, has

---

[18] Many pastors never become good orators, even though they are God-called, caring servants of Christ. In fact, is it being too harsh to say that many sermons by pastors are boring, or at least boring at times? What one church-critic refers to as "the thousand-yard stare" is very common among the pew sitters. But those same pastors who are boring orators are often very good conversationalists, and people rarely become bored while they are engaged in conversation with one another. That is why the interactive teaching at house churches is usually always interesting. Time flies during such times, as contrasted with the many covert glances at wristwatches during church sermons. House church pastors don't have to worry about being boring.

a teaching, has a revelation, has a tongue, has an interpretation" (1 Cor. 14:26). In house churches, no one is lost in the crowd or excluded by a church clique.

True believers desire to be used by God in service. In a house church, there is opportunity for everyone to be used to bless others, and responsibilities are shared among all, so that no one experiences the burnout that is common among committed members of institutional churches. At the minimum, everyone can bring food to share for the common meal, what Scripture seems to refer to as the "love feast" (Jude 1:12). For many house churches, that meal follows the example of the original Lord's Supper, which was part of an actual Passover meal. The Lord's Supper is not, as a little boy referred to it in a previous institutional church I pastored, "God's holy snack." The idea of eating a small wafer and drinking a little juice among strangers during a few seconds of a church service is utterly foreign to the Bible and to biblical house churches. The sacramental meaning of Communion is enhanced manifold during a shared meal among disciples who love each other.

In a house church, worship is simple, sincere and participatory, not a performance. True believers love to worship God in spirit and truth.

Doctrinal Balance and Toleration

In the casual and open forums of small church gatherings, all teaching can be scrutinized by anyone who can read. Brothers and sisters who know and love each other are inclined to consider respectfully viewpoints that differ from theirs, and even if the group doesn't reach a consensus, love, not doctrine, still binds them together. Any teaching by any person in the group, including elders/pastors/overseers, is subject to loving examination by anyone else, because the Teacher indwells every member (see 1 John 2:27). The built-in checks and balances of a biblical model help prevent it from becoming doctrinally derailed.

This is quite a contrast from the norm in modern institutional churches, where church doctrine is established from the start and not to be challenged. Consequently, bad doctrines endure indefinitely, and doctrine becomes the litmus test of acceptance. For this same reason, one point in a single sermon can result in the immediate exodus of dissenters, who all jump ship to temporarily find some "like-minded believers." They know there is no sense in even talking to the pastor about their doctrinal disagreement. Even if he was persuaded to change his viewpoint, he would have to keep it hidden from many in the church as well as from those of higher rank within his denomination. Doctrinal differences within institutional churches produce pastors who are some of the most skilled politicians in the world, orators who speak in vague generalities and avoid anything that could result in controversy, leading everyone to think he is in their camp.

A Modern Trend

Interestingly, more and more institutional churches are developing small group structures within their institutional models, recognizing their value in discipleship. Some churches go even further, basing their core structure on small groups, considering them to be the most important aspect of their ministry. Larger "celebratory meetings" are secondary in importance to the small groups (at least in theory).

These are steps in the right direction, and God blesses such steps, as His blessing upon us is proportionate to the degree that we line up with His will. Indeed, "cell churches" are better structured than standard institutional churches to facilitate disciple making. They stand halfway between the institutional church model and the house church model, combining elements of both.

How do modern institutional churches with small groups compare with ancient and modern house churches? There are some differences.

For example, small groups within institutional churches unfortunately sometimes serve to promote much that is wrong within institutional churches, especially when the real motive for starting small group ministry is to build the senior pastor's church kingdom. He consequently uses people for his own ends, and small groups fit that plan nicely. When this occurs, small group leaders are selected for their tested loyalty to the mother church, and they can't be too gifted or charismatic, lest the devil fill their heads with ideas that they can make it on their own. This kind of policy hinders the effectiveness of small groups and, just like in any other institutional church, drives off the truly called and aspiring leaders to Bible schools and seminaries, robbing the church of true gifts, and taking such people to a place where they will be lecture-taught rather than on-the-job discipled.

Small groups in institutional churches often evolve into little more than fellowship groups. Disciple making really doesn't occur. Since people are supposedly being spiritually fed on Sunday mornings, small groups sometimes focus on other things besides God's Word, not wanting a repeat of Sunday mornings.

Small groups in institutional churches are often organized by a staff member of the church, rather than birthed by the Spirit. They become one more program among many other church programs. People are put together based on ages, social status, background, interests, marital status or geographical location. Goats are often mixed with sheep. All of this fleshly organization does not help believers learn to love each other in spite of their differences. Remember that many of the early churches were a mixture of Jews and Gentiles. They regularly shared meals together, something forbidden by Jewish tradition. What a learning experience their meetings must have been! What opportunities to walk in love! What testimonies of the power of the gospel! So why do we think we must divide everyone into homogeneous groups to insure success of small groups?

Institutional churches with small groups still have the Sunday morning performance, where spectators watch the pros perform. Small groups are never permitted to meet when there are "real" church services, indicating to all that it is really the institutional services that are most important. Because of that message, many, if not the majority, of Sunday morning attendees will not get involved with a small group even if encouraged to do so, seeing them as optional. They are satisfied that they are attending the most important weekly service. So the small group concept may be promoted as being somewhat significant, but not nearly as significant as the Sunday institutional service. The best opportunity for real fellowship, discipleship and spiritual growth is effectively downplayed. The wrong message is sent. The institutional service is still king.

More Differences

Institutional churches with small groups are still structured like a corporation pyramid, where everyone knows his place in the hierarchy. The people at the top may call themselves "servant leaders," but they often are more like chief executive officers who are responsible to make executive decisions. The larger the church, the more distant the pastor is from the members of his flock. If he is a true pastor and you can get him to admit the truth in an unguarded moment, he will usually tell you he was happier when he pastored a smaller flock.

Similarly, institutional churches with small groups still promote the clergy-laity division. Small group leaders are always in a subordinate class to the paid professionals. Bible study lessons are often passed down or approved by clergy, since small group leaders can't be trusted with too much authority. Small groups are not permitted to practice the Lord's Supper or baptize. These sacred duties are reserved for the elite class with the titles and diplomas. Those who are called to vocational ministry within the body must go to a Bible school or seminary to be qualified for "real" ministry to join the elite group.

Small groups within institutional churches are sometimes nothing more than mini-church services, lasting no longer than 60 to 90 minutes, where one gifted person leads worship and another gifted person gives the approved teaching. There is little room for the Spirit to use others, distribute gifts, or develop ministers.

People are often not seriously committed to small groups in institutional churches, attending sporadically, and groups are sometimes designed to be temporary, and so the depth of community is lesser than in house churches.

Small groups in institutional churches ordinarily meet during the week so as not to crowd the weekend with another church meeting. Consequently, a midweek small group is normally time-limited to no longer than two hours for those who can attend, and prohibitive for those who have school-age children or who must travel any significant distance.

Even when institutional churches promote small group ministry, there is still a building on which to waste money. In fact, if the small group program adds people to the church, even more money ends up being wasted on building programs. Additionally, organized small groups within institutional churches often require at least one additional paid staff person. That means more money for another church program.

Perhaps worst of all, pastors of institutional churches with small groups are often extremely limited in their personal disciple making. They are so busy with their many responsibilities and find little time for one-on-one discipleship. About the closest they can get is discipling the small group leaders, but even that is often limited to a once-a-month meeting.

All of this is to say that house churches, in my opinion, are more biblical and effective in making and multiplying disciples and disciple-makers. I realize, however, that my opinion is not going to change hundreds of years of church tradition very quickly. So I urge institutional pastors to do *something* in the direction of moving their churches to a more biblical model of disciple-making.[19] They could consider personally discipling future leaders or initiating small group ministry. They could hold an "early-church Sunday" when the church building would be closed and everyone would share a meal in homes and attempt to meet like Christians did for the first three centuries.

Pastors who have small groups within their churches could consider releasing some of those small groups to form house churches and see what happens. If small groups are healthy and lead by God-called pastors/elders/overseers, they should be able to operate on their own. They don't need the mother church any more than any non-affiliated young church needs that mother church. Why not set them free?[20] The member's money that is going to the mother church could support the pastor of the house church.

Does my endorsement of house churches mean that there is nothing good to say about institutional churches? Absolutely not. To the degree that disciples who obey Christ are being made in institutional churches, they are to be commended. Their practices and structure, however, can sometimes be more of hindrance than a help to reaching the goal Christ has set before us, and they are often pastor killers.

---

[19] One of my favorite definitions of the word *insanity* is this: *Doing the same thing repeatedly and hoping for different results.* Pastors can teach for years about every member's responsibility to be involved in disciple-making, but unless they do something to change formats or structures, people will continue to come to church to sit, listen and go home. Pastor, if you continue to do what has not changed people in the past, it will not change people in the future. Change what you are doing!

[20] Of course, the primary reason that many pastors are adverse to this idea is because they are actually building their own kingdoms, not God's kingdom.

What Happens at a House Church Gathering?

Not every house church needs to be structured the same, and there is room for a lot of variation. Every house church should reflect its own cultural and social nuances—one reason why house churches can be very effective in evangelism, especially in countries that have no Christian cultural tradition. House church members don't invite their neighbors to a church building that is completely foreign to them where they would be involved in rituals that are completely foreign to them—major obstacles to conversions. Rather, they invite their neighbors to a meal with their friends.

The common meal is generally a major component of a house church meeting. For many house churches, that meal includes or is the Lord's Supper, and each individual house church can decide how to best bring out its spiritual significance. As previously mentioned, the *original* Lord's Supper began as an actual Passover meal that was packed with spiritual significance by itself. Celebrating the Lord's Supper as a meal or part of a meal is the apparent pattern followed when the early believers gathered. We read of the early Christians:

> And they were continually devoting themselves to the apostles' teaching and to fellowship, *to the breaking of bread* and to prayer....And day by day continuing with one mind in the temple, and *breaking bread from house to house, they were taking their meals together with gladness and sincerity of heart* (Acts 2:42, 46, emphasis added).

The early Christians were literally taking loaves of bread, breaking them, and sharing them together, something that was done at practically every meal in their culture. Could that breaking of bread during a meal have had some spiritual significance to the early Christians? The Bible doesn't say for certain. However, William Barclay writes in his book, *The Lord's Supper*, "It is not in doubt that the Lord's Supper began as a family meal or a meal of friends in a private house....The idea of a tiny piece of bread and a sip of wine bears no relation at all to the Lord's Supper as it originally was....The Lord's Supper was originally a family meal in a household of friends." It is amazing that every modern biblical scholar agrees with Barclay, yet the church still follows its tradition rather than God's Word on this issue!

Jesus commanded His disciples to teach their disciples to obey all that He had commanded them, so when He commanded them to eat bread and drink wine together in remembrance of Him, they would have taught their disciples to do the same. Could that have been done at common meals? It certainly seems as if it was when we read some of Paul's words to the Corinthians believers:

> Therefore when you *meet together* [and he is not talking about meeting in church buildings, because there were none] it is not to eat the *Lord's Supper*, for in your eating each one takes *his own supper* first; and one is hungry and another is drunk (1 Cor. 11:20-21, emphasis added).

How would such words make any sense if Paul was speaking about the Lord's Supper as it is practiced in modern churches? Have you ever heard of the problem of anyone in a modern church service taking his own supper first, and one being hungry while another one is drunk in conjunction with the Lord's Supper? Such words would only make sense if the Lord's Supper was done in conjunction with a real meal. Paul continues:

> What! Do you not have houses in which to eat and drink? Or do you despise the church of God [remember, Paul was not writing about a church building, but a gathering of people, the church of God], and shame those who have nothing? What shall I say to you? Shall I praise you? In this I will not praise you (1 Cor. 11:22).

How would people be shamed who had nothing if what was being done was not in the context of an actual meal? Paul was pointing out the fact that some of the Corinthian believers who arrived earliest at their gatherings ate their own meal without waiting for the others to arrive. When some arrived who were perhaps so poor that they brought no food to share at the common meal, they were not only left hungry, but also shamed because it was so obvious they had brought nothing.

Immediately after this, Paul wrote more about the Lord's Supper, a sacrament that he "received from the Lord" (1 Cor. 11:23), and he recounted what happened at the first Lord's Supper (see 1 Cor. 11:24-25). He then warned the Corinthians against partaking of the Lord's Supper in an unworthy manner, stating that if they didn't judge themselves, they could actually eat and drink judgment upon themselves in the form of weakness, sickness and even premature death (see 1 Cor. 11:26-32).

He then concluded,

> So then, my brethren, when you come together to eat, wait for one another. If anyone is hungry, let him eat at home, so that you may not come together for judgment (1 Cor. 11:33-34).

Contextually, the offense being committed at the Lord's Supper was inconsideration of other believers. Paul again warned that those who were eating their own supper first at what was supposed to be a shared, common meal, were in danger of being judged (or disciplined) by God. The solution was simple. If one was so hungry that he couldn't wait for the others, he should eat something before he came to the gathering. And those who arrived earliest should wait for those who arrived later for the meal, a meal that apparently included or was the Lord's Supper.

When we look at the entire passage, it seems clear Paul was saying that if it was the *Lord's* Supper that was being eaten, it would be done in a way that it was pleasing to the *Lord*, reflecting love and consideration for each other.

In any case, it is crystal clear that the early church practiced the Lord's Supper as part of a common meal in homes without an officiating clergy. Why don't we?

Bread and Wine

The nature of the elements of the Lord's Supper are not the most important thing. If we must strive for perfect imitation of the original Lord's Supper, we would have to know the exact ingredients of the bread and the exact kind of grapes from which the original wine was made. (Some of the church fathers during the first few centuries strictly prescribed that the wine had to be diluted with water, otherwise the Eucharist was being practiced improperly.)

Bread and wine were some of the most common elements of the ancient Jewish meals. Jesus gave profound significance to two things that were incredibly common, foods that practically everyone consumed each day. Had He visited another culture at a different time in history, the first Lord's Supper may have consisted of cheese and goat's milk, or rice cakes and pineapple juice. So any food and drink could potentially represent His body and blood at a common meal shared among His disciples. The important thing is the spiritual significance. Let us not neglect the spirit of the law while succeeding at keeping the letter of it!

It is not necessary that common meals be deathly solemn. The early Christians, as we already read, broke "bread from house to house…taking their meals together with *gladness* and sincerity of heart" (Acts 2:46, emphasis added). Seriousness, however, is certainly appropriate during that portion of the meal when Jesus' sacrifice is remembered and the elements are consumed. Self-examination is always appropriate before eating the Lord's Supper, as indicated by Paul's solemn words of warning to the Corinthian believers in 1 Corinthians 11:17-34. Any transgression of Christ's commandment to love one another is an invitation to God's discipline. Any and all strife and division should be resolved before the meal. Every believer should examine himself and confess any sins, which would be the equivalent of "judging yourself," to use Paul's words.

The Spirit Manifested Through the Body

The common meal could occur before or after a meeting in which worship, teachings and spiritual gifts are shared. It is up to each individual house church to determine its format, and formats can vary from gathering to gathering of the same house church.

It is very clear from Scripture that the early church gatherings were quite different from modern institutional church services. In particular, 1 Corinthians 11-14 gives us an abundance of insight into what happened when the early Christians gathered, and there isn't any reason to think that the same format cannot and should not be followed today. It is also clear that what occurred in the early church gatherings described by Paul could only have happened in small group settings. What Paul described could not have occurred logistically in a large meeting.

I will be the first to admit that I don't understand all that Paul wrote within those four chapters of 1 Corinthians. However, it seems obvious that the most outstanding characteristic of the gatherings described in 1 Corinthians 11-14 was the Holy Spirit's presence among them and His manifestation through members of the body. He gave gifts to individuals for the edification of the entire body.

Paul lists at least nine spiritual gifts: prophecy, tongues, interpretation of tongues, the word of knowledge, the word of wisdom, discerning of spirits, gifts of healings, faith, and working of miracles. He does not state that all of these gifts were manifested at every gathering, but certainly implies the possibility of their operation and seems to summarize some of the more common manifestations of the Spirit in 1 Corinthians 14:26:

> What is the outcome then, brethren? When you assemble, each one has a psalm, has a teaching, has a revelation, has a tongue, has an interpretation. Let all things be done for edification.

Let's consider all five of these common manifestations, and in a later chapter more thoroughly consider the nine gifts of the Spirit listed in 1 Corinthians 12:8-10.

First on the list is the psalm. Spirit-given psalms are mentioned by Paul in two of his other letters to churches, underscoring their place in Christian gatherings.

> And do not get drunk with wine, for that is dissipation, but be filled with the Spirit, speaking to one another in psalms and hymns and spiritual songs, singing and making melody with your heart to the Lord (Eph. 5:18-19).

> Let the word of Christ richly dwell within you, with all wisdom teaching and admonishing one another with psalms and hymns and spiritual songs, singing with thankfulness in your hearts to God (Col. 3:16).

The difference between psalms, hymns and spiritual songs is unclear, but the primary point is that all are based on Christ's words, are Spirit-inspired, and should be sung by believers to teach and admonish one another. Certainly many of the hymns and choruses that believers have sung throughout church history would fall into one of those categories. Unfortunately, too many modern hymns and choruses lack biblical depth, indicating they were not Spirit-given, and because they are so shallow, have no real value to teach and admonish believers. Nevertheless, believers who gather in house churches should expect that the Spirit will not only inspire individual members to lead well-known Christian songs, old and new, but will also give special songs to some of the members that can be utilized for the common edification. Indeed, how special it is for churches to have their own Spirit-given songs!

Teaching

Second on Paul's list is teaching. This again indicates that anyone might share a Spirit-inspired teaching at a gathering. Of course, every teaching would be judged to see if it lined up with the apostles' teaching (as everyone was devoted to that: see Acts 2:42) and we should do the same today. But note that there is no indication here or anywhere in the New Testament that the same person gave a sermon every week when local churches met, dominating the gathering.

There were, in Jerusalem, larger gatherings at the Temple at which the apostles taught. We know that elders were also given teaching responsibility in churches, and that some people are called to a teaching ministry. Paul did a lot of teaching, publicly and from house to house (see Acts 20:20). In the small gatherings of believers, however, the Holy Spirit might use others to teach besides apostles, elders or teachers.

When it comes to teaching, it would seem that we would be greatly advantaged over the early church to be able to bring personal copies of the Bible with us to our gatherings. On the other hand, perhaps our easy access to the Bible has helped us elevate doctrine above loving God with all our hearts and loving our neighbors as ourselves, robbing us of the very life that God's Word was meant to impart. We have been doctrinalized to death. Many small group Bible studies are every bit as irrelevant and boring as Sunday morning sermons. A good rule to follow in regard to house church teachings is this: If the older children aren't hiding their boredom, the adults are probably hiding theirs. Kids are great truth barometers.

Revelation

Third, Paul lists "revelation." That could mean anything that is revealed by God to some member of the body. For example, Paul specifically mentions how an unbeliever might visit a Christian gathering and have "the secrets of heart…disclosed" by means of gifts of prophecy. The result is that he would be "convicted" and "called to account" and "will fall on his face and worship God, declaring that God is certainly among you" (1 Cor. 14:24-25).

Here we once again see that the real presence of the Holy Spirit was an expected feature of church gatherings, and that supernatural things would occur because of His presence. The early Christians really believed Jesus' promise that, "Where two or three have gathered together in My name, there I am in their midst" (Matt. 18:20). If Jesus Himself was in their midst, miracles could happen. They literally "worshipped in the Spirit of God" (Phil. 3:3).

In any case, prophecy, which I will say more about shortly, might contain revelation about people's hearts. But revelation could be given about other things and by other means, such as through dreams or visions (see Acts 2:17).

Tongues and Interpretation

Fourth, Paul listed two gifts that work together, tongues and the interpretation of tongues. In Corinth, there was an overabundance and abuse of speaking in tongues. Namely, people were speaking in tongues during the church gatherings and there was no interpretation, so no one knew what was being said. We might wonder how the Corinthians could be blamed, as it would seem the fault of the Holy Spirit for giving people the gift of tongues without giving anyone the gift of interpretation. There is a very satisfactory answer to that question which I will address in a later chapter. In any case, Paul did not forbid speaking in tongues (as do many institutional churches). Rather, he forbade the forbidding of speaking in tongues, and declared this was the Lord's commandment (see 1 Cor. 14:37-39)![21] It was a gift that, when used properly, could edify the body and affirm God's supernatural presence in their midst. It was God speaking through people, reminding them of His truth and His will.

Paul did make a strong case in chapter 14 for the superiority of prophecy over non-interpreted tongues-speaking. He strongly encouraged the Corinthians to desire to prophesy, and this indicates that gifts of the Spirit are more likely to be manifested among those who desire them. Similarly, Paul admonished the Thessalonian believers, "Do not quench the Spirit; do not despise prophetic utterances" (1 Thes. 5:19). This indicates that believers can "quench" or "put out the fire of" the Spirit by harboring a wrong attitude towards the gift of prophecy. That is, no doubt, why the gift of prophecy is so rarely manifested among most believers today.

[21] I am aware, of course, that there are those who relegate all supernatural manifestations of the Spirit to the first century, at which time they supposedly ceased. Thus, we have no reason to seek what the early church experienced, and speaking in tongues is no longer valid. I have little sympathy with such people who are like modern-day Sadducees. As one who has on several occasions praised God in Japanese according to Japanese speakers who heard me, and having never learned Japanese, I know these gifts have not ceased to be given by the Holy Spirit. I also wonder why these modern Sadducees maintain the Holy Spirit still calls, convicts and regenerates sinners, but deny the Spirit's work beyond those miracles. This kind of "theology" is the product of human unbelief and disobedience, has no scriptural support, and actually works against Christ's goal. It is direct disobedience to Christ according to what Paul wrote in 1 Cor. 14:37.

How to Start

House churches are birthed by the Holy Spirit through the ministry of a house-church planter or an elder/pastor/overseer who is given a vision for a house church by God. Keep in mind that a biblical elder/pastor/overseer may be what the institutional church refers to as a mature layperson. No house church planter needs a formal ministry education.

Once the vision for a house church is given by the Spirit to the founder, he needs to seek the Lord regarding others who might join him. The Lord will bring him in contact with people with a similar vision, confirming his leading. Or he may be led to receptive unbelievers whom he can lead to Christ and then disciple in a house church.

Those who are just beginning a house church adventure should anticipate that it will take time for the members to feel comfortable with each other and learn to relate and flow with the Spirit. It will be trial and error along the way. The concepts of every-member participation, biblical servant leadership, equipping elders, the Holy Spirit's leading and gifts, a common meal, and a casual yet spiritual atmosphere are quite foreign to those who are only familiar with institutional church services. Thus the application of grace and patience is wise as a new house church is birthed. The initial format may be more a home Bible study, with one person leading worship, another sharing a prepared teaching, and then closing with an opportunity for corporate prayer, fellowship and a meal. However, as the biblical format for house churches is studied by the group, the elder/pastor/overseer should encourage the members to strive for God's best. Then, enjoy the ride!

House church meetings can circulate from one member's house to another each week, or one person can open his home each week. Some house churches occasionally move to scenic outdoor spots when the weather is nice. The meeting time and place does not have to be Sunday morning, but anytime that best works for the members. Finally, it is best to start small, with no more than twelve people.

How to Transition from Institution to House Church

Most likely, many of the pastors who are reading this are working within the structures of institutional churches, and perhaps you, dear reader, are one of them. If I've touched a chord within you that longs for the kind of church I've been describing, then you are already wondering how you can make the transition. Let me encourage you to take your time. Start by teaching only biblical truth and doing whatever you can within the framework of your existing structure to make disciples who obey Jesus' commandments. True disciples are much more likely to want to make the transition to a biblical church structure as they understand it. Goats and religious people are much more likely to resist any such transitions.

Second, study what Scripture says on the subject and teach your congregation about house church structures and their inherent blessings. You could eventually cancel your midweek or Sunday evening church service to begin weekly cell meetings in homes overseen by mature believers. Encourage everyone to attend. Increasingly pattern those meetings to follow the format of the biblical model of house churches as closely as possible. Then, allow time for the people to begin to fully enjoy the blessings of their small group.

Once everyone is enjoying the home meetings, you might announce that a certain Sunday in the next month is going to be "Early Church Sunday." That Sunday, the church building will be closed and everyone will go to homes to meet just as the early church did, enjoying full meals together, the Lord's Supper, fellowship, prayer, worship, shared teaching and spiritual gifts. If it is a success, you could start having such meetings one Sunday of every month, then eventually two Sundays, and then three Sundays. Eventually, you could release every group to be an independent house church, free to grow and multiply, and perhaps come together for larger meetings once every couple of months.

This whole transition process I've described could take from one to two years.

Or, if you want to go even more cautiously, you could begin just one home gathering with a few of your most interested members that you lead yourself. (Again, house churches don't have to meet on Sunday mornings.) It could be presented as an experiment and would certainly be a learning experience for all.

If it succeeds, then appoint an overseer and release the group to become an independent church that would only join the institutional Sunday service once per month. That way the new church would still be a part of the mother church, and would not be viewed so negatively by those still within the institutional congregation. That could also help influence others within the church to consider being part of another house church being planted by the institutional church.

If the first group grows, prayerfully divide it so that both groups have good leaders and sufficient gifts within their members. Both groups could meet together in a larger celebration on agreed-upon occasions, perhaps once a month or once every three months.

Regardless of the path you take, keep your eye on the goal even through the disappointments, of which there will likely be a few. House churches consist of people, and people cause problems. Don't give up.

It is highly unlikely that everyone in your entire institutional church congregation will make such a transition, so you would have to decide at what point you will personally begin to devote yourself completely to a house church or group of house churches, leaving the institution behind. That will be a significant day for you!

The Ideal Church

Could a pastor of a house church actually be more successful in God's eyes than a pastor of a mega-church with a huge building and thousands in attendance every Sunday? Yes, if he is multiplying obedient disciples and disciple-makers, following Jesus' model, as opposed to simply gathering spiritual goats once a week to watch a concert and listen to an entertaining speech sanctified by a few out-of-context scriptures.

A pastor who determines to follow the house church model will never have a large congregation of his own. In the long run, however, he will have much lasting fruit, as his disciples make disciples. Many pastors of "small" congregations of 40 or 50 people who are striving for more might need to adjust their thinking. Their churches might already be too large. Perhaps they should stop praying for a bigger building and start praying about who should be appointed to lead two new house churches. (Please, when that happens, don't give your new denomination a name and yourself the title of "bishop"!)

We need to eradicate the thinking that bigger is better when it comes to church. If we were to judge purely on a biblical basis, single congregations consisting of hundreds of undiscipled spectators who meet in special buildings would be considered quite strange. If any of the original apostles visited modern institutional churches, they would be scratching their heads!

A Final Objection

It is often said that in the Western world where Christianity has already become part of the culture that people will never accept the idea of churches meeting in homes. It is thus argued that we must stay with the institutional model.

First, this is proving not to be true, as the house church movement is gaining rapid momentum in the Western world.

Second, people already gladly meet in homes for parties, meals, fellowships, Bible studies and home cell groups. Accepting the idea of a church in a house takes a very small adjustment of thinking.

Third, it is true that religious people, "spiritual goats," will never accept the concept of house churches. They will never do anything that might potentially make them appear odd to their neighbors. But true disciples of Jesus Christ certainly accept the concept of house churches once they understand the biblical basis. They quickly realize how unnecessary church buildings are for discipleship. If you want to build a big church with "wood, hay and straw" (see 1 Cor. 3:12), you will need a building, but it will all burn in the end. But if you want to multiply disciples and disciple-makers, building the church of Jesus Christ with "gold, silver and precious stones," then you need not waste money and energy on buildings.

It is interesting that the greatest indigenous evangelistic movement in the world today, the "back to Jerusalem" movement of the Chinese house churches, has adopted a specific strategy to evangelize the 10/40 window. They say, "We have no desire to build a single church building anywhere! This allows the gospel to spread rapidly, is harder for authorities to detect, and enables us to channel all our resources directly into gospel ministry."[22] A wise and biblical example to follow indeed!

[22] Paul Hattaway, *Back to Jerusalem*, (Carlisle: Piquant, 2003), p. 58.

FIVE

Church Growth

So you are a pastor and you want your church to grow. That is a very common desire among pastors. But why do you want your church to grow? *What is the honest reason in your heart?*

Do you want your church to grow so that you can feel successful? Do you want to be respected and feel influential? Do you want to wield power over people? Do you hope to gain wealth? Those are all wrong reasons for wanting your church to grow.

If you want your church to grow so that God can be glorified as more and more lives are transformed by the Holy Spirit, then that is the right reason to desire church growth.

It is possible of course for us to fool ourselves, thinking our motives are pure when in fact they are actually selfish.

How can we know our true motives? How can we know if we truly want to build *God's* kingdom or simply build our *own* kingdom?

One way is by monitoring our inward reactions to the success of other pastors. If we think our motives are pure, if we think that we sincerely want God's kingdom and *His* church to grow, but we discover some envy or jealousy in our hearts when we hear of other churches' growth, it reveals that our motives are less than pure. It shows that we really aren't so interested in *the* church growing, but in *our* own church growing. And why is that? Because our motives are at least partially selfish.

We can also check our motives by monitoring our inward reaction when we hear of a new church that is starting in our area. If we feel threatened, that is a sign that we are more concerned about our own kingdom than God's kingdom.

Even pastors of large or growing churches can check their motives by this same means. Such pastors might also ask themselves some questions, such as, "Would I ever consider planting new churches by sending and relinquishing key leaders and people from my congregation, resulting in my church becoming smaller?" A pastor who is very resistant to such an idea is likely building his church for his own glory. (On the other hand, a pastor of a large church could plant new churches for his own glory as well, just so he can boast of how many churches have been birthed from his church.) Another question he could ask himself would be, "Do I associate with pastors of smaller churches or have I distanced myself from them, feeling above them?" Or, "Would I be willing to pastor just twelve to twenty people in a house church, or would that be too hard on my ego?"[23]

The Church Growth Movement

In Christian bookstores across America and Canada, there are often entire sections of shelves devoted to books on church growth. These books and the concepts within them have spread around the world. Pastors are hungry to learn how to increase attendance at their churches, and they are often quick to adopt the advice of American mega-church pastors who are deemed successful by virtue of the size of their buildings and the number of people who attend on Sundays.

Those who are a little more discerning, however, realize that attendance and building size are not necessarily an indication of the quality of disciple-making. Some American churches have grown due to appealing doctrines that are a perversion of biblical truth. I've spoken to pastors all over the world who have been shocked to learn that multitudes of American pastors believe and proclaim that once a person is saved, he can never forfeit his salvation regardless of what he believes or how he lives his life. Similarly, many American pastors proclaim a watered-down gospel of cheap grace, leading people to think that they can gain heaven without holiness. Quite a few more proclaim a gospel of prosperity, fueling the greed of people whose religion is a means to gain more treasures that they can lay up on earth. Those are pastors whose church-growth techniques certainly should not be imitated.

I've read my share of books on the subject of church growth, and I have mixed feelings about them. Many contain strategies and advice that are, to some degree, biblical, making them worthwhile to read. Almost all, however, are based on the 1700-year-old institutional church model, rather than on the biblical church model. Consequently, the focus is not on building the body of Christ through multiplying disciples and disciple-makers, but on building individual institutional congregations, which always requires bigger buildings, more specialized church staff and programs, and a structure that is more like a business corporation than a family.

Some modern church-growth strategies seem to suggest that, just for the sake of gaining numbers, church services be made more attractive for

---

[23] Here is another advantage of the house church model—pastors aren't striving to have large congregations for the wrong reasons, because congregation size is limited by house size.

people who don't want to follow Jesus. They advise short, positive sermons only, non-expressive worship, lots of social activities, that money never be mentioned, and so on. This does not result in the making of disciples who deny themselves and obey all of Christ's commandments. It results in professing Christians who are indistinguishable from the world and who are on the broad road to hell. This is not God's strategy to win the world but Satan's strategy to win the church. It is not "church growth" but "world growth."

The Seeker-Sensitive Model

The most popular American church-growth strategy is often referred to as the "seeker-sensitive" model. In this strategy, Sunday morning services are designed so that (1) Christians feel comfortable inviting unsaved friends, and (2) unsaved people hear the gospel in non-offensive terms to which they can relate and understand. Midweek services and small groups are reserved for discipling the believers.

By this means, some individual churches have grown quite large. Among American institutional churches, these may have the greatest potential to evangelize and disciple people, as long as everyone is incorporated into small groups (which they often are not) and discipled there, and as long as the gospel is not compromised (which it always is when the goal is to be non-offensive, because the true gospel is offensive to human pride). At least seeker-sensitive churches have implemented some strategy to reach unsaved people, something that most institutional churches do not have.

But how does the American seeker-sensitive model compare with the biblical model for church growth?

In the book of Acts, God-called apostles and evangelists preached the gospel publicly and from house to house, accompanied by signs and wonders that attracted the attention of unbelievers. Those who repented and believed in the Lord Jesus devoted themselves to the apostles' teaching, and regularly met together in houses where they learned God's Word, exercised spiritual gifts, celebrated the Lord's Supper, prayed together, and so on, all under the leadership of elders/pastors/overseers. God-called teachers and prophets circulated among the churches. Everyone shared the gospel with friends and neighbors. There were no buildings to construct that would slow the church's growth and rob God's kingdom of the resources that would help spread the gospel and make disciples. Leaders were quickly trained on the job rather than sent off to seminaries or Bible schools. All of this resulted in exponential church growth for a limited season, until all the receptive people in a given area were reached.

By comparison, the seeker-sensitive model is normally void of signs and wonders, thus it lacks that divine means of advertisement, attraction and conviction. It depends heavily on natural means of marketing and advertising to attract people to a building where they can hear the message. The preacher's oratory skills and his powers of persuasion are the primary means of conviction. How this differs from the methods of Paul, who wrote, "My message and my preaching were not in persuasive words of wisdom, but in demonstration of the Spirit and of power, that your faith should not rest on the wisdom of men, but on the power of God" (1 Cor. 2:4-5).

More Differences

The seeker-sensitive model is generally void of apostles and evangelists, because the primary figure is the pastor. A question: Does eliminating apostles and evangelists from their role of evangelization and giving that responsibility to pastors a superior means of obtaining church growth?[24]

The seeker-sensitive pastor preaches once a week in a Sunday service where Christians are encouraged to bring unsaved people. Thus, generally speaking, the gospel can be heard only once a week by unsaved associates of church members. Those unsaved people must be willing to come to church, and they must be invited by church members who are willing to invite them to church. In the biblical model, apostles and evangelists continually proclaim the gospel in public and private places, and all believers share the gospel with their friends and neighbors. Of these two models, through which would the most unsaved people hear the gospel?

The seeker-sensitive model requires an acceptable building that believers are not ashamed to invite their unsaved associates to and which their unsaved associates are not ashamed to visit. This always requires a substantial sum of money. Before the gospel can be "spread," an acceptable building must be obtained or constructed. In America that building must be in a good location, usually in wealthy suburbs. By contrast, the biblical model requires no special buildings, special locations or money. The spread of the gospel is not limited to the number of people who can fit into special buildings on Sundays.

Still More Differences

When comparing *some* seeker-sensitive churches with the biblical model, there are even more differences.

The apostles and evangelists in the book of Acts called people to repent, believe in the Lord Jesus and be baptized immediately. People were expected, at their conversion, to become disciples of Christ, meeting the conditions Jesus laid down for discipleship, enumerated in Luke 14:26-33

---

[24] This is much of the reason why today we have so many evangelists, teachers, prophets and even apostles pastoring churches. So many God-given ministries are not given a rightful place or any place within the institutional church structure, and so non-pastoral ministers end up pastoring churches, robbing the church of the greater blessing they could be to the larger body of believers within a biblical structure. It seems everyone has reverted to building his own kingdom in the form of an institutional church, regardless of his true calling. Because pastors supposedly have the right to "*their* peoples'" tithes, and much of that goes to constructing and maintaining buildings, non-pastoral ministers resort to pastoring churches just to gain financial support for the ministries to which they are actually called.

and John 8:31-32. They began loving Jesus supremely, living in His word, taking up their crosses, and giving up all their rights of possession, new stewards of that which now belonged to God.

The gospel that is often proclaimed in seeker-sensitive churches is different. Sinners are told how much God loves them, how He can meet their felt needs, and how they can be saved by "accepting Jesus as Savior." After they pray a short "salvation prayer," never having been told about counting the cost of discipleship, they are often assured that they are genuinely saved and solicited to join a class where they can begin to grow in Christ. If they do join such a class (many never return to church), they are often taken through a systematic learning process that focuses on gaining more knowledge of the church's particular doctrines rather than becoming more obedient to Christ's commandments. The pinnacle of this "discipleship" program is when the believer *eventually* starts to tithe his income to the church (to pay primarily for the mortgage and non-biblical staff salaries, which amounts to horrible stewardship, supporting much of which is not ordained of God and robbing that which God does want supported) and is led to believe that he has "found his ministry" when he begins performing some supportive role within the institutional church that is never once mentioned in Scripture.

What would happen if your nation's government, concerned because there were not enough men volunteering for its army, decided to become "seeker-sensitive"? Imagine that they promised potential recruits that if they joined, there was nothing expected of them—their paycheck would be a free gift, unearned and unmerited. They could get up in the morning whenever they wanted. They could practice the training drills if they wanted to, but they had the option to watch TV instead. If war broke out, they could chose if they wanted to participate in battles or go to the beach. What would be the result?

No doubt the army's ranks would swell! But the army would no longer be an army, unfit for its task. And that is what becomes of seeker-sensitive churches. Lowering the standards inflates Sunday attendance, but erodes discipleship and obedience. Those seeker-sensitive churches that attempt to "preach the gospel" on Sundays and "do discipleship" at midweek services find that they have a problem if they tell people at the midweek services that only Jesus' disciples are going to heaven. People then feel as if they've been lied to on Sunday mornings. Thus such churches must deceive people at the midweek services as well, presenting discipleship and obedience as options rather than requirements for heaven-bound people.[25]

---

[25] Remember that the requirements that Jesus enumerated to be His true disciple in Luke 14:26-33 were not spoken to people who were already believers, as if He was offering them a second step in their spiritual journey. Rather, He was speaking to the multitudes. Becoming His disciple was the *only* first step Jesus offered, which is nothing less than the step of salvation. This stands in contrast to what is taught in most seeker-sensitive churches.

I certainly understand that some institutional churches do incorporate aspects of the biblical model that others do not. Regardless, the biblical model is clearly the most effective in multiplying disciples and disciple-makers.

Why is the biblical model not followed today? The list of excuses seems endless, but in the final analysis, the reason the biblical model is not followed is because of tradition, unbelief and disobedience. Many say that the biblical model is an impossibility in our world today. But the fact is that the biblical model *is* being followed in many places around the world today. The explosive growth of the church in China over the past half-century, for example, is due to believers simply following the biblical model. Is God different in China than elsewhere?

All of this is to say that non-American pastors should beware of American church-growth methods that are being promoted around the globe. They would be much more successful in accomplishing Christ's goal of making disciples if they pursued the biblical model of church growth.

The Aftermath

It has been my observation that many proponents of modern church-growth teaching are out of touch with average pastors around the world. The very large majority of pastors shepherd flocks that consist of less than a hundred people. Many of these pastors become disheartened after trying church-growth techniques that don't work or that backfire through no fault of their own. No one seems to admit that there are several factors beyond the control of pastors that limit the growth of their churches. Let us consider some of them now.

First and foremost, *church growth is limited by the size of the local population.* It is obvious that most large institutional churches are found in large metropolitan areas. They often have millions of people from which to draw church members. If numbers, however, are a true determination of success, then a church should be judged, not by size, but by its *percentage* of the local population. On that basis, some churches of ten people are much more successful than other churches of ten thousand. A church with ten members in a village of fifty people is more successful than a church of ten thousand in a city of five million. (Yet those ten-people pastors will never be asked to speak at a church-growth convention.)

A Second Limiting Factor to Church Growth

Second, *church growth is limited by the degree of saturation among receptive people by all the churches in a given region.* At any certain time, there are only so many people in an area whose hearts are open to the gospel. Once those receptive ones are all reached, no church will grow, unless some already-churched people transfer to another church (which is how many large churches have grown—at the expense of other churches).

Of course, every current Christian was unreceptive to the gospel at one time but became receptive under the influence of the Holy Spirit. Thus, it is very possible that people who are currently unreceptive will become receptive. When they do, churches can grow. What we often refer to as "revival" occurs when *many* unreceptive people suddenly become receptive. We should not forget, however, that *one* person becoming receptive is also a revival, only on a smaller scale. Every big revival begins with just one person becoming receptive. So pastor, do not despise the day of small beginnings.

Jesus sent His disciples out to preach the gospel to cities that He knew would be possibly unreceptive, where not one single person would repent (see Luke 9:5). Yet Jesus still sent them to preach the gospel there. Were those disciples unsuccessful? No, even though they had no converts (and no church growth) they were successful, because they obeyed Jesus.

Likewise, Jesus still sends pastors to villages, cities and suburbs where He knows that only a small percentage of the people will ever be receptive to the gospel. Those pastors who faithfully serve their small congregations are successful in God's eyes, even though they may be failures in the eyes of some church-growth experts.

All pastors in every area should also be encouraged by the fact that, because of God's great mercy, and in answer to His peoples' intercession, He is working to help unreceptive people become receptive. He attempts to influence unsaved people by means of their consciences, His creation, circumstances, His temporal judgments, the living testimony of His church, the preaching of the gospel, and the conviction of the Holy Spirit. So pastor, take heart. Keep obeying, praying and preaching. Before every large-scale revival there first exists the great *need* for a revival. And there always exists someone who is *dreaming* of a revival. Keep dreaming!

A Third Limiting Factor to Church Growth

A third factor that limits the growth of individual churches is the ability of the pastor. The majority of pastors do not have the skills that are necessary to oversee a large congregation, and it is no fault of their own. They are simply not gifted organizationally, administratively or with the preaching/teaching skills that are necessary for a large congregation. Clearly, such pastors are not called by God to pastor large congregations, and they would be wrong to attempt to pastor anything but an average-size institutional church or house church.

I recently read a popular book on the subject of leadership by the senior pastor of one of America's largest churches. As I read the pages he had filled with his experienced advice for modern pastors, my overriding thought was this: "He isn't telling us how to be a pastor—he is telling us how to be a chief executive officer of a huge corporation." And there is no other choice for the American institutional mega-church senior pastor. He needs a large staff of helpers, and managing that staff is a full-time job. The author of the book I was reading was skilled enough to be the chief executive officer of a large secular corporation. (Indeed, in his book he often quoted famous big-business management consultants, applying their advice to his readership of pastors.) But many, if not most of his readers, do not have the leadership and management skills that he has.

In that same book, the author candidly related how, on several occasions as he built his huge congregation, he had made almost-fatal mistakes, errors that could have cost him his family or his future in the ministry. By the grace of God, he survived. His experiences, however, reminded me of the many instances when other institutional pastors, striving for the same kind of success, made similar errors and suffered total shipwreck. Some, devoting themselves to their churches, lost their children or ruined their marriages. Some suffered nervous breakdowns or severe ministerial burnout. Others became so disillusioned that they ultimately abandoned the ministry altogether. Many others survived, but that is about all that can be said. They continue living lives of quiet desperation, wondering if their super-human sacrifice is worth it.

As I read that particular book, it continually reinforced in my mind the wisdom of the early church, where there was nothing that resembled modern institutional churches, and no pastor was responsible for a flock larger than twenty-five or so people. As I stated in a previous chapter, many pastors who think their congregations are too small should reconsider their ministries in light of Scripture. If they have fifty people, their churches might actually be too large. If there is capable leadership within, they might prayerfully consider dividing into three house churches and selling their building, with the goal of making disciples and building God's kingdom God's way.

If this seems too radical, they might at least begin to disciple future leaders, or start small groups, or if they already have some small groups, set some free to be autonomous house churches to see what happens.

Other Modern Church-Growth Techniques

There are other techniques being promoted today as essential for church growth besides the seeker-sensitive church model. Many of these other techniques are unbiblical and fall under the category of "spiritual warfare." They are advertised using such names as "pulling down strongholds," "warfare prayer," and "spiritual mapping."

We'll consider some of these practices in a later chapter about spiritual warfare. In short, however, we might wonder why such practices that were completely unknown to the apostles would be considered necessary for church growth today.

Many of the new means of church growth are the result of the experiences of a few pastors who say, "I did this and that, and my church grew.

So if you do the same things, your church will also grow." The truth is, however, that there was no real connection between the growth of their churches and the peculiar things they did, even though they thought otherwise. This is proven repeatedly when other pastors follow those peculiar teachings, do the identical things, and their churches don't grow at all.

A church-growth pastor might be heard to say, "When we started screaming at the demons over our city, revival broke out in our church. So you need to start screaming at demons if you want revival to come to your church."

But why have there been so many wonderful revivals around the world in the past 2,000 years of church history where there was no one screaming at demons over cities? This shows that, even though that pastor *thought* the revival was a result of screaming at demons, he was mistaken. More likely, people within his city started becoming receptive to the gospel, perhaps as a result of the united *prayers* of the church, and that pastor happened to be there preaching the gospel when they became receptive. Most often, church growth is the result of *being at the right place at the right time*. (And the Holy Spirit helps us be at the right places at the right times.)

If screaming at demons over cities brought revival to a certain pastor's church, why, after a length of time, did the revival slow and then cease, as it always does? If screaming at demons is *the* key, then it stands to reason that if we just keep screaming at the demons, *everyone* in the city will come to Christ. But they don't.

The truth is obvious when we simply give it a little thought. The only biblical means of church growth are prayer, preaching, teaching, disciple-making, the help of the Holy Spirit, and so on. And even those biblical means don't guarantee church growth, because God has made people free moral agents. They can choose to repent or not repent. It could be said that even Jesus failed at church growth at certain times when cities He visited did not repent.

All of this is to say that we only need to practice *biblical* means for building the church. Anything else is a waste of time. They are works that consist of wood, hay, and straw that will one day be burned in the fire and go unrewarded (see 1 Cor. 3:12-15).

Finally, the goal should not be just growth in numbers, but disciple making. If the church grows as we make disciples, then praise God!

SIX

The Ministry of Teaching

In this chapter we will consider many aspects of the ministry of teaching. Teaching is the responsibility of apostles, prophets, evangelists,[26] pastors/elders/overseers, teachers (of course), and to some degree, all followers of Christ, as we are all supposed to be making disciples, teaching our disciples to obey all that Christ commanded.[27]

As I've previously emphasized, the disciple-making pastor or minister teaches first by his example, and second, verbally. *He preaches what he practices.* The apostle Paul, a very successful disciple-maker, wrote:

> Be imitators of me, just as I also am of Christ (1 Cor. 11:1).

This should be every minister's goal—to be able to honestly say to those he leads, "Act like me. If you want to know how a follower of Christ lives his life, just watch me."

By comparison, I can remember telling a former congregation that I pastored, "Don't follow me...follow Christ!" Although it didn't occur to me at the time, I was admitting that I was not a good example to follow. In fact, I was actually admitting that I was not following Christ as I should, and then telling everyone else to do what I wasn't doing! How different this was from what Paul said. In truth, if we can't tell people to imitate us because we are imitating Christ, we should not be in the ministry, because people use ministers as their role models. *The church is a reflection of its leaders.*

Teaching Unity by Example

Let's apply this concept to teaching by example to the teaching of one particular topic, the topic of unity. All pastors/elders/overseers desire that the flocks they lead be unified. They hate divisions within their local

---

[26] The preaching of the gospel by evangelists could be considered a form of teaching, and evangelists certainly need to proclaim a biblically-accurate gospel.

[27] All believers are not given responsibility to publicly teach groups of people, but all have the responsibility to teach on a one-to-one basis as they make disciples (see Matt. 5:19; 28:19-20; Col. 3:16; Heb. 5:12).

bodies. They know that factions are very displeasing to the Lord. After all, Jesus commanded us to love each other just as He loved us (see John 13:34-35). Our love for each other is what marks us as His disciples before the watching world. All this being so, most leaders of flocks admonish their sheep to love one another and strive for unity.

Yet, as ministers who are supposed to be teaching *foremost* by our example, we often fall far short in our teaching about love and unity by how we live. When we, for example, demonstrate a lack of love and unity with other pastors, we send a message that contradicts what we preach to our congregations. We expect them to do what we do not.

The fact is, *the most significant words Jesus spoke concerning unity were spoken to leaders regarding their relationships with other leaders.* For example, at the Last Supper, after He washed His disciples' feet, Jesus said to them,

> You call Me Teacher and Lord; and you are right, for so I
> am. If I then, the Lord and the Teacher, washed your feet,
> you also ought to wash one another's feet. For I gave you
> an example that you also should do as I did to you (John
> 13:13-15). [Note that Jesus taught by example.]

Pastors often use this passage of Scripture to teach their flocks about loving one another, which is certainly appropriate. The words in this passage, however, were addressed to leaders, the twelve apostles. Jesus knew that His future church had little hope of succeeding in its mission if its leaders were divided or if they competed with each other. So He made it clear that *He expects His leaders to humbly serve each other.*

In the context of the culture of His day, Jesus demonstrated humble service by means of doing one of the lowest tasks of a household servant, the washing of feet. If He had visited a different culture at a different time in history, He may have dug out the latrines or washed out the garbage cans of His disciples. *How many of His modern leaders are willing to demonstrate that kind of love and humility towards each other?*

Within the space of less than an hour, Jesus repeatedly underscored this important message. Minutes after He washed their feet, Jesus said to His group of future church leaders:

> A new commandment I give to you, that you love one an-
> other, even as I have loved you, that you also love one an-
> other. By this all men will know that you are My disciples,
> if you have love for one another (John 13:34-35).

These words certainly have application to all of Christ's disciples, *but they were originally spoken to leaders regarding their relationship with other leaders.*

Once again, just minutes later, Jesus said,

> This is My commandment, that you love one another, just

> as I have loved you. Greater love has no one than this, that
> one lay down his life for his friends (John 15:12-13).

Note that Jesus was again speaking to leaders.
Within seconds, He again said,

> This I command you, that you love one another (John
> 15:17).

Then, a few minutes later, Jesus' disciples heard Him pray on their behalf,

> And I am no more in the world; and yet they themselves
> are in the world, and I come to Thee. Holy Father, keep
> them in Thy name, the name which Thou hast given Me,
> *that they may be one,* even as We are (John 17:11, emphasis
> added).

Finally, just a few seconds later, as Jesus continued His prayer, His disciples heard Him say,

> I do not ask in behalf of these alone, but for those also who
> believe in Me through their word; *that they may all be one;*
> even as Thou, Father, art in Me, and I in Thee, that they
> also may be in Us; *that the world may believe that Thou didst
> send Me.* And the glory which Thou hast given Me I have
> given to them; *that they may be one,* just as We are one; I in
> them, and Thou in Me, *that they may be perfected in unity,
> that the world may know that Thou didst send Me,* and didst
> love them, even as Thou didst love Me (John 17:20-23, em-
> phasis added).

Thus, within the space of less then an hour, *six times* Jesus emphasized
to His future leaders the importance of their being unified and demonstrating their unity by humbly loving and serving one another. This was
obviously very important to Jesus. Their unity was a key factor in the
world believing in Him.

How Well Are We Doing?

Unfortunately, while we hope our flocks will be unified with love,
many of us compete with each other and use unethical means to build
our churches at the expense of other churches. Many of us avoid any fellowship with other pastors whose doctrine is different. We even advertise
our lack of unity on signs we post for the world to see in front of our
church buildings, sending a message to everyone: "We are not like those
other Christians in other church buildings." (And we've done a good job
at educating the world on our lack of unity, as most unbelievers know that
Christianity is a very divided institution.)

In short, we don't practice what we preach, and our example teaches our congregations much more than our sermons about unity do. It is foolish to think that average Christians are going to be unified and love each other when their leaders act differently.

The only solution, or course, is repentance. We must repent of setting the wrong example before believers and before the world. We must remove the barriers that divide us and start loving each other as Jesus commanded.

That means we must, first of all, meet with other pastors and ministers, including pastors of different doctrinal persuasions. I'm not speaking of fellowshipping with pastors who are not born again, who aren't striving to obey Jesus, or who are in ministry for personal profit. They are wolves in sheep's clothing, and Jesus told us exactly how to identify them. They are known by their fruit.

I am speaking, however, of pastors and ministers who are striving to keep Jesus' commandments, true brothers and sisters in Christ. If you are a pastor, you should be committed to loving other pastors, demonstrating that love in practical ways before your flock. One way to start is by going to other pastors in your vicinity and asking their forgiveness for not loving them as you should. That should break down some walls. Then commit to meeting together regularly to have a meal, encourage and admonish one another and to pray. When that occurs, you might eventually lovingly discuss the doctrines that tend to divide you, striving for unity whether you ultimately agree or not on everything you discuss. My life and ministry were enriched significantly when I finally became willing to listen to ministers who were not in my same doctrinal camp. I was missing so much blessing for so many years by shutting myself off.

You can also demonstrate your love and unity by inviting other pastors to preach at your church or house church gathering, or your church can have combined meetings with other churches or house church gatherings.

You can change the name of your church so that it doesn't advertise to the world your disunity with the rest of the body of Christ. You can pull out of your denomination or named association and identify only with the body of Christ, sending a message to everyone that you believe that Jesus is building only one church, not many different churches that can't get along with each other.

This, I know, sounds radical. But why do anything to uphold what Jesus clearly never intended? Why be involved in anything that displeases Him? There are no denominations or special associations mentioned in Scripture. When the Corinthians divided over their favorite teachers, Paul firmly rebuked them, saying that their divisions revealed their carnality and spiritual babyhood (see 1 Cor. 3:1-7). Do our divisions reveal anything less?

Anything that sets us apart from one another should be shunned. House churches should avoid giving themselves names or joining any associations that have names. In Scripture, individual churches were identified only by the houses in which they met. Groups of churches were identified only by the cities in which they were located. They all considered themselves to be part of the one church, the body of Christ.

There is only one King and one kingdom. *Anyone who sets himself up so that believers or churches identify with him is building his own kingdom within God's kingdom.* He had better get ready to stand before the King who says, "My glory I will not give to another" (Is. 48:11).

All of this is to again say that ministers should be setting the right example of obedience to Christ before everyone, because people are going to follow their example. The example they live before others is their most influential means of teaching. As Paul wrote to the believers in Philippi:

> Brethren, join in *following my example*, and *observe those who walk according to the pattern you have in us* (Phil. 3:17, emphasis added).

What to Teach

Like Paul, the disciple-making minister has a goal. That goal is to "present every man complete in Christ" (Col. 1:28b). So he, also like Paul, will "*admonish* every man and *teach* every man with all wisdom" (Col. 1:28a, emphasis added). Note that Paul didn't teach only to educate or entertain people.

The disciple-making minister can say with Paul, "The goal of our instruction is love from a pure heart and a good conscience and a sincere faith" (1 Tim. 1:5). That is, he wants to produce true Christ-likeness and holiness in the lives of the people he serves, which is why he teaches believers to obey all of Christ's commandments. He teaches the truth, admonishing his hearers to "pursue peace with all men, and the sanctification [holiness] without which no one will see the Lord" (Heb. 12:14).

The disciple-making minister knows that Jesus commanded His disciples to teach their disciples to obey *all*, and not just part, of what He had commanded them (see Matt. 28:19-20). He wants to be certain not to neglect teaching anything Christ commanded, and so he regularly teaches verse by verse through the Gospels and the epistles. That is where Jesus' commandments are recorded and re-emphasized.

This kind of expository teaching also insures that his instruction will remain balanced. When we teach only topical messages, we are more apt to focus on topics that are popular with people and likely to neglect those that are not so popular. The verse-by-verse teacher, however, will not only teach about God's love, but also about His discipline and wrath. He will not only teach about the blessings of being a Christian, but also about the responsibilities. He will be less likely to major on minor themes, emphasizing what is less important and neglecting what is most important. (According to Jesus, this was a fault of the Pharisees; see Matt. 23:23-24.)

Overcoming Fears of Expository Teaching

Many pastors are afraid to teach verse by verse because there is so much that they don't understand in Scripture, and they don't want their congregations to know how much they don't know! That, of course, is prideful. There is no one on earth who perfectly understands everything in Scripture. Even Peter said that some of the things that Paul wrote were difficult to understand (see 2 Pet. 3:16).

When a pastor who teaches verse by verse arrives at a verse or passage that he doesn't understand, he should simply tell his flock that he doesn't understand the next section and skip over it. He can also request that his flock pray that the Holy Spirit will help him understand. His humility will set a good example before his flock, *a sermon in itself.*

The pastor/elder/overseer of a house church has the extra advantage of teaching a small group in an informal setting, because questions can be asked during his teaching. This also opens up the possibility of the Holy Spirit giving insight to others in the group regarding scriptures that are being studied. The result can be much more effective learning for everyone.

A good place to start when teaching Christ's commandments is His Sermon on the Mount, found in Matthew 5-7. There, Jesus gave many commandments, and He helped his Jewish followers rightly understand the laws given through Moses. A little later in this book, I will teach through the Sermon on the Mount verse by verse to demonstrate how it can be done.

Sermon Preparation

There is no evidence in the New Testament that any pastor/elder/overseer ever prepared a weekly oration/sermon, complete with neatly-prepared points and illustrations all written down in outline form, as is the practice of many modern ministers. Certainly none of us could imagine Jesus doing such a thing! Teaching in the early church was more spontaneous and interactive, following the Jewish style, rather than oratory, as was the practice of the Greeks and Romans, a tradition that was eventually adopted by the church when it became institutionalized. If Jesus told His disciples not to prepare a defense when they were called into court, promising that the Holy Spirit would give them spontaneous, irrefutable words, we would expect that God would be able to help pastors in church gatherings to some degree!

This is not to say that ministers should not prepare *themselves* by praying and studying. Paul admonished Timothy:

> Be diligent to present yourself approved to God as a
> workman who does not need to be ashamed, handling ac-
> curately the word of truth (2 Tim. 2:15).

Ministers who follow Paul's instruction to "let the word of Christ richly dwell within you" (Col. 3:16) will be so full of God's Word that they will be able to teach from their "overflow." So dear pastor, the important thing is that you immerse yourself in the Bible. If you are knowledgeable and passionate about your topic, very little other preparation is really necessary to communicate God's truth. Additionally, if you teach verse by verse, you can simply use each consecutive verse as your outline. Your preparation should then consist of prayerfully meditating on the verses of Scripture you will be teaching. If you pastor a house church, the interactive nature of teaching will even more so lessen the need for sermon outlines.

The minister who has faith for God to help him as he teaches will be rewarded with God's help. So trust less in yourself, your preparation and your notes, and more on the Lord. Gradually, as you gain faith and confidence, prepare fewer sermon notes, until you can get along with just a skeleton outline or no outline at all.

The one who is self-conscious before others is the most likely to depend on prepared notes because he is so afraid of making a public mistake. He needs to realize that his fear is rooted in insecurity that is rooted in pride. He would be better to be less worried about how he appears in the eyes of people and be more concerned about how he and his audience appear in God's eyes. No prepared speech can move listeners like a heart-felt, Spirit-anointed teaching. Think of how communication would be hindered if everyone used prepared notes for all his or her conversations! Conversation would die! An unrehearsed conversational style comes across as much more sincere than a prepared oration. Teaching is not acting. It is imparting truth. We all know when we are just hearing a speech, and when we do, we have a tendency to automatically tune out.

Four More Thoughts

(1) Some ministers are like parrots, getting all their sermon material from books that others have written. They are missing out on a wonderful blessing of being personally taught by the Holy Spirit, and they are also likely to be propagating the errors of those writers they copy.

(2) Many pastors imitate the preaching and teaching styles of other preachers, styles that are often purely traditional. For example, it is thought in some circles that sermons are anointed only when they are loud and fast. Church attendees are thus subject to sermons that are shouted from beginning to end. The reality is that people usually tune out redundant shouting, just like they do when they hear monotone speaking. A varied voice is much more captivating. Moreover, *preaching* is naturally louder as

it is exhortational, whereas *teaching* is usually done in a more conversational tone because it is instructional.

(3) I've observed sermon-listeners in hundreds of church services, and it amazes me that so many preachers and teachers are oblivious to the many indications that people are bored and/or not listening. Pastor, the people who look bored *are* bored! Those who aren't looking at you while you speak are probably not listening. People who are not listening are not being helped in the least. If *sincere* people are being bored and/or not listening, then you need to improve your sermons. Give more examples. Tell relevant stories. Make up parables. Keep it simple. Teach the Word from your heart. Be sincere. Be yourself. Vary your voice. Make eye contact with as many listeners as possible. Use some facial expression. Use your hands. Move around. Don't speak too long. If the group is small, let people ask questions at any reasonable time.

(4) The idea that every sermon should have three points is just a human invention. The goal is to make disciples, not follow modern homiletic theories. Jesus said, "Feed My sheep," not "Impress My sheep."

Whom to Teach

Following Jesus' model, the disciple-making minister is, to some degree, selective with regard to *whom* he teaches. That may surprise you, but it is true. Jesus often spoke to the multitudes in *parables*, and He had a reason for doing so: He didn't want everyone to understand what He was saying. This is clear from Scripture:

> And the disciples came and said to Him, "Why do You speak to them in parables?" And He answered and said to them, "To you it has been granted to know the mysteries of the kingdom of heaven, but to them it has not been granted. For whoever has, to him shall more be given, and he shall have an abundance; but whoever does not have, even what he has shall be taken away from him. Therefore I speak to them in parables; because while seeing they do not see, and while hearing they do not hear, nor do they understand" (Matt. 13:10-13).

The privilege of understanding Christ's parables was reserved for only those who had repented and decided to follow Him. Those who turned down the opportunity to repent, resisting God's will for their lives, were likewise resisted by God. God resists the proud, but gives grace to the humble (see 1 Pet. 5:5).

Similarly, Jesus instructed His followers: "Do not give what is holy to dogs, and do not throw your pearls before swine, lest they trample them under their feet, and turn and tear you to pieces" (Matt. 7:6). Obviously, Jesus was speaking figuratively. He meant, "Don't give what is valuable to those who don't appreciate its value." Pigs don't realize that pearls are precious, and likewise spiritual pigs don't value God's Word when they hear it. If they believed it was actually God's Word that they were hearing, they would give it their utmost attention and obey it.

How do you know if someone is a spiritual pig? You cast one pearl his way and see what he does with that one pearl. If he disregards it, then you know he is a spiritual pig. If he obeys it, then you know he is not a spiritual pig.

Unfortunately, too many pastors are doing what Jesus told them not to do, continually casting their pearls before pigs, teaching people who are resisting or have rejected God's Word. *Those ministers are wasting their God-given time.* They should have shaken the dust off their feet and moved on long ago, just as Jesus commanded.

The Sheep, Goats and Pigs

The fact is, you can't disciple someone who doesn't want to be discipled, someone who doesn't want to obey Jesus. Many churches are full of people just like that, people who are only cultural Christians, many of whom think they are born again just because they have given a mental assent to a few theological facts about Jesus or Christianity. They are pigs and goats, not sheep. Yet many pastors spend 90% of their time trying to keep those pigs and goats happy, while neglecting the ones whom they could help spiritually and should be serving, the true sheep! Pastor, Jesus wants you to feed His *sheep*, not the goats and the pigs (see John 21:17)!

But how do you know who are the sheep? They are the ones who come to church earliest and leave the latest. They are hungry to learn the truth, because Jesus is their Lord and they want to please Him. They come to church not just on Sundays, but whenever there is a gathering. They get involved in small groups. They often ask questions. They are excited about the Lord. They are looking for opportunities to serve.

Pastor, devote the majority of your time and attention to those people. They are the disciples. To the goats and pigs who attend your church, preach the gospel as long as they can stand it. But if you preach the true gospel, they won't be able to stand it for long. Either they will leave the church, or if they have the power, they will attempt to remove you from your position. If they succeed, shake the dust off your feet as you leave. (In a house church setting, such a thing cannot happen, especially if your church meets in *your* house!)

Likewise, evangelists should feel no obligation to continually preach the gospel to the same people who have repeatedly rejected it. Leave the dead to bury the dead (see Luke 9:60). You are an ambassador for Christ, carrying the most important message from the King of kings! Your position is very high in God's kingdom and your responsibility is great! Don't waste your time telling anyone the gospel twice until everyone has heard it once.

If you are going to be a disciple-making minister, you should be selective in regard to whom you teach, not wasting your valuable time on people who don't want to obey Jesus. Paul wrote to Timothy,

> And the things which you have heard from me in the presence of many witnesses, these entrust to *faithful* men, who will be able to teach others also (2 Tim. 2:2, emphasis added).

Reaching the Goal

Imagine for a moment something that never could have happened under Jesus' ministry but happens all the time in modern churches. Imagine that Jesus, after His resurrection, stayed on the earth and started a church like a modern institutional church, and then pastored it for thirty years. Imagine Him giving sermons every Sunday to the same congregation. Imagine Peter, James and John sitting on the first pew during one of Jesus' sermons, where they had been sitting every Sunday for twenty years. Imagine Peter leaning toward John and whispering in his ear with a groan, "We've heard this same sermon ten times."

We know that such a scene is absurd, because we all know that Jesus would never have put Himself or His apostles into such a situation. Jesus came to make some disciples and do it a certain way within a certain amount of time. Over a period of about three years, He discipled Peter, James and John, and some others. He didn't do it by preaching to them once every Sunday in a church building. He did it by living His life before them, answering their questions, and giving them opportunities to serve. He completed His task and moved on.

So why do we do what Jesus would never have done? Why do we attempt to accomplish what God wants by preaching sermons to the same people for decades? When will we ever have completed our task? Why aren't our disciples, after a few years, ready to go make some disciples of their own?

My point is that, if we are doing our jobs correctly, there should come a time when our disciples are mature enough to not really need our ministry to them any longer. They should be turned lose to make disciples themselves. We are supposed to reach the goal God has set before us, and Jesus showed us how to do it. Incidentally, in a growing house church there is a continual need to disciple people and develop leaders. A healthy house church will not fall into the endless cycle of the same preacher preaching to the same people over decades.

Right Motives

To succeed at teaching that leads to the making of disciples, there is nothing more important than having the right motives. When someone is in the ministry for the wrong reasons, he'll do the wrong things. That is the primary reason why there is so much false and unbalanced teaching in the church today. When a minister's motives are to gain popularity, be successful in the eyes of others, or make lots of money, he is destined to fail in the eyes of God. The saddest thing is that he may succeed in reaching his goal of gaining popularity, becoming successful before others, or making lots of money, but the day will come when his wrong motives will be exposed at Christ's judgment seat, and he will receive no reward for his work. *If* he is permitted to enter the kingdom of heaven,[28] everyone there will know the truth about him, as his lack of reward and his low position in the kingdom will reveal it. There is no doubt that there are different ranks in heaven. Jesus warned:

> Whoever then annuls one of the least of these command-ments, and so teaches others, shall be called least in the kingdom of heaven; but whoever keeps and teaches them, he shall be called great in the kingdom of heaven (Matt. 5:19).

Of course those ministers who do obey and teach Christ's command-ments will suffer for it while on earth. Jesus promised suffering to those who obey Him (see Matt. 5:10-12; John 16:33). They are least likely to gain worldly success, popularity and wealth. What they do gain is future re-wards and praise from God. Which would you rather have? In this regard, Paul wrote:

> What then is Apollos? And what is Paul? Servants through whom you believed, even as the Lord gave opportunity to each one. I planted, Apollos watered, but God was caus-ing the growth. So then neither the one who plants nor the one who waters is anything, but God who causes the growth. Now he who plants and he who waters are one; but each will receive his own reward according to his own labor. For we are God's fellow workers; you are God's field, God's building.
>
> According to the grace of God which was given to me, as a wise master builder I laid a foundation, and another is building upon it. But let each man be careful how he builds upon it. For no man can lay a foundation other than the one which is laid, which is Jesus Christ. Now if any man builds upon the foundation with gold, silver,

---

[28] I say "if" because those who are wolves in sheep's clothing are clearly "ministers' who are selfishly moti-vated, and they will be cast into hell. I suppose what sets them apart from true ministers with wrong motives is the degree of their wrong motivations.

precious stones, wood, hay, straw, each man's work will become evident; for the day will show it, because it is to be revealed with fire; and the fire itself will test the quality of each man's work. If any man's work which he has built upon it remains, he shall receive a reward. If any man's work is burned up, he shall suffer loss; but he himself shall be saved, yet so as through fire (1 Cor. 3:5-15).

Paul likened himself to a master builder who lays a foundation. Apollos, a teacher who came to Corinth after Paul had established the church there, Paul likened to one who built upon the foundation already laid.

Note that both Paul and Apollos would ultimately be rewarded based upon the *quality*, not the *quantity*, of their work (see 3:13).

Figuratively speaking, Paul and Apollos could build God's building with six different kinds of materials, three of which are common, relatively inexpensive and combustible, and three of which are uncommon, very expensive, and not combustible. One day, their respective building materials would undergo the fire of God's judgment, and the wood, hay and straw would be consumed by the fire, revealing their worthless and temporal quality. The gold, silver and precious stones, representing works that were precious and eternal in God's eyes, would endure the testing flames.

We can be certain that unbiblical teaching will be burned to ashes at Christ's judgment. So will anything done in the power, methods, or wisdom of the flesh, as well as anything done for the wrong motives. Jesus warned that anything we might do that is motivated by the desire for the praise of people will not be rewarded (see Matt. 6:1-6, 16-18). These kinds of worthless works may not be evident to human eyes now, but will certainly be revealed to all in the future, as Paul warned. Personally, if my works were of the wood, hay and straw category, I'd rather discover it now than later. Now there is time to repent; then it will be too late.

Checking Our Motives

It is very easy to deceive ourselves about our motives. I certainly have. How can we know if our motives are pure?

The best way is to ask God to reveal to us if our motives are wrong, and then to monitor our thoughts and deeds. Jesus told us to do good works such as praying and giving to the poor in secret, and that is one way to assure ourselves that we are doing good because we desire the praise of God rather than the praise of people. If we are only obedient to God when people are watching us, that signals something is very wrong. Or, if we avoid scandalous sins that would ruin our reputation if we were caught, but indulge in lesser sins that no one would likely ever know about, this shows our motivations are wrong. If we are truly trying to please God—

who knows our every thought, word and deed—then we will strive to obey Him all the time, in things big and small, things known and unknown to others.

Similarly, if our motives are right, we will not follow church growth fads that serve only to increase church attendance at the expense of making disciples who obey all of Christ's commands.

We will teach all of God's Word and not just focus on popular topics that appeal to worldly and unspiritual people.

We will not twist God's Word or teach scriptures in a way that violates their context within the whole Bible.

We will not seek titles and places of honor for ourselves. We will not seek to be known.

We will not cater to the wealthy.

We will not lay up treasures on earth, but live simply and give all we can, setting an example of good stewardship before our flocks.

We will be more concerned with what God thinks of our sermons than what people think.

How are your motives?

A Doctrine that Defeats Disciple-Making

The disciple-making minister never teaches anything that works against the goal of making disciples. Thus, *he never says anything that would make people feel comfortable with disobeying the Lord Jesus.* He never presents God's grace as a means to sin without fear of judgment. Rather, he presents God's grace as a means to repent of sin and live an overcoming life. Scripture, as we know, declares that only overcomers will inherit God's kingdom (see Rev. 2:11; 3:5; 21:7).

Some modern ministers, unfortunately, hold to unbiblical doctrines that do great damage to the goal of making disciples. One such doctrine that has become very popular in the United States is that of *unconditional eternal security*, or "once saved always saved." This doctrine maintains that born again people can never forfeit their salvation regardless of how they live their lives. Because salvation is by grace, they say, the same grace that initially saves people who pray to receive salvation will keep them saved. Any other viewpoint, they maintain, is tantamount to saying that people are saved by their works.

Naturally, such a viewpoint is a great detriment to holiness. Since obedience to Christ is supposedly not essential for one to enter heaven, then there is little motivation to obey Jesus, especially when obedience is costly.

As I stated earlier in this book, the grace that God extends towards humanity does not relieve people of responsibility to obey Him. Scripture states that salvation is not just by grace, but also through faith (see Eph. 2:8). Both grace and faith are necessary for salvation. Faith is the proper response to God's grace, and true faith always results in repentance and obedience. Faith without works is dead, useless, and cannot save, according to James (see James 2:14-26).

That is why Scripture repeatedly declares that continued salvation is dependent upon continued faith and obedience. There are scores of scriptures that make this abundantly clear. For example, Paul states in his letter to the Colossian believers:

> And although you were formerly alienated and hostile in mind, engaged in evil deeds, yet He has now reconciled you in His fleshly body through death, in order to present you before Him holy and blameless and beyond reproach—*if indeed you continue in the faith firmly established and steadfast, and not moved away from the hope of the gospel* that you have heard, which was proclaimed in all creation under heaven (Col. 1:21-23, emphasis added).

It couldn't be clearer. Only a theologian could mistake or twist Paul's meaning. Jesus will confirm us blameless *if* we continue in the faith. This same truth is reiterated in Rom. 11:13-24, 1 Cor. 15:1-2 and Heb. 3:12-14; 10:38-39, where it is clearly stated that final salvation is contingent upon continuance in faith. All contain the conditional word *if*.

The Necessity of Holiness

Can a believer forfeit eternal life by sinning? The answer is found in many scriptures, such as the following, which all guarantee that those who practice various sins will not inherit God's kingdom. If a believer can return to the practice of the sins in the following lists compiled by Paul, then a believer can forfeit ultimate salvation:.

> Do you not know that the unrighteous shall not inherit the kingdom of God? Do not be deceived; neither *fornicators*, nor *idolaters*, nor *adulterers*, nor *effeminate*, nor *homosexuals*, nor *thieves*, nor the *covetous*, nor *drunkards*, nor *revilers*, nor *swindlers*, shall inherit the kingdom of God (1 Cor. 6:9-10, emphasis added).

> Now the deeds of the flesh are evident, which are: *immorality, impurity, sensuality, idolatry, sorcery, enmities, strife, jealousy, outbursts of anger, disputes, dissensions, factions, envying, drunkenness, carousing, and things like these*, of which I forewarn you just as I have forewarned you that those who practice such things shall not inherit the kingdom of God (Gal. 5:19-21, emphasis added).

> For this you know with certainty, that no *immoral* or *impure* person or *covetous* man, who is an idolater, has an

inheritance in the kingdom of Christ and God. Let no one deceive you with empty words, for because of these things the wrath of God comes upon the sons of disobedience (Eph. 5:5-6, emphasis added).

Notice that in every case, Paul was writing to believers, warning them. Twice he warned them to not be deceived, indicating that he was concerned that some believers might think that a person could practice the sins he listed and still inherit God's kingdom.

Jesus warned His closest disciples, Peter, James, John and Andrew of the possibility of their being cast into hell because of not being ready for His return. Note that the following words were addressed to them (see Mark 13:1-4), and not to a crowd of unbelievers:

> Therefore be on the alert, for you do not know which day *your Lord* is coming. But be sure of this, that if the head of the house had known at what time of the night the thief was coming, he would have been on the alert and would not have allowed his house to be broken into. For this reason *you* [Peter, James, John and Andrew] be ready too; for the Son of Man is coming at an hour when *you* [Peter, James, John and Andrew] do not think He will.

> Who then is the faithful and sensible slave whom his master put in charge of his household to give them their food at the proper time? Blessed is that slave whom his master finds so doing when he comes. Truly I say to you, that he will put him in charge of all his possessions. But if that evil slave says in his heart, "My master is not coming for a long time," and shall begin to beat his fellow slaves and eat and drink with drunkards; the master of that slave will come on a day when he does not expect him and at an hour which he does not know, and shall cut him in pieces and assign him a place with the hypocrites; weeping shall be there and the gnashing of teeth (Matt. 24:42-51, emphasis added).

The moral of the story? "Peter, James, John and Andrew, don't be like the unfaithful servant in this parable."[29]

To underscore what He just said to His closest disciples, Jesus immediately continued with the Parable of the Ten Virgins. All ten virgins were initially ready for the coming of the bridegroom, but five become unready

[29] Amazingly, some teachers, who can't escape the facts that Jesus was warning His closest disciples and that the unfaithful servant clearly represents one who was a believer, say that the place of weeping and gnashing of teeth is a place in the outer fringes of heaven. There, unfaithful believers will supposedly temporarily mourn their loss of rewards until Jesus wipes the tears from their eyes and then welcomes them into heaven!

and were excluded from the wedding feast. Jesus ended the parable with the words, "Be on the alert then [Peter, James, John and Andrew], for *you* [Peter, James, John and Andrew] do not know the day nor the hour" (Matthew 25:13). That is, "Don't be like the five foolish virgins, Peter, James, John and Andrew." If there were no possibility of Peter, James, John and Andrew not being ready, there would be no need for Jesus to have warned them.

Jesus then immediately told them the Parable of the Talents. It was the same message again. "Don't be like the one talent slave who had nothing to show for what his master entrusted to him when he returned." At the end of the parable, the master declared, "Cast out the worthless slave into the outer darkness; in that place there shall be weeping and gnashing of teeth" (Matt. 25:30). Jesus could not have made His message clearer. Only a theologian could twist His meaning. There was a danger that Peter, James, John and Andrew could all be cast into hell in the end if they weren't obedient when Jesus returned. If that possibility existed for Peter, James, John and Andrew, then that possibility exists for all of us. As Jesus promised, only those who do the will of His Father will enter the kingdom of heaven (see Matt. 7:21).[30]

Those who teach the false doctrine of unconditional eternal security clearly work against Christ and assist Satan, teaching the opposite of what Jesus and the apostles taught. They effectively neutralize Jesus' commandment to make disciples who will obey all He commanded, blocking the narrow road to heaven, and widening the broad highway to hell.[31]

Another Modern Doctrine that Defeats Disciple-Making

It is not just the teaching of unconditional eternal security that deceives people into thinking holiness is not essential for ultimate salvation. The love of God is often presented in a way that neutralizes disciple making. Preachers can often be heard saying to their audiences, "God loves you unconditionally." People interpret that to mean, "God accepts and approves of me regardless of whether I obey or disobey Him,." That, how-

[30] Of course, Christians who commit a single sin do not immediately forfeit their salvation. Those who ask forgiveness for their sins are forgiven by God (if they forgive those who sin against them). Those who don't ask for God's forgiveness place themselves in the danger of being disciplined by God. Only by hardening their hearts to God's on-going discipline do believers run the risk of forfeiting their salvation.

[31] Those who are still not persuaded that a Christian can forfeit his salvation should consider all of the following New Testament passages: Matt. 18:21-35; 24:4-5, 11-13, 23-26, 42-51; 25:1-30; Luke 8:11-15; 11:24-28; 12:42-46; John 6:66-71; 8:31-32, 51; 15:1-6; Acts 11:21-23; 14:21-22; Rom. 6:11-23; 8:12-14, 17; 11:20-22; 1 Cor. 9:23-27; 10:1-21; 11:29-32; 15:1-2; 2 Cor. 1:24; 11:2-4; 12:21-13:5; Gal. 5:1-4; 6:7-9; Phil. 2:12-16; 3:17-4:1; Col. 1:21-23; 2:4-8, 18-19; 1 Thes. 3:1-8; 1 Tim. 1:3-7, 18-20; 4:1-16; 5:5-6, 11-15, 6:9-12, 17-19, 20-21; 2 Tim. 2:11-18; 3:13-15; Heb. 2:1-3; 3:6-19; 4:1-16: 5:8-9; 6:4-9, 10-20; 10:19-39; 12:1-17, 25-29; Jas. 1:12-16; 4:4-10; 5:19-20; 2 Pet. 1:5-11; 2:1-22; 3:16-17; 1 John 2:15-2:28; 5:16; 2 John 6-9; Jude 20-21; Rev. 2:7, 10-11, 17-26; 3:4-5, 8-12, 14-22; 21:7-8; 22:18-19. The proof texts produced by those who teach the doctrine of unconditional eternal security are scriptures that simply emphasize God's faithfulness in salvation, and say nothing about human responsibility. Thus they must be interpreted to harmonize with the many scriptures I've just listed. Just because God promises His faithfulness is no guarantee of anyone else's faithfulness. Just because I promise my wife that I'll never leave her and keep my promise, that is no guarantee that she will never leave me.

ever, is simply not true.

Many of those same preachers believe that God casts people who are not born again into hell, and they are certainly correct in their belief. Now let us think about that. *Obviously*, God doesn't approve of people whom He casts into hell. So how can it be said that He loves them? Are people who are cast into hell loved by God? Do you think they would tell you that God loves them? Of course not. Would God say that He loves them? Certainly not! They are abhorrent to Him, which is why He is punishing them in hell. He doesn't approve of or love them.

This being so, God's love for earthly sinners is clearly a *merciful love* that is only temporary, not an *approving love*. He has mercy on them, forestalling His judgment and giving them an opportunity to repent. Jesus died for them, providing a way for them to be forgiven. To that degree and in that way, it could be said that God loves them. But He never *approves* of them. He never feels a love for them like a father feels for his child. Rather, Scripture declares, "Just as a father has compassion on his children, so the Lord has compassion on *those who fear Him*" (Ps. 103:13, emphasis added). Thus it can be said that God does *not* have the same compassion on those who *don't* fear Him. God's love for sinners is more akin to the mercy a judge has on a convicted killer who receives a life sentence rather than the death penalty.

There is not a single case in the book of Acts where anyone preaching the gospel said to an unsaved audience that God loved them. Rather, the biblical preachers often warned their audiences about God's wrath and called them to repent, letting them know that God *did not* approve of them, that they were in danger, and that they needed to make dramatic changes in their lives. Had they only told their audiences that God loved them (as do so many modern ministers), they may have misled their audiences into thinking that they were in no danger, that they were not storing up wrath for themselves, and that they had no need to repent.

God's Hatred of Sinners

Contrary to what is often proclaimed about God's love for sinners today, Scripture often states that God *hates* sinners:

> The boastful shall not stand before Your eyes; *You hate all who do iniquity.* You destroy those who speak falsehood; The Lord *abhors* the man of bloodshed and deceit (Ps. 5:5-6, emphasis added).

> The Lord tests the righteous and the wicked, and the one who loves violence *His soul hates* (Ps. 11:5, emphasis added).

> I have forsaken My house, I have abandoned My inheritance; I have given the beloved of My soul into the hand

of her enemies. My inheritance has become to Me like a lion in the forest; she has roared against Me; therefore *I have come to hate her* (Jer. 12:7-8, emphasis added).

All their evil is at Gilgal; Indeed, *I came to hate them there!* Because of the wickedness of their deeds I will drive them out of My house! *I will love them no more;* all their princes are rebels (Hos. 9:15).

Note that all of the above scriptures do not say that God only hates what people *do*—they say He hates *them*. This throws some light on the common cliché that God loves the sinner but hates the sin. We cannot separate a person from what he does. *What he does reveals what he is.* Thus God rightly hates people who commit sin, not just the sins people commit. If God approves of people who do what He hates, He is very inconsistent with Himself. In human courts, *people* are put on trial for their crimes, and *they* receive the just recompense. We don't hate the crime but approve of those who commit crimes.

People Whom God Abhors

Not only does Scripture affirm that God hates certain individuals, it also declares that God abhors some kinds of sinful people, or that they are an abomination to Him. Note once more that the following scripture quotations do not say that what these people *do* is an abomination to God, but that *they themselves* are an abomination to God. They do not say that God abhors their *sins*, but that God abhors *them*:[32]

A woman shall not wear man's clothing, nor shall a man put on a woman's clothing; for whoever does these things is an *abomination* to the Lord your God (Deut. 22:5, emphasis added).

For everyone who does these things, everyone who acts unjustly is an *abomination* to the Lord your God (Deut. 25:16, emphasis added).

Further, you will eat the flesh of your sons and the flesh of your daughters you will eat. I then will destroy your high places, and cut down your incense altars, and heap your remains on the remains of your idols, for My soul shall *abhor* you (Lev. 26:29-30, emphasis added).

[32] It could be argued that all of these scriptures that show God's hatred and abhorrence of sinners are from the Old Testament. God's attitude toward sinners has not changed, however, from Old to New Testaments. Jesus' encounter with the Canaanite woman in Matthew 15:22-28 is an excellent New Testament example of God's attitude toward sinners. At first, Jesus wouldn't even answer her pleadings, and He even referred to her as a dog. Her persistent faith resulted in Him showing her some mercy. Jesus' attitude toward the scribes and Pharisees can hardly be considered one of approving love (see Matt. 23).

> The boastful shall not stand before Your eyes; You hate all who do iniquity. You destroy those who speak falsehood; The Lord *abhors* the man of bloodshed and deceit (Ps. 5:5-6, emphasis added).

> For the devious are an *abomination* to the Lord; but He is intimate with the upright (Prov. 3:32, emphasis added).

> The perverse in heart are an *abomination* to the Lord, but the blameless in their walk are His delight (Prov. 11:20).

> Everyone who is proud in heart is an *abomination* to the Lord; assuredly, he will not be unpunished (Prov. 16:5, emphasis added).

> He who justifies the wicked and he who condemns the righteous, both of them alike are an *abomination* to the Lord (Prov. 17:15, emphasis added).

How are we to reconcile such scriptures with those that affirm God's love for sinners? How can it be said that God abhors and hates sinners, but that He also loves them?

It must be recognized that not all love is the same. Some love is not conditional. It could be called "merciful love." It is a love that says, "I love you in spite of." It loves people regardless of their actions. That is the kind of love God has for sinners.

Contrasted with *merciful love* is *conditional love*. It could be referred to as "approving love." It is a love that is earned or merited. It is a love that says, "I love you because of."

Some think that if love is conditional, it is not love at all. Or they belittle such a love, saying it is purely selfish, and unlike God's love.

The truth is, however, that God does possess conditional love, as we will soon see in Scripture. Thus *approving love* should not be sneered at. *Approving love* is the primary love that God has for His true children. We should much more desire God's *approving love* than His merciful love.

Is *Approving Love* an Inferior Love?

Stop and ask yourself this question: "Which kind of love would I rather people have for me—*merciful love* or *approving love*?" I'm sure you would prefer that people love you "because of," not "in spite of."

Would you rather hear your spouse say, "I have no reason to love you, and there is nothing about you that motivates me to show you my favor" or, "I love you for so many reasons, because there are so many things about you that I admire"? Of course, we would rather that our spouses love us with an *approving love*, and that is the primary kind of love that draws couples together and keeps them together. When there is nothing

The Disciple-Making Minister

that a person admires in his or her spouse, when all *approving love* has ceased to exist, few marriages last. If they do last, the credit goes to merciful love, which stems from the godly character of the giver of that love.

All this being so, we see that *approving*, or *conditional love*, is not an inferior love at all. While *merciful love* is the most praiseworthy love to *give*, *approving love* is the most praiseworthy love to *gain*. Moreover, the fact that *approving love* is the only kind of love that the Father has ever had for Jesus elevates it to its rightful place of respect. God the Father has never possessed even a drop of *merciful love* for Jesus, because there was never anything unlovely in Christ. Jesus testified:

> For this reason the Father loves Me, because I lay down My life so that I may take it again (John 10:17, emphasis added).

Thus we see that the Father loved Jesus *because of* Jesus' obedience to die. There must be nothing wrong and everything right about *approving love*. Jesus earned and deserved His Father's love.

Jesus also declared that he abided in His Father's love by keeping His Father's commandments:

> Just as the Father has loved Me, I have also loved you; abide in My love. If you keep My commandments, you will abide in My love; *just as I have kept My Father's commandments and abide in His love* (John 15:9-10, emphasis added).

Moreover, as this scripture indicates, we are to follow Jesus' example, and abide in His love by keeping His commandments. He is clearly speaking of *approving love* in this passage, telling us that we can and should earn His love, and that we may take ourselves out of His love through disobedience to His commandments. *We abide in His love only if we keep His commandments.* Such a thing is rarely taught today, but should be, because it is what Jesus said.

Jesus only affirmed God's *approving love* for those who keep His commandments:

> For *the Father Himself loves you, because you have loved Me* and have believed that I came forth from the Father (John 16:27, emphasis added).

> He who has My commandments and keeps them is the one who loves Me; and *he who loves Me will be loved by My Father*, and I will love him and will disclose Myself to him....*If anyone loves Me, he will keep My word; and My Father will love him*, and We will come to him and make Our abode with him (John 14:21, 23, emphasis added).

Note in the second quotation, Jesus was not making a promise to uncommitted believers that if they started keeping His words, He would draw closer to them in a special way. No, Jesus was promising that if anyone would start loving Him and keeping His word, then His Father would love that person, and both He and His Father would come to live in that person, a clear reference to being born again. Everyone who is born again has both the Father and Son living in him by the indwelling Holy Spirit (see Rom. 8:9). So we again see that those who are truly born again are those who repent and begin to obey Jesus, and they are the only ones who thus gain the *approving love* of the Father.

Of course, Jesus still reserves *merciful love* for those who believe in Him. When they disobey, He is ready to forgive them if they will confess their sin and forgive others.

The Conclusion

All of this is to say that God does not love His obedient children the same as He loves sinners. He loves sinners only with a *merciful love*, and that love is temporary, lasting only until they die. At the same time that He loves them with a *merciful love*, He hates them with a hatred that stems from His disapproval of their character. This is what Scripture teaches.

On the other hand, God loves His children much more than those who are not born again. He primarily loves them with an *approving love* because they have repented and are striving to obey His commandments. As they grow in holiness, He has less and less reason to love them with a *merciful love,* and more and more reason to love them with an *approving love*, which is exactly what they desire.

This is also to say that many portrayals of God's love by modern preachers and teachers are misleading and inaccurate. In light of what Scripture says, take a moment to evaluate the following familiar clichés about God's love:

> 1.) There isn't anything you could do to make God love you any more or less than He does right now.

> 2.) There is nothing you could do that would make God stop loving you.

> 3.) God's love is unconditional.

> 4.) God loves everyone the same.

> 5.) God loves the sinner but hates the sin.

> 6.) There is nothing you can do to earn or deserve God's love.

> 7.) God's love for us is not based upon our performance.

All of the above statements are potentially misleading or outright false, as the majority completely deny God's *approving love* and many misrepresent His *merciful love*.

Regarding (1), there is something believers can do that could make God *approvingly love* them more: they could be more obedient. And there is something they can do to make God *approvingly love* them less: disobedience. For sinners, there is something that they could do which could make God love them *much* more: repent. Then they would gain God's *approving love*. And there is something they could do that would make God love them less: die. Then they would lose the only love God had for them, His *merciful love*.

Regarding (2), a Christian could forfeit God's *approving love* by returning to the practice of sin, putting himself in a position to experience only God's *merciful love*. And, again, the non-believer could die, and that would stop God's *merciful love*, the only love God ever had for him.

Regarding (3), God's *approving love* is certainly conditional. And even His *merciful love* is conditional upon a person being physically alive. After death, God's *merciful love* ends, so it is conditional because it is temporary.

Regarding (4), it is more likely that God doesn't love anyone the same, because all, sinners and saints alike, He disapproves or approves to various degrees. Certainly it is true that God's love is not the same for sinners and saints.

Regarding (5), God hates sinners *and* their sins. It could be better said that He loves sinners with a *merciful love* and hates their sins. From a standpoint of His *approving love*, He hates them.

Regarding (6), anyone can and everyone should earn God's *approving love*. Of course, no one can earn His *merciful love*, as it is unconditional.

Finally, regarding (7), God's *merciful love* is not based upon performance, but God's *approving love* certainly is.

All of this is to say that the disciple-making minister should present God's love accurately, as it is described in the Bible, because he doesn't want anyone to be deceived. Only people whom God *approvingly loves* enter heaven, and God only approvingly loves those who have been born again and obey Jesus. The disciple-making minister would never teach what might lead people away from holiness. His goal is the same as God's goal, to make disciples who obey all of Christ's commandments.

SEVEN

Biblical Interpretation

Paul wrote to Timothy:

> Pay close attention to *yourself* and to *your teaching*; persevere in these things; for as you do this you will insure salvation both for yourself and for those who hear you (1 Tim. 4:16, emphasis added).

Every minister should take this admonition to heart, paying close attention, first of all, to *himself*, making certain that he is setting an example of godliness.

Second, he should pay close attention to his *teaching*, because his eternal salvation and the eternal salvation of those who listen to him are dependent on what he teaches, just as Paul wrote in the above-quoted verse.[33] If a minister embraces false doctrine or neglects to tell people the truth, the result can be eternally disastrous for him and others.

There is no excuse, however, for the disciple-making minister to teach false doctrine, as God has given him the Holy Spirit and His Word to guide him into the truth. In contrast, ministers with wrong motives often merely parrot the popular teachings of others, not studying the Word for themselves, and are apt to err in their doctrine and teaching. The safeguard against this is for the minister to purify his heart, making certain that his motive is to (1) please God and (2) help people be prepared to stand before Jesus, rather than to become personally wealthy, powerful or popular. Additionally, he must diligently study God's Word so that he has a thorough and balanced understanding of it. Paul also wrote to Timothy,

> Be diligent to present yourself approved to God as a workman who does not need to be ashamed, handling accurately the word of truth (2 Tim. 2:15).

[33] Obviously, Paul didn't believe in unconditional eternal security, otherwise he would not have told Timothy, a saved person, that he needed to do something in order to insure his salvation.

Reading, studying and meditating on God's Word should be a discipline that a minister practices continually. The Holy Spirit will help him better understand God's Word as he diligently studies, thus insuring that he will "handle accurately the word of truth." One of the greatest problems in the church today is that ministers misinterpret God's Word and consequently mislead the people they teach. This can be quite serious. James warned,

> Let not many of you become teachers, my brethren, knowing that as such we shall incur a stricter judgment (Jas. 3:1).

For this reason it is imperative that the disciple-making minister knows how to rightly interpret the Word of God, with the goal of accurately understanding and communicating the intending meaning of any given text.

Rightly interpreting God's Word is done the same way as rightly interpreting anyone else's words. If we want to understand accurately the intended meaning of any author or speaker, we must apply certain rules of interpretation, rules that are based on common sense. In this chapter, we will consider the three most important rules of sound Bible interpretation. They are, (1) *Read intelligently*, (2) *Read contextually*, and (3) *Read honestly*.

Rule #1: Read intelligently. Interpret what you read literally unless it is obviously intended to be understood as figurative or symbolic.

Scripture, like all literature, is full of figures of speech, such a *metaphors*, *hyperboles* and *anthropomorphisms*. They should be taken as such.

A *metaphor* is a comparison of similarities between two basically dissimilar things. Scripture contains many metaphors. One can be found in Christ's words during the Last Supper:

> And while they were eating, Jesus took some bread, and after a blessing, He broke it and gave it to the disciples, and said, "Take, eat; this is My body." And when He had taken a cup and given thanks, He gave it to them, saying, "Drink from it, all of you; for this is My blood of the covenant, which is poured out for many for forgiveness of sins" (Matt. 26:26-28).

Did Jesus mean that the bread He gave His disciples was *literally* His body and that the wine they drank was *literally* His blood? Common sense tells us *No*. Scripture plainly says that it was bread and wine that Jesus gave them, and it says nothing about them changing, literally, into flesh and blood at any point in time. Neither Peter nor John, present at the Last Supper, ever reported such a thing in their epistles, and it is very unlikely that the disciples would have had an easy time of playing the part of cannibals!

Some argue, "But Jesus said that the bread and wine were His body and blood, so I'm going to believe what Jesus said!"

Jesus also once said that He was the door (see John 10:9). Did He literally become a door with hinges and a doorknob? Jesus once said that He was the vine and that we are the branches (see John 15:5). Did Jesus literally become a grape vine? Have we literally become vine branches? Jesus once said that He was light of the world and the bread that came down out of heaven (see John 9:5; 6:41). Is Jesus also the sunlight and a loaf of bread?

Clearly, all of these expressions are figures of speech called *metaphors*, a comparison of two things that are basically dissimilar but which share some similarities. In some ways, Jesus was *like* a door and a grape vine. Jesus' statements at the Last Supper are obvious metaphors as well. The wine was *like* His blood (in some ways). The bread was *like* His body (in some ways).

Christ's Parables

Christ's parables are *similes*, which are the same as metaphors, but similes always include the word *like*, *as* or *so*. They teach spiritual lessons also by comparing similarities between two things that are essentially dissimilar. That is an important point to remember as we interpret them; otherwise we may make the error of looking for significance in each little detail of every parable. Metaphors and similes always reach a place where the similarities end and the dissimilarities begin. For example, if I say to my wife, "Your eyes are like pools," I mean that her eyes are blue, deep and inviting. I don't mean that fish swim in them, that birds land on them, and that they freeze over with ice during the winter.

Let us consider three of Jesus' parables, all similes, the first being the Parable of the Dragnet:

> The kingdom of heaven is like a dragnet cast into the sea, and gathering fish of every kind; and when it was filled, they drew it up on the beach; and they sat down, and gathered the good fish into containers, but the bad they threw away. So it will be at the end of the age; the angels shall come forth, and take out the wicked from among the righteous, and will cast them into the furnace of fire; there shall be weeping and gnashing of teeth (Matt. 13:47-50).

Are the kingdom of heaven and a dragnet *basically* the same? Absolutely not! They are *very much* different, but there are a *few* similarities. Just as fish are judged and separated into two categories, desirable and undesirable, when pulled from a dragnet, so it will be in God's kingdom. One day the wicked and the righteous, who are currently living together, will be separated. But that is where the similarities end. *Fish* swim; *people* walk. *Fishermen* separate fish. *Angels* will separate the wicked from the righteous. *Fish* are judged by how good they taste after they are cooked. *People* are judged by their obedience or disobedience to God. *Good fish* are put into containers and *bad fish* are thrown away. *Righteous people* inherit God's kingdom and *wicked people* are cast into hell.

This parable is a perfect example of how every metaphor and simile is ultimately an imperfect comparison because the things being compared are basically dissimilar. We don't want to go beyond the intention of the speaker, assuming that dissimilarities are actually similarities. For example, we all know that "good fish" actually end of being cooked in fire, and "bad fish" go back into the water to swim another day. Jesus didn't mention that! It would have worked against His purpose.

This particular parable does not teach (regardless of what anyone says) a strategy of "dragnet evangelism," where we try to drag everyone into the church, good and bad, whether they want to come or not! This parable does not teach that the beach is the best place to witness. This parable does not prove that the Rapture of the church occurs at the end of the tribulation period. This parable does not teach that our salvation is purely God's sovereign choice because the chosen fish in the parable had nothing to do with the reason for their selection. Don't force unwarranted significance into Jesus' parables!

Remaining Ready

Here is another familiar parable of Jesus, the Parable of the Ten Virgins:

> Then the kingdom of heaven will be comparable to [is like] ten virgins, who took their lamps, and went out to meet the bridegroom. And five of them were foolish, and five were prudent. For when the foolish took their lamps, they took no oil with them, but the prudent took oil in flasks along with their lamps. Now while the bridegroom was delaying, they all got drowsy and began to sleep. But at midnight there was a shout, "Behold, the bridegroom! Come out to meet him." Then all those virgins rose, and trimmed their lamps. And the foolish said to the prudent, "Give us some of your oil, for our lamps are going out." But the prudent answered, saying, "No, there will not be enough for us and you too; go instead to the dealers and buy some for yourselves." And while they were going away to make the purchase, the bridegroom came, and those who were ready went in with him to the wedding feast; and the door was shut. And later the other virgins also came, saying, "Lord, lord, open up for us." But he answered and said, "Truly I say to you, I do not know you." Be on the alert then, for you do not know the day nor the hour (Matt. 25:1-13).

What is the primary lesson of this parable? It is found in the final sentence: *Stay ready for the return of the Lord, because He might delay longer than you expect.* That's about it.

As I mentioned in a previous chapter, Jesus spoke this parable to some of His closest disciples (see Matt. 24:3; Mark 13:3), who were obviously obediently following Him at that time. So clearly implied in this parable is the fact that it was possible for Peter, James, John and Andrew *not* to be ready when Jesus returned. That is why Jesus was warning them. Thus this parable teaches there is a possibility that those who are currently ready for Christ's return may not be ready when He actually does return. All ten virgins were *initially* ready, but five became *unready.* Had the bridegroom returned sooner, all ten would have gained entrance into the wedding feast.

But what is the significance of there being *five* foolish and *five* wise virgins? Does that prove that only one-half of professing believers will be ready when Christ returns? No.

What is the significance of the oil? Does it represent the Holy Spirit? No. Does it reveal to us that only those who have been baptized in the Holy Spirit will make it into heaven? No.

Does the bridegroom's returning at midnight reveal that Jesus will return at midnight? No.

Why didn't the bridegroom ask the wise virgins to identify their foolish friends at the door? If the bridegroom had asked the wise to identify the foolish, it would have ruined the entire point of the parable, as the foolish would have ultimately gained entrance.

Perhaps it could be said that just as the foolish virgins no longer had light and went to sleep, so foolish believers begin to walk in spiritual darkness and go to sleep spiritually, thus ultimately leading to their condemnation. *Perhaps* a similarity could be found in the wedding feast of the parable and the future wedding feast of the Lamb, but that is about as far as one can go without forcing meaning into this parable or its various details.

Bearing Fruit

Perhaps the absolute worst interpretation I've ever heard of one of Christ's parables was one preacher's explanation of the Parable of the Wheat and the Tares. First, let's read that parable:

> He presented another parable to them, saying, "The kingdom of heaven may be compared to [is like] a man who sowed good seed in his field. But while men were sleeping, his enemy came and sowed tares also among the wheat, and went away. But when the wheat sprang up and bore grain, then the tares became evident also. And the slaves of the landowner came and said to him, "Sir, did you not sow good seed in your field? How then does

it have tares?" And he said to them, "An enemy has done this!" And the slaves said to him, "Do you want us, then, to go and gather them up?" But he said, "No; lest while you are gathering up the tares, you may root up the wheat with them. Allow both to grow together until the harvest; and in the time of the harvest I will say to the reapers, 'First gather up the tares and bind them in bundles to burn them up; but gather the wheat into my barn'" (Matt. 13:24-30).

Now here was that certain preacher's explanation:

It is a fact that when wheat and tares sprout, they look identical. No one can tell if they are wheat or tares. That is just how it is in the world and in the church. No one can tell who are the true Christians and who are the unbelievers. They cannot be identified by how they live their lives, because many Christians are not obeying Christ anymore than unbelievers. Only God knows their hearts, and He will sort them out in the end.

That, of course, is not the point of the Parable of the Wheat and Tares! In reality, it teaches that believers are indeed *very* distinguishable from non-believers. Notice that the slaves realized that tares had been planted when the wheat bore grain (see v. 26). Tares don't bear any fruit, and that is how they are easily identified as tares. I think it is significant that Jesus chose the *fruitless* tares to represent the wicked who will be gathered in the end and cast into hell.

The primary points of this parable are plain: *The truly saved bear fruit; the unsaved do not. Although God is not judging the wicked yet as they live among the saved, one day He will separate them from the righteous and cast them into hell.*

Jesus actually provided an explanation of this particular parable, so there is no need for anyone to search for any significance beyond what He explained:

The one who sows the good seed is the Son of Man, and the field is the world; and as for the good seed, these are the sons of the kingdom; and the tares are the sons of the evil one; and the enemy who sowed them is the devil, and the harvest is the end of the age; and the reapers are angels. Therefore just as the tares are gathered up and burned with fire, so shall it be at the end of the age. The Son of Man will send forth His angels, and they will gather out of His kingdom all stumbling blocks, and those who commit lawlessness, and will cast them into the furnace of fire; in that place there shall be weeping and gnashing of teeth. Then the righteous will shine forth as the sun in the kingdom of their Father. He who has ears, let him hear (Matt. 13:36-43).

Hyperbole

A second common figure of speech found within the Bible is *hyperbole*. A hyperbole is a deliberate exaggeration made for emphasis. When a mother tells her child, "I called you a thousand times to come home for dinner," that is hyperbole. An example of a hyperbole in the Bible would be Jesus' statement about cutting off your right hand:

And if your right hand makes you stumble, cut it off, and throw it from you; for it is better for you that one of the parts of your body perish, than for your whole body to go into hell (Matt. 5:30).

If Jesus literally meant that every one of us who sins in some way by using our right hand should cut that hand off, then all of us should be missing our right hands! Of course, the problem with sin is not really in our hands. More than likely, Jesus was teaching us that sin can send us to hell, and the way to avoid sin is to remove temptations and those things which cause us to stumble.

Anthropomorphism

A third figure of speech that we encounter within Scripture is *anthropomorphism*. Anthropomorphism is a metaphorical expression where human attributes are ascribed to God for the sake of helping us understand Him. For example, we read in Genesis 11:5:

And the Lord came down to see the city and the tower which the sons of men had built (Gen. 11:5).

This is a probable anthropomorphism because it seems unlikely that the all-knowing God literally had to journey from heaven down to Babel to investigate what people were building!

Many biblical scholars consider every biblical statement that describes parts of God's body, such as His arms, hands, nose, eyes and hair, to be anthropomorphisms. Surely, they say, almighty God does not actually have such parts as humans do.

I would disagree, however, for a number of reasons. First, because Scripture plainly teaches that *we* have been created in *God's* image and likeness:

Then God said, "Let Us make man in *Our image, according to Our likeness*" (Gen. 1:26, emphasis added).

Some would say we are created in God's image and likeness only in the sense that we possess self-awareness, moral responsibility, the capacity to reason and so on. However, let us read a statement that is very similar to Genesis 1:26, one that occurs just a few chapters later:

> When Adam had lived one hundred and thirty years, he became the father of a son *in his own likeness, according to his image,* and named him Seth (Gen. 5:3, emphasis added).

This surely means that Seth was similar in physical appearance to his father. If that is what it means in Genesis 5:3, certainly the identical expression means the same thing in Genesis 1:26. Common sense and sound interpretation say that it does.

Furthermore, we have some descriptions of God by biblical authors who saw Him. For example, Moses, along with seventy-three other Israelites, saw God:

> Then Moses went up with Aaron, Nadab and Abihu, and seventy of the elders of Israel, and *they saw the God of Israel*; and under *His feet* there appeared to be a pavement of sapphire, as clear as the sky itself. Yet He did not stretch out *His hand* against the nobles of the sons of Israel; and *they beheld God,* and they ate and drank (Ex. 24:9-11).

If you had asked Moses if God had hands and feet, what would he have said?[34]

The prophet Daniel also had a vision of God the Father *and* God the Son:

> I kept looking until thrones were set up, and the Ancient of Days [God the Father] *took His seat*; His vesture was like white snow, and *the hair of His head* like pure wool. His throne was ablaze with flames, its wheels were a burning fire. A river of fire was flowing and coming out from before Him; thousands upon thousands were attending Him, and myriads upon myriads were standing before Him; the court sat, and the books were opened….I kept looking in the night visions, and behold, with the clouds of heaven one like a Son of Man [God the Son] was coming, and He came up to the Ancient of Days and was presented before Him. And to Him was given dominion, glory and a kingdom, that all the peoples, nations, and men of every language might serve Him. His dominion is an everlasting dominion which will not pass away; and His kingdom is one which will not be destroyed (Dan. 7:9-10, 13-14).

---

[34] Moses also once also saw God's back as He "walked by." God held His hand in such a way so as to block Moses from seeing His face; see Ex. 33:18-23.

If you had asked Daniel if God had white hair and had a form whereby He was able to sit on a throne, what would He have said?

All of this being so, I'm convinced that God the Father has a glorious form that is somewhat similar to the form of a human being, although He is not made of flesh and blood, but is a spirit (see John 4:24).

How can you discern which portions of Scripture are meant to be interpreted literally and which should be interpreted figuratively or symbolically? That should be easy for anyone who can reason logically. Interpret everything literally unless there is no other intelligent alternative than to interpret what is written figuratively or symbolically. The Old Testament prophets and the book of Revelation, for example, are clearly full of symbolism, some of which is explained, some of which is not. But the symbolisms are not difficult to identify.

Rule #2: Read *contextually*. Every passage must be interpreted in light of the surrounding passages and the entire Bible. The historical and cultural context should also be considered whenever possible.

Reading scriptures without taking into consideration their immediate and biblical context is perhaps the primary cause of misinterpretation.

It is possible to make the Bible say anything you want it to say by isolating scriptures from their context. For example, did you know that the Bible says that God doesn't exist? In Psalm 14 we read, "There is no God" (Ps. 14:1). If we want to interpret those words accurately, however, we must read them within their context: *"The fool has said in his heart, 'There is no God'"* (Ps. 14:1, emphasis added). Now this verse takes on a whole different meaning!

Another example: I once heard a preacher give a sermon on the Christians' need to be "baptized in fire." He began his sermon by reading the words of John the Baptist from Matthew 3:11: "As for me, I baptize you with water for repentance, but He who is coming after me is mightier than I, and I am not fit to remove His sandals; He will baptize you with the Holy Spirit and fire."

Based on this one verse, he built a sermon. I remember his saying, "Just because you are baptized in the Holy Spirit, that is not enough! Jesus also wants to baptize you in fire, just like John the Baptist proclaimed!" He went on to explain that once we had been "baptized in fire," we would be full of zeal to work for the Lord. Finally he had an altar call for people who wanted to be "baptized in fire."

Unfortunately, that particular preacher had made the classic mistake of taking a scripture out of its context.

What did John the Baptist mean when he said that Jesus would baptize with fire? To find the answer, all we need to do is read the two verses before that verse, and one verse after it. Let's begin with the two preceding verses. There John said:

> And do not suppose that you can say to yourselves, "We have Abraham for our father"; for I say to you, that God is able from these stones to raise up children to Abraham. And the axe is already laid at the root of the trees; every tree therefore that does not bear good fruit is cut down and *thrown into the fire* (Matt. 3:9-10, emphasis added).

We first learn that at least part of John's audience that day consisted of Jews who thought their salvation was based upon their lineage. Thus, John's sermon was evangelistic.

We also learn that John was warning that unsaved people are in danger of being *cast into the fire*. It would seem reasonable to conclude that "the fire" of which John spoke in verse 10 is the same fire of which he spoke in verse 11.

This fact becomes even clearer when we read verse 12:

> "And His winnowing fork is in His hand, and He will thoroughly clear His threshing floor; and He will gather His wheat into the barn, *but He will burn up the chaff with unquenchable fire*" (Matt. 3:12, emphasis added).

In both verses 10 and 12, the fire of which John was speaking was the fire of hell. In verse 12, he metaphorically states that Jesus will divide people into two groups—wheat, which He will "gather into the barn," and chaff, which He will burn up "with unquenchable fire."

In light of the surrounding verses, John must have meant in verse 11 that Jesus will baptize people *either* with the Holy Spirit, if they are believers, or with fire, if they are unbelievers. Since that is the case, no one should preach to Christians that they need to be baptized in fire!

Moving beyond the immediate context of these verses, we should also look to the rest of the New Testament. Can we find an example in the book of Acts where Christians are said to have been "baptized in fire"? No. The closest thing is Luke's description of the day of Pentecost when the disciples were baptized in the Holy Spirit and tongues of fire temporarily appeared over their heads. But Luke never says that this was a "baptism in fire." Moreover, can we find an exhortation or any instruction in the epistles for Christians to be "baptized in fire"? No. Therefore, it is quite safe to conclude that no Christian should be seeking a baptism in fire.

A False Gospel Derived From Scripture

Oftentimes the gospel itself is misrepresented by preachers and teachers who, because they fail to consider context, misinterpret Scripture. False teaching regarding God's grace abounds for this very reason.

For example, Paul's statement about salvation being a product of grace and not works, found in Ephesians 2:8, has been abused to promote a false gospel, all because context has been ignored. Paul wrote:

> For by grace you have been saved through faith; and that
> not of yourselves, it is the gift of God; not as a result of
> works, that no one should boast (Eph. 2:8-9).

Many focus exclusively on Paul's statements about salvation being by grace, a gift, and not a result of works. From that, contrary to the testimony of hundreds of scriptures, they derive that there is no connection between salvation and holiness. Some even go so far to say that repentance is therefore not necessary for salvation to occur. This is a classic example of how Scripture is misinterpreted because context is ignored.

First, let us consider what the actual passage under consideration says in its *entirety*. Paul does *not* say that we have been *saved by grace*, but that we have been *saved by grace through faith*. Faith is every bit as much a part of the salvation equation as is grace. Scripture declares that faith without works is useless, dead, and cannot save (see Jas. 2:14-26). Thus Paul is not teaching that holiness is irrelevant in salvation. He is saying that our own efforts are not what save us; the basis of our salvation is God's grace. We could never be saved without God's grace, but it is only as we respond to God's grace with faith that salvation actually occurs in our lives. The result of salvation is always obedience, the fruit of genuine faith. By looking at the context no further away than the very next verse, this is substantiated. Paul says:

> For we are His workmanship, created in Christ Jesus for
> good works, which God prepared beforehand, that we
> should walk in them (Eph. 2:10).

The whole reason we have been regenerated by the Holy Spirit, now new creations in Christ, was so we could walk in good works of obedience. Thus Paul's salvation equation looks like this:

Grace + Faith = Salvation + Obedience

That is, grace plus faith equals (or results in) salvation plus obedience. When God's grace is responded to in faith, the result is always salvation and good works.

Yet those who have ripped Paul's words from their context have concocted a formula like this:

Grace + Faith – Obedience = Salvation

That is, grace plus faith without (or minus) obedience equals (or results in) salvation. That is heresy as far as the Bible is concerned.

If we read just a little more of the context of Paul's words, we also soon discover that the situation in Ephesus was the same as it was just about everywhere Paul preached. That is, Jews were teaching Paul's new Gentile converts that they had to be circumcised and keep some of the ceremonial aspects of the Mosaic Law if they wanted to be saved. It was within the context of circumcision and ceremonial works that Paul had in mind when he wrote about the "works" that don't save us (see Eph. 2:11-22).

If we read just a little further, taking in more of the context of Paul's entire letter to the Ephesians, we see very clearly that Paul believed that holiness was essential for salvation:

> But do not let immorality or any impurity or greed even be named among you, as is proper among saints; and there must be no filthiness and silly talk, or coarse jesting, which are not fitting, but rather giving of thanks. *For this you know with certainty, that no immoral or impure person or covetous man, who is an idolater, has an inheritance in the kingdom of Christ and God. Let no one deceive you with empty words, for because of these things the wrath of God comes upon the sons of disobedience* (Eph. 5:3-6, emphasis added).

If Paul believed that God's grace would ultimately save someone who was unrepentantly immoral, impure or covetous, he would never have written those words. Paul's intended meaning of his words recorded in Ephesians 2:8-9 can only be rightly understood in the context of his entire letter to the Ephesians.

The Galatian Fiasco

Paul's words in his letter to the Galatians have been similarly interpreted out of their context. The result has been the distortion of the gospel, the very thing that Paul was hoping to correct in his letter to the Galatians.

The entire theme of Paul's letter to the Galatians is "Salvation by faith, and not by works of the Law." But did Paul intend that his readers would conclude that holiness was not necessary to gain entrance into God's kingdom? Certainly not.

First, we note that Paul was once again combating Jews who had come to Galatia and were teaching the new converts that they could not be saved unless they were circumcised and kept the Law of Moses. Paul mentions the particular issue of circumcision repeatedly in his letter, as that seems to have been the primary emphasis of the Jewish legalists (see Gal. 2:3, 7-9, 12; 5:2-3, 6, 11; 6:12-13, 15). Paul was not concerned that the Galatian believers were becoming too obedient to Christ's commandments; he was concerned that they were no longer placing their faith in Christ for their salvation, but in circumcision and in their own feeble efforts at keeping the Mosaic Law.

As we consider the entire context of Paul's letter to the Galatians, we note that he writes in chapter 5:

> But if you are led by the Spirit, you are not under the Law. Now the deeds of the flesh are evident, which are: im-

morality, impurity, sensuality, idolatry, sorcery, enmities, strife, jealousy, outbursts of anger, disputes, dissensions, factions, envying, drunkenness, carousing, and things like these, of which I forewarn you just as I have forewarned you *that those who practice such things shall not inherit the kingdom of God* (Gal. 5:18-21, emphasis added).

If Paul wanted to convey to the Galatians that they could be unholy and gain heaven, then he would have never written such words. His message was not that unholy people could go to heaven, but that those who nullify God's grace and Christ's sacrifice by trying to earn their salvation through circumcision and the Mosaic Law cannot be saved. It is not circumcision that brings salvation. It is faith in Jesus that results in a salvation that changes believers into holy new creations:

For neither is circumcision anything, nor uncircumcision, but a new creation (Gal. 6:15).

All of this, again, shows how vital it is to consider context when interpreting Scripture. The only way that the gospel can be distorted by means of the Word of God is by ignoring context. We can only wonder about the hearts of "ministers" who do this in such a blatant way that it cannot be anything but deliberate.

For example, I once heard a preacher declare that we should never mention God's wrath when we preach the gospel, because the Bible says that, "it is the kindness of God that leads you to repentance" (Rom. 2:4). Thus, according to him, the proper way to proclaim the gospel was to speak only of God's love and goodness. That would supposedly lead people to repent.

But when we read the context of the solitary verse that preacher quoted from the second chapter of Romans, we discover that it is encased by scriptures about God's judgment and holy wrath! The immediate context reveals that there isn't any possibility that Paul's intended meaning was what that preacher said it was:

And we know that the *judgment of God* rightly falls upon those who practice such things. And do you suppose this, O man, when you pass judgment upon those who practice such things and do the same yourself, that you will escape *the judgment of God*? Or do you think lightly of the riches of His kindness and forbearance and patience, not knowing *that the kindness of God leads you to repentance*? But because of your stubbornness and unrepentant heart you are storing up wrath for yourself in the day of wrath and revelation of the righteous judgment of God, who will render to every man according to his deeds: to those who by perseverance in doing good seek for glory and honor and immortality, eternal life; but to those who are selfishly ambitious and do not obey the truth, but obey unrighteousness, *wrath and indignation. There will be tribulation and distress for every soul of man who does evil,* of the Jew first and also of the Greek (Rom. 2:2-9, emphasis added).

Paul's reference to God's kindness is about the kindness God shows in delaying His wrath! And one wonders how a minister could make such an absurd statement in light the greater context of the Bible, which is full of examples of preachers who publicly warned sinners to repent.

Scripture's Consistency

Because the Bible is inspired by one Person, its message is consistent throughout. That is why we can trust context to help us interpret God's intended meaning in any given passage. God would not say something in one verse that contradicts another verse, and if it appears that He has, we need to keep studying until our interpretation of both verses harmonizes. For example, in several places in Jesus' Sermon on the Mount, it may at first appear as if He was contradicting, even correcting, an Old Testament moral law. For example:

> You have heard that it was said, "An eye for an eye, and a tooth for a tooth." But I say to you, do not resist him who is evil; but whoever slaps you on your right cheek, turn to him the other also (Matt. 5:38-39).

Jesus quoted directly from the Mosaic Law and then made a statement that seemed to contradict the very law He quoted. How are we to interpret what He said? Has God changed His mind on an issue of basic morality? Was taking revenge acceptable behavior under the old covenant but not the new? The context is what will help us.

Jesus was speaking primarily to His disciples (see Matt. 5:1-2), people whose only previous exposure to God's Word was via the scribes and Pharisees who taught in their synagogues. There they had heard God's law quoted, "An eye for eye, and a tooth for a tooth," a commandment whose meaning the scribes and Pharisees had twisted by ignoring its context. God did not intend for that commandment to be interpreted as a requirement for His people to always gain personal revenge for petty wrongs. He, in fact, said in the Mosaic Law that vengeance was His (see Deut. 32:35), and that His people should do good to their enemies (see Ex. 23:4-5). But the scribes and Pharisees ignored those commandments and invented their own interpretation of God's "eye for an eye" law, one that gave them the convenient right of personal revenge.[35] They ignored context.

---

[35] It should also be noted that Jesus had said earlier in His sermon that unless His audience's righteousness surpassed that of the scribes and Pharisees, (continued on next page)

God's commandment about "an eye for an eye, and a tooth for a tooth" is found within the context of His commandments that prescribe due justice in Israel's courts (see Ex. 21:22-24; Deut. 19:15-21). Making provision for a court system is in itself a revelation of God's disproval of personal revenge. Impartial judges who examine evidence are much more able to administer justice than are offended, biased individuals. God expects that courts and judges will impartially dole out punishments that fit the crimes. Thus, "an eye for an eye, and a tooth for a tooth."

All this being so, we are able to harmonize what at first appears contradictory. Jesus was simply helping His audience, people who had sat under false teaching all their lives, understand God's true will for them regarding personal revenge, what had already been revealed in the Law of Moses but had been twisted by the Pharisees. Jesus was not contradicting the Law He gave to Moses. He was only revealing its originally-intended meaning.

This also helps us rightly understand what Jesus expects of us in regard to major disputes, the kind of which might lead to a court case. God did not expect the Israelites to overlook any and every offense suffered from fellow Israelites, otherwise He would not have established a court system. Likewise, God does not expect Christians to overlook any and every offense suffered by means of fellow believers (or non-believers). The New Testament prescribes that irreconcilable Christians use the mediatory help of fellow believers (see 1 Cor. 6:1-6). And there is nothing wrong with a Christian taking a non-believer to secular courts regarding disputes of major offense. Major offenses are such things as having your eye or tooth knocked out! Minor offenses are the kinds of things Jesus spoke of, like being slapped on the cheek, or being sued for a small settlement (like your shirt), or being forced to go one mile. God wants His people to imitate Him and show extraordinary grace to thoughtless sinners and evil people.

Along these same lines, there have been some well-meaning believers who, thinking they were obeying Jesus, refused to press legal charges against those who had been caught stealing from them. They thought they were "turning the other cheek," when in reality they were enabling a thief to steal again, teaching him that there are no consequences for crime. Such Christians are not walking in love towards everyone else who will have goods stolen by that same thief! God wants thieves to suffer justice and repent. But when someone offends you in some minor way, such as slapping your cheek, don't take him to court or slap him back. Show him mercy and love.

Interpreting the Old in Light of the New

Not only should we interpret New Testament scriptures in the light of the Old Testament, we should always interpret Old Testament scriptures in light of the New Testament. For example, some sincere believers have

(continued from previous page) they would not enter heaven (see Matt. 5:20). Jesus then continued by revealing a number of specific ways in which the scribes and Pharisees were falling short.

read the dietary laws of Moses and concluded that Christians should restrict their diets in accordance with those laws. If they would read just two passages in the New Testament, however, they would discover that Moses' dietary laws are not applicable to those under the New Covenant:

> And He [Jesus] said to them, "Are you too so uncomprehending? Do you not see that whatever goes into the man from outside cannot defile him; because it does not go into his heart, but into his stomach, and is eliminated?" (Thus He declared all foods clean) (Mark 7:18-19).

> But the Spirit explicitly says that in later times some will fall away from the faith, paying attention to deceitful spirits and doctrines of demons, by means of the hypocrisy of liars seared in their own conscience as with a branding iron, men who forbid marriage and advocate abstaining from foods, which God has created to be gratefully shared in by those who believe and know the truth. For everything created by God is good, and nothing is to be rejected, if it is received with gratitude; for it is sanctified by means of the word of God and prayer (1 Tim. 4:1-5).

Under the new covenant, we are not subject to the Law of Moses, but to the Law of Christ (see 1 Cor. 9:20-21). Although Jesus certainly endorsed the moral aspects of Mosaic Law (thus incorporating them into the Law of Christ), neither He nor the apostles taught that Christians are obligated to keep the Mosaic dietary laws.

It is clear, however, that the early Christians, all converted Jews, continued to keep the old covenant dietary laws because of their cultural convictions (see Acts 10:9-14). And as Gentiles began to believe in Jesus, the early Jewish Christians asked them to follow Mosaic dietary laws limitedly purely out of deference to neighboring Jews who might be otherwise offended (see Acts 15:1-21). Thus, there is nothing wrong with Christians keeping the dietary laws of Moses just as long as they aren't trusting that keeping those laws is what saves them.

Some of the early Christians were also persuaded that it was wrong to eat meats that had been sacrificed to idols. Paul instructed believers who thought otherwise (like himself) to walk in love towards their brethren of "weaker faith" (see Rom. 14:1), doing nothing to cause them to violate their consciences. If a person abstains from eating foods out of conviction before God (even if those convictions are unfounded), he is to be commended for his devotion, not condemned for his misunderstanding. Likewise, those who abstain from certain foods out of personal conviction should not pass judgment on those who don't abstain. Both groups should walk in love towards the other, as this is certainly commanded by God (see Rom. 14:1-23).

In any case, because the Bible is progressive revelation, we should always interpret the oldest revelation (the Old Testament) through the light of the newest revelation (the New Testament). None of the revelation that God has ever given is contradictory; it is always complimentary.

Cultural and Historical Context

Whenever possible, we should also consider the cultural and historical context of the scripture passages we are studying. Knowing something about the unique aspects of the culture, geography and history of a biblical setting often helps us to gain insight we might otherwise have missed. Of course, this requires some help from books besides the Bible. A good study Bible will usually contain help in this area.

Here are a few examples of how historical or cultural information can keep us from confusion when reading the Bible:

1.) We sometimes read in Scripture of people going up on housetops (see Acts 10:9) or digging through roofs (see Mark 2:4). It helps to know that roofs were generally flat in Israel in Bible days, and that there were stairways on the outside of most homes that led up to those flat roofs. If we don't know that, we might imagine some biblical character on a rooftop straddling the roof peak and clinging to the chimney!

2.) We read in Mark 11:12-14 that Jesus cursed a fig tree because it had no figs, even though "it was not the season for figs." It helps to know that fig trees usually have a few figs on them even when they are out of season, so Jesus was not unreasonable in His expectation.

3.) We read in Luke 7:37-48 about a woman who entered a Pharisee's house where Jesus was dining. Scripture says that as she stood behind Jesus weeping, she began to wet His feet with her tears, wipe them with her hair, and kiss and anoint them with perfume. We wonder how such a thing could be accomplished as Jesus was sitting around a table eating. Did she crawl under the table? How was she able to get though the legs of all the other diners?

The answer is found in Luke's statement that Jesus was "reclining at the table" (Luke 7:37). The customary way of eating in those days was to lie on one's side on the floor around a low table, propping oneself up with one arm and feeding one's mouth with the other arm and hand. In this posture was Jesus adored by the woman.

This also helps us understand how John could lean against Jesus' breast at the Last Supper to ask Him a question. John was lying on his side with his back facing Jesus, and he simply leaned back on Jesus' breast to ask his question discretely (see John 13:23-25). DaVinci's famous painting of the Last Supper, which shows Jesus seated at a table with six of His disciples on either side, reveals the painter's biblical ignorance. He needed some historical context!

A Common Question About Clothes

One question that I'm often asked by pastors around the world is this: "Is it acceptable for Christian women to wear trousers, considering that the Bible forbids women from wearing men's clothing?"

This is good question that we can answer by applying some sound rules of interpretation and through a little cultural context.

First, let's examine the Bible's prohibition against women wearing men's clothing (and visa-versa):

> A woman shall not wear man's clothing, nor shall a man
> put on a woman's clothing; for whoever does these things
> is an abomination to the Lord your God (Deut. 22:5).

We should begin by asking, "What was God's intention in giving this commandment?" Was His goal to keep women from wearing trousers?

No, that couldn't have been His intention, because no men in Israel wore trousers when God originally said this. Trousers were not considered to be men's clothing or anyone's clothing for that matter. In fact, what men wore in biblical days would seem more like women's clothing to most of us today! That is a little bit of historical and cultural information that helps us to interpret correctly what God is trying to say.

So what *was* God's intention?

We read that whoever wore clothing of the opposite sex was an *abomination* to the Lord. That sounds quite serious. If a man takes a woman's scarf and places it on his head for three seconds, does that make him an abomination to God? That seems very doubtful.

It would seem more likely that what God was opposed to was people intentionally dressing so that they would appear to be the opposite sex. Why would anyone want to do such a thing? Only because he or she was hoping to seduce someone of the same sex, a sexual perversion referred to as *transvestitism*. I think we can understand how *that* would be considered an abomination to God.

Thus one cannot rightfully conclude that it is wrong for women to wear trousers based on Deuteronomy 22:5, unless she is doing so as a transvestite. As long as she still looks like a woman, she is not sinning by wearing trousers.

Of course, Scripture teaches that women should dress modestly (see 1 Tim. 2:9), and so trousers that are skintight and revealing are inappropriate (as are skintight dresses and skirts) because they could lead men to lust. Much of the clothing that women wear publicly in Western countries is completely inappropriate and is the kind of clothing that only prostitutes wear in developing countries. No Christian woman should wear publicly clothing with the goal of appearing "sexy."

A Few Other Thoughts

It is interesting that I've never been asked the question regarding women wearing trousers by pastors in China. That is probably because most Chinese women have been wearing trousers for a long time. I've only been asked the question regarding women and trousers by pastors in countries where most women don't wear trousers. This shows their personal cultural bias.

It is also interesting to me that I've never been asked a similar question by female ministers in Myanmar, where men traditionally wear what we might call a skirt, but what they call a *longgi*. Again, what constitutes women's and men's clothing varies from culture to culture, so we must be careful not to force our cultural understanding on the Bible.

Finally, I wonder why so many men who expect women not to wear trousers based on Deuteronomy 22:5 feel no obligation to apply Leviticus 19:27 to themselves, which says,

> You shall not round off the side-growth of your heads, nor
> harm the edges of your beard (Lev. 19:27).

How can men, in defiance of Leviticus 19:27, completely shave their own God-given beards, beards that clearly distinguish them from women, and then accuse women who wear trousers of trying to look like men? That would seem to be a little bit hypocritical!

Incidentally, a little historical information helps us understand God's intention in Leviticus 19:27. Rounding off the side-growth of beards was part of an idolatrous pagan ritual. God didn't want His people to appear to be devoted to pagan idols.

Who is Speaking?

We should always note who is doing the speaking in any given biblical passage, as that bit of contextual information will help us rightly interpret it. Although everything in the Bible is inspired to be in the Bible, not everything in the Bible is the inspired Word of God. What do I mean?

In many passages of Scripture, the uninspired words of people are recorded. Therefore, we shouldn't think that everything spoken by people in the Bible is inspired by God.

For example, some make the error of quoting the words of Job and his friends as if they were the inspired words of God. There are two reasons why this is a mistake. First, Job and his friends *argued* for thirty-four chapters. They disagreed. Obviously not everything they said could be God's inspired Word because God doesn't contradict Himself.

Second, at the close of the book of Job, God Himself speaks, and He rebukes both Job and his friends for saying things that were not correct (see Job 38-42).

We must take the same precautions when reading the New Testament. In several cases, Paul plainly stated that certain portions of his writings were only his own opinions (see 1 Cor. 7:12, 25-26, 40).

Who is Being Addressed?

Not only should we ask who is doing the speaking in any given biblical passage, we should also take note of who is being addressed. If we don't, we might misinterpret something as applicable to us that isn't. Or we might interpret something that is applicable to us as not being applicable.

For example, some claim a promise found in Psalm 34, believing it applies to them:

> He will give you the desires of your heart (Psalm 37:4).

But does that promise apply to everyone who reads or knows it? No, if we read the context, we find that it only applies to certain people who meet five conditions:

> Trust in the Lord, and do good; dwell in the land and cultivate faithfulness. Delight yourself in the Lord; and He will give you the desires of your heart (Psalm 37:3-4).

So we see how important it is that we take note of who is being addressed.

Here is another example:

> Peter began to say to Him [Jesus], "Behold, we have left everything and followed You." Jesus said, "Truly I say to you, there is no one who has left house or brothers or sisters or mother or father or children or farms, for My sake and for the gospel's sake, but that he shall receive a hundred times as much now in the present age, houses and brothers and sisters and mothers and children and farms, along with persecutions; and in the age to come, eternal life" (Mark 10:28-30).

It is quite popular in some circles to claim the "hundred-fold return" when one gives money to support someone who is preaching the gospel. But does this promise apply to such people? No, it is addressed to people who actually leave their families, farms, or homes to preach the gospel, as did Peter, who asked Jesus what His and the other disciples' reward would be.

Interestingly, those who always preach about the hundred-fold return seem to focus primarily on the houses and farms, and never the children and persecutions that are also promised! Jesus, of course, was not promising that those who leave their homes will receive ownership of one-hundred homes in return. He was promising that when they leave their families and homes, the members of their new spiritual families will open up their homes for lodging. True disciples don't care about ownership because they don't own anything themselves—they are only stewards of that which is God's.

A Final Example

When people read what is known as Jesus' "Olivet Discourse," found in Matthew 24-25, some wrongly think He was speaking to unsaved people, and thus incorrectly conclude that what He said has no application to them. They read the Parable of the Unfaithful Servant and the Parable of the Ten Virgins as if they were addressed to unbelievers. But as I've already said, both were addressed to some of Jesus' closest disciples (see Matt. 24:3; Mark 13:3). Therefore, if Peter, James, John and Andrew needed to be warned of the possibility of not being ready when Jesus returned, so do we. Jesus' warnings in the Olivet Discourse are also applicable to every believer, even those who don't think so because of they fail to note who was being addressed by Jesus.

Rule #3 Read Honestly. Don't force your theology into a text. If you read something that contradicts what you believe, don't try to change the Bible; change what you believe.

Every one of us approaches the Scripture with some pre-conceived biases. For that reason, it is often very difficult for us to read the Bible honestly. We end up forcing our beliefs into Scripture, rather than letting the Bible mold our theology. We sometimes even hunt for scriptures that will support our doctrines, ignoring those that contradict our beliefs. This is known as "proof-texting."

Here is an example I recently encountered of forcing theology into a text. A particular teacher first read Matthew 11:28-29, a well-known quotation of Jesus:

> Come to Me, all who are weary and heavy-laden, and I will give you rest. Take My yoke upon you, and learn from Me, for I am gentle and humble in heart; and you shall find rest for your souls (Matt. 11:28-29)

The teacher then went on to explain that Jesus was offering *two different* rests. The first rest (supposedly) is the rest of salvation in 11:28, and the second rest is the rest of discipleship in 11:29. The first rest is received by coming to Jesus; the second rest is received by submitting to Him as Lord, or taking His yoke.

But was that the meaning Jesus intended? No, that is forcing a meaning into the text that is neither stated nor implied. Jesus didn't say He was offering two rests. He was offering one rest to those who are weary and heavy-laden, and the only way to receive that singular rest is by taking Jesus' yoke, that is, submitting to Him. That is Jesus' obvious meaning.

Why did that teacher come up with such an interpretation? Because the obvious meaning of the passage didn't fit his belief that there are two kinds of heaven-bound Christians—believers and disciples. So he did not interpret this passage honestly.

Of course, as we have seen from scores of other scriptures earlier in this book as we considered that particular theology, that teacher's interpretation doesn't fit the context of the rest of what Jesus taught. Nowhere does the New Testament teach that there are two kinds of heaven-bound Christians, the believers and the disciples. All true believers are disciples. Those who are not disciples are not believers. Discipleship is the fruit of genuine faith.

Let us strive to read the Bible honestly, with pure hearts. If we do, the result will be more devotion and obedience to Christ.

EIGHT

The Sermon on the Mount

Because of his desire to make disciples who obey all that Christ commanded, the disciple-making minister will be very interested in Jesus' Sermon on the Mount. There is no lengthier recorded sermon of Jesus, and it is full of His commandments. The disciple-making minister will want to obey as well as teach his disciples everything Jesus commanded in that sermon.

This being so, I'm going to share what I understand about that sermon contained in Matthew chapters 5-7. I encourage ministers to teach their disciples the Sermon on the Mount verse by verse. Hopefully what I've written will be helpful to that end.

Below is an outline of the Sermon on the Mount, just to give us a general overview and to highlight the primary themes.

    I.) Jesus gathers His audience (5:1-2)
    II.) Introduction (5:3-20)
        A.) The characteristics and blessings of the blessed (5:3-12)
        B.) Admonition to continue being salt and light (5:13-16)
        C.) The Law's relationship with Christ's followers (5:17-20)
    III.) The Sermon: Be more righteous than the scribes and Pharisees (5:21-7:12)
        A). Love each other, unlike the scribes and Pharisees (5:21-26)
        B.) Be sexually pure, unlike the scribes and Pharisees (5:27-32)
        C.) Be honest, unlike the scribes and Pharisees (5:33-37)
        D.) Don't take revenge, as do the scribes and Pharisees (5:38-42)
        E.) Don't hate your enemies, as do the scribes and Pharisees (5:43-48)
        F.) Do good for the right motives, unlike the scribes and Pharisees (6:1-18)
            1.) Give to the poor for the right motives (6:2-4)
            2.) Pray for the right motives (6:5-6)
            3.) A digression regarding prayer and forgiveness (6:7-15)

a.) Instructions concerning prayer (6:7-13)
b.) The necessity of forgiving each other (6:8-15)
4.) Fast for the right motives (6:16-18)
G.) Don't serve money, as do the scribes and Pharisees (6:19-34)
H.) Don't find little faults with your brothers (7:1-5)
I.) Don't waste your time giving truth to the unappreciative (7:6)
J.) Encouragement to pray (7:7-11)
IV.) Conclusion: A Summary of the Sermon
    A.) A summarizing statement (7:12)
    B.) An admonition to obey (7:13-14)
    C.) How to recognize false prophets and false believers (7:15-23)
    D.) A final warning against disobedience and a summary (7:24-27)

Jesus Gathers His Audience

And when He saw the multitudes, He went up on the mountain; and after He sat down, His disciples came to Him. And opening His mouth He began to teach them (Matt. 5:1-2).

It seems as if Jesus purposely reduced the size of His audience by walking away from the "multitudes" and up a mountain. We are told that "His disciples came to Him," as if to indicate that only those who were hungry to hear Him were willing to huff and puff up the mountain to where He finally rested. Apparently there were quite a few; they are called "the crowds" in 7:28.

Jesus then began His sermon, speaking to His disciples, and from the start we get a hint of what His overriding theme will be. He tells them that they are blessed if they possess certain characteristics, because those characteristics belong to the heaven-bound. That will be His overall theme for this sermon—*Only the holy will inherit God's kingdom*. The Beatitudes, as they are called, found in 5:3-12, abound with this theme.

Jesus enumerated a number of different traits that characterize the blessed people, and He promised a number of specific blessings to them. Casual readers often assume that each Christian should find himself in one, and only one, Beatitude. Careful readers, however, realize that Jesus was not listing different kinds of believers who will receive varied blessings, but *all true believers* who will receive *one* all-encompassing future blessing: inheriting the kingdom of heaven. There is no other intelligent way to interpret His words:

> Blessed are the poor in spirit, for theirs is the kingdom of heaven.
> Blessed are those who mourn, for they shall be comforted.
> Blessed are the gentle, for they shall inherit the earth.
> Blessed are those who hunger and thirst for righteousness,
> for they shall be satisfied.
> Blessed are the merciful, for they shall receive mercy.

Blessed are the pure in heart, for they shall see God.
Blessed are the peacemakers, for they shall be called sons of God.
Blessed are those who have been persecuted for the sake of righteousness, for theirs is the kingdom of heaven.
Blessed are you when people insult you and persecute you, and falsely say all kinds of evil against you because of Me. Rejoice and be glad, for your reward in heaven is great; for in the same way they persecuted the prophets who were before you (Matt. 5:3-12).

The Blessings and Character Traits

First, let's consider all the blessings promised. Jesus said that the blessed shall (1) inherit the kingdom of heaven, (2) receive comfort, (3) inherit the earth, (4) be satisfied, (5) receive mercy, (6) see God, (7) be called God's sons, and (8) inherit the kingdom of heaven (a repeat of #1).

Does Jesus want us to think that only the poor in spirit and those who have been persecuted for righteousness will inherit God's kingdom? Will only the pure in heart see God and only the peacemakers be called sons of God, while neither shall inherit God's kingdom? Will the peacemakers not receive mercy and the merciful not be called sons of God? Obviously these would all be wrong conclusions. Therefore, it is only safe to conclude that the many blessings promised are the manifold blessings of one big blessing—inheriting God's kingdom.

Now let's consider the different traits Jesus described: (1) poor in spirit, (2) mournful, (3) gentle, (4) hungering for righteousness, (5) merciful, (6) pure of heart, (7) peacemaking, and (8) persecuted.

Does Jesus want us to think that a person can be *pure in heart* yet *unmerciful*? Can one be *persecuted for the sake of righteousness* but not be one who *hungers and thirsts after righteousness*? Again, obviously not. The many character traits of the blessed are the manifold traits shared, to some degree, by *all* the blessed.

Clearly, the Beatitudes describe the character traits of Jesus' true followers. By enumerating those traits to His disciples, Jesus assured them that they were the blessed people who are saved and who would enjoy heaven one day. Currently, they might not feel so blessed because of their sufferings, and the on-looking world might not consider them blessed, but in God's eyes they were.

People who do *not* fit Jesus' description are not blessed and will not inherit the kingdom of heaven. Every disciple-making pastor feels an obligation to make sure the people within his flock know that.

The Character Traits of the Blessed

The eight traits of the blessed are subject to some degree of interpretation. For example, what is virtuous about being "poor in spirit"? I tend to think that Jesus was describing the first necessary trait a person must possess if he is going to be saved—he must realize his own spiritual poverty. One must first see his need for a Savior before he can be saved, and there were those kinds of people among Jesus' audience who had just realized their own wretchedness. How blessed were they compared to the proud in Israel who were so blind to their sins!

This first trait eliminates all self-sufficiency and any thought of meriting salvation. The truly blessed person is one who realizes that he has nothing to offer God and that his own righteousness is as "filthy rags" (Is. 64:6, KJV).

Jesus did not want anyone to think that purely by his own self-effort could he possess the traits of the blessed. No, people are blessed, that is, *blessed by God* if they possess the characteristics of the blessed. It all springs from God's grace. The blessed people Jesus was speaking of were blessed, not only because of what awaited them in heaven, but because of the work God had done in their lives on earth. When I see the traits of the blessed in my life, it should remind me not of what I've done, but of what God has done in me by His grace.

The Mournful

If the first characteristic is listed first because it is the first necessary trait of the heaven-bound, perhaps the second trait is also listed meaningfully: "Blessed are those who mourn" (Matt. 5:4). Could Jesus have been describing heartfelt repentance and remorse? I think so, especially since Scripture is clear that godly sorrow results in a repentance that is necessary for salvation (see 2 Cor. 7:10). The mournful tax collector of whom Jesus once spoke is an example of this kind of blessed person. He humbly bowed his head in the Temple, beating his breast and crying out for God's mercy. Unlike the nearby Pharisee who, as he prayed, proudly reminded God that he tithed and fasted twice a week, the tax gatherer left that place forgiven of his sins. In that story, the tax collector was blessed; the Pharisee was not (see Luke 18:9-14). I suspect that there were those among Jesus' audience who, under the conviction of the Holy Spirit, were mourning. Comfort from the Holy Spirit would soon be theirs!

If Jesus was not speaking of the initial mourning of the repentant person who is just coming to Christ, then perhaps He was describing the sorrow all true believers sense as they continually face a world that is in rebellion against the God who loves them. Paul expressed it as "great sorrow and unceasing grief in [his] heart" (Rom. 9:2).

The Gentle

The third characteristic, gentleness, is also listed in Scripture as one of the fruits of the Spirit (see Gal. 5:22-23). Gentleness is not a self-generated attribute. Those who have received the grace of God and the indwelling of the Spirit are also blessed to be made gentle. They will one day inherit the earth, since only the righteous will dwell on the new earth that God creates. Professing Christians who are harsh and violent should beware. They are not among the blessed.

Hungering for Righteousness

The fourth characteristic, hungering and thirsting for righteousness, describes the God-given inward longing that every true born-again person possesses. He is grieved by all the unrighteousness in the world and in what remains in himself. He hates sin (see Ps. 97:10; 119:128, 163) and loves righteousness.

Too often, when we read the word *righteousness* in Scripture, we immediately translate it, "the legal standing of righteousness imputed to us by Christ," but that is not always what the word means. Quite often it means, "the quality of living righteously by God's standards." That is obviously the meaning Jesus intended here, because there is no reason for a Christian to hunger for what he already possesses. Those who have been born of the Spirit long to *live* righteously, and they have assurance that they will "be satisfied" (Matt. 5:6), certain that God, by His grace, will complete the work He's begun in them (see Phil. 1:6).

Jesus' words here also foresee the time of the new earth, an earth "in which righteousness dwells" (2 Pet. 3:13). Then there will be no sin. Everyone will love God with all his heart and love his neighbor as himself. We who now hunger and thirst for righteousness will then be satisfied. Finally our heart-felt prayer will be fully answered, "Your will be done on earth as it is in heaven" (Matt. 6:10).

The Merciful

The fifth trait, mercifulness, is also one that every born-again person naturally possesses by virtue of his having the merciful God living within him. Those who possess no mercy are not blessed of God and reveal that they are not partakers of His grace. The apostle James concurs: "Judgment will be merciless to one who has shown no mercy" (Jas. 2:13). If one stands before God and receives a merciless judgment, do you think he would go to heaven or hell?[36] The answer is obvious.

Jesus once told a story of a servant who had received great mercy from his master, but who was then unwilling to extend some mercy to his fellow servant. When his master discovered what had happened, He "handed him over to the torturers until he should repay all that was owed him" (Matt 18:34). All his formerly-forgiven debt was reinstated. Then Jesus warned His disciples, "My heavenly Father will also do the same to you, if each of you does not forgive his brother from your heart" (Matt. 18:35). Thus to refuse to forgive a brother or sister in Christ who asks for for-

---

[36] Interestingly, the very next verse in the book of James is, "What use is it, my brethren, if a man says he has faith, but he has no works? Can that faith save him?" (Jas. 2:14).

giveness results in the reinstatement of our formerly-forgiven sins. That results in our being handed over to the torturers until we repay what we can never repay. That sure doesn't sound like heaven to me. Again, non-merciful people will not receive mercy from God. They are not among the blessed.

The Pure in Heart

The sixth trait of the heaven-bound is purity of heart. Unlike so many professing Christians, true followers of Christ are not just outwardly holy. By God's grace, their hearts have been made pure. They truly love God from their hearts, and it affects their meditations and motives. Jesus promised that they shall see God.

Again may I ask, are we to believe that there are true Christian believers who are *not* pure in heart and who therefore will *not* see God? Is God going to say to them, "You can come into heaven, but you can't ever see Me"? No, obviously *every* true heaven-bound person has a pure heart.

The Peacemakers

Peacemakers are listed next. They will be called sons of God. Again, Jesus must have been describing every true follower of Christ, because everyone who believes in Christ is a son of God (see Gal. 3:26).

Those who are born of the Spirit are peacemakers in at least three ways:

First, they've made peace with God, one who was formerly their enemy (see Rom. 5:10).

Second, they live in peace, as far as possible, with other people. They're not characterized by dissensions and strife. Paul wrote that those who practice strife, jealousy, outbursts of anger, disputes, dissensions and factions will not inherit God's kingdom (see Gal. 5:19-21). True believers will go the extra mile to avoid a fight and keep peace in their relationships. They do not claim to be at peace with God while not loving their brother (see Matt. 5:23-24; 1 John 4:20).

Third, by sharing the gospel, true followers of Christ also help others make peace with God and their fellow man. Perhaps alluding to this very verse of the Sermon on the Mount, James wrote, "And the seed whose fruit is righteousness is sown in peace by those who make peace" (Jas. 3:8).

The Persecuted

Finally, Jesus called *blessed* those who are persecuted for the sake of righteousness. Obviously, He was speaking of people who are *living* righteously, not just those who *think* that Christ's righteousness has been imputed to them. People who obey Christ's commandments are the ones whom nonbelievers persecute. They will inherit God's kingdom.

What kind of persecution was Jesus talking about? Torture? Martyrdom? No, He specifically listed being insulted and spoken against on His account. This again indicates that when a person is a true Christian, it is obvious to nonbelievers, otherwise nonbelievers wouldn't say evil things against him. How many so-called Christians are so indistinguishable from nonbelievers that not a single unbeliever speaks against them? They are not really Christians at all. As Jesus said, "Woe to you when all men speak well of you, for in the same way their fathers used to treat the false prophets" (Luke 6:26). When all men speak well of you, that's a sign that you're a false believer. The world hates true Christians (see also John 15:18-21; Gal. 4:29; 2 Tim. 3:12; 1 John 3:13-14).

Salt and Light

Once Jesus had assured His obedient disciples that they were indeed among the transformed and blessed people who were destined to inherit the kingdom of heaven, He raised a word of caution. Unlike many modern preachers who continually assure spiritual goats that they could never forfeit the salvation they supposedly possess, Jesus loved His true disciples enough to warn them that they could indeed remove themselves from the category of the blessed.

> You are the salt of the earth; but if the salt has become tasteless, how can it be made salty again? It is no longer good for anything, except to be thrown out and trampled under foot by men. You are the light of the world. A city set on a hill cannot be hidden; nor does anyone light a lamp and put it under a basket, but on the lampstand, and it gives light to all who are in the house. Let your light shine before men in such a way that they may see your good works, and glorify your Father who is in heaven (Matt. 5:13-16).

Notice that Jesus didn't exhort His disciples to *become* salt or *become* light. He said (metaphorically) that they already *were* salt, and He exhorted them to *remain* salty. He said (metaphorically) that they already *were* light, and exhorted them not to let their light be hidden, but to continue shining. How this stands in contrast to the many sermons given to professing Christians of their need to *become* salt and light. If people aren't already salt and light, they aren't Christ's disciples. They aren't among the blessed. They aren't going to heaven.

In Jesus' time, salt was used primarily as a preservative of meats. As obedient followers of Christ, we are what preserves this sinful world from becoming completely rotten and corrupt. But if we become like the world in our behavior, we are truly "no longer good for anything" (v. 13). Jesus warned the blessed to remain salty, preserving their unique characteristics. They must remain distinct from the world around them, lest they become "unsalty," deserving to be "thrown out and trampled under foot."

This is one of many clear warnings against backsliding found in the New Testament that is directed at true believers. If salt is truly salt, it is salty. Likewise, followers of Jesus act like followers of Jesus, otherwise they aren't followers of Jesus, even if they once were.

Christ's true followers are also the light of the world. Light *always* shines. If it isn't shining, it isn't light. In this analogy, light represents our good works (see Matt. 5:16). Jesus wasn't exhorting those who have no works to drum some up, but exhorting those who have good works not to hide their goodness from others. By so doing, they would glorify their heavenly Father because His work in them is the source of their goodness. Here we see a beautiful balance of God's gracious work and our cooperation with Him; both are needed for anyone to be holy.

The Law's Relationship to Christ's Followers

Now we begin a new paragraph (in the NASB). It is a pivotal section of enormous importance, an introduction to much of what Christ will say in the remainder of His sermon.

> Do not think that I came to abolish the Law or the Prophets; I did not come to abolish but to fulfill. For truly I say to you, until heaven and earth pass away, not the smallest letter or stroke shall pass from the Law until all is accomplished. Whoever then annuls one of the least of these commandments, and teaches others to do the same, shall be called least in the kingdom of heaven; but whoever keeps and teaches them, he shall be called great in the kingdom of heaven. For I say to you that unless your righteousness surpasses that of the scribes and Pharisees, you will not enter the kingdom of heaven (Matt. 5:17-20).

If Jesus warned His audience against thinking that He was abolishing the Law or the Prophets, then we can safely conclude that at least some in His audience were making that assumption. Why they were making such an assumption we can only guess. *Perhaps* it was Jesus' stern rebukes of the legalistic scribes and Pharisees that tempted some to think He was abolishing the Law and Prophets.

Regardless, Jesus clearly wanted His disciples to realize the error of such an assumption. He was the divine inspirer of the entire Old Testament, so certainly He was not going to abolish everything He'd said through Moses and the Prophets. On the contrary, He would, as He said, *fulfill* the Law and Prophets.

Exactly how would He fulfill the Law and Prophets? Some think that Jesus was talking only about fulfilling the messianic predictions. Although Jesus certainly did (or will yet) fulfill every messianic prediction, that is not entirely what He had in mind. Clearly, the context indicates He was also talking about *all* that was written in the Law and Prophets, down to "smallest letter or stroke" (v. 18) of the Law, and to the "least of" (v. 19) the commandments.

Others suppose Jesus meant that He would fulfill the Law by fulfilling its requirements on our behalf through His obedient life and sacrificial death (see Rom. 8:4). But that, as the context also reveals, is not what He had in mind. In the verses that follow, Jesus mentioned nothing about His life or death as being a reference point for the fulfilling of the Law. Rather, in the very next sentence, He stated that the Law would be relevant at least until "heaven and earth pass away" and "all is accomplished," reference points far after His death on the cross. He then declared that people's attitudes toward the Law would even affect their status in heaven (v. 19), and that people must obey the Law even better than the scribes or Pharisees or they will not enter heaven (v. 20).

Obviously, besides just fulfilling the messianic prophecies, types, and shadows of the Law, as well as fulfilling the requirements of the Law on our behalf, Jesus was also thinking about His audience *keeping* the commandments of the Law and *doing* what the Prophets said. In one sense, Jesus would fulfill the Law by revealing God's true and original intent in it, fully endorsing and explaining it, and completing what was lacking in His audience's understanding of it.[37] The Greek word translated *fulfill* in verse 17 is also translated in the New Testament as *complete, finish, fill,* and *fully carry out*. That is exactly what Jesus was about to do, beginning just four sentences later.

No, Jesus did not come to abolish the Law and Prophets, but to fulfill them, that is, "fill them to the full." When I teach this portion of the Sermon on the Mount, I often show everyone a half-full glass of water to serve as an example of the revelation God gave in the Law and Prophets. Jesus did not come to abolish the Law and Prophets (as I say this, I act as though I'm going to throw the half-full glass away). Rather, He would *fulfill* the Law and Prophets (at which time I take a bottle of water and fill the glass to the brim). That helps people understand what Jesus meant.

The Importance of Keeping the Law

Concerning the keeping of the commandments found in the Law and Prophets, Jesus couldn't have made His point more forcefully. He expect-

---

[37] This would be true of what is often referred to as the "ceremonial aspects of the Law" as well as the "moral aspects of the Law," although much of His fuller explanation concerning His fulfilling the ceremonial law would be given by His Holy Spirit to the apostles after His resurrection. We now understand why there is no need to sacrifice animals under the new covenant, because Jesus was the Lamb of God. Neither do we follow the old covenant dietary laws because Jesus declared all foods to be clean (see Mark 7:19). We don't need the intercession of an earthly high priest because Jesus is now our High Priest, and so on. Unlike the ceremonial law, however, no part of the moral law was ever altered by anything Jesus did or said, before of after His death and resurrection. Rather, Jesus expounded upon and endorsed God's moral law, as did the apostles by the inspiration of the Spirit after His resurrection. The moral aspects of the Mosaic Law are all included in the law of Christ, the law of the new covenant. Keep in mind also that Jesus was speaking that day to Jews under the Mosaic Law. Thus His words in Matt. 5:17-20 need to be interpreted in light of His ongoing revelation found in the New Testament.

ed His disciples to obey them. They were as important as ever. In fact, how they esteemed the commandments would determine their status in heaven: "Whoever then annuls one of the least of these commandments, and so teaches others, shall be called least in the kingdom of heaven; but whoever keeps and teaches them, he shall be called great in the kingdom of heaven" (5:19).

Then we come to verse 20: "For I say to you, that unless your righteousness surpasses that of the scribes and Pharisees, you shall not enter the kingdom of heaven."

Notice that this is not a new thought, but a concluding statement that is connected with previous verses by the conjunction *for*. How important is keeping the commandments? *One must keep them better than the scribes and Pharisees in order to enter the kingdom of heaven.* Again we see Jesus was keeping with His theme—*Only the holy will inherit God's kingdom.*

Lest he contradict Christ, the disciple-making minister would never assure anyone of possessing salvation whose righteousness did not surpass that of the scribes and Pharisees.

Of What Kind of Righteousness Was Jesus Speaking?

When Jesus stated that our righteousness must surpass that of the scribes and Pharisees, was He not alluding to the legal standing of righteousness that would be imputed to us as a free gift? No, He was not, and for good reason. First, the context does not fit this interpretation. Before and after this statement (and throughout the entire Sermon on the Mount), Jesus was talking about keeping the commandments, that is, living righteously. The most natural interpretation of His words is that we must *live* more righteously than the scribes and Pharisees. And how absurd it would be to think that Jesus was holding the scribes and Pharisees to a standard to which He was not holding His own disciples. How foolish to think that Jesus would condemn the scribes and Pharisees for committing sins for which He would not also condemn His disciples simply because they had prayed a "salvation prayer."[38]

Our problem is that we don't want to accept the obvious meaning of the verse, because it sounds to us like legalism. But our real problem is that we don't understand the inseparable correlation between imputed righteousness and practical righteousness. The apostle John did, however. He wrote: "Little children, let no one deceive you; the one who practices righteousness is righteous" (1 John 3:7). Nor do we understand the correlation between the new birth and practical righteousness as John also did: "Everyone also who practices righteousness is born of Him" (1 John 2:29).

---

[38] Moreover, if Jesus was talking about the imputed, legal righteousness that we receive as a gift for believing in Him, why didn't He at least hint at it? Why did He say something that would be so easily misunderstood by the uneducated people to whom He was speaking, who would never have guessed that He was talking about imputed righteousness?

Jesus could have added to His statement of 5:20, "And if you repent, are truly born again, and receive through a living faith My free gift of righteousness, your practical righteousness will indeed exceed that of the scribes and Pharisees as you cooperate with the power of My indwelling Spirit."

How to be Holier than the Scribes and Pharisees

The question that would naturally come to mind in response to Jesus' statement in 5:20 is this: How righteous, exactly, were the scribes and Pharisees? The answer is: *Not very.*

At another time, Jesus referred to them as "whitewashed tombs which on the outside appear beautiful, but inside they are full of dead men's bones and all uncleanness" (Matt. 23:27). That is, they appeared outwardly righteous, but were inwardly evil. They did a great job at keeping the *letter* of the Law, but ignored the *spirit* of it, often justifying themselves by twisting or even altering God's commandments.

This intrinsic flaw in the scribes and Pharisees was, in fact, Jesus' major focus in much of what remains in the Sermon on the Mount. We find that He quoted a number of God's well-known commandments, and after each quotation, revealed the difference between keeping the letter and spirit of each law. In so doing, He repeatedly exposed the false teaching and hypocrisy of the Scribes and Pharisees, and He revealed His true expectations for His disciples.

Jesus began each example with the words, "You have heard." He was speaking to people who had probably never read, but only heard the Old Testament scrolls read by the scribes and Pharisees in the synagogues. It could well be said that His audience had been sitting under false teaching all their lives, as they heard the scribes' and Pharisees' twisted commentary on God's Word and observed their unholy lifestyles.

Love Each Other, Unlike the Scribes and Pharisees

By using the sixth commandment as His first reference point, Jesus began teaching His disciples God's expectations for them, while at the same time exposing the hypocrisy of the scribes and Pharisees.

> You have heard that the ancients were told, "You shall not commit murder" and "Whoever commits murder shall be liable to the court." But I say to you that everyone who is angry with his brother shall be guilty before the court; and whoever shall say to his brother, "Raca," shall be guilty before the supreme court; and whoever shall say, "You fool," shall be guilty enough to go into the fiery hell (Matt. 5:21-22).

First, note that Jesus was warning about something that could cause a person to go to hell. That was His primary theme—*Only the holy will inherit God's kingdom.*

The scribes and Pharisees preached against murder, citing the sixth commandment, apparently warning that murder could land one in court.

Jesus, however, wanted his disciples to know what the scribes and Pharisees didn't seem to realize—there were much "lesser" infractions that could land one in court, apparently *God's* court. Because it is so important that we love one another (the second greatest commandment), when we become angry with a brother we should already consider ourselves found guilty in God's court. If we verbalize our anger by speaking in an unkind way to him, our infraction is even more serious, and we should consider ourselves guilty in God's highest court. And if we go beyond that, spewing out hatred for a brother with a second slur, we are guilty enough before God to be cast into hell![39] That is serious!

Our relationship with God is gauged by our relationship with our brothers. If we hate a brother, that reveals that we do not possess eternal life. John wrote,

> Everyone who hates his brother is a murderer; and you know that no murderer has eternal life abiding in him (1 John 3:15).

> If someone says, "I love God," and hates his brother, he is a liar; for the one who does not love his brother whom he has seen, cannot love God whom he has not seen (1 John 4:20).

How important it is that we love each other and, as Jesus commanded, work for reconciliation when we are offended by one another (see Matt. 18:15-17).

Jesus continued:

> If therefore you are presenting your offering at the altar, and there remember that your brother has something against you, leave your offering there before the altar, and go your way; first be reconciled to your brother, and then come and present your offering (Matt. 5:23-24).

This is to say that if our relationship with our brother is not right, then our relationship with God is not right. The Pharisees were guilty of majoring on what was of minor importance and minimizing what was of major importance, "straining out the gnat and swallowing the camel" as Jesus said (Matt. 23:23-24). They stressed the importance of tithing and giving offerings, but neglected what was *much* more important, the second great-

---

[39] This applies to our relationships with our brothers and sisters in Christ. Jesus called certain religious leaders *fools* (see Matt. 23:17), as does Scripture in general (see Prov. 1:7; 13:20).

est commandment, to love one another. How hypocritical it is to bring an offering, supposedly to show one's love for God, while violating His second most important commandment! This is what Jesus was warning against.

Still on the subject of the strictness of God's court, Jesus continued:

> Make friends quickly with your opponent at law while you are with him on the way, in order that your opponent may not deliver you to the judge, and the judge to the officer, and you be thrown into prison. Truly I say to you, you shall not come out of there, until you have paid up the last cent (Matt. 5:23-26).

It is best to stay out of God's courtroom altogether by living at peace with our brothers as much as is possible. If a brother or sister is angry with us and we stubbornly refuse to work for reconciliation "on the way to court," that is, on our journey through life to stand before God, we may certainly regret it. What Jesus said here is very similar to His warning regarding any imitation of the unforgiving servant in Matthew 18:23-35. The servant who was forgiven but who refused to forgive had his debt reinstated, and he was handed over to the torturers "until he should repay all that was owed" (Matt. 18:34). Here Jesus is likewise warning of the dire eternal consequences of not loving our brother as God expects.

Be Sexually Pure, Unlike the Scribes and Pharisees

The seventh commandment was the subject of Jesus' second example of how the scribes and Pharisees kept the letter while neglecting the spirit of the Law. Jesus expected His disciples to be more sexually pure than the scribes and Pharisees.

> You have heard that it was said, "You shall not commit adultery"; but I say to you, that everyone who looks on a woman to lust for her has committed adultery with her already in his heart. And if your right eye makes you stumble, tear it out, and throw it from you; for it is better for you that one of the parts of your body perish, than for your whole body to be thrown into hell. And if your right hand makes you stumble, cut it off, and throw it from you; for it is better for you that one of the parts of your body perish, than for your whole body to go into hell (Matt. 5:27-30).

Note *again* that Jesus was keeping with His primary theme—*Only the holy will inherit God's kingdom.* He warned again about hell and what one must do to stay out of it.

The scribes and Pharisees couldn't ignore the seventh commandment, so they outwardly obeyed it, remaining faithful to their wives. Yet they fantasized about making love to other women. They would mentally undress women they watched in the marketplace. They were adulterers at heart, and thus were transgressing the spirit of the seventh commandment. How many in the church today are no different?

God, of course, intended for people to be completely sexually pure. Obviously, if it is wrong to have a sexual relationship with your neighbor's wife, it is also wrong to meditate on having a sexual relationship with her. Jesus was not adding a stricter law to what was already required by the Law of Moses. The tenth commandment clearly contained a prohibition against lust: "You shall not covet your neighbor's wife" (Ex. 20:17).

Were any among Jesus' audience convicted? Probably they were. What should they have done? They should have immediately repented as Jesus instructed. Whatever it took, no matter what the cost, those who were lustful should stop lusting, because those who practice lust go to hell.

Of course, no reasonable person thinks Jesus meant that lustful people should literally pluck out an eye or cut off a hand. A lustful person who cuts out his eye simply becomes a one-eyed luster! Jesus was dramatically and solemnly emphasizing the importance of obeying the spirit of the seventh commandment. Eternity depended on it.

Following Christ's example, the disciple-making minister will admonish his disciples to "cut off" whatever it is that is causing them to stumble. If it's cable TV, the cable needs to be disconnected. If it's regular TV, the TV needs to be removed. If it's a magazine subscription, it should be canceled. If it's the Internet, it should be disconnected. If it is an open window, the shutters should be closed. None of those things are worth spending eternity in hell over, and because the disciple-making minister truly loves His flock, he will tell them the truth and warn them, just as Jesus did.

Another Way to Commit Adultery

Jesus' next example is very much related to the one that we just considered, which is probably why it is mentioned next. It should be considered a further elaboration rather than a new subject. The subject is, "Another thing Pharisees do that is equivalent to adultery."

> And it was said, "Whoever sends his wife away, let him give her a certificate of divorce"; but I say to you that everyone who divorces his wife, except for the cause of unchastity, makes her commit adultery; and whoever marries a divorced woman commits adultery (Matt. 5:31-32).

Here is an example of how the scribes and Pharisees twisted God's law to accommodate their sinful lifestyles.

Let's create an imaginary Pharisee in Jesus' day. Across the street from him lives an attractive woman after whom he is lusting. He flirts with her when he sees her each day. She seems attracted to him, and his desire for her grows. He would love to see her unclothed, and imagines her regularly in his sexual fantasies. Oh, if he could only have her!

But he has a problem. He is married, and his religion forbids adultery. He doesn't want to break the seventh commandment (even though he's already broken it every time he's lusted). What can he do?

There *is* a solution! If he were divorced from his present spouse, he could marry the mistress of his mind! But is it lawful to get a divorce? A fellow Pharisee tells him *Yes!* There is a scripture for it! Deuteronomy 24:1 says something about giving your wife a divorce certificate when you divorce her. Divorce *must* be lawful under certain circumstances! But what are those circumstances? He reads closely what God said:

> When a man takes a wife and marries her, and it happens that she finds no favor in his eyes because he has found some indecency in her, and he writes her a certificate of divorce and puts it in her hand and sends her out from his house... (Deut. 24:1).

Ahah! He *can* divorce his wife if he finds some indecency in her! And he has! She's not as attractive as the woman across the street! (This is not a far-fetched example. According to Rabbi Hillel, who had the most popular teaching regarding divorce in Jesus' day, a man could lawfully divorce his wife if he found someone who was more attractive, because that made his current wife "indecent" in his eyes. Rabbi Hillel also taught a man could divorce his wife if she put too much salt on his food, or spoke to another man, or didn't produce a son for him.)

So our lustful Pharisee lawfully divorces his wife by giving her the required certificate and quickly marries the woman of his fantasies. And all without incurring an ounce of guilt because God's Law has been obeyed!

A Different View

Of course, God sees things differently. He never stipulated what the "indecency" mentioned in Deuteronomy 24:1-4 actually was, or if it was even a legitimate reason to divorce. In fact, that passage says nothing in regard as to when divorce is lawful or not lawful. It contains only a prohibition against the twice-divorced or once-divorced/once widowed woman remarrying her first husband. To say that there must be some "indecency" in God's eyes that makes divorce legitimate based on this passage is to force meaning into the text.

In any case, in God's mind, the imaginary man I've just described is no different than an adulterer. He has broken the seventh commandment. In fact, he's even guiltier than the average adulterer, because he is guilty of "double adultery." How is that? First, he's committed adultery himself. Jesus later said, "Whoever divorces his wife, except for immorality, and marries another woman commits adultery" (Matt. 19:9).

Second, because his now-divorced wife must seek another husband to survive, in God's mind the Pharisee has done the equivalent of forcing his wife to have sex with another man. Thus, he incurs guilt for her "adultery."[40] Jesus said, "Everyone who divorces his wife, except for the cause of unchastity, *makes* her commit adultery" (Matt. 5:32, emphasis added).

Jesus may even have been charging our lustful Pharisee with "triple adultery" if His statement, "and whoever marries a divorced woman commits adultery" (Matt. 5:32), means that God holds the Pharisee accountable for the "adultery" of his former wife's new husband.[41]

This was a hot issue in Jesus' day, as we read in another place where some Pharisees questioned Him, "Is it lawful for a man to divorce his wife for any cause at all?" (Matt. 19:3). Their question reveals their hearts. Obviously, at least some of them wanted to believe divorce was lawful for any cause.

I must also add what a shame it is when Christians take these same scriptures about divorce, misinterpret them, and place heavy shackles on God's children. Jesus was not talking about the Christian who was divorced when he or she was unsaved, and who, upon finding a wonderful potential mate who also loves Christ, marries that person. That is not equivalent to adultery. If that is what Jesus meant, we'll have to change the gospel, because no longer does it provide forgiveness for all the sins of sinners. From now on we'll have to preach, "Jesus died for you, and if you repent and believe in Him, you can have all your sins forgiven. If you've been divorced, however, make sure you never get remarried or else you'll be living in adultery, and the Bible says that adulterers will go to hell. Also, if you've been divorced *and* remarried, before you come to Christ you need to commit one more sin and divorce your present spouse. Otherwise you'll continue to live in adultery, and adulterers aren't saved."[42] Is that the gospel?[43]

Be Honest, Unlike the Scribes and Pharisees

Jesus' third example of the unrighteous conduct and scriptural misapplication of the scribes and Pharisees is related to God's commandment to tell the truth. The scribes and Pharisees had developed a very creative way to lie. We learn from Matthew 23:16-22 that they did not consider

---

[40] Of course, God doesn't hold her accountable for adultery when she remarries; she was just the victim of her husband's sin. Obviously, Jesus' words make no sense unless she does remarry. Otherwise, there is no sense in which she could be considered to be an adulteress.

[41] Again, God would not hold the new husband accountable for adultery. He's doing a virtuous thing, marrying and providing for a divorced woman. However, if a man encouraged a woman to divorce her husband so he could marry her, then he would be guilty of adultery, and that is perhaps the sin Jesus had in mind here.

[42] There are, of course, other situations that could be addressed. For example, the Christian woman whose unsaved husband divorces her is certainly not guilty of adultery if she remarries a Christian man.

[43] In a later chapter about divorce and remarriage, I address this issue more thoroughly.

themselves obligated to keep their vows if they swore by the temple, the altar, or heaven. However, if they swore by the *gold* in the temple, the *offering* on the altar, or by *God* in heaven, they *were* obligated to keep their vow! It was an adult equivalent of a child thinking he is exempt from having to tell the truth as long as his fingers are crossed behind his back. Jesus expects His disciples to tell the truth.

> Again, you have heard that the ancients were told, "You shall not make false vows, but shall fulfill your vows to the Lord." But I say to you, make no oath at all, either by heaven, for it is the throne of God, or by the earth, for it is the footstool of His feet, or by Jerusalem, for it is the city of the great King. Nor shall you make an oath by your head, for you cannot make one hair white or black. But let your statement be, "Yes, yes" or "No, no"; and anything beyond these is of evil (Matt. 5:33-37).

God's original commandment concerning vows said nothing about making an oath by swearing on something else. God intended for His people to speak the truth at all times, so there would be no need to swear, ever.

There is nothing wrong with making an oath, because an oath is nothing more than a vow or promise. In fact, oaths to obey God are very good. Salvation begins with an oath to follow Jesus. But when people have to swear by something to convince others to believe them, *it is an outright admission that they normally lie*. People who always tell the truth do not need to swear, ever. Yet many churches today are full of liars, and the ministers are often the leaders in deceptiveness and guile.

The disciple-making minister sets an example of truthfulness and teaches his disciples to tell the truth always. He knows John warned that all liars will be cast into the lake that burns with fire and brimstone (see Rev. 21:8).

Don't Take Revenge, as do the Scribes and Pharisees

The next item on Jesus' list of grievances was a Pharisaic perversion of a very well-known verse in the Old Testament. We have already considered this passage in the chapter about biblical interpretation.

> You have heard that it was said, "An eye for an eye, and a tooth for a tooth." But I say to you, do not resist him who is evil; but whoever slaps you on your right cheek, turn to him the other also. And if anyone wants to sue you, and take your shirt, let him have your coat also. And whoever shall force you to go one mile, go with him two. Give to him who asks of you, and do not turn away from him who wants to borrow from you" (Matt. 5:38-42).

129

The Law of Moses declared that when a person was found guilty in court of injuring another person, his punishment should be equivalent to the harm he caused. If he knocked out someone's tooth, in fairness and justice, his tooth should be knocked out. This commandment was given to insure that justice would be served in court cases for major offenses. God instituted a system of courts and judges under the Law to deter crime, insure justice, and curb revenge. And God commanded judges to be impartial and just in their judgments. They were to mete out "an eye for and eye and a tooth for a tooth." But that phrase and commandment are always found in passages regarding justice in courts.

Once again, however, the scribes and Pharisees had twisted the commandment, turning it into a commandment that made obtaining personal revenge a holy obligation. Apparently, they had adopted a "zero tolerance" policy, seeking revenge for even the smallest offenses.

God, however, has always expected more from His people. Revenge is something He expressly forbade (see Deut. 32:35). The Old Testament taught that God's people should show kindness to their enemies (see Ex. 23:4-5; Prov. 25:21-22). Jesus endorsed this truth by telling His disciples to turn the other cheek and go the extra mile when dealing with evil people. When we are wronged, God wants us to be merciful, returning good for evil.

But does Jesus expect us to allow people to take gross advantage of us, allowing them to ruin our lives if they desire? Is it wrong to take a nonbeliever to court, seeking justice for an illegal act committed against us? No. Jesus was not talking about obtaining due justice for major offenses in court, but about getting personal revenge for petty infractions. Notice that Jesus did not say that we should offer our neck for strangling to someone who has just stabbed us in the back. He didn't say we should give someone our house when he demands our car. Jesus was simply telling us to show tolerance and mercy to a high degree when we daily encounter petty offenses and the normal challenges of dealing with selfish people. He wants us to be kinder than selfish people expect. To that standard, the scribes and Pharisees didn't come close.

Why are so many professing Christians so easily offended? Why are they so quickly upset by offenses that are ten times smaller than being slapped on the cheek? Are these people saved? The disciple-making minister sets an example of turning the other cheek, and he teaches his disciples to do the same.

Don't Hate Your Enemies, as do the Scribes and Pharisees

Finally, Jesus listed one more God-given commandment that the scribes and Pharisees had altered to accommodate their hateful hearts.

> You have heard that it was said, "You shall love your neighbor, and hate your enemy." But I say to you, love

your enemies, and pray for those who persecute you in order that you may be sons of your Father who is in heaven; for He causes His sun to rise on the evil and the good, and sends rain on the righteous and the unrighteous. For if you love those who love you, what reward have you? Do not even the tax-gatherers do the same? And if you greet your brothers only, what do you do more than others? Do not even the Gentiles do the same? Therefore you are to be perfect, as your heavenly Father is perfect (Matt. 5:43-48).

In the Old Testament, God had said, "Love your neighbor as yourself" (Lev. 19:18), but the scribes and Pharisees had conveniently defined neighbors as being only those people who loved them. Everyone else was an enemy, and since God said to love only our neighbors, it must be proper to hate our enemies. According to Jesus, however, that is not at all what God intended.

Jesus would later teach in the story of the Good Samaritan that we should consider *every* person to be our neighbor.[44] God wants us to love *everyone*, including our enemies. That is God's standard for His children, a standard by which He Himself lives. He sends crop-growing sun and rain, not only on good people, but also on evil people. We should follow His example, showing kindness to undeserving people. When we do, it shows that we are "sons of [our] Father who is in heaven" (Matt. 5:45). Authentic born-again people act like their Father.

The love that God expects us to show our enemies is not an emotion or an approval of their wickedness. God is not requiring us to foster warm feelings about those who oppose us. He is not telling us to say what is untrue, that our enemies are really wonderful people. But He does expect that we will be merciful towards them and take willful action to that end, at least by greeting them and praying for them.

Notice that Jesus once more reinforced His primary theme—*Only the holy will inherit God's kingdom*. He told His disciples that if they loved only those who loved them, they were no better than pagan Gentiles and tax collectors, two kinds of people whom every Jew would have agreed were hell-bound. It was another way of saying that people who only love those who love them are going to hell.

Do Good for the Right Motives, Unlike the Scribes and Pharisees

Not only does Jesus expect His followers to be holy, He expects them to be holy for the right reasons. It is quite possible to obey God's commandments and still be very displeasing to Him if one's obedience stems

---

[44] It was a Jewish teacher of the Law who, wishing to justify himself, asked Jesus the question, "Who is my neighbor?" You can be sure he already thought he had the right answer. Jesus answered him with the story of a Samaritan, a member of a race that was hated by the Jews, who proved himself to be a neighbor to a mistreated Jew (see Luke 10:25-37).

from a wrong motive. Jesus condemned the scribes and Pharisees because they did all their good deeds purely to impress others (see Matt. 23:5). He expects His disciples to be different.

> Beware of practicing your righteousness before men to be noticed by them; otherwise you have no reward with your Father who is in heaven. When therefore you give alms, do not sound a trumpet before you, as the hypocrites do in the synagogues and in the streets [Jesus' audience knew of whom He was speaking], that they may be honored by men. Truly I say to you, they have their reward in full. But when you give alms, do not let your left hand know what your right hand is doing that your alms may be in secret; and your Father who sees in secret will repay you (Matt. 6:1-4).

Jesus expected that His followers would give alms to the poor. The Law commanded it (see Ex. 23:11; Lev. 19:10; 23:22; 25:35; Deut. 15:7-11), but the scribes and Pharisees did it with the blowing of trumpets, ostensibly to call the poor to their generous public distributions. Yet how many professing Christians give *nothing* to the poor? They haven't even made it to the point of needing to examine their motives for alms giving. If selfishness motivated the scribes and Pharisees to advertise their alms giving, what is it that motivates professing Christians to *ignore* the plight of the poor? In this regard, does their righteousness surpass that of the scribes and Pharisees?

As Paul would echo in 1 Corinthians 3:10-15, we can do good things for the wrong reasons. If our motives are not pure, our good deeds will go unrewarded. Paul wrote that it is possible even to preach the gospel from impure motives (see Phil. 1:15-17). As Jesus prescribed, a good way to be sure our giving is purely motivated is to give as secretively as possible, not letting our left hand know what our right hand is doing. The disciple-making minister teaches his disciples to give to the poor (providing they have the means), and he quietly practices what he preaches.

Prayer and Fasting for the Right Reasons

Jesus also expected that His followers would pray and fast, and that they would do those things, not to be seen by people, but to please their Father. Otherwise they would be no different than the hell-bound scribes and Pharisees, who prayed and fasted only to gain the praise of people, a very temporary reward. Jesus admonished His followers:

> And when you pray, you are not to be as the hypocrites; for they love to stand and pray in the synagogues and on the street corners, in order to be seen by men [Jesus' audience certainly knew of whom He was speaking]. Truly I

say to you, they have their reward in full. But you, when you pray, go into your inner room, and when you have shut your door, pray to your Father who is in secret, and your Father who sees in secret will repay you.

And whenever you fast, do not put on a gloomy face as the hypocrites do, for they neglect their appearance in order to be seen fasting by men [Again, Jesus' audience certainly knew of whom He was speaking]. Truly I say to you, they have their reward in full. But you, when you fast, anoint your head, and wash your face, so that you may not be seen fasting by men, but by your Father who is in secret; and your Father who sees in secret will repay you (Matt. 6:5-6, 16-18).

How many professing Christians have a prayer life that is non-existent and have never fasted?[45] In this regard, how does their righteousness compare with that of the scribes and Pharisees, who practiced both (albeit for the wrong reasons)?

A Digression Regarding Prayer and Forgiveness

While on the subject of prayer, Jesus digressed a little to offer more specific instructions to His disciples regarding how they should pray. Jesus wants us to pray in such a way that we don't insult His Father by denying, through our prayers, what He has revealed about Himself. For example, since God knows what we need before we ask Him (He knows everything), there is no reason to use meaningless repetition when we pray:

And when you are praying, do not use meaningless repetition, as the Gentiles do, for they suppose that they will be heard for their many words. Therefore do not be like them; for your Father knows what you need, before you ask Him (Matt. 6:7-8).

Truly, our prayers reveal how well we know God. Those who know Him as He is revealed in His Word pray to the end that *His* will be done and that *He* be glorified. Their highest desire is to be holy, fully pleasing to Him. This is reflected in Jesus' model prayer, what we call the Lord's Prayer, included next in Jesus' instructions to His disciples. It reveals His expectations for our priorities and devotion:[46]

Pray, then, in this way: "Our Father who art in heaven, hallowed be Thy name. Thy kingdom come. Thy will be

---

[45] Later in this book, I have included an entire chapter on the subject of fasting.

[46] Some unfortunately claim that this is not a prayer that Christians should employ because it is not prayed "in Jesus' name." Applying this logic, however, we would have to conclude that many prayers of the apostles recorded in the book of Acts and epistles were not "Christian prayers."

done, on earth as it is in heaven. Give us this day our daily bread" (Matt. 6:7-11).

The foremost concern of Christ's disciples should be that God's name be hallowed, that it be respected, revered, and treated as holy.

Of course, those who pray that God's name be hallowed should be holy themselves, hallowing God's name. It would be hypocritical to do otherwise. Thus this prayer reflects our desire that others would submit themselves to God as we have.

The second request of the model prayer is similar: "Thy kingdom come." The idea of a kingdom implies that there is a King who rules His kingdom. The Christian disciple longs to see his King, the one who rules his life, rule over the whole earth. Oh, that everyone would bow his knee to King Jesus in obedient faith!

The third request echoes the first and second: "Thy will be done, on earth as it is in heaven." Again, how can we sincerely pray such a prayer without being submitted to God's will in our own lives? The true disciple desires that God's will be done on earth just as it is in heaven—perfectly and completely.

That God's name be hallowed, that His will be done, that His kingdom would come, should be more important to us than having sustaining food, our "daily bread." This fourth request is placed fourth for a reason. Even in itself, it reflects a right ordering of our priorities, and no hint of greed is found here. Christ's disciples serve God and not mammon. They aren't focused on laying up earthly treasures.

May I also add that this fourth request seems to indicate that this model prayer is one that should be prayed daily, at the beginning of each day.

The Model Prayer Continues

Do Christ's disciples ever sin? Apparently sometimes they do, since Jesus taught them to ask for forgiveness for their sins.

> "And forgive us our debts, as we also have forgiven our debtors. And do not lead us into temptation, but deliver us from evil. For Thine is the kingdom, and the power, and the glory, forever. Amen." For if you forgive men for their transgressions, your heavenly Father will also forgive you. But if you do not forgive men, then your Father will not forgive your transgressions (Matt. 6:12-15).

Jesus' disciples realize that their disobedience offends God, and when they sin, they feel ashamed. They want the stain to be removed, and thankfully their gracious heavenly Father is willing to forgive them. But they must ask for forgiveness, the fifth request found in the Lord's Prayer.

Their being forgiven, however, is conditional upon their forgiving others. Because they've been forgiven of so much, they have an obligation to forgive everyone who requests their forgiveness (and to love and work for reconciliation with those who don't). If they refuse to forgive, God won't forgive them.

The sixth and final request, too, is one that obviously reflects the true disciple's desire to be holy: "Do not lead us into temptation, but deliver us from evil [or 'the evil one']." So much does the true disciple long for holiness that he asks God not to lead him into a situation where he might be tempted, lest he succumb. Additionally, he requests that God would rescue him from any evil that might entrap him. Certainly this is a great prayer to pray at the beginning of each day, before we journey out into a world of evil and temptation. And certainly we can expect God to answer this prayer that He told us to pray!

Those who know God understand why all six requests of this prayer are so appropriate. The reason is revealed in the final line of the prayer: "For [or *because*] Thine is the kingdom, and the power, and the glory, forever" (Matt. 6:13). God is a great King who rules over His kingdom in which we are His servants. He is all-powerful, and no one should dare resist His will. All glory will belong to Him forever. He is worthy to be obeyed.

What is the dominant theme of the Lord's prayer? *Holiness.* Christ's disciples desire that God's name be hallowed, that His reign would be established over the earth, and that His will be done perfectly everywhere. This is more important to them than even their daily bread. They want to be pleasing in His sight, and when they fail, they want forgiveness from Him. As forgiven people, they extend forgiveness to others. They long to be perfectly holy, to the degree that they desire to avoid temptation, because temptation increases their chances of sinning. The disciple-maker teaches these things to his disciples.

The Disciple and His Material Possessions

The next topic of the Sermon on the Mount is potentially very disturbing for professing Christians whose primary motivation in life is the ever-increasing accumulation of material things:

> Do not lay up for yourselves treasures upon earth, where moth and rust destroy, and where thieves break in and steal. But lay up for yourselves treasures in heaven, where neither moth nor rust destroys, and where thieves do not break in or steal; for where your treasure is, there will your heart be also. The lamp of the body is the eye; if therefore your eye is clear, your whole body will be full of light. But if your eye is bad, your whole body will be full of darkness. If therefore the light that is in you is darkness, how great is the darkness! No one can serve two masters; for

either he will hate the one and love the other, or he will hold to one and despise the other. You cannot serve God and mammon (Matt. 6:19-24).

Jesus commanded that we not lay up for ourselves treasures on earth. What then constitutes a "treasure"? Literal treasures are normally kept in treasure chests, stored away somewhere, never used for anything practical. Jesus defined them as things that attract moths, rust and thieves. Another way of saying it would be, "non-essentials." Moths eat what is in the far ends of our closets, not what we wear frequently. Rust eats away at those things we rarely use. In more developed countries, thieves most often steal things people really don't need: art, jewelry, expensive gadgets, and what can be pawned.

True disciples have "given up all their possessions" (see Luke 14:33). They are simply stewards of God's money, so every decision to spend money is a spiritual decision. What we do with our money reflects who is controlling our lives. When we accumulate "treasures," hoarding money and buying what is not essential, we reveal that Jesus is not in control, because if He were, we would do better things with the money He's entrusted to us.

What are those better things? Jesus commands us to lay up treasure in heaven. How is that possible? He tells us in Luke's Gospel: "Sell your possessions and give to charity; make yourselves purses which do not wear out, an unfailing treasure in heaven, where no thief comes near, nor moth destroys" (Luke 12:33).

By giving money to help the poor and spread the gospel, we lay up treasure in heaven. Jesus is telling us to take what is sure to depreciate to the point of being worthless, and invest it in something that will never depreciate. That is what the disciple-making minister is doing, and he is teaching his disciples to do likewise.

The Bad Eye

What did Jesus mean when He spoke about people with clear eyes whose bodies are full of light and people with bad eyes whose bodies are full of darkness? His words must have something to do with money and material things, because that is what He was talking about before and after.

The Greek word translated "bad" in 6:23 is the same word translated in Matthew 20:15 as "envious." There we read of an employer who said to his worker, "Is your eye *envious* because I am generous?" Obviously an eye cannot literally be envious. Thus the expression "an envious (or bad) eye" speaks of a person with greedy desires. This helps us better understand what Christ meant in Matthew 6:22-23.

The person with a clear eye symbolizes the one who is pure in heart, allowing the light of the truth to come in to him. Thus he serves God and lays up treasure, not on earth, but in heaven where his heart is. The person with the bad eye shuts out the light of the truth from coming in, because he thinks he already has the truth, and thus he is full of darkness, believing lies. He lays up treasure on earth where his heart it. He believes that the purpose of his life is self-gratification. Money is his god. He is not heaven-bound.

What does it mean to have money as your god? It means that money has a place in your life that only God should rightfully have. Money is directing your life. It consumes your energy, thoughts and time. It is the main source of your joy. You love it.[47] That is why Paul equated greed with idolatry, stating that no greedy person will inherit God's kingdom (see Eph. 5:5; Col. 3:5-6).

Both God and money want to be masters of our lives, and Jesus said we can't serve them both. Again we see that Jesus stayed with His primary theme—*Only the holy will inherit God's kingdom.* He made it very clear that people who are full of darkness, whose god is money, whose heart is on the earth and who lay up earthly treasures, are not on the narrow road that leads to life.

The Covetous Poor

A preoccupation with material things is not only wrong when those things are luxury items. A person can be wrongly preoccupied with material things even when those things are basic necessities. Jesus continued:

> For this reason [that is, based upon what I just said] I say to you, do not be anxious for your life, as to what you shall eat, or what you shall drink; nor for your body, as to what you shall put on. Is not life more than food, and the body than clothing? Look at the birds of the air, that they do not sow, neither do they reap, nor gather into barns, and yet your heavenly Father feeds them. Are you not worth much more than they? And which of you by being anxious can add a single cubit to his life's span? And why are you anxious about clothing? Observe how the lilies of the field grow; they do not toil nor do they spin, yet I say to you that even Solomon in all his glory did not clothe himself like one of these. But if God so arrays the grass of the field, which is alive today and tomorrow is thrown into the furnace, will He not much more do so for you, O men of little faith? Do not be anxious then, saying, "What shall we eat?" or "What shall we drink?" or "With what shall we clothe ourselves?" For all these things the Gen-

---

[47] On another occasion, Jesus made the same statement about the impossibility of serving God and mammon, and Luke tells us, "Now the Pharisees, who were lovers of money, were listening to all these things, and they were scoffing at Him" (Luke 16:14). So again, here in the Sermon on the Mount, Jesus was clearly exposing the practice and teaching of the Pharisees.

tiles eagerly seek; for your heavenly Father knows that you need all these things. But seek first His kingdom and His righteousness; and all these things shall be added to you. Therefore do not be anxious for tomorrow; for tomorrow will care for itself. Each day has enough trouble of its own (Matt. 6:25-34).

Many readers of this book will not be able to relate at all to the people Jesus was addressing. When was the last time you worried about having food, drink or clothing?

Jesus' words certainly have application to all of us, however. If it is wrong to be preoccupied with the *essentials* of life, how much more wrong is it to be preoccupied with *nonessentials*? Jesus expects His disciples to be primarily focused on seeking two things: His kingdom and His righteousness. When a professing Christian can't afford to tithe (an old covenant commandment I might add), but *can* afford many non-essential material things, is he living up to Christ's standard of seeking first His kingdom and righteousness? The answer is obvious.

Don't be a Fault-Finder

Jesus' next set of commandments to His followers concerns the sins of judging and faultfinding:

Do not judge lest you be judged. For in the way you judge, you will be judged; and by your standard of measure, it will be measured to you. And why do you look at the speck that is in your brother's eye, but do not notice the log that is in your own eye? Or how can you say to your brother, "Let me take the speck out of your eye," and behold, the log is in your own eye? You hypocrite, first take the log out of your own eye, and then you will see clearly to take the speck out of your brother's eye (Matt. 7:1-5).

Although Jesus didn't directly or indirectly indict the scribes and Pharisees in this passage, they were certainly guilty of the sin under consideration; they found fault with Him!

What exactly did Jesus mean in this warning against judging others?

First, let us consider what He did not mean. He did not mean that we should not be discerning and make fundamental determinations about people's character by observing their actions. That is quite clear. Directly after this section, Jesus instructed His disciples not to cast their pearls to pigs or give what is holy to dogs (see 7:6). He was obviously speaking figuratively of certain kinds of people, referring to them as pigs and dogs, people who don't appreciate the value of the holy things, "pearls," they are being given. They are obviously unsaved people. And certainly, we must *judge* if people are pigs and dogs if we are to obey this commandment.

Moreover, Jesus shortly told His followers how to *judge* false teachers, "wolves in sheep's clothing" (see 7:15), by inspecting their fruit. Clearly, in order to obey Jesus' instructions we must observe people's lifestyles and make judgments.

Similarly, Paul told the Corinthian believers:

> I wrote to you not to associate with any so-called brother if he is an immoral person, or covetous, or an idolater, or a reviler, or a drunkard, or a swindler—not even to eat with such a one (1 Cor. 5:11).

To obey this instruction requires that we examine people's lifestyles and make judgments about them based on what we observe.

The apostle John also told us that we can easily discern who is of God and who is of the devil. By looking at people's lifestyles, it is obvious who is saved and who is unsaved (see 1 John 3:10).

All of this being so, discerning people's character by examining their actions and judging if they belong to God or the devil is not the sin of judging against which Christ warned. So what did Jesus mean?

Notice that Jesus was talking about finding small faults, *specks*, with a *brother* (note that Jesus uses the word *brother* three times in this passage). Jesus was not warning us against judging people to be unbelievers by observing their glaring faults (as He will shortly instruct us to do in this very sermon). Rather, these are instructions for how Christians should treat Christians. They should not be finding little faults with one another, and this is especially so when they themselves are blind to their own larger faults. In such cases, they are hypocritical. As Jesus once said to a crowd of hypocritical judges, "He who is without sin among you, let him be the first to throw a stone" (John 8:7).

The apostle James, whose epistle often parallels the Sermon on the mount, similarly wrote, "Do not complain, brethren, against one another, that you yourselves may not be judged; behold, the Judge is standing right at the door" (Jas. 5:9). Perhaps this also helps us to understand something of what Jesus was warning against—finding faults with fellow believers and then broadcasting what we've found, complaining against one another. This is one of the most prevalent sins in the church, and those who are guilty place themselves in a dangerous position of being judged. When we speak against a fellow believer, pointing out his faults to others, we're violating the golden rule, because we don't want others to speak ill of us in our absence.

We may lovingly approach a fellow believer about his or her fault, but only when we can do so without hypocrisy, certain that we are not guilty (or more guilty) of the same sin as the person we are confronting. It is, however, a complete waste of time to do so with an unbeliever, which seems to be the subject of the next verse. Jesus said,

> Do not give what is holy to dogs, and do not throw your pearls before swine, lest they trample them under their feet, and turn and tear you to pieces (Matt. 7:6).

Similarly, a proverb says, "Do not reprove a scoffer, lest he hate you; reprove a wise man, and he will love you" (Prov. 9:8). Jesus told His disciples at another time to shake the dust off their feet in protest against those who reject their gospel. Once the "dogs" have been identified by their lack of appreciation for the truth, God doesn't want His servants wasting their time trying to reach them while others have been given no opportunity yet.

Encouragement to Pray

Finally we come to the last section of the body of Jesus' sermon. It begins with some encouraging prayer promises:

> Ask, and it shall be given to you; seek, and you shall find; knock, and it shall be opened to you. For everyone who asks receives, and he who seeks finds, and to him who knocks it shall be opened. Or what man is there among you, when his son shall ask him for a loaf, will give him a stone? Or if he shall ask for a fish, he will not give him a snake, will he? If you then, being evil, know how to give good gifts to your children, how much more shall your Father who is in heaven give what is good to those who ask Him! (Matt. 7:7-11).

"Aha!" a reader somewhere might be saying. "Here's a part of the Sermon on the Mount that has nothing to do with holiness."

That all depends on what it is we're asking, knocking and seeking for in prayer. As those who "hunger and thirst for righteousness," we long to obey all that Jesus has commanded in His sermon, and that longing is certainly reflected in our prayers. In fact, the model prayer that Jesus previously shared in this same sermon was the expression of a desire for God's will to be done and for holiness.

Additionally, Luke's version of these same prayer promises under consideration ends with, "If you then, being evil, know how to give good gifts to your children, how much more shall your heavenly Father give the *Holy* Spirit to those who ask Him?" (Luke 11:13). Jesus was not thinking of luxury items when He promised us "good gifts." In His mind, the Holy Spirit is a "good gift," because the Holy Spirit makes us holy and helps us spread the gospel that makes other people holy. And holy people go to heaven.

Other good gifts are anything that are in within God's will. God is obviously most concerned about His will and His kingdom, and so we should expect that our prayers for anything that increase our usefulness in God's kingdom will always be answered.

A Summarizing Statement

Now we arrive at a verse that should be considered a statement that summarizes practically everything Jesus said up to this point. Many commentators miss this, but it is important that we don't. This particular verse is obviously a summarizing statement, as it begins with the word *therefore*. It is thus linked to previous instructions, and the question is: How much of what Jesus has said does it summarize? Let's read it and think:

> Therefore, however you want people to treat you, so treat
> them, for this is the Law and the Prophets (Matt. 7:12).

This statement can't be a summary of just the few verses before it concerning prayer, otherwise it would make no sense.

Remember that early in His sermon, Jesus had warned against the error of thinking that He had come to abolish *the Law or the Prophets* (see Matt. 5:17). From that point in His sermon until the verse at which we've now arrived, He did essentially nothing but endorse and explain God's Old Testament commandments. Thus, He now summarizes *everything* He's commanded, all of which He derived from the Law and Prophets: "Therefore, whatever you want others to do for you, do so for them, for this is *the Law and the Prophets*" (7:12). The phrase, "the Law and the Prophets," connects everything Jesus said between Matthew 5:17 and 7:12.

Now, as Jesus begins the conclusion of His sermon, He reiterates His primary theme once more—*Only the holy inherit God's kingdom:*

> Enter by the narrow gate; for the gate is wide, and the way
> is broad that leads to destruction, and many are those who
> enter by it. For the gate is small, and the way is narrow that
> leads to life, and few are those who find it (Matt. 7:13-14).

Obviously the narrow gate and the way that leads to life, which few find, is symbolic of salvation. The wide gate and broad way that leads to destruction, the route of the majority, symbolizes damnation. If everything Jesus said prior to this statement means anything, if this sermon has any logical progression, if Jesus possessed any intelligence as a communicator, then the most natural interpretation would be that the narrow way is the way of following Jesus, obeying His commandments. The broad way would be the opposite. How many professing Christians are on the narrow way described in this sermon? The disciple-making minister is certainly on the narrow way, and he is leading his disciples on that same way.

It is puzzling to some professing Christians that Jesus said nothing about faith or believing in Him in this sermon in which He said so much about salvation and damnation. To those who understand the inseparable correlation between belief and behavior, however, this sermon presents no problem. People who obey Jesus show their faith by their works. Those who don't obey Him don't believe He is the Son of God. Not only is our salvation an indication of God's grace toward us, so is the transformation that has taken place in our lives. Our holiness is really His holiness.

How to Recognize False Religious Leaders

As Jesus continued His concluding remarks, He next warned His disciples about false prophets who lead the undiscerning down the broad road to destruction. They are those who are not truly of God, yet disguised as so. All false teachers and leaders fall under this category. How can they be identified?

> Beware of the false prophets, who come to you in sheep's clothing, but inwardly are ravenous wolves. You will know them by their fruits. Grapes are not gathered from thorn bushes, nor figs from thistles, are they? Even so, every good tree bears good fruit; but the bad tree bears bad fruit. A good tree cannot produce bad fruit, nor can a bad tree produce good fruit. Every tree that does not bear good fruit is cut down and thrown into the fire. So then, you will know them by their fruits. Not everyone who says to Me, "Lord, Lord," will enter the kingdom of heaven; but he who does the will of My Father who is in heaven. Many will say to Me on that day, "Lord, Lord, did we not prophesy in Your name, and in Your name cast out demons, and in Your name perform many miracles?" And then I will declare to them, "I never knew you; depart from Me, you who practice lawlessness" (Matt. 7:15-23).

Clearly, Jesus indicated that false teachers are very deceptive. They have some exterior indications of being genuine. They may call Jesus their Lord, prophesy, cast out demons and perform miracles. But the "sheep's clothing" only hides the "ravenous wolf." They aren't of the true sheep. How can it be known if they are true or false? Their true character can be identified by examining their "fruits."

What are the fruits of which Jesus was speaking? Obviously, they are not fruits of miracles. Rather, they are the fruits of obedience to all Jesus taught. Those who are true sheep do the will of the Father. Those who are false "practice lawlessness" (7:23). Our responsibility, then, is to compare their lives with what Jesus taught and commanded.

False teachers abound today in the church, and we should not be surprised, because both Jesus and Paul forewarned us that, as the end approaches, we should expect nothing less (see Matt. 24:11; 2 Tim. 4:3-4). The most prevalent false prophets of our day are those who teach that heaven awaits the unholy. They are responsible for the eternal damnation of millions of people. Of them, John Wesley wrote,

> How terrible is this!—when the ambassadors of God turn agents for the devil!—when they who are commissioned to teach men the way to heaven do in fact teach them the way to hell....If it be asked, "Why, who ever did...this?"... I answer, Ten thousand wise and honourable men; even all those, of whatever denomination, who encourage the proud, the trifler, the passionate, the lover of the world, the man of pleasure, the unjust or unkind, the easy, careless, harmless, useless creatures, the man who suffers no reproach for righteousness' sake, to imagine he is in the way to heaven. These are false prophets in the highest sense of the word. These are traitors both to God and man.... They are continually peopling the realms of the night; and whenever they follow the poor souls they have destroyed, "hell shall be moved from beneath to meet them at their coming!"[48]

Interestingly, Wesley was specifically commenting about the false teachers whom Jesus warned against in Matthew 7:15-23.

Notice that Jesus again plainly said, contrary to what so many false teachers tell us today, that those who don't bear good fruit will be cast into hell (see 7:19). Moreover, this applies not just to teachers and prophets, but to everyone. Jesus said, "Not everyone who says to Me, 'Lord, Lord,' will enter the kingdom of heaven; but he who does the will of My Father who is in heaven" (Matt. 7:21). What is true for prophets is true for all. This is Jesus' main theme—*Only the holy will inherit God's kingdom*. People who aren't obeying Jesus are destined for hell.

Also notice the connection Jesus made between what a person is inwardly and what he is outwardly. "Good" trees produce good fruit. "Bad" trees *can't* produce good fruit. The source of the good fruit that shows up on the outside is the nature of the person. By His grace, God has changed the nature of those who have truly believed in Jesus.[49]

[48] *The Works of John Wesley* (Baker: Grand Rapids, 1996), by John Wesley, reprinted from the 1872 edition issued by the Wesleyan Methodist Book Room, London, pp. 441, 416.

[49] I can't resist taking the opportunity also to comment here about a common expression people use when trying to excuse sins in others: "We don't know what is in their hearts." In contradiction to this, Jesus said here that the outside reveals the inside. In another place, He said, "The mouth speaks out of that which fills the heart" (Matt. 12:34). When a person speaks words of hate, it indicates hatred fills his heart. Jesus also told us that "from within, out of the heart of men, proceed the evil thoughts, fornications, thefts, murders, adulteries, deeds of coveting and wickedness, as well as deceit, sensuality, envy, slander, pride and foolishness" (Mark 7:21-22). When a person commits adultery, we do know what is in his heart: adultery.

A Final Warning and Summary

Jesus concluded His sermon with a final warning and summarizing example. As you would expect, it is an illustration of His theme—*Only the holy will inherit God's kingdom.*

> Therefore everyone who hears these words of Mine, and acts upon them [literally, "does them"], may be compared to a wise man, who built his house upon the rock. And the rain descended, and the floods came, and the winds blew, and burst against that house; and yet it did not fall, for it had been founded upon the rock. And everyone who hears these words of Mine, and does not act upon them [literally, "does not do them"], will be like a foolish man, who built his house upon the sand. And the rain descended, and the floods came, and the winds blew, and burst against that house; and it fell, and great was its fall (Matt. 7:24-27).

Jesus' final illustration is not a formula for "success in life" as some use it. The context shows that He was not giving advice on how to prosper financially during tough times by having faith in His promises. This is the summary of all that Jesus had said in His Sermon on the Mount. Those who do what He says are wise and will endure; they need not fear the wrath of God when it falls. Those who don't obey Him are foolish and will suffer greatly, paying "the penalty of eternal destruction" (2 Thes. 1:9).

Answer to a Question

Is it not possible that Jesus' Sermon on the Mount was only applicable to those followers of His who lived prior to His sacrificial death and resurrection? Were they not under the Law as their temporary means of salvation, but after Jesus died for their sins, were then saved by faith, thus invalidating the theme expounded in this sermon?

This theory is a bad one. No one has ever been saved by his works. It has always been by faith, prior to and during the old covenant. Paul argues in Romans 4 that both Abraham (before the old covenant) and David (during the old covenant) were justified by faith and not works.

Moreover, it was an impossibility that any of Jesus' audience could be saved by works, because they had all sinned and fallen short of God's glory (see Rom. 3:23). Only God's grace could save them, and only faith could receive His grace.

Unfortunately, too many in the church today view Jesus' commandments as serving no higher purpose than to make us feel guilty so we'll see the impossibility of earning salvation by works. Now that we've "gotten the message" and have been saved by faith, we can ignore most of His commandments. Unless, of course, we want to get others "saved." Then we can pull out the commandments again to show people how sinful they are so they will be saved by a "faith" that is void of works.

Nevertheless, Jesus did not tell His disciples, "Go into all the world and make disciples, and make sure they realize that, once they've felt guilty and are then saved by faith, My commandments have served their purpose in their lives." Rather, He said, "Go therefore and make disciples of all the nations...*teaching them to observe all that I commanded you*" (Matt. 28:19-20, emphasis added). Disciple-making ministers are doing just that.

NINE

Jesus' Favorite Preacher

You may be surprised to learn that Jesus had a favorite preacher. You may be even more surprised to learn that Jesus' favorite preacher was not a Lutheran, Methodist, Pentecostal, Anglican, or Presbyterian. Rather, he was a Baptist! We know him as *John the Baptist*, of course! Jesus said of him,

> Truly, I say to you, among those born of women there has not arisen anyone greater than John the Baptist (Matt. 11:11a).

Since all people are "born of woman," this was another way of saying that, in Jesus' estimation, John the Baptist was the greatest person who had ever lived. Why Jesus felt that way is a matter of conjecture. It seems reasonable to think, however, that Jesus thought highly of John because of John's spiritual qualities. If so, we would certainly be wise to study and imitate those spiritual qualities. I've found at least seven spiritual qualities in John the Baptist that are praiseworthy. Although John's ministry best represents the ministry of a prophet and evangelist, all seven spiritual qualities are appropriate for any and every minister of the gospel. Let's consider the first of seven.

John's First Quality

> And this is the witness of John, when the Jews sent to him priests and Levites from Jerusalem to ask him, "Who are you?" And he confessed, and did not deny, and he confessed, "I am not the Christ." And they asked him, "What then? Are you Elijah?" And he said, "I am not." "Are you the Prophet?" And he answered, "No." They said then to him, "Who are you, so that we may give an answer to those who sent us? What do you say about yourself?" He

said, "I am a voice of one crying in the wilderness, 'Make straight the way of the Lord,' as Isaiah the prophet said" (John 1:19-23).

John knew his calling and pursued it.

How important it is for ministers to know their callings and pursue them. If you are an evangelist, you should not try to be a pastor. If you are a teacher, you should not try to be a prophet. Otherwise, you will only find frustration.

How do you know your calling? First, by seeking the Lord, the one who has called you. Second, by examining your gifting. If God has called you to be an evangelist, He will equip you for the task. And third, by the confirmation of others who will certainly notice your gifting.

Once you are certain of your calling, you should pursue it with all of your heart, letting no obstacle hinder you. Many are waiting around for God to do what He expects them to do. Noah didn't wait around for God to build an ark!

It has been said that the word *ministry* is spelled W O R K. Satan will surely try to stop you from fulfilling your calling, but you must resist him and forge ahead by faith. Even though Scripture doesn't tell us, you can be sure that there was one day when John *first started* preaching around the region of the Jordan. No doubt his first crowds were much smaller than his later crowds. You can be sure that people made fun of him and that he experienced persecution. But he would not be stopped. His sole aim was to please His God who had called him to his ministry. Ultimately, he succeeded.

John's first spiritual quality that is worthy of our imitation is this: *John knew his calling and pursued it.*

John's Second Quality

Now in those days John the Baptist came, preaching in the wilderness of Judea, saying, "Repent, for the kingdom of heaven is at hand" (Matt. 3:1-2).

Certainly Jesus highly approved of John's simple message, as it was the same message that Jesus preached wherever He went (see Matt. 4:17). John called people to repentance—to turn away from a life of sin and turn to a life of righteousness. He knew that a relationship with God begins with repentance, and that those who don't repent will be cast into hell.

Unlike so many modern evangelists, John never mentioned the love of God. Nor did he talk about people's "felt needs" as a means to entice them to pray a meaningless prayer of "accepting Jesus" so that they could begin to experience "the abundant life." He did not lead people to believe that they were basically good people whom God wanted to take to heaven if they could only realize that salvation was not of works. Rather, he saw them as God saw them—rebels in danger of facing eternal consequences for their sins. He solemnly warned them of the wrath to come. He made certain they understood that if they didn't change their hearts and actions, they were doomed.

So the second quality that John possessed that is worthy of every disciple-making minister's imitation is this: *John proclaimed that repentance was the first step in a relationship with God.*

John's Third Quality

> Now John himself had a garment of camel's hair, and a leather belt about his waist; and his food was locusts and wild honey (Matt. 3:4).

John certainly didn't fit the picture of the modern "prosperity preacher." They, in fact, would never allow such a man as John on their church platforms because he did not dress the part of success. John, however, was a true man of God who had no interest in pursuing earthly treasures or impressing people with his outward appearance, knowing that God looks at the heart. He lived simply, and his lifestyle caused no one to stumble, as they could see his motive was not money. How this stands in contrast to so many modern ministers around the world, who use the gospel primarily for personal gain. And as they misrepresent Jesus, they do great damage to Christ's cause.

John's third quality that contributed to his being Jesus' favorite preacher was this: *John lived simply.*

John's Fourth Quality

> He [John] therefore began saying to the multitudes who were going out to be baptized by him, "You brood of vipers, who warned you to flee from the wrath to come? Therefore bring forth fruits in keeping with repentance, and do not begin to say to yourselves, 'We have Abraham for our father,' for I say to you that God is able from these stones to raise up children to Abraham" (Luke 3:7-8).

As John's ministry began touching more people, he obviously did not compromise his message. John may have even become suspicious of people's motives when he noticed that it was becoming quite popular to be baptized. Even scribes and Pharisees were making the journey to the Jordan (see Matt. 3:7). He feared that many people were just going along with the crowd. So he did all he could to keep them from being self-deceived, knocking over any props that supported their deception. He didn't want anyone to think that just the act of baptism saved them, or that just a profession of repentance would keep them from hell. He warned that true repentance brings forth the fruit of obedience.

Moreover, because many Jews considered themselves to be saved due to their physical lineage from Abraham, John exposed the fallacy of that hope.

John's fourth praiseworthy quality is this: *He loved people enough to tell them the truth. He would never assure an unrepentant, unholy person that he was on the way to heaven.*

John's Fifth Quality

John would not baptize people who didn't appear repentant, not wanting to bolster anyone's self-deception. He baptized people "as they confessed their sins" (Matt. 3:6). He warned those who came:

> The axe is already laid at the root of the trees; every tree therefore that does not bear good fruit is cut down and thrown into the fire.... And His winnowing fork is in His hand, and He will thoroughly clear His threshing floor; and He will gather His wheat into the barn, but He will burn up the chaff with unquenchable fire (Matt. 3:10, 12).

John was not afraid to tell the truth about hell, a subject that is often avoided by preachers who are trying to win a popularity contest rather than win souls for God's kingdom. Neither did John fail to proclaim the same theme we discovered in Christ's Sermon on the Mount—only the holy inherit God's kingdom. Those who don't bear good fruit will be thrown into the fire.

If John were alive today, he would no doubt be castigated by many professing Christians as a "hellfire and brimstone preacher," a "gloom and doom prophet," "not seeker-sensitive," or worse, "negative," "condemning," "legalistic" or "self-righteous." Yet John was Jesus' favorite preacher. His fifth quality: *John preached about hell and made it clear what kinds of people are on their way there.* Interestingly, Luke referred to John's message as "the gospel" (Luke 3:18).

John's Sixth Quality

Although John was mightily used of God and became very popular with the multitudes, he knew that he was nothing in comparison to Jesus, and so he always exalted His Lord:

> As for me, I baptize you with water for repentance, but He who is coming after me is mightier than I, and I am not fit to remove His sandals; He will baptize you with the Holy Spirit and fire (Matt. 3:11).

How John's self-appraisal stands in contrast to the arrogance that is too often flaunted in our day by "ministers." Their color ministry magazines contain photos of them on every page, while Jesus is scarcely mentioned. They parade like peacocks across church platforms, exalting themselves in the eyes of their followers. They are untouchable and unreachable, filled with their own self-importance. Some even command angels and God! Yet John considered himself unworthy to remove Jesus' sandals, what would have been considered to be an act of a lowly slave. He objected when Jesus came to him to be baptized, and once he realized that Jesus was the Christ, he immediately pointed all to Him, declaring Him to be "the Lamb of God who takes away the sin of the world" (John 29). "He must increase, but I must decrease" (John 3:30) became John's humble motto.

This was John's sixth quality that helped make him Jesus' favorite preacher: *John humbled himself and exalted Jesus. He had no desire for self-exaltation.*

John' Seventh Quality

Modern preachers often speak in vague generalities lest they offend anyone. How easy it is to preach, "God wants us to do what is right!" True and false Christians alike will say "Amen" to such preaching. Many preachers also find it quite easy to continually harp on the scandalous sins of the world, avoiding any mention of similar sins within the church. They, for example, might rage against pornography, but dare not mention the R-rated and immoral videos and DVDs that are viewed and even collected by many of their parishioners. The fear of man has snared them.

John, however, didn't hesitate to preach *specifically*. Luke reports:

> And the multitudes were questioning him, saying, "Then what shall we do?" And he would answer and say to them, "Let the man who has two tunics share with him who has none; and let him who has food do likewise." And some tax-gatherers also came to be baptized, and they said to him, "Teacher, what shall we do?" And he said to them, "Collect no more than what you have been ordered to." And some soldiers were questioning him, saying, "And what about us, what shall we do?" And he said to them, "Do not take money from anyone by force, or accuse anyone falsely, and be content with your wages" (Luke 3:10-14).

It is interesting that five of the six specific directives John gave had something to do with money or material things. John was not afraid to preach about stewardship as it relates to the golden rule and the second greatest commandment. Neither did John wait several years until the new "believers" were ready for such "heavy" concepts. He believed that it was impossible to serve God and mammon, and so stewardship was of primary importance from the very beginning.

This brings up one other point. John did not major in the minors, continually harping on dress codes and other issues of holiness related to outward appearance. He focused on "the weightier provisions of the law" (Matt. 23:23). He knew that what is most important is loving our neighbors as ourselves and treating others just as we want to be treated. That means sharing food and clothing with those who lack such basic necessities, dealing honestly with others, and being content with what we have.

This was a seventh quality that endeared John to Jesus: *He preached not in vague generalities, but cited specific things people should do to please God, even things related to stewardship. And, he focused on what was most important.*

In Conclusion

A pastor or teacher's ministry would of course be characterized by a broader range of subject matter than was John's. John was preaching to the unrepentant. Pastors and teachers are supposed to be primarily teaching those who have already repented. Their teaching is based on those things Jesus said to His disciples and that are written in the New Testament epistles.

We often fail, however, to rightly identify our audiences, and it seems today that sinners are often preached to as if they were saints. Just because people are sitting in a church building does not mean our job is to assure them of their salvation, especially if their lives are essentially indistinguishable from those in the world. There is a crying need today for millions of "John the Baptists" to preach from church pulpits. Will you rise to the challenge? Will you become one of Jesus' favorite preachers?

TEN

The New Birth

When people repent and believe in the Lord Jesus Christ, they are "born again." What exactly does it mean to be born again? That is what this chapter is all about.

In order to understand what it means to be born again, it first helps to understand the nature of human beings. Scripture tells us that we are not just physical, but also spiritual beings. For example, Paul wrote,

> Now may the God of peace Himself sanctify you entirely; and may your *spirit* and *soul* and *body* be preserved complete, without blame at the coming of our Lord Jesus Christ (1 Thes. 5:23, emphasis added).

As Paul indicated, we can consider ourselves to be three-part beings consisting of spirit, soul and body. Scripture does not precisely define those three parts, so we do our best to differentiate between them by our understanding of the words themselves. We usually conclude that our *body* is our physical being—the flesh, bones, blood and so on. Our *soul* is our intellectual and emotional being—our mind. Our *spirit* is obviously our spiritual being, or as the apostle Peter describes him, "the hidden person of the heart" (1 Pet. 3:4).

Because the spirit is invisible to the physical eye, unregenerate people tend to discredit its existence. The Bible, however, is very clear that all of us are spiritual beings. Scripture tells us that when a person dies, it is only his body that ceases to function, while his spirit and soul continue to function as always. At death, they vacate the body (as one) to stand judgment before God (see Heb. 9:27). After judgment, they go to heaven or hell. Eventually every person's spirit and soul will be reunited with his or her body at its resurrection.

The Human Spirit More Defined

In 1 Peter 3:4, Peter referred to the spirit as the "hidden *person*," indicating that the spirit is a *person*. Paul, too, referred to the spirit as the "inner man," indicating his belief that the human spirit is not just a concept or a force, but a person:

> Therefore we do not lose heart, but though our *outer man*
> is decaying, yet our *inner man* is being renewed day by
> day (2 Cor. 4:16, emphasis added).

The "outer man" obviously describes the physical body, whereas the "inner man" defines the spirit. While the body grows older, the spirit is renewed daily.

Notice again that Paul refers to both body and spirit as *men*. So when you imagine your spirit, don't imagine a spiritual cloud. It is better to imagine a *person* with a form who looks like you. If your body is old, however, don't think that your spirit looks old. Imagine how you looked in the prime of your life because your spirit has never grown older! It is renewed day by day.

Your spirit is the part of you that is born again (if you have believed in the Lord Jesus). Your spirit is joined with God's Spirit (see 1 Cor. 6:17), and He is the one who guides you as you follow Jesus (see Rom. 10:14).

The Bible teaches that God is also a spirit (see John 4:24), and so are angels and demons. They all have forms and they all exist in the spiritual realm. The spiritual realm, however, cannot be perceived with our physical senses. Attempting to contact the spiritual world with our physical senses would be comparable to trying to feel radio signals with our hands. We cannot perceive with our physical senses that radio waves are traveling through a room, but that doesn't prove there are no radio waves present. The only way to tune in to the radio frequencies is to turn on a radio.

This is also true of the spiritual realm. Just because the spiritual realm can't be perceived with the physical senses does not disprove its existence. It does exist, and whether people realize it or not, they are part of the spiritual realm because they are spiritual beings. They are either spiritually related to Satan (if they have not repented) or spiritually related to God (if they are born again). Some spiritualists have learned how to relate to the spiritual world through their spirits, but they are contacting the realm of Satan's domain—the kingdom of darkness.

Eternal Bodies

While we are on the subject, let me take a moment to mention something about our bodies. Although they will eventually die, our physical deaths will not be permanent. There is a day coming when God Himself will resurrect every dead human body. Jesus said,

Do not marvel at this; for an hour is coming, in which all who are in the tombs will hear His voice, and will come forth; those who did the good deeds, to a resurrection of life, those who committed the evil deeds to a resurrection of judgment (John 5:28-29).

The apostle John wrote in the book of Revelation that the resurrection of the bodies of the unjust will occur at least one thousand years after the resurrection of the bodies of the righteous:

And they [the saints who were martyred during the tribulation period] came to life and reigned with Christ for a thousand years. The rest of the dead did not come to life until the thousand years were completed. This is the first resurrection.[50] Blessed and holy is the one who has a part in the first resurrection...they will be priests of God and of Christ and will reign with Him for a thousand years (Rev. 20:4b-6).

The Bible also informs us that when Jesus returns to catch away the church, all of the dead bodies of the righteous will be resurrected and joined together with their spirits as they return from heaven with Jesus to Earth's atmosphere:

For if we believe that Jesus died and rose again, even so God will bring with Him those [as spirits] who have fallen asleep in Jesus. For this we say to you by the word of the Lord, that we who are alive and remain until the coming of the Lord, will not precede those who have fallen asleep. For the Lord Himself will descend from heaven with a shout...and the dead in Christ [their bodies] will rise first. Then we who are alive and remain will be caught up together with them in the clouds to meet the Lord in the air, and so we shall always be with the Lord (1 Thes. 4:14-17).

God formed the original man from the dust of the ground, and it will be no trouble for Him to take the elements of every person's body and reform them into new individual bodies from the same materials.

Concerning the resurrection of our bodies, Paul wrote:

So also is the resurrection of the dead. It is sown a perishable body, it is raised an imperishable body; it is sown in

---

[50] Because John says that this is "the *first* resurrection," it leads us to believe there were no other mass resurrections prior to this. Because it takes place at the end of the world-wide tribulation when Jesus returns, it contradicts the idea of a pre-tribulation rapture, as we know there will be a mass resurrection when Jesus comes from heaven at the rapture of the church according to 1 Thes. 4:13-17. We will study this in more detail in a later chapter titled *The Rapture and End Times.*

dishonor, it is raised in glory; it is sown in weakness, it is raised in power; it is sown a natural body, it is raised a spiritual body....Now I say this, brethren, that flesh and blood cannot inherit the kingdom of God; nor does the perishable inherit the imperishable. Behold, I tell you a mystery; we shall not all sleep [die], but we shall all be changed, in a moment, in the twinkling of an eye, at the last trumpet; for the trumpet will sound, and the dead will be raised imperishable, and we shall be changed. For this perishable must put on the imperishable, and this mortal must put on immortality (1 Cor. 15:42-44a, 50-53).

Notice that the outstanding characteristic of our new bodies is that they will be immortal and imperishable. They will never grow old, get sick, or die! Our new bodies will be just like the new body that Jesus received after He was resurrected:

For our citizenship is in heaven, from which also we eagerly wait for a Savior, the Lord Jesus Christ; *who will transform the body of our humble state into conformity with the body of His glory,* by the exertion of the power that He has even to subject all things to Himself (Phil. 3:20-21, emphasis added).

The apostle John also affirmed this wonderful truth:

Beloved, now we are children of God, and it has not appeared as yet what we shall be. We know that, *when He appears, we shall be like Him,* because we shall see Him just as He is (1 John 3:2, emphasis added).

Although this is impossible for our minds to fully understand, we can believe it and rejoice in what lies ahead![51]

Jesus on the New Birth

Jesus once spoke to a Jewish leader named Nicodemus about the necessity of a rebirth of the human spirit by the action of the Holy Spirit:

Jesus answered and said to him [Nicodemus], "Truly, truly, I say to you, unless one is born again he cannot see the kingdom of God." Nicodemus said to Him, "How can a man be born when he is old? He cannot enter a second time into his mother's womb and be born, can he?" Jesus answered, "Truly, truly, I say to you, unless one is born of water and the Spirit, he cannot enter into the kingdom

[51] For further study on the subject of the resurrection, see Dan. 12:1-2; John 11:23-26; Acts 24:14-15; 1 Cor. 15:1-57.

156

of God. That which is born of the flesh is flesh; and that which is born of the Spirit is spirit. Do not marvel that I said to you, 'You must be born again'" (John 3:3-7).

At first, Nicodemus thought Jesus was talking about a physical rebirth when He said that a person must be born again to enter the kingdom of heaven. Jesus, however, made it clear that He was speaking of a spiritual rebirth. That is, a person's spirit must be reborn.

The reason that we need a spiritual rebirth is because our spirits have been infected with an evil, sinful nature. That sinful nature is often referred to in the Bible as *death*. For the sake of understanding, we will refer to that evil nature as *spiritual death* so we can differentiate between it and physical death (which is when the physical body ceases to function).

Spiritual Death Defined

Paul described what it means to be spiritually dead in Ephesians 2:1-3:

And you were *dead* in your trespasses and sins, in which you formerly walked according to the course of this world, according to the prince of the power of the air, of the spirit that is now working in the sons of disobedience. Among them we too all formerly lived in the lusts of our flesh, indulging the desires of the flesh and of the mind, and were by nature children of wrath, even as the rest (emphasis added).

Paul was obviously not referring to physical death because he was writing to physically alive people. Yet he said they were once "dead in their trespasses and sins." It is sin that opens the door to spiritual death (see Rom. 5:12). Being spiritually dead means having a sinful nature in your spirit. Notice Paul said that they were "*by nature* children of wrath."

In addition, being spiritually dead means possessing, in some sense, Satan's very nature in your spirit. Paul said that those who are spiritually dead have the spirit of the "prince of the power of the air" working *in* them. The "prince of the power of the air" is no doubt the devil (see Eph. 6:12), and his spirit is working in all of those who are unsaved.

Jesus, speaking to unregenerate Jews, said,

You are of your father the devil, and you want to do the desires of your father. He was a murderer from the beginning, and does not stand in the truth because there is no truth in him. Whenever he speaks a lie, he speaks from his own nature; for he is a liar and the father of lies (John 8:44).

From a spiritual standpoint, those who are not born again not only have

Satan's nature residing in their spirits, but Satan is their spiritual father as well. They naturally act like the devil. They are murderers and liars.

Not all unsaved people have committed murder, but they are motivated by the same hatred as murderers, and they would murder if they could get away with it. The legalization of abortion in many countries proves that fact. Unsaved people will murder even their own unborn babies.

This is why a person must experience a spiritual rebirth. When one does, that sinful, satanic nature is removed from his spirit and is replaced with God's holy nature. God's Holy Spirit comes to reside in his spirit. He is no longer "spiritually dead" but is made "spiritually alive." His spirit is no longer dead but alive unto God. Instead of being a spiritual child of Satan, he becomes a spiritual child of God.

Reformation is No Substitute for Regeneration

Because unsaved people are spiritually dead, they can never be saved by self-reformation, regardless of how hard they try. Unsaved people need a new nature, not just new outward actions. You can take a pig, wash it up nice and clean, spray some perfume on it, and tie a pink ribbon around its neck, but all you will have is a cleaned-up pig! His nature will still be the same. And it won't be long before he smells foul and is lying in mud again.

The same is true concerning religious people who have never been born again. They may be cleaned up on the outside a little bit, but inside they are as dirty as ever. Jesus said to some very religious people of His day,

> Woe to you, scribes and Pharisees, hypocrites! For you clean the outside of the cup and of the dish, but inside you are full of robbery and self-indulgence. You blind Pharisee, first clean the inside of the cup and of the dish, so that the outside of it may become clean also. Woe to you, scribes and Pharisees, hypocrites! For you are like whitewashed tombs which on the outside appear beautiful, but inside they are full of dead man's bones and all uncleanness. So you, too, outwardly appear righteous to men, but inwardly you are full of hypocrisy and lawlessness (Matt. 23:25-28).

Jesus' words are an apt description of all those who are religious but who have never experienced the new birth of the Holy Spirit. The new birth cleans up people on the inside and not just on the outside.

What Happens to the Soul When the Spirit is Reborn?

When a person's spirit is reborn, his soul initially remains essentially unaffected (other than the fact that he has made a decision in his mind to follow Jesus). God, however, expects us to do something with our souls once we become one of His children. Our souls (minds) should be renewed with God's Word so that we think as God wants us to think. It is through the renewing of our minds that a continued outward transformation is wrought in our lives, causing us to become progressively more like Jesus:

> And do not be conformed to this world, but *be transformed by the renewing of your mind,* so that you may prove what the will of God is, that which is good and acceptable and perfect (Rom. 12:2, emphasis added).

James also wrote of the same process in the life of the believer:

> In humility receive the word implanted, which is able to save your souls (Jas. 1:21b).

Notice that James was writing to Christians—people who already had their spirits reborn. But they needed to have their souls saved, and it would only happen as they humbly received the "word implanted." This is why new believers must be taught God's Word.

The Residue of the Old Nature

After their new birth, Christians soon discover that they are two-natured people, experiencing what Paul calls the war between "the Spirit and the flesh":

> For the flesh sets its desire against the Spirit and the Spirit against the flesh; for these are in opposition to one another, so that you may not do the things that you please (Gal. 5:17).

The residue of the old sinful nature that remains Paul refers to as "the flesh." These two natures within us produce different desires, which, if yielded to, produce different actions and lifestyles. Notice the contrast Paul makes between the "deeds of the flesh" and "the fruit of the Spirit":

> Now the deeds of the flesh are evident, which are: immorality, impurity, sensuality, idolatry, sorcery, enmities, strife, jealousy, outbursts of anger, disputes, dissensions, factions, envying, drunkenness, carousing, and things like these, of which I forewarn you just as I have forewarned you that those who practice such things shall not inherit the kingdom of God. But the fruit of the Spirit is love, joy, peace, patience, kindness, goodness, faithfulness, gentleness, self-control; against such things there is no law (Gal. 5:19-23).

Obviously it is possible for Christians to yield to the flesh; otherwise Paul would not have warned them that if they make a practice of following the flesh, they will not inherit God's kingdom. In his letter to the Romans, Paul also wrote of the two natures of every Christian and warned of the same consequence of yielding to the flesh:

> And if Christ is in you, though the body is dead because of sin, yet the spirit is alive because of righteousness....So then, brethren, we are under obligation, not to the flesh, to live according to the flesh—*for if you are living according to the flesh, you must die;* but if by the Spirit you are putting to death the deeds of the body, you will live. For all who are being led by the Spirit of God, these are sons of God (Rom. 8:10, 12-14, emphasis added).

This is clearly a warning to Christians. Living (that would indicate a regular practice) according to the flesh results in death. Paul must have been warning about spiritual death, because everyone eventually dies physically, even Christians who are "putting to death the deeds of the body."

A Christian might *temporarily* fall into one of the sins that Paul listed; but, when a believer does sin, he will feel convicted and hopefully repent. Anyone who confesses his sin and asks God's forgiveness will, of course, be cleansed (see 1 John 1:9).

When a Christian sins, it doesn't mean he has broken his *relationship* with God—it means he has broken his *fellowship*. He is still God's child, but he is now God's disobedient child. If the believer doesn't confess his sin, he places himself in a position to be disciplined by the Lord.

The War

If you've found yourself desiring to do things that you know are wrong, then you've experienced the "desire of the flesh." No doubt you've also discovered that when you are tempted by the flesh to do wrong, something on the inside of you resists that temptation. That is "the desire of the Spirit." And if you know the feeling of conviction that comes on the inside of you when you yield to temptation, then you recognize the voice of your spirit, which we call our "conscience."

God knew full well that our fleshly desires would tempt us to do wrong. That is not an excuse, however, for us to justify yielding to the desires of the flesh. God still expects us to act in obedience and holiness and to overcome the nature of the flesh:

> But I say, walk by the Spirit, and you will not carry out the desire of the flesh (Gal. 5:16).

There is no magical formula for overcoming the flesh. Paul simply said that we should "walk by the Spirit," and we "will not carry out the desires of the flesh" (Gal. 5:16). No Christian has any advantage over any other

Christian in this area. To walk after the Spirit is simply a decision we each must make, and our devotion to the Lord can be measured by the degree to which we do not yield to the desires of the flesh.

Paul similarly wrote:

> Now those who belong to Christ Jesus have crucified the
> flesh with its passions and desires (Gal. 5:24).

Notice Paul says that those who belong to Christ *have* (past tense) *crucified the flesh*. That happened when we repented and believed in the Lord Jesus Christ. We crucified the sinful nature, deciding to obey God and resist sin. So now it is not a matter of crucifying the flesh, but of keeping the flesh crucified.

It isn't always easy to keep the flesh crucified, but it is possible. If we will act upon the leadings of the inward person rather than yield to the impulses of the flesh, then we will manifest the life of Christ and walk in holiness before Him.

The Nature of our Recreated Spirits

There is one word that best describes the nature of our recreated spirits, and that word is *Christ*. Through the Holy Spirit, who has the identical nature as Jesus, we actually have the nature of Jesus living inside us. Paul wrote, "It is no longer I who live, but Christ lives in me" (Gal. 2:20).

Because we have His ability and nature in us, we have the wonderful potential to live like Christ. We don't really need *more* love, patience, or self-control—we have the most loving, patient, self-controlled Person living in us! All we need to do is allow Him to live through us.

We all have one major adversary, however, who fights against the nature of Jesus, hindering it from manifesting itself through us; and that is our flesh. No wonder Paul said we must *crucify* our flesh. It is our responsibility to do something with our flesh, and it's a waste of time to ask God to do anything about it. Paul, too, had troubles with his fleshly nature, but he took responsibility and overcame it:

> I buffet my body and make it my slave, lest possibly, after
> I have preached to others, I myself should be disqualified
> (1 Cor. 9:27).

You, too, will have to make your body a slave of your spirit if you want to walk holy before the Lord. You can do it!

ELEVEN

The Baptism in the Holy Spirit

As one reads through the book of Acts, the work of the Holy Spirit in the early church is evident on every page. If you remove the work of the Holy Spirit from the book of Acts you have virtually nothing left. Truly, He empowered the first disciples to "turn the world upside down" (see Acts 17:6; KJV).

The places in the world today where the church is expanding the fastest are those places where Jesus' followers are yielded to and empowered by the Holy Spirit. This should not surprise us. The Holy Spirit can accomplish more in ten seconds than we can accomplish in ten thousand years of our own efforts. Thus it is of vital importance that the disciple-making minister understand what Scripture teaches about the work of the Holy Spirit in the lives and ministries of believers.

In the book of Acts, we frequently find examples of believers being baptized in the Holy Spirit and empowered for ministry. We would be wise to study the subject so that we can, if possible, experience what they experienced and enjoy the miraculous help from the Holy Spirit that they enjoyed. Although some claim that such miraculous works of the Holy Spirit were confined to the age of the original apostles, I find no scriptural, historical or logical support for such an opinion. It is a theory born from unbelief. Those who believe what God's Word promises will experience the promised blessings. Like the unbelieving Israelites who failed to enter the Promised Land, those who don't believe God's promises today will fail to enter into all God has prepared for them. Which category are you in? Personally, I'm among the believers.

Two Works by the Holy Spirit

Every person who has truly believed in the Lord Jesus has experienced a work of the Holy Spirit in his life. His inward person, or spirit, has been regenerated by the Holy Spirit (see Tit. 3:5), and the Holy Spirit now lives within him (see Rom. 8:9; 1 Cor. 6:19). He has been "born of the Spirit" (John 3:5).

Not understanding this, many Charismatic and Pentecostal Christians have made the error of telling certain believers that they did not posses the Holy Spirit unless they had been baptized in the Holy Spirit and spoken in tongues. But this error is obvious from Scripture and from experience. Many non-Charismatic/Pentecostal believers have much more evidence of the indwelling Spirit than some Charismatic/Pentecostal believers! They manifest the fruits of the Spirit listed by Paul in Galatians 5:22-23 to a much greater degree, something that would be impossible apart from the indwelling Holy Spirit.

Just because a person has been *born* of the Spirit, however, does not guarantee that he has also been *baptized* in the Holy Spirit. According to the Bible, being born of the Holy Spirit and being baptized in the Holy Spirit are normally two distinct experiences.

As we begin to explore this subject, let us first consider what Jesus once said about the Holy Spirit to an unsaved woman at a well in Samaria:

> If you knew the gift of God, and who it is who says to you, "Give Me a drink," you would have asked Him, and He would have given you living water....Everyone who drinks of this water [from the well] will thirst again; but whoever drinks of the water that I will give him shall nev-er thirst; but the water that I will give him will become in him a well of water springing up to eternal life (John 4:10, 13-14).

It seems reasonable to conclude that the indwelling living water of which Jesus spoke represents the Holy Spirit who indwells those who believe. Later in John's Gospel, Jesus again used the same phrase, "living water," and there is no doubt that He was speaking about the Holy Spirit:

> Now on the last day, the great day of the feast, Jesus stood and cried out, saying, "If anyone is thirsty, let him come to Me and drink. He who believes in Me, as the Scripture said, 'From his innermost being shall flow rivers of living water.'" But *this He spoke of the Spirit,* whom those who believed in Him were to receive; for the Spirit was not yet given, because Jesus was not yet glorified (John 7:37-39, emphasis added).

In this instance Jesus did not speak of living water becoming "a well of water springing up to eternal life." Rather, this time the living water becomes *rivers* that flow from the recipient's innermost being.

These two similar passages from John's Gospel beautifully illustrate the difference between being born of the Spirit and being baptized in the Holy Spirit. Being born of the Spirit is primarily for the benefit of the one who is born again, that he might enjoy eternal life. When one is born again by the Spirit, he has a reservoir of Spirit within him that gives him eternal life.

Being baptized in the Holy Spirit, however, is primarily for the benefit of others, as it equips believers to minister to other people by the power of the Spirit. "Rivers of living water" will flow from their innermost beings, bringing God's blessings to others by the power of the Spirit.

Why the Baptism in the Holy Spirit is Needed

How desperately we need the help of the Holy Spirit to minister to others! Without His help, we can never hope to make disciples of all nations. That is, in fact, the very reason Jesus promised to baptize believers in the Holy Spirit—so the world would hear the gospel. He said to His disciples:

> Behold, I am sending forth the promise of My Father upon you; but you are to stay in the city until you are *clothed with power* from on high" (Luke 24:49, emphasis added).

Luke also records Jesus as saying:

> It is not for you to know times or epochs which the Father has fixed by His own authority; but *you will receive power when the Holy Spirit has come upon you*; and you shall be My witnesses both in Jerusalem, and in all Judea and Samaria, and even to the remotest part of the earth (Acts 1:7-8, emphasis added).

Jesus told His disciples not to leave Jerusalem until they were "clothed with power from on high." He knew they would be essentially powerless otherwise, sure to fail at the task He had given them. We note that once they were baptized in the Holy Spirit, however, God began to use them supernaturally to spread the gospel.

Many millions of Christians around the world, after being baptized in the Holy Spirit, have experienced a new dimension of power, particularly when witnessing to the unsaved. They found that their words were more convicting, and they sometimes quoted scriptures they didn't realize they knew. Some found themselves called and specifically gifted for a certain ministry, such as evangelism. Others discovered that God used them as He willed in various supernatural gifts of the Spirit. Their experience is thoroughly biblical. Those who oppose their experience have no biblical basis for their opposition. They are, in fact, fighting against God.

It should not surprise us that we who are called to imitate Christ are called to imitate His experience with the Holy Spirit. He was, of course, born of the Spirit when He was conceived in Mary's womb (see Matt. 1:20). He who was born of the Spirit was then baptized in the Spirit prior to the inauguration of His ministry (see Matt. 3:16). If Jesus needed to be baptized in the Holy Spirit to equip Him for ministry, how much more do we?

The Initial Evidence of the Baptism in the Spirit

When a believer is baptized in the Holy Spirit, the initial evidence of his experience will be that he speaks in a new language, what Scripture refers to as "new tongues" or "other tongues." Numerous scriptures support this fact. Let us consider them.

First, during the final moments before His ascension, Jesus said that one of the signs that would follow believers is that they would speak in new tongues:

> Go into all the world and preach the gospel to all cre-
> ation. He who has believed and has been baptized shall
> be saved; but he who has disbelieved shall be condemned.
> *These signs will accompany those who have believed:* in My
> name they will cast out demons, *they will speak with new
> tongues* (Mark 16:15-17, emphasis added).

Some commentators claim these verses should not be in our Bible because certain ancient manuscripts of the New Testament don't include them. Many of the ancient manuscripts, however, do include them, and none of the many English translations I've read omit them. Beyond that, what Jesus said in these verses correlates perfectly with the experience of the early church as recorded in the book of Acts.

There are five examples in the book of Acts of believers being initially baptized in the Holy Spirit. Let's consider all five, and as we do, we will continually ask two questions: (1) Was the baptism in the Holy Spirit an experience subsequent to salvation? and (2) Did the recipients speak in new tongues? This will help us to understand God's will for believers today.

Jerusalem

The first example is found in Acts 2, when the one hundred and twenty disciples were baptized in the Holy Spirit on the day of Pentecost:

> When the day of Pentecost had come, they were all togeth-
> er in one place. And suddenly there came from heaven a
> noise like a violent rushing wind, and it filled the whole
> house where they were sitting. And there appeared to
> them tongues as of fire distributing themselves, and they
> rested on each one of them. *And they were all filled with the*

Holy Spirit and began to speak with other tongues, as the Spirit was giving them utterance (Acts 2:1-4, emphasis added).

There is no doubt that the one hundred and twenty believers were already saved and born again before this time, so they definitely experienced the baptism in the Holy Spirit after salvation. It would have been impossible, however, for them to have received the baptism in the Holy Spirit prior to this time simply because the Holy Spirit was not given to the church until that day.

It is obvious the accompanying sign was that of speaking with other tongues.

Samaria

The second example of believers being baptized in the Holy Spirit is found in Acts 8, when Philip went down to the city of Samaria and preached the gospel there:

> But when they [the Samaritans] believed Philip preaching the good news about the kingdom of God and the name of Jesus Christ, they were being baptized, men and women alike....Now when the apostles in Jerusalem heard that Samaria had received the word of God, they sent them Peter and John, who came down and prayed for them that they might receive the Holy Spirit. For He had not yet fallen upon any of them; they had simply been baptized in the name of the Lord Jesus (Acts 8:12-16).

The Samaritan Christians clearly experienced the baptism in the Holy Spirit as a secondary experience after their salvation. The Bible plainly states that before Peter and John arrived, the Samaritans had already "received the word of God," believed the gospel, and been baptized in water. Yet when Peter and John came down to pray for them, Scripture says it was so "that they might receive the Holy Spirit." How could it be clearer?

Did the Samaritan believers speak with new tongues when they were baptized in the Holy Spirit? The Bible doesn't say, but it does say that something amazing happened to them. When a man named Simon witnessed what occurred as Peter and John laid their hands on the Samaritan Christians, he tried to purchase from them the same ability to impart the Holy Spirit:

> Then they began laying their hands on them, and they were receiving the Holy Spirit. Now when Simon saw that the Spirit was bestowed through the laying on of the apostles' hands, he offered them money, saying, "Give this authority to me as well, so that everyone on whom I lay my hands may receive the Holy Spirit" (Acts 8:17-19).

What did Simon see that impressed him so much? He had already seen a number of other miracles, such as people being delivered from demons and the paralyzed and lame being miraculously healed (see Acts 8:6-7). He himself had been previously involved in occult magic, astonishing all the people of Samaria (see Acts 8:9-10). This being so, what he witnessed when Peter and John prayed must have been quite spectacular. Although we can't say with absolute certainty, it seems quite reasonable to think that he witnessed the same phenomena that occurred every other time Christians received the Holy Spirit in the book of Acts—he saw and heard them speaking in other tongues.

Saul in Damascus

The third mention in the book of Acts of someone receiving the Holy Spirit is the case of Saul of Tarsus, later known as the apostle Paul. He had been saved on the road to Damascus, where he had also been temporarily blinded. Three days after his conversion, a man named Ananias was divinely sent to him:

> So Ananias departed and entered the house, and after laying his hands on him said, "Brother Saul, the Lord Jesus, who appeared to you on the road by which you were coming, has sent me so that you may regain your sight, and be filled with the Holy Spirit." And immediately there fell from his eyes something like scales, and he regained his sight, and he arose and was baptized (Acts 9:17-18).

There is no doubt that Saul was born again before Ananias arrived to pray for him. He believed in the Lord Jesus when he was on the road to Damascus, and he immediately obeyed His new Lord's instructions. Additionally, when Ananias first met Saul, he called him *"brother* Saul." Note that Ananias told Saul that he had come so that he would regain his sight *and* be filled with the Holy Spirit. Thus for Saul, being filled with, or baptized in, the Holy Spirit occurred three days after his salvation.

The Scriptures don't record the actual incident of Saul's being baptized in the Holy Spirit, but it must have happened shortly after Ananias arrived where Saul was staying. There is no doubt that Saul spoke with other tongues at some point, because he later stated in 1 Corinthians 14:18, "I thank God, I speak in tongues more than you all."

Caesarea

The fourth mention of believers being baptized in the Holy Spirit is found in Acts 10. The apostle Peter had been divinely commissioned to preach the gospel in Caesarea to the household of Cornelius. As soon as Peter revealed that salvation is received through faith in Jesus, his entire Gentile audience immediately responded in faith, and the Holy Spirit fell upon them:

While Peter was still speaking these words, the Holy
Spirit fell upon all those who were listening to the message. All the circumcised believers who came with Peter
were amazed, because the gift of the Holy Spirit had been
poured out on the Gentiles also. For they were hearing
them speaking with tongues and exalting God. Then Peter
answered, "Surely no one can refuse the water for these to
be baptized who have received the Holy Spirit just as we
did, can he?" And he ordered them to be baptized in the
name of Jesus Christ (Acts 10:44-48a).

In this case, it seems as if the members of Cornelius' household, who
became the first Gentile believers in Jesus, were born again and baptized
in the Holy Spirit simultaneously.

If we examine the surrounding scriptures and study the historical context, it is apparent why God didn't wait for Peter and his fellow believers to lay hands on the Gentile believers to receive the Holy Spirit. Peter
and the other Jewish believers had great difficulty believing that Gentiles
could even be saved, much less receive the Holy Spirit! They probably
would never have prayed for Cornelius' household to receive the baptism
in the Holy Spirit, so God sovereignly acted. God was teaching Peter and
his companions something about His marvelous grace toward Gentiles.

What convinced Peter and the other Jewish believers that Cornelius'
household had genuinely received the Holy Spirit? Luke wrote, "For they
were hearing them speaking with tongues" (Acts 10:46). Peter declared
that the Gentiles had received the Holy Spirit just as the one hundred and
twenty had on the day of Pentecost (see 10:47).

Ephesus

The fifth mention of believers being baptized in the Holy Spirit is found
in Acts 19. While traveling through Ephesus, the apostle Paul met some
disciples and asked them the following question: "Did you receive the
Holy Spirit when you believed?" (Acts 19:2).

Paul, the man who wrote the majority of the New Testament epistles,
clearly believed that it is possible to believe in Jesus but not have received
the Holy Spirit in some sense. Otherwise he would not have asked such
a question.

The men replied that they had never heard of the Holy Spirit. In fact,
they had only heard of the coming Messiah through John the Baptist, the
one who had baptized them. Paul immediately baptized them again in
water, and this time they experienced true Christian baptism. Finally, Paul
laid his hands on them that they might receive the Holy Spirit:

When they heard this, they were baptized in the name of
the Lord Jesus. And when Paul had laid his hands upon

them, the Holy Spirit came on them, and they began speaking with tongues and prophesying. There were in all about twelve men (Acts 19:5-7).

Again, it is obvious that the baptism in the Holy Spirit was subsequent to salvation, regardless of whether or not these twelve men were born again before they met Paul. Also, once again, the accompanying sign of their Holy Spirit baptism was speaking in tongues (and in this case also prophecy).

The Verdict

Let's review the five examples. In at least four of them, the baptism in the Holy Spirit was an experience that occurred after salvation.

In three of them, Scripture plainly states that the recipients spoke with other tongues. Moreover, in Paul's meeting with Ananias, his experience of being baptized in the Holy Spirit was not actually described, but we know that eventually he did speak in tongues. That represents the fourth case.

In the remaining case, something supernatural occurred when the believers in Samaria received the Holy Spirit because Simon tried to buy the power to impart the Holy Spirit.

Thus the evidence is quite clear. In the early church, born-again believers received a second experience with the Holy Spirit, and when they did, they spoke in other tongues. This should not surprise us, because Jesus said that those who believe in Him would speak in new tongues.

So we have conclusive evidence that every one who is born again should also experience another work of the Holy Spirit—that of being baptized in the Holy Spirit. Moreover, every believer should expect to speak with other tongues when he does receive the Holy Spirit baptism.

How to Receive the Baptism in the Holy Spirit

Like all of God's gifts, the Holy Spirit is received by faith (see Gal. 3:5). In order to have faith to receive, a believer must first be convinced that it is God's will for him to be baptized with the Holy Spirit. If he is wondering or doubting, he will not receive (see James 1:6-7).

No believer has any good reason not to believe that it is God's will for him to receive the Holy Spirit, because Jesus plainly stated God's will in the matter:

> If you then, being evil, know how to give good gifts to
> your children, how much more shall your heavenly Father
> give the Holy Spirit to those who ask Him (Luke 11:13).

That promise from the lips of Jesus should convince every child of God that it is God's will that he or she receive the Holy Spirit.

This same verse also supports the truth that being baptized in the Holy

Spirit occurs after salvation, because here Jesus promised God's children (the only people who have God as their "heavenly Father") that God will give them the Holy Spirit if they ask. Obviously, if the only experience one could have with the Holy Spirit was being born again at the moment of salvation, then Jesus' promise would make no sense. Unlike a certain breed of modern theologians, Jesus believes that it is very appropriate for people who are already born again to ask God for the Holy Spirit.

According to Jesus, there are only two conditions that must be met for one to receive the Holy Spirit. First, God must be one's Father, which He is if you are born again. Second, you must ask Him for the Holy Spirit.

Although receiving the Holy Spirit through the laying on of hands is scriptural (see Acts 8:17; 19:6), it is not an absolute necessity. Any Christian can receive the Holy Spirit by himself in his own place of prayer. He simply needs to ask, receive by faith, and begin to speak in tongues as the Spirit gives him utterance.

Common Fears

Some people worry that if they pray for the Holy Spirit, they might open themselves up to a demon spirit instead. There is, however, no basis for such a concern. Jesus promised,

> Now suppose one of you fathers is asked by his son for a fish; he will not give him a snake instead of a fish, will he? Or if he is asked for an egg, he will not give him a scorpion, will he? If you then, being evil, know how to give good gifts to your children, how much more will your heavenly Father give the Holy Spirit to those who ask Him? (Luke 11:11-13).

If we ask for the Holy Spirit, God will give us the Holy Spirit, and we should have no fear of receiving anything else.

Some are concerned that, when they speak in other tongues, it will just be themselves making up a nonsensical language rather than a supernatural language given by the Holy Spirit. If, however, you attempt to invent a credible language before being baptized in the Holy Spirit, you will see that it is impossible. On the other hand, you must understand that if you are going to speak in other tongues, you will consciously have to use your lips, tongue and vocal cords. The Holy Spirit does not do the speaking for you—He only gives you the utterance. He is our *helper*, not our *doer*. You must do the actual speaking, just as the Bible teaches:

> And *they* were all filled with the Holy Spirit and [they] began to speak with other tongues, *as the Spirit was giving them utterance* (Acts 2:4, emphasis added).

And when Paul had laid his hands upon them, the Holy

Spirit came on them, and *they* began speaking with
tongues (Acts 19:6, emphasis added).

After a believer has asked for the gift of the Holy Spirit, he should believe and expect to speak in other tongues. Because the Holy Spirit is received by faith, the recipient should not expect to experience any particular feelings or physical sensations. He should simply open his mouth and
begin to speak the new sounds and syllables that will make up the language that the Holy Spirit gives him. Unless the believer begins to *speak by
faith*, no utterance will come forth from his mouth. *He* must do the speaking, and the Holy Spirit will provide the utterance.

The Source of the Utterance

According to Paul, when a believer prays in tongues, it is not his mind
praying but rather his spirit:

> For if I pray in a tongue, my spirit prays, but my mind is
> unfruitful. What is the outcome then? I will pray with the
> spirit and I will pray with the mind also; I will sing with the
> spirit and I will sing with the mind also (1 Cor. 14:14-15).

Paul said that when he prayed in a tongue, his mind was unfruitful.
That means his mind had no part in it, and he did not understand what
he was praying in tongues. So, rather than praying all the time in tongues
without understanding what he was saying, Paul also spent time praying with his mind in his own language. He spent time singing in tongues
as well as singing in his own language. There is a place for both kinds of
praying and singing, and we would be wise to follow Paul's balanced
example.

Notice also that for Paul, speaking in tongues was just as much subject to his own will as was speaking in his known language. He said, "*I*
will pray with the spirit and *I* will pray with the mind also." Critics often
claim that if modern tongues speaking was truly a gift from the Spirit, one
would not be able to have control over it, lest he be guilty of controlling
God. But such a idea is unfounded. Modern and ancient tongues speaking
is under the control of the individual as God planned it would be. Critics
might as well say that people who have hands that are *truly* made by God
have no control over their hands, and that people who make conscious
decisions to use their hands are attempting to control God.

Once you have been baptized in the Holy Spirit, you can easily prove to
yourself that your utterance in tongues is coming from your spirit rather
than your mind. First, try to carry on a conversation with someone at the
same time as you read this book. You'll find that you can't do both at the
same time. You will discover, however, that you can continually speak
in tongues as you continually read this book. The reason is because you

aren't using your mind to speak in tongues—that utterance comes from your spirit. So as you use your spirit to pray, you can use your mind to read and understand.

Now That You Are Baptized in the Holy Spirit

Keep in mind the primary reason God gave you the Holy Spirit baptism—to empower you primarily for the purpose of being His witness, by means of the manifestation of fruit and gifts of the Spirit (see 1 Cor. 12:4-11; Gal. 5:22-23). By living a Christ-like life and demonstrating His love, joy, and peace to the world, as well as manifesting supernatural gifts of the Spirit, God will use you to draw others to Himself. The ability to speak in tongues is only one of the "rivers of living water" that should be flowing from your innermost being.

Also remember that God gave us the Holy Spirit to enable us to reach *all* the people of the earth with the gospel (see Acts 1:8). When we speak in other tongues, we should realize that the language we are speaking could well be the native tongue of some remote tribe or foreign nation. Every time we pray in tongues, we should be mindful that God wants people of every language to hear about Jesus. We should ask the Lord how He wants us to be involved in fulfilling Jesus' Great Commission.

Speaking in tongues is something we should do as much as possible. Paul, a spiritual powerhouse, wrote, "I thank God, I speak in tongues more than you all" (1 Cor. 14:18). He wrote those words to a church that did a lot of speaking in tongues (although usually at the wrong times). Therefore, Paul must have done a lot of speaking in tongues to do more than they did. Praying in tongues helps us to stay conscious of the Holy Spirit, who lives within us, and will help us to "pray without ceasing" as Paul taught in 1 Thessalonians 5:17.

Paul also taught that speaking in other tongues edifies the believer (see 1 Cor. 14:4). That means it builds us up spiritually. By praying in tongues, we can, in a way we may not fully understand, strengthen our inner man. Speaking in other tongues should provide daily enrichment in every believer's spiritual life and not be just a one-time experience at the initial filling of the Holy Spirit.

Once you have been baptized in the Holy Spirit, I encourage you to spend time every day praying to God in your new language. It will greatly enhance your spiritual life and growth.

Answers to a Few Common Questions

Can we say with certainty that all those who have never spoken in tongues have never been baptized in the Holy Spirit? Personally, I don't think so.

I've always encouraged people to expect to speak in tongues when I've prayed for them to be baptized in the Holy Spirit, and probably 95% of them have within seconds of my praying for them. It would amount to thousands of people over the years.

I would never say, however, that a Christian who has prayed to be baptized in the Spirit and who hasn't spoken in tongues is not baptized in the Holy Spirit, because the Spirit baptism is received by faith and speaking in tongues is voluntary. If I have an opportunity, however, to share with a believer who has prayed to be baptized in the Spirit but who has never spoken in tongues, I first show that person all the scriptures in the book of Acts on the subject. Then I also show that believer how Paul wrote that he was in control of when he spoke or did not speak in tongues. Like Paul, I can speak in tongues any time I desire, and thus I could decide, if I desired, never to speak in tongues again. That being so, I could conceivably have been baptized in the Holy Spirit and never spoken in tongues in the first place by not cooperating with the Spirit's utterance.

So again, when I have the opportunity to share with a Christian who has prayed in faith for the baptism in the Holy Spirit, but who has never spoken in tongues, I don't tell him (nor do I believe) that he isn't baptized in the Holy Spirit. I simply explain to him how speaking in tongues is not something that the Holy Spirit does apart from us. I explain that the Holy Spirit gives the utterance, but that we must do the speaking, just as when one speaks in his known language. Then I encourage that person to cooperate with the Holy Spirit and begin to speak in tongues. Almost without exception, all of them soon do.

Didn't Paul Write that Not All Speak with Tongues?

Paul's rhetorical question, "All do not speak with tongues, do they?" (1 Cor. 12:30) to which the obvious answer is "No," must be harmonized with the rest of the New Testament. His question is found within the context of his instruction about the spiritual gifts, which are all manifested only as the Spirit wills (see 1 Cor. 12:11). Paul was specifically writing about the spiritual gift of "various kinds of tongues" (1 Cor. 12:10) which, according to Paul, must always be accompanied by the spiritual gift of the interpretation of tongues. This particular gift could not have been what the Corinthians were always manifesting in their church, as they were speaking in tongues publicly without there being any interpretation. We should ask, *Why would the Holy Spirit impart the gift of tongues to someone in a public assembly without giving someone the gift of interpretation?* The answer is that He wouldn't. Otherwise, the Holy Spirit would be promoting something that is not God's will.

The Corinthians must have been *praying* in tongues out loud during their church services, without there being any interpretation. Thus, we learn that speaking in tongues has two different uses. One is praying in tongues, which Paul said should be done privately. That usage of speaking in tongues is not accompanied by interpretation, as Paul wrote, "My spirit prays, but my mind is unfruitful" (1 Cor. 14:14). Obviously, Paul didn't always know what he was saying when he spoke in tongues. There was no understanding on his part; neither was there interpretation.

There is also, however, a use of speaking in tongues that is for the public assembly of the church, which is always accompanied by the gift of the interpretation of tongues. That occurs when the Holy Spirit moves upon someone as He wills, giving him that gift. That person speaks out publicly, and then there is an interpretation given. God, however, doesn't use everyone like that. That is why Paul wrote that not all speak in tongues. Not all are used by God in the sudden, spontaneously-given gift of tongues, just as God doesn't use everyone in the gift of the interpretation of tongues. That is the only way to reconcile Paul's rhetorical question, "All do not speak with tongues, do they?" with the rest of what Scripture teaches.

I can speak in tongues any time I desire, just as Paul could. So obviously neither Paul nor myself would say that whenever we speak in tongues it is "only as the Spirit wills." It is as *we* will. So what we are doing whenever *we* desire *cannot* be the gift of speaking in tongues that only occurs "as the Spirit wills." Furthermore, Paul, like me, spoke in tongues privately without understanding what he was saying, so that *cannot* be the gift of tongues of which he wrote in 1 Corinthians, which he said would always be accompanied by the gift of the interpretation of tongues.

It has been only on rare occasions when I've spoken in tongues in a public assembly. That is only when I've sensed the Holy Spirit move upon me to do so, although I could (just like the Corinthians were doing) pray in tongues out loud anytime I wanted to in church without there being any interpretation. When I've sensed the Holy Spirit move upon me with that gift, there has always been an interpretation that has edified the body.

In conclusion, we must interpret the Bible harmoniously. Those who conclude, because of Paul's rhetorical question found in 1 Corinthians 12:30, that not all believers should speak with other tongues, are ignoring many other scriptures that do not harmonize with their interpretation. Because of their error, they are missing a great blessing from God.

TWELVE

Women in Ministry

Since it is common knowledge that women make up more than one-half of the church of the Lord Jesus Christ, it is important to understand their God-ordained role within the body. In most churches and ministries, women are viewed as valuable workers, as they often do the majority of the overall ministry.

Yet not all agree on women's roles. Women are often restricted from certain areas of ministry within the church that have to do with speaking and leadership. Some churches allow for female pastors; many do not. Some allow women to teach while others do not. Some restrict women from speaking at all during church services.

Most of these disagreements hinge on various interpretations of Paul's words regarding women's roles found in 1 Cor. 14:34-35 and 1 Tim. 2:11-3:7. These scriptures will be the focus of our study, particularly at the end of this chapter.

From the Beginning

As we begin, let us consider what Scripture reveals about women from its very first pages. Women, just like men, are created in God's image:

> And God created man in His own image, in the image of God He created him; male and female He created them (Gen. 1:27).

We know, of course, that God created Adam *before* He created Eve, and this is indeed a spiritually significant fact according to Paul (see 1 Tim. 2:3). We will later consider the significance of this order of creation as it is explained by Paul, but suffice it to say for now that it does not prove men's superiority over women. We know that God created animals before human beings (see Gen. 1:24-28), and no one would argue that animals are superior to people.[52]

The woman was created to be her husband's helper (see Gen. 2:18). This again does not prove her inferiority, but only reveals her role in marriage. The Holy Spirit is given as our helper, but He is certainly not inferior to us. Rather, the Holy Spirit is superior to us! And it could well be said that God's creation of the woman to be her husband's helper proves that men needed help! It was *God* who said that is wasn't good for the man to be alone (see Gen. 2:18). That truth has been proven countless times in history when men have been left without wives to help them.

Finally, we note from the very first pages of Genesis that the first woman was formed from the flesh of the first man. She was taken *from* him, pointing to the fact that he is missing something without her and that the two were originally one. Additionally, what God separated was intended by Him to become one again through sexual union, a means not only of procreation, but of expressing love and enjoying mutual pleasure upon which both are dependent upon the other.

Everything about these lessons from creation stands against the idea of one sex being superior to the other, or one having the right to dominate the other. And just because God has designed different roles for women in marriage or ministry has nothing to do with their equality with men in Christ, in whom "there is neither male nor female" (Gal. 3:28).

Women in Ministry in the Old Testament

With this foundation laid, let us now consider some of the women God used to accomplish His divine purposes in the Old Testament. It is obvious, of course, that God primarily called men into vocational ministry during the time of the Old Testament, just as He did during New Testament times. The stories of men such as Moses, Aaron, Joshua, Joseph, Samuel and David fill the pages of the Old Testament.

Many women, however, stand out as proof that God can call and use anyone He desires, and women equipped by God are sufficient for any task to which He calls them.

Before we consider any of those women specifically, it should be noted that every great man of God in the Old Testament was born and raised by a woman. There would have been no Moses without a woman named Jochebed (see Ex. 6:20). Nor would there have been any other great men of God if it weren't for the mothers of those men. Women have been given by God the weighty responsibility and praiseworthy ministry of raising children in the Lord (see 2 Tim. 1:5)

Jochebed was not only the mother of two God-called men, namely Moses and Aaron, but also of a God-called woman, their sister, a prophetess and worship leader named Miriam (see Exodus 15:20). In Micah 6:4, God

---

[52] It should also be noted that every man since Adam has been created by God *after* God created the women who gave him birth. Every man since Adam has come from a woman, as Paul reminds us in 1 Corinthians 11:11-12. Surely no one would argue that this divine order proves that men are inferior to their mothers.

categorized Miriam right with Moses and Aaron as being one of Israel's leaders:

> Indeed, I brought you up from the land of Egypt and ransomed you from the house of slavery, and *I sent before you Moses, Aaron, and Miriam* (emphasis added).

Of course, Miriam's leadership role in Israel was clearly not as dominant as Moses. Yet as a prophetess, Miriam spoke on God's behalf, and I think it is safe to assume God's messages through her were directed not at just the women, but the men of Israel as well.

A Female Judge Over Israel

Another woman whom God raised up as a leader in Israel was Deborah, who lived during the times of Israel's judges. She, too, was a prophetess, and was just as much a judge over Israel as were Gideon, Jeptha and Samson during their lives. We are informed that "the sons of Israel came up to her for judgment" (Judg. 4:5). So she rendered decisions for men, not just women. There can be no mistaking this: *A woman told men what to do, and God anointed her to do it.*

Like most women whom God calls into leadership, Deborah apparently faced at least one man who had difficulty receiving God's word through a female vessel. His name was Barak, and because he was skeptical about Deborah's prophetic instructions for him to go to war against Canaanite general Sisera, she informed him that the honor of killing Sisera would go to a woman. She was right, and a woman named Jael is remembered in Scripture as the lady who drove a tent peg through sleeping Sisera's head (see Judg. 4). The story ends with Barak singing a duet with Deborah! Some of the lyrics are full of praises for both Deborah and Jael (see Judg. 5), and so perhaps Barak became a believer in "women's ministry" after all.

A Third Prophetess

A third woman who is mentioned in the Old Testament as being a well-respected prophetess is Huldah. God used her to give reliable prophetic insight and instruction to a *man*, the troubled king of Judah, Josiah (see 2 Kin. 22). Again we see an example of God using a woman to instruct a man. Most likely, Huldah was used by God in such a ministry with some degree of regularity, otherwise Josiah would not have had such faith in what she said to him.

But why did God call Miriam, Deborah and Huldah as prophetesses? Couldn't He have called men instead?

Certainly God could have called men to do exactly what those three women did. But He didn't. And no one knows why. What we should learn from this is that we had better be careful about putting God in a box when it comes to whom He calls to ministry. Although God normally chose men for leadership tasks in the Old Testament, sometime He chose women.

Finally, it should be noted that all three preeminent examples of female ministers in the Old Testament were prophetesses. There are some Old Testament ministries to which no women were called. For example, there are no women who were called to be priests. Thus God might reserve some ministry offices exclusively for men.

Women in Ministry in the New Testament

Interestingly, we also find a woman being called of God as prophetesses in the New Testament. When Jesus was just a few days old, Anna recognized Him and began proclaiming His messiahship:

> And there was a *prophetess*, Anna the daughter of Phanuel, of the tribe of Asher. She was advanced in years, having lived with a husband seven years after her marriage, and then as a widow to the age of eighty-four. And she never left the temple, serving night and day with fastings and prayers. And at that very moment she came up and began giving thanks to God, and continued to speak of Him to all those who were looking for the redemption of Jerusalem (Luke 2:36-38, emphasis added).

Note that Anna spoke of Jesus to *all* those "who were looking for the redemption of Jerusalem." That would of course include men. Thus Anna could be said to have been teaching men about Christ.

There are other women in the New Testament whom God used in the gift of prophecy. Jesus' mother Mary is certainly in that group (see Luke 1:46-55). Every time Mary's prophetic words are read in a church service, it could be said that a woman is teaching the church. (And God unquestionably honored womanhood by sending His Son into the world by means of a woman, something He could have done by many other means.)

The list continues. God foretold by the mouth of the prophet Joel that when God poured out His Spirit, both sons and *daughters* in Israel would prophesy (see Joel 2:28). Peter confirmed that Joel's prophecy was certainly applicable to the new covenant dispensation (see Acts 2:17).

We are told in Acts 21:8-9 that Philip the evangelist had four daughters who were prophetesses.

Paul wrote of women prophesying in the church gatherings (see 1 Cor. 11:5). It is clear from the context that men were present.

With all of the scriptural examples of women being used by God as prophetesses and to prophecy, we certainly have no good reason to be closed to the idea that God might use women in such ministries! Moreover, there is nothing that would lead us to think that women can't prophesy to men on God's behalf.

Women as Pastors?

What about women serving as pastors? It seems clear that the office of pastor/elder/overseer is intended by God to be held by men:

> It is a trustworthy statement: if any *man* aspires to the office of overseer, it is a fine work he desires to do. An overseer, then, must be above reproach, the *husband* of one wife (1 Tim. 3:1-2, emphasis added).

> For this reason I left you in Crete, that you might set in order what remains, and appoint elders in every city as I directed you, namely, if any *man* be above reproach, the *husband* of one wife (Tit. 1:5-6, emphasis added).

Paul does not expressly say that women are forbidden from holding the office, and so we might exercise a little caution in making an absolute blanket conclusion. It seems that there are numerous very effective female pastors/elders/overseers around the world today, particularly in developing nations, yet they are still the overwhelming minority. Perhaps God does occasionally call women to this role when it serves His wise kingdom purposes or when there is a shortage of qualified male leadership. It is also possible that many of the female pastors in the body of Christ today are actually called to other ministry offices that are biblically valid for women, such as the office of prophetess, but current church structure only allows them to function in a pastoral role.

Why is the office of pastor/elder/overseer reserved for men? Understanding the function of that office might help us to understand. One of the scriptural requirements for the pastor/elder/overseer is that,

> He must be one who manages his own household well, keeping his children under control with all dignity (but if a man does not know how to manage his own household, how will he take care of the church of God?)" (1 Tim. 3:4-5).

This requirement makes perfect sense when we realize that the New Testament elder oversaw a small house church. His role was similar to that of a father overseeing his household. This helps us to understand why the pastoral office should be held by a man—because it so closely resembles the family structure which, if it is in line with God's design, should be headed by a husband, not a wife. More on this later.

Women as Apostles?

We have conclusively established that women can serve in the office of prophetess (if called by God). What about other types of ministries? It is enlightening to read Paul's salutations in Romans 16 where he praises a number of women who served in ministry for the sake of God's kingdom. One may even have been listed as an apostle. In the three consecutive quotations that follow, I've italicized all the female names:

> I commend to you our sister *Phoebe*, who is a servant of the church which is at Cenchrea; that you receive her in the Lord in a manner worthy of the saints, and that you help her in whatever matter she may have need of you; for she herself has also been a helper of many, and of myself as well (Rom. 16:1-2, emphasis added).

What an endorsement! We don't know exactly what ministry *Phoebe* fulfilled, but Paul called her "a servant of the church which is at Cenchrea" and "a helper of many," including himself. Whatever she was doing for the Lord, it must have been quite significant to warrant Paul's endorsement of her to the entire church in Rome.

Next we will read about *Prisca* (Priscilla), who, along with her husband, Aquila, had such a significant ministry that all the Gentile churches appreciated them:

> Greet *Prisca* and Aquila, my fellow workers in Christ Jesus, who for my life risked their own necks, to whom not only do I give thanks, but also all the churches of the Gentiles; also greet the church that is in their house. Greet Epaenetus, my beloved, who is the first convert to Christ from Asia. Greet *Mary*, who has worked hard for you. Greet Andronicus and Junias [or *Junia*, as the KJV translates it, which is feminine] my kinsmen, and my fellow prisoners, who are outstanding among the apostles, who also were in Christ before me (Rom. 16:3-7, emphasis added).

Regarding Junias, it would seem logical to think that a person who is "outstanding among the apostles" could only be an apostle. If the correct translation is *Junia*, then she was a female apostle. *Prisca* and *Mary* were workers for the Lord.

> Greet Ampliatus, my beloved in the Lord. Greet Urbanus, our fellow worker in Christ, and Stachys my beloved. Greet Apelles, the approved in Christ. Greet those who are of the household of Aristobulus. Greet Herodion, my kinsman. Greet those of the household of Narcissus, who are in the Lord. Greet *Tryphaena* and *Tryphosa*, workers in the Lord. Greet *Persis* the beloved, who has worked hard in the Lord. Greet Rufus, a choice man in the Lord, also *his mother and mine*. Greet Asyncritus, Phlegon, Hermes, Patrobas, Hermas and the brethren with them. Greet Philo-

logus and *Julia*, Nereus and *his sister*, and Olympas, and
all the saints who are with them (Rom. 16:8-15, emphasis
added).

Clearly, women can be "workers" in ministry.

Women as Teachers?

How about female teachers? The New Testament doesn't mention any.
Of course, the Bible doesn't mention any men called to be teachers either.
Priscilla (just mentioned above and also known as Prisca), wife of Aquila,
was involved in teaching at least on a small scale. For example, when she
and Aquila heard Apollos preaching a deficient gospel in Ephesus, "They
took him aside and explained to him the way of God more accurately"
(Acts 18:26). No one can debate that Priscilla helped her husband teach
Apollos, a man. Additionally, twice in Scripture Paul makes mention of
both Priscilla and Aquila when he writes of "the church their house"
(see Rom. 16:3-5; 1 Cor. 16:19), and he calls them *both* "fellow workers in
Christ" in Romans 16:3. There is little doubt that Priscilla had some active
role in ministry along side her husband.

When Jesus *Commanded* Women to Teach Men

Before we address Paul's words about women keeping silent in the
church and his forbidding women to teach men, lets consider one other
scripture that will help us balance those.

When Jesus was resurrected, an angel commissioned at least three
women to teach Jesus' male disciples. Those women were instructed to
tell the disciples that Jesus had risen and that He would appear to them
in Galilee. But that is not all. A short time later, Jesus Himself appeared to
the same women and commanded them to instruct the disciples to go to
Galilee (see Matt. 28:1-10; Mark 16:1-7).

First, I think it is significant that Jesus chose to appear first to women
and then to men. Second, if there was something fundamentally or morally wrong with women teaching men, one would think that Jesus wouldn't
have told women to teach men about His resurrection, hardly a trivial
piece of information, and one that He could have delivered on His own
(and in fact later did). No one can argue with this fact: the Lord Jesus instructed women to teach a vital truth and give some spiritual instructions
to some men.

The Problem Passages

Now that we have some understanding of what much of the Bible tells
us about women's roles in ministry, we are better able to interpret the
"problem passages" in Paul's writings. Let us first consider his words
about women keeping silent in the churches:

> Let the women keep silent in the churches; for they are not
> permitted to speak, but let them subject themselves, just
> as the Law also says. And if they desire to learn anything,
> let them ask their own husbands at home; for it is improp-
> er for a woman to speak in church (1 Cor. 14:34-35).

Some question, for several combined reasons, if these are Paul's actual instructions or simply his quotation of what the Corinthians had written to him. It is clear that in the second half of this letter, Paul was responding to questions the Corinthians had asked him in a letter they had sent (see 1 Cor. 7:1, 25; 8:1; 12:1; 16:1, 12).

Additionally, in the very next verse, Paul writes what could be considered his reaction to the Corinthians' blanket policy of silencing women in the churches:

> Was it from you that the word of God first went forth? Or
> has it come to you only? (1 Cor. 14:36).

The *King James Version* translates this verse in such a way that makes Paul sound even more amazed at the attitude of the Corinthians:

> What? came the word of God out from you? or came it
> unto you only? (1 Cor. 14:36).

In either case, Paul is obviously asking two rhetorical questions. The answer to both is *No*. The Corinthians were not originators of God's word, nor was God's word only given just to them. Paul's questions are obvious rebukes aimed at their pride. If they are his reaction to the two verses that immediately precede them, they seem to say, "Who do you think you are? Since when do you make the decrees regarding who God can use to speak His word? God can use women if He desires, and you are foolish to silence them."

This interpretation seems logical when we take into consideration that Paul had already, in the same letter, written about the proper way for women to prophesy in the churches (see 1 Cor. 11:5), something that re-quires them *not* to be silent. Moreover, just a few verses after those under consideration, Paul exhorts all the Corinthians,[53] women included, to "de-sire earnestly to prophesy" (1 Cor. 14:39). Thus he would seem quite con-tradictory to himself if he was indeed laying down a blanket command for women to keep silent in church gatherings in 14:34-35.

Other Possibilities

But let us assume for a moment that the words in 1 Corinthians 14:34-35 are Paul's original words, and that he *is* instructing women to keep silent.

---

[53] Paul's exhortation is addressed to the "brethren," a term that he uses 27 times in this letter, and which clearly refers to the entire body of Christians in Corinth, not just the men.

How then should we interpret what he says?

Again, we would have to wonder why Paul was making a blanket command for women to keep completely quiet in church gatherings when he said in the same letter that they can publicly pray and prophesy, apparently in church gatherings.

Moreover, surely Paul was aware of the many biblical instances we've already considered of God using women to speak His word publicly, even to men. Why would he completely silence those whom God has often anointed to speak?

Surely common sense dictates that Paul could not have meant for women to be *completely* silent whenever the church gathered. Keep in mind that the early church gathered in homes and shared common meals. Are we to think that the women said absolutely nothing from the time they entered the house until the time they left? That they didn't speak while they prepared or ate the common meal? That they said nothing to their children the entire time? Such a thought seems absurd.

If where "two or three are gathered" in Jesus' name He is among them (see Matt. 18:20), thus certainly constituting a church gathering, when two women come together in Jesus' name, must they not speak to one another?

No, if 1 Corinthians 14:34-35 is indeed Paul's instruction, he was simply addressing a small problem of order in the churches. Some women were out of order in some way in regard to asking questions. Paul did not mean for women to be completely silent for the entire meeting any more than he, when giving similar instructions a few verses earlier to prophets, intended for them to remain silent for the entire meeting:

> But if a revelation is made to another [prophet] who is
> seated, *let the first keep silent* (Cor. 14:30, emphasis added).

In this case, the words "keep silent" mean "temporarily refrain from speaking."

Paul also instructed those who spoke in tongues to remain silent if there was no interpreter in the gathering:

> But if there is no interpreter, *let him keep silent in the church*;
> and let him speak to himself and to God (1 Cor. 14:28, emphasis added).

Was Paul instructing such people to be *completely* silent during the *entire* meeting? No, he was only telling them to be silent in respect to their speaking in tongues when there was no interpreter. Note that Paul told them to "keep silent in the church," the same instruction he gave to women in 1 Cor. 14:34-35. So why should we interpret Paul's words to women to keep silent in the church to mean "keep silent for the entire meeting," and then interpret his words to out-of-order tongue-talkers to mean "refrain from speaking during specific moments in the meeting"?

Finally, note that Paul was not addressing *all* women in the passage under consideration. His words have application only to married women, because they are instructed to "ask their own husbands at home" if they have questions.[54] Perhaps part or all of the problem was that married women were asking questions of other men besides their *own* husbands. Such a scenario could certainly be considered inappropriate, and could reveal some degree of disrespect and lack of submission to their own husbands. If that was the problem Paul was addressing, that could be why he bases his argument on the fact that women should be submissive (obviously to their husbands), as the Law revealed in many ways from the earliest pages of Genesis (see 1 Cor. 14:34).

In summary, if Paul is indeed giving instruction regarding women keeping silent in 1 Corinthians 14:34-35, he is only telling married women to keep quiet in regard to asking questions at inappropriate times or in a way that was disrespectful to their husbands. Otherwise, they may prophesy, pray and speak.

The Other Problem Passage

Lastly, we come to the second "problem passage," found in Paul's first letter to Timothy:

> Let a woman quietly receive instruction with entire submissiveness. But I do not allow a woman to teach or exercise authority over a man, but to remain quiet. For it was Adam who was first created, and then Eve. And it was not Adam who was deceived, but the woman being quite deceived, fell into transgression (1 Tim. 2:11-14).

Surely Paul knew of Miriam, Deborah, Huldah and Anna, four prophetesses who spoke on God's behalf to men and women, effectively teaching them God's will. Surely he knew that Deborah, a judge over Israel, exercised some degree of authority over men and women. Surely he knew that God had poured out His Spirit on the day of Pentecost, partially fulfilling Joel's prophecy of the last days when God would pour out his Spirit on all flesh so that sons *and daughters* would prophesy the word of God. Surely he knew that Jesus commissioned some women to take a message from Him to His male apostles. Surely he knew of his own words of approval, written to the Corinthian church, regarding women praying and prophesying during church gatherings. Surely he remembered that he had told the Corinthians that any one of them might receive a teaching to share with the body from the Holy Spirit (see 1 Cor. 14:26). So what did he

[54] It should be noted that, in the original Greek, there were no different words for *women* and *wife*, or *man* and *husband*. Thus we must determine from context if the writer is speaking of men and women, or husbands and wives. In the passage under consideration, Paul is speaking to wives, as only they could ask their husbands anything at home.

intend to convey when he wrote these words to Timothy?

Notice that Paul appeals to two related facts from Genesis as the basis for his instruction: (1) Adam was created before Eve and (2) Eve and not Adam was deceived, and she fell into transgression. The first fact establishes the proper relationship between the husband and wife. As taught by the order of creation, the husband is to be the head, something that Paul teaches elsewhere (see 1 Cor. 11:3; Eph. 5:23-24).

The second fact Paul mentions is not meant to convey that women are more easily deceived than men, because they aren't. In fact, since there are more women and than men in the body of Christ, it could be argued that men are more likely to be deceived than women. Rather, the second fact shows that when God's intended order in the family is neglected, Satan can gain entrance. Humanity's entire problem began in the garden when the relationship between a man and his wife was out of order—Adam's wife was not submitted to him. Adam must have told his wife God's instruction regarding the forbidden fruit (see Gen. 2:16-17; 3:2-3). She, however, didn't follow his instruction. In a sense she even exercised authority over him when she gave him the forbidden fruit to eat (see Gen. 3:6). It wasn't Adam leading Eve in that case; it was Eve leading Adam. The result was disaster.

The Church—A Model of the Family

God's intended order for the family should certainly be demonstrated by the church. As I stated earlier, it is important to keep in mind that for the first three hundred years of church history, church congregations were small. They met in houses. The pastor/elder/overseers were like fathers of households. This God-ordained church structure so closely resembled the family, and in fact was a spiritual family, that female headship over it would have sent the wrong message to families inside and outside the church. Imagine a female pastor/elder/overseer regularly teaching in a house church, and her husband obediently sitting there, listening to her teaching and submitting to her authority. That would go against God's order in the family, and the wrong example would be set.

This is what Paul's words address. Note that they are found in the very close context of his requirements for elders (see 1 Tim. 3:1-7), one of which is that a person be a male. It should also be noted that elders are supposed to teach regularly in the church (see 1 Tim. 5:17). Paul's words regarding women quietly receiving instruction and not being allowed to teach or exercise authority over men are obviously related to the proper order in the church. What he describes as being improper is a woman, in part or whole, fulfilling the role of an elder/pastor/overseer.

This is not to say that a women/wife could not, under submission to her husband, pray, prophesy, receive a brief teaching to share with the body, or speak in general during a church gathering. All of these she could do in the church without violating God's divine order, just as she could do all those things at home without violating God's order. What she was forbidden to do in church was nothing more or less than what she was forbidden to do at home—exercise authority over her husband.

We also note from later verses that women could serve in the office of deacon just as well as men (see 1 Tim. 3:12). Serving in a church as a deacon, or *servant* as the word actually means, requires no violation of God's divine order between husbands and wives.

This is the only way I can see to harmonize Paul's words in 1 Timothy 2:11-14 with what the rest of Scripture teaches. In every other scriptural instance we've considered of God using women, none serve as models of the family as does the church, and thus none violate the God-ordained order. In none do we find an improper model of wives exercising authority over their husbands in a family setting. Again, picture a small gathering of several families in a house and a wife being in charge, teaching, and overseeing while her husband passively sits and submits to her leadership. This is not what God desires, as it goes against His order for the family.

Yet for Deborah to be a judge in Israel, for Anna to tell men about Christ, for Mary and her friends to tell the apostles about Christ's resurrection, none of these send a wrong message or in any way improperly model God's order in the family unit. The regular church gathering is a unique setting where danger exists for the wrong message to be sent if women/wives exercise authority and regularly teach men/husbands.

In Conclusion

If we just ask our selves, "What could be fundamentally wrong with women functioning in ministry, serving others from a heart of compassion and using their God-given gifts? What moral or ethical principle might that violate?" Then we shortly realize that the only possible violation of principle would be if a woman's ministry somehow violated God's order for the relationships between men and woman, husbands and wives. In both of the "problem passages" under consideration, Paul appeals to the divine order in marriage as the basis of his concern.

Thus we realize that women are restricted in ministry only in a very small sense. In so many other ways, God wants to use women for His glory, and He has been doing that for thousands of years. Scripture speaks of many positive contributions that women have made to God's kingdom, some of which we have already considered. Let us not forget that some of Jesus' closest friends were women (see John 11:5), and that women supported His ministry financially (see Luke 8:1-3), something that is not said of any men. The woman at the well of Samaria shared Christ with the men of her village, and many believed in Him (see John 4:28-30, 39). A female disciple named Tabitha is said to have been "abounding with deeds of kindness and charity which she continually did" (Acts 9:36). It was a woman who anointed Jesus for burial, and He commended her for it when certain men complained (see Mark 14:3-9). Finally, the Bible records that it was women who wept for Jesus as He carried His cross through the streets of Jerusalem, something not said of any men. These examples and many like them should encourage women to rise up and fulfill their God-ordained ministries. We need them all!

THIRTEEN

Divorce and Remarriage

The subject of divorce and remarriage is one that is often debated among sincere Christians. Two fundamental questions are the basis of that debate: (1) When, if ever, is divorce permissible in God's eyes? and (2) When, if ever, is remarriage permissible in God's eyes? Most denominations and independent churches have an official doctrinal stance on what is permissible and what is not, based on their particular interpretation of Scripture. We should respect them all for having convictions and living by them—if their convictions are motivated by their love for God. It would surely be best, however, if all of us held convictions that are 100% scriptural. The disciple-making minister does not want to teach what falls short of what God intends. Neither does he want to place burdens upon people that God never intended for them to carry. With that goal in mind, I'm going to do my best to interpret Scripture on this controversial topic and let you decide if you agree or disagree.

Let me begin by telling you that I am, like you, grieved that divorce is so rampant in the world today. Even more grievous is the fact that so many professing Christians are divorcing, including those in the ministry. This is a great tragedy. We need to do all we can to prevent this from happening more, and the best solution to the divorce problem is to preach the gospel and call people to repentance. When two married people are genuinely born again and both are following Christ, they'll never be divorced. The disciple-making minister will do all he can to make his own marriage strong, knowing that his example is his most influential means of teaching.

May I also add that I've been happily married for over twenty-five years and have never been previously married. I can't imagine ever being divorced. So I have no motive to soften difficult divorce scriptures for my own sake. I do, however, possess a strong sympathy for divorced people,

191

knowing that I could have easily made a bad decision as a young man myself, marrying someone whom I would have later been sorely tempted to divorce, or someone less tolerant of me than the wonderful woman I did marry. In other words, I could have ended up divorced, but I have not because of the grace of God. I think that most married people can relate to what I'm saying, and so we need to restrain ourselves from throwing stones at divorced people. Who are we, who have low-maintenance marriages, to condemn divorced persons, having no idea what they might have endured? God might consider them to be much more righteous than us, as He knows that we, under the same circumstances, might have divorced much sooner.

No one who marries expects to be ultimately divorced, and I don't think anyone hates divorce more than those who have suffered through it. So we should try to help married people stay married, and help divorced people find whatever grace God might be offering. It is in that spirit which I write.

I will do my best to allow scripture to interpret scripture. I've noticed that verses on this subject are often interpreted in such a way that they contradict other scriptures, which is a sure indication that those verses have been misunderstood, at least in part.

A Foundation

Let us begin with a foundational truth with which we can all agree. Most fundamentally, Scripture affirms that God is very much against divorce in general. During a time when some Israelite men were divorcing their wives, He declared through His prophet Malachi:

> I hate divorce...and him who covers his garment with wrong....So take heed to your spirit, that you do not deal treacherously (Mal. 2:16).

This should not surprise anyone who knows something about the loving and just character of God, or anyone who knows something about how divorce damages husbands, wives and children. We would have to question the moral character of anyone who was in favor of divorce in a general way. God is love (see 1 John 4:8), and thus He hates divorce.

Some Pharisees once asked Jesus a question regarding the lawfulness of divorce "for any cause." His response reveals His fundamental disapproval of divorce. In fact, divorce was never His intention for anyone:

> And some Pharisees came to Him, testing Him, and saying, "Is it lawful for a man to divorce his wife for any cause at all?" And He answered and said, "Have you not read, that He who created them from the beginning made them male and female, and said, 'For this cause a man

shall leave his father and mother, and shall cleave to his wife; and the two shall become one flesh'? Consequently they are no longer two, but one flesh. What therefore God has joined together, let no man separate" (Matt. 19:3-6).

Historically, we know that there were two schools of thought among Jewish religious leaders in Jesus' day. We'll explore those two schools of thought in more detail later, but suffice it to say for now that one was conservative and one was liberal. The conservatives believed that a man was permitted to divorce his wife only for very serious moral reasons. The liberals believed that a man could divorce his wife for just about any reason, including even finding a more attractive woman. These contradicting convictions were the very basis of the Pharisees' question to Jesus.

Jesus appealed to verses of Scripture from the earliest pages of Genesis that show how God's original plan was to join men and women together *permanently*, not temporarily. Moses declared that God made the two sexes with marriage in mind, and that marriage is such a significant relationship that it becomes the primary relationship. Once it is established, it ranks higher than one's relationship with his or her parents. Men *leave* their parents to *cleave* to their wives.

Moreover, the sexual union between man and wife points to their God-ordained oneness. Obviously, such a relationship, one that results in offspring, was not meant by God to be temporary, but meant to be permanent. I suspect that the tone of Jesus' response to the Pharisees indicated His grave disappointment that such a question was even being asked. God *certainly* did not intend that men would divorce their wives "for any cause."

Of course, God did not intend that anyone sin in any way, but all of us have. Mercifully, God made provision to rescue us from our slavery to sin. Moreover, He has some things to say to us *after* we have done what He did not want us to do. Likewise, God never intended for anyone to divorce, but divorce was inevitable among humans not submitted to God. God was not surprised at the first divorce or the millions of subsequent divorces. And so He not only declares His hatred of divorce, but He also has some things to say to people after they've been divorced.

In the Beginning

With this foundation laid, we can begin to explore more specifically what God has declared about divorce and remarriage. Since the most controversial statements about divorce and remarriage are those spoken by Jesus to Israelites, it will help us to first study what God said hundreds of years before on the same subject to earlier Israelites. If we find that what God said through Moses and what God said through Jesus are contradictory, we can be sure that either God's law changed or that we've misinterpreted something said by either Moses or Jesus. So let us begin with what God first revealed regarding divorce and remarriage.

I've already made mention of the passage in Genesis 2 that, according to Jesus, has some relevance to the subject of divorce. This time, let's read it straight from the Genesis account:

> And the Lord God fashioned into a woman the rib which He had taken from the man, and brought her to the man. And the man said, "This is now bone of my bones, and flesh of my flesh; she shall be called Woman, because she was taken out of Man." For this cause a man shall leave his father and his mother, and shall cleave to his wife; and they shall become one flesh (Gen. 2:22-24).

Here then is the origin of marriage. God made the first woman *from* the first man and *for* the first man, and *personally* brought her to him. In the words of Jesus, "*God*...joined [them] together" (Matt. 19:6, emphasis added). This first God-ordained marriage set the pattern for all subsequent marriages. God creates about the same number of women as men, and He creates them so that they are attracted to the opposite sex. So it could be said that God is still into arranging marriages on a grand scale (even though there are many more prospective mates for each individual than there were for Adam and Eve). Therefore, as Jesus pointed out, no *human* should separate what *God* joins together. It was not God's intention that the original couple live separate lives, but that they would find blessing in living together in mutual dependence. A violation of God's clearly revealed will would constitute sin. Thus, from the second chapter of the Bible, it is an established fact that divorce was not God's intention for any marriage.

God's Law Written in Hearts

I would also like to suggest that even those who have never read the second chapter of Genesis instinctively know that divorce is wrong, as the covenant of lifetime marriage is practiced in many pagan cultures where the people have no biblical knowledge. As Paul wrote in his letter to the Romans:

> For when Gentiles who do not have the Law do instinctively the things of the Law, these, not having the Law, are a law to themselves, in that they show the work of the Law written in their hearts, their conscience bearing witness, and their thoughts alternately accusing or else defending them (Rom. 2:14-15).

God's code of ethics is written on every human heart. In fact, that code of ethics that speaks through the conscience is all the law that God ever gave *anyone*, except the people of Israel, from Adam until the time of Jesus. *Anyone* even contemplating a divorce will find that he has to deal with his conscience, and the only way that he can overcome his conscience is to find some good justification for divorce. If he proceeds with a divorce without a good justification, his conscience will condemn him, although he may well suppress it.

As far as we know, for twenty-seven generations from Adam until the giving of the Law of Moses to Israel around 1440 BC, the law of the conscience was all the revelation that God gave to anyone, the Israelites included, regarding divorce and remarriage; God considered that to be sufficient. (Remember that Moses didn't pen the Genesis 2 creation account until the time of the Exodus.) It certainly seems reasonable to think that during those twenty-seven generations before the Mosaic Law, which included the time of Noah's flood, some of the millions of marriages during those hundreds of years ended in divorce. It also seems reasonable to conclude that God, who never changes, was willing to forgive those who incurred guilt from divorce if they confessed and repented of their sin. We are certain that people could be saved, or declared righteous by God, before the giving of the Law of Moses, as was Abraham, through his faith (see Rom. 4:1-12). If people could be declared righteous through their faith from Adam until Moses, that means they could be forgiven of anything, including sin incurred in divorce. Thus, as we begin to probe the subject of divorce and remarriage, I wonder: *Would people who incurred sin in divorce before the Mosaic Law and who received forgiveness from God then be convicted by their conscience (since there was no written law) that they would incur guilt if they remarried?* I only pose the question.

What about divorce *victims* who had not incurred sin, those who were divorced through no fault of their own, but only because of selfish spouses? Would their consciences have prohibited them from remarrying? That would seem unlikely to me. If a man abandoned his wife for another woman, what would ever lead her to conclude that she had no right to remarry? She had been divorced through no fault of her own.

The Law of Moses

It is not until we come to the third book of the Bible that we find divorce and remarriage specifically mentioned. Contained within the Law of Moses was a prohibition against priests marrying divorced women:

> They shall not take a woman who is profaned by harlotry,
> nor shall they take a woman divorced from her husband;
> for he is holy to his God (Lev. 21:7).

Nowhere within the Law of Moses is there such a prohibition addressed to the general population of Israelite men. Moreover, the just-quoted verse implies (1) that there were divorced Israelite women and (2) that there would be nothing wrong with non-priestly Israelite men marrying women who had been previously married. The above-quoted law applies only to priests and divorced women who might marry priests. There was nothing wrong, under the Law of Moses, with any divorced woman remarrying, just as long as she didn't marry a priest. There was nothing wrong with any man, other than a priest, marrying a divorced woman.

The high priest (perhaps as a supreme type of Christ) was required to live by even higher standards than regular priests. He was not even permitted to marry a *widow*. We read just a few verses later in Leviticus:

> A widow, or a divorced woman, or one who is profaned by harlotry, these he may not take; but rather he is to marry a virgin of his own people (Lev. 21:14).

Does this verse prove that it was sinful for any and *all* Israelite widows to ever remarry or that it was sinful for any and *all* Israelite men to marry widows? No, certainly not. In fact this verse strongly implies that it would not be sinful for *any* widow to marry *any* man as long as he wasn't the high priest, and it strongly implies that any man besides a high priest was permitted to marry a widow. Other scriptures affirm the complete legitimacy of widows remarrying (see Rom. 7:2-3; 1 Tim.5:14).

This verse also implies, along with the previous verse we considered (Lev. 21:7), that there would be nothing wrong for any Israelite man (other than a priest or high priest) to marry a divorced woman or even a woman who was not a virgin, "profaned by harlotry." It likewise implies that, under the Law of Moses, there was nothing wrong for a divorced woman to remarry or for a woman "profaned by harlotry" to marry, just as long as she didn't marry a priest. God graciously gave both fornicators and divorcees another chance, even though He was very opposed to both fornication and divorce.

A Second Specific Prohibition Against Remarriage

How *many* "second chances" did God give divorced women? Should we conclude that God gave divorced women just *one* more chance under the Law of Moses, permitting just one remarriage? That would be a wrong conclusion. We read later in the Law of Moses,

> When a man takes a wife and marries her, and it happens that she finds no favor in his eyes because he has found some indecency in her, and he writes her a certificate of divorce and puts it in her hand and sends her out from his house, and she leaves his house and goes and becomes another man's wife, and if the latter husband turns against her and writes her a certificate of divorce and puts it in her hand and sends her out of his house, or if the latter

196

husband dies who took her to be his wife, then her former
husband who sent her away is not allowed to take her
again to be his wife, since she has been defiled; for that is
an abomination before the Lord, and you shall not bring
sin on the land which the Lord your God gives you as an
inheritance (Deut. 24:1-4).

Note that in these verses, the sole prohibition was against the twice-
divorced woman (or once-divorced once-widowed woman) remarrying
her first husband. Nothing is said about her incurring guilt for remarrying
the second time, and once she was divorced the second time (or widowed
from her second husband), she was *only* prohibited from going back to her
first husband. The clear implication is that she would be free to remarry
any other man (who is willing to take the chance on her). If it were a sin for
her to remarry anyone else, then there would have been no need for God
to give this kind of specific instructions. All he would have had to say was,
"Divorced people are forbidden to remarry."

Moreover, if God permitted this woman to marry a second time, then
the man who married her after her first divorce could not have been incurring guilt either. And if she was permitted to be married a third time,
then any man who married her after she was twice divorced would not
be sinning (unless he had been her first husband). So the God who hated
divorce loved divorced people, and He mercifully offered them another
chance.

A Summary

Let me summarize what we've discovered so far: *Even though God declared His hatred of divorce, He gave no indication before or during the old covenant that remarriage was a sin, with these two exceptions: (1) the twice-divorced
or once-divorced once-widowed woman remarrying her first husband and (2) the
case of a divorced woman marrying a priest. Furthermore, God gave no indication
that marrying a divorced person was a sin for anyone except priests.*

This stands in apparent contrast to what Jesus stated about divorced
people who remarry and those who marry divorced persons. Jesus said
such people commit adultery (see Matt. 5:32). So we are either misunderstanding Jesus or Moses, or else God changed His law. My suspicion
is that we might be misinterpreting what Jesus taught, because it would
seem strange that God would suddenly declare something to be morally
sinful that was morally acceptable for fifteen hundred years under a Law
that *He* gave to Israel.

Before we tackle this apparent contradiction more fully, may I also point
out that God's permission of remarriage under the old covenant did not
carry any stipulations that were based on the reasons for one's divorce or
the degree of guilt one incurred in the divorce. God never said that certain
divorced people were disqualified from being remarried because their di-

vorce was not for legitimate reasons. He never said that some people were uniquely worthy to remarry because of the legitimacy of their divorce. Yet such judgments are often attempted by modern ministers based on one-sided testimony. For example, a divorced woman tries to convince her pastor that she is worthy to be permitted to be remarried because she was just the victim of her divorce. Her former husband divorced her—she didn't divorce him. But if that pastor was given an opportunity to hear her former husband's side of the story, he might become somewhat sympathetic for him. Perhaps she was a beast and shares some blame.

I've known a husband and wife who both tried to provoke the other to file for divorce so that each could avoid the guilt of being the person who filed for the divorce. They both wanted to be able to say after the divorce that it was their spouse, not they, who filed for divorce, thus making their subsequent second marriages lawful. We may be able to fool people, but we can't fool God. For example, what is His appraisal of the woman who, in disobedience to God's Word, continually withholds sex from her husband and then divorces him because he became unfaithful to her? Is she not at least partly responsible for the divorce?

The case of the twice-divorced woman we just read about from Deuteronomy 24 does not say anything about the legitimacy of her two divorces. Her first husband found some "indecency" in her. If that "indecency" had been adultery, she would have been worthy of death according to the Law of Moses, which prescribed that adulterers be stoned (see Lev. 20:10). So, if adultery is the only legitimate reason for divorce, perhaps her first husband did *not* have good reason to divorce her. On the other hand, perhaps she had committed adultery, and he, being a righteous man like Mary's Joseph, "desired to put her away secretly" (Matt. 1:19). There are many possible scenarios.

Her second husband is said to have simply "turned against her." Once again, we don't know who was to blame or if they shared the blame. But it doesn't make any difference. God's grace was extended to her to remarry anyone who would take the chance on a twice-divorced woman, with the exception of her first husband.

An Objection

"But if people are told that it is lawful for them to remarry after divorcing for any reason, that will encourage them to divorce for illegitimate reasons," it is often claimed. I suppose that *might* be true in some cases of religious people who are not truly attempting to please God, but trying to restrain people who are not submitted to God from sinning is a fairly useless exercise. People who are truly submitted to God in their hearts, however, are not trying to find ways to sin. They are trying to please God, and those kinds of people usually have strong marriages. Moreover, apparently God was not too concerned about people under the old covenant divorcing for illegitimate reasons due to a liberal law of remarriage, because He gave Israel a liberal law of remarriage.

Should we avoid telling people that God is willing to forgive them of any sin, lest they be encouraged to sin because they know that forgiveness is available? If so, we'll have to stop preaching the gospel. Again, it all comes down to the condition of people's hearts. Those who love God want to obey Him. I know very well that God's forgiveness would be available for me if I ask for it, no matter what sin I might commit. But that doesn't motivate me at all to sin, because I love God and have been born again. I've been transformed by God's grace. I want to please Him.

God knows there is no need to add one more negative consequence to the many unavoidable negative consequences of divorce in hopes of motivating people to remain married. Telling people with troubled marriages that they better not divorce because they will not ever be permitted to remarry provides very little motivation for staying married. Even if he believes you, the prospect of a life of singleness compared to a life of continual marital misery sounds like heaven to the miserably-married person.

Paul on Remarriage

Before we tackle the problem of harmonizing Jesus' words on remarriage with Moses', we need to realize there is one more biblical author who harmonizes with Moses, and his name is Paul the apostle. Paul clearly wrote that remarriage for those divorced is not a sin, identical to what the Law of Moses says:

> Now concerning virgins I have no command of the Lord, but I give an opinion as one who by the mercy of the Lord is trustworthy. I think then that this is good in view of the present distress, that it is good for a man to remain as he is. Are you bound to a wife? Do not seek to be released. Are you released from a wife? Do not seek a wife. *But if you should marry, you have not sinned*; and if a virgin should marry, she has not sinned. Yet such will have trouble in this life, and I am trying to spare you (1 Cor. 7:25-28, emphasis added).

There is no doubt that Paul was addressing divorced people in this passage. He advised the married, the never-married, and the divorced to remain in their current state because of the persecution that Christians were suffering at that time. However, Paul clearly stated that divorced people and virgins would not sin if they married.

Note that Paul didn't qualify the lawfulness of remarriage of divorced persons. He didn't say remarriage was only permitted if the divorced person shared no blame in his previous divorce. (And what person is qualified to judge such a thing as that other than God?) He didn't say remarriage was only permitted for those who had been divorced prior to their salvation. No, he simply stated that remarriage is not a sin for divorced persons.

Was Paul Soft on Divorce?

Because Paul endorsed a gracious policy on remarriage, does that mean he was also soft on divorce? No, Paul was clearly opposed to divorce in general. Earlier in the same chapter of his first letter to the Corinthians, he laid down a law on divorce that harmonizes with God's hatred of divorce:

> But to the married I give instructions, not I, but the Lord, that the wife should not leave her husband (but if she does leave, let her remain unmarried, or else be reconciled to her husband), and that the husband should not send his wife away. But to the rest I say, not the Lord, that if any brother has a wife who is an unbeliever, and she consents to live with him, let him not send her away. And a woman who has an unbelieving husband, and he consents to live with her, let her not send her husband away. For the unbelieving husband is sanctified through his wife, and the unbelieving wife is sanctified through her believing husband; for otherwise your children are unclean, but now they are holy. Yet if the unbelieving one leaves, let him leave; the brother or the sister is not under bondage in such cases, but God has called us to peace. For how do you know, O wife, whether you will save your husband? Or how do you know, O husband, whether you will save your wife? Only, as the Lord has assigned to each one, as God has called each, in this manner let him walk. And thus I direct in all the churches (1 Cor. 7:10-17).

Note that Paul first addressed believers who are married to believers. They should not divorce, of course, and Paul states that this is not his instruction, but the Lord's instruction. And that certainly agrees with everything we've considered in the Bible so far.

Here is where it gets interesting. Paul was obviously realistic enough to realize that even believers might divorce in rare cases. If that occurs, Paul stated that the person who divorced his or her spouse should remain unmarried or be reconciled to his or her spouse. (Although Paul gives these specific instructions to wives, I assume the same rules would apply to husbands.)

Again, what Paul writes does not surprise us. He first laid down God's law regarding divorce, but is intelligent enough to know that God's law might not always be obeyed. So when the sin of divorce occurs between two believers, he gives further instructions. The person who divorced his spouse should remain unmarried or be reconciled to his or her spouse. That would certainly be the best thing in the event of divorce between believers. As long as they both remain unmarried, there is hope of their reconciliation, and that would be best. Of course, if one remarries, that ends the hope and possibility of reconciliation. (And obviously, if they had committed an unpardonable sin by divorce, there would be little reason for Paul to tell them to remain unmarried or be reconciled.)

Do you suppose that Paul was intelligent enough to know that his second directive to divorced believers might not always be obeyed? I would think so. Perhaps he gave no further directive to divorced believers because he expected that true believers would follow his first directive not to divorce, and thus only for extremely rare cases was his second directive even needed. Surely true followers of Christ, if they had marital problems, would do all they could to preserve their marriage. And surely a believer who, after every attempt to preserve the marriage, felt he or she had no alternative but to divorce, surely that believer out of personal shame and desire to honor Christ would not consider remarrying anyone else, and would still hope for reconciliation. It seems to me that the real problem in the modern Church regarding divorce is that there is such a high percentage of false believers, people who have never truly believed in and thus submitted to the Lord Jesus.

It is quite clear from what Paul writes in 1 Corinthians 7 that God has higher expectations of believers, people who are indwelled by the Holy Spirit, than He does of unbelievers. Paul wrote, as we read, that believers should not divorce their unbelieving spouses as long as their unbelieving spouses are willing to live with them. Once again, this directive does not surprise us, as it lines up perfectly with everything else we've read in Scripture on the subject. God is against divorce. Paul goes on to say, however, that if the unbelieving one wants to divorce, the believer is to allow it. Paul knows that the unbeliever is not submitted to God, and so he doesn't expect the unbeliever to act like a believer. May I add that when a non-believer consents to live with a believer, it would be a good indication that either the non-believer is potentially open to the gospel, or the believer is backslidden or a phony Christian.

Now who would say that the believer who has been divorced by an unbeliever is not free to remarry? Paul *never* says such a thing, *as he did in the case of two believers who were divorced*. We would have to wonder why God would be opposed to the remarriage of the believer who had been divorced by an unbeliever. What purpose would that serve? Yet such an allowance apparently stands in opposition to what Jesus said about remarriage: "Whoever marries a divorced woman commits adultery" (Matt. 5:32). This, again, makes me suspect that we have misinterpreted what Jesus was trying to communicate.

The Problem

Jesus, Moses and Paul clearly all agree that divorce is an indication of sin on the part of one or both parties of the divorce. All are consistently against divorce in general. But here is our problem: How do we reconcile what Moses and Paul said about remarriage with what Jesus said about remarriage? Certainly we should expect that they should harmonize since all were inspired by God to say what they said.

Let's examine exactly what Jesus did say and consider to whom He was speaking. Twice in Matthew's Gospel we find Jesus addressing the subject of divorce and remarriage, once during the Sermon on the Mount and once when He was questioned by some Pharisees. Let's begin with Jesus' conversation with those Pharisees:

> Some Pharisees came to Jesus, testing Him and asking, "Is it lawful for a man to divorce his wife for any reason at all?" And He answered and said, "Have you not read that He who created them from the beginning made them male and female, and said, 'For this reason a man shall leave his father and mother and be joined to his wife, and the two shall become one flesh'? So they are no longer two, but one flesh. What therefore God has joined together, let no man separate." They said to Him, "Why then did Moses command to give her a certificate of divorce and send her away?" He said to them, "Because of your hardness of heart Moses permitted you to divorce your wives; but from the beginning it has not been this way. And I say to you, whoever divorces his wife, except for immorality, and marries another woman commits adultery" (Matt. 19:3-9).

During this conversation with Jesus, the Pharisees referred to a portion of the Mosaic Law that I mentioned earlier, Deuteronomy 24:1-4. There it was written, "When a man takes a wife and marries her, and it happens that she finds no favor in his eyes because he has found some *indecency* in her, and he writes her a certificate of divorce and puts it in her hand and sends her out from his house..." (Deut. 24:1, emphasis added).

In Jesus' day, there were two schools of thought concerning what constituted an "indecency." About twenty years before, a rabbi named Hillel taught that an indecency was an irreconcilable difference. By the time Jesus had His debate with the Pharisees, the "Hillel" interpretation had become even more liberal, allowing divorce for just about "any cause," as the Pharisees' question to Jesus indicates. One could divorce his wife if she burned his dinner, put too much salt on his food, spun around in public so her knees were exposed, took her hair down, spoke to another man, said something unkind about her mother-in-law, or was infertile. A man could even divorce his wife if he saw someone who was more attractive, thus making his wife "indecent."

Another famous rabbi, Shammai, who lived prior to Hillel, taught that an "indecency" was only something very immoral, such as adultery. As you might suspect, among the Pharisees of Jesus' day, Hillel's liberal interpretation was much more popular than Shammai's. The Pharisees lived and taught that divorce was lawful for any cause, and so divorce was rampant. The Pharisees, in their typical pharisaical way, emphasized the importance of giving your wife a divorce certificate when you divorced her, so as "not to break the Law of Moses."

Don't Forget that Jesus was Speaking to Pharisees

With this background in mind, we can better understand what Jesus was up against. Before Him stood a group of hypocritical religious teachers, many of whom, if not all, had divorced one or more times, and probably because they had found more attractive mates. (I think it is no coincidence that Jesus' words about divorce in the Sermon on the Mount directly follow His warnings regarding lust, also calling it a form of adultery.) Yet they were justifying themselves, claiming to have kept the Law of Moses.

Their question itself reveals their bias. They clearly believed one could divorce his wife for any cause at all. Jesus exposed their very flawed understanding of God's intention in marriage by appealing to Moses' words about marriage in Genesis chapter 2. God never intended that there be *any* divorces, much less divorce "for any cause," yet the leaders of Israel were divorcing their wives just as teenagers break up with their "steadies"!

I suspect that the Pharisees already knew Jesus' stand on divorce, as He had stated it publicly before, and so they were ready with their rebuttal: "Why then did Moses command to give her a certificate of divorce and send her away?" (Matt. 19:7).

This question again reveals their bias. It is phrased in such a way that makes it sound as if Moses was commanding men to divorce their wives when they discovered an "indecency," and requiring a proper divorce certificate, but as we know from reading Deuteronomy 24:1-4, that is not what Moses was saying at all. He was only regulating a woman's third marriage, prohibiting her from remarrying her first husband.

Since Moses mentioned divorce, it must have been permitted for some reason. But notice how the verb Jesus used in His response, *permitted*, contrasts with the Pharisees' choice of verb: *commanded*. Moses *permitted* divorce; he never *commanded* it. The reason Moses permitted divorce was because of the hardness of the hearts of the Israelites. That is, God permitted divorce as a merciful concession to people's sinfulness. He knew that people would be unfaithful to their spouses. He knew there would be immoralities. He knew people's hearts would be broken. So He made allowance for divorce. It wasn't what He had originally intended, but sin made it necessary.

Next, Jesus laid down God's law to the Pharisees, perhaps even defining what Moses' "indecency" was: "Whoever divorces his wife, except for *immorality*, and marries another woman commits adultery" (Matt. 19:9, emphasis added). In God's eyes, *immorality* is the only valid reason for a man to divorce his wife, and I can understand that. What could either a man or woman do that would be more offensive to his or her spouse? When one commits adultery or has an affair, he/she sends a brutal message. Jesus certainly was not just referring to adultery when He used the word "immorality." Surely passionate kissing and fondling someone else's mate would be an offensive immorality, as would the practice of viewing pornography, and other sexual perversions. Remember that Jesus equated lust with adultery during His Sermon on the Mount.

Let us not forget to whom Jesus was speaking—Pharisees who were divorcing their wives for any cause and quickly remarrying, but who would, God forbid, *never* commit adultery lest they break the seventh commandment. Jesus was telling them that they were only fooling themselves. What they were doing was no different than adultery, and that makes perfect sense. Anyone who is honest can see that a man who divorces his wife so that he can marry another woman is doing what an adulterer does, but under a guise of some legality.

The Solution

This is the key to harmonizing Jesus with Moses and Paul. Jesus was simply exposing the hypocrisy of the Pharisees. He was not laying down a law that forbids any remarriage. If He was, He was contradicting Moses and Paul and creating a confusing mess for millions of divorced and millions of remarried people. If Jesus was laying down a law of remarriage, then what should we tell those who have been divorced and remarried before they heard about Jesus' law? Shall we tell them that they are living in adulterous relationships, and knowing that the Bible warns that no adulterers will inherit God's kingdom (see 1 Cor. 6:9-10), instruct them to divorce again? *But doesn't God hate divorce?*

Shall we tell them to cease having sex with their spouses until their former spouses die so to avoid regularly committing adultery? *But does not Paul forbid married couples from withholding sex from each other?* Would not such a recommendation lead to sexual temptations and even foster desires for ex-spouses to die?

Shall we tell such people to divorce their current spouses and remarry their original spouses (as advocated by some), something that was forbidden under Mosaic Law in Deuteronomy 24:1-4?

What about divorced people who have not been remarried? If they are only permitted to remarry if their former spouse committed some immorality, who will take it upon himself to determine if an immorality was actually committed? In order to remarry, will some people be required to prove that their former spouse was only guilty of lust, while others will need to bring forth witnesses to their former spouses' affairs?

As I asked earlier, what about cases where a former spouse committed adultery due in part to being married to a person who withheld sex? Is it is fair that the person who withheld sex be permitted to remarry while the person who committed adultery not be permitted to be remarried?

What about the person who committed fornication prior to marriage? Is not his or her fornication an unfaithful act towards a future spouse? Would not that person's sin be equivalent to adultery had he or his sexual partner been married at the time of their sin? Why then is that person permitted to marry?

What about two people who live together, unmarried, who then "break up." Why are they permitted to marry someone else after their breakup, just because they weren't officially married? How are they any different than those who divorce and remarry?

What about the fact that "old things pass away" and "all things become new" when a person becomes a Christian (see 2 Cor. 5:17)? Does that really mean every sin committed *except* the sin of illegitimate divorce?

All of these and many more questions[55] could be asked that are strong reasons to think that Jesus was not laying down a new law concerning remarriage. Certainly Jesus was intelligent enough to realize the ramifications of His new law of remarriage if that is what it was. That in itself is enough to tell us that He was only exposing the hypocrisy of the Pharisees—lustful, religious, hypocritical men who were divorcing their wives for "any cause" and remarrying.

Surely the reason Jesus said they were "committing adultery" rather than simply saying that what they were doing was wrong is because He wanted them to see that divorce for any cause and subsequent remarriage is really no different than adultery, something they claimed never to do. Are we to conclude that the only thing Jesus was concerned about was the sexual aspect of a remarriage, and that He would approve of remarriage as long as there was abstinence from sex? Obviously not. So let us not make Him say what He never meant.

A Thoughtful Comparison

Let us imagine two people. One is a married man, religious, who claims to love God with all his heart, and who begins to lust for a younger woman next door. Soon he divorces his wife and then quickly marries the girl of his fantasies.

[55] For example, consider the comments of one divorced pastor who found himself cut off from the body of Christ when he remarried. He said, "It would have been better if I had murdered my wife than divorced her. If I had murdered her, I could have repented, received forgiveness, lawfully remarried, and continued in my ministry."

The other man is not religious. He has never heard the gospel and lives a sinful lifestyle, which ultimately costs him his marriage. Some years later, as a single man, he hears the gospel, repents, and begins following Jesus with all his heart. Three years later he falls in love with a very committed Christian woman whom he meets at his church. They both diligently seek the Lord and the counsel of others, and then decide to get married. They do get married, and serve the Lord and each other faithfully until death.

Now, let us *assume* that both men have sinned in getting remarried. Which of the two has the greater sin? Clearly, the first man. He is just like an adulterer.

But what about the second man? Does it really seem that he has sinned? Can it be said that he is *no different* than an adulterer, as can be said to the first man? I don't think so. Shall we tell him what Jesus said about those who divorce and remarry, informing him that he is now living with a woman whom God did not join him to, because God considers him still married to his first wife? Shall we tell him that he is living in adultery?

The answers are obvious. Adultery is committed by married people who get their eyes on someone other than their spouse. So divorcing one's spouse because one has found a more attractive mate is the same as adultery. But an unmarried person *cannot* commit adultery since he has no spouse to be unfaithful to, and neither can a divorced person commit adultery since he has no spouse to which he can be unfaithful. Once we understand the biblical and historical context of what Jesus said, we don't come up with conclusions that make no sense and that contradict the rest of the Bible.

Incidentally, when the disciples heard Jesus' response to the Pharisees' question, they responded by saying, "If the relationship of the man with his wife is like this, it is better not to marry" (Matt. 19:10). Realize that they had grown up under the teaching and influence of the Pharisees, and within a culture that was greatly influenced by the Pharisees. They had never considered that marriage was to be so permanent. In fact, up until a few minutes before, they too probably believed it was lawful for a man to divorce his wife for any cause. So they quickly concluded it might be best just to avoid marriage all together, and not risk committing divorce and adultery.

Jesus responded,

> Not all men can accept this statement, but only those to whom it has given. For there are eunuchs who were born that way from their mother's womb; and there are eunuchs who were made eunuchs by men; and there are also eunuchs who made themselves eunuchs for the sake of the kingdom of heaven. He who is able to accept this, let him accept it (Matt. 19:11-12).

That is, one's sexual drive and/or one's ability to control it is more of the determining factor. Even Paul said, "It is better to marry than to burn" (1 Cor. 7:9). Those who are born eunuchs or who are made eunuchs by men (as was done by men who needed other men whom they could trust to guard their harems) have no sexual desire. Those who make "themselves eunuchs for the sake of the kingdom of heaven" would seem to be those who are specially gifted by God with extra self-control, which is why "not all men can accept this statement, but only those to whom it has been given" (Matt. 19:11).

The Sermon on the Mount

We should keep in mind that the crowd to whom Jesus spoke during His Sermon on the Mount were also people who had spent their lives under the hypocritical influence of the Pharisees, the rulers and teachers in Israel. As we learned in our earlier study of the Sermon on the Mount, it is obvious that much of what Jesus said was nothing less than a correction of the false teaching of the Pharisees. Jesus even told the crowd that they would not get into heaven unless their righteousness exceeded that of the scribes and Pharisees (see Matt. 5:20), which was another way of saying that the scribes and Pharisees were going to hell. At the end of His sermon, the crowds were amazed, in part, because Jesus was teaching "not as their scribes" (Matt. 7:29).

Early in His sermon, Jesus exposed the hypocrisy of those who claim to have never committed adultery, but who lust or who divorce and remarry. He expanded the meaning of adultery beyond the physical sinful act between two people who are married to others. What He said would have been obvious to any honest person who would have just given it a little thought. Keep in mind that until Jesus' sermon, most of the people in the crowd would have thought that it was lawful to divorce for "any cause." Jesus wanted His followers and everyone else to know that God's intention from the beginning was a much higher standard.

> You have heard that it was said, "You shall not commit adultery"; but I say to you, that everyone who looks on a woman to lust for her has committed adultery with her already in his heart. And if your right eye makes you stumble, tear it out, and throw it from you; for it is better for you that one of the parts of your body perish, than for your whole body to be thrown into hell. And if your right hand makes you stumble, cut it off, and throw it from you; for it is better for you that one of the parts of your body perish, than for your whole body to go into hell. And it was said, 'Whoever sends his wife away, let him give her a certificate of divorce'; but I say to you that everyone

who divorces his wife, except for the cause of unchastity, makes her commit adultery; and whoever marries a divorced woman commits adultery (Matt. 5:27-32).

First, as I pointed out earlier, notice that Jesus' words about divorce and remarriage not only directly follow His words about lust, linking them to that degree, but that Jesus equates *both* as being adultery, linking them even more so. So we see the common thread that runs through this entire portion of Scripture. Jesus was helping His followers understand what obeying the seventh commandment actual entails. It means not committing lust and not divorcing and remarrying.

Everyone in His Jewish audience had heard the seventh commandment read in the synagogue (no one owned personal Bibles), and they had heard the exposition as well as observed its application in the lives of their teachers, the scribes and Pharisees. Jesus next said, "but I say to you," but He wasn't about to add new laws. He was only going to reveal God's original intent.

First, lust was clearly forbidden by the tenth commandment, and even without the tenth commandment, anyone who thought about it would have realized that it is wrong to long with desire to do what God condemns.

Second, from the earliest chapters of Genesis, God made it clear that marriage was to be a lifelong commitment. Moreover, anyone who thought about it would have concluded that divorce and remarriage is much like adultery, *especially* when one divorces with the intent to remarry.

But again in this sermon, it is clear that Jesus was only helping people to see the truth about lust and the truth about divorce for any cause and remarriage. He was not laying down a new law of remarriage that had heretofore not been "on the books."

It is interesting that very few in the church have ever taken Jesus' words about plucking out their eyes or cutting off their hands literally, as such ideas run so counter to the rest of Scripture, and they clearly serve only to make a strong point about avoiding sexual temptation. Yet so many in the church attempt to interpret quite literally Jesus' words about the remarried person committing adultery, even when such a literal interpretation contradicts so much of the rest of Scripture. Jesus' goal was to get His listeners to face up to the truth, with the hope that there would be fewer divorces. If His followers would take to heart what He said about lust, there would be no immorality among them. If there were no immorality, there would be no legitimate grounds for divorce, and there would be no divorce, just as God had intended from the beginning.

How Does a Man Make His Wife Commit Adultery?

Note that Jesus said, "Everyone who divorces his wife, except for the cause of unchastity, *makes her commit adultery*." This again leads us to believe that He was not laying down a new law of remarriage, but only revealing the truth about the sin of a man who divorces his wife without a good cause. He "makes her commit adultery." Some say that Jesus was thus prohibiting her remarriage, because He makes it to be adultery. But that is absurd. The emphasis is on the sin of the man doing the divorcing. Because of what *he* does, his wife will have no other choice but to remarry, which is no sin on her part as she was just the victim of her husband's selfishness. In God's eyes, however, because the man left his wife destitute with no other choice but to remarry, it was just as if he forced his wife into bed with another man. So the one who thinks he has *not* committed adultery is held guilty for a *double* adultery, his and his wife's.

Jesus could not have been saying that God held the victimized wife to be guilty of adultery, as that would be completely unfair, and in fact would be utterly meaningless if the victimized wife never remarried. How could God say she was an adulteress unless she remarried? It would make no sense whatsoever. Thus it is plain to see that God is holding the man guilty for his own adultery, and the "adultery" of his wife, which is really not adultery at all for her. It is lawful remarriage.

And what about Jesus' next statement that "whoever marries a divorced woman commits adultery"? There are only two possibilities that make any sense. Either Jesus was now adding a third count of adultery against the man who thinks he has never committed adultery (for a similar reason as He added the second count), or Jesus was speaking of the man who encourages a woman to divorce her husband in order to marry her so as "not to commit adultery." If Jesus was saying that any man on earth who marries a divorced woman is committing adultery, then every Israelite man during the previous hundreds of years committed adultery who, in complete compliance with the Law of Moses, married a divorced woman. In fact, every man in Jesus' audience that day who was presently married to a divorced woman in full compliance with the Mosaic Law suddenly became guilty of what he was not guilty just one minute before, and Jesus must have changed God's law at that moment. Moreover, every person in the future who married a divorced person, trusting Paul's words in his letter to the Corinthians that such was not a sin, was actually sinning, committing adultery.

The entire spirit of the Bible would lead me to admire a man who married a divorced woman. If she had been a blameless victim of her former husband's selfishness, I would admire him as much as I admire a man who marries a widow, taking her under his care. If she bore some blame for her previous divorce, I would admire him for his Christ-likeness in believing the best of her, and for his grace in offering to forget the past and take a risk. Why would anyone who has read the Bible and who has the Holy Spirit living in him conclude that Jesus was forbidding everyone from marrying any divorced person? How does such a view fit with God's justice, a justice that would never punish someone for being a victim, as is the case of the woman who is divorced through no fault of her own? How does such a view fit with the message of the gospel, which offers forgiveness and another chance to repentant sinners?

In Summary

The Bible consistently says that divorce always involves sin on the part of one or both parties. God never intended for anyone to divorce, but mercifully made provision for divorce when immorality occurs. He also mercifully made provision for divorced people to remarry.

If it wasn't for Jesus' words about remarriage, no one reading the Bible would have ever thought that remarriage was a sin (except for two very rare cases under the old covenant and for one rare case under the new, namely, remarriage after one was divorced from a Christian as a Christian). We have, however, found a logical way to harmonize what Jesus said about remarriage with what the rest of the Bible teaches. Jesus was not replacing God's law of remarriage with a stricter law that forbids all remarriage in every case, an impossible law for people who are already divorced and remarried to obey (like trying to unscramble eggs), and one that would create unlimited confusion and lead people to break other laws of God. Rather, He was helping people to see their hypocrisy. He was helping those who believed they would never commit adultery to see that they were committing adultery in other ways, by their lust and by their liberal attitude toward divorce.

As the entire Bible teaches, forgiveness is offered to repentant sinners regardless of their sin, and second and third chances are given to sinners, including divorced people. There is no sin in any remarriage under the new covenant, with the exception of the believer who has been divorced from another believer, which should never occur since true believers are not committing immoralities and there is thus no valid reason to divorce. In such a rare event that they do, both should remain single or be reconciled to each other.

FOURTEEN

Fundamentals of Faith

> And without faith it is impossible to please Him, for he
> who comes to God must believe that He is, and that He is
> a rewarder of those who seek Him (Heb. 11:6).

A s believers, our faith is built on the foundation that God exists, and
that He treats people who seek Him differently than He does people
who do not seek Him. As soon as we *truly* believe those two things, we
begin to please God, because we immediately begin to seek Him. Seeking
God implies (1) learning His will, (2) obeying Him, and (3) trusting His
promises. All three should be components of our daily walk.

This chapter focuses on our walk of faith. It is unfortunate that many
have emphasized faith to the point of unbiblical extremes, particularly
stressing the area of material prosperity. For that reason, some are appre-
hensive to approach the subject at all. But just because some people drown
in rivers is no reason for us to stop drinking water. We can remain balanced and scriptural. The Bible has plenty to teach on the subject, and God
wants us to exercise our faith in His many promises.

Jesus set an example of one who had faith in God, and He expected His
disciples to follow His example. Likewise, the disciple-making minister
strives to set an example of trust in God, and he teaches his disciples to
believe God's promises. This is vitally important. Not only is it impossible to please God without faith, it is impossible to receive answers to our
prayers without faith (see Matt. 21:22; Jas. 1:5-8). Scripture clearly teaches
that doubters are deprived of blessings that believers receive. Jesus said,
"All things are possible to him who believes" (Mark 9:23).

Faith Defined

The biblical definition of faith is found in Hebrews 11:1:

Now faith is the assurance of things hoped for, the conviction of things not seen.

From this definition, we learn several characteristics of faith. First, one who has faith possesses *assurance*, or confidence. This is different than hope, because faith is the "assurance of things *hoped for.*" Hope always leaves room for doubt. Hope always says "maybe." For example, I might say, "I sure *hope* it rains today so that my garden will be watered." I desire rain, but I'm not sure if it will rain. Faith, on the other hand, is always certain, the "assurance of things hoped for."

What people call *faith,* or *belief,* is often not faith by biblical definition. They might look at dark clouds in the sky, for example, and say, "I *believe* it's going to rain." They aren't, however, certain that it's going to rain—they just think that there is a good possibility that it *might* rain. That is not biblical faith. Biblical faith has no element of doubt. It leaves no room for any outcome other than what God has promised.

Faith is the Conviction of Things Not Seen

The definition found in Hebrews 11:1 also states that faith is the "conviction of things not seen." Thus, if we can see something or perceive it with our five physical senses, faith is not required.

Suppose someone said to you right now, "For some reason that I can't explain, I have faith that there is a book in your hands." You would, of course, think that something was wrong with that person. You would say, "Why, you don't need to *believe* I have a book in my hands, because you can plainly *see* that I'm holding a book."

Faith is of the unseen realm. For example, as I'm writing these words, I believe that there is an angel near me. I'm certain of it. How can I be so sure? Have I seen an angel? No. Have I felt or heard an angel fly by? No. If I had seen an angel or heard or felt one, then I wouldn't have to believe there was an angel near me—I'd *know* it.

So what makes me so certain of the angel's presence? My certainty stems from one of God's promises. In Psalm 34:7, He promised, "The angel of the Lord encamps around those who fear Him, and rescues them." I have no evidence for what I believe other than God's Word. That is true biblical faith—the "conviction of things not seen." The people of the world often use the expression, "Seeing is believing." But in the kingdom of God the opposite is true: "Believing is seeing."

When we exercise faith in one of God's promises, we often face circumstances that tempt us to doubt, or we go through a period of time when it looks as if God is not keeping his promise because our circumstances are not changing. In those cases, we simply need to resist doubts, persevere in faith, and remain convinced in our hearts that God always keeps His word. It is impossible for Him to lie (see Tit. 1:2).

How Do We Acquire Faith?

Because faith is based solely on God's promises, only one source exists for biblical faith—God's Word. Romans 10:17 says, "So *faith comes from hearing*, and hearing by the word of Christ" (Rom. 10:17, emphasis added). God's Word reveals His will. It is only when we know God's will that we can believe it.

So if you want to have faith, you must hear (or read) God's promises. Faith does not come by praying for it, fasting for it, or having someone lay hands on you to bestow it. It only comes from hearing God's Word, and once you hear it, you still must make a decision to believe it.

Beyond the acquiring of faith, our faith can also grow stronger. The Bible mentions various levels of faith—from little faith to mountain-moving faith. Faith grows stronger as it is fed and exercised, just like a human muscle. We should continue to feed our faith by meditating on God's Word. We should exercise it by acting and reacting to everything based on God's Word. This includes those times when we face problems, worries and concerns. God doesn't want His children to worry about anything, but rather to trust Him in every situation (see Matt. 6:25-34; Phil. 4:6-8; 1 Pet. 5:7). Refusing to worry is just one way we can exercise our faith.

If we truly believe what God has said, we will act and talk as if it's true. If you believe that Jesus is the Son of God, you will talk and act like a person who believes it. If you believe that God will supply all your needs, you will talk and act like it. If you believe that God wants you to be healthy, you will act and talk like it. The Bible is full of examples of people who, in the midst of adverse circumstances, acted on their faith in God and received miracles as a result. We'll consider a few later on in this chapter and in a later chapter about divine healing. (For some other good examples, see 2 Kings 4:1-7; Mark 5:25-34; Luke 19:1-10; and Acts 14:7-10.)

Faith is of the Heart

Biblical faith does not operate in our minds, but rather in our hearts. Paul wrote, "For with the heart a person believes" (Rom. 10:10a). Jesus said,

> Whoever says to this mountain, "Be taken up and cast into the sea," and *does not doubt in his heart*, but believes that what he says is going to happen, it shall be granted him (Mark 11:23, emphasis added).

It is quite possible to have doubts in your head but still have faith in your heart and receive what God has promised. In fact, most times when we endeavor to believe God's promises, our minds, influenced by our physical senses and Satan's lies, will be attacked with doubts. During those times we need to replace doubting thoughts with God's promises and hold fast in faith without wavering.

Common Faith Mistakes

Sometimes when we attempt to exercise faith in God, we fail to receive what we desire because we are not operating according to God's Word. One of the most common mistakes occurs when we try to believe for something that God has not promised us.

For example, it is scriptural for married couples to trust God for children because God's Word contains a promise upon which they can stand. I know of married couples who have been told by doctors that they could never bear children. They chose, however, to believe God instead, standing on the two promises listed below, and today they are parents of healthy children.

> But you shall serve the Lord your God, and He will bless your bread and your water; and I will remove sickness from your midst. There shall be no one miscarrying or barren in your land; I will fulfill the number of your days (Ex. 23:25-26).

> You shall be blessed above all peoples; there shall be no male or female barren among you or among your cattle (Deut. 7:14).

These promises should encourage childless couples! To attempt to believe specifically for a boy or a girl, however, is another story. In the Bible there are no specific promises that tell us we can pick the sex of our future children. We must stay within the boundaries of Scripture if our faith is to be effectual. We can only trust God for what He has promised us.

Let's consider a promise from God's Word and then determine what we can believe based on that promise:

> For the Lord Himself will descend from heaven with a shout, with the voice of the archangel and with the trumpet of God; and the dead in Christ will rise first (1 Thes. 4:16).

Based on this scripture, we can certainly trust that Jesus is going to return.

Could we pray, however, believing that Jesus will return tomorrow? No, because this scripture and no other scripture promises us that. In fact, Jesus said that no one knows the day or the hour of His return.

We could pray, of course, *hoping* that Jesus would return tomorrow, but we would not be guaranteed it would happen. When we pray in faith, we are certain that what we are praying for will happen because we have God's promise on it.

Based on this same scripture, we can trust that the bodies of those believers who have died will be resurrected at the return of Jesus. But can we have faith that those of us who are alive at Christ's return will receive resurrection bodies at the same moment as the "dead in Christ" do, or possibly even before they do? No, because this scripture promises us just the opposite: The "dead in Christ will rise first." In fact, the very next verse goes on to say, "Then we who are alive shall be caught up together in the air" (1 Thes. 4:17). Thus, there is no possibility that the "dead in Christ" won't be first to receive their resurrection bodies when Jesus returns. God's Word promises just that.

If we are going to trust God for something, we must be certain that it is God's will for us to receive what we desire. God's will can only be safely determined by examining His promises recorded in the Bible.

Faith works the same way in the natural realm. It would be foolish for you to believe that I was going to visit your home tomorrow at noon unless I had first promised you I would be there then.

Faith, without a promise on which to stand, is not really faith at all—it is foolishness. So before you ask God for anything, first ask yourself the question—which scripture in the Bible promises me what I desire? Unless you have a promise, you have no foundation for your faith.

A Second Common Mistake

Many times Christians attempt to trust for one of God's promises to come to pass in their lives without meeting all the conditions that accompany the promise. For example, I've heard Christians quote from Psalm 37 and say: "The Bible says that God will give me the desires of my heart. That's what I'm believing for."

However, the Bible doesn't only say that God will give us the desires of our hearts. Here's what it actually says:

> Do not fret because of evildoers, be not envious toward wrong doers. For they will wither quickly like the grass, and fade like the green herb. Trust in the Lord, and do good; dwell in the land and cultivate faithfulness. Delight yourself in the Lord; and He will give you the desires of your heart. Commit your way to the Lord, trust also in Him, and He will do it (Ps. 37:1-5).

Several conditions must be met if we are to believe that God will give us the desires of our heart. In fact, I counted at least eight conditions in the above promise. Unless we are meeting the conditions, we have no right to receive the blessing promised. Our faith has no foundation.

Christians also like to quote the promise found in Philippians 4:19: "My God shall supply all my needs according to His riches in glory." However, are there conditions to that promise? Decidedly, yes.

If you examine the context of the promise found in Philippians 4:19, you'll discover that it is not a promise given to all Christians. Rather, it is a promise given to those Christians who are givers themselves. Paul knew God would supply all the Philippians' needs because they had just sent him an offering. Because they were seeking first God's kingdom as Jesus commanded, God would supply all their needs, as Jesus promised (see Matt 6:33). Many of the promises in the Bible that relate to God's supplying our material needs carry the condition that we first be givers ourselves.

We really have no right to think we can trust God for our needs to be met if we're not obeying His commands concerning our money. Under the old covenant, God told His people that they were cursed because they were withholding their tithes, but He promised to bless them if they would obediently give their tithes and offerings (see Mal. 3:8-12).

Many of the blessings promised us in the Bible are contingent upon our obedience to God. Therefore, before we endeavor to believe God for something, we should first ask ourselves: "Am I meeting all the conditions accompanying that promise?"

A Third Common Mistake

In the New Testament, Jesus stated a condition that applies to every time we pray and ask for something:

> Have faith in God. Truly I say to you, whoever says to this mountain, "Be taken up and cast into the sea," and does not doubt in his heart, but believes that what he says is going to happen, it shall be granted him. Therefore I say to you, *all things for which you pray and ask, believe that you have received them, and they shall be granted you* (Mark 11:22-24, emphasis added).

The condition Jesus stated is to believe that we have received when we pray. Many Christians mistakenly try to exercise their faith by believing that they have received when they *see* the answer to their prayer. They believe that they are *going* to receive and not that they *have received*.

When we ask God for something that He has promised us, we should believe we receive the answer *when we pray* and begin thanking God for the answer right then. We must believe we have the answer *before* we see it and not *after* we see it. We should make our requests to God with thanksgiving, as Paul wrote:

> Be anxious for nothing, but in everything by prayer and supplication with thanksgiving let your requests be made known to God (Phil. 4:6).

As I previously stated, if we have faith in our hearts, naturally our words and our actions will correspond with what we believe. Jesus said, "The mouth speaks out of that which fills the heart" (Matt. 12:34).

Some Christians make the mistake of asking repeatedly for the same thing, which reveals they haven't yet believed they have received. If we have believed that we have received when we pray, then there is no need to repeat the same request. To ask repeatedly for the same thing is to doubt that God heard us the first time we asked.

Didn't Jesus Make the Same Request More Than Once?

Jesus, of course, made the same request three times in a row when He was praying in the Garden of Gethsemane (see Matt. 26:39-44). But keep in mind that He was not praying in faith according to God's revealed will. In fact, as He prayed three times for any possible escape from the cross, He knew that His request was contrary to God's will. That is why He submitted Himself to His Father's will three times in the same prayer.

That same prayer of Jesus is often wrongly used as a model for *all* prayer, as some teach that we should always end every prayer with the words, "If it be Thy will," or "Nevertheless not My will but Thy will be done," following Jesus' example.

Again, we must remember that Jesus was making a request that He knew was not God's will. To follow His example when we are praying according to God's will would be a mistake and display a lack of faith. To pray, for example, "Lord, I confess my sin to you and ask you to forgive me if it be Thy will," would imply that it may not be God's will to forgive my sin. We know, of course, that the Bible promises that God will forgive us when we confess our sins (see 1 John 1:9). Thus such a prayer would reveal one's lack of faith in God's revealed will.

Jesus didn't end every prayer with the words, "Nevertheless not My will, but Thy will done." There is only one example of His praying in that manner, and it was when He was committing Himself to do His Father's will, knowing the suffering He would endure because of it.

On the other hand, if we don't know God's will in a certain situation because He has not revealed it, then it is appropriate to end our prayer with the words, "If it be Thy will." James wrote,

> Come now, you who say, "Today or tomorrow, we shall go to such and such a city, and spend a year there and engage in business and make a profit." Yet you do not know what your life will be like tomorrow. You are just a vapor that appears for a little while and then vanishes away. Instead, you ought to say, "If the Lord wills, we shall live and also do this or that." But as it is, you boast in your arrogance; all such boasting is evil (Jas. 4:13-16).

What should we do once we've made our requests based on a promise from God and are meeting all the conditions? We should continually thank God for the answer that we have believed we have received until it actually comes to pass. It is through faith and patience that we inherit the promises of God (Heb. 6:12). Satan will surely try to defeat us by sending doubts, and we must realize that our mind is the battleground. When thoughts of doubt attack our minds, we simply need to replace those thoughts with thoughts based on God's promises and speak the Word of God in faith. As we do, Satan must flee (see Jas. 4:7; 1 Pet. 5:8-9).

An Example of Faith in Action

One of the classic biblical examples of faith in action is the story of Peter's walking on the water. Let's read his story and see what we can learn from it.

> And immediately [Jesus] made the disciples get into the boat, and go ahead of Him to the other side, while He sent the multitudes away. And after He had sent the multitudes away, He went up to the mountain by Himself to pray; and when it was evening, He was there alone. But the boat was already many stadia away from the land, battered by the waves; for the wind was contrary. And in the fourth watch of the night He came to them, walking on the sea. And when the disciples saw Him walking on the sea, they were frightened, saying, "It is a ghost!" And they cried out for fear. But immediately Jesus spoke to them, saying, "Take courage, it is I; do not be afraid." And Peter answered Him and said, "Lord, if it is You, command me to come to You on the water." And He said, "Come!" And Peter got out of the boat, and walked on the water and came toward Jesus. But seeing the wind, he became afraid, and beginning to sink, he cried out, saying, "Lord, save me!" And immediately Jesus stretched out His hand and took hold of him, and said to him, "O you of little faith, why did you doubt?" And when they got into the boat, the wind stopped. And those who were in the boat worshiped Him, saying, "You are certainly God's Son!" (Matt. 14:22-33).

It is significant that Jesus' disciples had been caught in another violent storm in a boat on the Sea of Galilee sometime earlier (see Matt. 8:23-27). During that incident, Jesus had been with them, and after He calmed the storm by His rebuke, He then rebuked His disciples for their lack of faith. Before they had embarked on their journey He had told them that it was His will that they go to the other side of the lake (see Mark 4:35). When the storm arose, however, they were more persuaded by their circumstances, and at one point believed they were all going to die. Jesus expected them at least not to be afraid.

This time, however, Jesus sent them across the Sea of Galilee on their own. Surely He was led by the Spirit to do so, and surely God knew that a contrary wind would arise that night. Thus the Lord allowed them to face a small challenge to their faith. Because of those contrary winds, what would have normally taken just a few hours took all night. We have to credit the disciples for their endurance, but can't help but wonder if any of them attempted to have faith for the winds to be calmed, something they had seen Jesus do just a few days earlier. Interestingly, Mark's Gospel reports that when Jesus came walking to them on the water, "He intended to pass by them" (Mark 6:48). He was going to leave them to face their problem alone as He miraculously walked right by! This seems to indicate that they weren't praying or looking to God. I wonder how many times the Miracle-Worker walks right by us as we strain at the oars of life against the winds of trouble.

Principles of Faith

Jesus responded to Peter's challenge with a single word: "Come." If Peter had attempted to walk on the water prior to that word, he would have sunk instantly, as he would have had no promise upon which to base his faith. He would have been stepping out by presumption rather than by faith. Similarly, even *after* Jesus spoke His word, had any of the other disciples tried to walk on the water, they also would have sunk immediately, as Jesus gave His promise only to Peter. None of them could have met the condition of the promise, as not one of them was Peter. Likewise, before any of us attempt to trust one of God's promises, we must make certain that the promise applies to us and that we are meeting the conditions of the promise.

Peter stepped out on the water. That was the point in time when he trusted, although there is no doubt that he who had been crying out for fear of a ghost just seconds before also had doubts in his head as he took his first step. But in order to receive the miracle, he had to act on his faith. Had he clung to the mast of the boat and dipped his big toe over the boat's side to see if the water would support his weight, he would never have experienced the miracle. Likewise, before we receive any miracles, we must commit ourselves to trust God's promise at some point in time and then act on what we believe. There is always a time when our faith is tested. Sometimes that time is short; sometimes it is long. But there is going to be some length of time when we have to disregard the testimony of our senses and act on God's word.

Peter progressed well at first. But as he considered the impossibility of what he was doing, taking note of the wind and waves, he became afraid. Perhaps he stopped walking, fearful of taking another step. And he who had been experiencing a miracle found himself sinking. We need to continue in faith once we have begun, continuing to act on our faith. Keep pressing on.

Peter sank because he doubted. People don't often like to blame themselves for their lack of faith. They would rather pass the blame on to God. But how do you suppose Jesus would have reacted if He had heard Peter, when he was safely back in the boat, saying to the other disciples, "It was really only God's will for me to walk part way to Jesus"?

Peter failed because he became afraid and lost his faith. Those are the plain facts. Jesus didn't condemn him, but immediately stretched out His hand to give Peter something steady to hold. And He immediately questioned Peter about why he doubted. Peter had no good reason to doubt, because the word of God's Son is more certain than anything. *None of us ever has any good reason to doubt God's Word, be afraid or worry.*

Scripture is full of victories that were the result of faith and failures that were the result of doubts. Joshua and Caleb possessed the Promised Land because of their faith while the majority of their peers died in the wilderness because of their doubts (see Num. 14:26-30). Jesus' disciples had their needs supplied as they journeyed two-by-two to preach the gospel (see Luke 22:35), but they once failed to cast out a demon because of their unbelief (see Matt. 17:19-20). Many received healing miracles under the ministry of Christ while most of the sick people in His hometown of Nazareth remained ill because of their unbelief (see Mark 6:5-6).

Like all of them, I've personally experienced success and failure according to my faith or doubts. But I'm not going to grow bitter over my failures or blame God. I'm not going to justify myself by condemning Him. I'm not going to search for some complicated theological explanation that re-invents God's clearly revealed will. I know it is impossible for God to lie. So when I've failed, I just repent of my unbelief and start walking on the water once again. I've noticed that Jesus always forgives me and rescues me from drowning!

The verdict is settled: Believers get blessed; doubters don't! The disciple-making minister follows Jesus' example. He is full of faith himself, and he admonishes his disciples, "Have faith in God!" (Mark 11:22).

FIFTEEN

Divine Healing

A lthough the subject of divine healing is somewhat controversial, it is certainly not one that is obscure in Scripture. In fact, one-tenth of all that was written in the four Gospels concerns Jesus' healing ministry. There are promises for divine healing in the Old Testament, in the Gospels and the New Testament epistles. Those who are ill can find great encouragement in a wealth of faith-building scriptures.

It has been my general observation around the world that where churches are full of highly-committed believers (true disciples), divine healing is much more commonplace. Where the church is lukewarm and sophisticated, divine healing is a very rare occurrence.[56] All of this should not surprise us, as Jesus told us that one of the signs that will follow *believers* is that they will lay hands on the sick and they shall recover (see Mark 16:18). If we were to judge churches by the signs that Jesus declared would follow the believers, we would have to conclude that many churches consist of no believers:

> And [Jesus] said to them, "Go into all the world and preach the gospel to all creation. He who has believed and has been baptized shall be saved; but he who has disbelieved shall be condemned. And these signs will accompany those who have believed: in My name they will cast out demons, they will speak with new tongues; they will pick up serpents, and if they drink any deadly poison, it shall not hurt them; they will lay hands on the sick, and they will recover" (Mark 16:15-18).

[56] In some churches in North America, a minister would take great risks to teach on this subject due to the heavy resistance he would encounter from the so-called believers. Jesus, too, met resistance and unbelief at times that hindered His healing ministry (see Mark 6:1-6).

221

The disciple-making minister, imitating the perfect ministry of Christ, will certainly use his gifts to promote the ministry of divine healing within his sphere of influence. He knows that divine healing furthers God's kingdom in at least two ways. First, healing miracles are a wonderful advertisement for the gospel, as any child who reads the Gospels or the book of Acts would understand (but which many ministers with advance degrees seemingly are unable to comprehend). Second, healthy disciples aren't hindered from ministry by personal sickness.

The disciple-making minister also needs to be sensitive to those members in the body of Christ who desire healing but who have had difficulty receiving. They often need tender instruction and gentle encouragement, especially if they have grown adverse to any healing message. The disciple-making minister faces a choice: he can avoid teaching on the subject of divine healing altogether, in which case no one will be offended and no one will be healed, or he can lovingly teach on the subject and risk offending some while helping others to experience healing. Personally, I've opted for the second option, believing that it follows Jesus' example.

Healing on the Cross

A good place to begin the study of divine healing is the fifty-third chapter of Isaiah, universally considered a messianic prophecy. Through the Holy Spirit, Isaiah graphically spoke of Jesus' sacrificial death and the work He would accomplish on the cross:

> Surely our griefs He Himself bore, and our sorrows He carried; yet we ourselves esteemed Him stricken, smitten of God, and afflicted. But He was pierced through for our transgressions, He was crushed for our iniquities; the chastening for our well-being fell upon Him, and by His scourging we are healed. All of us like sheep have gone astray, each of us has turned to his own way; but the Lord has caused the iniquity of us all to fall on Him (Is. 53:4-6).

By the Holy Spirit's inspiration, Isaiah declared that Jesus bore our *griefs* and *sorrows*. A better translation of the original Hebrew indicates that Jesus bore our *sicknesses* and *pains*, as many reliable translations indicate in their reference notes.

The Hebrew word translated *griefs* in Isaiah 53:4 is the word *choli*, which is also found in Deuteronomy 7:15; 28:61; 1 Kings 17:17; 2 Kings 1:2; 8:8, and 2 Chronicles 16:12; 21:15. In all those cases it is translated either *sickness* or *disease*.

The word translated *sorrows* is the Hebrew word *makob*, which can also be found in Job 14:22 and Job 33:19. In both those cases it is translated *pain(s)*.

All of this being so, Isaiah 53:4 is more accurately translated, "Surely our *sicknesses* He Himself bore, and our *pains* He carried." This fact is sealed by Matthew's direct quotation of Isaiah 53:4 in his Gospel: "He Himself took our infirmities and carried away our diseases" (Matt. 8:17).

Unable to escape these facts, some try to convince us that Isaiah was referring to our supposed "spiritual sickness" and "spiritual diseases." However, Matthew's quotation of Isaiah 53:4 leaves no doubt that Isaiah was referring to literal *physical* sickness and disease. Let's read it in context:

> When evening came, they brought to Him many who were demon-possessed; and He cast out the spirits with a word, and healed all who were ill. This was to fulfill what was spoken through Isaiah the prophet: *"He Himself took our infirmities and carried away our diseases"* (Matt. 8:16-17, emphasis added).

Matthew plainly stated that the physical healings performed by Jesus were a fulfillment of Isaiah 53:4. Thus there is no doubt that Isaiah 53:4 is a reference to Christ bearing our physical infirmities and diseases.[57] *Just as* Scripture says that Jesus *bore* our iniquities (see Isaiah 53:11), it also says that He *bore* our infirmities and diseases. That is news that should make any sick person glad. By His atoning sacrifice, Jesus has provided for our salvation *and* healing.

A Question Asked

But if that is true, some ask, then why isn't everyone healed? The answer to that question is best answered by asking another question: Why are not all people born again? All are not born again because they either haven't heard the gospel or else they haven't believed it. So, too, each individual must appropriate his healing through his own faith. Many have never yet heard the wonderful truth that Jesus bore their sicknesses; others have heard but rejected it.

God the Father's attitude toward sickness has been clearly revealed by the ministry of His beloved Son, who testified of Himself,

> Truly, truly, I say to you, the Son can do nothing of Himself, unless it is something He sees the Father doing; for whatever the Father does, these things the Son also does in like manner (John 5:19).

We read in the book of Hebrews that Jesus was the "exact representation of His [Father's] nature" (Heb. 1:3). There is no question that Jesus'

---

[57] Grasping for anything by which they can cling to their unbelief, some try to convince us that Jesus *completely* fulfilled Isaiah 53:4 by His healing of people that evening in Capernaum. But Isaiah said that Jesus bore *our* sicknesses, just as he also said that Jesus was crushed for *our* iniquities (compare Is. 53:4 and 5). Jesus bore the sicknesses of the very same people for whose iniquities He was crushed. Thus, Matthew was only indicating that Jesus' healing ministry in Capernaum validated that He was the Messiah spoken of in Isaiah 53, the one who would bear our iniquities and sicknesses.

attitude toward sickness was identical to His Father's attitude toward sickness.

What was Jesus' attitude? *Not once* did he turn away *anyone* who came to Him requesting healing. *Not once* did He say to a sick person who desired to be healed, "No, it's not God's will that you be healed, so you'll have to remain sick." Jesus *always* healed the sick who came to Him, and once they were healed, He often told them it was their faith that had healed them. Moreover, the Bible declares that God never changes (see Mal. 3:6) and that Jesus Christ "is the same yesterday and today and forever" (Heb. 13:8).

Healing Proclaimed

Unfortunately, salvation has been reduced today to little more than forgiveness of sins. But the Greek words most often translated "saved" and "salvation" imply the concepts not only of forgiveness, but complete deliverance and healing.[58] Let us consider a man in the Bible who experienced salvation in this fuller sense. He was healed by his faith as he listened to Paul preach the gospel in his city.

> They...fled to the cities of Lycaonia, Lystra and Derbe, and the surrounding region; and there they continued to preach the gospel. At Lystra a man was sitting who had no strength in his feet, lame from his mother's womb, who had never walked. This man was listening to Paul as he spoke, who, when he had fixed his gaze on him and had seen that he had faith to be made well, said with a loud voice, "Stand upright on your feet." And he leaped up and began to walk (Acts 14:6-10).

Notice that although Paul was preaching "the gospel," the man heard something that produced faith in his heart to receive physical healing. At bare minimum, he must have heard Paul say something about Jesus' healing ministry, and how Jesus healed everyone who asked in faith for healing. Perhaps Paul also mentioned Isaiah's prophecy of Jesus bearing our infirmities and diseases. We don't know, but since "faith comes from hearing" (Rom 10:17), the paralyzed man must have heard something that sparked faith in his heart to be healed. Something Paul said convinced him that God didn't want him to remain paralyzed.

Paul himself must have believed that God wanted the man to be healed, or his words could never have convinced the man to have faith for healing, nor would he have told the man to stand up. What would have hap-

---

[58] For example, Jesus said to a woman whom He had healed of internal bleeding, "Daughter, your faith has made you well" (Mark 5:34). The Greek word translated "made well" in this verse (*sozo*) and ten other times in the New Testament is translated "save" or "saved" over eighty times in the New Testament. It is, for example, the same word that is translated "saved" in Ephesians 2:5, "By grace you have been *saved* through faith." Thus we see that physical healing is implied within the meaning of the Greek word most often translated as "saved."

pened if Paul had said what so many modern preachers say? What if he had preached, "It isn't God's will for everyone to be healed"? The man would not have had faith to be healed. Perhaps this explains why so many are not healed today. The very preachers who should be inspiring people to have faith for healing are destroying their faith.

Again, notice that this man was healed by his *faith*. Had he not believed, he would have remained paralyzed, even though it was obviously God's will for him to be healed. Moreover, there probably were other sick people in the crowd that day as well, but we have no record of anyone else being healed. If that was so, why weren't they healed? For the same reason that many of the unsaved people in the crowd were not born again that day—because they didn't believe Paul's message.

We should never conclude that it is not God's will to heal everyone based on the fact that some people are never healed. That would be the same as concluding that it is not God's will for all to be born again just because some people are never born again. Every person must believe the gospel for himself if he is going to be saved, and every person must believe for himself if he is going to be healed.

Further Proof of God's Will to Heal

Under the old covenant, physical healing was included in Israel's covenant with God. Just a few days after the Exodus, God made Israel this promise:

> If you will give earnest heed to the voice of the Lord your God, and do what is right in His sight, and give ear to His commandments, and keep all His statutes, I will put none of the diseases on you which I have put on the Egyptians; for I, the Lord, am your healer (Ex. 15:26).

Anyone who is honest will have to agree that healing was included in Israel's covenant with God, contingent upon the people's obedience. (Incidentally, Paul makes it clear in 1 Corinthians 11:27-31 that physical health under the new covenant is also contingent upon our obedience.)

God also promised the Israelites:

> But you shall serve the Lord your God, and He will bless your bread and your water; and *I will remove sickness from your midst*. There shall be no one miscarrying or barren in your land; I will fulfill the number of your days (Ex. 23:25-26, emphasis added).

> You shall be blessed above all peoples; there will be no male or female barren among you or among your cattle. *The Lord will remove from you all sickness;* and He will not put on you any of the harmful diseases of Egypt which

you have known, but He will lay them on all who hate
you (Deut. 7:14-15, emphasis added).

If physical healing was included in the old covenant, one would wonder how it could not be included in the new covenant, if in fact the new
covenant is better than the old, as Scripture states:

> But now He [Jesus] has obtained a more excellent minis-
> try, by as much as He is also the mediator of a *better cov-
> enant, which has been enacted on better promises* (Heb. 8:6,
> emphasis added).

Yet Further Proof

The Bible contains many scriptures that offer indisputable proof that it
is God's will to heal everyone. Let me list three of the best:

> Bless the Lord, O my soul, and all that is within me, bless
> His holy name. Bless the Lord, O my soul, and forget none
> of His benefits; who pardons all your iniquities, *who heals
> all your diseases* (Ps. 103:1-3, emphasis added).

What Christian would dispute David's declaration that God wills to
pardon *all* our iniquities? David, however, believed that God also wills to
heal just as many of our diseases—all of them.

> My son, give attention to my words; incline your ear to
> my sayings. Do not let them depart from your sight; keep
> them in the midst of your heart. For they are life to those
> who find them and *health to all their body* (Prov. 4:20-22,
> emphasis added).

> Is anyone among you sick? Then he must call for the el-
> ders of the church and they are to pray over him, anoint-
> ing him with oil in the name of the Lord; and *the prayer
> offered in faith will restore the one who is sick*, and the Lord
> will raise him up, and if he has committed sins, they will
> be forgiven him (Jas. 5:14-15, emphasis added).

Notice that this last promise belongs to *any who are sick*. And notice that
it is not the elders or the oil that brings healing but the "prayer of faith."

Is it the faith of the elders or the sick person? It is the faith of both. The
faith of the sick person is expressed, at least in part, by his calling for the
elders of the church. The sick person's unbelief could nullify the effects
of the elders' prayers. The kind of prayer James wrote about is a good
example of the "prayer of agreement" that Jesus mentioned in Matthew
18:19. Both parties involved in this kind of prayer must "agree." If one
person believes and the other person does not believe, they are not in
agreement.

226

We also know that in several passages the Bible credits Satan for sickness (see Job 2:7; Luke 13:16; Acts 10:38; 1 Cor. 5:5). Thus it would stand to reason that God would be opposed to Satan's work in His children's bodies. Our Father loves us much more than any earthly father ever loved his children (see Matt. 7:11), and I've never yet met a father who desired that his children be sick.

Every healing performed by Jesus during His earthly ministry, and every healing recorded in the book of Acts, should encourage us to believe that God wants us to be healthy. Jesus frequently healed people who sought Him seeking healing, and He credited their faith for their miracle. That proves that Jesus did not single out certain exclusive people whom He wanted to heal. Any sick person could have come to Him in faith and be healed. He wanted to heal them all, but He required faith on their part.

Answers to Some Common Objections

Perhaps the most common objection to all of this is one that is not based on God's Word, but on people's experiences. It usually goes something like this: "I knew a wonderful Christian woman who prayed to be healed of cancer, yet she died. That proves it is not God's will to heal all."

We should never attempt to determine God's will by anything other than His Word. For example, if you traveled back in time and watched the Israelites wander in the wilderness for forty years while the land that flowed with milk and honey waited just across the Jordan River, you might have concluded that it wasn't God's will for Israel to enter the promised land. But if you know the Bible, then you know that was not the case. It *was* certainly God's will for Israel to enter the Promised Land, but they failed to enter because of their unbelief (see Heb. 3:19).

What about all the people who are now in hell? It was God's will for them to be in heaven, but they didn't meet the conditions of repentance and faith in the Lord Jesus. So, too, we cannot determine God's will concerning healing by looking at sick people. Just because a Christian prays for healing and fails to receive, that doesn't prove it isn't God's will to heal all. If that Christian had met God's conditions, he would have been healed, or else God is a liar. When we fail to receive healing and then blame God with the excuse that healing was not His will, we are no different than unbelieving Israelites who died in the wilderness claiming it wasn't God's will for them to enter the Promised Land. We would be better just to swallow our pride and admit that we are to blame.

As I stated in the previous chapter about faith, many sincere Christians have wrongfully ended their prayers for healing with the faith-destroying phrase, "If it be Thy will." This plainly reveals that they are not praying in faith because they aren't sure of God's will. When it comes to healing, God's will is very plain, as we have already seen. If you know God wants to heal you, there is no reason to add "if it be Thy will" to your prayer for healing. That would be equivalent to saying to the Lord, "Lord, I know you promised to heal me, but just in case you were lying about it, I ask you to heal me only if it is actually Your will."

It is also certainly true that God may discipline disobedient believers by allowing sickness to afflict them, even to the point of allowing their premature death in some cases. Such believers obviously need to repent before they can receive healing (see 1 Cor. 11:27-32). There are others who, by neglecting to take care of their bodies, open themselves up to sickness. Christians should be intelligent enough to maintain a healthy diet, to eat moderately, to exercise regularly, and to take necessary rest.

A Second Common Objection

It is often said, "Paul had a thorn in the flesh, and God didn't heal him."

The idea that Paul's thorn was sickness, however, is simply a bad theological theory in light of the fact that Paul told us exactly what His thorn was—an angel of Satan:

> Because of the surpassing greatness of the revelations, for this reason, to keep me from exalting myself, there was given me a thorn in the flesh, *a messenger of Satan* to torment me—to keep me from exalting myself! Concerning this I implored the Lord three times that it might leave me. And He has said to me, "My grace is sufficient for you, for power is perfected in weakness." Most gladly, therefore, I will rather boast about my weaknesses, so that the power of Christ may dwell in me (2 Cor. 12:7-9, emphasis added).

The word translated *messenger* is the Greek word "aggelos," which is translated *angel* or angels in over 160 places where it is found in the New Testament. Paul's thorn in the flesh was an angel of Satan sent to buffet him; it was not a sickness or disease.

Notice also that there is no mention of Paul's praying to be healed nor is there any indication that God refused to heal him. On three occasions, Paul simply asked God if He would remove the buffeting angel, and God said that His grace was sufficient.

Who is the one who gave Paul this thorn? Some believe it was Satan, since the thorn was called an "angel of Satan." Others believe it was God because the thorn was apparently given so Paul wouldn't be lifted up in pride. Paul himself said, "To keep me from exalting myself."

The *King James* version translates these verses a little differently. Rather than saying, "to keep me from exalting myself," it says, "lest I should be exalted above measure." This is an important difference because God is not opposed to our being exalted. In fact, He promises to exalt us if we will humble ourselves. So it is quite possible that God was the one doing the exalting and Satan was trying to stop Paul's exaltation by assigning a specific buffeting angel to stir up trouble wherever Paul traveled. Yet God said He would use the circumstances for His glory because His power could be manifested more in Paul's life as a result of his weaknesses.

Regardless, to say that Paul was sick and that God refused to heal him is a gross distortion of what the Bible actually states. In the passage about his thorn in the flesh, Paul never mentioned any sickness, and there is nothing resembling a refusal on God's part to heal him of his supposed sickness. If an honest person will read through Paul's listing of all his trials in 2 Corinthians 11:23-30, he will not find sickness or disease even mentioned once.

An Elaboration on the Same Theme

Some object to my explanation of Paul's thorn, saying, "But didn't Paul himself say to the Galatians that he was sick the first time he preached the gospel to them? Wasn't he speaking of his thorn in the flesh?"

Here is what Paul actually wrote in his letter to the Galatians:

> But you know that it was because of a bodily illness that I preached the gospel to you the first time; and that which was a trial to you in my bodily condition you did not despise or loathe, but you received me as an angel of God, as Christ Jesus Himself (Gal. 4:13-14).

The Greek word translated *illness* here in Galatians 4:13 is *asthenia*, which literally means "weakness." It *can* mean weakness because of sickness, but it doesn't have to.

For example, Paul wrote, "the *weakness* of God is stronger than men" (1 Cor. 1:25, emphasis added). The word that is translated *weakness* in this instance is also the word *asthenia*. It would not make any sense if the translators had translated it "the illness of God is stronger than men." (See also Matt. 26:41 and 1 Pet. 3:7, where the word *asthenia* is translated *weakness* and could not possibly be translated *sickness*).

When Paul first visited Galatia, as recorded in the book of Acts, there is no mention of his being ill. There is mention, however, of his being stoned and left for dead, and he was either raised from the dead or miraculously revived (see Acts 14:5-7, 19-20). Surely Paul's body, after he was stoned and left for dead, would have been in horrible condition with cuts and bruises all over it.

Paul did not have a sickness in Galatia that was a trial to his listeners. Rather, his body was weak from his recent stoning. Most likely, he still carried the reminders of his persecutions in Galatia when he wrote his letter to the Galatians, because he ended his epistle with these words:

> From now on let no one cause trouble for me, for I bear on my body the brand-marks of Jesus (Gal. 6:17).

229

Another Objection: "I'm Suffering for the Glory of God"

This objection is used by some who have taken a verse from the story of the raising of Lazarus as a basis to claim they are suffering sickness for God's glory. Jesus said concerning Lazarus:

> This sickness is not to end in death, but for the glory of God, so that the Son of God may be glorified by it (John 11:4).

Jesus wasn't saying that God was being glorified as a result of Lazarus' sickness, but that God would be glorified when Lazarus was healed and raised from the dead. In other words, the final result of the sickness wouldn't be death, but rather that God would be glorified. God isn't glorified in sickness; He is glorified in healing. (See also Matt. 9:8; 15:31; Luke 7:16; 13:13 and 17:15, where healing brought glory to God.)

Another Objection: "Paul Said He Left Trophimus Sick at Miletum"

I happen to be writing this sentence in a city in Germany. When I departed from my hometown in the United States last week, I left numerous sick people behind me. I left *hospitals* full of sick people. But that doesn't mean that it wasn't God's will for all of them to be healed. Just because Paul left one man sick in a city he visited is not proof that it wasn't God's will for that man to be healed. What about the hoards of unsaved people whom Paul also left behind? Does that prove it wasn't God's will for them to be saved? Absolutely not.

Another Objection: "I'm Just Like Job!"

Praise the Lord! If you've read the end of Job's story, you know he was healed. It wasn't God's will for Job to remain sick, and it isn't God's will for you to remain sick either. Job's story reaffirms that God's will is always healing.

Another Objection: Paul's Advice to Timothy About His Stomach

We know that Paul told Timothy to use a little wine for the sake of his stomach and his frequent ailments (see 1 Tim. 5:23).

Actually, Paul told Timothy to *stop drinking water* and to use a little wine for the sake of his stomach and frequent ailments. This would seem to indicate that something was wrong with the water. Obviously, if you are drinking contaminated water, you should stop drinking it and start drinking something else, or you will probably have stomach problems like Timothy.

Another Objection: "Jesus Only Healed to Prove His Deity."

Some people want us to believe that the only reason Jesus healed was to prove His deity. Now that His deity is well established, He supposedly no longer heals.

That is completely incorrect. It is true that Jesus' miracles did authenticate His deity, but that is not the only reason He healed people during his earthly ministry. Many times Jesus forbade people whom He healed to tell anyone what had happened to them (see Matt. 8:4; 9:6, 30; 12:13-16; Mark 5:43; 7:36; 8:26). If Jesus healed people for the singular purpose of proving His deity, He would have told those people to tell everyone what He had done for them.

What was the motivation behind Jesus' healings? Many times Scripture says He healed because He was "moved with compassion" (see Matt. 9:35-36; 14:14; 20:34; Mark 1:41; 5:19; Luke 7:13). The reason Jesus healed is because He loved people and was full of compassion. Has Jesus become less compassionate since His earthly ministry? Has His love diminished? Absolutely not!

Another Objection: "God Wants Me to be Sick for Some Reason."

That is impossible in light of all the scriptures we have considered. If you've been persisting in disobedience, it could be true that God has permitted your sickness in order to bring you to repentance. But it is still not His will for you to remain sick. He wants you to repent and be healed.

Additionally, if God wants you to be sick, then why are you going to the doctor and taking medication, hoping to be healed? Are you trying to get out of "God's will"?

A Final Objection: "If We Never Suffer Disease, How Will We Die?"

We know that the Bible teaches that our physical bodies are decaying (see 2 Cor. 4:16). There is nothing we can do to stop our hair from graying and our bodies from growing older. Eventually our sight and hearing are not as good as they were when we were younger. We can't run as fast. Our hearts are not as strong. We' re slowly wearing out.

But that doesn't mean we have to die of sickness or disease. Our bodies can simply wear out completely, and when we do, our spirits will leave our bodies when God calls us home to heaven. Many believers have died like that. Why not you?

SIXTEEN

The Healing Ministry of Jesus

It is often thought that because Jesus was the divine Son of God, He could work a miracle or heal anyone anytime He desired. But as we examine the Scriptures closely, we discover that although Jesus was certainly divine, He was apparently self-limited during His earthly ministry. He once said, "The Son can do nothing of Himself, unless it is something He sees the Father doing" (John 5:19). That clearly shows that Jesus was limited and dependent on His Father.

According to Paul, when Jesus became a human being He "emptied Himself" of certain things that He would have previously possessed as God:

> Have this attitude in yourselves which was also in Christ Jesus, who, although He existed in the form of God, did not regard equality with God a thing to be grasped, but *emptied Himself*, taking the form of a bond-servant, and being made in the likeness of men (Phil. 2:5-7, emphasis added).

Of what did Jesus "empty Himself"? It wasn't His divinity. It wasn't His holiness. It wasn't His love. It must have been His supernatural power. Obviously He was no longer omnipresent (existing everywhere). Likewise, He was no longer omniscient (all-knowing), and omnipotent (all-powerful). Jesus became a man. In His ministry, He operated as a man anointed by the Holy Spirit. This becomes abundantly clear as we look closely at the four Gospels.

For example, we might ask, *If Jesus was the divine Son of God, why was it necessary for Him to be baptized in the Holy Spirit when He began His ministry at age thirty?* Why would *God* need to be baptized with *God*?

Clearly, Jesus needed the baptism of the Holy Spirit in order to be anointed for ministry. That is why, soon after His baptism, we read of Him preaching these words: "The Spirit of the Lord is upon Me, *because He anointed Me* to preach….to proclaim…to set free…" (Luke 4:18, emphasis added).

That is also why Peter preached, "You know of Jesus of Nazareth, how *God anointed Him with the Holy Spirit and with power,* and how He went about doing good and healing all who were oppressed by the devil, for God was with Him" (Acts 10:38, emphasis added).

That is also why Jesus did no miracles until He was baptized in the Holy Spirit at about age thirty. Was He the Son of God at age twenty-five? Certainly. Then why did He do no miracles until age thirty? Simply because Jesus emptied Himself of the supernatural power that God possesses, and He had to wait for the time when He would be empowered by the Spirit.

More Proof that Jesus Ministered as a Man Anointed by the Spirit

We notice as we read the Gospels that there were times when Jesus possessed supernatural knowledge and other times when He didn't. In fact, Jesus often asked questions to obtain information.

For example, He told the woman at the well of Samaria that she had had five husbands and that she was living with a man now to whom she was not married (see John 4:17-18). How did Jesus know that? Was it because He was God and God knows everything? No, if that were the case, Jesus would have demonstrated that ability consistently. Although He was God and God knows everything, Jesus emptied Himself of His omniscience when He became a man. Jesus knew the marital history of the woman at the well because the Holy Spirit granted Him at that moment the gift of "the word of knowledge" (1 Cor. 12:8), which is the supernatural ability to know something about the present or past. (We will study in more detail the subject of the gifts of the Spirit in the next chapter).

Did Jesus know everything all the time? No, when the woman with the issue of blood touched the hem of Jesus' garment and He felt healing power proceed from Him, He asked, "Who touched My garments?" (Mark 5:30b). When Jesus saw a fig tree in the distance in Mark 11:13, He "went to see if perhaps He would find anything on it."

Why didn't Jesus know who had touched Him? Why didn't He know if the fig tree had figs on it? Because Jesus was operating as a man anointed by the Holy Spirit with gifts of the Spirit. Gifts of the Spirit operate as the Spirit wills (see 1 Cor. 12:11; Heb. 2:4). Jesus didn't know things supernaturally unless the Holy Spirit willed to give Him the gift of "the word of knowledge."

The same thing was true of Jesus' healing ministry. The Scripture makes it plain that Jesus couldn't heal anyone at any time at all. For example, we read in the Gospel of Mark that when Jesus visited His hometown of Nazareth, He was unable to accomplish everything He wanted to do.

And [Jesus] went out from there, and He came into His home town; and His disciples followed Him. And when the Sabbath had come, He began to teach in the synagogue; and the many listeners were astonished, saying, "Where did this man get these things, and what is this wisdom given to Him, and such miracles as these performed by His hands? Is not this the carpenter, the son of Mary, and brother of James, and Joses, and Judas, and Simon? Are not His sisters here with us?" And they took offense at Him. And Jesus said to them, "A prophet is not without honor except in his home town and among his own relatives and in his own household." And He *could do no miracle there* except that He laid His hands upon a few sick people and healed them. And He wondered at their unbelief (Mark 6:1-6, emphasis added).

Notice Mark didn't say that Jesus *wouldn't* do any miracle there, but that He *couldn't*. Why? Because the people of Nazareth were unbelieving. They didn't receive Jesus as being the anointed Son of God but only as a local carpenter's son. Just as Jesus Himself remarked, "A prophet is not without honor except in his hometown and among his own relatives and in his own household" (Mark 6:4). As a result, the most He could accomplish was to heal a few people "with minor ailments" (as one translation says). Surely, if there was any place where Jesus would have wanted to work miracles and dramatically heal people, it would have been the town He had lived most of His life. The Bible says, however, that He could not.

More Insight from Luke

Jesus healed primarily by two different methods: (1) by teaching the Word of God to encourage sick people to have faith to be healed, and (2) by operating in "gifts of healings" as the Holy Spirit willed. Therefore, Jesus was limited by two factors in His healing ministry: (1) by the unbelief of sick people, and (2) by the will of the Holy Spirit to manifest Himself through "gifts of healings."

Obviously, the majority of the people in Jesus' hometown did not have faith in Him. Even though they had heard of His healing miracles in other towns, they wouldn't believe He had power to heal, and consequently He couldn't heal them. Moreover, apparently the Holy Spirit didn't grant Jesus any "gifts of healings" in Nazareth—for what reason nobody knows.

Luke records in more detail than Mark exactly what happened when Jesus visited Nazareth:

And [Jesus] came to Nazareth, where He had been brought up; and as was His custom, He entered the synagogue on the Sabbath, and stood up to read. And the book of the prophet Isaiah was handed to Him. And He opened the book, and found the place where it was written, "The Spirit of the Lord is upon Me, because He anointed Me to preach the gospel to the poor. He has sent Me to proclaim release to the captives, and recovery of sight to the blind, to set free those who are oppressed, to proclaim the favorable year of the Lord." And He closed the book...and He began to say to them, "Today this scripture has been fulfilled in your hearing." And all were speaking well of Him, and wondering at the gracious words which were falling from His lips; and they were saying, "Is this not Joseph's son?" (Luke 4:16-22).

Jesus wanted His audience to believe that *He* was the promised anointed one of Isaiah's prophecy, hoping that they would believe and receive all the benefits of His anointing, which according to Isaiah, included freedom from captivity and oppression as well as sight for the blind.[59] But they didn't believe, and although they were impressed by His speaking ability, they wouldn't believe Joseph's son was anyone special. Recognizing their skepticism, Jesus responded,

No doubt you will quote this proverb to Me, "Physician, heal yourself! Whatever we heard was done at Capernaum, do here in your home town as well"....Truly I say to you, no prophet is welcome in his hometown (Luke 4:23-24).

The people in Jesus' hometown were waiting to see if He would do what they heard He had done in Capernaum. Their attitude was not one of expectant faith but skepticism. By their lack of faith they limited Him from performing any miracles or major healings.

Jesus' Other Limitation in Nazareth

Jesus' next words to the Nazareth crowd reveal that He was also limited by the will of the Holy Spirit to manifest Himself through "gifts of healings":

But I say to you in truth, there were many widows in Israel in the days of Elijah, when the sky was shut up for three years and six months, when a great famine came over all the land; and yet Elijah was sent to none of them, but only to Zarephath, in the land of Sidon, to a woman who was a widow. And there were many lepers in Israel in the time

---

[59] All of these could well refer to physical healing. Sickness can definitely be considered to be oppression, as Scripture says that "God anointed [Jesus] with the Holy Spirit and with power, and...He went about doing good, and healing all who were oppressed by the devil" (Acts 10:38).

of Elisha the prophet; and none of them was cleansed, but only Naaman the Syrian (Luke 4:25-27).

Jesus' point was that Elijah couldn't multiply oil and flour to sustain any widow *he* desired during Israel's three-year famine (see 1 Kin. 17:9-16). Although there were numerous suffering widows in Israel at that time, the Spirit anointed Elijah to help a single widow who wasn't even an Israelite. Likewise, Elisha couldn't cleanse just any leper *he* wanted to. This is proved by that fact that there were many lepers in Israel when Naaman was cleansed. If it had purely been his own choice, Elisha would naturally have cleansed fellow Israelites who were lepers before he cleansed Naaman, an idol worshipper (see 2 Kin. 5:1-14).

Both Elijah and Elisha were prophets—men anointed by the Holy Spirit who were used in various gifts of the Spirit as the Spirit willed. Why didn't God send Elijah to some other widows? I don't know. Why didn't God use Elisha to heal some other lepers? I don't know. Nobody knows, except God.

Those two familiar Old Testament stories do not prove, however, that it wasn't God's will to provide every widow's needs or heal every leper. The people of Israel could have brought an end to their famine during the time of Elijah if they and their wicked king (Ahab) would have repented of their sins. The famine was a form of God's judgment. And all the lepers in Israel could have been healed by obeying and believing the words of their God-given covenant, which, as we have already seen, included physical healing.

Jesus revealed to His audience in Nazareth that He was under the same limitations as were Elijah and Elisha. For some reason, the Holy Spirit didn't give Jesus any "gifts of healings" in Nazareth. That fact, coupled with the unbelief of the people of Nazareth, resulted in no major miracles being performed through Jesus in His hometown.

A Look at One "Gift of Healing" Through Jesus

If we study the Gospel accounts of the various healings performed by Jesus, we find that the majority of the people were healed, not through "gifts of healings," but through their faith. Let us consider the differences between those two types of healings by looking at examples of both. We will first study the story of the crippled man at the pool of Bethesda, healed not by his faith, but through a "gift of healing" through Jesus.

> Now there is in Jerusalem by the sheep gate a pool, which is called in Hebrew Bethesda, having five porticoes. In these lay a multitude of those who were sick, blind, lame, and withered, (waiting for the moving of the waters; for an angel of the Lord went down at certain seasons into the pool and stirred up the water; whoever then first, after the

stirring up of the water, stepped in was made well from whatever disease with which he was afflicted.) A man was there who had been ill for thirty-eight years. When Jesus saw him lying there, and knew that he had already been a long time in that condition, He said to him, "Do you wish to get well?" The sick man answered Him, "Sir, I have no man to put me into the pool when the water is stirred up, but while I am coming, another steps down before me." Jesus said to him, "Get up, pick up your pallet and walk." Immediately the man became well, and picked up his pallet and began to walk (John 5:2-9).

How do we know this man was healed, not by his faith, but through a "gift of healing"? There are several indications.

First, notice that this man hadn't been seeking Jesus. Rather Jesus found him sitting by the pool. If the man had been seeking Jesus, it would have been an indication of faith on his part.

Second, Jesus did not tell the man that his faith had healed him, as He often did when He healed other people.

Third, when the healed man was later questioned by the Jews as to who had told him to "arise and walk," he responded that he didn't even know who the Man was. So it definitely wasn't his faith in Jesus that effected his healing. This was a clear case of someone who was healed through a "gift of healing," manifested as the Spirit willed.

Notice also that even though there was a multitude of sick people waiting for the stirring of the waters, Jesus healed only one individual and left the remainder of the multitude sick. Why? Again, I don't know. This incident, however, does not prove that it is God's will for some to remain sick. Any and all of those sick people could have been healed through faith in Jesus. In fact, this could be the reason why this one man was supernaturally healed—to draw those sick people's attention to Jesus, the One who could and would heal them if they would only believe.

Many times, "gifts of healings" fall under the category of "signs and wonders," that is, miracles designed to draw attention to Jesus. That is why New Testament evangelists like Philip were equipped with various "gifts of healings," because the miracles they performed drew attention to the gospel they were preaching (see Acts 8:5-8).

Sick Christians shouldn't wait around for someone with "gifts of healings" to come by and heal them because that person and gift may never come. Healing is available through faith in Jesus, and, although not everyone will be healed through gifts of healings, everyone can be healed through his or her faith. Gifts of healings are placed in the church primarily so that unbelievers might be healed and attention might be drawn to the gospel. This is not to say that Christians won't ever be healed through gifts of healings. God, however, expects His children to receive healing by faith.

One Example of a Person Healed By His Faith

Bartimaeus was a blind man who was healed by his faith in Jesus. Let's read his story in Mark's gospel.

> Then they came to Jericho. And as [Jesus] was leaving Jericho with His disciples and a large crowd, a blind beggar named Bartimaeus, the son of Timaeus, was sitting by the road. When he heard that it was Jesus the Nazarene, he began to cry out and say, "Jesus, Son of David, have mercy on me!" Many were sternly telling him to be quiet, but he kept crying out all the more, "Son of David, have mercy on me!" And Jesus stopped and said, "Call him here." So they called the blind man, saying to him, "Take courage, stand up! He is calling for you." Throwing aside his cloak, he jumped up and came to Jesus. And answering him, Jesus said, "What do you want Me to do for you?" And the blind man said to Him, "Rabboni, I want to regain my sight!" And Jesus said to him, "Go; your faith has made you well." Immediately he regained his sight and began following Him on the road (Mark 10:46-52).

First notice that Jesus didn't seek Bartimaeus. (This is the exact opposite of what happened with the man at the Pool of Bethesda). In fact, Jesus was walking past him, and if Bartimaeus hadn't cried out, Jesus would have kept on walking. That means Bartimaeus wouldn't have been healed.

Now think about that. What if Bartimaeus had sat there and said to himself, "Well, if it's Jesus' will for me to be healed, then He'll come over and heal me." What would have happened? Bartimaeus never would have been healed, even though this story plainly reveals it was Jesus' will for him to be healed. The first sign of Bartimaeus' faith is that he cried out to Jesus.

Second, notice that Bartimaeus would not be discouraged by the ones who were trying to quiet him down. When the people tried to silence him, he just cried out "all the more" (Mark 10:48). That shows his faith.

Third, notice that Jesus didn't respond to Bartimaeus' initial cries. Of course, it is possible that He couldn't hear Bartimaeus' initial cries, but if He did, Jesus didn't respond. In other words, Jesus let the man's faith be tested.

If Bartimaeus had given up after crying out only one time, he would not have been healed. We, too, must sometimes persevere in faith because many times it looks as if our prayer will not be answered. That is when our faith is tested, so we need to continue to stand, refusing to be discouraged by contrary circumstances.

Further Indications of Bartimaeus' Faith

When Jesus finally called him to come, the Bible says that Bartimaeus "cast aside his cloak." It is my understanding that blind people in Jesus' day wore a certain kind of cloak that identified them to the public as being blind. If this is true, perhaps Bartimaeus cast his cloak aside when Jesus called him because he believed he would no longer need to be identified as blind. If that was so, his faith was evident again.

Furthermore, when Bartimaeus cast aside his cloak, the Bible says he "jumped up," an indication of his excited anticipation that something good was about to happen to him. People who have faith for healing are excited when they pray for God to heal them because they are expecting to receive their healing.

Notice that Jesus tested Bartimaeus' faith once more as he stood before Him. He asked Bartimaeus what he desired, and from Bartimaeus' response, it is clear he believed Jesus could and would heal him of his blindness.

Finally, Jesus told him it was his faith that made him well. If Bartimaeus could be healed by faith, so can anyone else because God is "no respecter of persons."

For Further Study

Below I have listed twenty-one specific cases of healings performed by Jesus as recorded in the four Gospels. Jesus, of course, healed many more than twenty-one people, but in all of these cases we know some details about the sick individual and how he or she was healed.

I've broken the list down into two major categories—those who were healed by faith and those who were healed through gifts of healings. I've noted that in a number of cases when people where healed by their faith, Jesus told them to keep quiet about their healing. This further indicates that these were not "gifts of healings" because the sick people were not cured in order to advertise Jesus or the gospel.

Cases Where Faith or Believing is Mentioned as the Cause of Healing:

1. The centurion's servant (or "boy"): Matt. 8:5-13; Luke 7:2-10 "Let it be done to you as you have believed."

2. The paralytic lowered through the roof: Matt. 9:2-8; Mark 2:3-11; Luke 5:18-26 "Seeing their faith....He said...'go home.'"

3. Jairus' daughter: Matt. 9:18-26; Mark 5:22-43; Luke 8:41-56 "'Do not be afraid—only believe'....And He gave them strict orders that no one should know about this."

4. The woman with the issue of blood: Matt. 9:20-22; Mark 5:25-34; Luke 8:43-48 "Your faith has made you well."

5. Two blind men: Matt. 9:27-31 "Be it done to you according to your faith....See here, let no one know about this!"

6. Blind Bartimaeus: Mark 10:46-52; Luke 18:35-43 "Your faith has made you well."

7. The ten lepers: Luke 17:12-19 "Your faith has made you well."

8. The Nobleman's son: John 4:46-53 "The man believed the word that Jesus spoke to him."

In the next four cases, the faith of the sick person is not specifically mentioned, but it is implied by his words or actions. For example, the two blind men (in number 10 below) cried out to Jesus as He was passing by just as blind Bartimaeus did. All of the sick persons in the next four examples sought out Jesus, a clear indication of their faith. In three of the next four cases, Jesus told the ones He healed not to tell anyone about what had happened to them, indicating further that these cases were not "gifts of healings."

9. The leper who didn't know God's will: Matt. 8:2-4; Mark 1:40-45; Luke 5:12-14 "See that you say nothing to anyone."

10. Two blind men (probably one was Bartimaeus): Matt. 20:30-34 "[They] cried out, saying, 'Lord, have mercy on us!'"

11. The deaf and dumb man: Mark 7:32-36 "And he gave them orders not to tell anyone."

12. A blind man: Mark 8:22-26 "Do not even enter the village."

These final two cases of people who were healed through faith were actually not healed—they were delivered from demons. But Jesus credited their faith for effecting their deliverance.

13. The lunatic boy: Matt. 17:14-18; Mark 9:17-27; Luke 9:38-42 "And Jesus said to him...'All things are possible to him who believes.' Immediately the boy's father cried out...'I do believe; help my unbelief.'"

14. The Syrophoenician woman's daughter: Matt. 15:22-28; Mark 7:25-30 "O woman, your faith is great; be it done for you as you wish."

Cases of People Healed Through "Gifts of Healings":

These final seven cases are people who apparently were healed through gifts of healings. In the first three cases, however, obedience to a specific command of Jesus was required before the sick person could be healed. In none of these cases did Jesus tell the healed person not to tell anyone of his healing. And in none of these cases did the sick person seek out Jesus.

15. The man with the withered hand: Matt. 12:9-13; Mark 3:1-5; Luke 6:6-10 "Arise and come forward....Stretch out your hand."

16. The man at the Pool of Bethesda: John 5:2-9 "Arise, take up your pallet, and walk."

17. The man blind from birth: John 9:1-38 "Go, wash in the Pool of Siloam."

18. Peter's mother-in-law: Matt. 8:14-15; Mark 1:30-31; Luke 4:38-39

19. The woman who was bent over for 18 years: Luke 13:11-16

20. The man healed of dropsy: Luke 14:2-4
21. The high priest's slave: Luke 22:50-51

Notice that in all of the twenty-one examples above, there are no cases of an adult being healed *solely* by another adult's faith. In every case when someone was healed by another person's faith, it was always a child being healed through his parent's faith (see examples 1, 3, 8, 13, and 14).

The only possible exceptions would be examples number 1 and 2, the Centurion's servant and the paralytic lowered through the roof. In the case of the Centurion's servant, the Greek word translated *servant* is the word *pais*, which can also be translated *boy* as it is in Matthew 17:18: "And the *boy* was cured at once" (emphasis added).

If it was actually the centurion's servant and not his son, his servant must have been a young boy. Therefore, the centurion was responsible for the boy as a legal guardian and could exercise faith on his behalf just as any parent could for his or her child.

In the case of the paralytic lowered through the roof, note that the paralytic himself must have also possessed faith, otherwise he would never have allowed his friends to lower him through the roof. Thus he was not healed *solely* by the faith of his friends.

All of this indicates that it is unlikely that one adult's faith can result in the healing of another adult if that sick adult does not have faith himself. Yes an adult can pray in agreement with another adult who needs healing, but the sick person's unbelief can potentially nullify the effects of the other adult's faith.

Our own children, however, can be healed through our faith, up to a certain age. Yet they will eventually reach an age when God expects them to receive from Him based on their own faith.

I encourage you to study closely every example listed above in your own Bible to strengthen your faith in the healing provision of our Lord.

The Healing Anointing

Finally, it is important to know that Jesus was anointed with tangible healing power during His earthly ministry. That is, He could actually feel that healing anointing leaving His body, and in some cases the sick person who was being healed could feel that anointing as it entered his body. For example, Luke 6:19 says, "And all the people were trying to touch Him, for power was coming from Him and healing them all."

Apparently that healing anointing even saturated Jesus' clothes so that, if a sick person touched His garment in faith, the healing anointing would flow into his body. We read in Mark 6:56:

> Wherever He entered villages, or cities, or countryside, they were laying the sick in the market places, and im-

ploring Him that they might just touch the fringe of His cloak; and as many as touched it were being cured.

The woman with the issue of blood (see Mark 5:25-34) was healed by simply touching the fringe of Jesus' garment and expecting by faith to be healed.

Not only was Jesus anointed with a tangible healing anointing but so was the apostle Paul during the later years of his ministry:

> God was performing extraordinary miracles by the hands
> of Paul, so that handkerchiefs or aprons were even carried
> from his body to the sick, and the diseases left them and
> the evil spirits went out (Acts 19:11-12).

The tangible healing anointing saturated any cloths that were attached to Paul's body, evidently indicating that cloth is a good conductor of healing power!

God hasn't changed since the days of Jesus or Paul, so we shouldn't be surprised if God anoints some of His servants today with such a healing anointing, as He did Jesus and Paul. These gifts, however, are not passed out to novices, but only to those who have proven themselves faithful and unselfishly motivated over a period of time.

SEVENTEEN

The Gifts of the Spirit

The Bible is full of instances when men and women were given sudden supernatural abilities by the Holy Spirit. In the New Testament, these supernatural abilities are called "gifts of the Spirit." They are gifts in the sense that they cannot be earned. We should not forget, however, that God does promote those whom He can trust. Jesus said, "He who is faithful in a very little thing is faithful also in much; and he who is unrighteous in a very little thing is unrighteous also in much" (Luke 16:10). Thus we would expect that gifts of the Spirit would be more likely to be given to those who have proven their trustworthiness before God. Being fully consecrated and yielded to the Holy Spirit is important, as God is more likely to use those kinds of people supernaturally. On the other hand, God once used a donkey to prophesy, so He can use anyone He pleases. If He had to wait until we were perfect to use us, then He couldn't use any of us!

In the New Testament, the gifts of the Spirit are listed in 1 Corinthians 12, and there are nine altogether:

> For to one is given the word of wisdom through the Spirit, and to another the word of knowledge according to the same Spirit; to another faith by the same Spirit, and to another gifts of healing by the one Spirit, and to another the effecting of miracles, and to another prophecy, and to another the distinguishing of spirits, to another various kinds of tongues, and to another the interpretation of tongues (1 Cor. 12:8-10).

Knowing how to define each individual gift is not crucial to being used by God in the spiritual gifts. The Old Testament prophets, priests, and kings, as well as the ministers of the early New Testament church, all operated in the gifts of the Spirit without knowledge of how to categorize or define them. Nevertheless, because the gifts of the Spirit are categorized for us in the New Testament, it must be something that God wants us to understand. Indeed, Paul wrote, "Now concerning spiritual gifts, brethren, I do not want you to be unaware" (1 Cor. 12:1).

The Nine Gifts Categorized

The nine gifts of the Spirit have been further categorized in modern times into three groupings: (1) the utterance gifts, which are: various kinds of tongues, the interpretation of tongues, and prophecy; (2) the revelation gifts, which are: the word of wisdom, the word of knowledge, and discerning of spirits; and (3) the power gifts, which are: working of miracles, special faith, and gifts of healing. Three of these gifts *say* something; three of them *reveal* something; and three of them *do* something. All of these gifts were manifested under the old covenant with the exception of various kinds of tongues and the interpretation of tongues. Those two are distinctive of the new covenant.

The New Testament offers no instruction concerning the proper use of any of the "power gifts" and very little instruction about the proper use of the "revelation gifts." A significant amount of instruction, however, is given by Paul concerning the proper use of the "utterance gifts," and the reason for this is probably two-fold.

First, the utterance gifts are those manifested most often in church gatherings, while the revelation gifts are manifested less often, and the power gifts are manifested the least. We would need, therefore, more instruction concerning the gifts that would tend to be manifested most often in church gatherings.

Second, the utterance gifts seem to require the greatest degree of human cooperation, and they are, therefore, the gifts most likely to be mishandled. It is much easier to add to and ruin a prophecy than it is to ruin a gift of healing.

As the Spirit Wills

It is important to realize that gifts of the Spirit are given as the Spirit wills and not as any person wills. The Bible makes this quite clear:

> But one and the same Spirit works all these things, distributing to each one individually *just as He wills* (1 Cor. 12:11, emphasis added).

> God also testifying with them, both by signs and wonders and by various miracles and by gifts of the Holy Spirit *according to His own will* (Heb. 2:4, emphasis added).

A person might be used frequently in certain gifts, but no one *possesses* any of the gifts. Just because you are anointed once to work a miracle is no indication that you can work a miracle any time you desire; nor is it any guarantee that you will ever be used again to work a miracle.

We will briefly study and consider a few biblical examples of each gift. Keep in mind, however, that God can manifest His grace and power in an infinite number of ways, so it is impossible to define exactly how each gift will operate every single time. Moreover, there are no definitions of the nine spiritual gifts in Scripture—all we have are their labels. Thus we can only look at examples in the Bible and attempt to determine under which label each one should fall, ultimately defining them by their apparent differences. Because there are so many ways that the Holy Spirit can manifest Himself through supernatural gifts, it may be unwise to try to be overly strict in our definitions. Some gifts might actually be more like combinations of several gifts. Along these lines Paul wrote:

> Now there are *varieties* of gifts, but the same Spirit. And there are *varieties* of ministries, and the same Lord. There are *varieties* of effects [or operations], but the same God who works all things in all persons. But to each one is given the manifestation of the Spirit for the common good (1 Cor. 12:4-7, emphasis added).

The Power Gifts

1) The gifts of healings: Gifts of healings obviously have something to do with sick people being healed. They are often defined as sudden supernatural endowments to heal physically sick people, and I can't see any reason to question that. In the previous chapter we considered one example of a gift of healing manifested through Jesus when He healed the crippled man at the Pool of Bethesda (see John 5:2-17).

God used Elisha to heal leprous Naaman the Syrian, who was an idol-worshiper (see 2 Ki. 5:1-14). As we learned when examining Jesus' words in Luke 4:27 concerning Naaman's healing, Elisha couldn't heal any leper any time he desired. He was suddenly supernaturally inspired to instruct Naaman to dip in the Jordan River seven times, and when Naaman ultimately obeyed, he was cleansed of his leprosy.

God used Peter to heal the crippled man at the gate called Beautiful through a gift of healing (Acts 3:1-10). Not only was the crippled man healed, but the supernatural sign drew many people to hear the gospel from Peter's lips, and about five thousand people were added to the church that day. Gifts of healings frequently serve a dual purpose of healing sick people *and* drawing the unsaved to Christ.

When Peter was delivering his message to those who gathered that day, he said:

> Men of Israel, why do you marvel at this, or why do you gaze at us, as if by our own power or piety we had made him walk? (Acts. 3:12).

Peter recognized that it wasn't because of any power that he possessed in himself, or because of his great holiness, that God used him to heal the crippled man. Remember that Peter, just two months prior to this miracle, had denied he ever knew Jesus. Just the fact that God used Peter so miraculously in the first pages of Acts should bolster our confidence that God will also use us as He wills.

When Peter tried to explain how the man had been healed, it is highly unlikely that he could have categorized it as a "gift of healing." All Peter knew was that he and John had been walking by a crippled man and he suddenly found himself anointed with faith for the man to be healed. So he commanded the man to walk in the name of Jesus, seized him by the right hand, and lifted him up. The crippled man began "walking and leaping and praising God." Peter explained it this way:

> And on the basis of faith in His name, it is the name of Jesus which has strengthened this man whom you see and know; and the faith which comes through Him has given him this perfect health in the presence of you all (Acts. 3:16).

It takes a special faith to seize a crippled man by the arm and lift him up and expect him to walk! Along with this particular gift of healing an impartation of faith would have also been needed to bring it to pass.

Some have suggested that the reason this gift is in the plural (that is, "gifts" of healings) is because there are different gifts that heal different kinds of sicknesses. Those who have been used frequently in gifts of healings sometimes discover that particular sicknesses are healed through their ministries more frequently than other sicknesses. For example, Philip the evangelist seemed to have particular success in getting paralyzed and lame people healed (Acts 8:7). There are some evangelists of the past century, for example, who have had greater success with blindness or deafness or heart problems, and so on, depending upon which gifts of healings were manifested through them most frequently.

2) The gift of faith and the working of miracles: The gift of faith and the gift of the working of miracles would seem to be very similar. With both gifts, the individual who is anointed suddenly receives faith for the impossible. The difference between the two is often described this way: With the gift of faith, the anointed individual is given faith to *receive* a miracle for himself, whereas with the gift of the working of miracles, the individual is given faith to *work* a miracle for another.

The gift of faith is sometimes referred to as "special faith" because it is a sudden impartation of faith that goes beyond *ordinary* faith. Ordinary faith comes from hearing a promise of God, whereas special faith comes from a sudden impartation by the Holy Spirit. Those who have experienced this gift of special faith report that things they would consider impossible suddenly become possible, and, in fact, they find it *impossible to doubt*. The same would be true for the gift of working of miracles.

The story of Daniel's three friends, Shadrach, Meshach, and Abed-nego provides an excellent example of how "special faith" makes it impossible to doubt. When they were cast into the fiery furnace for refusing to bow before the king's idol, they were all given the gift of special faith. It would take more than ordinary faith to survive being cast alive into white-hot flames! Let's look at the faith these three young men displayed before the king:

> Shadrach, Meshach and Abed-nego answered and said to the king, "O Nebuchadnezzar, we do not need to give you an answer concerning this. If it be so [if you are going to cast us into the furnace], our God whom we serve is able to deliver us from the furnace of blazing fire; and *He will deliver us out of your hand*, O king. But if not [if you don't throw us into the fiery furnace], let it be known to you, O king, that we are not going to serve your gods or worship the golden image that you have set up" (Dan. 3:16-18, emphasis added).

Notice that the gift was operating even before they were cast into the furnace. There was no doubt in their minds that God was about to deliver them.

Elijah operated in the gift of special faith when he was fed daily by ravens during the three-and-a-half year famine of evil King Ahab's reign (see 2 Kin. 17:1-6). It takes more than ordinary faith to trust God to use birds to bring you food morning and evening. Although God has not promised us anywhere in His Word that ravens will bring our food each day, we can use ordinary faith to trust God for our needs to be met—because that's a promise (see Matt. 6:25-34).

The working of miracles was in operation quite frequently through the ministry of Moses. He operated in this gift when he split the Red Sea (see Ex. 14:13-31) and when the various plagues came upon Egypt.

Jesus operated in the working of miracles when He fed the 5,000 by multiplying a few fish and a few loaves of bread (see Matt. 14:15-21).

When Paul caused Elymas the magician to be blind for a season because he was hindering Paul's ministry on the island of Cyprus, that too would be an example of the working of miracles (see Acts 13:4-12).

The Revelation Gifts

1). The word of knowledge and word of wisdom: The gift of the *word of knowledge* is often defined as a sudden supernatural impartation of certain information, past or present. God, who possesses all knowledge, will at times impart a small portion of that knowledge, which is perhaps why it is called a *word* of knowledge. A word is a fragmentary part of a sentence, and a word of knowledge would be a fragmentary portion of God's knowledge.

The *word of wisdom* is very similar to the word of knowledge, but it is often defined as a sudden supernatural impartation of the knowledge of *future* events. The concept of *wisdom* normally involves something regarding the future. Again, these definitions are somewhat speculative.

Let's look at an Old Testament example of the word of knowledge. After Elisha cleansed Naaman the Syrian of leprosy, Naaman offered Elisha a very large sum of money in gratitude for his healing. Elisha refused the gift, lest anyone think Naaman's healing was purchased rather than graciously granted by God. Elisha's servant, Gehazi, however, saw an opportunity to gain personal riches, and he secretively received some of Naaman's intended payment. After Gehazi had hidden his deceitfully acquired silver, he appeared before Elisha. We then read,

> And Elisha said to him, "Where have you been, Gehazi?" And he said, "Your servant went nowhere." Then he said to him, "Did not my heart go with you, when the man turned from his chariot to meet you?" (2 Kin. 5:25b-26a).

God, who knew full well Gehazi's dirty deed, revealed it supernaturally to Elisha. This story makes it obvious, however, that Elisha didn't "possess" the gift of the word of knowledge; that is, he didn't know everything about everyone all the time. If that had been the case, Gehazi would never have imagined he could conceal his sin. Elisha only knew things supernaturally when God occasionally revealed those things to him. The gift operated as the Spirit willed.

Jesus operated in the word of knowledge when He told the woman at the well of Samaria that she had had five husbands (see John 4:17-18).

Peter was used in this gift when he supernaturally knew that Ananias and Sapphira were lying to the congregation about giving the church the full price they had received for their recently-sold land (see Acts 5:1-11).

As for the gift of the word of wisdom, we see frequent manifestations of this gift throughout all of the Old Testament prophets. Whenever they predicted a future event, the word of wisdom was in operation. Jesus was granted this gift quite frequently, too. He predicted the destruction of Jerusalem, His own crucifixion, and events that would befall the world before His second coming (see Luke 17:22-36, 21:6-28).

The apostle John was used in this gift as the judgments of the Tribulation Period were revealed to him. These he recorded for us throughout the book of Revelation.

2). The gift of discerning of spirits: The gift of discerning of spirits is often defined as a sudden supernatural ability to see or otherwise discern what is occurring in the spiritual realm.

A vision, seen through the eyes or mind of a believer, could be classified as discerning of spirits. This gift might permit a believer to see angels, demons, or even Jesus Himself, as did Paul on several occasions (see Acts 18:9-10; 22:17-21; 23:11).

When Elisha and his servant were being pursued by the Syrian army, they found themselves trapped in the city of Dothan. At that point, Elisha's servant looked out over the city's walls and, seeing the masses of soldiers assembling, became quite concerned:

> So [Elisha] answered, "Do not fear, for those who are with us are more than those who are with them." Then Elisha prayed and said, "O Lord, I pray, open his eyes that he may see." And the Lord opened the servant's eyes, and he saw; and behold, the mountain was full of horses and chariots of fire all around Elisha" (2 Kin. 6:16-17).

Did you know that angels ride around on spiritual horses and in spiritual chariots? You'll see them one day in heaven, but Elisha's servant was granted the ability to see them on earth.

Through this gift, a believer might discern an evil spirit oppressing someone and have the ability to identify what kind of spirit it is.

This gift would include not only seeing into the spiritual realm but any other kind of discernment into the spiritual realm. It could involve, for example, hearing something from the spiritual realm, like the very voice of God.

Finally, this gift is not, as some have thought, "the gift of discernment." People who claim to have this gift sometimes think that they can discern the motives of others, but their gift could be more rightly described as the "gift of criticism and passing judgment on others." The truth is, you probably had that "gift" before you were saved, and now that you are saved, God wants to deliver you from it permanently!

The Utterance Gifts

1). The gift of prophecy: The gift of prophecy is the sudden supernatural ability to speak by divine inspiration in the speaker's known language. It can always begin with, "Thus says the Lord."

This gift is not preaching or teaching. Inspired preaching and teaching do contain an *element* of prophecy because they are anointed by the Spirit, but they are not prophecy in its strictest sense. Many times an anointed preacher or teacher will say things by sudden inspiration that he didn't plan on saying, but that is really not prophecy, although I suppose it could be considered *prophetic*.

The gift of prophecy by itself serves to edify, exhort and console:

> But one who prophesies speaks to men for edification and exhortation and consolation (1 Cor. 14:3).

Thus the gift of prophecy, by itself, contains no revelation. That is, it doesn't reveal anything about the past, present, or future, as do the word of wisdom and word of knowledge. As I stated previously, however, the gifts of the Spirit can work in conjunction with one another, and so the word of wisdom or word of knowledge can be conveyed by means of prophecy.

When we hear someone deliver a prophecy in a gathering that foretells future events, we really didn't hear *just* a prophecy; we heard a word of wisdom conveyed through the gift of prophecy. The simple gift of prophecy will sound very much as if someone were reading exhortations from the Bible, such as "Be strong in the Lord and in the strength of his might" and, "I will never leave you nor forsake you."

Some are convinced that New Testament prophecy should never contain anything "negative," otherwise it supposedly does not fit the parameters of "edification and exhortation and consolation." That, however, is not true. To limit what God may say to His people, only permitting Him to say what they consider "positive" even if they may deserve some rebuke, is to exalt oneself above God. Rebuke can definitely fall under the categories of both *edification* and *exhortation*. I noticed the Lord's messages to the seven churches in Asia, recorded in John's Revelation, certainly contain an element of rebuke. Shall we discard them? I don't think so.

2). The gift of various kinds of tongues and the interpretation of tongues: The gift of *various kinds of tongues* is the sudden supernatural ability to speak in a language that is unknown to the speaker. This gift would normally be accompanied by the gift of *the interpretation of tongues*, which is a sudden supernatural ability to interpret what was said in an unknown language.

This gift is called the *interpretation* of tongues and not the *translation* of tongues. So we should not expect word-for-word translations of messages in tongues. For that reason it is possible to have a short "message in tongues" and a longer interpretation, and vice versa.

The gift of the interpretation of tongues is very similar to prophecy because it also contains no revelation in itself and would normally be for edification, exhortation, and consolation. We could almost say that, according to 1 Corinthians 14:5, tongues plus interpretation of tongues equals prophecy:

> And greater is one who prophesies than one who speaks
> in tongues, unless he interprets, so that the church may
> receive edifying.

As I previously stated, there is no instruction given in the Bible regarding how to operate in the power gifts, very little instruction about how to operate in the revelation gifts, but quite a lot of instruction given on how to operate in the utterance gifts. Because there was some confusion in the Corinthian church regarding the operation of the utterance gifts, Paul devoted almost the entire fourteenth chapter of First Corinthians to that issue.

The foremost problem concerned the proper usage of speaking in other tongues, because as we have already learned in the chapter about the baptism in the Holy Spirit, every believer who is baptized in the Holy Spirit has the ability to pray in tongues any time he desires. The Corinthians were doing a lot of speaking in tongues during their church services, but much of it was out of order.

The Different Uses of Other Tongues

It is of utmost importance that we understand the difference between the public use of unknown tongues and the private use. Although every Holy Spirit-baptized believer can speak in tongues at any time, that does not mean God will use him in the public gift of various kinds of tongues. The *primary* use of speaking in tongues is in the private devotional life of each believer. The Corinthians, however, were coming together and speaking in tongues without any interpretation, and, of course, no one was being helped or edified by it (see 1 Corinthians 14:6-12, 16-19, 23, 26-28).

One way to differentiate between the public use of tongues and the private use of tongues is to classify the private use as *praying* in tongues and the public use as *speaking* in other tongues. Paul mentions both uses in the fourteenth chapter of his first letter to the Corinthians. What are the differences?

When we *pray* in tongues, our spirits are praying *to* God (see 1 Cor. 14:2, 14). Yet, when someone is suddenly anointed with the gift of various kinds of tongues, it is a message *from* God *to* the congregation (see 1 Cor. 14:5), and it is understood once the interpretation is given.

According to Scripture, we can pray in tongues as *we* will (see 1 Cor. 14:15), but the gift of various kinds of tongues only operates as the *Holy Spirit* wills (see 1 Cor. 12:11).

The gift of various kinds of tongues would normally be accompanied by the gift of the interpretation of tongues. The private use of praying in tongues, however, would normally not be interpreted. Paul said that when he prayed in tongues his mind was unfruitful (see 1 Cor. 14:14).

When an individual prays in tongues only *he* is edified (see 1 Cor. 14:4), but the *entire congregation* is edified when the gift of various kinds of tongues is in manifestation with the accompanying gift of the interpretation of tongues (see 1 Cor. 14:4b-5).

Every believer should pray in tongues every day as part of his daily fellowship with the Lord. One of the wonderful things about praying in tongues is that it doesn't require the use of your mind. That means you can pray in tongues even when your mind must be occupied with your work or other things. Paul said to the Corinthians, "I thank God, I speak in tongues *more than you all*" (1 Cor. 14:18, emphasis added). He must have spent a lot of time speaking in tongues to outdo the entire Corinthian Church!

Paul also wrote that when we pray in tongues, we are sometimes "blessing the Lord" (1 Cor. 14:16-17). Three times I have had my "prayer language" understood by someone present who knew the language in which I was praying. All three times I was speaking in Japanese. Once I said to the Lord in Japanese, "You are so good." Another time I said, "Thank you very much." On another occasion I said, "Come quickly, come quickly; I am waiting." Isn't that amazing? I've never learned a word of Japanese, but at least three times I've "blessed the Lord" in the Japanese language!

Paul's Instructions for Speaking in Tongues

Paul's instructions to the Corinthian church were very specific. In any given gathering, the number of people who were permitted to speak out publicly in tongues was limited to two or three. They should not all speak at once, but should wait and speak in turn (see 1 Cor. 14:27).

Paul did not necessarily mean that only three "messages in tongues" were permitted, but that no more than three people should speak out in tongues in any given service. It is thought by some that if there were more than three people who were frequently used in the gift of various kinds of tongues, any one of them could yield to the Spirit and given a "message in tongues" that the Spirit desired to be manifested in the church. If this is not so, Paul's instruction would actually limit the Holy Spirit by limiting the number of messages in tongues that could be manifested in any given meeting. If the Holy Spirit would never give any more than three gifts of various kinds of tongues in a gathering, there would be no need for Paul to give such intstructions.

The same could well be true for the interpretation of tongues. It is thought that perhaps more than one person in the assembly might be able to yield to the Spirit and give the interpretation of a "message in tongues." Such people would be considered "interpreters" (see 1 Cor. 14:28), as they would be used frequently in the gift of interpretation of tongues. If that is true, perhaps that is what Paul was referring to when he instructed, "let one interpret" (1 Cor. 14:27). Perhaps he was not saying that only one person should interpret *all* the messages in tongues; rather he was warning against "competitive interpretations" of the same message. If one interpreter interpreted a message in tongues, then another interpreter was not permitted to interpret the same message, even if he thought he could give a better interpretation.

In general, everything should be done "properly and in an orderly manner" in church gatherings—they should not be a hodgepodge of simultaneous, confusing and even competitive utterances. Additionally, believers should be sensitive to any unbelievers who may be present in their gatherings, just as Paul wrote:

> If therefore the whole church should assemble together and all speak in tongues, and ungifted men or unbelievers enter, will they not say that you are mad? (1 Cor. 14:23).

That was precisely the problem in Corinth—everyone was speaking in tongues simultaneously, and often there were no interpretations.

Some Instruction Concerning Revelation Gifts

Paul offered some instruction regarding the "revelation gifts" in regard to their manifestation through prophets:

> And let two or three prophets speak, and let the others pass judgment. But if a revelation is made to another who is seated, let the first keep silent. For you can all prophesy one by one, so that all may learn and all may be exhorted; and the spirits of prophets are subject to prophets; for God is not a God of confusion but of peace, as in all the churches of the saints (1 Cor. 14:29-33).

Just as there were members of the body in Corinth who apparently were frequently used in the gift of the interpretation of tongues who were known as "interpreters," so there were those who were frequently used in the gifts of prophecy and revelation who were considered "prophets." These would not be prophets in the same class as Old Testament prophets or even someone like Agabus in the New Testament (see Acts. 11:28; 21:10). Rather, their ministries would have been limited to their local church bodies.

Although there might be more than three such prophets present at a church gathering, again Paul placed limitations, specifically limiting prophetic ministry to "two or three prophets." This again suggests that when the Spirit was giving spiritual gifts in a gathering, more than one person might yield to receiving those gifts. If this is not so, Paul's instruction could result in the Spirit giving gifts that would never be enjoyed by the body, as he limited how many prophets could speak.

If there were more than three prophets present, the others, although restrained from speaking, could help by judging what was said. This also would indicate their ability to discern what the Spirit was saying and possibly imply that they could have yielded to the Spirit themselves to be used in the very gifts that were manifested through the other prophets. Otherwise they could have only judged prophecies and revelations in a general way, by making certain they were in agreement with revelation God has already given (such as in Scripture), something any mature believer could do.

Paul stated that these prophets could all prophesy sequentially (see 1

Cor. 14:31) and that "the spirits of prophets are subject to prophets" (1 Cor. 14:32), indicating that each prophet could restrain himself from interrupting another, even when given a prophecy or revelation from the Spirit to share with the congregation. This shows that the Spirit might give gifts at the same time to several prophets present in a gathering, but each prophet could and should control when his revelations or prophecies were to be shared with the body.

This is also true concerning any utterance gift that might be manifested through any believer. If a person receives a message in tongues or prophecy from the Lord, he can hold it until the proper time in the gathering. It would be wrong to interrupt someone else's prophecy or teaching to give your prophecy.

When Paul stated, "you can all prophesy one by one" (1 Cor. 14:31), remember that he was speaking in the context of prophets who had received prophecies. Some have unfortunately taken Paul's words out of context, saying that *every* believer can prophesy at *every* gathering of the body. The gift of prophecy is given as the Spirit wills.

Today, as much as ever, the church needs the Holy Spirit's help, power, presence and gifts. Paul instructed the Corinthian believers to "desire earnestly spiritual gifts, but especially that you may prophesy" (1 Cor. 14:1). This indicates that our level of desire has something to do with the manifestation of the Spirit's gifts, otherwise Paul would not have given such instructions. The disciple-making minister, desiring to be used by God for His glory, will indeed earnestly desire spiritual gifts and will teach his disciples to do the same.

EIGHTEEN

The Ministry Gifts

But to each one of us grace was given according to the measure of Christ's gift....And He gave some as *apostles*, and some as *prophets*, and some as *evangelists*, and some as *pastors* and *teachers*, for the equipping of the saints for the work of service, to the building up of the body of Christ; until we all attain to the unity of the faith, and of the knowledge of the Son of God, to a mature man, to the measure of the stature which belongs to the fullness of Christ (Eph. 4:7, 11-13, emphasis added).

And God has appointed in the church, first *apostles*, second *prophets*, third *teachers*, then *miracles*, then *gifts of healings, helps, administrations, various kinds of tongues* (1 Cor. 12:28, emphasis added).

The *ministry gifts*, as they are often called, are the callings and various abilities given to certain believers that enable them to stand in the offices of apostle, prophet, evangelist, pastor or teacher. No one can put himself or herself into one of these offices. Rather, one must be called and gifted by God.

It is possible that one person might occupy more than one of these five offices, but only certain combinations are feasible. For example, it is possible that a believer might be called to stand in the office of pastor and teacher or of prophet and teacher. It would be unlikely, however, that one could stand in the office of pastor and evangelist simply because the pastor's ministry requires that he remain in one place serving a local flock, and thus he could not fulfill the calling of an evangelist who must travel frequently.

Although these five offices are all gifted differently for different purposes, they have all been given to the church for one general purpose—for the "equipping of the saints for the work of service" (Eph. 4:12).[60] *The goal of every minister should be to equip holy people* (which is what the word "saints" means) *for acts of service.* Too often, however, those in ministry act as if they are called, not to equip holy people for service, but to entertain carnal people who sit in services—church services. Every person called to one of these offices should constantly evaluate his contribution to the "equipping of the saints for the work of service." If every minister did, many would eliminate numerous activities erroneously considered "ministry."

Were Some Ministry Gifts Only for the Early Church?

How long will these ministry gifts be given to the church? Jesus will give them as long as His holy people need to be equipped for service, which is at least until He returns. The church constantly takes in newborn Christians who need to grow, and the rest of us always have room to mature spiritually.

Some have unfortunately concluded that only two kinds of ministries exist today—pastors and evangelists—as if God has changed His plan. No, we still need apostles, prophets and teachers as much as the early church did. The reason we don't see examples of these gifts among much of the church around the world is simply because Jesus gives these gifts to *His* church, not the phony, unholy, false-gospel church. In the phony church can be found only those who make a feeble attempt to fulfill the roles of some of the ministry gifts (mostly pastors and perhaps a few evangelists), but they hardly resemble the God-called and anointed ministry gifts that Jesus gives to *His* church. They certainly aren't equipping the holy people for acts of service, because the very gospel they proclaim doesn't result in holiness; it only deceives people into thinking they are forgiven. And those people have no desire to be equipped for service. They have no intention of denying themselves and taking up their crosses.

How do You Know if You are Called?

How does a person know if he or she is called to one of these offices in the church? First and foremost, he will feel a divine calling from God. He will find himself burdened to fulfill a certain task. This is much more than simply seeing a need that could be filled. Rather, it is a God-given hunger within that *compels* a person into a certain ministry. If he is truly called of God, he cannot be satisfied until he begins to fulfill his calling. This has nothing to do with being appointed by a man or a committee of people. God is the one who does the calling.

Second, the truly-called person will find himself equipped by God to

---

[60] This is just another way of saying, "For making disciples of Jesus Christ."

fulfill his God-given task. Each of the five offices carries with it a supernatural anointing that enables the individual to do what God has called him to do. With the calling comes the anointing. *If there is no anointing, there is no calling.* One may aspire to function in a certain ministry, attend Bible School for four years educating himself and preparing for that ministry, but without the anointing from God, he has no chance of true success.

Third, he will find that God has opened some door of opportunity for him to exercise his particular gifts. In this way he can prove himself faithful, and eventually he will be entrusted with greater opportunities, responsibilities and gifts.

If a person hasn't felt a divine inner compulsion and calling to one of the five ministry gifts, or if he isn't aware of any special anointing to fulfill a God-given task, or if no opportunity has arisen to exercise the gifts he thinks he possesses, that person should not attempt to be something God has not called him to be. Rather, he should work to be a blessing among his local church body, his neighborhood, and at his workplace. Even though he isn't called to the "five-fold" ministry, he is called to serve using the gifts God has given him, and he should strive to prove himself faithful.

Although Scripture mentions five ministry gifts, this does not mean that every person who stands in a certain office will have an identical ministry. Paul wrote that "varieties of ministries" exist (1 Cor. 12:5), making variations between ministers who stand in the same office possible. Furthermore, there seem to be various levels of anointing resting upon those in these offices, so we could further categorize each office by degree of anointing. For example, there are some teachers that appear to be more anointed in certain ways than other teachers. The same is true of the other ministry gifts. I personally believe that any minister can do things that will result in an increased anointing upon his ministry, such as prove himself faithful over a period of time and deeply consecrate himself to God.

A Closer Look at the Office of Apostle

The Greek word translated *apostle* is *apostolos* and literally means "one who is sent." A true New Testament apostle is a believer divinely sent to a certain place or places to establish churches. He lays the spiritual foundation of God's "building" and is somewhat comparable to a "general contractor," as Paul, an apostle himself, wrote:

> For we are God's fellow-workers; you are God's field, God's building. According to the grace of God which was given to me, as a wise *master builder* I laid a foundation, and another is building upon it (1 Cor. 3:9-10a, emphasis added).

A "master builder," or general contractor, oversees the entire building process—he envisions the finished product. He's not a specialist like the carpenter or the bricklayer. He *may* be able to do the work of a carpenter or bricklayer, but probably not as well as they can. Likewise, the apostle has the ability to do the work of an evangelist or pastor, but only for a limited time as he establishes churches. (The apostle Paul usually remained in one place from six months to three years).

The apostle is best at establishing churches and then overseeing them to keep them on God's course. An apostle is responsible for installing elders/pastors/overseers to shepherd each congregation he plants (see Acts 14:21-23; Tit. 1:5).

True and False Apostles

It seems that some ministers today, longing for authority over churches, are quick to proclaim their supposed calling to be apostles, but most have a big problem. Since they've established no churches (or perhaps only one or two) and don't have the gifts and anointing of a biblical apostle, they must find gullible pastors who will allow them to have authority over their churches. If you are a pastor, don't be fooled by these self-exalted, power-hungry false apostles. They are usually wolves in sheep's clothing. Often they are after money. Scripture warns against false apostles (see 2 Cor. 11:13; Rev. 2:2). If they have to tell you that they are apostles, that is probably an indication that they are not apostles. Their fruit should speak for itself.

A pastor who establishes his own church and stays to pastor it for years is not an apostle. Such pastors, *perhaps*, could be referred to as "apostolic pastors" since they pioneered their own church. Still, they don't stand in the office of apostle because an apostle continually plants churches.

A truly God-sent and anointed "missionary," as they are often called today, whose main calling is to establish churches, would stand in the office of an apostle. On the other hand, missionaries who work at setting up Bible schools or training pastors would not be apostles but teachers.

A true apostle's ministry is characterized by supernatural signs and wonders, which are instrumental in helping him establish churches. Paul wrote:

> In no respect was I inferior to the most eminent apostles, even though I am a nobody. The signs of a true apostle were performed among you with all perseverance, by signs and wonders and miracles (2 Cor. 12:11b-12).

If a person doesn't have signs and wonders accompanying his ministry, he is not an apostle. Obviously, true apostles are rare, and they don't exist in the phony, unholy, false-gospel church. I find them mainly in the places of the world that still have virgin territory for the gospel.

The High Rank of the Apostle

In both New Testament lists of the ministry gifts, the office of apostle is listed first, indicating that it is the highest calling (see Eph. 4:11; 1 Cor. 12:28).

No one begins his ministry as an apostle. A person may be called to be an apostle *eventually*, but he won't start out in that office. He must first prove himself to be faithful over a period of years in preaching and teaching, then, eventually, he will stand in the office God has prepared for him. Paul was called from his mother's womb to be an apostle, but he spent many years in fulltime ministry before he finally stood in that office (see Gal. 1:15-2:1). He actually began as a teacher and a prophet (see Acts 13:1-2), and was later promoted to be an apostle when he was sent out by the Holy Spirit (see Acts 14:14).

We find mention of other apostles besides Paul and the original twelve in Acts 1:15-26; 14:14; Rom. 16:7; 2 Cor. 8:23; Gal. 1:17-19; Phil. 2:25 and 1 Thes. 1:1 with 2:6. (The word translated *messenger* in 2 Cor. 8:23 and Phil. 2:25 is the Greek word *apostolos*.) This dispels the theory that the apostolic office was limited to only twelve men.

Only twelve apostles, however, can be classified as "Apostles of the Lamb," and only those twelve will have a special place in the millennial reign of Christ (see Matt. 19:28; Rev. 21:14). We no longer need apostles like Peter, James and John who were uniquely inspired to write Scripture, because the Bible revelation is complete. Today, however, we still need apostles who establish churches by the power of the Holy spirit, just as Paul and other apostles did, as described in the book of Acts.

The Office of Prophet

A prophet is one who receives supernatural revelation and speaks by divine inspiration. Naturally, he is used frequently in the spiritual gift of prophecy as well as the revelation gifts: the word of wisdom, the word of knowledge, and discerning of spirits.

Any believer may be used of God in the gift of prophecy as the Spirit wills, but that does not make him a prophet. A prophet is, first of all, a minister who can preach or teach with an anointing. Because the prophet seems to be the second highest calling (see the order as it is listed in 1 Cor. 12:28), even a fulltime minister would not be placed in the office of a prophet until he has been in ministry for some years. If he does stand in that office, he will have the supernatural equipment that goes with it.

Two men who are named as prophets in the New Testament are Judas and Silas. We read in Acts 15:32 that they delivered a lengthy prophecy to the church in Antioch:

> And Judas and Silas, also being prophets themselves, encouraged and strengthened the brethren with a lengthy message.

Another New Testament example of a prophet would be Agabus. In Acts 11:27-28 we read:

> Now at this time some prophets came down from Jerusa-
> lem to Antioch. And one of them stood up and began to
> indicate by the Spirit that there would certainly be a great
> famine all over the world. And this took place in the reign
> of Claudius.

Notice that Agabus was given a word of wisdom—something about
the future was revealed to him. Of course, Agabus didn't know everything that would happen in the future, he only knew what the Holy Spirit
willed to reveal to him.

In Acts 21:10-11, there is another example of the word of wisdom operating through Agabus' ministry. This time it was on behalf of one person,
Paul:

> And as we were staying there for some days, a certain
> prophet named Agabus came down from Judea. And com-
> ing to us, he took Paul's belt and bound his own feet and
> hands, and said, "This is what the Holy Spirit says: 'In this
> way the Jews at Jerusalem will bind the man who owns this
> belt and deliver him into the hands of the Gentiles.'"

It is scriptural under the new covenant to seek personal guidance from
prophets? No. The reason is because all believers have the Holy Spirit
within them to guide them. A prophet should only *confirm* to a believer
what he already knows is God's direction in his own spirit. For example,
when Agabus prophesied to Paul, he gave him no direction as to what he
was supposed to do; he only confirmed what Paul had known for some
time.

As stated previously, Paul stood in the office of a prophet (and teacher)
before he was called to the ministry of an apostle (see Acts 13:1). We know
that Paul received revelations from the Lord according to Gal. 1:11-12, and
he also had a number of visions (see Acts 9:1-9; 18:9-10; 22:17-21; 23:11; 2
Cor. 12:1-4).

As with true apostles, we don't find true prophets within the false
church. The false church would (and does) shun true prophets like Silas,
Judas or Agabus. The reason is because true prophets would bring a revelation of God's displeasure of their disobedience (as did John to most of
the churches of Asia Minor in the first two chapters of Revelation). The
false church isn't open to that.

The Office of Teacher

According to the listed order in 1 Corinthians 12:28, the office of teacher
is the third highest calling. A teacher is one who is supernaturally anointed to teach the Word of God. Just because someone teaches the Bible does
not mean he is a New Testament teacher. Many teach simply because they
like to or feel obligated to, but a person who stands in the office of teacher

is supernaturally gifted to teach. He is often given supernatural revelation concerning the Word of God and can explain the Bible in a manner that makes it understandable and applicable.

Apollos is a New Testament example of one who stood in this office. Paul compared his apostolic ministry and the teaching ministry of Apollos in 1 Corinthians by saying:

> I planted, *Apollos watered,* but God was causing the growth....I laid a foundation, and *another is building upon it* (1 Cor. 3:6, 10b, emphasis added).

Apollos the teacher did not do the original planting or laying of the foundation. Instead, he watered the new sprouts with the Word of God and built walls on the existing foundation.

Apollos is also mentioned in Acts 18:27:

> And when he [Apollos] wanted to go across to Achaia, the brethren encouraged him and wrote to the disciples to welcome him; and when he arrived, he helped greatly those who had believed through grace; for he powerfully refuted the Jews in public, demonstrating by the Scriptures that Jesus was the Christ.

Notice that Apollos "helped greatly" people who were already Christians and that his teaching was described as "powerful." Anointed teaching is always powerful.

For the church, the teaching ministry is even more important than the working of miracles or gifts of healings. That is why it is listed before those gifts in 1 Corinthians 12:28:

> And God has appointed in the church, *first* apostles, *second* prophets, *third* teachers, *then* miracles, *then* gifts of healings (emphasis added).

Unfortunately, believers are sometimes more attracted to seeing healings than to listening to the clear teaching of the Word that will produce spiritual growth and holiness in their lives.

The Bible speaks of both preaching and teaching. Teaching is more logical and instructional, whereas preaching is more inspirational and motivational. Evangelists generally preach. Teachers and pastors generally teach. Apostles preach and teach. It is to be regretted that some believers don't recognize the value of teaching. Some even think that the only time speakers are anointed is if they are preaching loud and fast! That is just not so.

Jesus is the best example of an anointed teacher. His teaching was such a predominate part of His ministry that many addressed Him as "Teacher" (Matt. 8:19; Mark 5:35; John 11:28).

For further study about teachers and teaching, see Acts 2:42; 5:21, 25, 28, 42; 11:22-26; 13:1; 15:35; 18:11; 20:18-20; 28:30-31; Rom. 12:6-7; 1 Cor. 4:17; Gal. 6:6; Col. 1:28; 1 Tim. 4:11-16; 5:17; 6:2; 2 Tim. 1:11; 2:2 and Jas. 3:1. The last scripture listed tells us that teachers will incur a stricter judgment, and so they ought to be very cautious what they teach. They should only teach the Word.

The Office of Evangelist

The evangelist is one who is anointed to preach the gospel. His messages are designed to lead people to repentance and faith in the Lord Jesus Christ. They are accompanied by miracles that attract the attention of unbelievers and convict them of the truthfulness of his message.

No doubt there were many evangelists in the early church, but only one man is listed in the book of Acts as being an evangelist. His name was Philip: "And entering the house of *Philip the evangelist,* who was one of the seven, we stayed with him" (Acts 21:8, emphasis added).

Philip began his ministry as a servant (or perhaps "deacon") who waited on tables (see Acts 6:1-6). He was promoted to the office of evangelist around the time of the persecution of the church that arose in connection with Stephen's martyrdom. His first preached the gospel in Samaria:

> And Philip went down to the city of Samaria and began proclaiming Christ to them. And the multitudes with one accord were giving attention to what was said by Philip, as they heard and saw the signs which he was performing. For in the case of many who had unclean spirits, they were coming out of them shouting with a loud voice; and many who had been paralyzed and lame were healed. And there was much rejoicing in that city (Acts 8:5-8).

Notice that Philip had one message—Christ. His goal was to begin making disciples, that is, obedient followers of Christ. He proclaimed Christ as miracle worker, Son of God, Lord, Savior and soon-coming Judge. He urged people to repent and follow his Lord.

Also notice that Philip was equipped with supernatural signs and wonders that authenticated his message. One who stands in the office of evangelist will be anointed with gifts of healings and other spiritual gifts. The false church has only false evangelists who proclaim a false gospel. The world is full of such evangelists today, and it is obvious that God is not confirming their message with miracles and healings. The simple reason is because they are not preaching His gospel. They don't really preach Christ. They usually preach about people's needs and how Christ can give them abundant life, or they preach a formula of salvation that doesn't include repentance. They lead people into a false conversion that salves their guilt but doesn't save them. The results of their preaching is that people have even less of a chance of ever being born again, because now they see no need to receive what they think they already have. Such evangelists actually help build Satan's kingdom.

The office of evangelist is not listed with the other ministry gifts in 1 Corinthians 12:28 as it is in Ephesians 4:11. I assume, however, that the reference there to "miracles and gifts of healings" applies to the evangelist's office since those characterized Philip the evangelist's ministry, and they would naturally give supernatural authentication to any evangelist's ministry.

Many who travel from church to church calling themselves evangelists are not really evangelists because they preach only in church buildings to Christians, and they are not equipped with gifts of healings or miracles. (Some pretend to have such gifts, but they can fool only the naive. Their biggest miracles are getting people to fall over temporarily when they push them over.) These traveling ministers may be teachers or preachers or exhorters (see Rom. 12:8), but they do not stand in the office of evangelist. It is possible, however, that God might begin a person's ministry as an exhorter or preacher and later promote him to the office of evangelist.

For further study concerning the office of evangelist, read Acts 8:4-40, a record of Philip's ministry. Notice there the importance of the inter-dependence of the ministry gifts (see in particular verses 14-25) and how Philip not only preached the gospel to the multitudes but was led of God to minister to individuals as well (see Acts 8:25-39).

It seems that evangelists are commissioned to baptize their converts, but they are not necessarily commissioned to minister the baptism in the Holy Spirit to new believers. That would primarily be the responsibility of apostles or pastors/elders/overseers.

The Office of Pastor

In two earlier chapters, I compared the biblical role of the pastor with that of the average institutional pastor. There is, however, still more to say about the pastor's ministry.

In order to fully understand what Scripture teaches about the office of pastor, we need to understand three key Greek words. In the Greek language they are (1) *poimen*, (2) *presbuteros* and (3) *episkopos*. They are consecutively translated (1) *shepherd* or *pastor*, (2) *elder*, and (3) *overseer* or *bishop*.

The word *poimen* is found eighteen times in the New Testament and is translated *shepherd* seventeen times and *pastor* once. The verb form, *poimaino*, is found eleven times and is most often translated *shepherd*.

The Greek word *presbuteros* is found sixty-six times in the New Testament. Sixty of those times it is translated *elder* or *elders*.

Finally, the Greek word *episkopos* is found five times in the New Testament, and is translated *overseer* four of those times. The King James Version translates it as *bishop*.

All three of these words refer to the same position in the church, and they are used interchangeably. Whenever the apostle Paul established churches, he appointed elders (*presbuteros*) whom he left to take care of the local congregations (see Acts 14:23, Tit. 1:5). Their responsibility was to acts as overseers (*episkopos*) and shepherd (*poimaino*) their flocks. For example, in Acts 20:17 we read:

> And from Miletus he sent to Ephesus and called to him the *elders* [presbuteros] of the church (emphasis added).

And what did Paul say to those church elders?

> Be on guard for yourselves and for all the flock, among which the Holy Spirit has made you *overseers* [episkopos], to *shepherd* [poimaino] the church of God which He purchased with His own blood (Acts. 20:28, emphasis added).

Notice the interchangeable use of the three Greek words. They are not three different offices. Paul told the *elders* that they were *overseers* who were to act like *shepherds*.

Peter wrote in his first epistle:

> Therefore, I exhort the *elders* [presbuteros] among you, as your fellow-elder and witness of the sufferings of Christ, and a partaker also of the glory that is to be revealed, *shepherd* [poimaino] the flock of God among you, not under compulsion, but voluntarily, according to the will of God; and not for sordid gain, but with eagerness; nor yet as lording it over those allotted to your charge, but proving to be examples to the flock. And when the Chief Shepherd appears, you will receive the unfading crown of glory (1 Pet. 5:1-4, emphasis added).

Peter told the *elders* to *shepherd* their flocks. The verb that is here translated *shepherd* is translated (in its noun form) as *pastor* in Ephesians 4:11:

> And He [Jesus] gave some as apostles, and some as prophets, and some as evangelists, and some as *pastors* and teachers (emphasis added).

This also leads us to believe that elders and pastors are the same.

Paul also used the words *elder* (presbuteros) and *overseer* (episkopos) interchangeably in Titus 1:5-7:

> For this reason I left you in Crete, that you might set in order what remains, and appoint *elders* in every city as I directed you....For the *overseer* must be above reproach (emphasis added).

Thus it cannot be reasonably debated that the office of pastor, elder, and overseer are not all the same office. Anything written about overseers and elders in the New Testament epistles is therefore applicable to pastors.

Church Governance

It is also very clear from the above-quoted scriptures that not only have the elders/pastors/overseers been given the spiritual oversight of the church, they also have been given the governmental authority. Quite simply, the elders/pastors/overseers are in charge, and the members of the churches should submit to them:

> Obey your leaders, and submit to them; for they keep watch over your souls, as those who will give an account (Heb. 13:17).

Of course, no Christian should submit to a pastor who is not submitted to God, but he should also recognize that no pastor is perfect.

The pastors/elders/overseers have authority over their churches just as a father has authority over his family:

> An overseer [pastor/elder] must be above reproach....He must be one who manages his own household well, keeping his children under control with all dignity (but if a man does not know how to manage his own household, *how will he take care of the church of God?*) (1 Tim. 3:2-5, emphasis added).

Paul went on to say,

> Let the elders [pastors/overseers] *who rule well* be considered worthy of double honor, especially those who work hard at preaching and teaching (1 Tim. 5:17, emphasis added).

Clearly, elders are to govern the church.

Unscriptural Elders

Many churches believe their governing structure is biblical because they have a group of elders who govern, but their problem is that their concept of elders is incorrect. Their elders are regularly elected and rotated from within the congregation. They are often referred to as "The Board of Elders." But such people are not elders by biblical definition. If we simply examine the requirements that Paul enumerated for a man to be an elder, this becomes quite clear. Paul wrote that an elder occupies a fulltime, and thus paid, teaching/preaching and governing position in the church (see 1 Tim. 3:4-5; 5:17-18; Tit. 1:9). Very few, if any, of the people who sit on church "elder boards" fit those qualifications. They are not paid; they do not preach or teach; they do not work fulltime for the church; and they rarely know how to manage a church.

Unscriptural church government could very well be the cause of more problems in local churches than any other thing. When the wrong people are ruling a church, there is trouble coming. It can open the door for strife, compromise and the total demise of a church. An unscriptural church governing structure is like a welcome mat for the devil.

I realize that I'm writing to pastors of institutional churches as well as house churches. Some institutional church pastors may be pastoring churches that already have unscriptural governing structures in place where elders are elected from the congregation. These unscriptural governing structures usually cannot be altered without strife developing.

My advice to any such pastors is to do his best with God's help to alter the governing structure of the church and endure the possible inevitable temporary conflict, as future regular conflict is inevitable if he doesn't do anything. If he succeeds by enduring some temporary strife, he will have avoided all that future strife. If he fails, he can always start a new church and do it scripturally from the start.

Though painful, in the long run he will probably bear more fruit for God's kingdom. If those who are currently governing his church are true disciples of Christ, he does have a chance of successfully convincing them to change the structure if he can respectfully convince them from Scripture to make the needed changes.

The Plurality of Elders?

Some like to point out that elders are always spoken of in Scripture in the plural, thus purportedly showing that it is unscriptural to have a single elder/pastor/overseer leading a flock. This is, however, not conclusive proof in my opinion. The Bible does indeed mention that, in certain cities, more than one elder was overseeing the church, but it does not say that those elders were co-equal over one individual congregations. For example, when Paul gathered the elders from Ephesus (see Acts 20:17), it is quite obvious that those elders were from a city in which the overall body consisted of thousands and perhaps tens of thousands of people (see Acts 19:19). Thus there had to have been many flocks in Ephesus, and it is quite possible that each individual elder oversaw an individual house church.

There is no example in Scripture where God called a committee to do any task. When He wanted to deliver Israel from Egypt, He called one man, Moses, to be the leader. Others were called to help Moses, but all were subordinate to him, and like him, they each had individual responsibility over a certain sub-group of people. This pattern is repeatedly found in Scripture. When God has a task, He calls one person to take responsibility, and He calls others to help that person.

Thus it seems unlikely that God would call a committee of elders of equal authority to oversee every little house church of twenty people. It seems like an invitation for strife.

This is not to say that every house church should be overseen by one and only one elder. It is to say, however, that if there is more than one elder in a church, the younger and less spiritually mature elder(s) should submit to the oldest and most spiritually mature elder. Scripturally, it is the churches, not Bible Schools, that are supposed to be the training grounds for young pastors/elders/overseers, and so it is quite possible and even desirable for there to be several elders/pastors/overseers in a house church, with the spiritually younger being discipled by the spiritually older.

I have observed this phenomenon even in churches that are supposedly overseen by "equal" elders. There is always one who is looked up to by the others. Or there is one who is dominant while the others are more passive. Otherwise eventually there is strife. It is a fact that even committees always elect one chairperson. When a group of equals sets out to do a task, they recognize that there must be one leader. So it is in the church.

Additionally, the responsibility of elders is compared to the responsibility of fathers by Paul in 1 Timothy 3:4-5. Elders must manage their own households, otherwise they are not qualified to manage the church. But how well would a family with two equal fathers be managed? I suspect there would be problems.

Elders/pastors/overseers should be networked in the larger local body so there is mutual accountability among fellow-elders who can help if there is ever a problem that requires them. Paul wrote of a "presbytery" (see 1 Tim. 4:14), which must have been a meeting of *presbuteros* (elders) and possibly other men with ministry gifts. If there is a founding apostle, he too can be of service if there are problems in a local body that are the result of an elder who has erred. When institutional pastors go astray, it always results in big problems because of the structure of the church. There is a building and programs to maintain. But house churches can be instantly dissolved when a pastor goes astray. The members can simply join another body.

Authority to Serve

Because God gives the pastor spiritual and governmental authority in his church, this does not give him the right to dominate his flock. He is not their Lord—Jesus is. They are not his flock—they are God's flock.

> Shepherd the flock of God among you, not under compulsion, but voluntarily, according to the will of God; and not for sordid gain, but with eagerness; *nor yet as lording it over those allotted to your charge, but proving to be examples for the flock.* And when the Chief Shepherd appears, you will receive the unfading crown of glory (1 Pet. 5:2-4, emphasis added).

Each pastor will have to give an account for his ministry some day before the judgment seat of Christ.

Additionally, in financial matters, a single pastor/elder/overseer should not act alone. If there is money being collected regularly or sporadically for any reason, others within the body should provide accountability so that there will be no mistrust regarding the handling of funds (see 2 Cor. 8: 18-23). This could be an elected or appointed group.

Paying Elders

It is clear from Scripture that elders/overseers/pastors are to be paid, as they are fulltime workers in the church. Paul wrote,

> Let the elders who rule well be considered worthy of double honor, especially those who work hard at preaching and teaching. For the Scripture says, "You shall not muzzle the ox while he is threshing," and "The laborer is worthy of his wages" (1 Tim. 5:17-18).

The subject is clear—Paul even uses the word *wages*. His more vague phrase of letting the elders who rule well be considered worthy of double honor is easily understood when the context is considered. In the verses just before, Paul unmistakably wrote of the church's responsibility to support financially widows who otherwise would not be supported, and he began by using the same expression: "Honor widows who are widows indeed" (see 1 Tim. 5:3-16). So in this context, to "honor' means to financially support. Elders who rule well are to be considered worthy of double honor, receiving at least twice what is given to widows and more if they have children to support.

The institutional church around the world supports its pastors for the most part (and even in poor nations), but it seems that many house churches around the world, especially those in the West, do not. This, I believe, is due in part to the fact that many people's motives in the Western world for joining house churches is that they are really rebels at heart, and they are looking for and have found the least demanding form of Christianity that is available on the planet. They say they joined a house church because they wanted to escape the bondage of the institutional church, but they really wanted to escape any degree of commitment to Christ. They've found churches that ask for no financial commitment, churches that stand in sharp contrast to what Christ expects of His disciples. Those whose god is money and who prove it to be so by laying up their treasures on earth rather than in heaven are not true disciples of Christ (see Matt. 6:19-24; Luke 14:33). If one's Christianity doesn't affect what he does with his money, one is not a Christian at all.

House churches that claim to be biblical should be supporting their pastors, as well as taking care of the poor and supporting missions. In giving and in all financial matters, they should far excel institutional churches, since they have no buildings to pay for and no program staff to pay. It takes only ten people who do nothing more than tithe to support one pastor. Ten people who give 20% of their income can fully support one pastor and another missionary who lives at the same standard as their pastor.

What do Pastors do?

Imagine asking the average church attendee, "Whose job it is to do the following things?"

Who is supposed to share the gospel with unsaved people? Live a holy life? Pray? Admonish, encourage and help other believers? Visit the sick? Lay hands on and heal the sick? Bear the burdens of others? Exercise his gifts on behalf of the body? Deny himself, sacrificing for the sake of God's kingdom? Make and baptize disciples, teaching them to obey Christ's commandments?

Many church attendees would, without hesitation, answer by saying, "Those are all responsibilities of the pastor." But are they?

According to Scripture, every believer is supposed to share the gospel with unsaved people:

> But sanctify Christ as Lord in your hearts, always being ready to make a defense to everyone who asks you to give an account for the hope that is in you, yet with gentleness and reverence (1 Pet. 3:15).

Every believer is supposed to live a holy life:

> But like the Holy One who called you, be holy yourselves also in all your behavior; because it is written, "You shall be holy, for I am holy" (1Pet. 1:15-16)

Every believer is supposed to pray:

> Rejoice always; pray without ceasing (1 Thes. 5:16-17).

Every believer is expected to admonish, encourage and help other believers:

> And we urge you, *brethren*, admonish the unruly, encourage the fainthearted, help the weak, be patient with all men (1Thes. 5:14, emphasis added).

Every believer is supposed to visit the sick:

> I was naked, and you clothed Me; I was sick, and you visited Me; I was in prison, and you came to Me (Matt. 25:36).

More Responsibilities

But that is not all. Every believer is supposed to lay hands upon and heal the sick:

> And these signs will accompany *those who have believed*: in My name they will cast out demons, they will speak with new tongues; they will pick up serpents, and if they drink any deadly poison, it shall not hurt them; *they will lay hands on the sick, and they will recover* (Mark 16:17-18, emphasis added).

Every believer is to bear the burdens of fellow believers:

> Bear one another's burdens, and thus fulfill the law of Christ (Gal. 6:2).

Every believer is expected to exercise his or her gifts on behalf of others:

> And since we have gifts that differ according to the grace given to us, let each exercise them accordingly: if prophecy, according to the proportion of his faith; if service, in his serving; or he who teaches, in his teaching; or he who exhorts, in his exhortation; he who gives, with liberality; he who leads, with diligence; he who shows mercy, with cheerfulness (Rom. 12:6-8).

Every believer is supposed to deny himself, sacrificing for the sake of the gospel:

> And He summoned the multitude with His disciples, and said to them, "If *anyone* wishes to come after Me, *let him deny himself,* and take up his cross, and follow Me. For whoever wishes to save his life shall lose it; but whoever loses his life for My sake and the gospel's shall save it" (Mark 8:34-35, emphasis added).

And every believer is expected to make and baptize disciples, teaching them to obey Christ's commandments:

> Whoever then annuls one of the least of these commandments, and so teaches others, shall be called least in the kingdom of heaven; but whoever keeps *and teaches them,* he shall be called great in the kingdom of heaven (Matt. 5:19, emphasis added).

> For though by this time *you ought to be teachers*, you have need again for someone to teach you the elementary principles of the oracles of God, and you have come to need milk and not solid food (Heb. 5:12, emphasis added).

> Go therefore and *make disciples of all the nations, baptizing*
> *them* in the name of the Father and the Son and the Holy
> Spirit, teaching them to observe *all that I commanded you;*
> and lo, I am with you always, even to the end of the age
> (Matt. 28:19-20, emphasis added).[61]

All of these responsibilities are given to every believer, yet most church attendees think these tasks are given just to pastors! The reason is probably because pastors themselves so often think these tasks are solely their responsibility.

So What are Pastors Supposed to do?

If all these responsibilities are given to every believer, what then are pastors supposed to do? *Quite simply, they are called to equip the holy believers to do all those things* (see Eph. 4:11-12). *They are called to teach those holy believers to obey all of Christ's commandments* (see Matt. 28:19-20) *by precept and example* (see 1 Tim. 3:2; 4:12-13; 5:17; 2 Tim. 2:2; 3:16-4:4; 1Pet. 5:1-4).

Scripture couldn't make this clearer. The biblical role of the pastor is not to gather as many people as possible at Sunday-morning church services. It is to "present every man complete in Christ" (Col. 1:28). Biblical pastors don't tickle peoples' ears (see 2 Tim. 4:3); they teach, train, exhort, admonish, correct, reprove and rebuke, all based on God's Word (see 2 Tim. 3:16-4:4).

Paul listed some of the qualifications for a man to stand in the office of pastor in his first letter to Timothy. Fourteen of the fifteen have to do with his character, indicating that the example of his lifestyle is the most important thing:

> It is a trustworthy statement; if any man aspires to the
> office of overseer, it is a fine work he desires to do. An
> overseer, then, must be above reproach, the husband of
> one wife, temperate, prudent, respectable, able to teach,
> not addicted to wine or pugnacious, but gentle, uncontentious, free from the love of money. He must be one who
> manages his own household well, keeping his children
> under control with all dignity (but if a man does not know
> how to manage his own household, how will he take care
> of the church of God?); and not a new convert, lest he become conceited and fall into the condemnation incurred
> by the devil. And he must have a good reputation with
> those outside the church, so that he may not fall into reproach and the snare of the devil (1 Tim. 3:1-7).

[61] If Jesus' disciples were to expected to teach their disciples to obey everything He had commanded them, they consequently would have taught their disciples to make disciples themselves, baptizing and teaching them to obey all that Christ commanded. So the making, baptizing and teaching of disciples would have been a perpetual commandment that was binding upon every successive disciple.

Comparing these qualifications with those that are often listed by institutional churches that are searching for a new pastor reveals the primary problem with so many churches. They are looking for an employee manager/entertainer/short-speech-giver/administrator/psychologist/activities and program director/fund-raiser/friend-of-everyone/work horse. They want someone to "run the ministry of the church." The biblical overseer, however, above all else must be a man of great character and commitment to Christ, a true servant, because his goal is to reproduce himself. He must be able to say to his flock, "Be imitators of me, just as I also am of Christ" (1 Cor. 11:1).

For further study concerning the pastor's office, see also Acts 20:28-31; 1 Tim. 5:17-20; and Tit. 1:5-9.

The Office of Deacon

In closing, let me briefly mention something about deacons. The office of deacon is the only other office in the local church, and it is not among the five-fold ministry gifts. Deacons have no governing authority in the church as do elders. The Greek word translated *deacon* is *diakonos,* which literally means "servant."

The seven men appointed for the task of daily feeding the widows in the Jerusalem church are usually considered to be the first deacons (see Acts 6:1-6). They were chosen by the congregation and commissioned by the apostles. At least two of them, Philip and Stephen, were later promoted by God to be powerful evangelists.

Deacons are also spoken of in 1 Timothy 3:8-13 and Philippians 1:1. Apparently this office can be filled by a man or woman (see 1 Tim. 3:11).

NINETEEN

In-Christ Realities

Throughout the New Testament epistles, we find phrases such as "in Christ," "with Christ," "through Christ," and "in Him." These frequently reveal some benefit that we as believers possess because of what Jesus has done for us. When we see ourselves as God sees us, "in Christ," it will help us to live as God wants us to live. The disciple-making minister will want to teach his disciples who they are in Christ to help them grow to full spiritual maturity.

First, what does it mean to be "in Christ"?

When we are born again, we're placed into Christ's body and become one with Him, spiritually. Let's take a look at a few sample verses from the New Testament epistles that affirm this:

> So we, who are many, are one body *in Christ* (Rom. 12:5, emphasis added).

> But the one who joins himself to the Lord is one spirit *with Him* (1 Cor. 6:17, emphasis added).

> Now you are *Christ's body, and individually members of it* (1 Cor. 12:27, emphasis added).

We who have believed in the Lord Jesus Christ should see ourselves as joined to Him, members of His body and one spirit with Him. He is in us and we're in Him.

Here's a verse that tells us some of the benefits that we have by virtue of our being in Christ:

> But by His doing you are *in Christ Jesus*, who became to us wisdom from God, and righteousness and sanctification, and redemption (1 Cor. 1:30, emphasis added).

In Christ, we've been made righteous (declared "not guilty" and now do what is right), sanctified (set apart for God's holy use), and redeemed (purchased from slavery). We're not *waiting* to be made righteous, sanctified or redeemed at some point in the future. Rather, we have all those blessings right now because we are in Christ.

In Christ we've had our former sins forgiven:

> For He rescued us from the domain of darkness, and transferred us to the kingdom of His beloved Son, *in whom* we have redemption, *the forgiveness of our sins* (Col. 1:13-14, emphasis added).

Notice that this scripture also tells that that we're no longer in Satan's kingdom, the domain of darkness, but are now in the kingdom of light, the kingdom of Jesus.

> Therefore if anyone is *in Christ*, he is a new creature; the old things passed away; behold, new things have come (2 Cor. 5:17, emphasis added).

Praise God that if you are a follower of Christ, you are a "new creature," like a caterpillar changed into a butterfly! Your spirit has been given a new nature. Previously you possessed Satan's selfish nature in your spirit, but now all of your past life has "passed away."

More Blessings in Christ

> For you are all sons of God through faith *in Christ Jesus* (Gal. 3:26, emphasis added).

Isn't it wonderful to know that we are actually God's own sons, born of His Spirit? When we come to Him in prayer, we approach Him not only as our God but also as our Father!

> For we are His workmanship, created *in Christ Jesus* for good works, which God prepared beforehand so that we should walk in them (Eph. 2:10, emphasis added).

God has not only created us, He also recreated us *in Christ*. Moreover, God has predestined a ministry for each of us to fulfill, "good works... prepared beforehand." We each have an individual divine destiny.

> He made Him who knew no sin to be sin on our behalf, so that we might become the righteousness of God *in Him* (2 Cor. 5:21, emphasis added).

The righteousness that we possess because we are in Christ is actually God's own righteousness. That's because God has indwelt us and transformed us by the Holy Spirit. Our good deeds are really God's good deeds through us.

> But in all these things we overwhelmingly conquer *through Him* who loved us (Rom. 8:37, emphasis added).

What are "these things" of which Paul wrote? The verses in Romans that precede this verse reveal that they are the trials and sufferings that believers experience. Even in martyrdom we are the victors, although the world may consider us victims. We overwhelmingly conquer through Christ because when we die, we go to heaven!

> I can do all things *through Him* who strengthens me (Phil. 4:13, emphasis added).

Through Christ, nothing is impossible to us because God gives us ability and strength. We can accomplish any task He gives us.

> My God will supply all your needs according to His riches in glory *in Christ Jesus* (Phil. 4:19, emphasis added).

We can expect that God will meet our true needs if we seek first His kingdom. The Lord is our shepherd, and He takes care of His sheep!

Agreeing With What God Says

Some of us, unfortunately, don't believe what the Word of God says about us, as indicated by our making statements that contradict what the Bible says. Instead of saying, "I can do all things through Christ who strengthens me" we're saying, "I don't think I can make it."

Such statements are what the Bible calls "bad reports" because they disagree with what God says (see Num. 13:32). If, however, our hearts are full of God's Word, we will be full of faith, believing and saying only what agrees with Scripture.

Some Biblical Declarations

We should believe and say that we are who God says we are.
We should believe and say that we can do what God says we can do.
We should believe and say that God is who He says He is.
We should believe and say that God will do what He says He will do.
Here are some scriptural statements that all believers can boldly declare. Not all are necessarily "in Christ" realities, but all are true according to Scripture.

I am redeemed, sanctified and made righteous in Christ (see 1 Cor. 1:30).
I've been transferred out of the kingdom of darkness and into the kingdom of God's Son, the kingdom of light (see Col. 1:13).

All of my sins have been forgiven in Christ (see Eph. 1:7).

I am a new creation in Christ—my old life has passed away (see 2 Cor. 5:17).

God has prepared good works beforehand for me to walk in (see Eph. 2:10).

I've become the righteousness of God in Christ (see 2 Cor. 5:21).

I overwhelmingly conquer in all things through Christ who loved me (see Rom. 8:37).

I can do all things through Christ who strengthens me (see Phil. 4:13).

My God supplies all my needs according to His riches in glory in Christ (see Phil. 4:19).

I am called to be a saint (see 1 Cor. 1:2).

I am a child of God (see John 1:12, 1 John 3:1-2).

My body is the temple of the Holy Spirit (see 1 Cor. 6:19).

It is no longer I who live, but Christ who lives in me (see Gal. 2:20).

I have been delivered from Satan's authority (see Acts 26:18).

God's love has been shed abroad in my heart by the Holy Spirit (see Rom. 5:5).

Greater is He who is in me than he (Satan) who is in the world (see 1 John 4:4).

I am blessed with every spiritual blessing in the heavenly places in Christ (see Eph. 1:3).

I am seated with Christ in heavenly places, far above all of Satan's spiritual forces (see Eph. 2:4-6).

Because I love God and am called according to His purpose, He is causing all things to work together for good (see Rom. 8:28).

If God is for me, who can be against me? (see Rom. 8:31).

Nothing can separate me from Christ's love (see Rom. 8:35-39).

All things are possible for me because I'm a believer (see Mark 9:23).

I am a priest of God (see Rev. 1:6).

Because I am His child, God is leading me by His Spirit (see Rom. 8:14).

As I follow the Lord, the path of my life is getting brighter and brighter (see Prov. 4:18).

God has given me special gifts to use for His service (see 1 Pet. 4:10-11).

I can cast out demons and lay hands on the sick so that they will recover (see Mark 16:17-18).

God always leads me in triumph in Christ (see 2 Cor. 2:14).

I am an ambassador for Christ (see 2 Cor. 5:20).

I have eternal life (see John 3:16).

Everything I ask in prayer, believing, I receive (see Matt. 21:22).

By Jesus' stripes, I am healed (see 1 Pet. 2:24).

I am the salt of the earth and the light of the world (see Matt. 5:13-14).

I am an heir of God and a joint-heir with Jesus Christ (see Rom. 8:17).

I am part of a chosen race, a royal priesthood, a holy nation, and a people for God's own possession (see 1 Pet. 2:9).

I am a member of the body of Christ (see 1 Cor. 12:27).

The Lord is my shepherd, I shall not want (see Ps. 23:1).

The Lord is the defense of my life—whom shall I fear? (see Ps. 27:1).

God will satisfy me with long life (see Ps. 91:16).

Christ bore my sicknesses and carried my pains (see Is. 53:4-5).

The Lord is my helper, so I will not be afraid (see Heb. 13:6).

I cast all my cares upon the Lord because He cares for me (see 1 Pet. 5:7).

I resist the devil, and he flees from me (see Jas. 4:7).

I am finding my life by losing if for Jesus' sake (see Matt. 16:25).

I am the Lord's bondslave (see 1 Cor. 7:22).

For me, to live is Christ, and to die is gain (see Phil. 1:21).

My citizenship is in heaven (see Phil. 3:20).

God will complete the good work He has begun in me (see Phil. 1:6).

God is at work within me, to do His good pleasure (see Phil. 2:13).

This is just a small sampling of positive declarations that we can make based on the Word of God. It would be a good idea to make a habit of saying these declarations until the truths they affirm become deeply rooted in our hearts. And we should monitor every word that comes out of our mouths to make sure we aren't taking sides against what God has said.

TWENTY

Praise and Worship

> The woman said to [Jesus], "Sir, I perceive that You are a prophet. Our fathers worshiped in this mountain; and you people say that in Jerusalem is the place where men ought to worship." Jesus said to her, "Woman, believe Me, an hour is coming when neither in this mountain, nor in Jerusalem, shall you worship the Father....But an hour is coming, and now is, when the true worshipers shall worship the Father in spirit and truth; for such people the Father seeks to be His worshipers. God is spirit, and those who worship Him must worship in spirit and truth" (John 4:19-24).

These words from the lips of Jesus lay the foundation for our understanding of the most important aspects of worship. He spoke of "true worshippers" and described their qualifications. This indicates that there are people who are worshippers but not *true* worshippers. They may think they are worshiping God but really aren't because they aren't meeting His requirements.

Jesus declared what characterizes true worshippers—they worship "in spirit and truth." Thus it could be said that false worshippers are those who worship "in flesh and insincerity." Fleshly, false worshippers may go though the motions of worship, but it is all a show, as it does not stem from a heart that loves God.

True worship of God can only come from a heart that loves God. Worship, therefore, is not just something we do when the church gathers, but something we do every moment of our lives as we obey Christ's commandments. Amazingly, the woman Jesus with whom was speaking had been married five times and was now living with a man, and she wanted to

281

debate about the proper location to worship God! How representative she is of so many religious people who attend worship services while living daily lives that are in rebellion to God. They are not true worshippers.

Jesus once rebuked the Pharisees and scribes for their false and heart-less worship:

> You hypocrites, rightly did Isaiah prophesy of you, say-ing, *"This people honors Me with their lips, but their heart is far away from Me.* But in vain do they worship Me, teach-ing as their doctrines the precepts of men" (Matt. 15:7-9, emphasis added).

Although the Jews and Samaritans in Jesus' day obviously placed great emphasis on the location where people worshiped, Jesus said that the lo-cation was unimportant. Rather, it is the condition of each person's heart and his attitude toward God that determines the quality of his worship.

Much of what is called "worship" in churches today is nothing more than dead ritual acted out by dead worshipers. People are mindlessly parroting someone else's words about God as they sing "worship songs," and their worship is in vain, because their lifestyles betray what is really in their hearts.

God would rather hear a simple, heart-felt "I love You" from one of His true obedient children than endure the heartless droning of a thousand Sunday-morning Christians singing "How Great Thou Art."

Worshipping in Spirit

Some say that to worship "in spirit" means to pray and sing in other tongues, but that seems to be a strained interpretation in light of Jesus' words. He said that "an hour is coming, *and now is,* when the true wor-shipers shall worship the Father in spirit and truth," indicating that there were *already* those who met the conditions for worship "in spirit" when He made His statement. Of course, no one spoke in tongues until the day of Pentecost. Therefore, any believer, whether he can speak in tongues or not, can worship God in spirit and in truth. Praying and singing in other tongues can certainly aid a believer in his worship, but even praying in tongues can become a heartless ritual.

An interesting insight into the worship of the early church is found in Acts 13:1-2:

> Now there were at Antioch, in the church that was there, prophets and teachers; Barnabas, and Simeon who was called Niger, and Lucius of Cyrene, and Manaen who had been brought up with Herod the tetrarch, and Saul. And while they were *ministering to the Lord* and fasting, the Holy Spirit said, "Set apart for Me Barnabas and Saul for the work to which I have called them" (emphasis added).

Notice this passage said they were "ministering to the Lord." It seems reasonable to think that means they were worshiping Him, and thus we learn that true worship actually ministers to the Lord. That is only true, however, when the Lord is the object of our love and affection.

Ways to Worship

The book of Psalms, which could be said to have been Israel's hymn-book, exhorts us to worship God in a number of different ways. For example, in Psalm 32 we read:

> "*Shout* for joy all you who are upright in heart" (Ps 32:11b, emphasis added).

Although quiet, reverent, worship has its place, so does shouting for joy.

> *Sing for joy* in the Lord, O you righteous ones; praise is becoming to the upright. Give thanks to the Lord with the lyre; sing praises to Him with a harp of ten strings. Sing to Him a new song; play skillfully with a shout of joy (Ps. 33:1-3, emphasis added).

We should, of course, sing to the Lord in worship, but our singing should be *joyful*, which is another outward indication of one's heart condition. We can also accompany our joyful singing with various musical instruments. I must mention, however, that in many church gatherings, the electrical musical instruments are often so loud that they drown out the singing completely. They should be turned down or turned off. The psalmists never had that problem!

> So I will bless Thee as long as I live; I will *lift up my hands* in Thy name (Ps. 63:4, emphasis added).

As a sign of surrender and reverence, we can lift our hands to God.

> Shout joyfully to God, all the earth; sing the glory of His name; make His praise glorious. *Say* to God, *"How awesome are Thy works!* Because of the greatness of Thy power Thine enemies will give feigned obedience to Thee. All the earth will worship Thee, and will sing praises to Thee" (Ps. 66:1-4, emphasis added).

We should tell the Lord how awesome He is and praise Him for His many wonderful attributes. The Psalms are an excellent place to find appropriate words with which to praise God. We need to go beyond the continual repetition of "I praise you, Lord!" There is so much more to say to Him.

> Come, let us worship and *bow down;* let us kneel before the Lord our Maker (Ps. 95:6).

Even our posture can be an expression of worship, whether it be standing, kneeling or bowing.

> Let the godly ones exult in glory; let them sing for joy *in their beds* (Ps. 149:5, emphasis added).

But we don't have to be standing or kneeling to worship—we can even be lying in bed.

> Enter His gates with *thanksgiving*, and His courts with praise. Give *thanks* to Him; bless His name (Ps. 100:4, emphasis added).

Giving of thanks should certainly be a part of our worship.

> Let them praise His name with *dancing* (Ps. 149:3, emphasis added).

We can even praise the Lord with dancing. But it should be dancing that is not fleshly, sensual or purely entertaining.

> Praise Him with trumpet sound; praise Him with harp and lyre. Praise Him with timbrel and dancing; praise Him with stringed instruments and pipe. Praise Him with loud cymbals; praise Him with resounding cymbals. Let everything that has breath praise the Lord (Ps. 150:3-6).

Thank God for those who are musically gifted. Their gifts can be used to glorify God if they play their instruments from a heart of love.

Spiritual Songs

> O *sing to the Lord a new song*, for he has done wonderful things (Ps. 98:1a, emphasis added).

There is nothing wrong with singing an old song, unless it becomes a ritual. Then we need a new song that comes from our hearts. In the New Testament, we learn that the Holy Spirit will help us compose new songs:

> Let the word of Christ richly dwell within you, with all wisdom teaching and admonishing one another with psalms and hymns and spiritual songs, singing with thankfulness in your hearts to God (Col. 3:16).

> And do not get drunk with wine, for that is dissipation, but be filled with the Spirit, speaking to one another in psalms and hymns and spiritual songs, singing and making melody with your heart to the Lord; always giving thanks for all things in the name of our Lord Jesus Christ to God, even the Father (Eph. 5:18-20).

Paul wrote that we should be singing to one another with "psalms, hymns, and spiritual songs," so there must be a difference between all three. A study of the original Greek words offers little help, but perhaps "psalms" meant an actual singing of psalms from the Bible accompanied by musical instruments. "Hymns," on the other hand, may have been general songs of thanksgiving composed by various believers in the churches. "Spiritual songs" were probably spontaneous songs given by the Holy Spirit and similar to the simple gift of prophecy, except that the utterances would be sung.

Praise and worship should be a part of our everyday lives—not just something we do when the church gathers. Throughout every day we can minister to the Lord and experience close fellowship with Him.

Praise—Faith in Action

Praise and worship are a normal expression of our faith in God. If we truly believe the promises of God's Word, then we will be joyful people, full of praise to God. Joshua and the people of Israel had to shout *first*; then the walls fell. The Bible admonishes us to "rejoice in the Lord always" (Phil. 4:4) and "in everything give thanks" (1 Thes. 5:18a).

One of the most outstanding examples of the power of praise is found in 2 Chronicles 20 when the nation of Judah was being invaded by the armies of Moab and Ammon. In response to King Jehoshaphat's prayer, God instructed Israel:

> Do not fear or be dismayed because of this great multitude, for the battle is not yours but God's. Tomorrow go down against them....You need not fight in this battle; station yourselves, stand and see the salvation of the Lord on your behalf, O Judah and Jerusalem (2 Chron. 20:15b-17).

The narrative continues:

> And they rose early in the morning and went out to the wilderness of Tekoa; and when they went out, Jehoshaphat stood and said, "Listen to me, O Judah and inhabitants of Jerusalem, put your trust in the Lord your God, and you will be established. Put your trust in His prophets and succeed." And when he had consulted with the people, he appointed those who sang to the Lord and those who praised Him in holy attire, as they went out before the army and said, "*Give thanks to the Lord, for His lovingkindness is everlasting.*" *And when they began singing and praising, the Lord set ambushes against the sons of Ammon, Moab, and Mount Seir, who had come against Judah; so they were routed.* For the sons of Ammon and Moab rose

up against the inhabitants of Mt. Seir destroying them completely, and when they had finished with the inhabitants of Seir, they helped to destroy one another. When Judah came to the look-out of the wilderness, they looked toward the multitude; and behold, they were corpses lying on the ground, and no one had escaped. And when Jehoshaphat and his people came to take their spoil, they found much among them, including goods, garments, and valuable things which they took for themselves, more than they could carry. And they were three days taking the spoil because there was so much" (2 Chron. 20: 20-25, emphasis added).

Faith-filled praise brings protection and provision!

For further study on the subject of the power of praise, see Phil. 4:6-7 (praise brings peace), 2 Chron. 5:1-14 (praise brings God's presence), Acts 13:1-2 (praise brings God's purposes and plans to light), and Acts 16:22-26 (praise brings God's preservation and prison release).

TWENTY-ONE

The Christian Family

God, or course, is the one who came up with the idea of families. It stands to reason then that He could offer us insight into how the families should function and can warn us of those pitfalls that destroy families. Indeed, the Lord has given us many principles in His Word regarding the structure of the family and the role that each individual member should perform. When these biblical instructions are followed, families will experience all the blessings God intended for them to enjoy. When they are violated, havoc and heartache are the result.

The Role of Husband and Wife

God has designed that the Christian family conform to a certain structure. Because this framework provides the stability for family life, Satan works hard to pervert God's intended design.

First, God has ordained that the husband be the head of the family unit. This does not give the husband the right to selfishly dominate his wife and children. God has called husbands to love, protect, provide for, and lead their families as the head. God also intended that wives be submissive to the leadership of their husbands. This is clear from Scripture:

> Wives, be subject to your own husbands, as to the Lord. For the husband is the head of the wife, as Christ also is head of the church, He Himself being the Savior of the body. But as the church is subject to Christ, so also the wives ought to be to their husbands in everything (Eph. 5:22-24).

The husband is not the *spiritual* head of his wife—Jesus is the one who fulfils that role. Jesus is the spiritual head of the church, and the Christian wife is just as much a member of the church as her Christian husband is. In the family, however, the Christian husband is the head of his wife and children, and they should be submitted to his God-given authority.

To what degree should the wife submit to her husband? She should submit to him in *everything*, just as Paul said. The only exception to that rule would be if her husband expects her to disobey the Word of God or to do something that violates her conscience. Of course, no Christian husband would ever expect his wife to do anything to violate God's word or her conscience. The husband is not his wife's lord—only Jesus has that place in her life. If she must choose whom to obey, she should choose Jesus.

Husbands should remember that God is not necessarily always "on the husband's side." God once told Abraham to do what his wife Sarah told him (see Gen. 21:10-12). Scripture also records that Abigail disobeyed her foolish husband Nabal and averted a catastrophe (see 1 Sam. 25:2-38).

God's Word to Husbands

To husbands, God says:

> Husbands, love your wives, just as Christ also loved the church and gave Himself up for her....So husbands ought also to love their own wives as their own bodies. He who loves his own wife loves himself; for no one ever hated his own flesh, but nourishes and cherishes it, just as Christ also does the church, because we are members of His body....Nevertheless let each individual among you also love his own wife even as himself; and let the wife see to it that she respect her husband (Eph. 5:25, 28-30, 33).

Husbands are commanded to love their wives as Christ loves the church. That is no small responsibility! Any wife will gladly submit to someone who loves her as much as Jesus does—who gave His own life in sacrificial love. Just as Christ loves his own body, the church, so also a husband ought to love the woman with whom he is "one flesh" (Eph. 5:31). If a Christian husband loves his wife as he should, he will provide for her, care for her, honor her, help her, encourage her, and spend time with her. If he fails in his responsibility to love his wife, the husband is in danger of hindering the answer to his own prayers:

> You husbands likewise, live with your wives in an understanding way, as with a weaker vessel [body], since she is a woman; and *grant her honor as a fellow-heir of the grace of life, so that your prayers may not be hindered* (1 Pet. 3:7, emphasis added).

There has never been, of course, a marriage that is completely void of conflicts and disagreements. Through commitment and the development of the fruit of the spirit in our lives, however, husbands and wives can learn to live harmoniously and experience the ever-increasing blessedness of Christian marriage. Through the inevitable problems that arise in all marriages, each partner can learn to grow to greater maturity in Christ-likeness.

For further study on the duties of husbands and wives, see Gen. 2:15-25; Prov. 19:13; 21:9, 19; 27:15-16; 31:10-31; 1 Cor. 11:3; 13:1-8; Col. 3:18-19; 1 Tim. 3:4-5; Tit. 2:3-5; 1 Pet. 3:1-7.

Sex in Marriage

God is the one who invented sex, and He obviously created it for plea-sure as well as for procreation. The Bible, however, plainly states that sex-ual relations are to be enjoyed only by those who have joined themselves together in a life-long marriage covenant.

Sexual relations that take place outside the bonds of marriage are clas-sified as either fornication or adultery. The apostle Paul stated that those who practice such things will not inherit the kingdom of God (see 1 Cor. 6:9-11). Although a Christian might be tempted and might possibly com-mit an act of fornication or adultery, he will feel great condemnation in his spirit that will lead him to repentance. And repent he should!

Paul also gave some specific instruction regarding the sexual responsi-bilities of husbands and wives:

> But because of immoralities, let each man have his own wife, and let each woman have her own husband. Let the husband fulfill his duty to his wife, and likewise also the wife to her husband. The wife does not have authority over her own body, but the husband does; and likewise also the husband does not have authority over his own body, but the wife does. Stop depriving one another, ex-cept by agreement for a time that you may devote your-selves to prayer, and come together again lest Satan tempt you because of your lack of self-control (1 Cor. 7:2-5).

These verses make it very plain that sex should not be used as a "re-ward" by either husband or wife because neither has authority over his own body.

Moreover, sex is a God-given gift and not unholy or sinful as long as it stays within the confines of marriage. Paul encouraged married Christian couples to engage in sexual relations. Furthermore, we find this advice to Christian husbands in the book of Proverbs:

> Let your fountain be blessed, and rejoice in the wife of your youth. As a loving hind and a graceful doe, let her breasts satisfy you at all times; be exhilarated always with her love (Prov. 5:18-19).[62]

---

[62] For more proof that God is not prudish, see Song of Solomon 7:1-9 and Leviticus 18:1-23.

If Christian couples are to enjoy a mutually satisfying sexual relationship, husbands and wives should understand that there is a vast difference between the sexual nature of men and women. By comparison, a man's sexual nature is more physical, whereas a woman's sexual nature is connected with her emotions. Men become sexually excited by visual stimulation (see Matt. 5:28), whereas women tend to be sexually excited by relationships and by touch (see 1 Cor. 7:1). Men are sexually attracted to women who appeal to their eyes; whereas women tend to be sexually attracted to men they admire for more reasons than just physical attractiveness. Thus wise wives look their best to please their husbands all the time. And wise husbands show their affection for their wives all the time by hugs and thoughtful acts of kindness, rather than expecting their wives to be "turned on" in an instant at the end of the day.

A man's degree of sexual desire tends to increase with the build-up of semen in his body, whereas a woman's sexual desire increases or decreases depending upon her menstrual cycle. Men have the capacity to be sexually excited and experience sexual climax within a matter of seconds or minutes; women take much longer. Although he is normally physically ready for actual intercourse in seconds, her body may not be physically ready for as much as half an hour. Thus wise husbands take their time in sexual foreplay with caresses, kisses and manual stimulation of those areas of her body that will result in her becoming ready for intercourse. If he doesn't know where those parts of her body are, he should ask her. Additionally, He should know that although he has the capacity for reaching only one sexual climax, his wife has the capacity for more. He should see that she receives what she desires.

It is vital for Christian husbands and wives to discuss their needs honestly with one another and learn as much as they can about how the opposite sex differs. Through months and years of communication, discovery and practice, sexual relationships between husbands and wives can result in ever-increasing blessedness.

Children of a Christian Family

Children should be taught to be submitted and fully obedient to their Christian parents. And if they will, long lives and other blessings are promised to them:

> Children, obey your parents in the Lord, for this is right.
> "Honor your father and mother" (which is the first commandment with a promise), "that it may be well with you,
> and that you may live long on the earth" (Eph. 6:1-3).

Christian fathers, as heads of their families, are given the primary responsibility for the training of their children:

> And, fathers, do not provoke your children to anger, but
> bring them up in the discipline and instruction of the Lord
> (Eph. 6:4).

Note that the father's responsibility is two-fold: to bring his children up in the *discipline* and *instruction* of the Lord. Let us first consider the need to discipline children.

Child Discipline

The child who is never disciplined will grow up to be selfish and rebellious toward authority. Children should be disciplined any time they *defiantly* disobey reasonable rules that have been established beforehand by their parents. Children should not be punished for mistakes or childish irresponsibility. They should, however, usually be required to face the consequences of their mistakes and irresponsibilities, thus helping to prepare them for the realities of adult life.

Young children should be disciplined by means of spanking, as God's Word instructs. New babies, of course, should not be spanked. This does not mean that babies should always be given their own way. In fact, from the day of birth it should be clear to them that mother and father are in charge. They can be taught at a very young age what the word "no" means by simply restraining them from doing what they are doing or about to do. Once they begin to understand what "no " means, a light slap on their buttocks will help them understand even better during those times that they don't obey. If this is done consistently, children will learn to be obedient at a very young age.

Parents can also establish their authority by not reinforcing undesirable behavior in their children, such as immediately giving them what they want every time they cry. To do so is to teach children to cry in order to gain their desires. Or, if parents yield to the demands of their children every time they throw a temper tantrum or whine, such parents are actually encouraging such undesirable behavior. Wise parents only reward behavior that is desirable in their children.

Spankings should not be physically harmful but should certainly generate enough pain to cause the disobedient child to cry for a short time. In this way, the child will learn to associate disobedience with pain. This the Bible affirms:

> He who spares his rod hates his son, but he who loves him
> disciplines him diligently....Foolishness is bound up in the
> heart of a child; the rod of discipline will remove it far
> from him....Do not hold back discipline from the child, although you punish him with the rod, he will not die. You
> shall punish him with the rod, and deliver his soul from
> Sheol....The rod and reproof give wisdom, but a child who

gets his own way brings shame to his mother (Prov. 13:24; 22:15; 23:13-14; 29:15).

When parents simply enforce their rules, they do not need to threaten children to make them obedient. If a child defiantly disobeys, he should be spanked. If a parent only *threatens* to spank his disobedient child, he is only reinforcing his child's continued disobedience. As a result, the child learns not to be concerned about being obedient until his parents' verbal threats reach a certain volume.

After the spanking has been administered, the child should be hugged and reassured of his parent's love.

Train Up a Child

Christian parents must realize they have a responsibility to train their children, just as we read in Proverbs 22:6: *"Train* up a child in the way he should go, even when he is old he will not depart from it" (emphasis added).

Training involves not only punishment for disobedience but reward for good behavior. Children need to be consistently praised by their parents to reinforce their good behavior and desirable traits. Children need to be reassured often that they are loved, accepted and appreciated by their parents. Parents can convey their love by praises, hugs and kisses, and through the time they spend with their children.

To "train" means to "make to obey." Christian parents, therefore, should not give their children the option of whether or not they will attend church or pray every day and so on. Children are not responsible enough to know what is best for them—that is why God gave them parents. To the parents who invest the effort and energy to see that their children are properly trained, God promises that their children will not depart from going the right way when they are older, as we read in Proverbs 22:6.

Children should also be given increasing responsibilities as they grow older. The goal of effective parenting is to gradually prepare the child for the full responsibilities of adulthood. As the child grows older, he should be given progressively more freedom to make his own decisions. In addition, the teenager should understand that he will accept responsibility for the consequences of his decisions and that his parents will not always be there to "bail him out" of trouble.

Parents' Responsibility to Instruct

As we read in Ephesians 6:4, fathers are not only responsible to discipline their children but also expected to *instruct* them in the Lord. It is not the church's responsibility to give the child instruction in biblical morality, Christian character, or theology—it is the father's job. The parents who relegate all the responsibility to the Sunday School teacher to teach their children about God are making a very serious error. God commanded Israel through Moses:

> And these words, which I am commanding you today, shall be on your heart; and *you shall teach them diligently to your sons* and shall talk of them when you sit in your house and when you walk by the way and when you lie down and when you rise up (Deut. 6:6-7, emphasis added).

Christian parents should introduce their children, from an early age, to God, telling them who He is and how much He loves them. Young children should be taught the story of Jesus' birth, life, death, and resurrection. Many children can understand the gospel message by age five or six and can make a decision to serve the Lord. Soon after (by age six or seven, and sometimes even younger), they can receive the baptism in the Holy Spirit with the evidence of speaking in tongues. Of course, no ironclad rules can be laid down because every child is different. The point is that Christian parents should make the spiritual training of their children their highest earthly priority.

Ten Rules for Loving Your Children

1). Don't exasperate your children (see Eph. 6:4). Children can't be expected to act like adults. If you expect too much from them, they'll quit trying to please you, knowing it's impossible.

2). Don't compare your children with other children. Let them know how much you appreciate their unique qualities and gifts from God.

3). Give them responsibilities around your home so they will know they are an important part of the family unit. Accomplishments are the building blocks of healthy self-esteem.

4). Spend time with your children. That lets them know they are important to you. Giving them material things is no substitute for giving them yourself. Furthermore, children are influenced the most by those who spend the most time with them.

5). If you must say something negative, try to say it in a positive way. I never told my children they were "bad" when they disobeyed me. Instead, I'd say to my son, "You're a good boy, and good boys don't do what you just did!" (Then I'd spank him.)

6). Realize the word "no" means "I care about you." When children always get their way, they intuitively know you don't care enough to restrict them.

7). Expect your children to imitate you. Children learn from the example of their parents. The wise parent will never say to his child, "Do as I say, not as I do."

8). Don't bail your children out of all their problems. Only remove stumbling-stones; let stepping stones remain on their path.

9). Serve God with all of your heart. I've noticed that children of parents who are spiritually lukewarm rarely continue to serve God in their adulthood. Christian children of unsaved parents and children of fully-committed Christian parents normally continue to serve God once "out of the nest."

10). Teach your children the Word of God. Parents often prioritize the education of their children but fail to give them the most important education they could get, an education in the Bible.

The Priorities of Ministry, Marriage and Family

Perhaps the most common error made by Christian leaders is that of neglecting their marriages and families due to devotion to their ministries. They justify themselves by saying that their sacrifice is "for the Lord's work."

This error is remedied when the disciple-making minister realizes that His *true* obedience and devotion to God is reflected by His relationships with His spouse and children. A minister cannot claim to be devoted to God if he does not love his wife like Christ loves the church, or if he neglects to spend the time necessary with his children to bring them up in the nurture and admonition of the Lord.

Moreover, neglecting one's spouse and children for the sake of "the ministry" is usually a sure sign of fleshly ministry that is being done in the power of one's own strength. Many institutional pastors who carry heavy work burdens exemplify this, as they exhaust themselves in order to keep all the church programs running.

Jesus promised that His burden is light and His yoke is easy (see Matt. 11:30). He is not calling any minister to show his devotion for the world or the church at the expense of loving his family. In fact, a requirement for an elder is that he "must be one who manages his own household well" (1 Tim. 3:4). His relationship with his family is a test of his fitness for ministry.

Those who are called to traveling ministries and who must be away at times should spend extra time focused on their families when they are home. Fellow-members of the body of Christ should do what is within their power to make such an arrangement possible. The disciple-making minister realizes that his own children are his primary disciples. If he fails at that task, he has no right to attempt to make disciples outside of his home.

TWENTY-TWO

How to be Led by the Spirit

John's gospel records a number of Jesus' promises concerning the Holy Spirit's role in the life of believers. Let's read a few of them:

> And I will ask the Father, and He will give you another Helper, that He may be with you forever; that is the Spirit of truth, whom the world cannot receive, because it does not behold Him or know Him, but you know Him because He abides with you, and will be in you (John 14:16-17).

> But the Helper, the Holy Spirit, whom the Father will send in My name, He will teach you all things, and bring to your remembrance all that I said to you (John 14:26).

> But I tell you the truth, it is to your advantage that I go away; for if I do not go away, the Helper shall not come to you; but if I go, I will send Him to you....I have many more things to say to you, but you cannot bear them now. But when He, the Spirit of truth, comes, He will guide you into all the truth; for He will not speak on His own initiative, but whatever He hears, he will speak; and He will disclose to you what is to come. He shall glorify Me; for He shall take of Mine, and shall disclose it to you. All things that the Father has are Mine; therefore I said, that He takes of Mine, and will disclose it to you (John 16:7, 12-15).

Jesus promised His disciples that the Holy Spirit would abide in them. He would also help them, teach them, guide them and show them things to come. As Christ's disciples today, we have no reason to think the Holy Spirit would do any less for us.

Amazingly, Jesus told His disciples that it was to their advantage that He go away or else the Holy Spirit wouldn't come! That indicated to them that their fellowship with the Holy Spirit could be just as intimate as if Jesus were physically present with them all the time. Otherwise it wouldn't be to their advantage to have the Holy Spirit with them rather than Jesus. Through the Holy Spirit, Jesus is always with us and in us.

In what ways should we expect the Holy Spirit to lead us?

His very name, *Holy* Spirit, indicates that His primary role in leading us will be in leading us to be holy and obedient to God. So everything that pertains to holiness and the accomplishing of God's will on earth is within the realm of the Holy Spirit's guidance. He will lead us to obey all of Christ's general commandments as well as in Christ's specific commandments that pertain to the unique ministry God has called us to. So if you want to be led by the Spirit in regard to your specific ministry, you must also be led by the Spirit in general holiness. You can't have one without the other. Too many ministers want the Holy Spirit to lead them into great ministry exploits and miracles, but don't want to bother with the "smaller" aspects of general holiness. That is a great error. How did Jesus lead His disciples? Primarily by giving them general instructions in holiness. His specific leadings for their ministerial responsibilities were rare by comparison. So it is with the Holy Spirit who indwells us. So if you want to be led by the Spirit, you must first of all follow His leadings to be holy.

The apostle Paul wrote, "For all who are being led by the Spirit of God, these are sons of God" (Rom. 8:14). It is our being led by the Spirit that marks us as being among those who are God's children. Thus all of God's children are being led by the Spirit. It is up to us of course, as free moral agents, to obey the Spirit's leadings.

All of this being so, no Christian really needs to be taught how to be led by the Holy Spirit, because the Holy Spirit is already leading every Christian. On the other hand, Satan is trying to mislead God's children, and we still have the old nature of the flesh within us that attempts to lead us contrary to God's will. So believers do need to learn to discern the Spirit's leading from those other leadings. That is a process on the road to maturity. But the foundational fact is this: The Spirit will always lead us in line with God's written Word, and He will always lead us to do what is right and pleasing to God, what will bring Him glory (see John 16:14).

The Voice of the Holy Spirit

Although Scripture tells us that the Holy Spirit may sometimes lead us in spectacular ways, such as through visions, prophecy, or the audible voice of God, the more usual way that the Holy Spirit communicates to us is in our spirits by "impressions." That is, if the Spirit wants us to do something, He will "tug" at us—in our spirits—and we will sense a "leading" to follow a certain direction.

We could call the voice of our spirit our "conscience." All Christians know what their conscience sounds like. If we are tempted to sin, we don't hear an audible voice within us saying, "Don't give in to that temptation." Rather, we simply feel something within us *resisting* that temptation. And if we do yield to a temptation, after a sin is committed, we don't hear an audible voice saying, "You sinned! You sinned!" We simply sense a conviction on the inside, now leading us to repent and confess our sin.

In the same manner the Spirit will teach us and lead us into general truth and understanding. He will teach us by imparting a sudden revelation (always in line with the Bible) within us. Those revelations may take ten minutes to describe to someone else, but they can come by the Holy Spirit in a matter of seconds.

In the same manner the Holy Spirit will lead us in the affairs of ministry. We must simply make a conscious effort to be sensitive to those inner leadings and impressions, and we will slowly learn (by trial and error) to follow the Spirit in regard to things pertaining to ministry. It is when we allow our heads (our rational or irrational thinking) to get in the way of our hearts (where the Spirit is leading us) that we find ourselves making errors in regard to God's will.

How the Spirit Led Jesus

Jesus was led by the Holy Spirit by inward impressions. For example, Mark's Gospel describes what happened directly after Jesus was baptized in the Holy Spirit following His baptism by John:

> And immediately the Spirit *impelled* Him to go out into the wilderness" (Mark 1:12, emphasis added).

Jesus didn't hear an audible voice or see a vision that led Him into the wilderness—He was simply *impelled* to go. That is how the Holy Spirit normally leads us. We will sense a drawing, a leading, a conviction, within us to do a certain thing.

When Jesus told the paralyzed man who had been lowered through the roof that his sins were forgiven, Jesus knew that the scribes who were present thought He was blaspheming. How did He know what they were thinking? We read in Mark's gospel:

> And immediately Jesus, *perceiving in His spirit* that they were reasoning that way within themselves, said to them, "Why are you reasoning about these things in your hearts?" (Mark 2:8, emphasis added).

Jesus perceived in His spirit what they were thinking. If we will be sensitive to our spirits, we too can know how to answer those who oppose the work of God.

The Spirit's Leading in the Ministry of Paul

After at least twenty years of serving in ministry, the apostle Paul had learned well how to follow the leading of the Holy Spirit. To some degree, the Spirit showed him "things to come" relative to his future ministry. For example, as Paul was concluding his ministry in Ephesus, He had some conception of the course that his life and ministry would follow for the next three years:

> Now after these things were finished, Paul purposed in the spirit to go to Jerusalem after he had passed through Macedonia and Achaia, saying, "After I have been there, I must also see Rome" (Acts 19:21).

Notice that Paul didn't purpose this intended direction in his *mind* but in his *spirit*. That indicates that the Holy Spirit was leading him in his spirit to go first to Macedonia and Achaia (both located in modern day Greece), then to Jerusalem, and finally to Rome. And that is precisely the course he followed. If you have a map in your Bible showing Paul's third missionary journey and his journey to Rome, you can follow his path from Ephesus (where he purposed his route in his spirit) through Macedonia and Achaia, onto Jerusalem, and several years later, to Rome.

More precisely, Paul traveled through Macedonia and Achaia, then he backtracked through Macedonia once again, circling the coast of the Aegean Sea, and then he traveled down the Aegean coast of Asia Minor. During that journey he stopped at the city of Miletus, called for the elders of the church of nearby Ephesus, and delivered a farewell address to them in which he said:

> And now, behold, *bound in spirit,* I am on my way to Jerusalem, not knowing what will happen to me there, except that the Holy Spirit solemnly testifies to me in every city, saying that bonds and afflictions await me (Acts 20:22-23, emphasis added).

Paul said he was "bound in spirit," meaning he had a conviction in his spirit that was leading him to Jerusalem. He didn't have the complete picture regarding what would happen when he arrived in Jerusalem, but he stated that in every city in which he stopped on his journey, the Holy Spirit testified that bonds and afflictions awaited him there. How did the Holy Spirit "testify" of those bonds and afflictions that awaited him in Jerusalem?

Two Examples

In the 21st chapter of Acts, we find two recorded incidents that answer that question. The first example is when Paul landed at the Mediterranean port city of Tyre:

> And after looking up the disciples, we stayed there seven
> days; and they kept telling Paul through the Spirit not to
> set foot in Jerusalem (Acts 21:4).

Because of this one verse, some commentators conclude that Paul disobeyed God by continuing on his way to Jerusalem. In the light of the rest
of the information given to us in the book of Acts, however, we cannot
rightly make that conclusion. This will become clear as we progress in the
story.

Apparently the disciples in Tyre were spiritually sensitive and dis-
cerned that trouble awaited Paul in Jerusalem. They subsequently tried to
convince him not to go. William's translation of the New Testament bears
this out, as it translates this same verse: "Because of impressions made by
the Spirit they kept on warning Paul not to set foot in Jerusalem."

The disciples in Tyre met with no success, however, because Paul continued his journey toward Jerusalem in spite of their warnings.

This teaches us that we must be very careful not to add our own interpretation to revelations we receive in our spirits. Paul knew full well that
trouble awaited him in Jerusalem, but he also knew it was God's will for
him to journey there regardless. If God reveals something to us by the
Holy Spirit, that doesn't necessarily mean we are supposed to go and tell
it, and we must also be careful not to add our own interpretation to what
the Spirit has revealed.

Caesarea Stop Over

The next stop on Paul's journey to Jerusalem was the port city of Caesarea:

> And as we were staying there for some days, a certain
> prophet named Agabus came down from Judea. And
> coming to us, he took Paul's belt and bound his own feet
> and hands, and said, "This is what the Holy Spirit says;
> 'In this way the Jews at Jerusalem will bind the man who
> owns this belt and deliver him into the hands of the Gen-
> tiles'" (Acts 21:10-11).

Here is yet another example of the Holy Spirit testifying to Paul that
"bonds and afflictions" awaited him in Jerusalem. But notice that Agabus didn't say, "Therefore, thus says the Lord, 'Do not go to Jerusalem!'"
No, God was leading Paul to Jerusalem and was simply preparing him
through Agabus' prophecy for the troubles that awaited him there. Notice
also that Agabus' prophecy only confirmed what Paul already knew in
his spirit months before. We should never be led by prophecy. If prophecy
doesn't confirm what we already know, we shouldn't follow it.

Agabus' prophecy is what we might consider to be "spectacular guidance," because it went beyond just an inward impression within Paul's

spirit. When God grants "spectacular guidance," such as a vision or hearing an audible voice, it is usually because God knows our way is not going to be easy. We will need the extra assurance that spectacular guidance brings. In Paul's case, he was nearly going to be killed by a mob and spend several years in prison before his journey to Rome as a prisoner. Because of the spectacular guidance he received, however, he could maintain perfect peace through it all, knowing the outcome would be favorable.

If you don't receive spectacular guidance you shouldn't be concerned because if you need it, God will see that you get it. We should, however, always strive to be sensitive to and be led by the inward witness.

In Chains and in God's Will

When Paul arrived in Jerusalem, he was seized and incarcerated. Once again he received some spectacular guidance in the form of a vision of Jesus:

> But on the night immediately following, the Lord stood at his [Paul's] side and said, "Take courage; for as you have solemnly witnessed to My cause at Jerusalem, so you must witness at Rome also" (Acts. 23:11).

Notice that Jesus did not say, "Now Paul, what are you doing here? I tried to warn you not to come to Jerusalem!" No, Jesus actually confirmed the leading that Paul had perceived in his spirit months before. Paul was in the center of God's purpose in Jerusalem in order to testify on behalf of Jesus. He would eventually proclaim Christ in Rome as well.

We must keep in mind that part of Paul's original calling was to testify not only before Jews and Gentiles but also before kings (see Acts 9:15). In the course of Paul's imprisonment in Jerusalem and later in Caesarea, he was given the opportunity to testify before Governor Felix, Porcius Festus, and King Agrippa, who was "almost persuaded" (Acts 26:28) to believe in Jesus. Finally, Paul was sent to Rome to testify before the Roman Emperor himself, Nero.

On the Way to See Nero

While on board a ship that was carrying him to Italy, Paul once again received God's guidance by being sensitive to his spirit. As the ship's captain and pilot were trying to determine at which port they should winter on the island of Crete, Paul received a revelation:

> And when considerable time had passed and the voyage was now dangerous, since even the fast was already over, Paul began to admonish them, and said to them, "Men, I *perceive* that the voyage will certainly be attended with damage and great loss, not only of the cargo and the ship, but also of our lives" (Acts 27:9-10, emphasis added).

Paul *perceived* what was about to occur. Obviously his perception was though an impression given by the Spirit.

Unfortunately, the captain didn't listen to Paul and attempted to reach another harbor. As a result, the ship was caught in a violent storm for two weeks. The situation was so perilous that the ship's crew jettisoned all the cargo on the second day, and on the third day even threw the ship's tackle overboard. Sometime later, Paul received further guidance:

> And since neither sun nor stars appeared for many days, and no small storm was assailing us, from then on all hope of our being saved was gradually abandoned. And when they had gone a long time without food, then Paul stood up in their midst and said, "Men, you ought to have followed my advice and not to have set sail from Crete, and incurred this damage and loss. And yet now I urge you to keep up your courage, for there shall be no loss of life among you, but only of the ship. For this very night an angel of God to whom I belong and whom I serve stood before me, saying, 'Do not be afraid, Paul; you must stand before Caesar; and behold, God has granted you all those who are sailing with you.' Therefore, keep up your courage, men, for I believe God, that it will turn out exactly as I have been told. But we must run aground on a certain island" (Acts 27:20-26).

I think it is obvious why God granted Paul more "spectacular guidance" in light of his present predicament. Beyond that ordeal, Paul would soon face the plight of shipwreck. Shortly after that he would be bitten by a deadly snake (see Act 27:41-28:5). It's nice to have an angel let you know in advance that everything is going to be OK!

Some Practical Advice

Begin to look to your spirit for those perceptions and impressions that are the Holy Spirit's leadings. You will probably make some mistakes at first thinking that the Holy Spirit is leading you when He isn't, but that's normal. Don't be discouraged; just keep at it.

It also helps to spend time in a quiet place, praying in tongues and reading the Bible. When we pray in other tongues, it is our spirit that prays, and we naturally tend to be more sensitive to our spirits then. By reading and meditating in the Word of God, we also become more sensitive to our spirits because God's Word is spiritual food.

When God leads you in a certain direction, His leading won't diminish. That means you should continue praying about major decisions for some time to be certain that it is *God* who is leading you and not your own ideas or emotions. If you don't have peace in your heart when you pray about a certain direction, then don't take that direction until you do have peace.

If you receive spectacular guidance, that is fine, but don't try to "believe" to see a vision or hear an audible voice. God hasn't promised to lead us by those means (although He does at times according to His sovereign will). We can, however, always trust that He will lead us by the inward witness.

Finally, don't add to what God says to you. God may reveal to you some ministry He has prepared for you in the future, but you may assume the time of fulfillment is weeks away when it may be years. I know this from experience. Don't make assumptions. Paul knew a little bit of what his future held but didn't know everything, because God didn't reveal everything. God wants us to continue to walk by faith always.

TWENTY-THREE

The Sacraments

Jesus gave the church only two sacraments: water baptism (see Matt. 28:19) and the Lord's Supper (see 1 Cor. 11:23-26). We will first study water baptism.

Under the new covenant, every believer should experience three different baptisms. They are: baptism into the body of Christ, baptism in water, and baptism in the Holy Spirit.

When a person is born again, he is automatically baptized into the body of Christ. That is, he becomes a member of Christ's body, the church:

> For by one Spirit we were all baptized into one body (1 Cor. 12:13; see also Rom. 6:3; Eph. 1:22-23; Col. 1:18, 24).

Being baptized in the Holy Spirit is an experience subsequent to salvation, and this baptism can and should be received by every believer.

Finally, every believer should be baptized in water as soon as possible after he repents and believes in the Lord Jesus. Baptism should be the first act of obedience of the new believer:

> And [Jesus] said to them, "Go into all the world and preach the gospel to all creation. He who has believed and *has been baptized* shall be saved; but he who has disbelieved shall be condemned" (Mark 16:15-16, emphasis added).

The early church regarded Jesus' command to baptize as very important. Almost without exception, new converts were baptized immediately after their conversion (see Acts 2:37-41; 8:12-16, 36-39; 9:17-19; 10:44-48; 16:31-33; 18:5-8; 19:1-5).

Some Unscriptural Ideas About Baptism

Some practice baptism by sprinkling the new convert with a few drops of water. Is this correct? The verb translated *baptize* in the New Testament is the Greek word *baptizo*, which literally means "to immerse." Those who are baptized in water should, therefore, be immersed under the water and not simply sprinkled with a few drops. The symbolism of Christian baptism, which we will study shortly, also supports the idea of immersion.

Some practice the baptism of infants, yet there are no scriptural examples of infant baptism in the Bible. Such a practice has its origins in the false doctrine of "baptismal regeneration"—the idea that a person is born again the moment he is baptized. Scripture clearly teaches that people should first believe in Jesus before they are baptized. Thus, children who are old enough to repent and follow Jesus qualify for baptism, but not babies and small children.

Some teach that, although a person may believe in Jesus, he is not saved until he is baptized in water. That is not true according to Scripture. In Acts 10:44-48 and 11:17, we read that the household of Cornelius was saved and baptized in the Holy Spirit *before* any of them were baptized in water. It is impossible for anyone to be baptized in the Holy Spirit unless he is first saved (see John 14:17).

Some teach that unless a person is baptized according to their particular formula, he is not really saved. Scripture provides no specific ritual to be followed for correct baptism. For example, some say that a believer is not saved if he has been baptized "in the name of the Father, and the Son, and the Holy Spirit" (Matt. 28:19) rather than "in the name of Jesus" (Acts 8:16). These people demonstrate the same spirit that dominated the Pharisees, straining out gnats and swallowing camels. What a tragedy it is that Christians debate over the correct words to say during baptism while the world waits to hear the gospel.

The Scriptural Symbolism of Baptism

Water baptism symbolizes several things that have already occurred in the new believer's life. Most simply, it represents that we have had our sins washed away, and now we stand clean before God. When Ananias was sent to Saul (Paul) soon after his conversion, he said to him:

> And now why do you delay? Arise, and be baptized, and *wash away your sins,* calling on His name (Acts 22:16, emphasis added).

Second, water baptism symbolizes our identification with Christ in His death, burial and resurrection. Once we have been born again and placed into the body of Christ, we are considered by God to be "in Christ" from that point on. Because Jesus was our substitute, God attributes all that Jesus did to our account. So "in Christ," we have died, been buried, and have been raised from the dead to live as new persons:

> Or do you not know that all of us who have been baptized into Christ Jesus have been baptized into His death?

> Therefore we have been buried with Him through baptism into death, in order that as Christ was raised from the dead through the glory of the Father, so we too might walk in newness of life (Rom. 6:3-4).

> Having been buried with Him in baptism, in which you were also raised up with Him through faith in the working of God, who raised Him from the dead (Col. 2:12).

Every new believer should be taught these important truths when he is baptized in water, and he should be baptized as soon as possible after he believes in Jesus.

The Lord's Supper

The Lord's Supper has its origins in the Old Testament Passover Feast. On the night when God delivered Israel from Egyptian slavery, He instructed each household to slay a one-year-old lamb and sprinkle its blood on the lintel and doorposts of their houses. When the "death angel" passed through the nation that night, killing all the first-born in Egypt, he would see the blood on the Israelites' houses and "pass over."

Furthermore, the Israelites were to celebrate a feast that night by eating their Passover lamb and also by eating unleavened bread for seven days. This was to be a permanent ordinance for Israel, celebrated the same time each year (see Ex. 12:1-28). Obviously, the Passover lamb was representative of Christ, who is called "our Passover" in 1 Corinthians 5:7.

When Jesus instituted the Lord's Supper, He and His disciples were celebrating the Passover Feast. Jesus was crucified during the Passover feast, truly fulfilling His calling as the "Lamb of God who takes away the sin of the world" (John 1:29).

The bread that we eat and the juice we drink are symbolic of Jesus' body, which was broken for us, and His blood, which was shed for the remission of our sins:

> And while they were eating, Jesus took some bread, and after a blessing, He broke it and gave it to the disciples, and said, "Take, eat; this is My body." And He took a cup and gave thanks, and gave it to them, saying, "Drink from it, all of you; for this is My blood of the covenant, which is to be shed on behalf of many for forgiveness of sins. But I say to you, I will not drink of this fruit of the vine from now on until that day when I drink it new with you in My Father's kingdom" (Matt. 26:26-29).

The apostle Paul told the story this way:

> For I received from the Lord that which I also delivered to you, that the Lord Jesus in the night in which He was

betrayed took bread; and when He had given thanks, He broke it, and said, "This is My body, which is for you; do this in remembrance of Me." In the same way He took the cup also, after supper, saying, "This cup is the new covenant in My blood; do this, as often as you drink it, in remembrance of Me." For as often as you eat this bread and drink the cup, you proclaim the Lord's death until He comes (1 Cor. 11:23-26).

When and How

Scripture does not tell us how often to partake of the Lord's Supper, but it is clear that in the early church, it was done with regularity in the house church meetings as a full meal (see 1 Cor. 11:20-34). Because the Lord's Supper has its roots in the Passover Meal, it was part of a full meal when instituted by Jesus, and was eaten as a full meal by the early church, that is how it should be practiced today. Still much of the church follows "the traditions of men."

We should approach the Lord's Supper with reverence. The apostle Paul taught that it was a serious offense to partake of the Lord's Supper in an unworthy manner:

> Therefore whoever eats the bread or drinks the cup of the Lord in an unworthy manner, shall be guilty of the body and the blood of the Lord. But let a man examine himself, and so let him eat of the bread and drink of the cup. For he who eats and drinks, eats and drinks judgment to himself, if he does not judge the body rightly. For this reason many among you are weak and sick, and a number sleep. But if we judged ourselves rightly, we should not be judged. But when we are judged, we are disciplined by the Lord in order that we may not be condemned along with the world (1 Cor. 11:27-32).

We are admonished to examine and judge ourselves before partaking of the Lord's Supper, and if we discover any sin, we need to repent and confess it. Otherwise, we can be "guilty of the body and the blood of the Lord."

Because Jesus died and shed His blood to free us from sin, we certainly don't want to partake of the elements, which represent His body and blood, with any known unconfessed sin. If we do, we can eat and drink judgment upon ourselves in the form of sickness and premature death, as did the Corinthian Christians. The way to avoid God's discipline is to "judge ourselves," that is, acknowledging and repenting of our sins.

The primary sin of the Corinthian Christians was their lack of love; they were bickering and fighting with one another. In fact, their lack of consideration even manifested itself during the Lord's Supper when some ate while others went hungry, and some were even drunk (see 1 Cor. 11:20-22).

The bread we eat represents the body of Christ, which is now the church. We partake of one loaf, representing our unity as one body (see 1 Cor. 10:17). What a crime it is to partake of that which represents the one body of Christ while involved in fighting and disharmony with other members of that body! Before we partake of the Lord's Supper, we need to make certain we are in right relationship with our brothers and sisters in Christ.

TWENTY-FOUR

Confrontation, Forgiveness and Reconciliation

When we studied Jesus' Sermon on the Mount in an earlier chapter, we learned how important it is that we forgive those who sin against us. If we don't forgive them, Jesus solemnly promised that God will not forgive us (see Matt. 6:14-15).

What does it mean to forgive someone? Let's consider what Scripture teaches.

Jesus compared forgiveness to erasing someone's debt (see Matt. 18:23-35). Imagine someone owing you money and then releasing that person from his obligation to repay you. You destroy the document that recorded his debt. You no longer expect payment, and you are no longer angry with your debtor. You now see him differently than you did when he owed you money.

We can also better understand what it means to forgive if we consider what it means to be forgiven by God. When He forgives us of a sin, He no longer holds us accountable for what we did that displeased Him. He is no longer angry with us because of that sin. He will not discipline or punish us for what we did. We are reconciled with Him.

Likewise, if I truly forgive someone, I release that person in my heart, overcoming the desire for justice or revenge by means of showing mercy. I am no longer angry with the person who sinned against me. We are reconciled. *If I am harboring anger or a grudge against someone, I haven't forgiven him.*

Christians often fool themselves in this regard. They say they have forgiven someone, knowing that is what they are supposed to do, but they still harbor a grudge against the offender deep inside. They avoid seeing the offender because it causes that suppressed anger to surface again. I know what I'm talking about, because I've done just that. Let us not fool ourselves. Remember that Jesus does not want us even to be angry with a fellow believer (see Matt. 5:22).

Now let me ask a question: Who is easier to forgive, an offender who asks for forgiveness or an offender who does not ask forgiveness? Of course, we all agree that is it much easier to forgive an offender who admits his wrong and asks for our forgiveness. In fact, it seems infinitely easier to forgive someone who asks for it than someone who doesn't. To forgive someone who doesn't request it seems practically impossible.

Let's consider this from another angle. If refusing to forgive an offender who repents and refusing to forgive an offender who *does not* repent are both wrong, which is the greater sin? I think we would all agree that if both are wrong, to refuse to forgive an offender who repents would be a greater evil.

A Surprise from Scripture

All of this leads me to another question: Does God expect us to forgive everyone who sins against us, even those who don't humble themselves, admit their sin, and request forgiveness?

As we study Scripture closely, we discover that the answer is "No." To the surprise of many Christians, Scripture clearly states that, although we are commanded to love everyone, we are not required to forgive everyone.

For example, does Jesus simply expect us to forgive a fellow believer who sins against us? No, He doesn't. Otherwise, He would not have told us to follow the four steps to reconciliation outlined in Matthew 18:15-17, steps that end with excommunication if the offender does not repent:

> And if your brother sins, go and reprove him in private;
> if he listens to you, you have won your brother. But if he
> does not listen to you, take one or two more with you, so
> that by the mouth of two or three witnesses every fact may
> be confirmed. And if he refuses to listen to them, tell it to
> the church; and if he refuses to listen even to the church,
> let him be to you as a Gentile and a tax-gatherer.

Obviously, if the fourth step is reached (excommunication), forgiveness is not granted to the offender, as forgiveness and excommunication are incompatible actions. It would seem strange to hear someone say, "We forgave him and then we excommunicated him," because forgiveness results in reconciliation, not severance. (What would you think if God said, "I forgive you, but I will have nothing to do with you from now on"?) Jesus told us treat the excommunicated person "as a Gentile and a tax-gatherer," two kinds of people that Jews had no relationships with and actually abhorred.

In the four steps that Jesus outlined, forgiveness is not granted after the first, second or third steps unless the offender repents. If he doesn't repent after any step, he is taken to the next step, still treated as an unrepentant offender. Only when the offender "listens to you" (that is, repents), can it be said that you "have won your brother" (that is, been reconciled).

The purpose for confrontation is so that forgiveness can be granted. Forgiveness is predicated, however, upon the repentance of the offender. So we (1) confront with the hope that the offender will (2) repent so we can (3) forgive him.

All this being so, we can say with certainty that God does not expect us simply to forgive fellow believers who have sinned against us and who are unrepentant after confrontation. This, of course, does not give us the right to hate an offending believer. On the contrary, we confront because we love the offender and want to forgive him and be reconciled.

Yet once every effort is made for reconciliation by means of the three steps Jesus outlined, the fourth step terminates the relationship in obedience to Christ.[63] Just as we are not to have any fellowship with so-called Christians who are adulterers, drunkards, homosexuals and so on (see 1 Cor. 5:11), we are not to have any fellowship with the so-called Christians who refuse to repent at the consensus of the entire body. Such people prove that they are not true followers of Christ, and they bring reproach on His church.

God's Example

As we further consider our responsibility to forgive others, we might also wonder why God would expect us to do something that He Himself does not do. Certainly God loves guilty people and extends His merciful hands in an offer to pardon them. He withholds His wrath and gives them time to repent. But their actually being forgiven is contingent upon their repentance. *God does not forgive guilty people unless they repent.* So why should we think that He expects more of us?

All of this being so, is it not possible that the sin of unforgiveness that is so grievous in God's eyes is specifically the sin of not forgiving those who request our forgiveness? It is interesting that just after Jesus outlined the four steps of church discipline, Peter asked ,

> "Lord, how often shall my brother sin against me and I forgive him? Up to seven times?" Jesus said to him, "I do not say to you, up to seven times, but up to seventy times seven" (Matt. 18:21-22).

Did Peter think that Jesus was expecting him to forgive an *unrepentant* brother hundreds of times for hundreds of sins when Jesus had just told him moments before to treat an *unrepentant* brother like a Gentile or tax collector because of *one* sin? That seems very unlikely. Again, you don't treat a person as being abhorrent if you've forgiven him.

Another question that should provoke our thinking is this: If Jesus ex-

---

[63] It would stand to reason that if the excommunicated one later repented, Jesus would expect that forgiveness would be granted then.

pects us to forgive a believer hundreds of times for hundreds of sins of which he never repents, thus maintaining our relationship, why does He allow us to terminate a marriage relationship for only one sin committed against us, the sin of adultery, if our spouse does not repent (see Matt. 5:32)?[64] That would seem rather inconsistent.

An Elaboration

Directly after Jesus told Peter to forgive a brother four-hundred and ninety times, He told a parable to help Peter understand what He meant:

> For this reason the kingdom of heaven may be compared to a certain king who wished to settle accounts with his slaves. And when he had begun to settle them, there was brought to him one who owed him ten thousand talents [This would have been equivalent to over 5,000 years of wages for the average laborer in Jesus' day.] But since he did not have the means to repay, his lord commanded him to be sold, along with his wife and children and all that he had, and repayment to be made. The slave therefore falling down, prostrated himself before him, saying, "Have patience with me, and I will repay you everything." And the lord of that slave felt compassion and released him and forgave him the debt. But that slave went out and found one of his fellow slaves who owed him a hundred denarii [equivalent to one hundred day's wages]; and he seized him and began to choke him, saying, "Pay back what you owe." So his fellow slave fell down and began to entreat him, saying, "Have patience with me and I will repay you." He was unwilling however, but went and threw him in prison until he should pay back what was owed. So when his fellow slaves saw what had happened, they were deeply grieved and came and reported to their lord all that had happened. Then summoning him, his lord said to him, "You wicked slave, I forgave you all that debt because you entreated me. Should you not also have had mercy on your fellow slave, even as I had mercy on you?" And his lord, moved with anger, handed him over to the torturers until he should repay all that was owed him. So shall My heavenly Father also do to you, if each of you does not forgive his brother from your heart (Matt. 18:23-35).

[64] If an adulterous spouse is a Christian, we should take that spouse through the three steps Jesus outlined for reconciliation before going through with a divorce. If that adulterous spouse repents, we are expected to forgive according to Jesus' commandment.

Notice that the first slave was forgiven because he asked his master for it. Then notice that the second slave also humbly asked the first slave for forgiveness. The first slave did not grant the second slave what he had been granted, and that is what so angered his master. This being so, would Peter have thought that Jesus was expecting him to forgive an unrepentant brother who never asked for forgiveness, something not illustrated at all by Jesus' parable? That seems unlikely, and even more so since Jesus had just told him to treat an unrepentant brother, after he had been properly confronted, like a Gentile and tax collector.

It seems even more unlikely that Peter would have thought that he was expected to forgive an unrepentant brother in light of the punishment that Jesus promised us if we don't forgive our brothers from our hearts. Jesus promised to reinstate all of our formerly-forgiven debt and hand us over to the torturers until we repay what we can never repay. Would that be a just punishment for a Christian who does not forgive a brother, *a brother whom God does not forgive either?* If a brother sins against me, he sins against God, and God does not forgive him unless he repents. Can God justly punish me for not forgiving someone whom He does not forgive?

A Synopsis

Jesus' expectations for our forgiving fellow believers is succinctly stated by His words recorded in Luke 17:3-4:

> Be on your guard! If your brother sins, rebuke him; *and if he repents*, forgive him. And if he sins against you seven times a day, and returns to you seven times, saying, "*I repent*," forgive him (emphasis added).

How much clearer could it be? Jesus expects us to forgive fellow believers when they repent. When we pray, "Forgive us our debts as we also have forgiven our debtors," we're *asking* God to do for us what we have done for others. We would never expect Him to forgive us unless we *ask.* So why would we think He expects us to forgive those who *don't* ask?

Again, all of this does not give us the right to harbor a grudge against a brother or sister in Christ who has sinned against us. We are commanded to love one another. That is why we are commanded to confront a fellow believer who sins against us, so that there might be reconciliation with him, and that he might be reconciled to God against whom he has also sinned. *That is what love would do.* Yet too often, Christians say they forgive an offending fellow believer, but it is only an excuse to avoid confrontation. They actually don't forgive, and it is clear by their actions. They avoid the offender at all costs and often speak of their hurt. There is no reconciliation.

When we sin, God confronts us by His Holy Spirit within us because He loves us and wants to forgive us. We should imitate Him, lovingly

313

confronting fellow believers who sin against us so that there will be repentance, forgiveness and reconciliation.

God has always expected His people to love one another with a genuine love, a love that allows for rebuke, but a love that does not allow for bearing a grudge. Contained within the Law of Moses is the commandment:

> You shall not hate your fellow countryman in your heart; *you may surely reprove your neighbor,* but shall not incur sin because of him. You shall not take vengeance, *nor bear any grudge* against the sons of your people, but *you shall love your neighbor as yourself;* I am the Lord (Lev. 19:17-18, emphasis added).

An Objection

But what about Jesus' words in Mark 11:25-26? Do they not indicate that we must forgive everyone of everything regardless of whether or not they request forgiveness?

> And whenever you stand praying, forgive, if you have anything against anyone; so that your Father also who is in heaven may forgive you your transgressions. But if you do not forgive, neither will your Father who is in heaven forgive your transgressions.

This one verse does not supersede all the other verses we've already considered on the subject. We already know that what is so grievous to God is our refusal to forgive someone who requests our forgiveness. So we can interpret this verse in light of that well-established fact. Jesus is only emphasizing here that we must forgive others if we want God's forgiveness. He is not telling us the more specific mechanics of forgiveness and what one must do to receive it from another.

Notice that Jesus also does not say here that we must ask God for forgiveness in order to receive it from Him. Shall we then ignore everything else that Scripture teaches about God's forgiveness being predicated upon our asking for it (see Matt. 6:12; 1 John 1:9)? Shall we assume that we don't need to ask for forgiveness from God when we sin because Jesus doesn't mention it here? That would be an unwise assumption in light of what Scripture tells us. It is equally unwise to ignore everything else Scripture teaches about our forgiving others being based on their asking for it.

Another Objection

Did not Jesus pray for the soldiers who were dividing His garments, "Father, forgive them; for they do not know what they are doing" (Luke 23:34)? Does this not indicate that God forgives people without their asking for it?

It does, but only to a certain degree. It indicates that God shows mercy to the ignorant, a measure of forgiveness. Because God is perfectly just, He holds people accountable only when they know they are sinning.

Jesus' prayer for the soldiers didn't guarantee their place in heaven—it only insured that they would not be held accountable for dividing the garments of God's Son, and only because of their ignorance of who He was. They considered Him to be just one more criminal to execute. So God extended mercy for a deed that would have deserved certain judgment had they known what they were actually doing.

We should likewise show mercy to those who are ignorant of what they've done to us, such as in the case of unbelievers like the ignorant soldiers who divided Jesus' garments. Jesus expects us to show unbelievers extraordinary mercy, loving our enemies, doing good to those who hate us, blessing those who curse us and praying for those who mistreat us (see Luke 6:27-28). We should attempt to melt their hatred with our love, overcoming evil with good. This concept was prescribed even under the Mosaic Law:

> If you meet your enemy's ox or his donkey wandering away, you shall surely return it to him. If you see the donkey of one who hates you lying helpless under its load, you shall refrain from leaving it to him, you shall surely release it with him (Ex. 23:4-5).

> If your enemy is hungry, give him food to eat; and if he is thirsty, give him water to drink; for you will heap burning coals on his head, and the Lord will reward you (Prov. 25:21-22).

It is interesting that, although Jesus commanded us to love our enemies, do good to those who hate us, bless those who curse us, and pray for those who mistreat us (see Luke 6:27-28), He never told us to forgive any of them. We can actually love people without forgiving them—just as God loves people without forgiving them. Not only *can* we love them, but we *should* love them, as we are commanded by God to do so. And our love for them should be manifested by our actions.

Just because Jesus prayed for His Father to forgive the soldiers who were dividing His garments does not prove that God expects us to ignore everything else we have studied from Scripture on this subject and forgive everyone who sins against us. It only teaches us that we should automatically forgive those who are ignorant of their sin against us and show extraordinary mercy towards unbelievers.

The Practice of Matthew 18:15-17

Although the four steps of reconciliation listed by Jesus are quite simple to understand, they actually can be more complex to practice. When Jesus outlined the four steps, He did so from a perspective of when brother A is convinced, and rightly so, that brother B has sinned against him. In reality, however, brother A could be wrong. So let's imagine a situation in which every possible scenario is considered.

If brother A is convinced that brother B has sinned against him, he should first make sure that he is not being overly critical, finding a speck in brother B's eye. Many small offenses should just be overlooked and mercy extended (see Matt. 7:3-5). If, however, brother A finds himself feeling resentment towards brother B for a significant offense, he should confront him.

He should do it privately, obeying Jesus' command, demonstrating his love for brother B. His motive should be love and his goal reconciliation. He shouldn't tell anyone else about the offense. "Love covers a multitude of sins" (1 Pet. 4:8). If we love someone, we won't expose his sins; we'll hide them.

His confrontation should be gentle, demonstrating his love. He should say something like, "Brother B, I really value our relationship. But something has happened that has created a wall in my heart against you. I don't want that wall to be there, and so I must tell you why I feel you have sinned against me so that we can work to be reconciled. And if I have done anything that has contributed to this problem, I want you to tell me." And then he should gently tell brother B what the offense is.

In most cases, brother B will not even have realized that he offended brother A, and as soon as he learns that he has, he will ask forgiveness. If that is what happens, brother A should immediately forgive brother B. Reconciliation has taken place.

Another possible scenario is that brother B will try to justify his sin against brother A by telling him that he was only reacting to an offense already committed by brother A against him. If that is the case, brother B should have already confronted brother A. But at least now there is finally some dialogue and a hope of reconciliation.

In such cases, the offended parties should discuss what happened, admit their blame to the degree of each one's guilt, and then offer and receive forgiveness from each other. Reconciliation has been accomplished.

A third scenario is that A and B are unable to reconcile. They thus need help, and it is time to go to step two.

Step Two

It would be best if brother A and brother B both agreed on who should now join them to assist in working towards reconciliation. Ideally, brothers C and D should know and love both A and B, thus insuring their impartiality. And only brothers C and D should be told of the dispute out of love and respect for A and B.

If brother B is not cooperative at this point, it will be up to brother A to find one or two others who can help.

If brothers C and D are wise, they will not render a judgment until they have heard the viewpoints of both A and B. Once C and D have rendered their judgment, A and B should submit to their decision and make the apologies and restitutions that are recommended to one or the other or both.

Brothers C and D should not try to appear more impartial and take less personal risk by recommending that both brothers A and B need to repent when in fact only one actually does. They should know that if either A or B reject their judgment, it will be appealed before the entire church and their cowardly judgment will become evident to everyone. This temptation faced by C and D to attempt to maintain their friendships with both A and B by compromising the truth is a good reason why two judges are better than one, as they can strengthen each other in the truth. Additionally, their decision is more likely to carry weight before A and B.

Step Three

If either A or B reject the judgment of C and D, the matter is to be taken up with the entire church. This third step is never done in institutional churches—and for good reason—it would inevitably result in church splits as people took sides. Jesus never intended that local churches would be larger than what could fit in a house. This smaller congregational family where everyone knows and cares about A and B is the intended scriptural setting for step three. In an institutional church, step three should be done in the context of a small group consisting of people who know and love both A and B. If A and B are members of different local bodies, several of the best-suited members from both bodies could serve as the decision-making body.

Once the church renders its judgment, brothers A and B should both submit to it, knowing the consequences of defiance. Apologies should be made, forgiveness granted and reconciliation occur.

If either A or B refuses to make the recommended apologies, he should be put out of the church and none within the church should fellowship with him any longer. Often, by this time, an unrepentant person will have already voluntarily removed himself, and he may have done so long before if he didn't get his way at any step of the process. This reveals his lack of genuine commitment to love his spiritual family.

A Common Problem

In institutional churches, people normally solve their disputes by simply leaving one church and going to another, where the pastor, who wants to build his kingdom at any cost and who has no real relationship with other pastors, welcomes such people and sides with them as they relate their woeful tales. This pattern effectively neutralizes Christ's commanded steps of reconciliation. And normally, it is just a matter of months or years before the offended person, whom such pastors welcomed into their church, has left to find another church, offended once again.

Jesus expected that churches would be small enough to fit into homes, and that local pastors/elders/overseers would be working together in one body. Thus the excommunication of a member of one church would effectively be an excommunication from all the churches. It is the responsibility of each pastor/elder/overseer to ask incoming Christians about their former church background and then contact the leadership of their former church to determine if such people should be welcomed.

God's Intention for a Holy Church

Another common problem in institutional churches is that they often consist of many people who attend just for the show, having little if any accountability to anyone because their relationships are purely social in nature. Thus no one, and especially the pastors, have any idea how they live their lives, and unholy people continually bring a stain on the churches they attend. Outsiders then judge people whom they deem to be Christians as being no different than unbelievers.

This by itself should be proof enough to anyone that the structure of institutional churches is not God's intention for His holy church. Unholy and hypocritical people are always hiding in large institutional churches, bringing a reproach to Christ. Yet from what we've read in Matthew 18:15-17, Jesus clearly intended that His church would consist of holy people who were committed members of a self-cleansing body. The world would look at the church and see His pure bride. Today, however, they see a great harlot, one that is unfaithful to her Husband.

This divinely-intended self-cleansing aspect of the church was evident when Paul addressed a critical situation in the Corinthian church. An accepted member of the body was actually living in an adulterous relationship with his stepmother:

> It is actually reported that there is immorality among you, and immorality of such a kind as does not exist even among the Gentiles, that someone has his father's wife. And you have become arrogant, and have not mourned instead, in order that the one who had done this deed might be removed from your midst. For I, on my part, though absent in body, but present in spirit, have already judged him who has so committed this, as though I were present. In the name of our Lord Jesus, when you are assembled, and I with you in spirit, with the power of our Lord Jesus, deliver such a one to Satan for the destruction of his flesh, that his spirit might be saved in the day of the

> Lord Jesus....I wrote you in my letter not to associate with
> immoral people; I did not at all mean with the immoral
> people of this world, or with the covetous and swindlers,
> or with idolaters; for then you would have to go out of the
> world. But actually, I wrote to you not to associate with
> any so-called brother if he should be an immoral person,
> or covetous, or an idolater, or a reviler, or a drunkard, or a
> swindler—not even to eat with such a one. For what have
> I to do with judging outsiders? Do you not judge those
> who are within the church? But those who are outside,
> God judges. Remove the wicked man from among your-
> selves (1 Cor. 5:1-5, 9-13).

There was no need to take this particular man through the steps of reconciliation because he was clearly not a true believer. Paul referred to him
as a "so-called brother" and a "wicked man." Moreover, a few verses later,
Paul wrote,

> Or do you not know that the unrighteous shall not inherit
> the kingdom of God? Do not be deceived; neither fornica-
> tors, nor idolaters, nor adulterers, nor effeminate, nor ho-
> mosexuals, nor thieves, nor the covetous, nor drunkards,
> nor revilers, nor swindlers, shall inherit the kingdom of
> God (1 Cor. 6:9-10).

Clearly, Paul rightly believed that those who are immoral, like the man
in the Corinthian church, betray the falseness of their faith. Such people
should not be treated as brothers and taken through the four steps to reconciliation. They should be excommunicated, "turned over to Satan," so
that the church does not strengthen their self-deception, and so they have
hope of seeing their need of repentance in order to "be saved in the day of
the Lord Jesus" (1 Cor. 5:5).

In large churches around the world today, there are sometimes hundreds of people posing as Christians, who by biblical standards are non-
believers and who should be excommunicated. Scripture clearly shows
us that the church has the responsibility to remove those within it who
are unrepentant fornicators, adulterers, homosexuals, drunkards and so
on. Yet such people, under the banner of "grace," are today often placed
into church support groups where they can be encouraged by other "believers" with similar problems. This is an affront to the life-transforming
power of the gospel of Jesus Christ.

Fallen Leaders

Finally, should a repentant leader be immediately restored to his position if he has fallen into serious sin (such as adultery)? Although the Lord

will immediately forgive the repentant leader (and so should the church), the fallen leader will have lost the trust of the ones to whom he ministers. *Trust is something that must be earned.* Therefore, fallen leaders should voluntarily remove themselves from their leadership positions and submit to spiritual oversight until they can prove their trustworthiness. They must start over. Those who are unwilling to humbly serve in smaller ways in order to regain trust should not be submitted to as leaders by anyone within the body.

In Summary

As disciple-making ministers who are called to "reprove, rebuke, exhort, with all patience and instruction" (2 Tim. 4:2), let us not shy away from our calling. Let us teach our disciples to truly love one another by means of merciful forbearance always, gentle confrontation when necessary, additional confrontation with the help of others when needed, and forgiveness whenever it is requested. How much better this is than false forgiveness that brings no true healing to broken relationships. And let us strive to obey the Lord in every aspect to keep His church pure and holy, a praise to His name!

For further study concerning confrontation and church discipline, see Rom. 16:17-18; 2 Cor. 13:1-3; Gal. 2:11-14; 2 Thes. 3:6, 14-15; 1 Tim. 1:19-20, 5:19-20; Tit. 3:10-11; Jas. 5:19-20; 2 John 10-11.

TWENTY-FIVE

God's Discipline

For consider Him who has endured such hostility by sinners against Himself, so that you may not grow weary and lose heart. You have not yet resisted to the point of shedding blood in your striving against sin; and you have forgotten the exhortation which is addressed to you as sons, "My son, do not regard lightly the discipline of the Lord, nor faint when you are reproved by Him; for those whom the Lord loves He disciplines, and He scourges every son whom He receives." It is for discipline that you endure; God deals with you as with sons; for what son is there whom his father does not discipline? But if you are without discipline, of which all have become partakers, then you are illegitimate children and not sons. Furthermore, we had earthly fathers to discipline us, and we respected them; shall we not much rather be subject to the father of spirits, and live? For they disciplined us for a short time as seemed best to them, but He disciplines us for our good, that we might share His holiness. All discipline for the moment seems not to be joyful, but sorrowful; yet to those who have been trained by it, afterwards it yields the peaceful fruit of righteousness. Therefore, strengthen the hands that are weak and the knees that are feeble, and make straight paths for your feet, so that the limb which is lame may not be put out of joint, but rather be healed (Heb. 12:3-13).

According to the inspired author of the book Hebrews, our heavenly Father disciplines all of His children. If we are never disciplined by Him, it indicates that we aren't one of His children. We therefore need to be aware of and sensitive to His discipline. Some professing Christians, whose only focus is God's blessings and goodness, interpret all negative circumstances as being attacks from the devil void of any divine purpose. This can be a great error if God is trying to bring them to repentance by His discipline.

Good earthly parents discipline their children with the hope that their children will learn, mature, and be prepared for responsible adult life. God likewise disciplines us so that we grow spiritually, become more useful in His service, and are prepared to stand before His judgment seat. He disciplines us because He loves us, and because He desires that we share His holiness. Our loving heavenly Father is dedicated to our spiritual growth. Scripture says, "He who began a good work in you will perfect it until the day of Christ Jesus" (Phil 1:6).

No child ever enjoys his parents' spankings, and when we are disciplined by God, the experience is not "joyful, but sorrowful," as we just read. In the end, however, we are better for it because discipline yields "the peaceful fruit of righteousness."

When and How Does God Discipline Us?

Like any good father, God only disciplines His children when they are disobedient. Any time we disobey Him, we are in danger of suffering His discipline. The Lord is very merciful, however, and He normally gives us ample time to repent. His discipline usually comes after our repeated acts of disobedience and His repeated warnings.

How does God discipline us? As we learned in a previous chapter, God's discipline may come in the form of weakness, sickness or even premature death:

> For this reason many among you are weak and sick, and a number sleep. But if we judged ourselves rightly, we should not be judged. But when we are judged, we are disciplined by the Lord in order that we may not be condemned along with the world (1 Cor. 11:30-32).

We shouldn't automatically conclude that all sickness is a result of God's discipline (the case of Job comes to mind). If sickness does strike, however, it is wise to do a spiritual checkup to see if we may have opened the door to God's discipline through disobedience.

We can avoid God's judgment if we judge ourselves—that is, acknowledge our sin and repent. It would be logical to conclude that we would candidates for healing once we have repented if our sickness is a result of God's discipline.

By means of God's judgment, Paul said that we actually avoid being condemned along with the world. What did he mean? He could only have meant that God's discipline leads us to repent so that we ultimately aren't sent to hell with the world. This is difficult to accept by those who think holiness is optional for those on the way to heaven. But for those who have read Jesus' Sermon on the Mount, they know that only those who obey God will enter His kingdom (see Matt. 7:21). Thus, if we persist in sin and don't repent, we risk forfeiting eternal life. Praise God for His discipline that leads us to repent and saves us from hell!

Satan as a Tool of God's Judgment

It is clear from a number of scriptures that God may use Satan for His disciplinary purposes. For example, in the parable of the unforgiving servant found in Matthew 18, Jesus said that the servant's master was "moved with anger" when he learned that his forgiven servant had not in turn forgiven his fellow servant. Consequently, he handed his unforgiving servant "over to the torturers until he should repay all that was owed him" (Matt. 18:34). Jesus ended this parable with the solemn words:

> So shall my heavenly Father also do to you, if each of you does not forgive his brother from your heart (Matt. 18:35).

Who are "the torturers"? It would seem likely that they would be the devil and his demons. God may turn one of His disobedient children over to the devil in order to bring him to repentance. And if he doesn't repent then, God will turn him over eternally. Hardship and calamity have a way of bringing people to repentance—as the prodigal son learned (see Luke 15:14-19).

In the Old Testament, we find examples of God's using Satan or evil spirits to bring about His discipline or judgment in the lives of people who deserve His wrath. One example is found in the ninth chapter of Judges, where we read that "God sent an evil spirit between Abimelech and the men of Shechem" (Judg. 9:23) in order to bring judgment upon them for their wicked deeds against the sons of Gideon.

The Bible also says that "an evil spirit from the Lord" afflicted King Saul in order to bring him to repentance (1 Sam 16:14). Saul never did repent, however, and he eventually died in battle because of his rebellion.

In both of these Old Testament examples, the Scripture says that the evil spirits were "sent from God." This is not to say that God has evil spirits in heaven who are waiting there to serve Him. More likely, God simply allows Satan's evil spirits to limitedly work their ill in hopes that sinners will repent under their affliction.

Other Means of God's Discipline

Under the old covenant, we also find that God frequently disciplined His people by permitting troubles such as famines or foreign enemies to dominate them. Eventually they would repent and He would deliver them from their enemies. When they refused to repent after years of oppression and warnings, God ultimately permitted a foreign power to overcome them completely and deport them from their land as exiles.

Under the new covenant, it is certainly possible that God might discipline His disobedient children by permitting troubles in their lives, or He may permit their enemies to afflict them. For example, the scripture quoted at the start of this chapter about God's discipline (Heb. 12:3-13) is found within the context of Hebrew believers who were being persecuted for their faith. Not all persecution, however, is permitted because of disobedience. Every case must be judged separately.

Rightly Reacting to God's Discipline

According to the admonition quoted at the beginning of this chapter, we can react wrongly to God's discipline in one of two ways. We may either "regard lightly the discipline of the Lord" or we may "faint when [we] are reproved by Him" (Heb. 12:5). If we "regard lightly" God's discipline, that means that we don't recognize it, or we ignore its warning. To faint from God's discipline is to give up trying to please Him because we think His discipline is too severe. Either reaction is wrong. We should recognize that God loves us, and that He disciplines us for our good. When we recognize His loving hand of discipline, we should repent and receive His forgiveness.

Once we've repented, we should expect relief from God's discipline. We should not, however, necessarily expect relief from the inevitable consequences of our sin, although we may well ask the Lord for mercy and help. God responds to a humble and contrite spirit (see Isaiah 66:2). The Bible promises, "For His anger is but for a moment, His favor is for a lifetime; weeping may last for the night, but a shout of joy comes in the morning" (Ps. 30:5).

After His judgment fell upon the Israelites, God promised:

> For a brief moment I forsook you, but with a great compassion I will gather you. In an outburst of anger I hid My face from you for a moment; but with everlasting lovingkindness I will have compassion on you (Is. 54:7-8).

God is good and merciful!

For further study concerning God's discipline, see 2 Chron. 6:24-31, 36-39; 7:13-14; Ps. 73:14; 94:12-13; 106:40-46; 118:18; 119:67, 71; Jer. 2:29-30; 5:23-25; 14:12; 30:11; Hag. 1:2-13; 2:17; Acts 5:1-11; Rev. 3:19.

TWENTY-SIX

Fasting

Fasting is the voluntarily act of abstaining from eating food and or liquid for a period of time.

The Bible records many examples of people who fasted. Some abstained from eating *all* foods, and others abstained from eating only *certain kinds of foods* for the duration of their fast. An example of the latter would be Daniel's three-week fast, when he ate no "tasty food...meat or wine" (Dan. 10:3).

There are also a few examples in Scripture of people who fasted both food and water, but this kind of total fast was rare and should be considered supernatural if it lasted longer than three days. When Moses, for example, went for forty days without eating or drinking anything, he was in the presence of God Himself, to the extent that his face shined (see Ex. 34:28-29). He repeated a second 40-day fast shortly after his first one (see Deut. 9:9, 18). His were two very supernatural fasts, and no one should attempt to imitate them. It is impossible, apart from the supernatural help of God, for a person to survive more than a few days without water. Dehydration leads to death.

Going without water is not the only potential danger to one's health. To abstain from food for long periods of time can also be dangerous, especially for those who are already partially malnourished, and even healthy individuals should exercise caution if they are planning on fasting for more than a week.

Why Fast?

The primary purpose of fasting is to provide oneself extra time to pray and seek the Lord. There is hardly a reference to fasting in the Bible that does not also contain a reference to prayer, leading us to believe that it is pointless to fast without praying. Both references to fasting in the book of

Acts, for example, mention praying. In the first case (see Acts 13:1-3), the prophets and teachers in Antioch were simply "ministering to the Lord and fasting." As they did, they received prophetic revelation, and consequently sent Paul and Barnabas on their first missionary journey. In the second case, Paul and Barnabas were appointing elders over new churches in Galatia. We read,

> When they had appointed elders for them in every church,
> having prayed with fasting, they commended them to the
> Lord in whom they had believed (Acts 14:23).

Perhaps in this second case, Paul and Barnabas were following Jesus' example, as He prayed all night long before choosing the twelve (see Luke 6:12). Important decisions, such as appointing spiritual leaders, need to be prayed about until one is certain he has the leading of the Lord, and fasting could give more time for prayer to that end. If the New Testament commends temporary abstinence from sexual relations between marriage partners in order to increase devotion to prayer (see 1 Cor. 7:5), then we could easily understand how temporary abstinence from eating could serve the same purpose.[65]

Thus when we need to pray for God's direction for important spiritual decisions, fasting lends itself to that end. Prayers for other needs can be made in a relatively short time (we don't need to fast in order to pray the Lord's prayer). Prayers for guidance take longer because of our difficulty in "hearing God's voice." Gaining assurance in guidance can require an extended period of prayer, and that is where fasting is beneficial.

Wrong Reasons to Fast

Now that we have established the scriptural reason for fasting under the New Covenant, we should also consider some unscriptural reasons for fasting.

Some people fast hoping that it will increase the chance of God answering their prayer requests. Jesus, however, told us that the primary means to answered prayer is faith, not fasting (see Matt. 21:22). Remember that fasting doesn't change God at all. He is the same before our fast, during our fast, and after our fast. Fasting is not a means to "twist God's arm," or a way of saying to Him, "You better answer my prayer or I will starve myself to death!" That is not a biblical fast—that is a hunger strike! Remember that David fasted and prayed for several days for his sick baby by Bathsheba to live, but the baby died because God was disciplining David. Fasting didn't change his situation. David was not praying in faith

---

[65] The *King James Version* of 1 Corinthians 7:5 commends the mutual consent of husbands and wives to abstain from sexual relations in order that they might devote themselves to "*fasting* and prayer." Most modern translations of this verse only mention prayer.

because he had no promise on which to stand. In fact, he was praying and fasting contrary to God's will, as evidenced by the outcome.

Fasting is not a prerequisite to having a revival, as some think. There is no example of anyone in the New Testament fasting for a revival. Rather, the apostles simply obeyed Jesus by preaching the gospel. If a city was unresponsive, they obeyed Jesus again, sweeping the dust off of their feet and journeying to the next city (see Luke 9:5; Acts 13:49-51). They didn't stay around and fast, waiting for a revival.

Fasting is not a means of "putting the flesh under," as the desire to eat is a legitimate and non-sinful desire, unlike the obvious "desires of the flesh" listed in Galatians 5:19-21. Yet fasting is an exercise in self-control, and the same virtue is needed to walk after the Spirit and not after the flesh.

Fasting for the purpose of proving one's spirituality or advertising one's devotion to God is a waste of time and an indication of hypocrisy. This was the reason why the Pharisees fasted, and Jesus condemned them for it (see Matt. 6:16; 23:5).

Some people fast to get victory over Satan. But that is also unscriptural. Scripture promises that if we resist Satan by faith in God's Word, then he will flee from us (see Jas. 4:7; 1 Pet. 5:8-9). Fasting is not necessary.

But did not Jesus say that some demons can only be cast out by means of "prayer and fasting"?

That statement was made in reference to getting someone delivered from a demon that possessed him, not in reference to a believer who needed to gain victory over Satan's attacks against him.

But does not Jesus' statement indicate that we can gain a greater authority over demons by fasting?

Remember that when some of Jesus' disciples asked Him why they had failed to cast a demon out of a young boy, He first replied that it was because of the littleness of their faith (see Matt. 17:20). He *may* also have added as a footnote, "But this kind does not go out except by prayer and fasting" (Matt. 17:21), but that statement may not have actually been included in Matthew's original Gospel.

Even if Jesus actually did say those words, we would be wrong to conclude that fasting can increase one's authority over demons. If Jesus gives someone authority over demons, as He did His twelve disciples (see Matt. 10:1), then he has it, and fasting can't increase it. Fasting, however, could give one more time to pray and meditate, thereby increasing his faith in his God-given authority.

Keep in mind that if Jesus did actually make the statement under consideration, it was only in reference to *one* kind of demon. Fasting would still play a very small part in the overall ministry of deliverance, if any part at all.

Overemphasis Regarding Fasting

Some Christians have unfortunately made a religion out of fasting, giving it the dominant place in their Christian life. There is, however, not a single reference to fasting in the New Testament epistles.[66] There are no instructions given to believers on how or when to fast. There is no encouragement given to fast. This shows us that fasting is a relatively minor aspect of following Jesus.

Under the old covenant, it seems that fasting did hold a more predominant place. It was most often associated with either times of mourning, such as in connection with someone's death or a time of repentance, or with fervent prayer during times of national or personal crises (see Judg. 20:24-28; 1 Sam. 1:7-8; 7:1-6; 31:11-13; 2 Sam. 1:12; 12:15-23; 1 Kin. 21:20-29; 2 Chron. 20:1-3; Ezra 8:21-23; 10:1-6; Neh. 1:1-4; 9:1-2; Est. 4:1-3, 15-17; Ps. 35:13-14; 69:10; Is. 58:1-7; Dan. 6:16-18; 9:1-3; Joel 1:13-14; 2:12-17; Jonah 3:4-10; Zech. 7:4-5).

The Old Testament also teaches that devotion to fasting at the neglect of obedience to more important commandments, such as caring for the poor, is wrong (see Is. 58:1-12; Zech. 7:1-14).

Jesus, who ministered under the old covenant, certainly cannot be accused of overly promoting fasting. He was accused by the Pharisees of under-emphasizing it (see Matt. 9:14-15). He chided them for overemphasizing it (see Luke 18:9-12).

On the other hand, Jesus did speak of fasting to His followers during His Sermon on the Mount. He instructed them to fast for the right reasons, indicating that He anticipated His followers would fast at times. He also promised them that God would reward them for their fasting. He Himself practiced fasting to some extent (see Matt. 17:21).

How Long Should One Fast?

All of the forty-day fasts recorded in the Bible can be classed as supernatural. We've already considered Moses two forty-day fasts in God's presence. Elijah also fasted for forty days, but he was fed by an angel beforehand (see 1 Kin. 19:5-8). There were also some very supernatural elements to Jesus' forty-day fast. He was supernaturally led by the Holy Spirit into the wilderness. He experienced supernatural temptations from Satan near the end of His fast. He was also visited by angels at the end of His fast (see Matt. 4:1-11).

Although it is possible for some people to fast for forty days without supernatural assistance, many could be jeopardizing their health. Forty-day fasts are not the biblical norm.

---

[66] The only exception would be Paul's mentioning of fasting by married couples in 1 Cor. 7:5, but this is found only in the *King James Version*. *Involuntary* fasting is mentioned Acts 27:21, 33-34, 1 Cor. 4:11 and 2 Cor. 6:5; 11:27. These were fasts done not for spiritual purposes however, but only because of trying circumstances or because no food was available to eat.

If a person voluntarily abstains from eating one meal for the purpose of spending time seeking the Lord, he has fasted. The idea that fasts can only be measured in terms of days is erroneous.

The two fasts mentioned in the book of Acts that we have already considered (see Acts 13:1-3; 14:23) were apparently not very long fasts. They may have only been one-meal fasts.

Because fasting is primarily for the purpose of having more time to seek the Lord in prayer for His direction, my recommendation is that you fast for as long as you need to, until you have the clear direction you are seeking. Remember, fasting doesn't force God to talk to you. Fasting can only improve your sensitivity to the Holy Spirit. God is speaking to you whether you fast or not. Our difficulty is sorting out His leading from our own desires.

Some Practical Advice

Fasting normally affects the physical body in various ways. One may experience weakness, tiredness, headaches, nausea, light-headedness, stomach cramps, and so on. If one has a habit of drinking coffee, tea, or other caffeinated beverages, some of these symptoms can be attributed to withdrawal from caffeine. In such cases, it is wise for those individuals to eliminate those beverages from their diets several days before their fast begins. If a person fasts on a regular or semi-regular basis, he will discover that his fasts become progressively easier, although he will usually experience some weakness.

Fasts should be broken slowly, and the longer the fast, the more careful one should be as he breaks his fast. If a person's stomach has digested no solid foods for three days, it would be unwise for him to break his fast by eating foods that are difficult to digest. He should start with foods that are easy to digest. Longer fasts require more time for the digestive system to adjust to eating again, but missing one or two meals needs no special breaking-in period.

TWENTY-SEVEN

The Afterlife

Most Christians know that when people die, they either go to heaven or hell. Not all realize, however, that heaven is not the final habitation of the righteous, and that *Hades* is not the final habitation of the unrighteous.

When followers of Jesus Christ die, their spirits/souls immediately go to heaven where God lives (see 2 Cor. 5:6-8; Phil. 1:21-23; 1 Thes. 4:14). Sometime in the future, however, God will create a new heaven and earth, and the New Jerusalem will come down from heaven to earth (see 2 Pet. 3:13; Rev. 21:1-2). There the righteous will live forever.

When the unrighteous die, they immediately go to *Hades*, but Hades is only a place where they will temporarily wait for their bodies to be resurrected. When that day arrives, they will stand before God's judgment seat and then be cast into the lake that burns with fire and brimstone, referred to as *Gehenna* in the Bible. All of this we will consider in much more detail from Scripture.

When the Unrighteous Die

In order to better understand what happens to the unrighteous after death, we must study one Old Testament Hebrew word and three New Testament Greek words. Although these Hebrew and Greek words actually describe three different places, they are often all translated *hell* in certain Bible translations, which can be misleading to readers.

First, let's consider the Old Testament Hebrew word *Sheol*.

The word *Sheol* is mentioned more than sixty times in the Old Testament. It clearly refers to the after-death abode of the unrighteous. For example, when Korah and his followers rebelled against Moses in the wilderness, God punished them by opening up the ground, which swallowed them and all their possessions. Scripture says they fell into Sheol:

> So they and all that belonged to them went down alive to
> *Sheol*; and the earth closed over them, and they perished
> from the midst of the assembly (Num. 16:33, emphasis
> added).

Later in Israel's history, God warned them that His wrath kindled a fire
that burns in Sheol:

> For a fire is kindled in My anger, and burns to the lowest
> part of *Sheol*, and consumes the earth with its yield, and
> sets on fire the foundations of the mountains (Deut. 32:22,
> emphasis added).

King David declared that,

> The wicked will return to *Sheol*, even all the nations who
> forget God (Ps. 9:17, emphasis added).

And he prayed against the unrighteous by requesting,

> Let death come deceitfully upon them; let them go down
> alive to *Sheol*, for evil is in their dwelling, in their midst
> (Ps. 55:15, emphasis added).

Warning young men of the wiles of the harlot, wise Solomon wrote,

> Her house is the way to *Sheol*, descending to the chambers
> of death....he does not know that the dead are there, that
> her guests are in the depths of *Sheol* (Prov. 7:27; 9:18, em-
> phasis added).

Solomon wrote other proverbs that lead us to believe that it is certainly
not the righteous who end up in Sheol:

> The path of life leads upward for the wise, that he may keep
> away from *Sheol* below (Prov. 15:24, emphasis added).

> You shall beat him [your child] with the rod, and deliver
> his soul from *Sheol* (Prov. 23:14, emphasis added)

Finally, foreshadowing Jesus' description of hell, Isaiah prophetically
spoke to the king of Babylon, who had exalted himself but who would be
thrust down into Sheol:

> *Sheol* from beneath is excited over you to meet you when
> you come; it arouses for you the spirits of the dead, all the
> leaders of the earth; it raises all the kings of the nations
> from their thrones. They will all respond and say to you,
> "Even you have been made weak as we, you have become
> like us. Your pomp and the music of your harps have been

brought down to *Sheol*; maggots are spread out as your bed beneath you, and worms are your covering." How you have fallen from heaven, O star of the morning, son of the dawn! You have been cut down to the earth, you who have weakened the nations! But you said in your heart, "I will ascend to heaven; I will raise my throne above the stars of God, and I will sit on the mount of assembly in the recesses of the north. I will ascend above the heights of the clouds; I will make myself like the Most High." Nevertheless you will be thrust down to *Sheol*, to the recesses of the pit. Those who see you will gaze at you, they will ponder over you, saying, "Is this the man who made the earth tremble, who shook kingdoms, who made the world like a wilderness and overthrew its cities, who did not allow his prisoners to go home?" (Isa. 14:9-17, emphasis added).

These scriptures and others like them lead us to believe that Sheol has always been and still is the tormenting place where the unrighteous are incarcerated after their deaths. And there is more proof.

Hades

It is clear that the New Testament Greek word, *Hades*, refers to the same place as the Old Testament Hebrew word *Sheol*. For proof of this, all we need do is compare Psalm 16:10 with Acts 2:27 where it is quoted:

Thou wilt not abandon my soul to *Sheol*; neither wilt Thou allow Thy Holy One to undergo decay (Ps. 16:10, emphasis added).

Because Thou wilt not abandon my soul to *Hades*, nor allow Thy Holy One to undergo decay (Acts 2:27, emphasis added).

This being so, it is interesting that in all ten instances where *Hades* is mentioned in the New Testament, it is always spoken of in a negative sense and often as a tormenting place where the wicked are incarcerated after death (see Matt. 11:23; 16:18; Luke 10:15; 16:23; Acts 2:27; 2:31; Rev. 1:18; 6:8; 20:13-14). Again, all of this indicates that Sheol/Hades was and is an after-death abode for the unrighteous, a place of torment.[67]

Did Jesus Go to Sheol/Hades?

Let us further consider Psalm 16:10 and its quotation by Peter recorded

---

[67] Some try to make a case by means of a few scriptures, such as Gen. 37:35, Job 14:13, Ps. 89:48, Eccl. 9:10 and Isa. 38:9-10, that Sheol was a place that the *righteous* also went after their deaths. The scriptural evidence for this idea is not very compelling. If Sheol was a place where both unrighteous and righteous went at death, then Sheol must have consisted of two separate compartments, one a hell and one a paradise, which is what is usually argued by the proponents of this idea.

in Acts 2:27, two verses that indicate that Sheol and Hades are the same place. According to Peter's Pentecost sermon, David was not speaking in Psalm 16:10 of himself, but prophetically speaking of Christ, because David's body, unlike Christ's, did undergo decay (see Act 2:29-31). This being so, we realize that it was actually Jesus speaking to His Father in Psalm 16:10, declaring His belief that His Father would not abandon His soul to Sheol or allow His body to undergo decay.

Some interpret this declaration of Jesus as proof that His soul went to Sheol/Hades during the three days between His death and resurrection. That, however, is not actually implied. Note again exactly what Jesus said to His Father:

> Thou wilt not abandon my soul to Sheol; neither wilt Thou allow Thy Holy One to undergo decay (Ps. 16:10).

Jesus was not saying to His Father, "I know that my soul will spend a few days in Sheol/Hades, but I believe You won't abandon Me there." Rather He was saying, "I believe that when I die I will not be treated like the unrighteous, my soul being abandoned to Sheol/Hades. I won't even spend a minute there. No, I believe Your plan is to resurrect Me in three days, and You won't even allow My body to undergo decay."

This interpretation is certainly warranted. When Jesus said, "Neither wilt Thou allow Thy Holy One to undergo decay," we don't interpret that to mean that Jesus' body progressively decayed for three days until it was restored at His resurrection. Rather, we interpret it to mean that His body never went through *any* decay *whatsoever* from the time of His death until His resurrection.

Likewise, His statement that His soul would not be abandoned to Sheol/Hades does not need to be interpreted that He was left in Sheol/Hades for a few days but was ultimately not abandoned there. [68] Rather, it should be interpreted to mean that His soul would not be treated like an unrighteous soul that would be abandoned to Sheol/Hades. His soul would never spend a single minute there. Notice also that Jesus said, "Thou wilt not abandon my soul *to* Sheol," not, "Thou wilt not abandon my soul *in* Sheol."

Where Was Jesus' Soul During the Three Days?

Remember that Jesus told His disciples that He would spend three days and nights in the heart of the earth (see Matt. 12:40). This does not seem to

---

[68] Those who do subscribe to this particular interpretation must then subscribe to one of two other theories. One is the theory that Sheol/Hades was the name for an after-death abode of the unrighteous *and* righteous that was divided into two compartments, a place of torment and a place of paradise to which Jesus went. The other theory is that Jesus endured the torments of the damned for three days and nights in the fires of Sheol/Hades as He suffered the full extent of the penalty of sin as our substitute. Both of these theories are difficult to prove from Scripture, and neither are necessary if Jesus never spent any time in Sheol/Hades. That is what His declaration actually means. In regard to the second theory, Jesus did not suffer the torments of the damned for three days and nights between His death and resurrection, because our redemption was purchased through His sufferings on the cross (see Col. 1:22), not through his alleged sufferings in Sheol/Hades.

be a likely reference to His body being in a tomb for three days, as a tomb would hardly be considered to be at "the heart of the earth." Rather, Jesus must have been speaking of His spirit/soul being deep in the earth. Therefore we can conclude that His spirit/soul was not in heaven between His death and resurrection. Jesus affirmed this at His resurrection when He told Mary that He had not yet ascended to His Father (see John 20:17).

Keep in mind that Jesus also told the repentant thief on the cross that he would be with Him that very day in Paradise (see Luke 23:43). Putting all these facts together, we know that Jesus' spirit/soul spent three days and nights in the heart of the earth. At least part of that time He was in a place He called "Paradise," which certainly doesn't sound like an acceptable synonym for the place of torment called Sheol/Hades!

All of this leads me to think that there must be a place in the heart of the earth besides Sheol/Hades, a place called *Paradise*. This idea is certainly buttressed by a story Jesus once told of two people who died, one unrighteous and one righteous, the rich man and Lazarus. Let's read the story:

> Now there was a certain man, and he habitually dressed in purple and fine linen, gaily living in splendor every day. And a certain poor man named Lazarus was laid at his gate, covered with sores, and longing to be fed with the crumbs which were falling from the rich man's table; besides, even the dogs were coming and licking his sores. Now it came about that the poor man died and he was carried away by the angels to *Abraham's bosom*; and the rich man died and was buried. And in *Hades* he lifted up his eyes, being in torment, and saw Abraham far away, and Lazarus in his bosom. And he cried out and said, "Father Abraham, have mercy on me, and send Lazarus, that he may dip the tip of his finger in water and cool off my tongue; for I am in agony in this flame." But Abraham said, "Child, remember that during your life you received the good things, and likewise Lazarus bad things; but now he is being comforted here, and you are in agony. And besides all this, between us and you there is a great chasm fixed, in order that those who wish to come over from here to you may not be able, and that none may cross over from there to us" (Luke 16:19-26, emphasis added).

Of course, both Lazarus and the rich man were not in their bodies once they died, but they had traveled to their respective places as spirits/souls.

Where Was Lazarus?

Notice that the rich man found himself in *Hades*, but he could see Lazarus in *another place* with Abraham. In fact, Lazarus is spoken of as being in "Abraham's bosom," not a name for the place but probably a reference to the comfort Lazarus was receiving from Abraham upon his arrival in that place.

How great of a distance was there between the rich man and Lazarus after they had died?

Scripture says the rich man saw Lazarus "far away," and we are told there was a "great chasm fixed" between them. So the distance between them is a matter of speculation. It seems reasonable to conclude, however, that the distance between them was not so great as the distance between the heart of the earth and heaven. Otherwise, it would seem that it would have been quite impossible for the rich man to have been able to see Lazarus (apart from divine help), and there would hardly have been a need to mention or even have a "great chasm fixed" between the two locations specifically to prevent anyone from crossing from one to the other. Moreover, the rich man "cried out" to Abraham and Abraham spoke back to him. This would lead us to think they were fairly close to one another as they spoke across the "great chasm."

All of this leads me to believe that Lazarus was not in what we call heaven, but rather in a separate compartment within the earth.[69] It must have been the place that Jesus referred to as *Paradise* to the repentant thief. It was to this Paradise in the heart of the earth that the Old Testament righteous went after their deaths. It was where Lazarus went and where Jesus and the repentant thief went.

It is also apparently where the prophet Samuel went after his death. We read in 1 Samuel 28 that when God permitted the spirit of the dead prophet Samuel to appear and speak prophetically to Saul, the medium of En-dor described Samuel as "a divine being *coming up out of the earth*" (1 Sam. 28:13, emphasis added). Samuel himself said to Saul, "Why have you disturbed me by *bringing me up?*" (1 Sam. 28:15, emphasis added). Apparently, Samuel's spirit/soul had been in Paradise in the earth.

Scripture seems to support the fact that at Christ's resurrection, Paradise was emptied, and those righteous people who died during the time of the Old Testament were taken to heaven with Jesus. The Bible says that when Jesus ascended to heaven from the lower parts of the earth, "He led captive a host of captives" (Eph. 4:8-9; Ps. 68:18). Those captives I assume to be all those who were living in Paradise. Jesus certainly didn't release people from Sheol/Hades![70]

---

[69] Notice also that both Lazarus and the rich man, although separated from their bodies, were conscious and possessed all their faculties such as sight, touch and hearing. They could experience pain and comfort and remember past experiences. This disproves the theory of "soul sleep," the idea that people go into an unconscious state when they die, awaiting to regain consciousness at the resurrection of their bodies.

[70] It is thought by some, and perhaps rightfully, that the captives spoken of in Ephesians 4:8-9 are all of us where were captive to sin, now made free through Christ's resurrection.

Jesus Preached to Spirits in Prison

Scripture also tells us that Jesus made a proclamation to a group of people, disembodied spirits, at some point in time between His death and resurrection. We read in 1 Peter 3:

> For Christ also died for sins once for all, the just for the unjust, in order that He might bring us to God, having been put to death in the flesh, but made alive in the spirit; in which also He went and made proclamation to the spirits in prison, who once were disobedient, when the patience of God kept waiting in the days of Noah, during the construction of the ark, in which a few, that is, eight persons, were brought safely through the water (1 Pet. 3:18-20).

This passage of Scripture certainly raises some questions to which I don't have answers. Why would Jesus make a proclamation specifically to some disobedient people who died during Noah's flood? What did He tell them?

In any case, this scripture does seem to support the fact that Jesus did not spend the entire three days and nights from His death to His resurrection in Paradise.

Gehenna

Today when the bodies of the righteous die, their spirits/souls go immediately to heaven (see 2 Cor. 5:6-8; Phil. 1:21-23; 1 Thes. 4:14).

The unrighteous still go to Sheol/Hades where they are tormented and await the resurrection of their bodies, their final judgment, and their being cast into "the lake of fire," a place that is different and separate from Sheol/Hades.

This lake of fire is described by a third word that is also sometimes translated *hell*, the Greek word *Gehenna*. This word was derived from the name of a garbage dump outside of Jerusalem in the valley of Hinnom, a rotting heap that was infested with worms and maggots, and part of which perpetually smoked and burned with fire.

When Jesus spoke of Gehenna, He spoke of it as a place where people would be cast *bodily*. For example, He said in Matthew's gospel:

> And if your right hand makes you stumble, cut if off, and throw it from you; for it is better for you that one of the parts of your body perish, than for your whole *body* to go into hell [Gehenna]....And do not fear those who kill the body, but are unable to kill the soul; but rather fear Him who is able to destroy both soul and *body* in hell [Gehenna] (Matt. 5:30, 10:28, emphasis added).

Gehenna and Hades couldn't be the same place because Scripture says that the unrighteous are sent to Hades as disembodied spirits/souls. It is only after the thousand-year reign of Christ when the bodies of the unrighteous will be resurrected and face judgment before God that they will then be cast into *the lake of fire*, or Ghenna (see Rev. 20:5, 11-15). Moreover, one day Hades itself will be cast into that lake of fire (see Rev. 20:14), so it must be a different place than the lake of fire.

Tartaros

The fourth word often translated *hell* in Scripture is the Greek word *tartaros*. It is found only once in the New Testament:

> For if God did not spare angels when they sinned, but cast them into hell [tartaros] and committed them to pits of darkness, reserved for judgment (2 Pet. 2:4).

Tartaros is normally thought of as a special prison for certain angels who sinned; therefore, it is not Sheol/Hades or Gehenna. Jude also wrote of angels who are being detained:

> And angels who did not keep their own domain, but abandoned their proper abode, He has kept in eternal bonds under darkness for the judgment of the great day (Jude 6).

The Horrors of Hell

Once an unrepentant person dies, he is given no further opportunity for repentance. His fate in sealed. The Bible says, "It is appointed for men to die once and after this comes judgment" (Heb. 9:27).

Hell is eternal, and those who are confined there have no hope of escape. Speaking of the future condemnation of the unrighteous, Jesus said, "And these will go away into *eternal* punishment, but the righteous into eternal life" (Matt. 25:46, emphasis added). The punishment of the unrighteous in hell is just as much eternal as is eternal life for the righteous.

Similarly, Paul wrote:

> For after all it is only just for God to repay with affliction those who afflict you...when the Lord Jesus shall be revealed from heaven with His mighty angels in flaming fire, dealing out retribution to those who do not know God and to those who do not obey the gospel of our Lord Jesus. These will pay the penalty of *eternal* destruction, away from the presence of the Lord and from the glory of His power (2 Thes. 1:6-9, emphasis added).

Hell is a place of indescribable agony because it will be a *never-ending* punishment. Confined there forever, the unrighteous will bear their eternal guilt and suffer the wrath of God in an unquenchable fire.

Jesus described hell as a place of "outer darkness," where there will be "weeping and gnashing of teeth," and a place "where their worm does not die, and their fire is not quenched" (Matt. 22:13; Mark 9:44). Oh, how we need to warn people of that place and tell them of the salvation provided only in Christ!

One particular denomination teaches the concept of purgatory, a place where believers will suffer for a time to be purged of their sins and thus be made worthy for heaven. This idea, however, is nowhere taught in the Bible.

The Righteous After Death

When a believer dies, his spirit goes immediately to heaven to be with the Lord. Paul made this fact very clear when he wrote of his own death:

> For to me, to live is Christ, and *to die is gain.* But if I am to live on in the flesh, this will mean fruitful labor for me; and I do not know which to choose. But I am hard-pressed from both directions, having the desire *to depart and be with Christ,* for this is very much better (Phil. 1:21-23, emphasis added).

Notice that Paul said he had the desire to depart and that if he did depart, he would then be with Christ. His spirit would not go into some unconscious state, waiting for the resurrection (as some unfortunately think).

Also notice that Paul said that for him, to die would be *gain.* That would only be true if he went to heaven when he died.

Paul also declared in his second letter to the Corinthians that if a believer's spirit left his body, he was then "at home with the Lord":

> Therefore, being always of good courage, and knowing that while we are at home in the body we are absent from the Lord...and prefer to be absent from the body and to be at home with the Lord (2 Cor. 5:6-8).

In further support, Paul also wrote:

> But we do not want you to be uninformed, brethren, about those who are asleep, that you may not grieve, as do the rest who have no hope. For if we believe that Jesus died and rose again, even so God will bring with Him those who have fallen asleep in Jesus (1 Thes. 4:13-14).

If Jesus is going to bring back from heaven with Him at His return "those who have fallen asleep," they must then be in heaven with Him now.

Heaven Foreseen

What is heaven like? In our finite minds we could never fully grasp all of the glories that await us there, and the Bible gives us only a glimpse. The most exciting fact about heaven for believers is that we will see our Lord and Savior, Jesus, and God our Father face to face. We will live in "the Father's house":

> In My Father's house are many dwelling places; if it were not so, I would have told you; for I go to prepare a place for you. And if I go and prepare a place for you, I will come again, and receive you to Myself; that where I am, there you may be also (John 14:2-3).

When we get to heaven, many mysteries that our minds cannot currently comprehend will be understood. Paul wrote,

> For now we see in a mirror dimly, but then face to face; now I know in part, but then I shall know fully just as I have been fully known (1 Cor. 13:12).

The book of Revelation gives us the best picture of what heaven is like. Described as a place of great activity, wonderful beauty, unlimited variation, and inexpressible joy, heaven won't be a place where the people just sit around on clouds and strum harps all day!

John, who was once given a vision of heaven, first noticed the throne of God, the center of the universe:

> Immediately I was in the Spirit; and behold, a throne was standing in heaven, and One sitting on the throne. And He who was sitting was like a jasper stone and a sardius in appearance; and there was a rainbow around the throne, like an emerald in appearance. And around the throne were twenty-four thrones; and upon the thrones I saw twenty-four elders sitting, clothed in white garments, and golden crowns upon their heads. And from the throne proceed flashes of lightning and sounds and peals of thunder. And there were seven lamps of fire burning before the throne, which are the seven spirits of God; and before the throne there was, as it were, a sea of glass like crystal; and in the center and around the throne, four living creatures full of eyes in front and behind. And the first creature was like a lion, and the second creature like a calf, and the third creature had a face like that of a man, and the fourth creature was like a flying eagle. And the four living creatures, each one of them having six wings, are full of eyes around and within; and day and night they do not cease to say, "Holy, Holy, Holy, is the Lord God Almighty, who was and who is and who is to come." And when the living

creatures give glory and honor and thanks to Him who sits on the throne, to Him who lives forever and ever, the twenty-four elders will fall down before Him who sits on the throne, and will worship Him who lives forever and ever, and will cast their crowns before the throne, saying, "Worthy art Thou, our Lord and our God, to receive glory and honor and power; for Thou didst create all things, and because of Thy will they existed, and were created" (Rev. 4:2-11).

John did his best to describe in earthly terms what can hardly be compared to anything on earth. Obviously, there is no way we are going to comprehend everything he saw until we see it ourselves. But it certainly makes for inspiring reading.

The most inspiring passages about heaven are found in Revelation chapters 21 and 22, where John described the New Jerusalem, which is presently in heaven but will come down to earth after the thousand-year reign of Christ:

And he carried me away in the Spirit to a great and high mountain, and showed me the holy city, Jerusalem, coming down out of heaven from God, having the glory of God. Her brilliance was like a very costly stone, as a stone of crystal-clear jasper. It had a great and high wall, with twelve gates, and at the gates twelve angels....And the one who spoke with me had a gold measuring rod to measure the city, and its gates and its wall. And the city is laid out as a square, and its length is as great as the width; and he measured the city with the rod, fifteen hundred miles; its length and width and height are equal....And the material of the wall was jasper; and the city was pure gold, like clear glass....And the twelve gates were twelve pearls; each one of the gates was a single pearl. And the street of the city was pure gold, like transparent glass. And I saw no temple in it, for the Lord God, the Almighty, and the Lamb, are its temple. And the city had no need of the sun or of the moon to shine upon it, for the glory of God has illumined it, and its lamp is the Lamb.....And he showed me a river of the water of life, clear as crystal, coming from the throne of God and of the Lamb, in the middle of its street. And on either side of the river was the tree of life, bearing twelve kinds of fruit, yielding its fruit every month; and the leaves of the tree were for the healing of the nations. And there shall no longer be any curse; and the throne of God and of the Lamb shall be in it, and His bond-servants shall serve Him; and they shall see His face, and His name shall be on their foreheads. And there shall no longer be any night; and they shall not have need of the light of a lamp nor the light of the sun, because the Lord God shall illumine them; and they shall reign forever and ever (Rev. 21:10-22:5).

Every follower of Jesus can look forward to all of these wonders, as long as he continues in the faith. No doubt, we'll spend our first few days in heaven saying to one another, "Oh! So that's what John was trying to describe in the book of Revelation!"

TWENTY-EIGHT

God's Eternal Plan

Why did God create us? Has He had some goal in mind from the beginning? Didn't He know that everyone would rebel against Him? Didn't He foresee the consequences of our rebellion, all the suffering and sadness that humanity has since faced? Then why did He create anyone in the first place?

The Bible answers these questions for us. It tells that even before God created Adam and Eve, He knew that they and everyone after them would sin. Amazingly, He had already formed a plan to redeem fallen humanity through Jesus. Of God's pre-creation plan Paul wrote,

> God, who has saved us, and called us with a holy calling, not according to our works, but *according to His own purpose and grace which was granted us in Christ from all eternity* (2 Tim. 1:8b-9, emphasis added).

God's grace was granted us in Christ *from* all eternity, not just *to* all eternity. That indicates that Jesus' sacrificial death is something God had planned from ages past.

Similarly, Paul wrote in his letter to the Ephesians:

> This was in accordance with the *eternal purpose* which He carried out in Christ Jesus our Lord (Eph. 3:11, emphasis added).

Jesus' death on the cross was not an afterthought, a quickly-devised plan to fix what God had not foreseen.

Not only did God have an eternal purpose in granting us His grace from all eternity, but He also foreknew from eternity past who would choose to receive His grace, and He even wrote their names in a book:

And all who dwell on the earth will worship him [the beast of Revelation], every one *whose name has not been written from the foundation of the world in the book of life* of the Lamb who has been slain [Jesus] (Rev. 13:8, emphasis added).

The fall of Adam didn't catch God by surprise. Neither did your fall or my fall. God knew we would sin, and He also knew who would repent and believe in the Lord Jesus.

The Next Question

If God foreknew that some would believe in Jesus and others would reject Him, why did He create people whom He knew would reject Him? Why not simply create people whom He knew would repent and believe in Jesus?

The answer to that question is a little more difficult to understand, but not impossible.

First, we must understand that God created us with free wills. That is, all of us have the privilege of deciding for ourselves whether or not we will serve God. Our decisions to obey or disobey, repent or not repent, are not predetermined by God. They are our choice.

This being so, every one of us must be tested. God, of course, foreknew what we would do, but *we had to do something at some point in time in order for Him to foreknow it.*

By way of example, God knows the outcome of every football game before it is played, but there must be football games that are played with outcomes if God is going to foreknow the outcomes. God doesn't (and can't) foreknow the outcomes of football games that are never played because there are no outcomes to foreknow.

Similarly, God can only foreknow the decisions of free moral agents if those free moral agents are given an opportunity to make decisions and do make them. They must be tested. And that is why God didn't (and couldn't) create only people whom He foreknew would repent and believe in Jesus.

Another Question

It could also be asked, "If all God wants are people who are obedient, why then did He create us with free wills? Why didn't He create a race of eternally obedient robots?"

The answer is because God is a Father. He wants to have a father-child relationship with us, and there can be no father-child relationship with robots. God's desire is to have an eternal family of children who have chosen, by their own free will, to love Him. According to Scripture, that was His predestined plan:

In love He predestined us to *adoption as sons* through Jesus

Christ to Himself, according to the kind intention of His will (Eph. 1:4b-5, emphasis added).

If you want to have some idea how much pleasure God would have derived from robots, just place a puppet on your hand and have that puppet tell you that he loves you. Most likely, you won't get a warm feeling in your heart! That puppet is only saying what you make him say. He doesn't really love you.

What makes love so special is that it is based on the choice of someone with a free will. Puppets and robots know nothing about love because they can't decide anything for themselves.

Because God wanted a family of children who would *choose* to love and serve Him from their own hearts, He *had* to create free moral agents. That decision involved His taking the risk that some free moral agents would choose *not* to love and serve Him. And those free moral agents, after a lifetime of resisting God who reveals Himself and draws all people through His creation, their conscience and the call of the gospel, would have to face their rightful punishment, having proved themselves worthy of God's wrath.

No person in hell can rightfully point a finger of accusation against God because He provided a way whereby every person can escape the penalty of his sins. God desires for every person to be saved (see 1 Tim. 2:4; 2 Pet. 3:9), but each person must decide for himself.

Biblical Predestination

But what about those scriptures in the New Testament that speak of God predestining us, choosing us before the foundation of the world?

Some unfortunately think that God has specifically chosen certain people to be saved and chosen the rest to be damned, basing His decision on nothing those individuals have done. That is, God supposedly chose who would be saved or damned. This idea obviously eliminates the concept of free will and it is certainly not taught in Scripture. Let's consider what the Bible does teach about predestination.

Indeed, Scripture teaches that God has chosen us, but this fact must be qualified. God has chosen from the foundation of the world to redeem the people whom He foreknew would repent and believe the gospel under the influence of His drawing, but *by their own choice*. Read what the apostle Paul says about the people God chooses:

God has not rejected His people whom He foreknew. Or do you not know what the Scripture says in the passage about Elijah, how he pleads with God against Israel? "Lord, they have killed Thy prophets, they have torn down Thine altars, and I alone am left and they are seeking my life." But what is the divine response to him? "I have kept for Myself seven thousand men who have not bowed the knee to Baal." *In the same way then, there has also come to be at the present time a remnant according to God's gracious choice* (Rom. 11:2-5, emphasis added).

Notice that God said to Elijah that He had "kept for Himself seven thousand men," but those seven thousand men had *first* made a choice not to "bow the knee to Baal." Paul said that *in the same way,* there was also a remnant of believing Jews *according to God's choice.* So we can say that yes, God has chosen us, but God has chosen those who have first made the right choice themselves. God has chosen to save all who believe in Jesus, and that was His plan even before creation.

God's Foreknowledge

Along these same lines, Scripture also teaches that God also *foreknew* all those who would choose to make the right choice. Peter, for example, wrote:

> To those who reside as aliens...*who are chosen according to the foreknowledge of God the Father* (1 Pet. 1:1-2a, emphasis added).

We are chosen according to God's foreknowledge. Paul also wrote of foreknown believers:

> For whom He foreknew [us], He also predestined to become conformed to the image of His Son, that He [Jesus] might be the first-born among many brethren; and whom He predestined, these He also called; and whom He called, these He also justified; and whom He justified, these He also glorified (Rom. 8:29-30).

God foreknew those of us who would choose to believe in Jesus, and He predestined that we would become conformed to the image of His Son, becoming regenerated children of God in His big family. In keeping with that eternal plan, He called us through the gospel, justified us (made us righteous) and will ultimately glorify us in His future kingdom.

Paul wrote in another letter:

> Blessed be the God and Father of our Lord Jesus Christ, who has blessed us with every spiritual blessing in the heavenly places in Christ, *just as He chose us in Him before the foundation of the world, that we should be holy and blameless before Him. In love He predestined us to adoption as sons through Jesus Christ* to Himself, according to the kind intention of His will, to the praise of the glory of His grace, which He freely bestowed on us in the Beloved (Eph. 1:3-6, emphasis added).

The same truth is presented here—God predestined us (whom He foreknew would repent and believe) before the foundation of the world to become His holy sons through Jesus Christ.

As already mentioned, some twist the meaning of such scriptures by ignoring everything else the Bible teaches, claiming that we really had no choice in our salvation—the choice was supposedly all God's. This they call the doctrine of "unconditional election." But who ever heard of such a thing as an "unconditional election," that is, an election that is not made on the basis of certain conditions being met? In free countries, we elect political candidates based on conditions they meet in our minds. We elect spouses based on conditions they meet, characteristics about them that make them desireable. Yet some theologians want us to believe that God's supposed choice of who is saved and who is not saved is an "unconditional election," not based on any conditions people have met! Thus the salvation of individuals is by *pure chance*, the whims of a cruel, unrighteous, hypocritical and unintelligent monster named God! The very phrase, "unconditional election" contradicts itself, as the very word *election* implies conditionality. If it is an "unconditional election,' it is no election at all; it is pure chance.

The Big Picture

Now we see the big picture. God knew all of us would sin, but He made a plan to redeem us before any of us were born. That plan would reveal His amazing love and justice, as it would require that His sinless Son die for our sins as our substitute. And God not only predestined that we who repented and believed would be forgiven, but that we would become like His Son Jesus, as Paul said, "It is no longer I who live, but Christ lives in me" (Gal. 2:20).

We who are born-again children of God will one day be given incorruptible bodies, and we will live in a perfect society, serving, loving and fellowshipping with our wonderful heavenly Father! We will live on a new earth and in the New Jerusalem. All of this will have been made possible through the sacrificial death of Jesus! Praise God for His predestined plan!

This Present Life

Once we understand God's eternal plan, we can more fully comprehend what this present life is all about. Primarily, this life serves as a test for every person. Each person's choice determines if he or she will be enjoy the blessed privilege of being one of God's own children who will live with Him for eternity. Those who humble themselves by yielding to God's drawing, then repenting and believing, will be exalted (see Luke 18:14). *This life is primarily a test for that future life.*

This also helps us understand some of the mysteries that surround this present life. For example, many have wondered, "Why are Satan and his demons permitted to tempt people?" or, "When Satan was cast out of heaven, why was he permitted to have access to the earth?"

We can see now that even Satan serves a divine purpose in God's plan. Primarily, Satan serves as the alternate choice for humanity. If the only choice were to serve Jesus, then everyone would serve Jesus whether he wanted to or not.

It would be similar to an election in which everyone was required to vote, but there was only one candidate. That candidate would be unanimously elected, but he could never have the confidence that he is loved or even liked by any of his electors! They had no choice but to vote for him! God would be in a similar situation if there were no one competing with Him for the hearts of people.

Consider it from this angle: What if God had placed Adam and Eve in a garden where nothing was forbidden? Then Adam and Eve would have been robots by reason of their environment. They couldn't have said, "We've chosen to obey God," because they would have had no opportunity to disobey Him.

More importantly, God would not have been able to say, "I know Adam and Eve love Me," because Adam and Eve would have had no opportunity to obey and prove their love for God. *God must give free moral agents the opportunity to disobey in order for Him to determine if they want to obey Him.* God doesn't tempt anyone (see Jas. 1:13), but He tests everyone (see Ps. 11:5; Prov. 17:3). One way that He tests them is to allow them to be tempted by Satan, who thus serves a divine purpose in His eternal plan.

A Perfect Example

We read in Deuteronomy 13:1-3:

> If a prophet or a dreamer of dreams arises among you and gives you a sign or a wonder, and the sign or the wonder comes true, concerning which he spoke to you, saying, "Let us go after other gods (whom you have not known) and let us serve them," you shall not listen to the words of that prophet or that dreamer of dreams; for *the Lord your God is testing you to find out if you love the Lord your God* with all your heart and with all your soul (emphasis added).

It seems reasonable to conclude that it wasn't God who gave that false prophet the supernatural ability to work a sign or wonder—it must have been Satan. Yet God permitted it and used Satan's temptation as His own test to find out what was in the hearts of His people.

This same principle is also illustrated in Judges 2:21-3:8 when God permitted Israel to be tempted by the surrounding nations in order to determine whether or not they would obey Him. Jesus, too, was led by the

Spirit into the wilderness for the purpose of being tempted by the devil (see Matt. 4:1) and thus tested by God. He had to be proven sinless, and the only way to be proven sinless is to be tested by temptation.

Satan Does Not Deserve All the Blame

Satan has already deceived a great number of people in the world by blinding their minds to the truth of the gospel, but we must realize that Satan can't blind just anyone. He can only deceive those who allow themselves be deceived, people who reject the truth.

Paul declared that unbelievers are "darkened in their understanding" (Eph. 4:18) and ignorant, but he also revealed the root reason for their darkened understanding and ignorance:

> That you walk no longer just as the Gentiles also walk, in the futility of their mind, being darkened in their understanding, excluded from the life of God because of the ignorance that is in them, *because of the hardness of their heart;* and they, *having become callous,* have given themselves over to sensuality, for the practice of every kind of impurity with greediness (Eph. 4:17b-19, emphasis added).

The unsaved are not just unfortunate people who have been sadly tricked by Satan. Rather, they are rebellious sinners who are willfully ignorant and who want to remain deceived because their hearts are so hard.

No person has to remain deceived, as your own life proves! Once you softened your heart toward God, Satan couldn't keep you deceived.

Ultimately, Satan will be bound during the thousand-year reign of Christ, and he will then have no influence on anyone:

> And he [an angel] laid hold of the dragon, the serpent of old, who is the devil and Satan, and bound him for a thousand years, and threw him into the abyss, and shut it and sealed it over him, so that he should not deceive the nations any longer, until the thousand years were completed; after these things he must be released for a short time (Rev. 20:2-3).

Note that before Satan's incarceration he "deceived the nations," but when he is bound he will no longer deceive them. Once released, however, he will deceive the nations again:

> And when the thousand years are completed, Satan will be released from his prison, and will come out to *deceive the nations* which are in the four corners of the earth...to gather them together for the war....And they came up on the broad plain of the earth and surrounded the camp of

the saints and the beloved city, and fire came down from heaven and devoured them (Rev. 20:7-9, emphasis added).

Why will God release Satan for this short period of time? The reason is so that all those who hate Christ in their hearts but have been feigning obedience to Him during His rule will be manifested. Then they can be rightfully judged. That will be the final test.

For the same reason, Satan is permitted to operate on the earth now—that those who hate Christ in their hearts might be manifested and ultimately judged. Once God no longer has any use for Satan to fulfill His divine purposes, the deceiver will be cast into the lake of fire to be tormented there forever (see Rev. 20:10).

Preparing For the Future World

If you've repented and believed the gospel, you've passed the initial and most important test of this life. Don't think, however, that you will not continue to be tested in order that God might determine your continued devotion and faithfulness to Him. Only those who "continue in the faith" will be presented before God as "holy and blameless" (Col. 1:22-23).

Beyond this, it is clear from Scripture that all of us will one day stand at God's judgment seat, at which time we will be individually rewarded according to our obedience on earth. So we are still being tested in order to determine our worthiness of future special rewards in God's kingdom. Paul wrote,

> But you, why do you judge your brother? Or you again, why do you regard your brother with contempt? *For we shall all stand before the judgment seat of God.* For it is written, "As I live, says the Lord, every knee shall bow to Me, and every tongue shall give praise to God." So then *each one of us shall give account of himself to God* (Rom. 14:10-12, emphasis added).

> For we must all appear before the judgment seat of Christ, that each one may be recompensed for his deeds in the body, according to what he has done, whether good or bad (2 Cor. 5:10).

> Therefore do not go on passing judgment before the time, but wait until the Lord comes who will both bring to light the things hidden in the darkness and *disclose the motives of men's hearts; and then each man's praise will come to him from God* (1 Cor. 4:5, emphasis added).

What Will be the Rewards?

What, exactly, will be the rewards given to those who prove their love and devotion to Jesus?

Scripture speaks of at least two different rewards—praise from God, and more opportunity to serve Him. Both are revealed in Jesus' parable of the nobleman:

> He said therefore, "A certain nobleman went to a distant country to receive a kingdom for himself, and then return. And he called ten of his slaves, and gave them ten minas, and said to them, 'Do business with this until I come back.' But his citizens hated him, and sent a delegation after him, saying, 'We do not want this man to reign over us.' And it came about that when he returned, after receiving the kingdom, he ordered that these slaves, to whom he had given the money, be called to him in order that he might know what business they had done. And the first appeared, saying, 'Master, your mina has made ten minas more.' And he said to him, 'Well done, good slave, because you have been faithful in a very little thing, be in authority over ten cities.' And the second came, saying, 'Your mina, master, has made five minas.' And he said to him also, 'And you are to be over five cities.' And another came, saying, 'Master, behold your mina, which I kept put away in a handkerchief; for I was afraid of you, because you are an exacting man; you take up what you did not lay down, and reap what you did not sow.' He said to him, 'By your own words I will judge you, you worthless slave. Did you know that I am an exacting man, taking up what I did not lay down, and reaping what I did not sow? Then why did you not put the money in the bank, and having come, I would have collected it with interest?' And he said to the bystanders, 'Take the mina away from him, and give it to the one who has the ten minas.' And they said to him, 'Master, he has ten minas already.' 'I tell you, that to everyone who has shall more be given, but from the one who does not have, even what he does have shall be taken away. But these enemies of mine, who did not want me to reign over them, bring them here, and slay them in my presence'" (Luke 19:12-27).

Obviously, Jesus is represented by the nobleman who was absent but who eventually returned. When Jesus returns, we will have to give account for what we did with the gifts, abilities, ministries, and opportunities He gave us, represented by the one mina given to each servant in the parable. If we've been faithful, we'll be rewarded with praise from Him and be given authority to help Him rule and reign over the earth (see 2 Tim. 2:12; Rev. 2:26-27; 5:10; 20:6), represented by the cities each faithful servant was authorized to oversee in the parable.

The Fairness of Our Future Judgment

Another parable Jesus told illustrates the perfect fairness of our future judgment:

> For the kingdom of heaven is like a landowner who went out early in the morning to hire laborers for his vineyard. And when he had agreed with the laborers for a denarius for the day, he sent them into his vineyard. And he went out about the third hour and saw others standing idle in the market place; and to those he said, "You too go into the vineyard, and whatever is right I will give you." And so they went. Again he went out about the sixth and the ninth hour, and did the same thing. And about the eleventh hour he went out, and found others standing; and he said to them, "Why have you been standing here idle all day long?" They said to him, "Because no one hired us." He said to them, "You too go into the vineyard." And when evening had come, the owner of the vineyard said to his foreman, "Call the laborers and pay them their wages, beginning with the last group to the first." And when those hired about the eleventh hour came, each one received a denarius. And when those hired first came, they thought that they would receive more; and they also received each one a denarius. And when they received it, they grumbled at the landowner, saying, "These last men have worked only one hour, and you have made them equal to us who have borne the burden and the scorching heat of the day." But he answered and said to one of them, "Friend, I am doing you no wrong; did you not agree with me for a denarius? Take what is yours and go your way, but I wish to give to this last man the same as to you. Is it not lawful for me to do what I wish with what is my own? Or is your eye envious because I am generous?" Thus the last shall be first, and the first last (Matt. 20:1-16).

Jesus was not teaching in this parable that all of God's servants will receive the same reward in the end, as that would not only be unfair, but would also contradict many other scriptures (see, for example, Luke 19:12-27; 1 Cor. 3:8).

Rather, Jesus was teaching that each of God's servants will be reward-ed, not only on the basis on what they did for Him, but on the basis of how much opportunity He gave them. The one-hour workers in the Christ's parable would have worked all day had the landowner given them the opportunity. So those who made the most of their one-hour opportunity were rewarded equally with those who were given the opportunity to work all day.

So, too, God gives different opportunities to each of His servants. To some He gives great opportunities to serve and bless thousands of people using the amazing gifts He has given them. To others He gives lesser op-portunities and gifts, yet they can receive the same reward in the end if they are equally as faithful with what God has given them.[71]

The Conclusion

There is nothing more important than obeying God, and one day every-one will know that. Wise people know it now and act accordingly!

> The conclusion, when all has been heard, is: fear God and keep His commandments, because this applies to every person. For God will bring every act to judgment, every-thing which is hidden, whether it is good or evil (Eccl. 12:13-14).

The disciple-making minister obeys God with all his heart and is doing everything he can to motivate his disciples to do likewise!

For further study concerning this important topic of our future judg-ment, see Matt. 6:1-6, 16-18; 10:41-42; 12:36-37; 19:28-29; 25:14-30; Luke 12:2-3; 14:12-14; 16:10-13; 1 Cor. 3:5-15; 2 Tim. 2:12; 1 Pet. 1:17; Rev. 2:26-27; 5:10; 20:6.

---

[71] This parable also does not teach that those who repent at a young age and faithfully labor for many years will be rewarded the same as those who repent during the last year of their life and faithfully serve God only one year. That would be unfair, and would not be based on the opportunity that God gave each one, as God gave each one opportunity to repent all through their lives. Thus those who labor longer will receive more reward than those who labor for less time.

TWENTY-NINE

The Rapture and End Times

When Jesus walked on the earth in human form, He plainly told His disciples that He would depart and then return for them one day. When He did return, He would take them back to heaven with Him (what modern Christians refer to as "the Rapture"). For example, on the night before His crucifixion, Jesus said to His eleven faithful apostles:

> Let not your heart be troubled; believe in God, believe also in Me. In My Father's house are many dwelling places; if it were not so, I would have told you; for I go to prepare a place for you. And if I go and prepare a place for you, *I will come again, and receive you to Myself*; that where I am, there you may be also (John 14:1-3, emphasis added).

Clearly implied by Jesus' words was the possibility of His return during the lifetimes of the eleven. In fact, after hearing what Jesus said, they simply would have assumed that He would be returning for them within their lifetimes.

Jesus also repeatedly warned His disciples to be *ready* for His return, again implying the possibility of His return within their lifetimes (see, for example, Matt. 24:42-44).

Jesus' Imminent Return in the Epistles

The apostles who wrote New Testament letters certainly affirmed their belief that Jesus might return within the lifetimes of their first-century readers. For example, James wrote:

> Be patient, therefore, brethren, until the coming of the Lord. Behold, the farmer waits for the precious produce of the soil, being patient about it, until it gets the early

and late rains. You too be patient; strengthen your hearts, *for the coming of the Lord is at hand* (Jas. 5:7-8, emphasis added).

There would have been no reason for James to admonish his readers to be patient for what could not happen within their lifetimes. He believed, however, that the coming of the Lord was "at hand." Contextually, James wrote at a time when the church had been suffering persecution (see Jas. 1:2-4), a time when believers would naturally long for the return of their Lord.

Similarly, Paul certainly believed that Jesus might return within the lifetimes of many of his contemporaries:

> But we do not want you to be uninformed, brethren, about those who are asleep, that you may not grieve, as do the rest who have no hope. For if we believe that Jesus died and rose again, even so God will bring with Him those who have fallen asleep in Jesus. For this we say to you by the word of the Lord, *that we who are alive, and remain until the coming of the Lord,* shall not precede those who have fallen asleep. For the Lord Himself will descend from heaven with a shout, with the voice of the archangel, and with the trumpet of God; and the dead in Christ shall rise first. *Then we who are alive and remain shall be caught up together with them in the clouds to meet the Lord in the air,* and thus we shall always be with the Lord. Therefore comfort one another with these words (1 Thes. 4:13-18, emphasis added).[72]

From this we learn also that when Jesus returns from heaven, the bodies of deceased believers will be resurrected and, along with believers who are alive at His coming, will be "caught up to meet the Lord in the air" (the Rapture). Because Paul also stated that Jesus would bring with Him from heaven those who had died "in Him," we can only conclude that at the Rapture, the spirits of the heavenly believers will be joined with their just-resurrected bodies.

Peter also believed that the coming of Christ was imminent when he wrote his first epistle:

> Therefore, gird your minds for action, keep sober in spirit, *fix your hope completely on the grace to be brought to you at the revelation of Jesus Christ....The end of all things is at hand;* therefore, be of sound judgment and sober spirit for the purpose of prayer....but to the degree that you share the

---

[72] A few other scriptures that show Paul's belief that Jesus could possibly return within the lifetimes of his contemporaries are Phil. 3:20; 1 Thes. 3:13; 5:23; 2 Thes. 2:1-5; 1 Tim. 6:14-15; Tit. 2:11-13; Heb. 9:28.

sufferings of Christ, keep on rejoicing; *so that also at the revelation of His glory, you may rejoice* with exultation (1 Pet. 1:13, 4:7, 13, emphasis added).[73]

Finally, when John wrote his letters to the churches, he too believed the end was near and that the readers of his day might well see Jesus' return:

Children, *it is the last hour;* and just as you heard that anti-christ is coming, even now many antichrists have arisen; from this *we know that it is the last hour*....And now, little children, abide in Him, *so that when He appears, we may have confidence and not shrink away from Him in shame at His coming*....Beloved, now we are children of God, and it has not appeared as yet what we shall be. *We know that, when He appears, we shall be like Him, because we shall see Him* just as He is. And everyone who has this hope fixed on Him purifies himself, just as He is pure (1 John 2:18, 28; 3:2-3, emphasis added).

His Delay

Looking back over the last 2,000 years, we realize that Jesus did not return as soon as the apostles had hoped. Even back in their day, there were those who were beginning to doubt that Jesus would *ever* return in light of how long it had been since His departure. As Peter's earthly life drew to a close, for example (see 2 Pet. 1:13-14), Jesus still had not come back, and so Peter addressed those with doubting thoughts in his final letter:

Know this first of all, that in the last days mockers will come with their mocking, following after their own lusts, and saying, "Where is the promise of His coming? For ever since the fathers fell asleep, all continues just as it was from the beginning of creation." For when they maintain this, it escapes their notice that by the word of God the heavens existed long ago and the earth was formed out of water and by water, through which the world at that time was destroyed, being flooded with water. But the present heavens and earth by His word are being reserved for fire, kept for the day of judgment and destruction of ungodly men. But do not let this one fact escape your notice, be-loved, that with the Lord one day is as a thousand years, and a thousand years as one day. The Lord is not slow about His promise, as some count slowness, but is patient toward you, not wishing for any to perish but for all to

---

[73] Other scriptures that indicate Peter's conviction that Jesus' could return within the lifetimes of his contemporaries are 2 Pet. 1:15-19; 3:3-15.

> come to repentance. But the day of the Lord will come like
> a thief, in which the heavens will pass away with a roar
> and the elements will be destroyed with intense heat, and
> the earth and its works will be burned up (2 Pet. 3:3-10).

Peter affirmed that Jesus' delay was due to His love and mercy—He wants to give more time for people to repent. But He also affirmed that there was absolutely no doubt Jesus would return. When He does, He will come in great wrath.

Scripture is also very clear, as we will see, that Christ's wrathful return will be preceded by years of unprecedented worldwide tribulation and the pouring out of God's wrath upon the wicked. Much of the subject matter of the book of Revelation covers that future period of time. As we will see later in our study, Scripture indicates that there will be seven years of future tribulation. There is no doubt that the Rapture of the church takes place at some point within or near those seven years.

When Exactly Does the Rapture Occur?

A question that often divides Christians is that of the exact time of the Rapture. Some say that the Rapture will occur just before seven years of tribulation, and can therefore occur at any time. Others say that it will occur right at the middle point of the seven years of tribulation. Still other says it will occur at some point after the middle of the seven years of tribulation. And still others say the Rapture will occur at the time of Jesus' wrathful return at the end of the Tribulation.

This issue is certainly not worth dividing over, and all four camps should remember that they all agree that the Rapture will occur at some point within or very near that future seven-year time period. That's a fairly narrow window in thousands of years of history. So rather than divide over our disagreement, we would be better off to rejoice in our agreement! And regardless of what we each may believe, it is not going to change what is actually going to occur.

That being said, I must tell you that for the first twenty-five years of my Christian life, I believed the Rapture would occur prior to the seven-year Tribulation. I believed that because that is what I had been taught, and I also didn't want to go through what I read about in the book of Revelation! As I studied Scripture for myself, however, I began to adopt a different view. So let's take a look together at what the Bible says and see what conclusions can be drawn. Even if I don't persuade you to join my camp, we must still love each other!

The Olivet Discourse

Let's begin by considering the 24th chapter of Matthew's Gospel, a section of Scripture that is foundational in regard to the events of the end times and the return of Jesus. Coupled with the 25th chapter of Matthew, they are known as the *Olivet Discourse,* because those two chapters are the record of a sermon Jesus delivered to some of His closest disciples[74] on the Mount of Olives. As we read it, we'll learn about many events of the end times, and we'll consider what Jesus' disciples, those to whom His discourse was addressed, would have concluded about the timing of the Rapture:

> And Jesus came out from the temple and was going away when His disciples came up to point out the temple build-ings to Him. And He answered and said to them, "Do you not see all these things? Truly I say to you, not one stone here shall be left upon another, which will not be torn down." And as He was sitting on the Mount of Olives, the disciples came to Him privately, saying, "Tell us, when will these things be, and what will be the sign of Your coming, and of the end of the age?" (Matt 24:1-3).

Jesus' disciples wanted to know about the future. They specifically wanted to know when the temple buildings would be destroyed (as Jesus had just foretold), and what would be the sign of His return and the end of the age.

Looking at it in retrospect, we know that the temple buildings were completely demolished in 70 A.D. by general Titus and the Roman armies. We also know that Jesus has not returned yet to gather the church to Him-self, so those two events are hardly simultaneous.

Jesus Answers Their Questions

It seems that Matthew did not record Jesus' answer to the first question about the future destruction of the temple buildings, whereas Luke did in his Gospel (see Luke 21:12-24). In Matthew's Gospel, Jesus immediately began speaking of the signs that would precede His return and the end of the age:

> And Jesus answered and said to them, "See to it that no one misleads *you.* For many will come in My name, say-ing, 'I am the Christ,' and will mislead many. And *you* will be hearing of wars and rumors of wars; see that *you* are not frightened, for those things must take place, but that is not yet the end. For nation will rise against nation, and kingdom against kingdom, and in various places there will be famines and earthquakes. But all these things are merely the beginning of birth pangs" (Matt. 24:4-8, em-phasis added).

---

[74] Mark 13:3 names four who were present: Peter, James, John and Andrew. Incidentally, we find the Olivet Discourse also recorded in Mark 13:1-37 and Luke 21:5-36. Luke 17:22-37 also contains similar information.

It is clear from the start of this sermon that Jesus believed His first-century disciples could very well be alive during the events that lead up to His return. Notice how many times He used the personal pronoun *you*. Jesus used the personal pronoun *you* at least twenty times in the 24th chapter alone, so all His listeners would have believed that they would live to see what Jesus foretold.

We know, of course, that every disciple who listened to Jesus that day died long ago. We should not conclude, however, that Jesus was deceiving them, but that He Himself did not know the exact time of His return (see Matt. 24:36). It was indeed quite possible then for those who heard His Olivet Discourse to be alive at His return.

Jesus' foremost concern was that His disciples would not be deceived by false Christs, as so many will be during the last days. We know that the antichrist himself will be a false Christ, deceiving much of the world. They will consider him to be a wonderful savior.

Jesus said that there will be wars, famines and earthquakes, but He indicated that those events are *not* signs of His return, but only "the beginning of birth pangs." It would be safe to say that those signs have been occurring for the last two thousand years. However, Jesus next speaks of something that has not yet occurred.

Worldwide Tribulation Begins

> Then they will deliver *you* to tribulation, and will kill *you*, and *you* will be hated by all nations on account of My name. And at that time many will fall away and will deliver up one another and hate one another. And many false prophets will arise, and will mislead many. And because lawlessness is increased, most people's love will grow cold. But the one who endures to the end, he shall be saved. And this gospel of the kingdom shall be preached in the whole world for a witness to all the nations, and then the end shall come (Matt. 24:9-14, emphasis added).

Again, had you asked those who originally heard Jesus that day, "Do you expect that you will be alive to see the fulfillment of these things?" they certainly would have answered in the affirmative. Jesus kept using the personal pronoun *you*.

As we just read, after the "birth pangs" will come an event that certainly has not yet occurred, a time of unprecedented, worldwide persecution of Christians. We will be hated by "*all* nations," or literally, "*all* ethnic groups and tribes." Jesus was speaking of a certain specific time when that would occur, not a general time over hundreds of years, because He said in the very next sentence, "And *at that time* many will fall away and will deliver up one another and hate one another."

His statement obviously speaks of the falling away of Christian believers who will then hate other believers, as non-believers can't "fall away," and they already hate one another. Thus, when worldwide persecution begins, the result will be a great apostasy of many who claim to be followers of Christ. Whether they are genuine or false believers, sheep or goats, *many* will fall away, and they in turn will reveal the identities of other believers to the persecuting authorities, hating those they once professed to love. The result will be the purification of the church all over the world.

Then there will also be a rise of false prophets, one of whom is prominently featured in the book of Revelation as the antichrist's accomplice (see Rev. 13:11-18; 19:20; 20:10). Lawlessness will increase to the degree of draining what little love remains in people's hearts, and sinners will become utterly heartless.

Martyrs and Survivors

Although Jesus foretold that believers would lose their lives (see 24:9) not all apparently will, because He promised that those who endure to the end will be saved (see 24:13). That is, if they don't allow themselves to be deceived by the false Christs or false prophets and resist the temptation to abandon their faith and fall away, they will be saved, or rescued, by Christ when He comes back to gather them in the sky. This future time of tribulation and rescue was also succinctly revealed to the prophet Daniel, who was foretold,

> And there will be a time of distress such as never occurred since there was a nation until that time; and at that time your people, everyone who is found written in the book, will be rescued. And many of those who sleep in the dust of the ground will awake, these to everlasting life" (Dan. 12:1-2).

Salvation will still be graciously offered even during those days, as Jesus promised that the gospel would be proclaimed to all the nations (literally, "ethnic groups and tribes"), giving one final opportunity to repent, and then the end would come.[75] It is interesting that we read in the book of Revelation what could very well be the fulfillment of Jesus' promise:

> And I saw another angel flying in midheaven, having an eternal *gospel to preach* to those who live on the earth, and *to every nation and tribe and tongue and people*; and he said with a loud voice, "Fear God, and give Him glory, *because the hour of His judgment has come*; and worship Him who made the heaven and the earth and sea and springs of waters" (Rev. 14:6-7, emphasis added).

---

[75] This promise is often pulled from its context, and it is frequently said that before Jesus will return, we must complete the task of world evangelism. But within its context, this promise is speaking of a final proclamation of the gospel to the entire world just before the end.

It is thought by some that the reason an angel will proclaim the gospel then is because by that time in the seven-year tribulation, the Rapture will have occurred and all the believers will be gone. But that is, of course, speculative.

The Antichrist

The prophet Daniel revealed that the antichrist will actually take a seat in the rebuilt temple in Jerusalem during the midpoint of the seven years of tribulation and proclaim himself to be God (see Dan. 9:27, which we will study later). It is this event that Jesus had in mind as He continued His Olivet Discourse:

> Therefore when you see the abomination of desolation which was spoken of through Daniel the prophet, standing in the holy place (let the reader understand), then let those who are in Judea flee to the mountains; let him who is on the housetop not go down to get the things out that are in his house; and let him who is in the field not turn back to get his cloak. But woe to those who are with child and to those who nurse babes in those days! But pray that your flight may not be in the winter, or on a Sabbath; for then there will be a great tribulation, such as has not occurred since the beginning of the world until now, nor ever shall.[76] And unless those days had been cut short, no life would have been saved; but for the sake of the elect those days shall be cut short (Matt. 24:15-22).

This is a more specific elaboration concerning the tribulation Jesus had spoken of earlier (see 24:9). When the antichrist declares that he is God from Jerusalem's temple, unimaginable persecution will break out against believers in Jesus. In declaring himself to be God, the antichrist will expect everyone to acknowledge his deity. Consequently, all true followers of Christ will immediately become official enemies of the state to be hunted down and killed. That is why Jesus said the believers in Judea should flee for the mountains without any delay, praying that their escape not be hindered for any reason.

My guess is that it would be a good idea for believers all over the world to flee to remote places when that event occurs, as it probably will be one that is televised around the globe. Scripture tells us that the whole world will be deceived by the antichrist, thinking he is their Christ, and they will give him their allegiance. When he declares himself to be God, they will believe him and worship him. When he speaks blasphemies against the true God—the God of the Christians—he will influence the entire de-

---

[76] If the rapture of the church occurs at this precise point in the seven-year Tribulation as some say, there would be no need for Jesus' instructions for believers to flee for their lives because they would all be raptured.

ceived world to hate those who refuse to worship him (see Rev. 13:1-8).

Jesus promised eventual deliverance for His own people by "cutting short" those days of tribulation; otherwise "no life would have been saved" (24:22). His "cutting short" those days for "the sake of the elect" must be a reference to His delivering them when He appears and gathers them in the sky. Jesus does not tell us here, however, how long after the antichrist's declaration of deity that deliverance will occur.

In any case, we note once more that Jesus left His listeners that day with the impression that they would live to see the antichrist declare his deity and wage war against the Christians. This stands in contrast to those who say that believers will be raptured to heaven prior to that event. If you had asked Peter, James or John if Jesus would be returning to rescue them prior to the antichrist's declaration of his deity, they would have responded, "Apparently not."

War Against the Saints

Scripture foretells in other places of the antichrists' persecution of believers. For example, it was revealed to John, as he recorded it in the book of Revelation:

> And there was given to him [the antichrist] a mouth speaking arrogant words and blasphemies; and authority to act for forty-two months was given to him. And he opened his mouth in blasphemies against God, to blaspheme His name and His tabernacle, that is, those who dwell in heaven. *And it was given to him to make war with the saints and to overcome them;* and authority over every tribe and people and tongue and nation was given to him (Rev. 13:5-7, emphasis added).

Note that the antichrist will be given "authority to act" for forty-two months, or exactly three-and-a-half years. It is interesting that this is exactly one-half the time of the seven-year Tribulation. It seems reasonable to think that it will be the final forty-two months of the Tribulation that the antichrist will be given his "authority to act," since his authority will certainly be completely taken away from him when Christ returns to wage war against him and his armies at the close of the Tribulation.

Obviously, this "authority to act" for forty-two months speaks of some *special* authority, as the antichrist will certainly be given *some* authority by God during his rise to power. This special "authority to act" could well be a reference to the time he is given to overcome the saints, because we read in the book of Daniel:

> I kept looking, and that horn [the antichrist] was waging war with the saints and overpowering them until the An-

cient of Days [God] came, and judgment was passed in favor of the saints of the Highest One, and the time arrived when the saints took possession of the kingdom....And he [the antichrist] will speak out against the Most High and wear down the saints of the Highest One, and he will intend to make alterations in times and in law; and *they will be given into his hand for a time, times, and half a time* (Dan. 7:21-22, 25, emphasis added).

Daniel foretold that the saints will be given into the hand of the antichrist for "a time, times, and half a time." This cryptic phrase should be interpreted *three-and-a-half years*, according to a comparison of Revelation 12:6 and 14. We are told in Revelation 12:6 that a certain symbolic woman will be given a place to hide in the wilderness to be "nourished" for 1,260 days, which amounts to three-and-a-half years of 360-day years. Then, just eight verses later, she is spoken of again, and it is said that she will be given a place in the wilderness to be "nourished" for "a time and times and half a time." Thus "time and times and half a time" is the equivalent of 1,260 days or three-and-a-half years.

So the word "time" in this context means *year*, "times" means *two years*, and "half a time" means *half a year*. This unusual expression found in Revelation 12:14 must mean the same thing as it did in Daniel 7:21. Thus we now know that the saints will be given into the hand of the antichrist for three-and-a-half years, the same time that we were told in Revelation 13:5 that the antichrist would be given "authority to act."

I think it goes without saying that both of these forty-two month periods will be identical periods of time. If they begin at the antichrist's declaration of deity at the middle of the seven-year Tribulation, then the saints will be given into his hands for the next three-and-a-half years, and Jesus will deliver them when He appears in the sky and gathers them to himself at or near the close of the seven-year Tribulation. If, however, those forty-two months begin at some other point during the seven-year Tribulation, then we could conclude that the Rapture will occur at some point before the end of the seven-year Tribulation.

The difficulty with the latter of those two possibilities is that it requires that the saints will be given into the hands of the antichrist *before* they are in danger and need to flee for the mountains at his declaration of deity. That seems illogical.

The difficulty with the former of those two possibilities is that it would seem to mean that the saints will still be on the earth during many of God's cataclysmic and worldwide judgments of which we read in the book of Revelation. We will consider this difficulty later.

Now let's return to the Olivet Discourse.

False Messiahs

Jesus next more fully elaborated to His disciples the importance of not being misled by reports of false Christs:

> Then if anyone says to you, "Behold, here is the Christ," or "There He is," do not believe him. For false Christs and false prophets will arise and will show great signs and wonders, so as to mislead, if possible, even the elect. Behold, I have told you in advance. If therefore they say to you, "Behold, He is in the wilderness," do not go forth, or, "Behold, He is in the inner rooms," do not believe them. For just as the lightning comes from the east, and flashes even to the west, so shall the coming of the Son of Man be. Wherever the corpse is, there the vultures will gather (Matt. 24:23-28).

Notice again Jesus' many uses of the personal pronoun *you*. His audience on the Mount of Olives would have expected to live to see the rise of false Christs and false prophets who would perform great miracles. And they would have expected to see Jesus return in the sky like lightning.

Of course, the danger of falling away at that time will be very great, because persecution against believers will be so horrific and false Christs and false prophets will be so convincing due to their miracles. That is why Jesus repeatedly warned His disciples about what would occur just prior to His return. He did not want them to be misled like so many will be. True and steadfast believers will wait for Jesus to return in the sky like lightning, whereas those who are not His true followers will be drawn to false Christs like vultures are drawn to a carcass in the wilderness.

Signs in the Sky

Jesus continued:

> But immediately after the tribulation of those days the sun will be darkened, and the moon will not give its light, and the stars will fall from the sky, and the powers of the heavens will be shaken, and then the sign of the Son of Man will appear in the sky, and then all the tribes of the earth will mourn, and they will see the Son of Man coming on the clouds of the sky with power and great glory. And He will send forth His angels with a great trumpet and they will gather together His elect from the four winds, from one end of the sky to the other (Matt. 24:29-31).

The images of this section of Jesus' Olivet Discourse would have been familiar to the Jews of His day, as they are images right from Isaiah and

Joel that speak of God's final judgment at the end of the world, what is often referred to as "the day of the Lord," when the sun and moon will be darkened (see Is. 13:10-11; Joel 2:31). Then all the world's inhabitants will see Jesus return in the sky in His glory, and they will mourn. Then Jesus' angels will "gather together His elect from the four winds, from one end of the sky to the other," indicating that believers will actually be caught up and gathered to meet Jesus in the air, and it will all happen at the sound of "a great trumpet."

Again, had you asked Peter, James or John at this point in the Olivet Discourse if Jesus would return for them before or after the time of the antichrist and the great tribulation, they would have certainly replied, "After."

The Return and the Rapture

This section of the Olivet Discourse all sounds very familiar to an event of which Paul wrote, one that is undoubtedly the Rapture of the church, yet one which many commentators say occurs *before* the tribulation period begins. Consider the following scripture that we examined earlier in this chapter:

> But we do not want you to be uninformed, brethren, about those who are asleep, that you may not grieve, as do the rest who have no hope. For if we believe that Jesus died and rose again, even so God will bring with Him those who have fallen asleep in Jesus. For this we say to you by the word of the Lord, that we who are alive, and remain until *the coming of the Lord*, shall not precede those who have fallen asleep. For the *Lord Himself will descend from heaven* with a shout, with the voice of the archangel, and *with the trumpet of God*; and the dead in Christ shall rise first. Then we who are alive and remain *shall be caught up together with them in the clouds to meet the Lord in the air*, and thus we shall always be with the Lord. Therefore comfort one another with these words. Now as to the times and the epochs, brethren, you have no need of anything to be written to you. For you yourselves know full well that *the day of the Lord* will come just like a thief in the night. While they are saying, "Peace and safety!" then destruction will come upon them suddenly like birth pangs upon a woman with child; and they shall not escape (1 Thes. 4:13 – 5:3, emphasis added).

Paul wrote of Jesus coming from heaven with the trumpet of God and of believers being caught up "in the clouds to meet the Lord in the air." It sounds just like what Jesus was describing in Matthew 24:30-31, what clearly occurs after the rise of the antichrist and tribulation.

Moreover, as Paul continued writing about Christ's return, he mentioned the subject of when it would occur, "the times and epochs," and he reminded his readers that they already knew full well that "the day of the Lord [would] come just like a thief in the night." Paul believed that Christ's return and the Rapture of believers would occur on "the day of the Lord," a day when terrible wrath and destruction would fall upon those who were expecting "peace and safety." As Christ returns to catch away His church, His wrath will fall on the world.

This harmonizes perfectly with what Paul wrote in a later letter to the Thessalonians concerning Christ's wrathful return:

> For after all it is only just for God to repay with affliction those who afflict you, and to give relief to you who are afflicted and to us as well *when the Lord Jesus shall be revealed from heaven* with His mighty angels in flaming fire, dealing out retribution to those who do not know God and to those who do not obey the gospel of our Lord Jesus. And these will pay the penalty of eternal destruction, away from the presence of the Lord and from the glory of His power, when He comes to be glorified in His saints on that day, and to be marveled at among all who have believed—for our testimony to you was believed (2 Thes. 1:6-10, emphasis added).

Paul stated that when Jesus returned to give relief to the persecuted Thessalonian Christians (see 1 Thes. 1:4-5), He would appear "with His mighty angels in flaming fire" to afflict those who had afflicted them, dealing out just retribution. This hardly sounds like what so many describe as the pre-tribulation Rapture, when the church is supposedly caught up by Christ *before* the seven-year tribulation period begins, and what is normally described as a *secret* appearance of Jesus and a *quiet* catching away of the church. No, this sounds exactly like what Jesus described in Matthew 24:30-31, His return at or near the *end* of the tribulation period, when He catches away believers and pours out His wrath on unbelievers.

The Day of the Lord

Later in that same letter, Paul wrote:

> Now we request you, brethren, *with regard to the coming of our Lord Jesus Christ, and our gathering together to Him*, that you may not be quickly shaken from your composure or be disturbed either by a spirit or a message or a letter as if from us, to the effect that *the day of the Lord* has come (2 Thes. 2:1-2).

First, note that Paul's subject was Christ's return and the Rapture. He wrote of our "gathering together" to Him, using the identical words as Jesus used in Matthew 24:31, when He spoke of the angels who would "gather together" His elect from "one end of the sky to the other."

Second, note that Paul equated those events with "the day of the Lord," just as He did in 1 Thessalonians 4:13 – 5:2. That couldn't be more obvious.

Paul then continued:

> Let no one in any way deceive you, for *it will not come unless the apostasy comes first, and the man of lawlessness is revealed*, the son of destruction, who opposes and exalts himself above every so-called god or object of worship, so that he takes his seat in the temple of God, displaying himself as being God (2 Thes. 2:3-4, emphasis added).

The Thessalonian Christians were being somehow misled that the day of the Lord, which according to Paul must begin with the Rapture and the return of Christ, had already come. But Paul plainly stated that it *could not come* until *after* the apostasy (perhaps the great falling away of which Jesus spoke in Matt. 24:10) and *after* the antichrist declares his deity from the Jerusalem temple. So Paul clearly told the Thessalonian believers that they should not expect Christ's return, the Rapture, or the day of the Lord, until after the antichrist's declaration of deity.[77]

Paul next describes Christ's return and His subsequent destruction of the antichrist:

> Do you not remember that while I was still with you, I was telling you these things? And you know what restrains him now, so that in his time he may be revealed. For the mystery of lawlessness is already at work; only he who now restrains will do so until he is taken out of the way. And then that lawless one will be revealed whom the Lord will slay with the breath of His mouth and bring to an end by the appearance of His coming; that is, the one whose coming is in accord with the activity of Satan, with all power and signs and false wonders, and with all the deception of wickedness for those who perish, because they did not receive the love of the truth so as to be saved (2 Thes. 2:5-10).

Paul stated that the antichrist will be brought to an end "by the appear-

---

[77] This dispels the theory that Jesus' words in the Olivet Discourse only have application to Jewish believers who are born-again during the Tribulation because all those who were born again before the Tribulation will supposedly be already raptured. No, Paul told the gentile Thessalonian believers that their Rapture and return of Christ would not occur until after the antichrist makes his declaration of deity, what occurs in the middle of the seven-year Tribulation.

ance of His coming." If this "appearance" is the same as His appearance at the Rapture mentioned just nine verses earlier (see 2:1), then the antichrist will be slain at the same time that the church is gathered to meet the Lord in the air. Corroborating with this is the record of Revelation chapters 19 and 20. We read there of Christ's return (see Rev. 19:11-16), the destruction of the antichrist and his armies (see 19:17-21), the binding of Satan (see 20:1-3) and the "first resurrection" (see 20:4-6), in which believers who were martyred during the seven-year Tribulation come back to life. If this truly is the *first* resurrection in the sense that it is the first general resurrection of the righteous, then there is less doubt that the Rapture and Christ's wrathful return occur at the same time as the destruction of the antichrist, as Scripture plainly tells us that all those who have died in Christ will be bodily resurrected at the Rapture (see 1 Thes. 4:15-17).[78]

Being Ready

Let's return once again to the Olivet Discourse.

> "Now learn the parable from the fig tree: when its branch has already become tender, and puts forth its leaves, you know that summer is near; even so you too, when you see all these things, recognize that He is near, right at the door. Truly I say to you, this generation will not pass away until all these things take place.[79] Heaven and earth will pass away, but My words shall not pass away" (Matt. 24:32-35).

Jesus didn't want His disciples to be caught off guard, which was the primary point of the Olivet Discourse. They would know that He was "right at the door" when they began to "see all these things"—worldwide tribulation, the apostasy, the rise of many false prophets and Christs, the antichrist's declaration of deity, and then even closer to the time of His return, the sun and moon being darkened along with falling stars.

However, directly after telling them of signs that will precede His coming by a few years, months or days, He then told them that the *precise* time of His return would remain a mystery:

> But of that day and hour no one knows, not even the angels of heaven, nor the Son, but the Father alone (Matt. 24:36).

[78] Some say that this resurrection spoken of in Revelation 20:4-6 is actually the *second* part of the *first* resurrection, the resurrection that occurred during Christ's *first* return at the Rapture. What warrant is there for this interpretation? If the resurrection of Revelation 20:4-6 is actually a second resurrection, why wasn't it called "the second resurrection"?

[79] Although those who heard Jesus that day may have thought that their generation would be the generation to see all those things take place, we know they weren't. Thus we must interpret Jesus' words in 24:34 to mean that all those things would happen in one generation, or perhaps that the *race* (as the word *generation* is sometimes translated) of Christians (or Jews) would not pass away until all those things take place.

How often this scripture is quoted out of its context! It is usually quoted to support the concept that we have *no idea* when Jesus will return, because He could return at any time and rapture the church. Yet within its context, that is not at all what Jesus meant. He had just made quite an effort to insure that His disciples would be ready for His return by telling them of many signs that would occur just before He returned. Now He simply tells them that the exact day and hour will not be revealed to them. Moreover, Jesus was obviously not referring in this passage to His supposed *first* return before the seven-year Tribulation begins, when the church supposedly would be secretly raptured, but of His return at or near the end of the Tribulation. That is not debatable from an honest look at the context.

His Return—A Complete Surprise?

An argument that is often used against the idea of the Rapture occurring near or at the end of the Tribulation is that such a return would not be a surprise as Jesus (supposedly) said it would be, because such a return could be anticipated by the events of the Tribulation. There must be a pre-tribulation Rapture, they say, otherwise the believers would not need to be ready and stay alert as Scripture says they should, knowing that it could be seven years or more before Jesus returns.

Against this objection, however, is the fact that the entire point of Jesus' Olivet Discourse was to insure that His disciples would be ready for His return at or near the end of the Tribulation, and He revealed to them numerous signs that would precede His coming. Why is the Olivet Discourse punctuated with so many admonitions to be ready and to stay alert even when Jesus knew that His return had to be at least several years away from the time He originally spoke those words? *Apparently Jesus believed that Christians need to be ready and stay alert even if His return is still years away.* The apostles who in their letters admonished believers to be ready and stay alert for Jesus' coming were only imitating Jesus Himself.

Additionally, those who believe that it is only a pre-tribulation Rapture that justifies any admonitions to stay ready have another problem. According to them, Christ's first return precedes the end of the Tribulation by seven years. So Jesus' first alleged return really can't happen at just *any* time—it must happen exactly seven years before the end of the Tribulation. Thus in reality, there is no need to expect that Jesus will return until world events are in place to begin the seven years of Tribulation, events that can certainly be anticipated and ascertained.

Most who subscribe to a pre-tribulation Rapture, if they are honest, will say that they know Jesus will not return today or tomorrow due to the political situation in the world. There are still prophesied events that must be fulfilled before the seven years of the Tribulation can begin. For example, as we will soon learn from the book of Daniel, the antichrist will make a covenant with Israel for seven years, and that will mark the beginning of the Tribulation. Thus the Rapture, if it occurs seven years before the end of the Tribulation, must occur when the antichrist makes his seven-year agreement with Israel. Until there is something on the political horizon that will make that scenario possible, there is no need for pre-tribulation Rapture theorists to expect that Jesus will return.

Moreover, for those pre-tribulation Rapture proponents who believe that Jesus will also return at the *end* of the Tribulation, that means the exact day of Jesus' alleged second return could be calculated. Once the Rapture occurs, what Jesus said only the Father knows, could be calculated just by counting ahead seven years.

Again, from what Jesus actually did say, He clearly did not want His return to be a complete surprise. In fact, He *wanted* it to be anticipated by certain events of the Tribulation. Simply put, Jesus did not want His disciples caught off guard, as would the world. He continued His Olivet Discourse:

> For the coming of the Son of Man will be just like the days of Noah. For as in those days which were before the flood they were eating and drinking, they were marrying and giving in marriage, until the day that Noah entered the ark, and they did not understand until the flood came and took them all away; so shall the coming of the Son of Man be. Then there shall be two men in the field; one will be taken, and one will be left. Two women will be grinding at the mill; one will be taken, and one will be left.[80] Therefore be on the alert, for you do not know which day your Lord is coming. But be sure of this, that if the head of the house had known at what time of the night the thief was coming, he would have been on the alert and would not have allowed his house to be broken into. For this reason you be ready too; for the Son of Man is coming at an hour when you do not think He will (Matt. 24:37-44)

Again, Jesus' obvious concern was that His disciples be ready for His return. That in fact, was the primary reason for everything He said before and after this point in the Olivet Discourse. *His many admonitions for them to stay ready and alert are not so much of an indication that His return would be a complete surprise, but an indication of how difficult it will be under the adversity of the time to remain ready and alert.* This being so, those who are expecting an any-time, pre-Tribulation Rapture, thinking they are more ready than other Christians, may actually *not* be ready for what they may well

---

[80] It doesn't really make any difference if the person who is suffering judgment in these examples is the one taken or the one left to remain, as is often debated. The point is that some will be ready for Christ's return and some will not. Their readiness will determine their eternal destiny.

face. If they expect no tribulation and then find themselves in the midst of worldwide persecution under the reign of the antichrist, the temptation to fall away may overwhelm them. Better to be prepared for what Scripture actually teaches will occur.

And again, if you asked Peter, James or John when they could expect to see Jesus return, they would have told you of all the signs that Jesus told them would occur just prior to His return. They would *not* have expected to see Him before the tribulation period or the rise of the antichrist.

A Thief in the Night

Notice that even Jesus' "thief in the night" analogy is contained within the context of His revealing many signs whereby His disciples would not be caught off guard by His return. So the "thief in the night" analogy cannot be rightly used to prove that none should expect to have *any* idea of when Jesus will return.

Both Paul and Peter used Jesus' "thief in the night" analogy when they were writing about "the day of the Lord" (see 1 Thes. 5:2-4, 2 Pet. 3:10). They believed the analogy had application to Jesus' wrathful return at or near the end of the seven-year Tribulation. Interestingly, however, Paul told his readers, "But you, brethren, are not in darkness, that the day should overtake you like a thief" (1 Thes. 5:4). He correctly interpreted Jesus' analogy, realizing that those who were alert to the signs and obediently following Jesus were not in the darkness, so that Christ's coming would not catch them by surprise at all. For them, Jesus would *not* come like a thief in the night. Only those in darkness would be surprised, which is exactly what Jesus taught. (See also Jesus' use of the "thief in the night" phrase in Rev. 3:3 and in 16:15, where He uses it in reference to His coming at the battle of Armageddon).

From this point on in the Olivet Discourse, Jesus repeatedly admonished His disciples to be ready for His return. At the same time, He also told them how they could be ready, as He recited the parables of the unfaithful slave, the ten virgins, and the talents, and then foretold the judgment of the sheep and goats (all worth reading). In almost every case, He warned them that hell awaited those who were not ready for His return (see Matt. 24:50-51; 25:30, 41-46.) The way to be ready is to be found doing God's will when He returns.[81]

Another Objection

Some object to a Rapture near or at the end of the Tribulation on the basis that biblically, the righteous are never punished with the unrighteous,

---

[81] Clearly, for Jesus to warn His closest disciples of not being ready at His return, there existed the possibility of their not being ready. If He warned them of the penalty of eternal punishment for not being ready because of sin, then it was possible for them to forfeit their salvation because of sin. How this should speak to us of the importance of holiness, and the folly of those who say that it is impossible for believers to forfeit their salvation.

proven by such examples as Noah, Lot, and the Israelites in Egypt.

Indeed, we certainly have good reason to believe that the righteous will not suffer God's wrath during the seven-year Tribulation, as that would stand in contrast to many biblical precedents and promises (see, for example, 1 Thes. 1:9-10; 5:8).

Jesus, however, foretold of the great tribulation that the righteous will suffer during that time. It will be not at the hands of God, but at the hands of the unrighteous. Christians are not exempt from persecution—they are promised persecution. During the seven-year Tribulation, many believers will forfeit their lives (see Matt. 24:9; Rev. 6:9-11; 13:15; 16:5-6; 17:6; 18:24; 19:2). Many will be beheaded (see Rev. 20:4).

Thus, if every believer in a certain nation is martyred, there will be nothing to prevent God's wrath from falling on everyone in that entire nation. And certainly if there are believers within a nation, God is able to protect them from His judgments as they fall on the wicked. During His judgments upon Egypt in Moses' time, He proved that. God wouldn't even let a dog bark against an Israelite, while judgment after judgment fell on the neighboring Egyptians (see Ex. 11:7). Similarly, we read in the book of Revelation of stinging locusts that will be released to afflict the wicked people of the earth for five months, but they are specifically not permitted to afflict the 144,000 Jewish bond-servants who will be sealed with a special mark on their foreheads (see Rev. 9:1-11).

The Rapture in Revelation

Nowhere in the book of Revelation do we read of the Rapture of the church, and neither do we read of any other appearance of Christ except the one mentioned in Revelation 19, when He comes to slay the antichrist and his armies at the battle of Armageddon. The Rapture is not written as occurring even then. The resurrection of Tribulation martyrs, however, is mentioned as occurring in that same time period (see 20:4). Because Paul wrote that the dead in Christ will rise at Christ's return, which is the same time the church will also be raptured, this, along with other scriptures we've already considered, leads us to believe that the Rapture will not occur until the end of the seven-year Tribulation, depicted in Revelation 19 and 20.

But there are other views.

Some find the Rapture in Revelation 6 and 7. In Revelation 6:12-13, we read of the sun becoming "black as sackcloth" and of stars falling from the sky, two signs that Jesus said would immediately precede His appearing and His gathering of the elect (see Matt. 24:29-31). Then, a little later in chapter 7, we read of a great multitude in heaven from every nation, tribe and tongue who have "come out of the great tribulation" (7:14). They are not mentioned as being martyrs as is another group just one chapter earlier (see 6:9-11), leading us to speculate that they are raptured rather than martyred—believers who are *rescued* out of the great tribulation.

It is certainly right to assume that the Rapture will occur sometime soon after the cosmic events depicted in Revelation 6:12-13, simply because of what Jesus similarly said in Matthew 24:29-31. We are given no conclusive indication, however, as to when the cosmic events of Revelation 6:12-13 will actually occur during the seven years of the Tribulation. If the events described in Revelation 6:1-13 are sequential, and if the Rapture occurs right after 6:13, it would lead us to believe that the Rapture will *not* occur until after the appearance of the antichrist (see 6:1-2), worldwide war (see 6:3-4), famine (see 6:5-6), death of one-fourth of the earth by means of war, famine, pestilence and wild beasts (see Rev. 6:7-8), and many martyrs being made (see Rev. 6:9-11). Certainly all of those events described could occur *before* the end of the seven-year Tribulation, but they could also describe the entire seven-year period, placing the Rapture at the very end.

Adding some weight to the idea of the Rapture occurring *before* the end of the seven years is the fact that Revelation describes two sets of seven judgments after Revelation 8: the "trumpet judgments" and the "bowl judgments." The latter of these two is said to finish God's wrath (see 15:1). Just before the bowl judgments begin, however, John sees "those who had come off victorious from the beast and from his image and from the number of his name, standing on the sea of glass" (15:2). These victorious saints *could* have been raptured. On the other hand, they could have been martyred. Scripture doesn't tell us which. Moreover, we don't know if 15:2 bears any chronological relationship to the scenes described near it.

Another fact found in Revelation that may add weight to the idea of the Rapture occurring before the end of the seven years is this: At the occasion of the fifth "trumpet judgment" recorded in Revelation 9:1-12, we are told that the stinging locusts will be permitted to hurt only those who "do not have the seal of God on their foreheads" (9:4). The only ones of whom we are told will have that seal are 144,000 descendants of Israel (see Rev. 7:3-8). Thus it seems that all other believers will have to be raptured before that fifth trumpet judgment; otherwise they would not be exempt from the power of the stinging locusts. Additionally, because the locusts will hurt people for five months (9:5, 10), it is thought that the Rapture must occur at least five months before the end of the seven-year Tribulation.

There are, of course, ways around this logic. Perhaps there are others who are sealed and are simply not mentioned in Revelation's condensed synopsis. In any case, if this does prove that the Rapture occurs prior to the fifth trumpet judgment, it also indicates that there will be one group of believers who will *not* be raptured before the release of the stinging locusts—the 144,000 specially-marked descendants of Israel. Yet they will thankfully be protected from being harmed by God's wrath as it is manifested by those stinging locusts.

The conclusion to all of this? I can only conclude that the Rapture occurs either *near* the end or *at* the end of the seven-year Tribulation. Believers need not fear suffering God's wrath, but they should be prepared for severe persecution and possible martyrdom.

The Tribulation Period

Let's spend some time looking a little more closely at what Scripture teaches about the seven-year Tribulation. How do we arrive at a figure of seven years as being the length of the Tribulation? We must study the book of Daniel, which, besides the book of Revelation, is probably the most revealing book of the Bible relative to the end times.

In the ninth chapter of his book, we find that Daniel is a captive in Babylon with his fellow Jews. While studying the book of Jeremiah, Daniel discovered that the length of Jewish captivity in Babylon would be seventy years (see Dan. 9:2; Jer. 25:11-12). Realizing that this seventy-year period was almost completed, Daniel began to pray, confessing the sins of his people and asking for mercy. In response to his prayer, the angel Gabriel appeared to him and revealed Israel's future right through the time of the Tribulation to the return of Christ. The prophecy contained in Daniel 9:24-27 is one of the most amazing in Scripture. I've quoted it below along with my bracketed comments:

> Seventy weeks [these are obviously weeks of years, as we will see, or a total of 490 years] have been decreed for your people [Israel] and your holy city [Jerusalem], to finish the transgression [*possibly* the culminating act of Israel's sins—the crucifixion of their own Messiah], to make an end of sin [*probably* a reference to Christ's redemptive work on the cross], to make atonement for iniquity [*no doubt* a reference to Jesus' redemptive work on the cross], to bring in everlasting righteousness [the beginning of the earthly reign of Jesus in His kingdom], to seal up vision and prophecy [*perhaps* a reference to the end of the writing of Scripture, or to a fulfilling of all pre-millennial prophecy], and to anoint the most holy place [*possibly* a reference to the establishing of the millennial temple]. So you are to know and discern that from the issuing of a decree to restore and rebuild Jerusalem [this decree was be made by King Artaxerxes in 445 B.C.], until Messiah the Prince [the Lord Jesus Christ] there will be seven weeks and sixty-two weeks [a total of 69 weeks, or 483 years]; it will be built again, with plaza and moat, even in times of distress [that is the rebuilding of Jerusalem, previously destroyed by the Babylonians]. Then after the sixty-two weeks [that is, 483 years after the decree of 445 B.C.] the Messiah

will be cut off and have nothing [Jesus will be crucified in 32 A.D., if we calculate by the Jewish calendar of 360 days per year], and the people [the Romans] of the prince who is to come [the antichrist] will destroy the city and the sanctuary [a reference to the destruction of Jerusalem in 70 A.D. by Titus and the Roman legions]. And its end will come with a flood; even to the end there will be war; desolations are determined. And he [the "prince who is to come"—the antichrist] will make a firm covenant with the many [Israel] *for one week* [or seven years—this is the Tribulation period], but in the middle of the week [at about three and a half years] he will put a stop to sacrifice and grain offering; and on the wing of abominations [when the antichrist sets himself in the Jewish temple in Jerusalem, calling himself God; see 2 Thes. 2:1-4] will come one who makes desolate [Jesus will return], even until a complete destruction, one that is decreed, is poured out on the one who makes desolate [the defeat of the antichrist by Jesus] (Dan. 9:24-27, emphasis added).

490 Special Years

From the decree of 445 B.C. by King Artaxerxes to rebuild Jerusalem, God allocated 490 special years of future history. But those 490 years were not sequential; rather, they were divided into two segments of 483 years and seven years. When the first 483 years of that allocated time were completed (on the year Jesus was crucified), the clock stopped. Daniel probably never would have dreamed that the clock would stop for what is now almost 2,000 years. At some point in the future, that clock will start up again and run for seven final years. That final seven years is referred to, not only as "the Tribulation," but also as "Daniel's seventieth week."

Those seven years are divided into two periods of three-and-a-half years. At the mid-point, as we just read in Daniel's prophecy, the antichrist will break his covenant with Israel and "put a stop to sacrifice and grain offering." He will then, as Paul told us, seat himself in the Jerusalem temple and declare that he is God.[82] That is the "abomination of desolation" to which Jesus referred (see Matt. 24:15). That is why believers in Judea should "flee to the mountains" (Matt. 24:16), as that marks the beginning of the worst tribulation the world has ever witnessed (see Matt. 24:21).

It is possible that the "Judean flight" was symbolically seen by John in his vision, recorded in the twelfth chapter of the book Revelation. If so, the Judean believers will find a special place of safety prepared for them in the wilderness where they will be "nourished" for exactly three-and-a-half

---

[82] This indicates to us, of course, that the Jerusalem temple must be rebuilt, as currently, there is no temple in Jerusalem (as of the year 2005 when this is being written).

years, the remaining period of the seven-year Tribulation (see Rev. 12:6, 13-17). John foresaw Satan's rage over their escape, and his subsequent war with the rest of those who "keep the commandments of God and hold to the testimony of Jesus" (Rev. 12:17). That is why I think it would be a good idea for believers all around the world to run for safety in remote locations when the antichrist declares his deity in Jerusalem.

Daniel's Last Revelation

One other interesting passage from Daniel that we have not yet considered is found in the final thirteen verses of his amazing book. They are words spoken by an angel to Daniel. I have quoted it below along with my bracketed comments:

> Now at that time Michael [the angel], the great prince who stands guard over the sons of your people, will arise. And there will be a time of distress such as never occurred since there was a nation until that time [this would be the same distress of which Jesus spoke in Matthew 24:21]; and at that time your people, everyone who is found written in the book, will be rescued [this could be a reference to the Judean flight or the rescue of believers at the Rapture]. And many of those who sleep in the dust of the ground will awake, these to everlasting life, but the others to disgrace and everlasting contempt [the resurrection of the righteous and the wicked]. And those who have insight will shine brightly like the brightness of the expanse of heaven, and those who lead the many to righteousness, like the stars forever and ever. [After their resurrection, the righteous will receive new bodies that will shine with God's glory.] But as for you, Daniel, conceal these words and seal up the book until the end of time; many will go back and forth, and knowledge will increase." [The amazing advances in transportation and knowledge over the past century are seemingly fulfilling this foretelling.]
>
> Then I, Daniel, looked and behold, two others were standing, one on this bank of the river, and the other on that bank of the river. And one said to the man dressed in linen, who was above the waters of the river, "How long will it be until the end of these wonders?" And I heard the man dressed in linen, who was above the waters of the river, as he raised his right hand and his left toward heaven, and swore by Him who lives forever that it would be for a time, times, and half a time [three-and-a-half years accord-

ing to the deciphering revelation of Rev. 12:6 and 12:14];
and as soon as they finish shattering the power of the holy
people, all these events will be completed. [Just as Daniel
7:25 told us that the saints would be given into the hands
of the antichrist for three-and-a-half years, here it seems
obvious that they are the final three-and-a-half years of
the seven years of Tribulation. The end of all the events
spoken of by the angel will occur when "the power of the
holy people" is "shattered."] As for me, I heard but could
not understand; so I said, "My lord, what will be the outcome of these events?" And he said, "Go your way, Daniel,
for these words are concealed and sealed up until the end
time. Many will be purged, purified and refined [through
tribulation, no doubt]; but the wicked will act wickedly,
and none of the wicked will understand, but those who
have insight will understand. And from the time that the
regular sacrifice is abolished, and the abomination of desolation is set up, there will be 1,290 days. [This should
not be interpreted to be the time *between* those two events,
because they both occur in the middle of the seven years.
Rather, it should be interpreted that from the time those
two events take place, it will be 1,290 days until *something*
very significant occurs at the end. 1,290 days is 30 days
more than three-and-a-half years of 360-day years, a time-
period that is repeatedly mentioned in prophetic scripture of Daniel and Revelation. Why this extra thirty days
is added is a matter of speculation. To add to the mystery,
the angel next told Daniel:] How blessed is he who keeps
waiting and attains to the 1,335 days! [So now we have another forty-five days of mystery.] But as for you, go your
way to the end; then you will enter into rest and rise again
[Daniel's own promised resurrection] for your allotted
portion at the end of the age" (Dan. 12:1-13)

Obviously, something very wonderful will happen at the end of those
extra 75 days! We'll have to wait and see.

We know from reading the final chapters of Revelation that there are
many events that apparently occur soon after Christ's return, one being
the Marriage Supper of the Lamb, concerning which an angel told John,
"Blessed are those who are invited to the marriage supper of the Lamb"
(Rev. 19:9). Perhaps this is the same blessing referred to by the angel who
spoke to Daniel. If so, that glorious supper will occur about two-and-a-
half months after Jesus returns.

Perhaps those seventy-five days are filled with other things that we know will occur according to what is written in the final chapters of Revelation, such as the casting of the antichrist and the false prophet in the lake of fire, the binding of Satan, and the setting up of the administration of Christ's worldwide kingdom (see Rev. 19:20 – 20:4).

The Millennium

The *Millennium* is a term that refers to the time when Jesus will personally reign over the entire earth for a period of one thousand years (see Rev. 20:3, 5, 7), which occurs after the seven-year Tribulation. Isaiah foresaw Christ's governmental reign over the earth almost three thousand years ago:

> For a child will be born to us, a son will be given to us; and *the government will rest on His shoulders;* and His name will be called...Prince of Peace. *There will be no end to the increase of His government or of peace,* on the throne of David and over his kingdom, to establish it and to uphold it with justice and righteousness from then on and forevermore (Is. 9:6-7, emphasis added).

Similarly, the angel Gabriel announced to Mary that her Son would reign over a never-ending kingdom:

> And the angel said to her, "Do not be afraid, Mary; for you have found favor with God. And behold, you will conceive in your womb, and bear a son, and you shall name Him Jesus. He will be great, and will called the Son of the Most High; and the Lord God will give Him the throne of His father David; *and He will reign over the house of Jacob forever; and His kingdom will have no end*" (Luke 1:30-33, emphasis added).[83]

During the Millennium, Jesus will personally reign from Jerusalem's Mt. Zion, which will be raised in elevation above its present height. His rule will be one of perfect justice for all nations, and there will peace over the whole earth:

> In the last days, the mountain of the house of the Lord will be established as the chief of the mountains, and will be raised above the hills; and all the nations will stream to it. And many peoples will come and say, "Come, let us go up

---

[83] This scripture illustrates how easy it can be to make a wrong assumption about the timing of prophetic events by misconstruing what scripture actually says. Mary could have easily and logically assumed that her special Son would be reigning on David's throne within a few decades. Gabriel told her she would give birth to a son who would reign over the house of Jacob, making it sound as if Jesus' birth and reign would be two seamless events. Mary would never have imagined that there would be at least 2,000 years between them. We also should be cautious of making similar assumptions as we try to interpret prophetic scripture.

to the mountain of the Lord, to the house of the God of Jacob; that He may teach us concerning His ways, and that we may walk in His paths." For the law will go forth from Zion, and the word of the Lord from Jerusalem. And He will judge between the nations, and will render decisions for many peoples; and they will hammer their swords into plowshares, and their spears into pruning hooks. Nation will not lift up sword against nation, and never again will they learn war (Is. 2:2-4).

Zechariah predicted the same:

Thus says the Lord of hosts, "I am exceedingly jealous for Zion, yes, with great wrath I am jealous for her." Thus says the Lord, "I will return to Zion and will dwell in the midst of Jerusalem. Then Jerusalem will be called the City of Truth, and the mountain of the Lord of Hosts will be called the Holy Mountain"....Thus says the Lord of hosts, "It will yet be that peoples will come, even the inhabitants of many cities; and the inhabitants of one will go to another saying, 'Let us go at once to entreat the favor of the Lord, and to seek the Lord of hosts; I will also go.' So many peoples and mighty nations will come to seek the Lord of hosts in Jerusalem and to entreat the favor of the Lord." Thus says the Lord of hosts, "In those days ten men from the nations of every language will grasp the garment of a Jew saying, 'Let us go with you, for we have heard that God is with you'" (Zech. 8:2-3, 20-23).

The Bible teaches that believers will actually be ruling and reigning with Christ during those one thousand years. Their level of responsibility in His kingdom will be based upon their faithfulness now (see Dan. 7:27; Luke 19:12-27; 1 Cor. 6:1-3; Rev. 2:26-27; 5:9-10; and 22:3-5).

We will be clothed in our resurrected bodies, but there apparently will be natural people living in mortal bodies who will populate the earth at that time. Furthermore, it seems that the longevity of the patriarchs will be restored, and that wild animals will lose their ferocity:

I will also rejoice in Jerusalem, and be glad in My people; and there will no longer be heard in her the voice of weeping and the sound of crying. No longer will there be in it an infant who lives but a few days, or an old man who does not live out his days; for the youth will die at the age of one hundred. And the one who does not reach the age of one hundred shall be thought accursed....The wolf and the lamb shall graze together, and the lion shall eat straw like the ox; and dust shall be the serpent's food. They shall do no evil or harm in all My holy mountain. (Is. 65:19-20, 25; see also Is. 11:6-9).

There are many references to the future Millennium in the Bible, especially in the Old Testament. For further study, see Is. 11:6-16; 25:1-12; 35:1-10; Jer. 23:1-5; Joel 2:30-3:21; Amos 9:11-15; Mic. 4:1-7; Zeph. 3:14-20; Zech. 14:9-21; and Rev. 20:1-6.

Many of the Psalms also apply prophetically to the Millennium. For example, read this passage of Psalm 48:

Great is the Lord, and greatly to be praised, in *the city of our God, His holy mountain. Beautiful in elevation, the joy of the whole earth, is Mt. Zion in the far north, the city of the great King. God, in her palaces, has made Himself known as a stronghold.* For, lo, the kings assembled themselves, they passed by together. They saw it, then they were amazed; they were terrified, they fled in alarm. Panic seized them there, anguish, as of a woman in childbirth (Ps. 48:1-6, emphasis added).

When Jesus sets up His administration in Jerusalem at the beginning of the Millennium, apparently many of the rulers of the earth who survive the Tribulation will hear the report of Jesus' reign and will travel to see it for themselves! They will be shocked by what they see.[84]

For other Psalms that refer to the millennial reign of Christ, see Ps. 2:1-12; 24:1-10; 47:1-9; 66:1-7; 68:15-17; 99:1-9; and 100:1-5.

The Eternal State

The end of the Millennium marks the beginning of what Bible scholars refer to as the "Eternal State," which begins with a new heavens and new earth. Jesus will then turn everything over to the Father, according to 1 Corinthians 15:24-28:

Then comes the end, when He [Jesus] delivers up the kingdom to the God and Father, when He has abolished all rule and all authority and power. For He must reign until He has put all His enemies under His feet. The last enemy that will be abolished is death. For "He has put all things in subjection under His feet" [Ps. 8:6]. But when He says, "All things are put in subjection," it is evident that He [the Father] is excepted who put all things in subjection to Him. And when all things are subjected to Him [the Father], then the Son Himself will also be subjected

[84] From looking at other scriptures, it seems that the Millennium will begin, not only with believers populating the earth, but with unbelievers as well (see Is. 2:1-5; 60:1-5; Dan. 7:13-14).

to the One who subjected all things to Him, that God may be all in all.

Satan, who had been bound for the duration of the thousand years, will be released at the end of the Millennium. He will then deceive those who are inwardly rebellious toward Jesus but who have been feigning obedience to Him (see Ps. 66:3).

God will permit Satan to deceive them in order to reveal the true condition of their hearts so that they can be rightfully judged. Under his deception, they will gather together to attack the holy city, Jerusalem, intending to overthrow the government of Jesus. The battle won't last long because fire will come down from heaven to consume the surrounding armies, and Satan will be cast permanently into the lake of fire and brimstone (see Rev. 20:7-10).

That future gathering for battle is foretold in Psalm 2:

> Why are the nations in an uproar, and the peoples devising a vain thing? The kings of the earth take their stand, and the rulers take counsel together against the Lord and against His Anointed [Christ]; "Let us tear their fetters apart, and cast away their cords from us!" He who sits in the heavens laughs, the Lord scoffs at them. Then He will speak to them in His anger and terrify them in His fury; "But as for Me, I have installed My King upon Zion, My Holy mountain." "[Jesus now speaks] I will surely tell of the decree of the Lord; He said to Me, 'Thou art My Son, today I have begotten Thee. Ask of Me, and I will surely give the nations as Thine inheritance, and the very ends of the earth as Thy possession. Thou shalt break them with a rod of iron, Thou shalt shatter them like earthenware.'" Now therefore, O kings, show discernment; take warning, O judges of the earth. Worship the Lord with reverence, and rejoice with trembling. Do homage to the Son, lest He become angry, and you perish in the way. For His wrath may soon be kindled. How blessed are all who take refuge in Him!

A Final Judgment

Just preceding the Eternal State, one final judgment will take place. All the unrighteous of all the ages will be bodily resurrected to stand before God's throne and be judged according to their deeds (see Rev. 20:5, 11-15). Everyone who is now in Hades will be brought before that judgment, referred to as the "Great White Throne of Judgment," and will then be cast into Gehenna, the lake of fire. This is referred to as "the second death" (Rev. 20:14).

The Eternal State begins with a passing away of the first heavens and earth, fulfilling Jesus' two-thousand-year-old promise: "Heaven and earth will pass away, but My words shall not pass away" (Matt. 24:35).

Then God will create a new heavens and earth just as Peter foretold in his second epistle:

> But the day of the Lord will come like a thief, in which the heavens will pass away with a roar and the elements will be destroyed with intense heat, and the earth and its works will be burned up. Since all these things are to be destroyed in this way, what sort of people ought you to be in holy conduct and godliness, looking for and hastening the coming of the day of God, on account of which the heavens will be destroyed by burning, and elements will melt with intense heat! But according to His promise we are looking for new heavens and a new earth, in which righteousness dwells (2 Pet. 3:10-14; see also Is. 65:17-18).

Finally, the New Jerusalem will come down out of heaven to the earth (see Rev. 21:1-2). Our minds can hardly begin to grasp the glories of that city, which covers an area one-half the size of the United States (see Rev. 21:16), or the wonders of that never-ending age. We will be living in the perfect society forever, under the rule of God, to the glory of Jesus Christ!

THIRTY

Modern Myths About Spiritual Warfare, Part 1

The subject of spiritual warfare has become increasingly popular in the church in recent years. Unfortunately, much of what is being taught contradicts Scripture. Consequently, many ministers around the world are teaching and practicing a kind of spiritual warfare that the Bible never prescribes. Certainly there is such a thing as *scriptural* spiritual warfare, and that is what disciple-making ministers should be practicing and teaching.

In this chapter and the next I'll address some of the most common misconceptions regarding Satan and spiritual warfare. This is a condensation of an entire book I wrote on this subject titled, *Modern Myths About Satan and Spiritual Warfare*. That book can be read in its entirety in English on our website at www.shepherdserve.org.

> **Myth #1: "In eternity past, God and Satan engaged in a great battle. Today, the cosmic struggle still rages between them."**

This particular myth contradicts one of the most well-established, fundamental truths about God that is revealed in Scripture—that He is all-powerful, or *omnipotent*.

Jesus told us that *all things* are possible with God (see Matt. 19:26). Jeremiah affirmed that there is *nothing* too difficult for Him (see Jer. 32:17). No person or force can stop Him from fulfilling His plans (see 2 Chron. 20:6; Job 41:10; 42:2). Through Jeremiah God asks, "For who is like Me.... And who then...can stand against Me?" (Jer. 50:44). The answer is *no one*, not even Satan.

If God is truly all-powerful as the above-mentioned scriptures affirm, then to say that God and Satan were or are in a battle is to imply that He is not all-powerful. If God lost even a single round, was slightly overcome by Satan even to a small degree or had to struggle against him for even a short time, then He is not all-powerful as He declares Himself to be.

385

Christ's Commentary on Satan's Power

Jesus once said something concerning Satan's fall from heaven that will help us understand how much power Satan has in comparison to our omnipotent God:

> And the seventy returned with joy, saying, "Lord, even the demons are subject to us in Your name." And He said to them, "I was watching Satan fall from heaven like lightning" (Luke 10:17-18).

When the all-powerful God decreed Satan's expulsion from heaven, *Satan could not resist.* Jesus chose the metaphor, *like lightning,* to emphasize the speed with which Satan fell. He fell, not *like molasses,* but *like lightning.* Satan was in heaven one second, and in the next—BOOM!—he was gone!

If God can so quickly and easily expel Satan himself, it should have been no surprise that His commissioned servants could also quickly and easily expel demons. Like Christ's first disciples, too many Christians today have a great respect for the power of the devil and have not yet grasped that God's power is far, far, *far* greater. God is the Creator, and Satan is only a creation. *Satan is no match for God.*

The War That Never Was

As strange as it may seem to some of our ears, we need to understand that *God and Satan are not, have never been, and never will be in a battle.* Yes, they do have differing agendas, and it could be said that they are in opposition. But when two parties are in opposition to one another, and one is immensely more powerful than the other, their conflicts are not considered battles. Could an earthworm fight with an elephant? Satan, like an earthworm, made a feeble attempt to oppose One who was immensely more powerful. His opposition was quickly dealt with, and he was expelled from heaven "like lightning." There was no battle—there was only an expulsion.

If God is all-powerful, then Satan doesn't have a ghost of a chance at even slightly hindering God from doing what He wants to do. And if God does permit Satan to do anything, ultimately it is only to accomplish His own divine will. This truth will become abundantly clear as we continue to examine the scriptures on this subject.

Interestingly, God's supreme authority over Satan was not only demonstrated in eternity past, but will also be demonstrated in the future. We read in Revelation that *one solitary angel* will bind Satan and incarcerate him for a thousand years (see Rev. 20:1-3). That future incident could not be considered a battle between God and Satan any more than Satan's original expulsion from heaven could be considered a battle. Note also that Satan will not have the power to break out of his prison and will only be released when it suits God's purposes (see Rev. 20:7-9).

What About the Future "War in Heaven"?

If it is true that God and Satan are not, have never been, and never will be in a battle, then why do we read in the book of Revelation of a future war in heaven that involves Satan (see Rev. 12:7-9)? That's a good question, and one that can be answered easily.

Notice that this war will be between *Michael and his angels* and *Satan and his angels*. God Himself is not mentioned as being involved in the battle. If He were, the conflict could hardly be described as a war, because God, being all-powerful, could easily squelch any opposition in a moment of time as He has already proven.

Angels, including Michael, are not all-powerful, and thus their conflict with Satan and his angels can be described as a war because there will be some actual conflict for a portion of time. Still, being more powerful, they will overcome Satan and his hordes.

Why would God not become personally involved in this particular battle, leaving it to His angels? I have no idea. Certainly God, being all-knowing, knew that His angels could win the war, and so perhaps He figured there was no need for Him to be involved personally.

I have no doubt that God could have easily and quickly annihilated the wicked Canaanites in the days of Joshua, but He chose to give the task to the Israelites. What God could have done effortlessly in seconds, He required them to do, expending great efforts over a period of months. Perhaps this was more pleasing to God as it required faith on the part of the Israelites. Perhaps that is the reason He will not personally be involved in that future war in heaven. The Bible, however, does not tell us.

Just because there is going to be a war someday in heaven between Michael and his angels and Satan and his angels, that is no reason for us to think that God is not all-powerful—any more than Israel's battles in Canaan are reason for us to think that God is not all-powerful.

Was Not Satan Defeated by Jesus on the Cross?

Finally, in regard to this first myth of God and Satan's reputed battles, I would like to conclude by considering the commonly-used statement: *Jesus defeated Satan on the cross.* Scripture never actually states that Jesus *defeated* Satan on the cross.

When we say that Jesus *defeated* Satan, we make it sound as if Jesus and Satan were in a battle, which implies that God is not all-powerful and that Satan was not already under the complete authority of God. There are more biblical ways of describing what happened to Satan when Jesus gave His life on Calvary. For example, Scripture tells us that through His death, Jesus rendered "powerless him who had the power of death" (see Heb. 1:14-15).

To what extent did Jesus render Satan powerless? Obviously, Satan is not completely powerless now, or else the apostle John would never have written, "The whole world lies in the *power* of the evil one" (1 John 5:19, emphasis added). According to Hebrews 1:14-15, Satan was rendered powerless in regard to "*the power of death.*" What does that mean?

Scripture makes reference to three kinds of death: *spiritual death, physical death,* and *the second death.*

As we learned in an earlier chapter, the *second death* (or *eternal death*) is referred to in Revelation 2:22; 20:6,14; 21:8, and it is the time when unbelievers will be thrown into the lake of fire.

Physical death occurs when a person's spirit departs from his body, which then ceases to function.

Spiritual death describes the condition of a human spirit that has not been born again by the Holy Spirit. A spiritually dead person has a spirit that is alienated from God, a spirit that possesses a sinful nature, a spirit that is, to some degree, joined to Satan. Ephesians 2:1-3 paints for us a picture of the spiritually dead person:

> And you were dead in your trespasses and sins, in which you formerly walked according to the course of this world, according to the prince of the power of the air, of the spirit that is now working in the sons of disobedience. Among them we too all formerly lived in the lusts of our flesh, indulging the desires of the flesh and of the mind, and were by nature children of wrath, even as the rest.

Paul wrote that the Ephesian Christians were *dead* in their trespasses and sins. Obviously he was not referring to physical death because he was writing to physically alive people. Therefore, he must have been saying that they were *dead, spiritually speaking.*

What killed them, spiritually? It was their "trespasses and sins." Remember God told Adam that in the day he disobeyed, he would die (see Gen. 2:17). God was not speaking of physical death, but spiritual death, because Adam did not die physically on the day he ate the forbidden fruit. Rather, he died spiritually that day, and did not die physically until hundreds of years later.

Paul continued by saying that the Ephesians, as spiritually dead people, had walked in (or practiced) those trespasses and sins, following the "course of the world" (that is, doing what everyone else was doing) and following "the prince of the power of the air."

Who is "the prince of the power of the air"? He is Satan, who rules his dark domain as commander-in-chief over other evil spirits who inhabit the atmosphere. Those evil spirits are listed by various ranks in a later chapter of Ephesians (see Eph. 6:12).

Paul said that dark prince is a "spirit that is now working in the sons of disobedience." The expression, "sons of disobedience," is just another description for all unbelievers, emphasizing that their nature is sinful. Paul later said that they *"were by nature* children of wrath" (Eph. 2:3, emphasis added). Additionally, he said that Satan was working *in* them.

The Devil for a Dad

Whether unsaved people realize it or not, they are following Satan and are his subjects in the kingdom of darkness. They have his evil, selfish nature residing in their spiritually-dead spirits. Satan is actually their spiritual lord and father. That is why Jesus once said to some unsaved religious leaders: "You are of your father the devil, and you want to do the desires of your father" (John 8:44).

This is the bleak picture of the person who has not been born again! He is walking through life spiritually dead, full of Satan's nature, heading for an inevitable physical death that he greatly fears; and whether he realizes it or not, he will one day experience the worst death of all, eternal death, as he is cast into the lake of fire.

It is extremely important that we understand that spiritual, physical, and eternal death are all manifestations of God's wrath upon sinful humanity and that Satan has a part in all of it. God has permitted Satan to rule over the kingdom of darkness and over all those who "love the darkness" (John 3:19). In effect, God said to Satan, "You may hold in captivity through your power those who are not submitted to Me." Satan became a subordinate instrument of God's wrath upon human rebels. Because all have sinned, all are under Satan's power, filled with his nature in their spirits and held captive to do his will (see 2 Tim. 2:26).

The Ransom for Our Captivity

We can thank God, however, that He had mercy on humanity, and because of His mercy, no one has to remain in his or her pitiful condition. Because Jesus' substitutionary death satisfied the claims of divine justice, all those who believe in Christ can escape from spiritual death and Satan's captivity because they are no longer under God's wrath. When we believe in the Lord Jesus, the Holy Spirit comes into our spirits and eradicates Satan's nature from it, causing our spirits to be born again (see John 3:1-16) and allowing us to become partakers of God's divine nature (see 2 Pet. 1:4).

Now back to our original question. When the writer of Hebrews stated that Jesus, through His death, rendered "powerless him who had the power of death, that is, the devil," he meant that the power of *spiritual* death, which Satan holds over every unsaved person, has been broken for all those who are "in Christ." We are made spiritually alive because of

Christ who has paid the penalty for our sins.

Moreover, because we are no longer spiritually dead and under Satan's dominion, we no longer have to fear *physical death*, since we know what awaits us—a glorious eternal inheritance.

Finally, because of Jesus, we have been delivered from suffering the *second death*, being cast into the lake of fire.

Did Jesus *defeat* the devil on the cross? No, He did not, because there was no battle between Jesus and Satan. Jesus did, however, render Satan powerless in regard to Satan's power over spiritual death, by which he holds unsaved people captive in sin. Satan still holds the power of spiritual death over unsaved people, but as far as those who are in Christ are concerned, Satan is powerless over them.

The Disarming of the Powers

This also helps us understand Paul's statement about the "disarming of rulers and authorities" found in Colossians 2:13-15:

> And when you were [spiritually] dead in your transgressions...He made you alive together with Him, having forgiven us all our transgressions, having canceled out the certificate of debt consisting of decrees against us and which was hostile to us; and He has taken it out of the way, having nailed it to the cross. *When He had disarmed the rulers and authorities, He made a public display of them, having triumphed over them through Him* (emphasis added).

Paul uses obvious metaphorical language in this passage. In the first part, he compares our guilt to a "certificate of debt." What we could not pay was paid for us by Christ, who took our sin-debt to the cross.

In the second part, just as ancient kings stripped their defeated foes of their weapons and triumphantly paraded them through their city streets, so Christ's death was a triumph over "rulers and authorities," that is, the lower ranks of demons who rule over rebellious humans, holding them captive.

Could we not say, based upon this passage, that Christ *defeated* Satan? Perhaps, but with some qualification. We must keep in mind that in this passage, Paul was writing metaphorically. And every metaphor has a point where the similarities turn to dissimilarities, as we learned in the chapter about biblical interpretation.

In interpreting Paul's metaphors in Colossians 2:13-15, we must be cautious. Obviously, there wasn't an actual "certificate of debt" that had all our sins written on it that was nailed to the cross. That is, however, symbolic of what Jesus accomplished.

Similarly, the demons who ruled over unsaved humanity were not literally disarmed of their swords and shields and paraded publicly through the streets by Jesus. The language Paul uses is symbolic of what Jesus accomplished for us. We were held captive by those evil spirits. By dying for our sins, however, Jesus released us from our captivity. Jesus didn't literally fight against those evil spirits and they were not at war with Him. They, by God's righteous permission, held *us* in their power all of our lives. Their "armaments," as it were, were pointed, not at Christ, but at us. Jesus, however, "disarmed" them. They can't keep us captive any longer.

Let us not think that there was some age-long fight between Jesus and Satan's evil spirits, and finally, Jesus won the battle on the cross. If we are going to say that Jesus defeated the devil, let us be certain we understand that He defeated the devil *for us,* and not for Himself.

I once chased away a small dog in my yard who was terrifying my baby daughter. I might say I *defeated* that little dog, but I hope you understand that dog was never any threat to me, only to my daughter. It was the same with Jesus and Satan. Jesus chased a dog away from us that never bothered Him at all.

How did He chase away that Satan-dog? He did it by bearing the punishment for our sins, thus releasing us from our guilt before God, thus delivering us from God's wrath, and thus the evil spirits whom God righteously permits to enslave human rebels no longer had any right to enslave us. Praise God for that!

This leads us to an appropriate place to examine a second related myth.

Myth #2: "There are constant battles in the spiritual realm between God's angels and Satan's angels. The outcome of those battles is determined by our spiritual warfare."

We've already learned from the book of Revelation that there will one day be a war in heaven between Michael and his angels and Satan and his angels. Other than that, there is only *one* other angelic battle that Scripture mentions, found in the tenth chapter of Daniel.[85]

Daniel tells us that he had been mourning for three weeks during the third year of the reign of Cyrus, king of Persia, when an angel appeared to him by the Tigris River. The purpose of the angel's visit was to impart understanding to him concerning Israel's future, and we've already briefly studied what Daniel was told in a previous chapter about the Rapture and End Times. During their conversation, the unnamed angel said to Daniel:

---

[85] Two possible objections answered: (1) Jude mentions a dispute between Michael and Satan about the body of Moses, but there is no mention of an actual battle. In fact, Jude tells us that Michael would "not dare pronounce against him [Satan] a railing judgment, but said, 'The Lord rebuke you'" (Jude 1:9). (2) When Elisha and his servant were surrounded by a Syrian army in the city of Dothan, Elisha prayed for God to open his servant's eyes (2 Kings 6:15-17). Consequently, his servant saw "horses and chariots of fire" which we assume were mounted and occupied by an army of angels in the spiritual realm. This is not, however, a definite indication that these angels had been or were about to be involved in a battle with demonic angels. Angels are used at times by God to execute His wrath against wicked human beings, an example being the slaughter of 185,000 Assyrian soldiers by one angel, recorded in 2 Kings 19:35.

> Do not be afraid, Daniel, for from the first day that you set your heart on understanding this and on humbling yourself before your God, your words were heard, and I have come in response to your words. But the *prince of the kingdom of Persia* was withstanding me for twenty-one days; *then behold, Michael, one of the chief princes, came to help me,* for I had been left there with the kings of Persia (Dan. 10:12-13, emphasis added).

Daniel learned that his prayer had been heard three weeks prior to his encounter with this angel, but that it had taken the angel three weeks to get to him. The reason for the angel's delay was because "the prince of the kingdom of Persia" had withstood him. He was able to break through, however, when Michael, "one of the chief princes," came to help him.

When the angel was about to depart from Daniel, he said to him,

> I shall now return to fight against the prince of Persia; so I am going forth, and behold, the prince of Greece is about to come. However, I will tell you what is inscribed in the writing of truth. Yet there is no one who stands firmly with me against these forces except Michael your prince (Dan. 10:20-21).

Several interesting facts can be learned from this passage of Scripture. Again we see that God's angels are not all-powerful, and that they can actually be involved in fighting wicked angels.

Second, we learn that some angels (such as Michael) are more powerful than others (such as the one who spoke with Daniel).

Questions for Which We Have No Answers

We may ask "Why didn't God send *Michael* with the message for Daniel in the first place so that there would not have been a three-week delay?" The fact is that the Bible doesn't tell us why God sent an angel whom He undoubtedly knew would not be able to break past the "prince of Persia" without the help of Michael. In fact, we have no idea why God would use *any* angel to deliver a message to someone! Why didn't He go personally, or speak to Daniel audibly, or bring Daniel temporarily to heaven to tell him? We just don't know.

But does this passage prove that there are constant battles in the spiritual realm between God's angels and Satan's angels? No, it only proves that, several thousand years ago, there was one three-week struggle between one of God's weaker angels and one of Satan's angels named "the prince of Persia," a battle, which, if God had so willed, would never have occurred. *The only other angelic battle mentioned in the entire Bible is the one future war in heaven, recorded in the book of Revelation.* That's it. There *may* have been other angelic battles that have occurred, but it would be an assumption on our part to so conclude.

A Myth Based Upon a Myth

Does this story of Daniel and the prince of Persia prove that our spiritual warfare can determine the outcome of angelic battles? Again, this idea *assumes* (based upon a few scriptures) that there *are* regular angelic battles. But let's take a leap in the dark and say that, yes, there are regular angelic battles. Does this story about Daniel prove that our spiritual warfare can determine the outcome of angelic battles that perhaps do occur?

The question is often asked by those who promote this particular myth, "What if Daniel had given up after one day?" The answer to that question, of course, no one actually knows, because the fact is that Daniel didn't stop seeking God in prayer until the unnamed angel arrived. The implication in asking it, however, is to convince us that Daniel, through continued spiritual warfare, was the key to the unnamed angel's breakthrough in the heavenlies. If Daniel had quit doing spiritual battle, supposedly the angel would never have made it past the prince of Persia. They want us to believe that we, like Daniel, must continue in spiritual battle, or else some evil angel may triumph over one of God's angels.

First, may I point out that Daniel was not "doing spiritual warfare"—he was *praying to God*. There is no mention of him saying anything to any demonic angels, or binding them, or "warring" against them. Daniel, in fact, *had no knowledge that there was any on-going angelic battle until three weeks had passed and the unnamed angel appeared to him*. He spent those three weeks fasting and seeking God.

So let us rephrase the question: If Daniel had quit praying and seeking God after one or two days, would that unnamed angel have failed to get God's message through to him? We don't know. May I point out, however, that the unnamed angel never said to Daniel, "It's a good thing you kept praying, or else I would never had made it." No, the angel gave credit to *Michael* for his breakthrough. Obviously it was *God* who sent the unnamed angel *and* Michael, and He sent them in response to Daniel's prayer for understanding of what was to take place in Israel's future.

It would be an assumption to think that if Daniel had stopped fasting or seeking God, God would have said, "O.K. you two angels, Daniel has stopped fasting and praying, so even though I sent one of you to take a message to him on the first day he started praying, forget about getting that message to Daniel. It looks like there never will be an eleventh or twelfth chapter in Daniel's book."

Daniel obviously did persevere in *prayer* (not "spiritual warfare"), and God responded by sending angels. We, too, should persevere in prayer to God, and if God so wills, our answer could come by the agency of an angel. But don't forget that there are plenty of examples of angels delivering important messages to biblical people where no mention is made of any-one praying a single prayer, much less praying for three weeks.[86] We need to remain balanced. Furthermore, there are scores of instances of angels who gave messages to biblical people that include no mention of those angels having to fight demonic angels on the way from heaven. Those angels *may* have had to fight evil angels in order to deliver their messages, but if they did, we don't know about it, because the Bible doesn't tell us.

So on we go to a third commonly-believed myth.

Myth #3: "When Adam Fell, Satan Got Adam's Lease to Control the World."

What exactly did happen to Satan at the fall of humanity? Some think that Satan gained a big promotion when Adam fell. They say Adam was originally "the god of this world," but at Adam's fall *Satan* gained that position, thus giving him the right to do whatever he wanted to do on the earth. Even God was supposedly powerless to stop him from then on, because Adam had the "legal right" to give his position to Satan, and God had to honor His agreement with Adam which now belonged to Satan. Satan supposedly now possesses "Adam's lease," and God can't stop Satan until "Adam's lease runs out."

Is this theory true? Did Satan gain "Adam's lease" at the fall of humanity?

Absolutely not. Satan gained nothing at the fall of humanity except a curse from God and a divine promise of his total demise.

The fact is that the Bible never says that Adam was the original "god of this world." Second, the Bible never says that Adam had a legal right to give anyone else his supposed authority over the world. Third, the Bible never says that Adam had a lease that would one day expire. All of these ideas are unscriptural.

What authority did Adam originally possess? We read in Genesis that God told Adam and Eve to "be fruitful and multiply, and fill the earth, and *subdue* it; and *rule over the fish of the sea and over the birds of the sky, and over every living thing that moves on the earth*" (Gen. 1:28, emphasis added).

God said nothing to Adam about being a "god" over the earth, or that he could control *everything*, such as the weather, and all the future people who would be born, and so on. He simply gave both Adam and Eve, as the first humans, dominion over the fish, birds and animals and commanded them to fill the earth and subdue it.

When God pronounced judgment upon the man, He said nothing about Adam losing his supposed position as "god of this world." Moreover, He said nothing to Adam or Eve about losing their dominion over fish, birds and cattle. In fact, I think it is obvious that humanity is still ruling over the fish and birds and "every creeping thing." The human race is still fill-

---

[86] See, for example, Matt. 1:20; 2:13,19; 4:11; Luke 1:11-20, 26-38.

ing the earth and subduing it. Adam lost none of his original, God-given authority at the fall.

Isn't Satan "God of This World"?

But didn't Paul refer to Satan as the "god of this world," and Jesus refer to him as "ruler of this world"? Yes they did, but neither made any intimation that Adam was formerly "the god of this world" or that Satan gained the title from Adam when he fell.

Additionally, Satan's title as "god of this world" does not prove that Satan can do anything he wants on the earth or that God is powerless to stop him. Jesus said, "*All* authority has been given to Me in heaven *and on earth*" (Matt. 28:18, emphasis added). If Jesus has *all* authority on the earth, then Satan can operate only with *His* permission.

Who gave Jesus all authority in heaven and on earth? It must have been God the Father, who possessed it Himself in order to give it to Jesus. That is why Jesus spoke of His Father as "Lord of heaven *and earth*" (Matt 11:25; Luke 10:21, emphasis added).

God has had all authority over the earth since He created it. He gave a little authority to humans at the beginning, and humanity has never lost what God originally gave.

When the Bible speaks of Satan being the god or ruler of this world, it simply means that the people of the world (who are not born again) are following Satan. He is the one they are serving, whether they realize it or not. He is their god.

Satan's Real-Estate Offer?

Much of the Satan-Gained theory is built upon the story of Satan's temptation of Jesus in the wilderness, recorded by Matthew and Luke. Let's examine Luke's account to see what we can learn:

> And he [Satan] led Him [Jesus] up and showed Him all the kingdoms of the world in a moment of time. And the devil said to Him, "I will give You all this domain and its glory; for it has been handed over to me, and I give it to whomever I wish. Therefore if You worship before me, it shall all be Yours." And Jesus answered and said to him, "It is written, 'You shall worship the Lord your God and serve Him only'" (Luke 4:5-8).

Does this incident prove that Satan has control over *everything* in the world, or that Adam handed it over to him, or that God is powerless to stop the devil? No, and for a number of good reasons.

First, we should be careful basing our theology on a statement made by someone whom Jesus called "the father of lies" (John 8:44). Satan sometimes does tell the truth, but in this case, our warning flag should be waving furiously, because what Satan said apparently contradicts something that God has said.

In the fourth chapter of the book of Daniel, we find the story of King Nebuchadnezzar's humiliation. Nebuchadnezzar, full of pride over his position and accomplishments, was told by the prophet Daniel that he would be given the mind of an animal until he recognized that *"the Most High is ruler over the realm of mankind, and bestows it on whomever He wishes"* (Dan. 4:25, emphasis added). Four times this same declaration is made in connection with this story, underscoring its importance (see Dan. 4:17, 25, 32; 5:21).

Notice that Daniel said, *"the Most High is ruler over the realm of mankind."* That indicates God has some control on the earth, doesn't it?

Notice also that Daniel's claim seems to be a direct contradiction of what Satan said to Jesus. Daniel said God "bestows it on whomever He wishes," and Satan said, "I give it to whomever I wish" (Luke 4:6).

So who are you going to believe? Personally, I'm going to believe Daniel.

There is, however, a possibility that Satan was telling the truth—if we look at what he said from a different angle.

Satan is "the god of this world," which, as I have already stated, means that he is ruling over the kingdom of darkness, which includes people in every nation who are in rebellion against God. The Bible states that "the whole world lies in the power of the evil one" (1 John 5:19). When Satan claimed he could give authority over the kingdoms of the earth to whomever he wished, he could very well have been speaking *only of his own domain, the kingdom of darkness*, which is made up of sub-kingdoms that roughly correspond to geopolitical kingdoms. We are informed by Scripture that Satan has several ranks of evil spirits through which he rules his kingdom (see Eph. 6:12), and could assume that he is the one who promotes or demotes those spirits within his ranks, as he is the chief. In that case, Satan was legitimately offering Jesus the position of number two evil spirit—after himself—to help him rule his dark kingdom. All Jesus had to do was fall before Satan and worship him. Thankfully, Jesus passed that opportunity for "advancement."

Who Gave Satan His Authority?

But what about Satan's claim that the authority of those kingdoms had been "handed over" to him?

Again, there is the very real possibility that Satan was lying. But let's give him the benefit of the doubt and assume he was telling the truth.

Notice Satan did not say that *Adam* had handed it over to him. As we have already seen, Adam couldn't have handed it over to Satan because Adam never had it to give. Adam ruled fish, birds, and cattle, not kingdoms. (There were, in fact, no kingdoms of people to rule when Adam fell.) Additionally, if Satan was offering Jesus rule over the kingdom of darkness, which consisted of all evil spirits and unsaved people, then there is absolutely no way that Adam could have handed that jurisdiction over to Satan. *Satan was ruling over fallen angels before Adam was created.*

Satan *may* have meant that all the people of the world had handed him authority over them, as they were not submitted to God and thus were, knowingly or unknowingly, submitted to him.

An even better possibility is that *God* handed it over to him. It is very possible, in the light of Scripture, that God said to Satan, "You and your evil spirits have My permission to rule over everyone who is not submitted to Me." That may seem hard for you to swallow now, but you will later see that is probably the best explanation of Satan's claim. If God truly is "ruler over the realm of mankind" (Dan. 4:25), then any authority Satan has over mankind *must* have been granted by God.

Satan is only ruling the kingdom of darkness, which could also be called the "kingdom of rebellion." He was ruling over that kingdom since the day he was expelled from heaven, which was prior to Adam's fall. Up until Adam's fall, the kingdom of darkness consisted only of angelic rebels. But when Adam sinned, he joined the kingdom of rebellion, and Satan's kingdom ever since then has included not just rebellious angels, but rebellious humans.

Satan had rule over his dark domain before Adam was even created, and so let us not think that when Adam fell, Satan gained something that Adam previously possessed. No, when Adam sinned, he joined a kingdom of rebellion that had existed for some time, a kingdom ruled by Satan.

Was God Surprised by the Fall?

Another flaw in the "Satan's-Gain theory" is that it makes God look rather stupid, as if He was caught off-guard by the events of the fall and as a result found Himself in a sad predicament. Did God not know that Satan would tempt Adam and Eve and that the fall of man would result? If God is all-knowing, and He is, then He must have known what was going to happen. That is why the Bible informs us that He made plans to redeem humanity even before He created humanity (see Matt. 25:34; Acts 2:2-23; 4:27-28; 1 Cor. 2:7-8; Eph. 3:8-11; 2 Tim. 1:8-10; Rev. 13:8).

God created the devil knowing he would fall, and He created Adam and Eve knowing they would fall. There is absolutely no way that Satan could have tricked God and gained something that God would rather Satan not have.

Am I saying that God *wants* Satan to be "the god of this world?" Yes, for as long as it suits His divine purposes. If God didn't want Satan to operate, He would simply stop him, as we are told in Revelation 20:1-2 He will one day do.

I am not saying, however, that God wants *anyone* to remain under Satan's rule. God wants *everyone* to be saved and escape the domain of Satan (Acts 26:18; Col. 1:13; 1 Tim. 2:3-4; 2 Pet. 3:9). Yet God permits Satan to rule over everyone who loves darkness (see John. 3:19)—those who continue in their rebellion against Him.

But isn't there anything we can do to help people escape Satan's dark kingdom? Yes, we can pray for them and call them to repent and believe the gospel (as Jesus has commanded us). If they do, they'll be delivered from Satan's authority. But to think that we can "pull down" the wicked spirits that hold people in their grasp is erroneous. If people want to stay in darkness, God will let them. Jesus told His disciples that if people in certain cities did not receive their message, they should shake the dust off their feet and go to another city (Matt 10:14). He did not tell them to stay and pull down the strongholds over the city so that the people would become more receptive. God allows wicked spirits to hold in bondage those who refuse to repent and turn to Him.

Further Proof of God's Supreme Authority Over Satan

There are many other scriptures that abundantly prove that God did not lose any control over Satan at the fall of man. The Bible repeatedly affirms that God always has had and always will have complete control over Satan. The devil can do only what God permits. Let's first examine some Old Testament illustrations of this fact.

The first two chapters of the book of Job include a classic example of God's authority over Satan. There we read of Satan, before the throne of God, accusing Job. Job was obeying God more than any other person on the earth at the time, and so naturally, Satan targeted him. God knew Satan had "set his heart" on Job (Job 1:8, see note in margin of NASB), and He listened as Satan accused Job of serving Him only because of all the blessings he enjoyed (see Job 1:9-12).

Satan said that God had put a hedge around Job and requested that He take away Job's blessings. Consequently, God permitted Satan to afflict Job to a limited degree. Initially, Satan could not touch Job's body. Later, however, God did allow Satan to afflict Job's body, yet forbade Satan to kill him (Job 2:5-6).

This one passage of scripture clearly proves that Satan cannot do anything he wants. He couldn't touch Job's possessions until God permitted him. He couldn't steal Job's health until God permitted him. And he couldn't kill Job because God would not allow it.[87] God has control over Satan, even since the fall of Adam.

Saul's Evil Spirit "From God"

There are several examples of God using Satan's evil spirits as agents of His wrath in the Old Testament. We read in 1 Samuel 16:14: "Now the

---

[87] This entire passage is also proof that Job did not "open the door to Satan through his fear" a myth believed by some. God Himself said to Satan concerning Job in 2:3: "And he [Job] still holds fast his integrity, although you incited Me against him, to ruin him *without cause*" (emphasis added). I discuss this in detail in my book, *God's Tests*, pp. 175-181, which is also available to read in English on our website (www.shepherdserve.org).

Spirit of the Lord departed from Saul, and an evil spirit from the Lord terrorized him." This situation obviously occurred because of God's discipline upon disobedient King Saul.

The question is, what is meant by the phrase "an evil spirit from God"? Does it mean that God sent an evil spirit who lived with Him in heaven, or does it mean that God sovereignly permitted one of Satan's evil spirits to afflict Saul? I think that most Christians would tend to accept the second possibility in light of the rest of what the Bible teaches. The reason the scripture says that the evil spirit was "from God" was because that evil spirit's harassment was a direct result of God's divine discipline of Saul. Thus we see that evil spirits are under God's sovereign control.

In Judges 9:23 we read, "God sent an evil spirit between Abimelech and the men of Shechem," in order that divine judgment might come upon them for their wicked deeds. Again, this evil spirit was not from God's heaven, but from Satan's realm, and was divinely permitted to work evil plans against certain deserving persons. Evil spirits cannot successfully work their evil plans against anyone without God's permission. If that is not true, then God is not all-powerful. Thus we can once more safely conclude that when Adam fell, Satan did not gain authority that was beyond God's control.

New Testament Examples of God's Power Over Satan

The New Testament provides additional evidence that refutes the Satan-Gained theory.

For example, we read in Luke 9:1 that Jesus gave His twelve disciples "authority over all the demons." Additionally, in Luke 10:19, Jesus told them, "Behold, I have given you authority to tread upon serpents and scorpions, and over *all the power of the enemy*, and nothing shall injure you" (emphasis added).

It Jesus gave them authority over *all the power* of Satan, He first must have had that authority Himself. Satan is under God's authority.

Later in Luke's gospel we read of Jesus saying to Peter, "Simon, Simon, behold, Satan has demanded *permission* to sift you like wheat" (Luke 22:33). The text indicates that Satan could not sift Peter without first obtaining permission from God. Again, Satan is under God's control.[88]

Satan's Thousand-Year Prison Term

When we read of the binding of Satan by one angel in Revelation 20, there is no mention of Adam's lease expiring. The reason given for his incarceration is simply "that he should not deceive the nations any longer" (Rev. 20:3).

Interestingly, after Satan is imprisoned for 1,000 years, he will be re-

---

[88] See also 1 Corinthians 10:13, which indicates that God limits our temptation, which indicates that He limits the tempter.

leased and "will come out to deceive the nations which are in the four corners of the earth" (Rev. 20:8). Those deceived nations will then muster their armies to attack Jerusalem, where Jesus will be ruling. When they have surrounded the city, fire will come down from heaven and "devour them" (Rev. 20:9).

Would anyone be so foolish as to say that Adam's lease included one final short period of time after those 1,000 years, and so God was obligated to release Satan for that reason? Such an idea is absurd.

No, what we learn once more from this section of Scripture is that God has complete control of the devil and permits him to work his deception only to fulfill His own divine purposes.

During the future thousand-year rule of Jesus, Satan will be out of operation, unable to deceive anyone. There will be, however, people on the earth who are only outwardly obedient to Christ's rule, but who inwardly would love to see Him overthrown. Yet they will not attempt a coup knowing that they have no chance to overthrow the one who will "rule with a rod of iron" (Rev. 19:15).

But when Satan is released, he will be able to deceive those who, in their hearts, hate Christ, and they will foolishly attempt the impossible. As Satan is permitted to deceive potential rebels, the condition of people's hearts will be revealed, and then God will righteously judge those who are unfit to live in His kingdom.

That, of course, is one of the reasons God permits Satan to deceive people today. We will later investigate God's fuller purposes for Satan, but suffice it for now to say that God does not want anyone to *remain* deceived. He does, however, want to know what is in people's hearts. Satan can't deceive those who know and believe the truth. But God allows the devil to deceive those who, because of their callous hearts, reject the truth.

Speaking of the time of the antichrist, Paul wrote;

> And then that lawless one will be revealed whom the Lord will slay with the breath of His mouth and bring to an end by the appearance of His coming; that is, the one whose coming is in accord with the activity of Satan, with all power and signs and false wonders, and *with all the deception of wickedness for those who perish, because they did not receive the love of the truth so as to be saved. And for this reason God will send upon them a deluding influence so that they might believe what is false, in order that they all may be judged who did not believe the truth, but took pleasure in wickedness* (2 Thes. 2:8-12, emphasis added).

Notice that *God* is the one given the credit for sending a "deluding influence so that they might believe what is false." But also notice that these people who will be deluded are people who "did not believe the truth," indicating they had an opportunity, but still rejected the gospel. God will allow Satan to empower the antichrist with false signs and wonders so that Christ-rejecters will be deceived, and God's ultimate purpose is that "they may all be judged." For that same reason, God permits Satan to deceive people today.

If God had no reason to permit Satan to operate on the earth, He could have easily banished him to some other place in the universe when he fell. We are told in 2 Peter 2:4 that there are certain sinful angels whom God has *already* cast into hell and committed "to pits of darkness, reserved for judgment." Our omnipotent God could have done the same thing to Satan and to any of his angels if it suited His divine purposes. But for a while longer, God has good reasons to permit Satan and his angels to operate on the earth.

The Demons' Fear of Torment

As we close our study of this particular myth, one final scriptural example to consider is the story of the Gadarene demoniacs:

> And when He [Jesus] had come to the other side into the country of the Gadarenes, two men who were demon-possessed met Him as they were coming out of the tombs; they were so exceedingly violent that no one could pass by that road. And behold, they cried out, saying, "What do we have to do with You, Son of God? *Have You come here to torment us before the time*?" (Matt. 8:28-29, emphasis added).

This story is often used by the proponents of the Satan-Gained theory to support their ideas. They say, "Those demons appealed to Jesus' justice. They knew He had no right to torment them before the time when Adam's lease expires, the time when they and Satan will be cast into the lake of fire to be tormented day and night forever."

But actually just the opposite is true. They knew Jesus had the power and every right to torment them any time He desired, which is why they begged Him for mercy. They obviously were very afraid that the Son of God might send them to be tormented much sooner. Luke tells us they entreated Him "not to command them to depart to the abyss" (Luke 8:31). If Jesus didn't have that right because of some supposed legal right of the devil, they wouldn't have been concerned at all.

Those demons knew they were completely at the mercy of Jesus, as illustrated by their plea not to be sent out of the country (Mark 5:10), their entreaty to be permitted to enter the nearby herd of pigs (Mark 5:12), their begging to not be cast into "the abyss" (Luke 8:31), and their imploring Christ not to be tormented before "the time."

Myth #4: "Satan, as 'the god of this world' has control over everything on the earth, including human governments, natural disasters, and the weather."

Satan is spoken of in Scripture as being "the god of this world" by the apostle Paul (2 Cor. 4:4) and "the ruler of this world" by Jesus (John 12:31; 14:30; 16:11). Based on these titles for Satan, many have assumed that Satan has total control over the earth. Although we have already considered enough scriptures to expose the error of this particular myth, it will do us well to study even further so that we can have a full understanding of just how limited Satan's power really is. We must be cautious that our entire understanding of Satan is not built upon only four scriptures that refer to him as god, or ruler, of the world.

As we examine more of the Bible, we discover that not only did Jesus refer to Satan as "ruler of this world," but He also referred to His heavenly Father as "Lord of heaven *and earth*" (Matt. 11:25; Luke 10:21, emphasis added). Additionally, not only did the apostle Paul refer to Satan as "the god of this world," but he, like Jesus, referred to God as "Lord of heaven *and earth*" (Acts 17:24, emphasis added). This proves to us that neither Jesus nor Paul would want us to think that Satan has complete control over the earth. Satan's authority must be limited.

A very important distinction between these contrasting scriptures is to be found in the words *world* and *earth*. Although we often use these two words synonymously, in the original Greek the two are usually not the same. Once we understand how they differ, our understanding of God and Satan's authority on the earth increases dramatically.

Jesus referred to God the Father as Lord of the *earth*. The word translated *earth* is the Greek word *ge*. It refers to the physical planet upon which we live, and from it the English word *geography* is derived.

Contrariwise, Jesus said that Satan is the ruler of this *world*. The Greek word for *world* here is *kosmos*, and it refers primarily to order or arrangement. It speaks of *people* rather than of the physical planet itself. That is why Christians often speak of Satan as the "god of this world's *system*."

Presently, God does not have complete control over the *world*, because He does not have complete control over all the *people* of the world. The reason for this is that He has given all people a choice regarding who will be their master, and many have chosen to give their allegiance to Satan. Humanity's free will, of course, is a part of God's plan.

Paul used a different word for *world*, the Greek word *aion*, when he wrote of the god of this *world*. *Aion* can and often is translated as *age*, that is, a marked period of time. Satan is the god of this present age.

What does all this mean? The *earth* is the physical planet upon which we live. The *world* speaks of the people who presently live upon the earth, and more specifically, those who are not serving Jesus. They are serving

Satan, and are caught up in his perverted, sinful system. We, as Christians, are said to be "in the world" but not "of the world" (John 17:11,14). We live among the citizens of the kingdom of darkness, but we are actually in the kingdom of light, the kingdom of God.

So now we have our answer. To put it simply: God sovereignly controls the entire earth. Satan, by God's permission, only has control of the "world's system," which is control over those who are citizens of his dark kingdom. For this reason, the apostle John wrote that the "whole *world* (not the whole *earth*) lies in the power of the evil one" (1 John 5:19).

This is not to say that God has no authority over *the world*, or the world's *system*, or the people of the world. He is, as Daniel stated, "ruler over the realm of mankind, and bestows it on whomever He wishes" (Dan. 4:25). He still can exalt or humble any person He desires. However, as supreme "ruler over the realm of mankind," He has sovereignly permitted Satan to rule over the portion of mankind that is in rebellion against Him.

Satan's Offer Considered

This distinction between the earth and the world is also helpful in understanding Jesus' temptation in the wilderness. There Satan showed Jesus "all the kingdoms of the *world* in a moment's time." Satan could not have been offering Jesus a political position over earthly human governments, what we might call a president or prime minister. Satan is *not* the one who exalts and humbles earthly human rulers—God is.

Rather, Satan must have shown Jesus all the sub-kingdoms of his worldwide kingdom of darkness. He showed Jesus the hierarchy of evil spirits who, in their respective territories, reign over the kingdom of darkness, as well as the rebel humans who are their subjects. Satan offered Jesus control over *his* domain—if Jesus would join Satan's rebellion against God. Jesus would then have become second-in-command over the kingdom of darkness.

God's Control Over Earthly, Human Governments

Let's establish even more specifically the limits of Satan's authority by first examining scriptures that affirm God's authority over earthly, human governments. Satan has *some* authority in human governments only because he has some authority over unsaved people, and governments are often controlled by unsaved people. But ultimately, God is sovereign over human governments, and Satan can only manipulate them to the degree that God allows.

We've already examined Daniel's statement to King Nebuchadnezzar, but because it is so illuminating, let us briefly consider it once more.

Great King Nebuchadnezzar was lifted up in pride because of his power and accomplishments, and so God decreed that he would be brought down to a low estate in order that he might learn that "the Most High is ruler over the realm of mankind, and bestows it on whom He wishes, and sets over it the lowliest of men" (Dan. 4:17). Obviously God deserved the credit for Nebuchadnezzar's rise to political greatness. This is true of every earthly leader. The apostle Paul, speaking of earthly rulers, declared that "there is no authority except from God, and those which exist are established by God" (Rom. 13:1).

God is the original and supreme authority of the entire universe. If anyone has any authority, it can only be because God delegated some of His or permitted someone to have some.

But what about evil rulers? Did Paul mean that even they are established by God? Yes he did. Earlier in the same letter, Paul wrote, "For the Scripture says to Pharaoh, 'For this very purpose I raised you up, to demonstrate My power in you, and that My name might be proclaimed throughout the whole earth'" (Rom. 9:17). God exalted hard-hearted Pharaoh for the purpose of glorifying Himself. God would show forth His great power though His delivering miracles—an opportunity afforded by a stubborn man whom He exalted.

Is this fact not also apparent in Jesus' conversation with Pilate? Amazed that Jesus would not answer his questions, Pilate said to Jesus, "You do not speak to me? Do You not know that I have authority to release You, and I have authority to crucify You?" (John 19:10).

Jesus replied, "You would have no authority over Me, *unless it had been given you from above*" (John 19:11, emphasis added). Knowing Pilate's cowardly character, God had exalted him in order that His preordained plan for Jesus to die on the cross would be consummated.

Just a cursory reading of the Old Testament books of history reveals that God sometimes uses evil human rulers as agents of His wrath upon deserving people. Nebuchadnezzar was used by God to bring His judgment upon many Old Testament nations.

There are numerous examples of rulers whom God exalted or brought down in the Bible. In the New Testament, for example, we read of Herod, who failed to give glory to God when some of his subjects cried out before him, "The voice of a god and not of a man!" (Acts 12:22).

The result? "And immediately an angel of the Lord struck him...and he was eaten by worms and died" (Acts 12:23).

Keep in mind that Herod was definitely a citizen of Satan's kingdom, but he was not out of God's jurisdiction. Obviously, God could bring down any present earthly leader if He desired.[89]

---

[89] Does this mean that we should not pray for governmental leaders, or vote in elections, knowing that God exalts whomever He wants over us? No, in a democracy, God's wrath is practically built in. We get whom we vote for, and wicked people usually elect other wicked people. For this reason, the righteous should cast their vote. Additionally, in both Old and New Testaments, we are instructed to pray for our governmental leaders (Jer. 29:7; 1 Tim. 2:1-4), which indicates that we can influence God as He determines who will be put into office. Because God's judgment sometimes comes in the form of wicked governmental leaders, and because most nations are so deserving of judgment, we can ask for and obtain some mercy from Him, so that our particular country does not get *everything* it deserves.

God's Personal Testimony

Finally, let us read what God Himself once said through the prophet Jeremiah in regard to His sovereignty over earthly, human kingdoms.

> "Can I not, O house of Israel, deal with you as this potter does?" declares the Lord. "Behold, like the clay in the potter's hand, so are you in My hand, O house of Israel. At one moment I might speak concerning a nation or concerning a kingdom to uproot, to pull down, or to destroy it; if that nation against which I have spoken turns from its evil, I will relent concerning the calamity I planned to bring on it. Or at another moment I might speak concerning a nation or concerning a kingdom to build up or to plant it; if it does evil in My sight by not obeying My voice, then I will think better of the good with which I had promised to bless it" (Jer. 18:6-10).

Can you see that there is no way that Satan, when he tempted Jesus in the wilderness, could have been legitimately offering Jesus rule over earthly, human, political kingdoms? If he was telling the truth (as he sometimes does), then all he could have been offering Jesus was control over his kingdom of darkness.

But does Satan have *influence* in human governments? Yes, but only because he is the spiritual lord of unsaved people, and unsaved people are involved in human governments. Yet he only has as much influence as God permits him to have, and God can foil any of Satan's schemes any time He desires. The apostle John wrote of Jesus as being "the ruler of the kings of the earth" (Rev. 1:5).

Does Satan Cause Natural Disasters and Adverse Weather?

Because Satan is "the god of this world," many have also assumed that he controls the weather and is the one who causes all natural disasters, such as droughts, floods, hurricanes, earthquakes and so on. But is this what Scripture teaches us? Again, we must be careful that we don't base our entire theology of Satan upon one scripture that says that, "the thief comes only to steal, and kill, and destroy" (John 10:10). How often I've heard people quote this verse as proof that anything that steals, kills or destroys is from Satan. When we examine more of the Bible, however, we learn that God Himself sometimes kills and destroys. Consider these three passages out of many possible examples:

> There is only one Lawgiver and Judge, the One who is able to save and to *destroy* (James 4:12, emphasis added).

> But I will warn you whom to fear: fear the One who after

He has *killed* has authority to cast into hell; yes, I tell you, fear Him! (Luke 12:5, emphasis added.)

And do not fear those who kill the body, but are unable to kill the soul; but rather fear Him who is able to *destroy* both soul and body in hell (Matt. 10:28, emphasis added).

If we say that *everything* that involves killing or destroying is the work of Satan, we are mistaken. There are scores of examples in the Bible of God killing and destroying.

We should ask ourselves, *When Jesus spoke of the thief who comes to kill, steal, and destroy, was He actually speaking about the devil?* Again, all we need to do is read His statement contextually. One verse prior to His statement about the thief coming to kill, steal, and destroy, Jesus said, "All who came before Me are *thieves* and robbers, but the sheep did not hear them" (John 10:8). When we read Jesus' entire discourse in John 10:1-15 stating He is the good Shepherd, it becomes even more obvious that His terms *thief* and *thieves* are references to false teachers and religious leaders.

Various Views of Adverse Weather and Natural Disasters

When a hurricane or earthquake strikes, it raises a theological question in the minds of people who believe in God: "Who is causing this?" There are only two possibilities for Bible-believing Christians: Either God or Satan causes them.

Some may object: "Oh no! God is not to blame! People are to blame. God is judging them for *their* sins."

If God is *causing* hurricanes and earthquakes because of His judgment upon sin, then certainly we can lay the *blame* on rebel humans rather than on God, but still, God bears *responsibility*, as the natural disasters would not occur without His decree.

Or, if it is true that God *allows Satan* to send hurricanes and earthquakes to bring His judgment upon sinners, then we could say that *Satan* causes them, but still, God bears responsibility. The reason is because *He* is the one who permitted Satan to cause the destruction and because those disasters occur as a result of *His* reaction to sin.

Some say that neither God nor Satan are responsible for hurricanes and earthquakes, but that they are simply a "natural phenomena in our fallen world of sin." In a vague way, they are also attempting to lay the blame on humankind for natural disasters, but still missing the point. This explanation does not take God out of the picture. If hurricanes are simply a "natural phenomena in our fallen world of sin," who decided that they would be? Obviously hurricanes are not man-*made*. That is, hurricanes don't develop whenever a certain volume of lies are spoken into the atmosphere. Earthquakes don't occur when a certain number of people commit adultery.

No, if there is a relationship between hurricanes and sin, then God is involved, because hurricanes are a manifestation of His judgment upon sin. Even if they occur randomly, it would have to be God who decreed that they would occur randomly, and thus He is involved.

Even if there is *no* relationship between sin and natural disasters, and God goofed when He designed the world, so that there are faults in the earth's crust that sometimes shift and weather systems that occasionally go berserk, still God would bear responsibility for earthquakes and hurricanes as He is the Creator, and His mistakes harm people.

There is No "Mother Nature"

So we have only two possible answers for the question of natural disasters. Either God or Satan is responsible. Before we look at specific scriptures to determine which answer is correct, let's think further about those two possible answers.

If Satan is the one who causes natural disasters, then either God can or cannot stop him. If God *can* stop Satan from causing natural disasters but doesn't, then He again bears some responsibility. The disaster never would have occurred without His permission.

And now on the other side. Let's assume, for a moment, that God *can't* stop Satan, but He would like to stop him. Is that really a possibility?

If God can't stop Satan from causing a natural disaster, then either Satan is more powerful than God, or Satan is smarter than God. This is, in effect, what adherents to the "Satan gained control over the world at Adam's fall" theory are saying. They claim that Satan has a legal right to do whatever he pleases on the earth because he stole Adam's lease. Now, supposedly, God would like to stop Satan but can't because He must honor Adam's lease that Satan now possesses. In other words, God was too stupid to foresee what would happen at the fall, but Satan, being more intelligent than God, has now gained power that God wishes he didn't have. Personally, I'm not about to say that Satan is wiser than God.

If the "Satan-Gained" theory were true, we would want to know why Satan doesn't cause more earthquakes and hurricanes than he presently does, and why he doesn't target large populations of Christians. (If you say "because God won't let him target populations of Christians," then you've just admitted that Satan cannot operate without God's permission.)

When we narrow it down specifically, the only two possible answers to our question are these: Either (1) God causes earthquakes and hurricanes or (2) Satan does *with God's permission*.

Can you see that regardless of which answer is correct, God is the one who is ultimately responsible? When people say, "God didn't send that hurricane—Satan did with God's permission," they are not totally letting God "off the hook" as they might hope. If God could have stopped Satan from causing the hurricane, regardless of whether He wanted to or not, then He bears responsibility. Human rebels may be the ones to *blame* because of their sin (if the hurricane was sent by God or permitted by God as judgment), but still, it is foolish to say that God is in no way involved or responsible.

Scripture's Testimony

What, specifically, does Scripture say about "natural disasters"? Does the Bible say that God or the devil causes them? Let's look at earthquakes first because the Bible speaks of many.

According to Scripture, earthquakes might occur due to God's judgment upon deserving sinners. We read in Jeremiah: "At His [God's] wrath *the earth quakes*, and the nations cannot endure His indignation" (Jer. 10:10, emphasis added).

Isaiah warns,

> From the Lord of hosts you will be punished with thunder and *earthquake* and loud noise, with whirlwind and tempest and the flame of a consuming fire (Is. 29:6, emphasis added).

You may recall that during the days of Moses, the earth opened up and swallowed Korah and his rebellious followers (see Num. 16:23-34). This was clearly an act of God's judgment. Other examples of God's judgment by earthquakes can be found in Ezek. 38:19; Ps. 18:7; 77:18; Hag. 2:6; Luke 21:11; Rev. 6:12; 8:5; 11:13; 16:18.

Some earthquakes that are recorded in Scripture are not necessarily acts of God's judgment, but nevertheless, were caused by God. For example, according to the Gospel of Matthew, there was an earthquake when Jesus died (Matt. 27:51,54), and one when He was resurrected (Matt. 28:2). Did Satan cause those?

When Paul and Silas were singing praises to God at midnight in a Philippian jail, "suddenly there came a great *earthquake*, so that the foundations of the prison house were shaken; and immediately all the doors were opened, and everyone's chains were unfastened" (Acts 16:26, emphasis added). Did Satan cause that earthquake? I don't think so! Even the jailer was saved after he witnessed God's power. And that is not the only God-caused earthquake in the book of Acts (see Acts 4:31).

I recently read of some well-meaning Christians who, upon hearing of a prediction of an earthquake in a certain area, traveled to the site to do "spiritual warfare" against the devil. Can you see the error in their assumption? It would have been scriptural for them to *pray* to *God* for *His mercy* upon the people who lived in that area. And if they had done that, there would have been no need to waste their time and money traveling to the potential earthquake site—they could have prayed to God right where they lived. But to battle the devil in order to stop an earthquake is unscriptural.

How About Hurricanes?

The word *hurricane* is not found in Scripture, but we can definitely find some examples of strong winds there. For example:

> Those who go down to the sea in ships, who do business on great waters; they have seen the works of the Lord, and His wonders in the deep. For *He spoke and raised up a stormy wind*, which lifted up the waves of the sea (Ps. 107:23-25, emphasis added).

> And *the Lord hurled a great wind on the sea* and there was a great storm on the sea so that the ship was about to break up (Jonah 1:4, emphasis added).

> After this I saw four angels standing at the four corners of the earth, holding back the four winds of the earth, so that no wind should blow on the earth or on the sea or on any tree (Rev. 7:1).

Obviously, God can start winds and stop them.[90]

In the entire Bible, there is only one scripture that gives Satan credit for sending a wind. It was during Job's trials, when a messenger reported to him: "A great wind came from across the wilderness and struck the four corners of the house, and it fell on the young people and they died" (Job 1:19).

We know from reading the first chapter of the book of Job that it was Satan who caused Job's misfortunes. We must not forget, however, that Satan could do nothing to harm Job or his children without God's permission. So, again, we see that God is sovereign over the wind.

The Gale on Galilee

What about the "fierce gale" that assailed Jesus and His disciples when they were once boating across the Sea of Galilee? Surely it must have been Satan who caused that storm, as God would never send a wind that would capsize a boat that contained His own Son. "A kingdom divided against itself will fall," and so why would God ever send a wind that could potentially harm Jesus and the twelve disciples?

These are good arguments, but let us stop and think for a moment. If God didn't send the storm and Satan did, then we still must admit that God *allowed* Satan to send it. So the same question must still be answered: Why would God allow Satan to send a storm that might potentially harm Jesus and the twelve?

Is there an answer? Perhaps God was teaching the disciples something

---

[90] Other scriptures which prove that God is in control of the wind are: Gen. 8:11; Ex. 10:13,19; 14:21; 15:10; Num. 11:31; Ps. 48:7; 78:76; 135:7; 147:18; 148:8; Is. 11:15; 27:8; Jer. 10:13; 51:16; Ezek. 13:11,13; Amos 4:9,13; Jonah 4:8; Hag. 2:17. In many of these examples, God used the wind as a means of judgment.

about faith. Perhaps He was testing them. Perhaps He was testing Jesus, who had to be "tempted in all things as we are, yet without sin" (Heb. 4:15). To be fully tested, Jesus had to have an opportunity to be tempted to fear. Perhaps God wanted to glorify Jesus. Perhaps He wanted to do all of the above.

God led the children of Israel to the edge of the Red Sea knowing full well that they were trapped by Pharaoh's advancing army. But wasn't God *delivering* the Israelites? Then was He not working against Himself by leading them to a place where they would be massacred? Is this not an example of a "kingdom divided against itself"?

No, because God had no intention of letting the Israelites be massacred. And He had no intention, in either sending or allowing Satan to cause a gale on the Sea of Galilee, of letting Jesus and the twelve be drowned.

Regardless, the Bible doesn't say that Satan sent that gale on the Sea of Galilee, and it doesn't say God did either. Some say it had to be Satan because Jesus *rebuked* it. Perhaps, but that is not a watertight argument. Jesus didn't rebuke *God*—He rebuked the wind. God the Father could have done the same thing. That is, He could have stirred up the wind with a word, and then calmed it by rebuking it. Just because Jesus rebuked the gale is no proof that Satan caused it.

Again, we shouldn't base our entire theology on one verse that really proves nothing. I have already made reference to scores of scriptures that prove God is sovereignly in control of the wind, and He is most often given credit for sending it. My main point is that Satan, even though he is "god of this world," definitely does not have independent control over the wind or the right to cause a hurricane anytime or anywhere he desires.

Therefore, when hurricanes occur, we should not view it as something that is beyond God's control, something He would like to stop but can't. Jesus' rebuke of the gale on the Sea of Galilee should be proof enough that God can stop a hurricane if He desires.

And if God is sending (or allowing) a hurricane, then He must have some reason, and the most intelligent answer why He would send or allow a storm that causes widespread *catastrophic* devastation is that He is warning and judging disobedient people.

"But Hurricanes Sometimes Harm Christians"

But what about Christians who are affected by natural disasters? When a hurricane hits, it doesn't just demolish the homes of non-Christians. Aren't Christians exempt from God's wrath due to Jesus' sacrificial death? Then how can we say that God is the one ultimately behind natural disasters when they might very well harm His own children?

These are indeed difficult questions. We must realize, however, that the answers aren't any easier if we base them upon the false premise that Satan causes natural disasters. If Satan causes all natural disasters, then why does God *allow* him to cause things that might harm God's own children? We still face the same problem.

The Bible does state plainly that those who are in Christ are "not destined for wrath" (1 Thes. 5:9). At the same time, the Bible says that "the wrath of God abides on" those who don't obey Jesus (John 3:36). Yet how can God's wrath abide upon the unsaved without affecting the saved, when the saved live right among the unsaved? The answer is that, sometimes it can't, and we should face up to that fact.

In the days of the exodus, all the Israelites were living together in one location, and the plagues which God sent as judgment upon the Egyptians did not harm them (see Ex. 8:22-23; 9:3-7; 24-26; 12:23). But with us, we live and work side-by-side with the "Egyptians." If God is to judge them by means of a natural disaster, then how are we to escape?

Escape is definitely the key word in understanding the answer to this question. Although Noah escaped God's full wrath when God flooded the earth, he still was adversely affected, as he had to labor to build the ark and then had to spend a year on board with a multitude of smelly animals. (Incidentally, both Old and New Testaments give *God* the credit for the flood of Noah, not Satan; see Gen. 6:17; 2 Pet. 2:5).

Lot escaped with his life when God's judgment fell upon Sodom and Gomorrah, but he still lost everything he had in the destruction of the fire and brimstone. God's judgment upon wicked people affected a righteous man.

Years in advance, Jesus had forewarned the believers in Jerusalem to flee when they saw their city surrounded by armies, because those would be "days of vengeance" (Luke 21:22-23)—clearly indicating God's wrathful purpose for allowing the Roman siege of Jerusalem in 70 A.D. Praise God that the Christians who heeded Christ's warning escaped with their lives, but they still lost what they had to leave behind in Jerusalem.

In all three of the above examples, we see that God's people may very well suffer to some degree when God's judgment falls upon the wicked. We cannot, therefore, jump to the conclusion that God is not responsible for natural disasters because they sometimes affect Christians.

What Then Shall We Do?

We live in a world that is cursed by God, a world that is experiencing the wrath of God all the time. Paul wrote, "the wrath of God is revealed [not "*going to be* revealed"] from heaven against all ungodliness and unrighteousness of men" (Rom. 1:18). As those who are living among an evil, God-cursed world, we cannot completely escape the effects of God's wrath upon it, even though that wrath is not aimed specifically at us.

Knowing this, what should we do? First, we should trust God. Jeremiah wrote:

> Blessed is the man who trusts in the Lord and whose trust
> is the Lord. For he will be like a tree planted by the water,
> that extends its roots by a stream and will not fear when
> the heat comes; but its leaves will be green, and it will not
> be anxious in a year of drought nor cease to yield fruit (Jer.
> 17:7-8).

Notice Jeremiah did not say that the man who trusts in the Lord will
never be faced with a drought. No, when the heat and the famine come,
the man who trusts in the Lord is like a tree that extends its roots by a
stream. He has another source of supply, even while the world languishes
around him. The story of Elisha being fed by ravens during the famine
in Israel comes to mind as an example (see 1 Kings 17:1-6). David wrote
of the righteous, "In the days of famine they will have abundance" (Ps.
37:19).

But aren't famines caused by the devil? No, not according to Scripture.
God always takes the responsibility, and famine is often spoken of as a
consequence of His wrath upon deserving people. For example:

> Therefore, thus says the Lord of hosts, "Behold, *I am about
> to punish them*! The young men will die by the sword, *their
> sons and daughters will die by famine*" (Jer. 11:22, emphasis
> added).

> Thus says the Lord of hosts, "Behold, *I am sending* upon
> them the sword, *famine*, and pestilence, and I will make
> them like split-open figs that cannot be eaten due to rot-
> tenness" (Jer. 29:17).

> "Son of man, if a country sins against Me by committing
> unfaithfulness, and *I stretch out My hand against it, destroy
> its supply of bread, send famine against it*, and cut off from it
> both man and beast..." (Ezek. 14:13, emphasis added).

> "You look for much, but behold, it comes to little; when
> you bring it home, I blow it away. Why?" declares the Lord
> of hosts, "Because of My house which lies desolate, while
> each of you runs to his own house. Therefore, because of
> you the sky has withheld its dew, and the earth has with-
> held its produce. And *I called for a drought* on the land, on
> the mountains, on the grain, on the new wine, on the oil,
> on what the ground produces, on men, on cattle, and on all
> the labor of your hands" (Hag. 1:9-11, emphasis added).

In the fourth example above, we read that the Israelites were given the blame for the drought because of their sin, but still, God claimed responsibility for sending it.[91]

If God sends a famine upon evil people, and we happen to live among those evil people, then we should trust that He will provide for our needs. Paul affirmed that famine cannot separate us from the love of Christ!: "Who shall separate us from the love of Christ? Shall tribulation, or distress, or persecution, or *famine*, or nakedness, or peril, or sword?" (Rom. 8:35, emphasis added). Notice Paul did not say that Christians will never be faced with a famine, but rather implied that they might, even though he as a student of the Scriptures, knew that famines can be sent by God to judge the wicked.

Obedience and Wisdom

Second, we should be obedient and use godly wisdom to avoid being caught in any of God's wrath that is aimed at the world. Noah had to build his ark, Lot had to head for the hills, the Jerusalem Christians had to flee from their city; all of these had to obey God in order to avoid getting caught in His judgment upon the wicked.

If I lived in a hurricane zone, I'd build a strong house that could not be blown down or a cheap house that could easily be replaced! And I'd pray. Every Christian should pray and remain sensitive to the One whom Jesus promised would "disclose to you what is to come" (John 16:13) so that he can avoid God's wrath upon the world.

We read in Acts 11 of the prophet Agabus who warned of an impending famine that could have been potentially disastrous to Christians living in Judea. Consequently, an offering was received by Paul and Barnabas for their relief (see Acts 11:28-30).

Can such things happen today? Certainly, because the Holy Spirit hasn't changed, nor has God's love waned. It is unfortunate, however, that some in the body of Christ are not open to such gifts and manifestations of the Holy Spirit, and thus, because they "quench the Spirit" (1 Thes. 5:19) miss out on some of God's best.

In his autobiography, the late president and founder of the Full Gospel Businessmen, Demos Shakarian, recounts how God spoke through an illiterate boy-prophet to the Christians living in Armenia in the late 1800's. He warned them of an impending holocaust, and as a result, thousands of Pentecostal Christians who believed in such supernatural manifestations fled the country, including Shakarian's own grandparents. Shortly thereafter, a Turkish invasion of Armenia resulted in the slaughter of over a million Armenians, including those Christians who refused to heed God's warning.

[91] For additional references to God causing famine, see Deut. 32:23-24; 2 Sam. 21:1; 24:12-13; 2 Kin. 8:1; Ps. 105:16; Is. 14:30; Jer. 14:12,15-16; 16:3-4; 24:10; 27:8; 34:17; 42:17; 44:12-13; Ezek. 5:12,16-17; 6:12; 12:16; 14:21; 36:29; Rev. 6:8; 18:8). Jesus Himself said that God "sends rain on the righteous and the unrighteous" (Matt. 5:45). God controls the rain.

We would be wise to remain open to the Holy Spirit and be obedient to God, or else it is quite possible that we might experience a dose of God's wrath that He really doesn't want us to experience. Elisha once instructed a woman: "Arise and go with your household, and sojourn wherever you can sojourn; for the Lord has called for a famine, and it shall even come on the land for seven years" (2 Kin. 8:1). What if that woman hadn't listened to the prophet?

In the book of Revelation we read an interesting warning to God's people to come out of "Babylon" lest they be caught in God's judgment upon her:

> And I heard another voice from heaven, saying, "Come out of her [Babylon], my people, that you may not participate in her sins and *that you may not receive of her plagues;* for her sins have piled up as high as heaven, and God has remembered her iniquities....For this reason in one day her plagues will come, pestilence and mourning and famine, and she will be burned up with fire; for the Lord God who judges her is strong" (Rev. 18:4-5,8, emphasis added).

In summary, God is sovereign over the weather and natural disasters. God has repeatedly proven Himself as Lord over nature in the Bible, from His causing forty days of rain during Noah's day, to His raining hailstones as well as sending other natural plagues upon Israel's enemies, to His stirring up the wind against Jonah's boat, to His rebuking the storm in the Sea of Galilee. He is, as Jesus said, "Lord of heaven and earth" (Matt. 11:25). For additional specific scriptural proof of God's lordship over nature, see Josh. 10:11; Job 38:22-38; Jer. 5:24; 10:13; 31:35; Ps. 78:45-49; 105:16; 107:33-37; 135:6-7; 147:7-8,15-18; Matt. 5:45; Acts 14:17.

A Few Questions Answered

If God is judging people through famines, floods, and earthquakes, then is it wrong for us, as God's representatives, to assist and relieve the suffering of those whom God is punishing?

No, absolutely not. We should realize that God loves everyone, including people He judges. As strange as it may seem to our ears, His judgment through natural disasters is actually an indication of His love. How can that be? Through the hardship and difficulties that natural disasters cause, God is warning people whom He loves that He is holy and judgmental, and that there is a consequence for sin. God allows temporal suffering in order to help people wake up to see their need for a Savior—in order that they might escape the lake of fire. That is love!

As long as people are still breathing, God is still showing them undeserved mercy and there is time for them to repent. Through our compassion and assistance, we can demonstrate God's love for people who are experiencing His temporal wrath, but who can be saved from His eternal wrath. Natural disasters are opportunities to reach out to the world for which Jesus died.

Isn't reaching people with the gospel the most important thing in this life? When we have an eternal perspective, the suffering of those caught in natural disasters is nothing in comparison to the suffering of those who will be cast into the lake of fire.

It is a fact the people generally become more receptive to the gospel when they are suffering. There are numerous biblical examples of this phenomenon, from the repentance of Israel during the oppression of neighboring nations, to Jesus' story of the prodigal son. Christians should view natural disasters as times when the harvest is potentially very ripe.

Let's Tell the Truth

But what should our message be to those picking up the pieces of their lives after a hurricane or earthquake? How shall we answer if they ask for a theological answer to their predicament? Let's be honest with what the Bible teaches, and tell people that God is holy and that their sin does have consequences. Let's tell them that the ferocious roar of the hurricane is but a small sampling of the power that the almighty God possesses, and the fear they felt as their house shook is nothing in comparison to the terror that will grip them as they are thrown into hell. And let's tell them that even though we all deserve to be cast into hell, God is mercifully giving us time to repent and believe in Jesus, through whom we can be saved from God's wrath.

"But we shouldn't scare people about God, should we?" some ask. The answer is found in Scripture: "The fear of the Lord is the beginning of knowledge" (Prov. 1:7). Until people fear God, they really don't know anything.

What if People Become Angry With God?

But might not people become angry at God because of their suffering? Perhaps they will, but we gently need to help them see their pride. None have a right to complain at God for His treatment of them, because we all deserve to have been cast into hell a long time ago. Rather than cursing God for their calamity, people should be praising Him for loving them so much to warn them. God has every right to ignore everyone, leaving them to follow their selfish paths to hell. But God loves people and is calling out to them every day. He quietly calls them through the flowering of apple trees, the songs of birds, the majesty of mountains, and the twinkling of a myriad of stars. He calls to them through their consciences, through His body the church, and through His Holy Spirit. But they ignore His call.

Certainly it is not God's will for people to have to suffer, but when they keep ignoring Him, He loves them enough to use more drastic measures to get their attention. Hurricanes, earthquakes, floods and famines are some of those more drastic measures. God hopes that such calamities will humble people's pride and bring them to their senses.

Is God Unfair in His Judgment?

When we look at God and our world from a biblical perspective, then and only then are we thinking rightly. The biblical perspective is that everyone deserves God's wrath, but that God is merciful. When suffering people say they deserve better treatment from God, surely He must groan. Everyone is receiving much more mercy than he or she deserves.

In keeping with this theme, Jesus once commented on two contemporary calamities. We read in Luke's gospel:

> Now on the same occasion there were some present who reported to Him [Jesus] about the Galileans, whose blood Pilate had mingled with their sacrifices. And He answered and said to them, "Do you suppose that these Galileans were greater sinners than all other Galileans, because they suffered this fate? I tell you, no, but unless you repent, you will all likewise perish. Or do you suppose that those eighteen on whom the tower in Siloam fell and killed them, were worse culprits than all the men who live in Jerusalem? I tell you, no, but unless you repent, you will all likewise perish" (Luke 13:1-5).

The Galileans who died at Pilate's hand could not say, "God has treated us unfairly by not saving us from Pilate!" No, they were sinners who deserved to die. And, according to Jesus, those Galileans who survived would be wrong to jump to the conclusion that they were less sinful than their murdered neighbors. They had not *earned* greater favor from God—they had been *granted* greater mercy.

Christ's message was clear: "You are *all* sinners. Sin has consequences. For now, you live because of God's mercy. So repent before it is too late for you as well."

Jesus concluded His comments on those tragedies with a parable about God's mercy:

> And He began telling this parable: "A certain man had a fig tree which had been planted in his vineyard; and he came looking for fruit on it, and did not find any. And he said to the vineyard-keeper, 'Behold, for three years I have come looking for fruit on this fig tree without finding any. Cut it down! Why does it even use up the ground?' And he answered and said to him, 'Let it alone, sir, for this year too, until I dig around it and put in fertilizer; and if it bears fruit next year, fine; but if not, cut it down'" (Luke 13:6-9).

Here are the justice and mercy of God illustrated. God's justice cries out, "Cut down the worthless tree!" But His mercy pleads, "No, give it more time to bring forth fruit." Every person who is without Christ is like that tree.

Can We Rebuke Hurricanes and Floods?

One final question about natural disasters: Is it not true that if we have enough faith, we can rebuke and stop natural disasters from occurring?

To have faith means to believe God's revealed will. Faith, therefore, must be founded on God's own word or it is not faith at all, but rather hope or presumption. There is no place in the Bible where God gives us the promise that we can rebuke and calm hurricanes, and so there is no way a person could have faith to do so (apart from God sovereignly granting him faith).

Let me explain further. The only way a person could have faith to rebuke a hurricane is if he was certain God did not want that hurricane to strike a certain geographical area. As we have learned from Scripture, God is the one who controls the wind and is thus responsible for hurricanes. Therefore, it would be impossible for someone to have confident faith that he could stop a hurricane when God Himself has decreed its occurrence! The only exception to this would be if God changed His mind about the hurricane, which He might do in response to someone's prayer that He show mercy, or in response to the repentance of the people whom He was about to judge (the story of Nineveh in Jonah's day comes to mind as an example). Yet even if God changed His mind, still no one could have faith to rebuke and calm a hurricane unless that person *knew* God had changed His mind and also knew that God wanted him to rebuke and calm the storm.

The only person who ever rebuked and calmed a great wind was Jesus. The only way any of us could do it would be if God gave us the "gift of faith," (or the gift of "special faith" as it is sometimes called), one of the nine gifts of the Spirit listed in 1 Corinthians 12:7-11. As with all the gifts of the Spirit, the gift of faith operates not as we might will, but only as the Spirit wills (see 1 Cor. 12:11). Therefore, unless God gives you special faith to rebuke an oncoming hurricane, you should not remain in its path, supposedly acting in faith. You should get out of the way! I would also suggest that you pray for God's protection, and ask Him to have mercy upon the people He was judging, asking Him to spare their lives that they might have more time to repent.

Notice that when Paul was bound for Rome on a boat that was driven for two weeks by gale-force winds, he did not calm it by a rebuke (see Acts 27:14-44). The reason he didn't is because he couldn't. Also notice that God did have mercy upon every person on board, as all 276 of them survived the resulting shipwreck (see Acts 27:24, 34, 44). I would like to think that God had mercy upon them because Paul prayed for God to have mercy on them.

THIRTY-ONE

Modern Myths About Spiritual Warfare, Part 2

We continue this chapter by considering additional erroneous but popular teachings regarding Satan and spiritual warfare. At the conclusion, we will consider what Scripture actually says in regard to spiritual warfare that every believer should practice.

Myth #5: "We can pull down demonic strongholds in the atmosphere through spiritual warfare."

There is, according to Scripture, no doubt that Satan rules over a hierarchy of evil spirits who inhabit the earth's atmosphere and who assist him in ruling the kingdom of darkness. That those evil spirits are "territorial," ruling over certain geographical areas, is a concept that is also contained in the Bible (see Dan. 10:13, 20-21; Mark 5:9-10). That Christians have the authority to cast demons out of other people and the responsibility to resist the devil is scriptural (see Mark 16:17; Jas. 4:7; 1 Pet. 5:8-9). But can Christians pull down evil spirits over cities? The answer is that they can't, and to attempt to do so is a waste of their time.

Just because we can cast demons out of people, we should not assume that we can pull down evil spirits over cities. There are numerous examples of casting demons out of people in the Gospels and the book of Acts, but can you think of even one example in the Gospels or the book of Acts where someone pulled down an evil spirit that was ruling over a city or geographical area? You can't because there are no such examples. Can you think of one instruction anywhere in the epistles about our responsibility to pull down evil spirits from the atmosphere? No, because there are none. For this reason, we have no biblical basis to believe that we can or should be waging "spiritual warfare" against evil spirits in the atmosphere.

Pushing Parables Too Far

Reading more meaning into the Bible than God intended is an error Christians often make when they read scripture passages containing metaphorical language. A classic example of misinterpreting metaphorical language is how many interpret Paul's words about "pulling down strongholds":

> For though we walk in the flesh, we do not war according to the flesh, for the weapons of our warfare are not of the flesh, but divinely powerful for the destruction of fortresses. We are destroying speculations and every lofty thing raised up against the knowledge of God, and we are taking every thought captive to the obedience of Christ, and we are ready to punish all disobedience, whenever your obedience is complete (2 Cor. 10:3-6).

The *King James Version*, rather than saying "we are destroying speculations," says we are "pulling down strongholds." From this one metaphorical phrase, practically an entire theology has been built to defend the idea of doing "spiritual warfare" in order to "pull down the strongholds" consisting of evil spirits in the atmosphere. But as the *New American Standard Version* clearly conveys, Paul is speaking, not of evil spirits in the atmosphere, but of strongholds of false beliefs that exist in people's minds. *Speculations* are what Paul was destroying, not wicked spirits in high places.

This becomes even clearer as we read contextually. Paul said, "We are destroying speculations and every lofty thing raised up against *the knowledge of God*, and we are taking every *thought* captive to the obedience of Christ" (emphasis added). The battle of which Paul symbolically writes is a battle against thoughts, or ideas, that are contrary to the true knowledge of God.

Using military metaphors, Paul explains that we are in a battle, a battle for the minds of people who have believed the lies of Satan. Our primary weapon in this battle is the truth, which is why we've been commanded to go into the entire world and preach the gospel, invading enemy territory with a message that can set captives free. The fortresses we are destroying have been built with bricks of lies joined by the mortar of deception.

The Whole Armor of God

Another passage in Paul's writings that is often misinterpreted is found in Ephesians 6:10-17, where he wrote about our responsibility to put on God's armor. Although this passage is definitely about the Christian's struggle with the devil and evil spirits, there is no mention of pulling down evil spirits over cities. As we study the passage closely, it becomes clear that Paul was primarily writing about each individual's responsibility to resist Satan's schemes in his personal life by applying the truth of God's Word.

As we read this particular passage, notice also the evident metaphorical language. Paul was obviously not speaking of a literal, material armor that Christians should put on their bodies. Rather, the armor of which he wrote is figurative. Those pieces of armor represent the various scriptural truths that Christians should use for protection against the devil and evil spirits. By knowing, believing, and acting upon God's Word, Christians are, figuratively speaking, clothed in God's protective armor.

Let's examine this passage in Ephesians verse by verse, while asking ourselves, *What was Paul really trying to convey to us?*

The Source of Our Spiritual Strength

First, we are told to "be strong in the Lord, and in the strength of His might" (Eph. 6:10). The emphasis is on the fact that we should *not* derive our strength from ourselves but God. This is further brought out in Paul's next statement: "Put on the full armor of God" (Eph. 6:11a). This is *God's* armor, not ours. Paul is not saying that God Himself wears armor, but that we need the armor that God has supplied for us.

Why do we need this armor that God has supplied? The answer is, "That you may be able to stand firm against the schemes of the devil" (Eph. 6:11b). This armor is primarily for *defensive*, not offensive use. It is not so we can go out and pull down evil spirits over cities; it is so we can *stand firm against* Satan's schemes.

We learn that the devil has evil plans to attack us, and unless we are wearing the armor that God supplies, we are vulnerable. Notice also that it is *our* responsibility to put on the armor, not God's.

Let's continue:

> For our struggle is not against flesh and blood, but against the rulers, against the powers, against the world forces of this darkness, against the spiritual forces of wickedness in the heavenly places (Eph. 6:12).

Here it becomes crystal clear that Paul is not talking about a physical, material battle, but a spiritual one. We are struggling against the schemes of various ranks of evil spirits whom Paul lists. Most readers assume that Paul listed those evil spirits as they are ranked from bottom to top, "rulers" being the lowest class and "spiritual forces of wickedness in the heavenly places" being the highest class.

How can we struggle against spiritual beings? That question can be answered by asking, *How can spiritual beings attack us?* They attack us primarily with temptations, thoughts, suggestions, and ideas that contradict

God's Word and will. Therefore, our defense is knowing, believing, and obeying God's Word.

> Therefore, take up the full armor of God, that you may be able to resist in the evil day, and having done everything, to stand firm (Eph. 6:13).

Notice, once again, that Paul's purpose is to equip us to *resist* and *stand* against Satan's attacks. His purpose is not to equip us to go out and attack Satan and pull down evil spirits from the atmosphere. Three times in this passage Paul tells us to *stand firm*. Our position is one of defense, not offense.

Truth—Our Primary Defense

> Stand firm therefore, having girded your loins with truth (Eph. 6:14a).

Here is what keeps our armor in place—the truth. What is the truth? Jesus said to His Father, "Thy word is truth" (John 17:17). We cannot successfully stand firm against Satan unless we know the truth with which we can counter his lies. Jesus beautifully demonstrated this during His temptation in the wilderness as He responded to Satan's every suggestion with, "It is written."

Paul continued:

> And having put on the breastplate of righteousness (Eph. 6:14b).

As Christians, we should be familiar with two kinds of righteousness. First, we have been given, as a gift, the righteousness of Christ (see 2 Cor. 5:21). His righteous standing has been imputed to those who believe in Jesus, who bore their sins on the cross. That righteous standing has delivered us from Satan's dominion.

Second, we should be living righteously, obeying Jesus' commands, and that is probably what Paul had in mind regarding the breastplate of righteousness. By obedience to Christ, we give no place to the devil (see Eph. 4:26-27).

Firm Footing in Gospel Shoes

> And having shod your feet with the preparation of the gospel of peace (Eph. 6:15)

Knowing, believing and acting upon the truth of *the gospel* gives us firm footing to stand against Satan's attacks. The shoes that Roman soldiers wore had spikes on the bottom that gave them a firm grip on the battlefield. When Jesus is our Lord, we have firm footing to stand against Satan's lies

> In addition to all, taking up the shield of faith with which

you will be able to extinguish all the flaming missiles of
the evil one (Eph. 6:16).

Notice again Paul's emphasis here on our defensive posture. He is not
talking about our pulling down demons over cities. He is talking about
our using faith in God's Word to resist the devil's lies. When we believe
and act upon what God has said, it is like having a shield that protects us
from Satan's lies, represented figuratively as the "flaming missiles of the
evil one."

Our Spiritual Sword—God's Word

And take the helmet of salvation, and the sword of the
Spirit, which is the word of God (Eph. 6:17).

Salvation, as the Bible describes it, includes our deliverance from Satan's captivity. God has "delivered us from the domain of darkness, and
transferred us to the kingdom of His beloved Son" (Col. 1:13). Knowing
this is like having a helmet that guards our minds from believing Satan's
lie that we are still under his dominion. Satan is no longer our master—Jesus is.

Additionally, we are to take "the sword of the Spirit" which, as Paul
explains, is figurative for the Word of God. As I already mentioned, Jesus
was the perfect example of a spiritual warrior who skillfully yielded His
spiritual sword. During His temptation in the wilderness He responded
to Satan each time by quoting directly from God's Word. So too, if we are
to defeat the devil in spiritual combat, we must know and believe what
God has said, lest we fall for his lies.

Also notice that *Jesus* used "the sword of the Spirit" *defensively*. Some
like to point out, to those of us who maintain that the armor of which
Paul wrote is primarily defensive, that a sword is definitely an offensive
weapon. Thus, with a very weak argument, they try to justify their theory
that this passage in Ephesians 6:10-12 is applicable to our supposed responsibility to offensively "pull down strongholds" of evil spirits in the
heavenly places.

Obviously, from reading Paul's own reason why Christians should put
on God's armor (that they may "stand firm against the schemes of the
devil"), we know that he is speaking primarily of a defensive use of the
armor. Additionally, although a sword can be thought of as an offensive
weapon, it can also be thought of as defensive, as it blocks and protects
from the thrusts of the opponent's sword.

Moreover, we must be careful that we don't strain the entire metaphor,
as we attempt to wrench from the various pieces of armor significance
that really doesn't exist. When we begin to argue about the defensive and
offensive nature of a sword, we are very likely "pushing the parable too
far" as we carve into pieces a simple metaphor that was never meant to
be so dissected.

423

But Didn't Jesus Instruct Us to "Bind the Strong Man"?

Three times in the Gospels we find Jesus making mention of "binding the strong man." In none of those three cases, however, did He tell His followers that "binding the strong man" was something they should practice. Let's examine exactly what Jesus did say, and let's read what He said contextually:

> And the scribes who came down from Jerusalem were saying, "He is possessed by Beelzebul," and "He casts out the demons by the ruler of the demons." And He called them to Himself and began speaking to them in parables, "How can Satan cast out Satan? And if a kingdom is divided against itself, that kingdom cannot stand. And if a house is divided against itself, that house will not be able to stand. And if Satan has risen up against himself and is divided, he cannot stand, but he is finished! *But no one can enter the strong man's house and plunder his property unless he first binds the strong man, and then he will plunder his house.* Truly I say to you, all sins shall be forgiven the sons of men, and whatever blasphemies they utter; but whoever blasphemes against the Holy Spirit never has forgiveness, but is guilty of an eternal sin"—because they were saying, "He has an unclean spirit" (Mark 3:23-30, emphasis added).

Notice that Jesus was not teaching His followers to bind any strong men. Rather, He was responding to the criticism of the Jerusalem scribes with unassailable logic and a clear metaphor.

They accused Him of casting out demons by using demonic power. He responded by saying that Satan would be insane to work against himself. No one can intelligently argue with that.

If it wasn't Satan's power that Jesus used to cast out demons, then whose power was He using? It had to be a power stronger than Satan's. It had to be *God's* power, the power of the Holy Spirit. Thus Jesus spoke metaphorically of Satan, comparing him to a strong man guarding his possessions. The only one able to take the strong man's possessions would be someone even stronger, namely, Himself. This was the true explanation as to how He cast out demons.

This passage that mentions the strong man, as well as the similar ones found in Matthew and Luke, cannot be used to justify our "binding strong men" over cities. Additionally, when we examine the rest of the New Testament, we do not find any examples of anyone "binding strong men" over cities, or any instruction for anyone to do so. We can thus safely conclude that it is unscriptural for any Christian to attempt to bind and render powerless some supposed "strong man-evil spirit" over a city or geographic area.

What About "Binding on Earth and in Heaven"?

Only twice in the Gospels do we find Jesus' words, "Whatever you shall bind on earth shall be [or 'have been'] bound in heaven, and whatever you shall loose on earth shall be [or 'have been'] loosed in heaven." Both instances are recorded in Matthew's gospel.

Was Jesus teaching us that we can and should "bind" demonic spirits in the atmosphere?

First, let's consider His words, *binding* and *loosing*. Jesus' use of those words is obviously figurative, as He certainly did not mean that His followers would be taking physical ropes or cords and literally binding anything or literally loosing anything that was bound with physical ropes or cords. So what did Jesus mean?

For the answer, we should look at His use of the words *binding* and *loosing* within the context of whatever He was speaking of at the time. Was He talking on the subject of evil spirits? If so, we could conclude that His words about binding have application to the binding of evil spirits.

Let's examine the first passage where Jesus mentioned binding and loosing:

> He [Jesus] said to them, "But who do you say that I am?" And Simon Peter answered and said, "Thou art the Christ, the Son of the living God." And Jesus answered and said to him, "Blessed are you, Simon Barjona, because flesh and blood did not reveal this to you, but My Father who is in heaven. And I also say to you that you are Peter, and upon this rock I will build My church; and the gates of Hades shall not overpower it. I will give you the keys of the kingdom of heaven; and *whatever you shall bind on earth shall have been bound in heaven, and whatever you shall loose on earth shall have been loosed in heaven.* (Matt. 16:15-19, emphasis added).

No doubt the reason this passage has been interpreted in so many ways is that it contains at least five metaphorical expressions: (1) "flesh and blood," (2) "rock," (3) "gates of Hades," (4) "keys of the kingdom of heaven," and (5) "binding/loosing." All of these expressions are figurative, speaking of something else.

Hades' Gates

Regardless of the precise meaning of the metaphors, you can see that, in this passage, Jesus did not mention evil spirits. The closest He came was His mention of the "gates of Hades," which are of course symbolic, as there is no way that the literal gates of Hades could do anything to hinder the church.

What do the "gates of Hades" represent? Perhaps they are symbolic of Satan's power, and Jesus meant that Satan's power would not stop His church from being built. Or, perhaps Jesus meant that the church He would build would save people from the fate of being imprisoned behind Hades' gates.

Notice that Jesus actually made reference to two sets of gates: the gates of Hades, and the gates to heaven, implied by His giving Peter the "keys to heaven." This contrast further supports that idea that Jesus' statement about Hades' gates is representative of the church's role in saving people from going to Hades.

Even if Jesus did mean that "all the power of Satan would not stop His church," we cannot jump to the conclusion that His comments about binding and loosing are instructions as to what we should be doing with evil spirits over cities, for the simple reason that we can find no examples in the Gospels or Acts of anyone binding evil spirits over cities, nor can we find any instructions in the epistles for doing such a thing. However we interpret Christ's words about binding and loosing, our interpretation must be supported contextually within the rest of the New Testament.

In light of the absence of *any* scriptural example, it is amazing how often Christians say such things as, "I bind the devil in Jesus name," or "I loose the angels over that person" and so on. You don't find anyone saying such things anywhere in the New Testament. The emphasis in Acts and the epistles is not on speaking to the devil or binding and loosing evil spirits, but on preaching the gospel and praying to God. For example, when Paul was being continually buffeted by a messenger (literally, "angel") of Satan, he didn't try to "bind" it. He prayed to God about it (see 2 Cor. 12:7-10).

The Keys to Heaven

Let's look further at the immediate context of Jesus' words about binding and loosing. Note that directly before He mentioned binding and loosing, Jesus said that He would give Peter the "keys to the kingdom of heaven." Peter was never given any literal keys to heaven's gates, and so Jesus' words must be taken as being figurative. What do "keys" represent? Keys represent *the means of access to something that is locked.* One who has the keys has means that others do not have to open certain doors.

As we consider Peter's ministry as reported in the book of Acts, what is it that we find him doing that could be considered comparable to opening doors that are locked to others?

Primarily, we find him proclaiming the gospel, the gospel that opens heaven's doors for all who will believe (and the gospel which shuts the gates of Hades). In that sense, all of us have been given the keys to the kingdom of heaven, as we are all Christ's ambassadors. *The keys to the kingdom of heaven can only be the gospel of Jesus Christ, the message that can open heaven's gates.*

And Now, Binding and Loosing

Finally, after promising to give Peter the keys to the kingdom of heaven, Jesus made His statement about binding and loosing, His fifth figurative expression in the passage under consideration.

Within the context of the statements we've already examined, what did Jesus mean? How does Peter's binding and loosing have application to Jesus building His church, to the saving of people from Hades, and to proclaiming the gospel?

There is really only one possibility. Jesus simply meant, "I'm authorizing you as heaven's representative. Fulfill your responsibility on earth, and heaven will back you up."

If an employer said to his salesman, "Whatever you do in Bangkok will be done in the home office," how would that salesman interpret his boss's words? He would take them to mean that he was authorized to represent his company in Bangkok. All that Jesus meant was that Peter, on earth, was authorized to represent God in heaven. This promise to Peter would be a buttress to his confidence when he began proclaiming God's message in Jerusalem under the critical eye of the scribes and Pharisees—people who thought that they were God's authorized representatives, and people whom Peter would have previously revered as such.

This particular interpretation of Jesus' words harmonizes well with His second use of the same expression, found two chapters after the first passage in Matthew's gospel:

> And if your brother sins, go and reprove him in private; if he listens to you, you have won your brother. But if he does not listen to you, take one or two more with you, so that by the mouth of two or three witnesses every fact may be confirmed. And if he refuses to listen to them, tell it to the church; and if he refuses to listen even to the church, let him be to you as a Gentile and a tax-gatherer. Truly I say to you, *whatever you shall bind on earth shall be bound in heaven; and whatever you loose on earth shall be loosed in heaven.* Again I say to you, that if two of you agree on earth about anything that they may ask, it shall be done for them by My Father who is in heaven. For where two or three have gathered together in My name, there I am in their midst (Matt. 18:15-20, emphasis added).

In this second passage that mentions binding and loosing, there is absolutely *nothing* within the text that would lead us to believe that Jesus was speaking of binding evil spirits. Here Christ spoke of binding and loosing directly after speaking on the subject of church discipline.

This would seem to indicate that in reference to binding and loosing in this passage, Jesus meant something like, "I'm giving *you* responsibility to determine who should be in the church and who should not. It is your job. As you fulfill your responsibilities, heaven will back you up."

In a broader application, Jesus was simply saying, "You are authorized on earth as heaven's representatives. You have responsibilities, and as you fulfill your responsibilities on earth, heaven will always support you."

Binding and Loosing in Context

This interpretation fits well within the immediate context as well as the wider context of the rest of the New Testament.

In regard to the immediate context, we note that directly after His statement about binding and loosing, Jesus said: "Again I say to you, that if two of you agree *on earth* about anything that they may ask, it shall be done for them by My Father who is *in heaven*" (Matt. 18:19; emphasis added).

There again is the theme of "what you do on earth will be supported in heaven." We on earth are authorized and responsible to pray. When we do, heaven will respond. Jesus' words, "*Again* I say..." seem to indicate He is expanding upon His prior statement about binding and loosing.

Jesus' final statement in this passage, "For where two or three have gathered together in My name, there I am in their midst," also supports the "heaven will back you up" theme. When believers gather in His name, He who lives in heaven shows up.

Even if you totally disagree with my interpretation of the passages in consideration, you are going to be hard pressed to present a sound, scriptural argument that Jesus was speaking about binding evil spirits over cities!

God's Divine Plan Includes Satan

Satan and his angels are a rebel army, but not an army that is beyond God's control. This rebel army was *created by God*, (although they were not rebellious when first created). Paul wrote:

> For by Him [Christ] all things were created, both *in the heavens* and on earth, visible and *invisible*, whether *thrones or dominions or rulers or authorities*—all things have been created by Him and for Him (Col. 1:16, emphasis added).

Jesus created every angelic spirit of every rank, including Satan. Did He know that some would rebel? Of course He did. Then why did He create them? Because He would use those rebel spirits to help fulfill His plan. If He had no purpose for them, He would simply have incarcerated them, as we are told He has already done with some rebellious angels (see 2 Pet. 2:4) and as He will one day do with Satan (see Rev. 20:2).

God has reasons for allowing Satan and every evil spirit to operate upon the earth. If He didn't, they would be completely out of commission. What are God's reasons for allowing Satan to operate upon the earth? I don't think anyone understands every reason, yet God has revealed some of the reasons in His Word.

First, God allows Satan to operate limitedly on the earth to fulfill His plan to test humans. Satan serves as the alternate choice for humanity's allegiance. Whether they realize it or not, people are in subjection either to God or Satan. God permitted Satan to tempt Adam and Eve, two people who possessed God-given free wills, in order to test them. All those with free wills must be tested to reveal what is in their hearts, either obedience or disobedience.[92]

Second, God allows Satan to operate limitedly on the earth as an agent of His wrath upon evildoers. I have already previously proved this by showing several specific instances in Scripture when God brought judgment upon deserving people through evil spirits. Just the fact that God has allowed Satan to rule over the unsaved people of the world is an indication of His wrath upon them. God judges groups of evil people by allowing wicked humans to rule over them, and also by allowing wicked spiritual beings to rule over them, making their lives all the more miserable.

Third, God allows Satan to operate limitedly on the earth to glorify Himself. "The Son of God appeared for this purpose, that He might destroy the works of the devil" (1 John 3:8). Every time God destroys one of Satan's works, it glorifies His power and wisdom.

Jesus is the Head Over Principalities and Powers

As Christians, our scriptural responsibility to deal with Satan and evil spirits is two-fold: to resist them in our own lives (Jas. 4:7), and to cast them out of others who want to be delivered (Mark 16:17). Any Christian who has experience in casting demons out of other people knows that, as a general rule, unless the demonized person wants to be delivered, he will be unable to cast the demon out.[93] God honors every person's free will, and if a person wants to yield to evil spirits, God won't stop him.

This is yet another reason why we can't pull down territorial spirits over geographic areas. Those evil spirits are there holding people in bondage because that is what those people have chosen. Through proclaiming the gospel to them, we offer them a choice. If they make the right choice, it will result in their freedom from Satan and evil spirits. But if they make the wrong choice, choosing not to repent, God will allow Satan to hold them captive.

Jesus is spoken of in Scripture as being "the head over all rule and authority" (Col. 2:10). Although the Greek words for *rule* (arche) and *author-*

[92] This concept is discussed much more thoroughly in my book, *God's Tests*, available to read in English on our website, www.shepherdserve.org

[93] The exception to this rule would be in cases of people who are so controlled by demons that they have no way of communicating their desire for freedom. In those cases, special gifts of the Spirit would be necessary to bring deliverance, and gifts of the Spirit operate as the Spirit wills.

ity (exousia) are sometimes used in describing human political leaders, they are also used in the New Testament as titles for demonic spiritual rulers. The classic passage about the Christian's struggle against rulers (arche) and powers (exousia) in Ephesians 6:12 is one example.

When we read contextually what Paul wrote about Jesus being the head over all rule and authority in Colossians 2:10, it seems clear that he is speaking of spiritual powers. For example, in the same passage just four verses later, Paul writes of Jesus, "When He had disarmed the *rulers* and *authorities*, He made a public display of them, having triumphed over them through Him" (Col. 2:15).

If Jesus is the head of the spiritual rulers and authorities, then He is sovereign over them. This is a wonderful revelation to Christians living in pagan, animistic cultures, who spent their former lives worshipping idols in fear of the evil spirits whom they knew ruled over them.

The Only Way of Escape

The only way to escape the captivity of evil spirits is to repent and believe the gospel. That is the escape God has provided. No one can bind the demonic forces over a city and set you free or set you partially free. Until a person repents and believes the gospel, He is abiding in God's wrath (see John 3:36), which includes being held by demonic powers.

That is why there are no measurable changes in the cities where the big spiritual warfare conferences and sessions have taken place, because nothing has happened that has really affected the demonic hierarchies that rule in those areas. Christians can scream at principalities and powers all day and night; they can attempt to torment the devil by so-called "warring tongues"; they can say "I bind you evil spirits over this city" a million times; they can even do all these things up in airplanes and on the top floors of skyscrapers (as some actually do); and the only way the evil spirits will be affected is that they will get a good laugh at the foolish Christians.

Let's proceed to a sixth modern myth about spiritual warfare.

Myth #6: "Spiritual warfare against territorial spirits opens the door for effective evangelism."

The driving motivation for many Christians who are heavily involved in doing spiritual warfare against territorial spirits is their desire to see God's kingdom expanded. For this they are to be commended. Every Christian should desire to see more people escape from Satan's grasp.

It is important, however, that we use God's methods to build God's kingdom. God knows what works and what is a waste of time. He has told us exactly what our responsibilities are in regard to the expansion of His kingdom. To think we can do something not found in Scripture that will multiply the effectiveness of our evangelism, something that Jesus,

Peter, or Paul never practiced in their ministries, is foolish.

Why do so many Christians think that spiritual warfare can open the door to effective evangelism? Their line of reasoning usually sounds something like this: "Satan has blinded the minds of unsaved people. We must therefore do spiritual warfare against Satan to stop him from blinding them. Once the blinders are removed, more people will believe the gospel." Is this true?

There is certainly no doubt that Satan has blinded the minds of unsaved people. Paul wrote:

> And even if our gospel is veiled, it is veiled to those who are perishing, in whose case the god of this world has blinded the minds of the unbelieving, that they might not see the light of the gospel of the glory of Christ, who is the image of God (2 Cor. 4:3-4).

The question is, *Did Paul give this piece of information to the Corinthian Christians with the intent of motivating them to do spiritual warfare and pull down territorial spirits so that unsaved people would become more receptive?*

The answer is *No* for several obvious reasons.

First, because Paul did not go on to say, "Therefore Corinthians, because Satan has blinded the minds of unbelievers, I want you to do spiritual warfare and pull down territorial spirits so those blinders will be removed." Rather, the very next thing he mentioned was his preaching of Christ, which *is* the way that spiritual blindness *is* removed.

Second, in *none* of his letters did Paul instruct any believers to be involved in pulling down strongholds over their cities that evangelistic results might increase.

Third, we know from reading all of Paul's letters that he did not believe Satan's blinding was the *primary* reason why unbelievers remained unbelieving. Satan's blinding is a contributing factor, but not the main or only factor. *The primary factor that keeps people unsaved is the hardness of their hearts.* This is obvious for the simple reason that Satan is not able to keep everyone blinded. Some people, when they hear the truth, believe it, and thus reject any lies they formerly believed. It is not so much Satan's blinding that causes their unbelief, as it is their unbelief that allows Satan's blinding.

Callous Hearts

In his letter to the Ephesians, the apostle Paul explained precisely why non-Christians remain in unbelief:

> This I say therefore, and affirm together with the Lord, that you walk no longer just as the Gentiles also walk, in the futility of their mind, being *darkened in their understanding* [perhaps a reference to Satan's blinding], exclud-

ed from the life of God, because of the ignorance that is in them, *because of the hardness of their heart*; and they, having become *callous*, have given themselves over to sensuality, for the practice of every kind of impurity with greediness (Eph. 4:17-19, emphasis added).

Paul said that the unsaved are excluded from the life of God because of "the ignorance that is in them." But why are they ignorant? Why has their "understanding been darkened"? The answer is, "because of the hardness of their hearts." They have become "callous." That is the root and primary reason why people remain unsaved.[94] They bear the blame themselves. Satan only supplies the lies they want to believe.

Jesus' parable of the sower and the soils illustrates this concept perfectly:

The sower went out to sow his seed; and as he sowed, some fell beside the road; and it was trampled under foot, and the birds of the air ate it up....Now the parable is this: the seed is the word of God. And those beside the road are those who have heard; then the devil comes and takes away the word from their heart, so that they may not believe and be saved (Luke 8:5, 11-12).

Notice that the seed, which represents the gospel, fell beside the road and was trampled. It couldn't penetrate the hard soil where people frequently walked. Thus it was easy for birds, which represent the devil, to steal the seeds.

The point of the entire parable is to compare the condition of people's hearts (and their receptivity to God's Word) with various types of soil. Jesus was explaining why some people believe and why others do not: It all depends upon them.

How does Satan figure into the picture? He is only able to steal the Word from those with hardened hearts. The birds in the parable were only a secondary cause as to why the seeds did not germinate. The primary problem was with the soil; in fact, it was the soil's hardness that made it possible for the birds to get the seeds.

The same thing is true with the gospel. The real problem is with the hardened hearts of free moral agents. When people reject the gospel, they make a choice to remain blinded. They would prefer to believe lies rather than the truth. As Jesus put it, "The light is come into the world, and *men loved the darkness* rather than the light; for their deeds were evil" (John 3:19, emphasis added).

The Bible does not lead us to believe that people are sincere, good-hearted folks, who would surely believe the gospel if Satan would only stop blinding them. On the contrary, the Bible paints a very dim picture

---

[94] Paul's description of unbelievers in Romans 1:18-32 also supports this same concept.

of human character, and God will hold every individual responsible for his sinful choices. Sitting on His throne of judgment, God will not accept anyone's excuse that "the devil made me do it."

How Satan Blinds People's Minds

Exactly how does Satan blind people's minds? Does he possess some mystical spiritual power that he pours like a potion into people's heads to dull their understanding? Does a demon dig its talons into their brains, effectively short-circuiting their rational thinking processes? No, Satan blinds people's minds *by supplying them with lies to believe.*

Obviously, if people really believed the truth that Jesus is the Son of God who died for their sins, if they really believed that they will one day have to stand before Him to give an account of their lives, then they would repent and become His followers. But they don't believe those things. They do, however, believe *something.* They may believe that there is no God, or that there is no life after death. They may believe in reincarnation, or that God would never send anyone to hell. They may think that their religious works will get them into heaven. But whatever they believe, if it is not the gospel, it can be summed up in one word: *lies.* They don't believe the truth, and thus Satan keeps them blinded through lies. If, however, they humble themselves and believe the truth, Satan will not be able to blind them any longer.

The Lies of Darkness

Satan's kingdom is referred to in Scripture as the "domain of *darkness*" (Col. 1:13). Darkness, of course, represents the absence of truth—the absence of light or enlightenment. When you are in darkness, you navigate by your imagination and usually end up being hurt. That is how it is in Satan's kingdom of darkness. Those who are in it are navigating their lives by their imaginations, and their imaginations have been filled with Satan's lies. They are in spiritual darkness.

Satan's kingdom is best defined then, not as a geographical kingdom with clearly defined borders, but as a kingdom of belief—belief, that is, in lies. The kingdom of darkness is located in the same place as the kingdom of light. Those who believe the truth live right among those who believe lies.[95] Our primary job is to proclaim the truth to people who already believe lies. When someone believes the truth, Satan loses another one of his subjects because he is no longer able to deceive him.

Thus we set unsaved people free from Satan, not by "binding" evil spirits over them but by proclaiming the truth. Jesus said, "You shall know the truth, and *the truth shall make you free*" (John 8:32, emphasis added). Spiritual blindness is removed by truth.

Within that same passage of Scripture in John's Gospel, Jesus said to an unsaved audience:

[95] It is true, of course, that in various geographical areas, there are greater or lesser percentages of people in either kingdom.

> You are of your father the devil, and you want to do the desires of your father. He was a murderer from the beginning, and *does not stand in the truth, because there is no truth in him. Whenever he speaks a lie, he speaks from his own nature; for he is a liar, and the father of lies.* But because I speak the truth, you do not believe Me (John 8:44-45, emphasis added).

Notice the contrast Jesus made between Himself and the devil. He speaks the truth; Satan is the ultimate liar.

Notice also that even though Jesus told His listeners that they were of their father the devil, and even though He exposed Satan as a liar, He still placed responsibility on them to believe the truth He spoke. It was not the devil's fault that they were blinded—it was their own fault. *Jesus held them responsible.* Satan assists people who "love darkness" to stay in the darkness by supplying them with lies to believe. But Satan can't fool anyone who will believe the truth.

All this being so, the primary way we can push back the kingdom of darkness is by spreading the light—the truth of God's Word. That is why Jesus did *not* tell us, "Go into all the world and bind the devil" but rather, "Go into all the world and preach the gospel." Jesus told Paul that the purpose of his preaching would be to open people's "eyes *so that they may turn* from darkness to light and from the dominion of Satan to God" (Acts 26:18, emphasis added). This makes it clear that people escape Satan's dominion when they are exposed to the truth of the gospel and then make a decision to turn from darkness to light, believing the truth rather than a lie. The only strongholds we are "pulling down" are strongholds of lies built in people's minds.

This is God's Plan

Don't forget that God is the one who cast Satan out of heaven to the earth. He could have put Satan anywhere in the universe or incarcerated him forever. But He didn't. Why? Because God wanted to use Satan to accomplish His ultimate goal—the goal one day to have a big family of free moral agents who would love Him, having chosen to serve Him.

If God wanted a family of children who would love Him, then two things were required. First, He had to create people with free wills, because the foundation of love is free will. Robots and machines can't love.

Second, He had to test them in an environment where they would be faced with a choice to obey or disobey, to love or hate Him. Free moral agents *must* be tested. *And if there is going to be a test of loyalty, there must exist a temptation to disloyalty.* Thus, we begin to understand why God placed Satan on the earth. Satan would serve as the alternate choice for humanity's allegiance. He would be permitted (with certain limitations) to influence anyone who was receptive to his lies. Everyone would be faced with the choice: *Will I believe God or Satan? Will I serve God or Satan?* Whether people realize it or not, they have all made a decision already. Our job is to encourage people who have made the wrong decision to repent and believe the gospel, making the right decision.

Is this not what happened in the Garden of Eden? God placed the tree of the knowledge of good and evil there and then forbade Adam and Eve to eat from it. If God didn't want them to eat from it, why did He place it there? The answer is that it served as a test.

We also note that Satan was permitted by God to tempt Eve. Again, if loyalty is to be tested, there must exist the temptation to be disloyal. Satan lied to Eve and she believed him, and so at the same time, she decided *not* to believe what God had said. The result? The first free moral agents revealed the disloyalty that was in their hearts.

In a similar manner, every free moral agent is tested throughout his or her lifetime. God has revealed Himself through His creation, and so everyone can see that there is an awesome God who exists (see Rom. 1:19-20). God has given every one of us a conscience, and in our hearts, we know right from wrong (see Rom. 2:14-16). Satan and his evil spirits are permitted, in a limited manner, to lie to and tempt people. The result is that every free moral agent is tested.

The sad truth of the matter is that every free moral agent has rebelled and "exchanged the truth of God for a lie" (Rom. 1:25). We can thank God, however, that He has provided a ransom for our sins and a way to be born into His family. Jesus' sacrificial death is the only and all-sufficient answer to our problem.

Satan's Deception, Now and Later

So we understand at least one reason why the devil and his rebel army are permitted to work on this planet: for the purpose of deceiving those who love darkness.

This truth is further validated when we consider that according to the book of Revelation, Satan will one day be bound by an angel and incarcerated for a thousand years. The reason for his incarceration? "That he should not deceive the nations any longer" (Rev. 20:3). During that Millennium, Jesus will personally rule the world from Jerusalem.

But after those thousand years, Satan will be released for a short period of time. The result? He "will come out to deceive the nations which are in the four corners of the earth" (Rev. 20:8).

If God doesn't want Satan to deceive people at that time, why will He release him? Especially in light of the fact that God originally incarcerated Satan "that he should not deceive the nations any longer"?

God, of course, would prefer that Satan never deceive anyone. But He knows that the only people whom Satan can deceive are those who don't believe what He Himself has said. Satan can only deceive those who reject the truth, and that is why God permits him to operate now, and why He will permit Satan to operate then. As Satan deceives people, the condition of people's hearts is made apparent, and then God can sort the "wheat from the tares" (see Matt. 13:24-30).

This is exactly what will happen at the end of the Millennium when Satan is released. He will deceive all those who love darkness, and they will then gather their armies around Jerusalem in an attempt to overthrow Christ's rule. God will know exactly who loves Him and who hates Him, and thus He will immediately send "fire from heaven" that will "devour them" (Rev. 20:10). Satan will serve God's purposes then just as he does now. For this reason among others, it is foolish to think that we can "pull down territorial spirits." God allows them to operate for His own reasons.

Biblical Evangelism

The plain fact is that neither Jesus nor any of the New Testament apostles practiced the kind of spiritual warfare that some are claiming is the missing key to effective evangelism today. We never find Jesus, Peter, John, Stephen, Philip, or Paul "pulling down strongholds" or "binding the strong men" over the cities in which they preached. Rather, we find that they followed the Holy Spirit in regard to where He wanted them to preach; we find them proclaiming the simple gospel—calling people to repentance and faith in Christ—and we find them enjoying marvelous results. And in those cases where they preached to unreceptive people who rejected the gospel, we don't find them "doing spiritual warfare so that Satan wouldn't be able to continue blinding their minds." Rather, we find them "shaking the dust off their feet" as Jesus commanded and going to the next city (see Matt. 10:14; Acts 13:5).

It is amazing that anyone could claim that "pulling down strongholds" and "binding the strong men" is a prerequisite to successful evangelism when there are so many thousands of examples of great revivals in church history where such "spiritual warfare" was never practiced.

"But our techniques work!" someone will say. "Since we started doing this kind of spiritual warfare, more people have been getting saved than ever before."

If that is true, I'll tell you why. It is because there has been more scriptural prayer and evangelism done at the same time, or because a group of people has suddenly become more receptive to the gospel.

What would you say if an evangelist told you, "Tonight, before I preached at the revival service, I privately ate three bananas. And when I preached, sixteen people were saved! I've finally found the secret to effective evangelism! From now on, I'm going to make sure I eat three bananas before I preach!"?

Surely you would say to that evangelist, "Your eating three bananas had nothing to do with those sixteen people being saved. The key to your success is that you preached the gospel, and there were sixteen people listening who were receptive."

God honors His Word. If God gives a promise, and someone meets the conditions to that particular promise, God will keep His promise, even if that person is doing other things that are unscriptural.

This is true with the present spiritual warfare practices. If you start passing out tracts and "binding the strong man" over your city, a certain percentage of people will be saved. And if you just start passing out tracts without binding the strong man, the same percentage of people will be saved.

How to Pray Scripturally for a Spiritual Harvest

How should we pray for unsaved people? First, we should understand that there is no instruction in the New Testament that tells us to pray that God will save people, nor is there any record of any early Christians praying that way. The reason is because from God's standpoint, He has done everything He needs to do in order for everyone in the world to be saved. He so much desires for them to be saved that He gave His Son to die on the cross.

But why isn't everyone saved yet? Because not everyone has believed the gospel. And why have they not believed? There are only two reasons: (1) Either they have never yet heard the gospel, or (2) they've heard the gospel and rejected it.

That is why the scriptural way to pray for the unsaved is to pray that they will have opportunities to hear the gospel. For example, Jesus told us "The harvest is plentiful, but the laborers are few; therefore *beseech the Lord of the harvest to send out laborers into His harvest*" (Luke 10:2, emphasis added). In order for people to hear the gospel and be saved, someone has to tell them the gospel. That is why we should pray for God to send people to them.

When the early church prayed regarding a spiritual harvest, they prayed, "Grant that Thy bond-servants may *speak Thy word with all confidence*, while Thou dost extend Thy hand to heal, and signs and wonders take place through the name of Thy holy servant Jesus" (Acts 4:29-30, emphasis added).

They were asking either for (1) opportunities to proclaim the gospel boldly or (2) boldness to proclaim the gospel during the opportunities they knew they would have. They also expected God to confirm the gospel with healings, signs and wonders. Those are scriptural prayers, and notice the objective was to give people the opportunity to hear the gospel. God answered their prayer: "And when they had prayed, the place where they had gathered together was shaken, and they were all filled with the Holy Spirit, and began to speak the word of God with boldness" (Acts 4:31).

How did Paul think Christians should pray in regard to producing a spiritual harvest? Did he instruct them to ask God to save more people? No, let's read what he said:

Finally, brethren, *pray for us that the word of the Lord may spread rapidly and be glorified,* just as it did also with you (2 Thes. 3:1, emphasis added).

Pray on my behalf, *that utterance may be given to me* in the opening of my mouth, *to make known with boldness the mystery of the gospel,* for which I am an ambassador in chains; *that in proclaiming it I may speak boldly,* as I ought to speak (Eph. 6:19-20, emphasis added).

Whether or not people are saved now depends more upon them than it does upon God, and so our prayers should be for people to hear the gospel and for God to help us proclaim it. God will answer our prayers, but that still doesn't guarantee that anyone will be saved, because God gives people the right to make their own choices. Their salvation depends on their response to the gospel.

Myth #7: "When a Christian sins, he opens the door for a demon to come and live in him."

It is true that when a Christian sins, it may be because he has yielded to temptation from an evil spirit. Yielding to the suggestion of an evil spirit, however, does not mean that the evil spirit himself is then able to come inside the believer. When we sin as Christians, we break our fellowship with God because we have disobeyed Him (see 1 John 1:5-6). We feel guilty. We have not, however, broken our *relationship* with Him, as we are still His children.

If we confess our sins, "He is faithful and righteous to forgive us our sins and cleanse us from all unrighteousness" (1 John 1:9). Then our fellowship with Him is restored. Notice John did not say that we needed to be cleansed from any indwelling demons when we are guilty of sin.

Every Christian is faced with daily temptations from the world, the flesh and the devil. Paul wrote that we do indeed have a struggle against various evil spirits (see Eph 6:12). Therefore, to some degree, every believer is harassed by demon spirits. That is normal, and it is our responsibility to resist the devil and demons by faith in God's Word (see 1 Pet. 5:8-9). When we believe and act upon what God has said, that is resisting the devil.

For example, if Satan brings thoughts of depression, we should think on a scripture that counteracts depression, and obey God's Word to "rejoice always" (1 Thes. 5:16) and "give thanks in everything" (1 Thes. 5:18). It is our responsibility to act upon God's Word and replace Satan's thoughts with God's thoughts.

We must recognize that as free moral agents, we can think about whatever we want to think. If a believer continually *chooses* to listen and yield to the suggestions of evil spirits, he can certainly open his mind to being *oppressed*, which is simply a state of being more receptive to and more dominated by wrong thoughts. If he chooses to yield even more, he could become *obsessed* with a certain kind of wrong thinking, which is very rare for a Christian, but can occur. Yet even then, if the obsessed Christian desires to be free, all he needs to do is determine to think about and yield to God's Words and resist the devil.

But could he ever become *possessed*? Only if he willfully decided, from his heart, without being pressured, to reject Christ and turn His back upon Him completely. Then, of course, he would no longer be a Christian[96] and thus potentially could become possessed—if he yielded himself all the more to the evil spirit that was oppressing him. But that is a far cry from the idea of opening the door for an evil spirit to inhabit you through committing one sin.

It is a fact that there is not a single example in the New Testament of any Christian being possessed by a demon. Nor is there any warning addressed to Christians about the dangerous possibility of their being inhabited by demons. Nor is there any instruction regarding how to cast out demons from fellow-Christians.

The truth is that as Christians, we don't need demons cast out of us—what we need is to have our minds renewed upon the Word of God. That is scriptural. Paul wrote:

> And do not be conformed to this world, but be transformed
> by the renewing of your mind, that you may prove what
> the will of God is, that which is good and acceptable and
> perfect (Rom. 12:2).

Once our minds have been cleansed of old thinking patterns and been renewed with the truth of God's Word, we gain victory over sinful habits and live in a consistent Christ-like manner. The truth is what sets us free (John 8:32). We are transformed as we renew our minds, not as we have all the demons exorcised.

Why then are there so many Christians who testify that they have had a demon (or demons) cast out of them? One possibility is that they just imagined that they had a demon in them that has since been cast out. Many Christians are gullible and lack knowledge of God's Word, and so they are easy prey for "ministers of deliverance" who psychologically manipulate people into thinking they have demons. Once people are convinced they have a demon living in them, they will naturally cooperate with anyone who appears confident of his ability to exorcise the demon.

Another real possibility is that such people who have had demons cast of out them were not true believers in Christ at the time of their deliverance, even though they thought they were believers. The modern gospel,

---

[96] Those who hold to the position of "once saved, always saved" will no doubt disagree. I would encourage them to read Rom. 11:22; 1 Cor. 15:1-2; Phil. 3:18-19; Col. 1:21-23 and Heb. 3:12-14, paying special attention to the word "if" whenever it is found.

which stands in stark contrast to the biblical gospel, has deceived many into thinking they are Christians even though they are indistinguishable from non-Christians and Jesus is not their Lord. In Scripture, we find that when people believed the gospel and were born again, demons that lived in them automatically came out (see Acts 8:5-7). Demons can't possess people who are indwelt by the Holy Spirit, and the Holy Spirit indwells all people who are born again.

Myth 8: "Through studying the history of a city, we can determine which evil spirits are dominating it, and thus be more effective in spiritual warfare and ultimately in evangelization."

This myth is based upon several ideas that cannot be supported by Scripture. One such idea is that territorial spirits stay around for a long time. That is, the ones that lived over a region hundreds of years ago are supposedly the ones still there. Thus, if we find that a city was founded by greedy people, we can then conclude that there are spirits of greed dominating the city today. If the city was once an old Indian village, we can conclude that spirits of shamanism and witchcraft dominate the city today. And on and on it goes.

But is it true that the same evil principalities and powers that lived over a geographical area hundreds of years ago are still there today? Perhaps, but not necessarily.

Consider the story we've previously considered from the tenth chapter of the book of Daniel. The unnamed angel who was assisted by Michael to fight "the prince of Persia" said to Daniel, "I shall now return to fight against the prince of Persia; so I am going forth, and behold, *the prince of Greece is about to come*" (Dan. 10:20, emphasis added). History tells us that the Persian Empire fell to the Greeks through the conquests of Alexander the Great. Yet this unnamed angel was aware of imminent corresponding changes in the spiritual realm—the "prince of Greece" was coming.

When the prince of Greece did come, did he rule in the spiritual realm over the Greek Empire just as the prince of Persia ruled in the spiritual realm over the Persian Empire? That would seem to be a reasonable conclusion, and if so, then some high-ranking evil spirits changed geographical locations, as the Greek Empire included practically all the territory of the Persian Empire. When there are political changes on earth, there is a possibility that there are changes in the kingdom of darkness. The fact is, however, that we just don't know unless God would reveal it to us.

Regardless, it makes little difference what particular evil spirits are ruling over any given geographical area, as there is nothing we can do about it through "spiritual warfare," as proven earlier.

Over-Categorizing Evil Spirits

Moreover, it is an assumption on our part to think that there are ruling spirits that specialize in specific sins. The whole concept of there being "spirits of greed," "spirits of lust," "religious spirits," "spirits of strife," and so on, cannot be supported by Scripture, much less the idea that those different kinds of spirits exist in the higher ranks of evil spirits who rule the kingdom of darkness.

Amazing as it is to those who have never studied the four Gospels closely, there are only three *specific* kinds of demons that Jesus cast out: Once a "dumb demon" is mentioned (Luke 11:14), once we read of a "deaf and dumb spirit" (Mark 9:25), and more than once we find reference to "unclean spirits," which seem to include all demons that Jesus exorcised, including even the "deaf and dumb" one (see Mark 9:25).

Is it not possible that the "deaf and dumb spirit" was able to do something other than make someone deaf and dumb? There is no doubt it could, because it caused the boy of Mark 9 to have terrible seizures as well. Therefore "deaf and dumb" may not be a reference to the specific *type* of spirit it was but rather a simple reference as to *how it was harming* a certain individual. Some of us have become "category-crazy" when it comes to demons, going way beyond biblical revelation.

In the entire Old Testament, the only specific spirits that are named that could perhaps be considered specific evil spirits are a "deceiving spirit" (1 Kings 22:22-23), a "spirit of distortion" (Is. 19:14), and a "spirit of harlotry" (Hos. 4:12; 5:4). In regard to the first and the second, certainly all evil spirits could be referred to as "deceiving spirits" and "spirits of distortion." In regard to the third, the phrase "spirit of harlotry" is not necessarily a reference to a specific evil spirit, but simply a prevailing attitude.[97]

In the whole book of Acts, the only time a specific evil spirit is mentioned is in Acts 16:16, where we read about a young girl who had a "spirit of divination." And in all the epistles, the only kind of specific evil spirits that are mentioned are "deceitful spirits" (1 Tim. 4:1) which, again, could be a description of any evil spirit.

In light of the few references to specific kinds of demons in the Bible, it is amazing to read through some of the modern lists which contain hundreds of various kinds of demons that might inhabit people or control cities.

We should not assume there is any categorization, by specific sin, of any higher ranks of evil spirits. It is an assumption to say, "Because there is so much gambling in that city, there must be gambling spirits over it."

Smoking Spirits?

Think how foolish someone would appear who said, "There must be many smoking spirits over that city, because so many people in that city

[97] The "spirit of jealousy" spoken of in Numbers 5:14-30 and the "spirit of haughtiness" of Proverbs 16:18 are good examples of the word *spirit* being used to convey a certain kind of predominant attitude, rather than an actual demon. In Numbers 14:24 we read that Caleb had a "different spirit," which is obviously referring to Caleb's good attitude.

smoke cigarettes." What were those "smoking spirits" doing before those cities existed? Where were they then? What were they doing before tobacco was ever used for smoking? Is the reason fewer people are now smoking is because some of those old "smoking demons" are dying off or moving to new territories?

Do you see how foolish it is when we say such things as, "That city is controlled by spirits of lust, which is why there are so many houses of prostitution there"? The truth is that wherever people are not serving Christ, there exists the kingdom of darkness. Many evil spirits operate in that dark realm who entice their subjects to sin and continue in their rebellion against God. Those spirits will tempt people in every area of sin, and in some places, people yield more to one sin than other sins. Their only hope is the gospel that we are called to proclaim.

Even if there were specific kinds of evil spirits who specialized in certain sins and who ruled certain geographical areas, it wouldn't help us to know about it, because there is nothing we can do to remove them. Our responsibility is to pray (in a scriptural manner) for the people there who are deceived and to preach the gospel to them.

The only good it would do to find out about the most predominate sins in a certain city would be so that we can preach more convicting messages to the unsaved living there—by specifically naming the sins that hold them guilty before God. But there is no need to research a city's history to determine that. One only needs to visit for a short while and keep his eyes and ears open. The predominant sins will soon become evident.

Finally, there is no example in the New Testament of anyone doing "spiritual mapping" as a means of preparing for spiritual warfare or evangelization. Nor are there any instructions in the epistles to do so. In the New Testament, the apostles followed the Holy Spirit in regard to where they should preach, faithfully proclaimed the gospel and called for people to repent, and relied upon the Lord to confirm the word with signs following. Their method worked quite well.

Myth 9: "Some Christians need to be set free from generational or satanic curses."

The whole of idea of "generational curses" is derived from four passages of Scripture found in the Old Testament that all say essentially the same thing. They are Exodus 20:5; 34:7; Numbers 14:8 and Deuteronomy 5:9. Let's consider Numbers 14:18:

> The Lord is slow to anger and abundant in lovingkindness, forgiving iniquity and transgression; but He will by no means clear the guilty, *visiting the iniquity of the fathers on the children to the third and the fourth generations* (emphasis added).

How are we to interpret this passage of Scripture? Does it mean that

God will put a curse on or punish someone for the sins of his parents, grandparents, great grandparents, or great, great grandparents? Are we to believe that God might forgive someone of his sins when he believes in Jesus but then punish that same person for his great-grandparents' sins?

Absolutely not, otherwise God could rightfully be accused of being grossly unjust and hypocritical. He Himself has stated that punishing someone for his parents' sins would be morally wrong:

> Yet you [the Israelites] say, "Why should the son not bear the punishment for the father's iniquity?" [God responds:] When the son has practiced justice and righteousness, and has observed all My statutes and done them, he shall surely live. The person who sins will die. *The son will not bear the punishment for the father's iniquity, nor will the father bear the punishment for the son's iniquity*; the righteousness of the righteous will be upon himself, and the wickedness of the wicked will be upon himself (Ezek. 18:19-20, emphasis added).

Moreover, under the Law of Moses, God commanded that neither father nor son should bear the punishment for the sins of the other:

> Fathers shall not be put to death for their sons, nor shall sons be put to death for their fathers; everyone shall be put to death for his own sin (Deut. 24:16).

There is no possibility that a God of love and righteousness might curse or punish someone for his ancestor's sins.[98] So then what does Scripture mean when it says that God will "by no means clear the guilty, visiting the iniquity of the fathers on the children to the third and the fourth generations"?

It can only mean that God holds people responsible for the sinful example they set in front of their offspring, and He thus holds them partly responsible for the sins their offspring commit because of their influence. God holds people partly responsible, because of their evil influence, for the sins of their great grandchildren! That is how holy God is. And no one can say that He is unfair in doing so.

Notice that the passage under consideration states that God will "visit the iniquity of the fathers on the children." It is the iniquity *of fathers on their children* that is being *visited*.

---

[98] This is not to say that children don't suffer because of their parents' sins, because they often do. When they do, however, it is not an indication that God is punishing those children for their parents' sins, but an indication that people are so evil that they practice certain sins that they know will cause their own children to suffer. It is also clear from Scripture that God may mercifully withhold judgment on one individual that He may later pour out upon a subsequent and equally- or more-deserving offspring. Similarly, He might mercifully withhold His judgment upon a wicked generation yet pour it out upon a subsequent and equally- or more-deserving generation (see Jer. 16:11-12). That is much different than punishing a person for his grandparents' sins.

Thus, the whole idea of "generational curses" is a superstition, and a bad one at that, as it makes God appear unrighteous.

Satanic Curses?

But what about "satanic curses"?

First, there is nothing in the entire Bible that indicates Satan is able to "put a curse" on anyone, nor are there any examples of his doing so. Certainly we find Satan afflicting people in the Bible, but never do we find him "putting a curse" on a family which then results in continual bad luck upon them and their successive generations.

Every Christian is harassed by Satan and evil spirits (to a limited extent) all of his life, but this does not mean that any of us need someone to "break a satanic curse" over us that has been passed down to us from our parents. What we need to do is stand on God's Word and resist the devil by faith, as we are told to do in the Scriptures (see 1 Pet. 5:8-9).

In the Bible, *God* is the one who has the power to bless and curse (see Gen. 3:17; 4:11; 5:29; 8:21 ; 12:3; Num. 23:8; Deut. 11:26; 28:20; 29:27; 30:7; 2 Chron. 34:24; Ps. 37:22; Prov. 3:33; 22:14; Lam. 3:65; Mal. 2:2; 4:6). Others may curse us with their mouths, but their curses are powerless to harm us:

> Like a sparrow in its flitting, like a swallow in its flying, so
> a curse without cause does not alight (Prov. 26:2).

Balaam had it right when, after being hired by Balak to curse the children of Israel, he said, "How shall I curse, whom God has not cursed? And how can I denounce, whom the Lord has not denounced?" (Num. 23:8).

Some Christians have gone overboard on the idea of people placing curses on other people based on Jesus' words in Mark 11:23: "Truly I say to you, whoever says to this mountain, 'Be taken up and cast into the sea,' and does not doubt in his heart, but believes that what he says is going to happen, it shall be granted him."

Notice, however, that there is no power in just speaking words, but rather in speaking words that are believed from the heart. There is no way a person could have faith that his curse against someone could actually bring harm to that person, because faith is a confident assurance (Heb. 11:1), and faith only comes from hearing God's Word (Rom. 10:17). A person might *hope* his curse against someone will bring misfortune, but he could never *believe* it, because God has given no faith-supplying promise about cursing people.

The only exception to this would be if God gave someone "the gift of faith" along with a "gift of prophecy" (two of the nine gifts of the Spirit), that would be spoken in the form of a blessing or curse, as we see He occasionally did in the lives of some Old Testament characters (see Gen. 27:27-29, 38-41; 49:1-27; Josh. 6:26 with 1 Kin. 16:34; Judg. 9:7-20, 57; 2 Kin.

2:23-24). Even in those cases, the blessings or curses originated from *God*, not man. Thus, the whole idea of someone being able to "place a curse" on another person is just a superstition. This is why Jesus did not instruct us to "break curses that have been spoken against us," but rather to simply "bless those who curse us." We do not need to be afraid of any person's curses. To be afraid of someone's curse is to display a lack of faith in God. Unfortunately, I meet pastors all the time who seemingly have more faith in the power of Satan than the power of God. Although I travel to different countries every month doing a lot of damage to Satan's kingdom, I am not the least bit afraid of Satan or any curses being placed on me. There is no reason to be afraid.

Occult Curses?

Is it possible to have some satanic curse upon us because of past involvement in the occult?

We must not forget that when we are born again, we are delivered from Satan's power and the kingdom of darkness (see Acts 26:18; Col. 1:13). Satan no longer has any hold on us unless we give it to him. Although the Bible indicates that the Ephesian Christians were heavily involved in practicing magic before their conversion (see Acts 19:18-19), there is no record of Paul breaking any "Satanic curses" or binding Satan's power over them after they were born again. The reason is because they were automatically set free from Satan's dominion the moment they first believed in Jesus.

Additionally, when Paul wrote to the Ephesian Christians, he gave no instructions regarding setting anyone free from generational or satanic curses. All he told them was "do not give the devil an opportunity" (Eph. 4:27), and to "put on the full armor of God" that they might "be able to stand firm against the schemes of the devil" (Eph. 6:11). Those are every Christian's responsibilities.

But why, in some cases, have Christians apparently been helped when someone broke a "generational" or "satanic curse" over them? Possibly because the individual who needed help had faith that the devil would flee once the "curse" was broken. Faith is what puts the devil on the run, and every Christian can and should have faith that when he resists the devil, the devil will flee. There is no need, however, to call in a "deliverance specialist" in order to send Satan running.

Finally, the Bible tells us that Christ "became a *curse* for us," and in so doing, "redeemed us from the *curse* of the Law" (Gal 3:13, emphasis added). All of us were formerly under God's curse because we had sinned, but since Jesus bore our punishment, we have been released from that curse. Praise God! No longer cursed, we can rejoice that we have now been *blessed* "with every spiritual blessing in the heavenly places in Christ" (Eph. 1:3).

Myth 10: "We can break demonic bondages through fasting."

Some Christians seem to regard fasting as one of the most preeminent aspects of Christian life and responsibility. This is quite amazing in light of the fact that in all of the epistles of the New Testament, there is not one instruction given to Christians regarding fasting. Nowhere in the epistles are Christians even encouraged to fast. In fact, the epistles have nothing at all to say about fasting, other than Paul's mention of a few times when he had to go hungry, examples of involuntary fasting.

In the book of Acts, there are only two examples of voluntary fasting:

> And while they were ministering to the Lord and *fasting*, the Holy Spirit said, "Set apart for Me Barnabas and Saul for the work to which I have called them." Then, when they had *fasted* and prayed and laid their hands on them, they sent them away (Acts 13:2-3, emphasis added).

> And when they had appointed elders for them in every church, having prayed with *fasting*, they commended them to the Lord in whom they had believed (Acts 14:23, emphasis added)

We learn that the primary benefit of fasting under the new covenant is to give us more time to concentrate on prayer. This is especially important when we are seeking God for specific direction as we wait for His guidance to become clear within our own spirits.

As every Christian knows, probably the most difficult thing about spending extended time in prayer is finding the time to do it. Sometimes the only way to find a few hours to pray is to eliminate something else. That is probably why Jesus once prayed all night (notice it was before He chose His apostles), and why He often rose early in the morning to pray. That is why Paul wrote to married Christians and told them not to deprive their spouses of sexual relations, "except by agreement for a time *that you may devote yourselves to prayer*" (1 Cor. 7:5, emphasis added). In order to spend an extended time of prayer, we may have to temporarily abstain from some of the legitimate pleasures of life, such as sleep, sex or food.

Fast or Hunger Strike?

Fasting, of course, does not change God. We shouldn't think that because we are afflicting ourselves by fasting, God will more readily listen to our prayers. That would be more like a hunger strike.

Fasting does not give us more spiritual power or give us authority over demons. As members of Christ's body, we already are "seated in heavenly places, far above all rule and authority and power and dominion, and every name that is named" (Eph. 1:21). We already have the authority to cast out demons according to Jesus' promise in Mark 16:17: "And these signs will accompany those who have believed: in My name they will cast out demons."

But what about Jesus' statement concerning a demon He once exorcised: "But this kind does not go out except by prayer and fasting" (Matt. 17:21)?

First, my Bible indicates that many of the original manuscripts of Matthew's Gospel do not contain this particular verse, which means it is possible that Jesus never said, "This kind does not go out except by prayer and fasting."

In Mark's account of the same incident, Jesus is recorded as saying, "This kind cannot come out by anything but prayer" (Mark 9:29), and it is noted in the margin that many manuscripts add "and fasting" to the end of the verse.

So did Jesus say that fasting is a necessary ingredient in exercising a particular kind of demon? The answer is that we don't know. Nevertheless, if Jesus did actually make the statement regarding fasting, that is the only time He or any of the New Testament writers associated fasting with deliverance from a demon.

Perhaps it would be helpful to ask ourselves how fasting could be an aid in exorcising demons. Certainly fasting could not increase anyone's authority over demons. If God has given one authority to cast out demons, he has it. The only thing that fasting could do is provide one with more time to meditate on God's promise of his authority, thus increasing his faith in what God has said, and faith is definitely a factor in bringing deliverance.

In the case under consideration, the disciples had previously been given authority to cast out unclean spirits (see Matt. 10:1), but they failed to cast out a demon from a young boy. When Jesus heard of their failure, He immediately lamented their unbelief (see Matt. 17:17), and when they asked Him why they failed, He responded, "Because of the littleness of your faith" (Matt. 17:20). It is a few verses later that we find Jesus' questionable statement concerning fasting.

Thus we can conclude the reason for their failure as being one of two possibilities: Either they didn't have faith in their God-given authority *plus* they didn't pray and fast beforehand, or they didn't have faith in their God-given authority, and time spent in fasting and prayer could have helped them build their faith. I would prefer to accept the second scenario, as it makes more sense, while the first seems to make Jesus contradict Himself. Keep in mind that both possibilities are predicated upon the assumption that Jesus actually made the statement about fasting.

Regardless of the correct interpretation, we must not forget that the overwhelming majority of references to spiritual warfare and deliverance from demons make no mention of fasting. There is no mention at all of fasting in connection with our *personal warfare* against Satan and evil spirits, and to say that we must fast to gain personal victory over the devil is entirely unscriptural.

The Fast That God Chooses

One other passage of Scripture that is often misconstrued to prove that fasting can break demonic bondages is Isaiah 58:6:

> Is this not the fast which I choose, to loosen the bonds of wickedness, to undo the bands of the yoke, and to let the oppressed go free, and break every yoke? (Is. 58:6).

Does this verse of Scripture teach that we can break demonic bondages over people by fasting? It can only when it is taken out of context and assumptions are made. Let's beat Satan at one of his games (taking scriptures out of context), and read most of the fifty-eighth chapter of Isaiah to learn what God was actually saying there:

> Cry loudly, do not hold back; raise your voice like a trumpet, and declare to My people their transgression, and to the house of Jacob their sins (Is. 58:1)

God was speaking to Isaiah, commissioning him to declare to Israel their sins. In the very next verse, God began to enumerate those sins:

> Yet they seek Me day by day, and delight to know My ways, as a nation that has done righteousness, and has not forsaken the ordinance of their God. They ask Me for just decisions, they delight in the nearness of God (Is. 58:2).

Clearly, the people of Israel claimed to be righteous, but their religion was just a façade. They were only going through the motions of devotion. They asked God,

> "Why have we fasted and Thou dost not see? Why have we humbled ourselves and Thou dost not notice?" (Is. 58:3a).

And God responded:

> Behold, on the day of your fast you find *your desire, and drive hard all your workers*. Behold, you fast for *contention* and *strife* and to *strike with a wicked fist*. You do not fast like you do today to make your voice heard on high. Is it a fast like this which I choose, a day for a man to humble himself? Is it for bowing one's head like a reed, and for spreading out sackcloth and ashes as a bed? *Will you call this a fast, even an acceptable day to the Lord*? (Is. 58:3b-5, emphasis added).

Apparently, the Israelites had been fasting to gain God's attention or favor, and they wondered why their situation hadn't improved. God responded by reminding them of their selfish lifestyles, exhibited even during the days of their fasting. Even their reasons for fasting were selfish, making it entirely unacceptable to God. Then He told them about the kind of fast He was looking for—a fast from selfishness:

> Is this not the fast which I choose, to loosen the bonds of wickedness, to undo the bands of the yoke, and to let the oppressed go free, and break every yoke? Is it not to divide your bread with the hungry, and bring the homeless poor into the house; when you see the naked, to cover him; and not to hide yourself from your own flesh? (Is. 58:6-7).

Was God saying that the act of fasting will set people free from demonic bondage? No, not at all. God wanted them to abstain, not from food, but from being selfish. He wanted them to love their neighbor as themselves. He wanted them to break yokes, "let the oppressed go free," divide their bread with the hungry, bring the homeless poor into their houses, and cover the naked. The act of abstaining from food by itself will not result in any of those things. Those are things *people* must do.

This interpretation becomes even clearer as we continue reading. If the Israelites would begin to fast from their self-centered lifestyles, God promised,

> Then your light will break out like the dawn, and your recovery will speedily spring forth; and your righteousness will go before you; the glory of the Lord will be your rear guard. Then you will call, and the Lord will answer; you will cry, and He will say, 'Here I am.' If _you_ *remove the yoke from your midst, the pointing of the finger, and speaking wickedness, and if _you_ give yourself to the hungry, and satisfy the desire of the afflicted*, then your light will rise in darkness, and your gloom will become like midday (Is. 58:8-10, emphasis added).

Verse 9 makes it very clear that God was not talking about Himself removing some demonic yoke in response to their fasting. Rather, He was telling them that *they* were the ones who should be removing, not demonic, but human yokes from people, such as injustice and poverty.

God was much more interested in the Israelites abstaining from selfishness than He was in their abstaining from food. This is no doubt true for us as well. The second greatest commandment is not, "Make sure you fast often" but, "You shall love your neighbor as yourself" (Mark 12:31).

The idea that we can break people free from Satan's grasp by the act of fasting is erroneous. The primary way to get people set free from Satan is to tell them the gospel. If they respond with faith, they'll be set free. Then we can teach them how to resist the devil by faith in God's Word.

Scriptural Spiritual Warfare

So we have covered many of the modern myths regarding spiritual warfare. But is there a form of spiritual warfare that is scriptural? Yes, and that will now be our focus.

Perhaps the first thing we need to know about spiritual warfare is that it should not be the focus of our Christian life. We should be focused on Christ, to follow and obey Him, as we progressively grow to be more like Him. Only a small percentage of the New Testament writings address the subject of spiritual warfare, indicating to us that it should be a minor focus in the Christian life.

The second thing we need to know about spiritual warfare is that the Bible tells us what we need to know. We don't need any special discernment (or a preacher who claims to have special discernment) into the "deep things of Satan." Biblical spiritual warfare is simple. Satan's schemes are clearly revealed in Scripture. Our responsibilities are straightforwardly outlined. Once you know and believe what God has said, you are guaranteed to be a winner in this spiritual struggle.

Back to the Beginning

Let's go back to the book of Genesis, where we are first introduced to the devil. In the first chapters there, Satan appears in the form of a serpent. If there is any doubt that this serpent is the devil, Revelation 20:2 removes it: "And he laid hold of the dragon, *the serpent of old*, who is the devil and Satan" (emphasis added).

Genesis 3:1 tells us, "The serpent was more crafty than any beast of the field which the Lord God had made." When you think about how crafty some of God's creatures are as they compete to survive and stalk their prey, it makes you realize how cunning Satan must be. On the other hand, Satan is not all-knowing or all-wise as God is, and we should not assume that we are at a mental disadvantage in our struggle against him. Jesus instructed *us* to be as "shrewd as *serpents*" (Matt. 10:16, emphasis added). Paul claimed that he was not ignorant of Satan's schemes (see 2 Cor. 2:11) and that we have the "mind of Christ" (1 Cor. 2:16).

Satan launched his first-recorded fiery dart by questioning Eve about what God has said. Her response would reveal to him whether he had a chance of deceiving her into disobeying God. *Satan has no avenue to deceive anyone who believes and obeys what God has said, which is why his entire strategy revolves around ideas that contradict God's Word.*

Satan asked her, "Indeed, has God said, 'You shall not eat from any tree of the garden'?" (Gen. 3:1.) It almost sounds like an innocent question from a casual inquirer, but Satan knew exactly what his goal was.

Eve responded, "From the fruit of the trees of the garden we may eat; but from the fruit of the tree which in the middle of the garden, God has said, 'You shall not eat from it or touch it, lest you die'" (Gen. 3:2-3).

Eve almost had it right. Actually, God never forbade them to *touch* the tree of the knowledge of good and evil, but only forbade them to eat from it.

Eve certainly did know enough of the truth to recognize the lie of Satan's response: "You surely shall not die!" (Gen. 3:4). That, of course, is a blatant contradiction of what God said, and it would be unlikely that Eve would believe it outright. So Satan then sugarcoated his lie with some truth, as he often does, making it much easier to swallow. He continued: "For God knows that in the day you eat from it your eyes will be opened, and you will be like God, knowing good and evil" (Gen. 3:5).

Satan actually said three things that were true after he lied. We know that once Adam and Eve ate the forbidden fruit, their eyes *were* opened (see Gen. 3:7) as Satan had said. Additionally, God Himself later said that the man *had* become like God and that he *had* come to know good and evil (see Gen. 3:22). Take note: *Satan often mixes truth with error in order to deceive people.*

Notice also that Satan maligned God's character. God didn't want Adam and Eve to eat the forbidden fruit for their own wellbeing and happiness, but Satan made it sound as if God was withholding something from them that was good. The majority of Satan's lies malign God's character, will, and motives.

Unfortunately, Earth's first couple rejected the truth to believe a lie, and they suffered the consequences. But notice all the elements of modern spiritual warfare in their story: Satan's only weapon was a lie couched in truth. The humans were faced with a choice to believe what God had said or what Satan had said. Believing the truth could have been their "shield of faith," but they never lifted it.

Jesus' Spiritual Warfare

As we read of Jesus' encounter with Satan during His wilderness temptation, we quickly see that Satan had not changed his methods over thousands of years. His avenue of attack was to discredit what God had said, as he knew that his only way of defeating his enemy was to dissuade Him from believing or obeying the truth. *God's Word is again at the center of the battle.* Satan volleyed his lies, and Jesus deflected them with truth. Jesus believed and obeyed what God had said. That is biblical spiritual warfare.

Jesus was faced with the same situation as Eve, Adam, and all the rest of us. He had to decide if He would listen to God or Satan. Jesus fought His spiritual battle with the "sword of the Spirit," the Word of God. Let's see what we can learn from spiritual warfare with Satan.

Recounting Jesus' second temptation, Matthew tells us:

> Then the devil took Him into the holy city; and he had
> Him stand on the pinnacle of the temple, and said to Him,
> "If You are the Son of God throw Yourself down; for it is
> written, 'He will give His angels charge concerning You';
> and 'On their hands they will bear You up, lest You strike
> Your foot against a stone.'" Jesus said to him, "On the oth-
> er hand, it is written, 'You shall not put the Lord your God
> to the test'" (Mark 4:5-7).

Here the central issue is again what God has said. Satan even quoted from the ninety-first Psalm, but He twisted it in an attempt to make it mean something that God did not intend.

Jesus responded by quoting a scripture that brought a balanced understanding of God's promise of protection found in Psalm 91. God will protect us, but not if we act foolishly, "putting Him to the test," as the note in the margin of my Bible indicates.

This is why it is so vital that we not wrench Bible verses out of context from the rest of the Bible. Every scripture must be balanced with what the rest of Scripture says.

Twisting Scripture is one of Satan's most common tactics in spiritual warfare, and sadly, he has been very successful using that tactic against many Christians who are caught up in the modern spiritual warfare movement. A classic example of such twisting is the use of the biblical phrase "pulling down strongholds" to support the idea of pulling down evil spirits in the atmosphere. As I pointed out earlier, that particular phrase, when read in context, has absolutely no application to the pulling down of evil spirits in the atmosphere. Yet the devil would love for us to think it does, so we can waste our time screaming at the principalities and powers in the sky.

In Matthew's account of Jesus third temptation we read,

> Again, the devil took Him to a very high mountain, and
> showed Him all the kingdoms of the world, and their glo-
> ry; and he said to Him, "All these things will I give You, if
> You fall down and worship me." Then Jesus said to him,
> "Begone, Satan! For it is written, 'You shall worship the
> Lord your God, and serve Him only.'" (Matt. 4:8-10).

This was a temptation for power. If Jesus had worshipped Satan, and if Satan then kept his promise to Him, Jesus would have gained the second-in-command position over the kingdom of darkness. He would have ruled over every unsaved human being and every evil spirit, having worldwide authority as only Satan had previously. We can only speculate in our nightmares what would have happened had Jesus yielded to that temptation.

Notice again that Jesus countered Satan's suggestion with the written Word of God. During each of the three temptations, Jesus overcame by saying, "It is written." We, too, must know God's Word and believe it if we want to avoid being deceived and fall into Satan's traps. That is what spiritual warfare is all about.

The Battle Ground

For the most part, the only power that Satan and his demons have is to plant thoughts in people's hearts and minds (and even that is limited by God; see 1 Cor. 10:13). With that thought in mind, consider the following sampling of scriptures:

> But Peter said, "Ananias, why has *Satan filled your heart to lie to the Holy Spirit, and to keep back some of the price of the land?*" (Acts 5:3, emphasis added).

> And during supper, *the devil having already put into the heart of Judas Iscariot, the son of Simon, to betray Him...* (John 13:2, emphasis added).

> But the Spirit explicitly says that in later times some will fall away from the faith, *paying attention to deceitful spirits and doctrines of demons...* (1 Tim. 4:1, emphasis added).

> But I am afraid, lest *as the serpent deceived* Eve by his craftiness, *your minds should be led astray* from the simplicity and purity of devotion to Christ (2 Cor. 11:3, emphasis added).

> Stop depriving one another, except by agreement for a time that you may devote yourselves to prayer, and come together again *lest Satan tempt you* because of your lack of self-control (1 Cor. 7:5, emphasis added).

> For this reason, when I could endure it no longer, I also sent to find out about your faith, for fear that *the tempter might have tempted you, and our labor should be in vain* (1 Thes. 3:5, emphasis added).

> ...in whose case *the god of this world has blinded the minds of the unbelieving*, that they might not see the light of the gospel of the glory of Christ, who is the image of God (2 Cor. 4:4, emphasis added).

> And the great dragon was thrown down, the serpent of old who is called the devil and Satan, *who deceives the whole world*; he was thrown down to the earth, and his

angels were thrown down with him (Rev. 12:9, emphasis added).

You are of your father the devil, and you want to do the desires of your father. He was a murderer from the beginning, and *does not stand in the truth, because there is no truth in him. Whenever he speaks a lie, he speaks from his own nature; for he is a liar, and the father of lies* (John 8:44, emphasis added).

These scriptures and others make it clear that the primary battleground in biblical spiritual warfare is our hearts and minds. Satan attacks with thoughts—evil suggestions, wrong ideas, false philosophies, temptations, various lies and so on. Our means of defense is knowing, believing, and acting upon God's Word.

It is vitally important that you understand that every thought you think does not necessarily originate from within yourself. Satan has many spokespersons who help him plant his thoughts in people's minds. He works to influence us through newspapers, books, television, magazines, radio, through friends and neighbors, and even through preachers. Even the apostle Peter was once unwittingly used as a spokesman for Satan, suggesting to Jesus that it was not God's will for Him to die (see Matt. 16:23).

But Satan and evil spirits also work directly on human minds, without any human intermediary, and all Christians will at times find themselves under direct assault. That is when the warfare begins.

I remember a dear Christian woman who once came to me to confess a problem. She said that whenever she prayed, she found that blasphemous thoughts and swear words would come to her mind. She was one of the sweetest, kindest, dearest, most dedicated women in my church, yet she had this problem with terrible thoughts.

I explained to her that those thoughts did not originate within her, but that she was being attacked by Satan, who was attempting to ruin her prayer life. She then told me she has stopped praying every day because she was so afraid she might think those thoughts again. Satan had succeeded.

So I told her to start praying again, and if those blasphemous thoughts came to her mind, she should counteract them with truth from God's Word. If a thought said to her, "Jesus was just a -------, she should say, "No, Jesus was and is the divine Son of God." If a thought came that was a swear word, she should replace that thought with a thought of praise for Jesus, and so on.

I also told her that by being afraid that she might think wrong thoughts, she was actually inviting them, as fear is somewhat of a reverse faith—a faith in the devil. By trying not to think about something, we have to think about it in order to try not to think about it.

For example, if I say to you, "Don't think about your right hand," you will immediately think about your right hand as you attempt to obey me. The harder you try, the worse it gets. The only way not to think about your right hand is to consciously think about something else, for example, your shoes. Once you have your mind on your shoes, you are not thinking about your hand.

I encouraged that dear woman to "fear not," just as the Bible commands us. And whenever she recognized a thought that was contrary to God's Word, she should replace it with one that agreed with God's Word.

I'm happy to report that she followed my advice, and, although attacked a few more times during her prayer times, she gained complete victory over her problem. She triumphed in biblical spiritual warfare.

It has also been interesting for me to discover, upon taking surveys in a number of churches, that her problem was very common. Usually more than half of the Christians I survey indicate that at one time or another, they have had blasphemous thoughts while praying. Satan is not so original.

"Take Care What You Listen To"

We cannot stop Satan and evil spirits from attacking our minds, but we don't have to allow *their* thoughts to become *our* thoughts. That is, we don't have to dwell upon demonic ideas and suggestions, taking possession of them. As it has been said, "You can't keep the birds from flying over your head, but you can keep them from making a nest in your hair."

Additionally, we should be careful not to subject our minds to ungodly influences whenever it is within our control. When we sit down in front of the television for an hour, or read the newspaper, we are putting out the welcome mat to be influenced with thoughts that may be satanic. Directly after He told the parable of the sower and the soils, Jesus warned, "Take care what you listen to" (Mark 4:24). Jesus knew the destructive effects of listening to lies, allowing Satan to plant his "seeds" in our hearts and minds. Those seeds may grow up into "thorns and thistles" which will ultimately choke the Word of God from our lives (see Mark 4:7, 18-19).

Peter on Spiritual Warfare

The apostle Peter understood true, biblical spiritual warfare. Never in his epistles did he instruct Christians to pull down principalities and powers over cities. He did, however, instruct them to resist Satan's attacks against their personal lives, and he told them exactly how they should resist:

> Be of sober spirit, be on the alert. Your adversary, the devil, prowls about like a roaring lion, seeking someone to devour. But resist him, firm in your faith, knowing that the same experiences of suffering are being accomplished by your brethren who are in the world (1 Pet. 5:8-9).

Notice first that Peter indicated our position is one of defense, not offense. Satan is the one who is prowling around, not us. He is looking for us; we're not looking for him. Our job is not to attack but to resist.

Second, notice that Satan, like a lion, is seeking someone to *devour*. How could he possibly devour Christians? Did Peter mean that Satan could literally eat their flesh like a lion would? Obviously not. The only way Satan could devour a Christian is to deceive him into believing a lie that destroys his faith.

Third, notice Peter tells us to resist the devil through our faith. Our struggle is not a physical battle, and we can't fight Satan by swinging our fists in the air. He attacks us with lies, and we resist those lies by standing firm in our faith in God's Word. That, again, is scriptural spiritual warfare.

The Christians to whom Peter was writing were suffering some severe persecution, and thus were being tempted to renounce their faith in Christ. It is often when we are in the midst of adverse circumstances that Satan will attack with his doubts and lies. That is the time to stand firm in your faith. That is the "evil day" of which Paul wrote when you need to "put on the full armor of God, that you may be able to *stand firm* against the schemes of the devil (Eph. 6:11, emphasis added).

James on Spiritual Warfare

The apostle James also mentioned something about spiritual warfare in his epistle. Did he tell the Christians that their prayers could determine the outcome of angelic battles? No. Did he tell them to pull down the spirits of lust, apathy, and drunkenness over their cities? No. Did he tell them to study the history of their cities so they could determine which kind of evil spirits have been there since the beginning? No.

James believed in scriptural, spiritual warfare, and so he wrote:

> Submit therefore to God. Resist the devil and he will flee from you (James 4:7, emphasis added).

Once again, notice that the Christian's posture is one of defense—we are to resist, not attack. When we do, James promises us that Satan will flee. He has no reason to stick around a Christian who will not be persuaded to believe his lies, follow his suggestions, or yield to his temptations.

Notice also that James first instructed us to submit to God. We submit to God by submitting to His Word. Our resistance against Satan is predicated upon our submission to God's Word.

John on Spiritual Warfare

The apostle John also wrote about spiritual warfare in his first epistle. Did he tell us to go up to the high places in order to tear down the devil's strongholds? No. Did he tell us how to cast the demon of anger out of Christians who sometimes get angry? No.

Rather, John, like Peter and James, only believed in biblical, spiritual warfare, and so his instructions are the same:

> Beloved, do not believe every spirit, but test the spirits to see whether they are from God; because many false prophets have gone out into the world. By this you know the Spirit of God: every spirit that confesses that Jesus Christ has come in the flesh is from God; and every spirit that does not confess Jesus is not from God; and this is the spirit of the antichrist, of which you have heard that it is coming, and now it is already in the world. You are from God, little children, and have overcome them; because greater is He who is in you than he who is in the world. They are from the world; therefore they speak as from the world, and the world listens to them. We are from God; he who knows God listens to us; he who is not from God does not listen to us. By this we know the spirit of truth and the spirit of error (1 John 4:1-6).

Notice that John's entire discussion in these verses revolves around Satan's lies and God's truth. We are to test the spirits to see if they are from God, and the test is based on truth. Evil spirits will not admit that Jesus Christ came in the flesh. They are liars.

John also told us that we have overcome evil spirits. That is, as citizens of the kingdom of light, we are not under their dominion any longer. The greater one, Jesus, lives in us. People who have Christ living in them should not be afraid of demons.

John also said that the world listens to the evil spirits, which indicates that those evil spirits must be speaking. We know that they are not speaking audibly, but are planting lies in people's minds.

As followers of Christ, we should not be listening to the lies of evil spirits, and John states that those who know God are listening to us, because we have the truth; we have God's Word.

Again, notice that Satan's strategy is to persuade people to believe his lies. Satan cannot defeat us if we know and believe the truth. That is what scriptural, spiritual warfare is all about.

Faith is the Key

Knowing God's Word is not enough to win in spiritual battle. The key is *truly believing* what God has said. This is true in resisting the devil and in casting out of demons. For example, consider again an example we have examined previously, when Jesus gave His twelve disciples "authority over unclean spirits, to cast them out" (Matt. 10:1). We find them, seven chapters later, unable to cast a demon out of an epileptic boy.[99] When Jesus learned of their failure, He lamented:

"O *unbelieving* and perverted generation, how long shall I be with you? How long shall I put up with you?" (Matt. 17:17, emphasis added).

It was their unbelief that Jesus bemoaned. Moreover, when His disciples later questioned Him as to why they were unable to cast the demon out, Jesus responded, "Because of the littleness of your faith" (Matt. 17:20). Thus we see that their authority to cast out demons did not work apart from their faith.

Our success in casting out demons and resisting the devil is dependent on our faith in God's Word. If we truly do believe what God has said, then we will talk like it and act like it. Dogs chase people who run from them, and it is the same with the devil. If you run, the devil will chase you. If you'll stand firm in your faith, however, the devil will flee from you (see Jas. 4:7).

No doubt the apostles' lack of faith would have been very evident to any observer, as they tried, but failed, to deliver that boy from a demon. If that demon put on the same show for the disciples as it performed in front of Jesus, throwing the boy into a "violent convulsion" (Luke 9:42) and causing him to foam at the mouth (see Mark 9:20), it is possible that the disciples' faith turned to fear. They were perhaps paralyzed by what they witnessed.

One who has faith, however, is not moved by what he sees, but rather, is moved only by what God has said. "We walk by faith, *not by sight*" (2 Cor. 5:7, emphasis added). God cannot lie (see Tit. 1:2), and so even if our circumstances seemingly contradict what God has said, we should remain steadfast in faith.

Notice that Jesus delivered the boy in just a few seconds. He did it by faith. He did not waste His time conducting a "deliverance session." Those who have faith in their God-given authority don't need to spend hours casting out a demon.

Moreover, there is no record that Jesus screamed at the demon. Those who have faith don't need to scream. Neither did Jesus repeatedly command the demon to come out. One command was sufficient. A second command would have been an admission of doubt.

In Summary

The disciple-making minister teaches, by his example and with his words, biblical spiritual warfare, so that his disciples are able to stand firm against Satan's schemes and walk in obedience to Christ's commands. He does not lead his disciples to follow the current "winds of doctrine" that promote unbiblical methods of spiritual warfare, knowing that those who practice such methods are wrongly focused and are actually deceived by Satan, the very one they are victoriously claiming to engage.

---

[99] We should be very cautious in assuming that all epilepsy is caused by an indwelling evil spirit.

THIRTY-TWO

Stewardship

In an earlier chapter about Jesus' Sermon on the Mount, we considered some words Jesus spoke to His disciples regarding stewardship. He told them not to lay up treasures on the earth, but in heaven. He pointed out, not only the foolishness of those who invest in temporal treasures, but also the darkness that is in their hearts (see Matt. 6:19-24).

Money is the true god of those who lay up earthly treasures, because they serve it and it rules their lives. Jesus declared that it is impossible to serve God and money, clearly indicating that if God is our true Master, then He is also Master of our money. *Money, more than anything else, competes with God for the hearts of people.* That is no doubt why Jesus taught that we cannot be His disciples unless we give up all our own possessions (see Luke 14:33). Christ's disciples own nothing. They are simply stewards of that which is God's, and God likes to do things with *His* money that reflect *His* character and furthers *His* kingdom.

Jesus had much to say about stewardship, but it seems His words are often ignored by those who profess to be His followers. Much more popular is the twisting of Scripture to fabricate the modern "prosperity doctrine" in its many forms, subtle and blatant. The disciple-making minister, however, desires to teach people to obey all of Christ's commandments. He will thus teach, by his example and by his words, *biblical* stewardship.

Let us consider what Scripture teaches about stewardship, and at the same time, expose some of the more common examples of false teaching about prosperity. This will by no means be an exhaustive study. I've written an entire book on this subject that is available to read in English at our website (ShepherdServe.org). It is found under the heading of "Biblical Topics" and the subheading, "Jesus on Money."

The Supplier of Needs

Beginning on a positive note, we remember that Paul, under the inspira-

459

tion of the Holy Spirit, wrote, "God shall supply all your needs according to His riches in glory in Christ Jesus" (Phil. 4:19). That familiar promise is often quoted and claimed by Christians, but what was its context? As we read contextually, we soon discover the reason Paul was so confident that God would supply all the needs of the Philippian believers:

> Nevertheless, you have done well to *share with me in my affliction*. And you yourselves also know, Philippians, that at the first preaching of the gospel, after I departed from Macedonia, no church shared with me in the matter of giving and receiving but you alone; for even in Thessalonica *you sent a gift more than once for my needs*. Not that I seek the gift itself, but I seek for the profit which increases to your account. But I have received everything in full, and have an abundance; I am amply supplied, *having received from Epaphroditus what you have sent*, a fragrant aroma, an acceptable sacrifice, well-pleasing to God. And my God shall supply all your needs according to His riches in glory in Christ Jesus (Phil. 4:14-19, emphasis added).

Paul was certain that Jesus would indeed supply the needs of the Philippians because they had met Jesus' condition: They were seeking first the kingdom of God, proven by their sacrificial gifts to Paul so he could continue planting churches. Remember that in His Sermon on the Mount, Jesus said,

> For your heavenly Father knows that you need all these things. But seek first His kingdom and His righteousness; and all these things shall be added to you (Matt. 6:32-33).

So we see that Paul's promise in Philippians 4:19 doesn't apply to every Christian who quotes and claims it. Rather, it only has application to those who are seeking first God's kingdom.

What Do We Really Need?

There is something else we can learn from Jesus' promise in Matthew 6:32-33. We sometimes have difficulty distinguishing our needs from our wants. Jesus, however, defined what our needs are. He said, "Your heavenly Father knows that you *need* all these things."

What are those "things" Jesus was referring to that would be added to those who sought first His kingdom and righteousness? They are food, drink and clothing. No one can debate that, because that is what Jesus said just prior to the promise under consideration (see Matt. 6:25-31). Food, drink and clothing, are our only real material needs. Those are, in fact, the only things that Jesus and His traveling band of disciples possessed.

Paul also evidently agreed with Jesus' definition of our needs, as he wrote to Timothy:

But godliness actually is a means of great gain, when accompanied by contentment. For we have brought nothing into the world, so we cannot take anything out of it either. *And if we have food and covering, with these we shall be content.* But those who want to get rich fall into temptation and a snare and many foolish and harmful desires which plunge men into ruin and destruction. For the love of money is a root of all sorts of evil, and some by longing for it have wandered away from the faith, and pierced themselves with many a pang (1 Tim. 6:6-10, emphasis added).

Paul believed that food and covering were all that we really needed materially, otherwise he would not have said we should be content with just those things. That leads us to a little different perspective regarding his promise to the Philippians that God would supply all their needs! The way some preachers expound on that verse, you would think it said, "My God shall supply all your greeds!" Moreover, if we should be content with just food and covering, should we not be much more content with what we actually do have, which for most of us is much more than just food and covering?

Discontentment

Our problem is that we think we need so much more than we really do. Consider the fact that when God created Adam and Eve they owned nothing, and yet they were living in a paradise. Obviously, God did not intend for us to derive our happiness from collecting material things. Have you ever considered the fact that Jesus never once turned on a faucet or stood under a shower in a bathroom? He never washed His clothing in a washing machine; He never opened the door of a refrigerator. He never drove a car or even a bicycle for that matter. Not once did He listen to a radio, speak to someone over a phone, cook a meal on a stove, or preach through a public address system. He never watched a video or a television show, turned on an electric lamp, or cooled off in front of an air conditioner or electric fan. He never owned a wristwatch. He didn't have a closet full of clothing. How could He have been happy?

In the United States (and perhaps in your country as well), we are bombarded with advertisements that show us how happy people are as they enjoy their new material possessions. Consequently, we are brainwashed (or "brain-dirtied") into thinking that happiness comes from acquiring more, and regardless of how much we accumulate, we're never content. This is what Jesus referred to as "the deceitfulness of riches" (Matt. 13:22). Material things promise happiness but rarely deliver on their promise. And as we join the world's frenzied race to acquire more material things, we actually become idolaters, slaves to mammon, who forget God and His most important commandments to love Him with all our hearts and our neighbor as ourselves. God warned about this very thing to Israel:

> Beware lest you forget the Lord your God by not keeping
> His commandments and His ordinances and His statutes
> which I am commanding you today; lest, when you have
> eaten and are satisfied, and have built good houses and
> lived in them, and when your herds and your flocks mul-
> tiply, and your silver and gold multiply, and all that you
> have multiplies, then your heart becomes proud, and you
> forget the Lord your God who brought you out from the
> land of Egypt, out of the house of slavery (Deut. 8:11-14).

Similarly, Jesus warned that "the deceitfulness of riches" could potentially choke spiritual life from a true believer who allows himself to become distracted (see Matt. 13:7, 22). Paul warned that "the love of money
is a root of all sorts of evil," saying that "some by longing for it have wandered away from the faith, and pierced themselves with many a pang" (1
Tim. 6:10). We are admonished by the author of the book of Hebrews, "Let
your character be free from the love of money, being content with what
you have; for He Himself has said, 'I will never desert you, nor will I ever
forsake you'" (Heb. 13:5). These are just a sampling of Scripture's warnings regarding the dangers of wealth.

When Money is Master

Perhaps there is no better barometer of our relationship with God than
our interaction with money. Money—the time and the means we use to
acquire it, and what we do with it after we acquire it—reveals much about
our spiritual lives. Money, when we possess it and even when we possess none, fuels temptation perhaps like nothing else. Money can easily
stand in utter contempt of the two greatest commandments, because it can
become a god above the only God, and it can entice us to love ourselves
more and our neighbors less. On the other hand, money can be used as a
means to prove our love for God and our neighbors.

Jesus once told a parable about a man who allowed money to rule him
rather than God:

> The land of a rich man was very productive. And he began
> reasoning to himself, saying, "What shall I do, since I have
> no place to store my crops?" Then he said, "This is what I
> will do: I will tear down my barns and build larger ones,
> and there I will store all my grain and my goods. And I
> will say to my soul, 'Soul, you have many goods laid up
> for many years to come; take your ease, eat, drink and be
> merry.'" But God said to him, "You fool! This very night
> your soul is required of you; and now who will own what
> you have prepared? "So is the man who stores up treasure
> for himself, and is not rich toward God (Luke 12:16-21).

Jesus portrayed this wealthy man as being very foolish. Although blessed with health, productive land and farming skills, he didn't know God, otherwise he would not have stored up his excess and retired to a life of selfish pleasure and ease. Rather, he would have sought the Lord regarding what he should do with his blessing, knowing that he was but God's steward. God, of course, would have wanted him to share his abundance and continue working so he could continue to share his abundance. Perhaps the only other acceptable alternative would have been to stop farming and devote himself to some self-supporting ministry, if that is what God called him to do.

The wealthy farmer in Jesus' parable made a major miscalculation regarding the date of his death. He assumed he had many years remaining, when he was just hours away from eternity. Jesus' point is unmistakable: We should live each day as if it were our last, always ready to stand before God to give an account.

Two Perspectives

How different is God's perspective from man's! The wealthy man in Jesus' parable would have been the envy of most people who knew him, yet God pitied him. He was rich in the eyes of men, but poor in the sight of God. He could have laid up treasure in heaven where it would have been his forever, but he chose to lay it up on earth where it was of no profit to him the moment he died. And in light of what Jesus taught about greedy people, it seems quite unlikely that Jesus wanted us to think the wealthy man went to heaven when he died.

This parable should help us all to remember that everything we have is a gift from God, and He expects us to be faithful stewards. It has application, not only to those who have material wealth, but to anyone and everyone who is tempted to make material things too important. This Jesus made clear as He continued speaking to His disciples:

> For this reason [that means what He was about to say was based on what He just said] I say to you, do not worry about your life, as to what you will eat; nor for your body, as to what you will put on. For life is more than food, and the body more than clothing. Consider the ravens, for they neither sow nor reap; they have no storeroom nor barn, and yet God feeds them; how much more valuable you are than the birds! And which of you by worrying can add a single hour to his life's span? If then you cannot do even a very little thing, why do you worry about other matters? Consider the lilies, how they grow: they neither toil nor spin; but I tell you, not even Solomon in all his glory clothed himself like one of these. But if God so clothes the grass in the field, which is alive today and tomorrow is

thrown into the furnace, how much more will He clothe you? You men of little faith! And do not seek what you will eat and what you will drink, and do not keep worrying. For all these things the nations of the world eagerly seek; but your Father knows that you need these things. But seek His kingdom, and these things will be added to you. Do not be afraid, little flock, for your Father has chosen gladly to give you the kingdom.

Sell your possessions and give to charity; make yourselves money belts which do not wear out, an unfailing treasure in heaven, where no thief comes near nor moth destroys. For where your treasure is, there your heart will be also (Luke 12:22-34).

How Jesus' words stand in contrast to those of modern "prosperity preachers"! Today we are being told that God wants us to have more, whereas Jesus told His disciples to sell what they already possessed and give it to charity! Again He exposed the foolishness of those who lay up their treasures on earth—where those treasures are destined to perish, and where the hearts of the treasure-owners reside.

Notice that Jesus applied the lesson of the rich fool to those who had so little that they were tempted to be concerned about food and clothing. Being worried about such things betrays that our focus is wrong. If we trust our caring Father as we should, we won't worry, and that carefree attitude liberates us to focus on building God's kingdom.

Christ's Example

Jesus had many other things to say about money. He taught, however, as every disciple-making minister should, by His example. He preached what He practiced. How did Jesus live?

Jesus did not amass earthly riches, even though He could have easily exploited His situation and become extremely wealthy. Many gifted ministers have wrongly assumed that if their ministries attract money, God must want them to be personally wealthy. Jesus, however, did not use His anointing for personal gain. Money that was given to Him was used to make disciples. He even provided the needs of His traveling band whom He discipled.[100] In our day, young disciples most often have to pay their own way to be lectured to by older ministers in Bible schools. Yet Jesus modeled the exact opposite!

Jesus also lived a life of trust, believing that His Father would supply all His needs and bless Him so He could supply the needs of others.

---

[100] Prosperity preachers often use this fact to prove that Jesus' ministry was prosperous. There is no doubt that God supplied Jesus' needs so He could accomplish His mission. The difference between Jesus and the prosperity preachers is that Jesus wasn't selfish, and He didn't spend his ministry's money to enrich Himself personally.

Sometimes He was invited to banquets to dine, and other times we find Him eating raw standing grain from a field (see Luke 6:1).

On at least two occasions He provided food for thousands of people who came to hear Him. How different this is from modern Christian conferences where everyone who wants to hear the speaker must pay an entrance fee! We who provide free food for those who attend our ministers' conferences are sometimes even mocked for "paying people to listen to us." In reality, we're just following Jesus' model.

Jesus also cared for the poor, as His group kept a moneybox from which distributions were made. Giving to the poor was such a regular feature of Jesus' ministry that when He told Judas to work quickly as he departed from the Last Supper, all the other disciples assumed that Judas was either going to buy food for their group or taking money to the poor (see John 13:27-30).

Jesus truly loved His neighbor as Himself, and so He lived simply and shared. He didn't need to repent at the preaching of John the Baptist who said, "Let the man who has two tunics share with him who has none" (Luke 3:11). Jesus only had one tunic. Yet some prosperity preachers try to convince us that Jesus was wealthy because He wore a seamless inner garment (see John 19:23), something supposedly only worn by wealthy people. It is amazing what significance can be found in a biblical text if someone wants to prove what contradicts numerous other scriptures! We might just as well draw the equally-absurd conclusion that Jesus was attempting to *hide* His wealth, as He didn't also wear a seamless *outer* garment.

Jesus had much more to say about money that we don't have space to consider. Let us, however, consider a few more of the common teachings of modern prosperity preachers who are so adept at twisting scriptures and deceiving the gullible.

"God Made Solomon Rich"

This is the justification that many prosperity preachers use to disguise their greed. They fail to remember that God gave Solomon wealth for a reason. The reason was because, when God promised Solomon that He would grant any request, Solomon asked for wisdom to rule the people. God was so pleased that Solomon didn't ask for wealth (among other things) that along with wisdom He also gave him wealth. Solomon, however, didn't use His divinely-given wisdom as God intended, and he consequently became the most foolish man who ever lived. Had he been wise, he would have heeded what God said to Israel in the Law long before he was born:

> When you enter the land which the Lord your God gives
> you, and you possess it and live in it, and you say, "I will

465

> set a king over me like all the nations who are around me,"
> you shall surely set a king over you whom the Lord your
> God chooses, one from among your countrymen you shall
> set as king over yourselves; you may not put a foreigner
> over yourselves who is not your countryman. Moreover,
> he shall not multiply horses for himself, nor shall he cause
> the people to return to Egypt to multiply horses, since the
> Lord has said to you, "You shall never again return that
> way." Neither shall he multiply wives for himself, lest his
> heart turn away; nor shall he greatly increase silver and
> gold for himself (Deut. 17:15-17).

Here is another scripture that prosperity preachers always ignore, following the example of Solomon who also ignored it to his own demise. And just like him, they also become idolaters. Remember that Solomon's heart was led astray to worship idols by his many wives, wives he could only have afforded because of the misuse of his wealth.

God intended that Solomon would use his God-given wealth to love his neighbor as himself, but Solomon used it to love only himself. He multiplied gold, silver, horses and wives for himself, in direct disobedience to God's commandment. He ultimately married seven hundred wives and possessed three hundred concubines, effectively robbing one thousand men of wives. Rather than giving to the poor, Solomon indulged himself. It is a great wonder that prosperity preachers hold up Solomon as a role model for every New Testament Christian in light of his selfishness and gross idolatry. Isn't our goal to become like *Christ*?

"God Made Abraham Rich, and Abraham's Blessings Are Promised To Us"

This common justification is fabricated from Paul's words found in the third chapter of Galatians. I will quote the oft-misquoted verse, but within its context:

> The Scripture, foreseeing that God would justify the Gen-
> tiles by faith, preached the gospel beforehand to Abraham,
> saying, "All the nations will be blessed in you." *So then
> those who are of faith are blessed with Abraham, the believer.*
>
> For as many as are of the works of the law are under a
> curse; for it is written, "Cursed is everyone who does
> not abide by all things written in the book of the law, to
> perform them." Now that no one is justified by the law
> before God is evident; for, "The righteous man shall live
> by faith." However, the law is not of faith; on the con-
> trary, "He who practices them shall live by them." Christ

redeemed us from the curse of the law, having become a curse for us—for it is written, "Cursed is everyone who hangs on a tree"—*in order that in Christ Jesus the blessing of Abraham might come to the Gentiles*, so that we would receive the promise of the spirit through faith (Gal. 3:8-14, emphasis added).

The "blessing of Abraham" of which Paul wrote in verse 14 was God's promise to Abraham to bless all the nations *in him* (which Paul quoted in verse 8), or more specifically, as Paul explained just a few verses later, *in Abraham's singular seed*, Jesus (Gal. 3:16). According to what we just read, Jesus provided that promised blessing to all the nations by being cursed by God, dying for the sins of the world on the cross. So the "blessing of Abraham coming to the Gentiles" is not about God making Gentiles materially wealthy like Abraham, but about God's promise to Abraham to bless the Gentile nations through his seed—and its fulfillment by Jesus through His death on the cross for them. (Paul's overriding theme here is that Gentiles can be saved by faith, just like Jews, through faith in Jesus.)

Another Twisting

This same passage is often used in another way by prosperity preachers to justify their doctrine. They say that, because the law promised the curse of poverty to those who didn't keep it (see Deut. 28:30-31, 33, 38-40, 47-48, 51, 68), and because Paul wrote, "Christ redeemed us from the curse of the law" in Galatians 3:13, we who are in Christ have been redeemed from the curse of poverty.

First, it is debatable that Paul was thinking of the specific curses found in Deuteronomy 28 when he wrote about "the curse of the law" from which Christ redeemed us. Notice that Paul didn't say Christ redeemed us from the "curses" (plural) of the law, but rather the "curse" of the law, singular, perhaps implying that the whole law was a curse to those who tried to find salvation by keeping it. Once we are redeemed by Christ, we no longer would make the error of trying to save ourselves by keeping the law, and so we are in that sense "redeemed from the curse of the law."

If Paul was actually saying that Christ redeemed us from every disasterous thing listed in Deuteronomy 28, thus guaranteeing our material prosperity, we would have to wonder why Paul once wrote of himself, "To this present hour we are both hungry and thirsty, and are poorly clothed, and are roughly treated, and are homeless" (1 Cor. 4:11). We would also have to wonder why Paul would write,

Who will separate us from the love of Christ? Will tribulation, or distress, or persecution, or famine, or nakedness, or peril, or sword? Just as it is written, "For Your sake we are being put to death all day long; we were considered as sheep to be slaughtered" (Rom. 8:35-36).

Obviously, Paul would not have written those words if all Christians were exempt from suffering persecution, famine, nakedness, peril or sword by virtue of Christ's having redeemed us from the curse of the law.

We would also have to wonder why Jesus foretold the following heavenly scene,

> Then the King will say to those on His right, "Come, you who are blessed of My Father, inherit the kingdom prepared for you from the foundation of the world. For I was hungry, and you gave Me something to eat; I was thirsty, and you gave Me something to drink; I was a stranger, and you invited Me in; naked, and you clothed Me; I was sick, and you visited Me; I was in prison, and you came to Me." Then the righteous will answer Him, 'Lord, when did we see You hungry, and feed You, or thirsty, and give You something to drink? And when did we see You a stranger, and invite You in, or naked, and clothe You? When did we see You sick, or in prison, and come to You?" The King will answer and say to them, "Truly I say to you, *to the extent that you did it to one of these brothers of Mine,* even the least of them, you did it to Me." (Matt. 25:34-40, emphasis added).

Thus there is little doubt that some believers who are "redeemed from the curse of the law" will find themselves in less-than-prosperous circumstances. Notice, however, that in the trying circumstances Jesus described, God met the needs of the suffering believers, and He did it through other believers who had more than they needed. *We can always expect that God will supply our needs, even if it temporarily seems otherwise.*

Finally, those prosperity preachers who want to be rich like Abraham should sincerely question if they want to live in a tent all of their lives without electricity or running water! Those whom God blessed with any degree of wealth in the Old Testament were expected to use their wealth for God's glory, sharing their abundance and providing for others. This Abraham did, providing employment for hundreds of people which then supplied their needs (see Gen. 14:14). Job too did this, and also testified of using his wealth to care for widows and orphans (Job 29:12-13, 31:16-22). Those who are gifted to build businesses should make sure their chief business is to obey God and love their neighbor as themselves.

"Scripture Says That Jesus Became Poor So That We Could Become Rich"

Indeed the Bible does say,

> For you know the grace of our Lord Jesus Christ, that though He was rich, yet for your sake He became poor, so that you through His poverty might become rich (2 Cor. 8:9).

It is argued that since this scripture obviously means that Jesus was *materially* rich in heaven and became *materially* poor on earth, then *material wealth* is what Paul had in mind when he wrote that his readers might become *rich* through Christ's poverty. Surely, they say, if Paul was speaking of *material* wealth and poverty in the first part of the verse, he wouldn't have been speaking of *spiritual* riches in the second part.

If Paul actually meant, however, that we would become materially rich because of Christ' material poverty, we would have to wonder why he wrote just a few verses later in the very same letter,

> I have been in labor and hardship, through many sleepless nights, in hunger and thirst, often without food, in cold and exposure (2 Cor. 11:27).

If Paul meant in 2 Corinthians 8:9 that Christ became materially poor so that we could become materially rich, Christ's intention was certainly not being done in Paul's life! So obviously Paul did *not* mean that Christ became materially poor so that we could become materially rich on this earth. He meant that we would become spiritually rich, "rich toward God," to borrow an expression Jesus used (see Luke 12:21), and rich in heaven where our treasures and hearts are.

Is it really safe to assume that because Paul was speaking of *material* wealth in one part of a sentence that he could not possibly be speaking of *spiritual* wealth in another part or that sentence, as prosperity preachers claim? Consider the following words of Jesus addressed to some of His followers in the city of Smyrna:

> I know your tribulation and your poverty (but you are rich)…(Rev. 2:9a).

Clearly, Jesus was speaking of the *material* poverty that the Smyrnan believers were facing, and then just four words later, He was speaking of the *spiritual* wealth of those same believers.

"Jesus Promised a Hundred-Fold Return on Our Giving"

Jesus did promise a hundred-fold return to those who make certain sacrifices. Let's read exactly what He said:

> Truly I say to you, there is no one who has left house or brothers or sisters or mother or father or children or farms, for My sake and for the gospel's sake, but that he will receive a hundred times as much now in the present age, houses and brothers and sisters and mothers and children and farms, along with persecutions; and in the age to come, eternal life (Mark 10:29-30).

Notice that this is not a promise to those who give money to preachers, as is often claimed by prosperity preachers. Rather, this is a promise to those who leave their homes, farms and relatives to go preach the gospel far and wide. Jesus promised such people "a hundred times as much now in the present age."

But was Jesus promising that such people would become literal owners of one hundred houses or farms as some prosperity preachers claim? No, not any more than He was promising that such people would acquire one hundred literal mothers and one hundred literal children. Jesus was only saying that those who leave their homes and families would find that fellow believers would open their homes to them and welcome them as family among their families.

Notice Jesus also promised persecution and eternal life to such people. This reminds us of the context of the entire passage, in which the disciples had watched a rich young ruler who wanted eternal life walk sadly away as Jesus declared, "It is easier for a camel to go through the eye of a needle than for a rich man to enter the kingdom of God" (Mark 10:25).

The disciples were shocked at Jesus' statement, and wondered then about their own chances of entering God's kingdom. They reminded Jesus of what they had left behind to follow Him. That is when Jesus spoke His "hundred-fold" promise.

All of this being so, it is incredible that any prosperity preacher would attempt to persuade us that Jesus was promising a literal hundred-fold material return that would soon make us incredibly wealthy in a short time, in light of the fact that seconds before, Jesus had told a rich man to sell everything and give the proceeds to charity if he wanted eternal life!

There are many other scriptures that prosperity preachers twist besides the ones we've considered, but space limits us in this book. Beware!

A Maxim to Remember

John Wesley, founder of the Methodist movement in the Church of England, coined a wonderful maxim regarding the proper perspective of money. It is, "Make all you can; save all you can; give all you can."

That is, Christians should first work hard, using their God-given abilities and opportunities to make money, but making sure they do so honestly and without violating any of Christ's commandments.

Second, they should live frugally and simply, spending as little as possible on themselves, which enables them to "save all they can."

Finally, having followed the first two steps, they should then "give all they can," not limiting themselves to a tenth, but denying themselves as much as possible so that widows and orphans might be fed and the gospel proclaimed around the world.

The early church certainly practiced such stewardship, and sharing with the needy among them was a regular feature of New Testament life. Those first believers took seriously Jesus' command to His followers, "Sell your possessions and give to charity; make yourselves purses which do not wear out, an unfailing treasure in heaven, where no thief comes near, nor moth destroys" (Luke 12:33). We read in Luke's account of the early church:

> And all those who had believed were together, and had all things in common; and they began selling their property and possessions, and were sharing them with all, as anyone might have need. And the congregation of those who believed were of one heart and soul; and not one of them claimed that anything belonging to him was his own; but all things were common property to them....and abundant grace was upon them all. For there was not a needy person among them, for all who were owners of land or houses would sell them and bring the proceeds of the sales, and lay them at the apostles' feet; and they would be distributed to each, as any had need (Acts 2:44-45; 4:32-35).

Scripture is also clear that the early church fed and provided for the pressing needs of poor widows (see Acts 6:1; 1 Tim. 5:3-10).

Paul, the greatest apostle ever to have lived, entrusted by God to take the gospel to the Gentiles, human author of a large majority of New Testament epistles, considered ministering to the material needs of the poor an essential part of his ministry. Among the churches he founded, Paul raised large sums of money for poor Christians (see Acts 11:27-30; 24:17; Rom. 15:25-28; 1 Cor. 16:1-4; 2 Cor. 8-9; Gal. 2:10). At least seventeen years after his conversion, Paul journeyed to Jerusalem to submit the gospel he had received to the scrutiny of Peter, James and John. None of them could find anything wrong with the message he had been preaching, and as Paul recounted the occasion in his Galatian letter, he remembered, "They only asked us to remember the poor—the very thing I also was eager to do" (Gal. 2:10). In the minds of Peter, James, John and Paul, showing compassion to the poor was second only to the proclamation of the gospel.

In Summary

On this subject, the best advice to disciple-making ministers comes from the apostle Paul, who after warning Timothy that the "love of money is a root of all sorts of evil," and saying that "some by longing for it have wandered away from the faith and pierced themselves with many a pang," then admonished him,

> Flee from these things, you man of God, and pursue righteousness, godliness, faith, love, perseverance and gentleness (1 Tim. 6:11).

THIRTY-THREE

Secrets of Evangelism

When Abraham proved his willingness to offer up his beloved son, Isaac, God made a promise to him:

> In your seed all the nations of the earth shall be blessed, because you have obeyed My voice (Gen. 22:18).

The apostle Paul points out that this promise was made to Abraham and to his *seed*, singular, not *seeds*, plural, and that the singular seed was Christ (see Gal. 3:16). In Christ all the nations, or more accurately, all the ethnic groups of the earth would be blessed. This promise to Abraham foretold the inclusion of the thousands of Gentile ethnic groups around the globe into the blessings of being in Christ. Those ethnic groups are distinct from each other in that they live in different geographical areas, are of different races, conform to different cultures and speak different languages. God wants them all to be blessed in Christ, which is why Jesus died for the sins of the entire world (see 1 John 2:2).

Although Jesus said that the way is narrow that leads to life, and few find it (see Matt. 7:14), the apostle John left us with good reason to believe that there will be representatives from all of the world's ethnic groups in the future kingdom of God:

> After these things I looked, and behold, a great multitude, which no one could count, *from every nation and all tribes and peoples and tongues,* standing before the throne and before the Lamb, clothed in white robes, and palm branches were in their hands; and they cry out with a loud voice, saying, "Salvation to our God who sits on the throne, and to the Lamb" (Rev. 7:9-10, emphasis added).

So it is with great anticipation that the children of God look forward to

473

joining a multi-ethnic multitude before God's throne one day!

Many contemporary missionary strategists have placed great emphasis on reaching the remaining thousands of "hidden" ethnic groups around the world, with the hopes of planting a viable church in every one of them. This is certainly commendable, as Jesus commanded us to go into the whole world and "make disciples of all the nations (or literally, *ethnic groups*)" (Matt. 28:19). The plans of men, however, no matter how well-intentioned, especially when void of the Holy Spirit's guidance, can often do more harm than good. It is vital that we follow the wisdom of God as we seek to build His kingdom. He gave us more information and instruction regarding how we are to make disciples around the world than what is found in Matthew 28:19.

Perhaps the most overlooked fact by those who strive to fulfill the Great Commission is that *God* is the greatest evangelist of all, and we are supposed to be working *with* Him, not *for* Him. He cares much more about reaching the world with the gospel than anyone, and He is working to that end much more diligently than anyone. He was, and is, so devoted to the cause that He died for it, and was thinking about it before He even created anyone, and still is! That is commitment!

"Wining the World For Christ"

It is interesting that when we read the New Testament epistles, we don't find any impassioned pleas (as we often do today) for the believers to "get out there and reach the world for Christ!" The early Christians and Christian leaders realized that *God* was working with great effort to redeem the world, and their job was to cooperate with Him as He led them. If anyone knew this, it was the apostle Paul, whom no one "led to the Lord." Rather, he was converted by a direct act of God as he journeyed to Damascus. And throughout the book of Acts, we find the church expanding because Spirit-anointed and Spirit-led people cooperated with the Holy Spirit. The book of Acts, although often referred to as "The Acts of the Apostles," should really be referred to as "The Acts of God." In Luke's introduction to Acts, he stated that his first account (the Gospel that bears his name) was a record of "all that Jesus *began* to do and teach" (Acts 1:1, emphasis added). Luke obviously believed that the book of Acts was an account of what Jesus *continued* to do and teach. He worked through Spirit-anointed and Spirit-led servants who cooperated with Him.

If the early Christians were not encouraged to "get out there and witness to their neighbors and help win the world for Christ," what was their responsibility in regard to building God's kingdom? Those who were not specifically called and gifted to proclaim the gospel publicly (apostles and evangelists) were called to live obedient and holy lives, and to be ready to make a defense to anyone who reviled or questioned them. Peter wrote, for example,

But even if you should suffer for the sake of righteousness, you are blessed. And do not fear their intimidation, and do not be troubled, but sanctify Christ as Lord in your hearts, always being ready to make a defense to everyone who asks you to give an account for the hope that is in you, yet with gentleness and reverence; and keep a good conscience so that in the thing in which you are slandered, those who revile your good behavior in Christ will be put to shame (1 Pet. 3:14-16).

Note that the Christians Peter wrote to were enduring persecution. Unless Christians are different than the world, however, the world (of course) won't persecute them. This is one reason there is so little persecution of Christians in many places today—because the so-called Christians act no differently than anyone else. They aren't really Christians at all, and so no one persecutes them. Yet many of these kinds of "Christians" are being exhorted on Sundays to "share their faith with their neighbors." When they do witness to their neighbors, those neighbors are surprised to learn that they are (supposedly) born-again Christians. Worse, the "gospel" they share amounts to little more than telling their neighbors the "good news" that they are mistaken if they think that good works or obedience to God has anything to do with salvation. All that matters is that they just "accept Jesus as their personal Savior."

Contrasted with that, the early Christians (whose Lord truly was Jesus) stood out like lights in darkness, and so they didn't need to take classes on witnessing or get up the courage to tell their neighbors that they were followers of Christ. They had plenty of opportunities to share the gospel as they were questioned or reviled for their righteousness. They only needed to set apart Jesus as Lord in their hearts and be ready to make a defense, just as Peter said.

Perhaps the primary difference between modern Christians and the early Christians is this: Modern Christians tend to think that a Christian is characterized by what he knows and believes—we call it "doctrine," and we thus focus on learning it. In contrast, the early Christians believed that a Christian was characterized by what he did—and thus they focused on obedience to Christ's commandments. It is interesting to realize that practically no Christian for the first fourteen centuries owned a personal Bible, thus making it impossible for him to "read his Bible every day," what has become one of the cardinal rules of a contemporary Christian responsibility. I am certainly not saying that modern Christians shouldn't read their Bibles every day. I'm only saying that too many Christians have made studying the Bible more important than obeying it. We ultimately pride ourselves for having correct doctrine (as opposed to those members of the other 29,999 denominations who aren't quite up to our level) yet still gossip, lie, and lay up earthly treasures.

If we hope to soften people's hearts so that they become more receptive to the gospel, we are more likely to do it by our deeds than our doctrines.

God, the Greatest Evangelist

Let's consider in more detail God's work in building His kingdom. The better we understand His working, the better we can cooperate with Him.

When people believe in Jesus, it is something they do with their hearts (see Rom. 10:9-10). They believe in the Lord Jesus and thus they repent. They dethrone their own will and put Jesus on the throne of their will. *Believing involves a change of heart.*

Similarly, when people *don't* believe in Jesus, it is something they do with their hearts. They *resist* God, so they don't repent. By a conscious decision, they keep Jesus off the throne of their heart. *Unbelief involves a continual decision not to change one's heart.*

Jesus indicated that all people's hearts are so hard that no one would come to Him unless they were drawn by the Father (see John 6:44). God is mercifully and continually drawing everyone to Jesus by various means, all of which touch their hearts, and through which they must continually decide either to soften or harden their hearts.

What means does God use to touch people's hearts in hopes of drawing them to Jesus?

First, He uses His creation. Paul wrote,

> For the wrath of God is revealed from heaven against all ungodliness and unrighteousness of men, who suppress the truth in unrighteousness, because that which is known about God is evident within them; for God made it evident to them. *For since the creation of the world His invisible attributes, His eternal power and divine nature, have been clearly seen, being understood through what has been made,* so that they are without excuse (Rom. 1:18-20, emphasis added).

Notice Paul said that people "suppress the truth" that is "evident within them." That is, the truth rises up within them and confronts them, yet they push it back down and resist that inward conviction.

What exactly is the truth that is inwardly evident to every person? Paul said they are the truths of God's "invisible attributes, His eternal power and divine nature," revealed through "what has been made." People inwardly know from looking at God's creation that He obviously exists,[101] that He is extremely powerful, amazingly creative and incredibly intelligent and wise, to name a few.

---

[101] That is why Scripture declares, "The fool has said in his *heart*, "There is no God" (Psalm 14:1, emphasis added). Only fools suppress such obvious truth.

Paul's conclusion is that such people "are without excuse," and he is right. God is continually shouting at everyone, revealing Himself and trying to get them to soften their hearts, but most close their ears. God, however, never stops shouting throughout all of their lives, with a constant display of miracles—through flowers, birds, babies, snowflakes, bananas, apples, and a million other things.

If God exists and He is as great as His creation reveals, then obviously He should be obeyed. That inward revelation shouts one overriding message: *Repent!* For this reason, Paul maintains that everyone has already heard God's call to repent:

> But I say, surely they have never heard, have they? Indeed they have; "Their voice has gone out into all the earth, and their words to the ends of the world" (Rom. 10:18).

Paul was actually quoting a well-known verse from Psalm 19, of which the fuller text says,

> The heavens are telling of the glory of God; and their expanse is declaring the work of His hands. Day to day pours forth speech, and night to night reveals knowledge. There is no speech, nor are there words; their voice is not heard. *Their line [voice] has gone out through all the earth, and their utterances to the end of the world* (Psalm 19:1-4a, emphasis added).

This again indicates that God is speaking to everyone, day and night, through His creation. If people reacted rightly to God's creation message, they would fall on their faces and cry out something like, "Great Creator, you have created me, and obviously you have created me to do Your will. So I submit to You!"

Another Means by Which God Speaks

Related to this outward/inward revelation is another inward revelation, one that is also God-given, and one that is not dependent upon one's exposure to the miracles of creation. That inward revelation is each person's conscience, a voice that continually reveals God's law. Paul wrote,

> For when Gentiles who do not have the Law do instinctively the things of the Law, these, not having the Law, are a law to themselves, in that they show the work of the Law written in their hearts, their conscience bearing witness, and their thoughts alternately accusing or else defending them, on the day when, according to my gospel, God will judge the secrets of men through Christ Jesus (Rom. 2:14-16).

Thus, everyone knows right from wrong. Or to say it more strongly, everyone knows what pleases God and what does not please Him, and He will hold each person accountable on the day of judgment for doing what he or she knows displeases Him. As people grow older, they certainly become more adept at justifying their sin and ignoring the voice of their conscience, but God never stops speaking His law within them.

A Third Means

But that is not all. God, the great evangelist who is working to bring everyone to repentance, speaks to people through yet another means. Once again, we read the words of Paul:

> For *the wrath of God is revealed from heaven against all ungodliness and unrighteousness of men*, who suppress the truth in unrighteousness (Rom. 1:18, emphasis added).

Notice Paul said God's wrath *is* revealed, not *is going to be revealed* someday. God's wrath is evident to everyone in the many sorrowful and tragic events, large and small, that plague humanity. If God is all-powerful, able to do anything and prevent anything, then such things, when they strike those who ignore Him, can only be a manifestation of His wrath. Only senseless theologians and foolish philosophers can't see this. Yet even in His wrath God's mercy and love are revealed, as the objects of His wrath often receive much less wrath than they deserve, and are thus lovingly warned of the eternal wrath that awaits the unrepentant after death. This is another means that God uses to get the attention of people who need to repent.

A Fourth Means

Finally, God not only attempts to draw people through creation, conscience and calamity, but also through the calling of the gospel. As His servants obey Him and proclaim the good news, the same message of creation, conscience and calamity is reaffirmed once again: *Repent!*

You can see that what we do in evangelization in comparison to what God does is of no comparison. He is continually evangelizing *every* person *every* moment of *every* day of his or her life, whereas even the greatest human evangelists might speak to a few hundred thousand people over the process of decades. And those evangelists generally preach to any given group of people only once for just a short period of time. In fact, that single opportunity is all such evangelists are really permitted to offer people in light of Jesus' command to wipe the dust from their feet whenever a city, village or house does not receive them (see Matt. 10:14). All of this is to say that when we compare God's never ceasing, universal, dramatic, inwardly-convicting evangelism with our very limited evangelism, there is really no comparison.

This perspective helps us to understand better our responsibility in evangelization and in building God's kingdom. However, before we consider our role more specifically, there is one other important factor that we must not overlook.

As stated previously, repenting and believing are things people do with their hearts. God desires that everyone humble himself, soften his heart, repent and believe in the Lord Jesus. Toward that end, God continually works on people's hearts in the numerous ways just described.

God also knows of course, the condition of every person's heart. He knows whose hearts are softening and whose are hardening. He knows who is listening to His never-ceasing messages and who is ignoring them. He knows whose hearts are such that a certain calamity in their life will cause them to open their hearts and repent. He knows whose hearts are so hard that there is no hope of their repentance. (He told Jeremiah three times, for example, not even to pray for Israel because their hearts were beyond repentance; see Jer. 7:16; 11:14; 14:11.)[102] He knows whose hearts are softening to the point that just a little more conviction by His Spirit will result in their repenting.

Keeping all of this in mind, what can we learn about the churches' responsibility to proclaim the gospel and build God's kingdom?

Principle #1

First, does it not seem reasonable that God, the Great Evangelist who is doing 95% of the overall work and who has already been relentlessly shouting at everyone every day, would probably send His servants to proclaim the gospel to those whose hearts are the most receptive rather than those who are least receptive? I would think so.

Does it not also seem possible that God, the Great Evangelist who has already been preaching to all people every moment of their lives, might chose *not* even to bother sending the gospel to those who are completely ignoring everything else He has been saying to them for years? Why should He waste His efforts telling people the last 5% of what He would like them to know if they have been completely ignoring the first 95% of what he is trying to say to them? I would think that it is more likely that God would send judgment upon such people hoping that they would soften their hearts. If and when they did, then it would seem logical to think that He would send His servants to proclaim the gospel.

Some might say that God will send His servants to those He knows will not repent so that they will be without excuse when they stand in judgment before Him. Keep in mind, however, that according to Scripture, such people are already without excuse before God because of His never-ceasing revelation of Himself through His creation (see Rom. 1:20). Thus if God does send one of His servants to such people, it is not so they will be-

---

[102] Beyond this, Scripture teaches that God may even actively further harden the hearts of those who continually harden their hearts against Him (like Pharoah). It would seem unlikely that there is any hope of such people repenting.

come accountable, but so that they will become all the more accountable.

If it is in fact true that God would more likely lead His servants to receptive people, then we, His servants, should prayerfully ask for His wisdom so we might be led to those He knows are ripe for harvest.

A Scriptural Example

This principle is beautifully demonstrated in the ministry of Philip the evangelist as recorded in the book of Acts. Philip had preached to receptive crowds in Samaria, but was later directed by an angel to journey to a specific road. There he was led to an incredibly receptive seeker:

> But an angel of the Lord spoke to Philip saying, "Get up and go south to the road that descends from Jerusalem to Gaza." (This is a desert road.) So he got up and went; and there was an Ethiopian eunuch, a court official of Candace, queen of the Ethiopians, who was in charge of all her treasure; and he had come to Jerusalem to worship, and he was returning and sitting in his chariot, and was reading the prophet Isaiah. Then the Spirit said to Philip, "Go up and join this chariot." Philip ran up and heard him reading Isaiah the prophet, and said, "Do you understand what you are reading?" And he said, "Well, how could I, unless someone guides me?" And he invited Philip to come up and sit with him. Now the passage of Scripture which he was reading was this:

> He was led as a sheep to slaughter; and as a lamb before its shearer is silent, so He does not open his mouth. In humiliation His judgment was taken away; who will relate His generation? For His life is removed from the earth.

> The eunuch answered Philip and said, "Please tell me, of whom does the prophet say this? Of himself or of someone else?" Then Philip opened his mouth, and beginning from this Scripture he preached Jesus to him. As they went along the road they came to some water; and the eunuch said, "Look! Water! What prevents me from being baptized?" And Philip said, "If you believe with all your heart, you may." And he answered and said, "I believe that Jesus Christ is the Son of God." And he ordered the chariot to stop; and they both went down into the water, Philip as well as the eunuch, and he baptized him. When they came up out of the water, the Spirit of the Lord

snatched Philip away; and the eunuch no longer saw him, but went on his way rejoicing (Acts. 8:26-39).

Philip was divinely directed to minister to a man who was so spiritually hungry that he had journeyed from Africa to Jerusalem to worship God and had purchased at least a portion of a copy of the scrolls of Isaiah's prophecies. As he was reading the 53rd chapter of Isaiah, the most explicit scripture in the Old Testament that details the atoning sacrifice of Christ, and wondering whom Isaiah was writing about, there was Philip, ready to explain what he was reading! There was a man ripe for conversion! God knew his heart and sent Philip.

A Better Way

How much more rewarding it is to be led by the Spirit to receptive people than to randomly or systematically approach people who are unreceptive because we guiltily think they won't be evangelized otherwise. Don't forget—every person you encounter is being relentlessly evangelized by God. We would do better to ask people how their conscience is treating them to determine first if they are receptive to God or not, because everyone is dealing with guilt by some means.

Another example of this same principle is the conversion of the household of Cornelius under the ministry of Peter, who was supernaturally led to preach the gospel to this very receptive group of Gentiles. Cornelius was certainly a man who was listening to his conscience and seeking God, as illustrated by his alms-giving and prayer life (see Acts 10:2). God connected him with Peter, and he listened to Peter's message with an open heart and was gloriously saved.

How much wiser we would be to pray and ask the Holy Spirit to lead us to those whose hearts are open rather than formulating extensive and time-wasting plans to divide our cities into quadrants and organize witnessing teams to visit every home and apartment. If Peter had been attending a meeting on missionary strategies in Jerusalem or if Philip had continued preaching in Samaria, the household of Cornelius and the Ethiopian eunuch would have remained unreached.

Evangelists and apostles, of course, will be led to proclaim the gospel before mixed crowds of receptive and unreceptive people. But even they should seek the Lord regarding where He wants them to preach. Again, the record found in the book of Acts is one of Spirit-led and Spirit-anointed people cooperating with the Holy Spirit as He built the kingdom of God. How different were the methods of the early church compared to the modern church. How different are the results! Why not imitate what was so successful?

Principle #2

How else do the biblical principles considered in the first part of this chapter help us understand our role in evangelization and building God's kingdom?

If God has so designed that creation, conscience and calamity are all calling humanity to repentance, then those who preach the gospel need to be certain they aren't proclaiming a contradictory message. Yet so many are! *Their preaching directly contradicts everything that God is already trying to say to sinners!* Their message of unbiblical grace promotes the idea that holiness and obedience are unimportant for ultimately obtaining eternal life. By not mentioning the necessity of repentance for salvation, by emphasizing that salvation is not of works (in a way that Paul never meant it to be understood), they actually work against God, leading people into a deeper deception that often seals their eternal doom, because they are now certain they are saved when they in fact are not. What a tragedy, when God's messengers actually work against the God they claim to represent!

Jesus commanded us to preach "repentance for forgiveness of sins" (Luke 24:47). That message reaffirms what God has been saying to the sinner all of his life. The preaching of the gospel cuts people to their hearts and offends those whose hearts are hard. Yet the soft modern gospel that informs people how much God loves them (something no apostle ever mentioned when preaching the gospel in the book of Acts), misleads them to think that God is not angry or offended at them. They are often told that they simply need to "accept Jesus." But the King of kings and Lord of lords does not need our acceptance. The question is not, "Do you accept Jesus?" The question is, "Does Jesus accept you?" The answer is, unless you repent and begin to follow Him, you are abhorrent to Him, and only His mercy forestalls your destiny in hell.

In light of the modern gospel that so cheapens God's grace, I cannot help but wonder why so many nations, ruled by leaders who have been given their authority to rule by God (and this is not debatable; see Dan. 4:17, 25, 32l 5:21; John 19:11; Acts 12:23; Rom. 13:1), have closed their nations completely to Western missionaries. Could it be because God is trying to keep the false gospel out of those countries?

Principle #3

The principles considered earlier in this chapter also help us to understand better how God views people who are following false religions. Are they ignorant people to be pitied because they've never heard the truth? Does all the blame lie at the feet of the church for not having effectively evangelized them?

No, such people are not ignorant of the truth. The may not know everything that a Bible-believing Christian knows, but they know all that God is revealing about Himself through creation, conscience and calamity. They are people whom God has been calling to repentance all of their lives, even if they have never seen a Christian or heard the gospel. Furthermore, they have either been softening their hearts toward God or hardening them.

Paul wrote of the ignorance of unbelievers and revealed the reason for their ignorance:

> This I say therefore, and affirm together with the Lord, that you walk no longer just as the Gentiles also walk, in the futility of their mind, being darkened in their understanding, excluded from the life of God, because of the ignorance that is in them, *because of the hardness of their heart*; and they, having become *callous*, have given themselves over to sensuality, for the practice of every kind of impurity with greediness (Eph. 4:17-19).

Notice that the reason that the Gentiles are ignorant is "because of the hardness of their heart." Paul also declared that they have "become callous." He was obviously speaking of the condition of their hearts. Calluses develop on people's hands from continual contact with what is abrasive against soft skin. Calloused skin becomes less sensitive. Likewise, as people continually resist God's call through creation, conscience and calamity, their hearts become calloused, making them progressively less sensitive to that divine call. This is why statistics indicate that people generally become less receptive as they grow older. The older a person is, the less likely it is that he will repent. *Wise evangelists mostly target younger people.*

The Guilt of the Unbelieving

Further proof that God holds people guilty even if they have never heard a Christian evangelist is the fact that He actively judges them. If God wasn't holding them accountable for their sins He would not punish them. Because He does punish them, however, we can be sure that He holds them accountable, and if He holds them accountable, they must know that what they are doing is displeasing to Him.

One manner by which God punishes those who resist His call to repentance is through "giving them over" to their sinful desires so that they become slaves to even deeper degradation. Paul wrote:

> For even though *they knew God*, they did not honor Him as God, or give thanks; but they became futile in their speculations, and their foolish heart was darkened. Professing to be wise, they became fools, and exchanged the glory of the incorruptible God for an image in the form of corruptible man and of birds and four-footed animals and crawling creatures.
>
> Therefore *God gave them over* in the lusts of their hearts to

impurity, that their bodies might be dishonored among them. For they exchanged the truth of God for a lie, and worshiped and served the creature rather than the Creator, who is blessed forever. Amen.

For this reason *God gave them over* to degrading passions; for their women exchanged the natural function for that which is unnatural, and in the same way also the men abandoned the natural function of the woman and burned in their desire toward one another, men with men committing indecent acts and receiving in their own persons the due penalty of their error.

And just as they did not see fit to acknowledge God any longer, *God gave them over* to a depraved mind, to do those things which are not proper, being filled with all unrighteousness, wickedness, greed, evil; full of envy, murder, strife, deceit, malice; they are gossips, slanderers, haters of God, insolent, arrogant, boastful, inventors of evil, disobedient to parents, without understanding, untrustworthy, unloving, unmerciful; and, although they know the ordinance of God, that those who practice such things are worthy of death, they not only do the same, but also give hearty approval to those who practice them. (Rom. 1:21-32, emphasis added).

Notice how Paul stressed the facts of human guilt and accountability before God. The unregenerate "knew God," but "they did not honor Him as God, or give thanks." They "exchanged the truth of God for a lie," so they must have encountered God's truth. Thus God "gave them over" to ever-increasing degradation, to the point where people do the most bizarre, unnatural and perverted things as they become more deeply enslaved to sin. In effect God says, "So you want to serve sin as you should serve Me? Then go ahead. I won't stop you, and you'll become progressively more enslaved to the god you love."

I suppose one could even consider this form of judgment to be an indication of God's mercy, in that it would be reasonable to think that as people became more perverse and sinful, they would realize it and wake up. One wonders why more homosexuals don't ask themselves the question, "Why do I find myself sexually attracted to people of the same sex with whom I can't actually have a full sexual relation? This is bizarre!" In a sense it can be argued that God indeed did "make them that way" (as they themselves often argue to justify their perversion), but only in a permissive sense, and only because He hopes to wake them up in order that they might repent and experience His amazing mercy.

It is not only homosexuals who should be asking themselves such questions. Paul listed numerous enslaving sins that are the evidence of God's judgment on those who refuse to serve Him. Billions of people should question themselves about their bizarre behavior. "Why do I hate my own family?" "Why do I find satisfaction is spreading gossip?" "Why am I never content with what I own?" "Why am I compelled to look at increasingly more explicit pornography?" God has given them all over to be enslaved to their god.

Of course, anyone at any point can soften his heart, repent and believe in Jesus. Some of the most hardened sinners on earth have done just that, and God has cleansed and freed them from their sins! As long as people are still breathing, God is still giving them an opportunity to repent.

No Excuses

According to Paul sinners have no excuse. They reveal that they know what is right and what is wrong as they condemn others, and thus they are worthy of God's condemnation:

> Therefore you are without excuse, every man of you who passes judgment, for in that you judge another, you condemn yourself; for you who judge practice the same things. And we know that the judgment of God rightly falls upon those who practice such things. And do you suppose this, O man, when you pass judgment upon those who practice such things and do the same yourself, that you will escape the judgment of God? Or do you think lightly of the riches of His kindness and forbearance and patience, not knowing that the kindness of God leads you to repentance? (Rom. 2:1-4).

Paul said the reason for God's forbearance and patience is to give people opportunity to repent. Furthermore, as Paul continued, he revealed that only those who repent and live holy lives will inherit God's kingdom:

> But because of your stubbornness and unrepentant heart you are storing up wrath for yourself in the day of wrath and revelation of the righteous judgment of God, who will render to every man according to his deeds: to those who by perseverance in doing good seek for glory and honor and immortality, eternal life; but to those who are selfishly ambitious and do not obey the truth, but obey unrighteousness, wrath and indignation. There will be tribulation and distress for every soul of man who does evil, of the Jew first and also of the Greek, but glory and honor and peace to every man who does good, to the Jew first and also to the Greek (Rom. 2:5-10).

Clearly, Paul would not agree with those who teach that people who just "accept Jesus as Savior" are guaranteed eternal life. Rather, it is those who repent and "who by perseverance in doing good seek for glory and honor and immortality."

But does this not indicate that people can continue to practice religions other than Christianity and be saved as long as they repent and obey God?

No, there is no salvation apart from Jesus for a number of reasons, one of which is that only Jesus can set people free from their enslavement to sin.

But if they want to repent, how will they know to call on Jesus if they have never heard of Him?

God, who knows the hearts of all people, will reveal Himself to anyone who is sincerely seeking. Jesus promised, "Seek and you will find" (Matt. 7:7), and God expects everyone to seek Him (see Acts 17:26-27). When He sees a person whose heart is responding to His relentless evangelization, He will send the gospel to that person, just as He did for the Ethiopian eunuch and Cornelius' household. God is not even limited by the church's participation, as He proved in the conversion of Saul of Tarsus. If there is no one to take the gospel to a sincere seeker, God will go Himself! I've heard numerous contemporary instances where people in closed countries have been converted by visions they had of Jesus.

Why People Are Religious

The fact is that most of those who practice false religions are not sincere seekers of truth. Rather, they are religious because they are only looking for a justification or a covering for their sins. As they continually violate their consciences, they hide behind the guise of religion. By their religiosity, they convince themselves that they are not worthy of hell. This is just as true for religious "Christians" (including cheap-grace evangelical Christians) as it is for Buddhists, Muslims and Hindus. Even as they practice their religion, their conscience condemns them.

When the Buddhist bows reverently before his idols or before monks who sit proudly before him, his conscience tells him he is doing wrong. When the Hindu justifies his lack of compassion for a diseased street beggar, believing that the beggar must be suffering for sins committed in a previous life, his conscience condemns him. When a Muslim extremist beheads an "infidel" in the name of Allah, his conscience is screaming at him for his own murderous hypocrisy. When the evangelical "Christian" lays up earthly treasure, regularly views sexually-explicit television, and gossips about fellow church members, trusting that he is saved by grace, his heart condemns him. All of these are examples of people who want to keep on sinning and who have found religious lies to believe by which they can continue sinning. The "righteousness" of unregenerate yet religious people falls far, far, far short of God's expectations.

All of this is to say that God does not consider people who are following false religions to be ignorant people who are to be pitied because they've never heard the truth. Neither does the blame for their ignorance lie at the feet of the church for not having effectively evangelized them.

Again, although we know that God wants the church to preach the gospel all over the world, we should follow the leading of His Spirit to where "the fields are ripe for harvest" (see John 4:35), where people are receptive because they've been softening their hearts to God's relentless effort to reach them.

Principle #4

One final principle that we can learn from the biblical truths considered earlier in this chapter is this: If God is actively judging sinners in hopes that they will soften their hearts, we should expect that some sinners, after enduring God's judgment or observing others endure it, will be softening their hearts. Thus after calamities there are opportunities to reach people who were previously unreachable.

Christians should look for opportunities to share the gospel in places where people are suffering. Those who have recently lost loved ones, for example, may well be more open to what God wants them to hear. When I served as a pastor, I always seized the opportunity to proclaim the gospel at funerals, remembering that Scripture says, "It is better to go to a house of mourning than to go to a house of feasting, because that is the end of every man, *and the living takes it to heart* (Eccl. 7:2, emphasis added).

When people suffer from sickness, financial loss, broken relationships, natural disasters and the many consequences of sin and judgments upon sin, they need to know that their sufferings are a wake up call. Through temporal sufferings God is trying to save sinners from eternal judgment.

In Summary

God does most of the work of building His kingdom. Our responsibility is to cooperate intelligently with Him.

All believers are to live holy and obedient lives that gain the attention of those in darkness, and they should always be ready to make a defense for the hope within them.

God is always working to motivate all persons to soften their hearts and repent, continually speaking to them through creation, conscience and calamity, and sometimes through the call of the gospel.

Sinners know they are disobeying God, and are accountable to Him even if they never hear the gospel. Their sin is evidence of the hardness of their hearts. Their increasingly deeper degradation and slavery to sin is an indication of God's wrath towards them.

Religious people area not necessarily seeking for truth. They are more likely justifying their sin through believing the lies of their religion.

God knows the condition of every person's heart. Although He may lead us to share the gospel with those who are not receptive, He is more likely to lead us to those who are receptive to the gospel.

As God works to soften people's hearts through their sufferings, we should seize those opportunities to proclaim the gospel.

God wants us to take the gospel into the whole world, but He wants us to follow His Spirit as we seek to fulfill the Great Commission, as illustrated in the book of Acts.

God will reveal Himself to anyone who sincerely seeks to know Him.

God wants our message to agree with His message.

One day there will be representatives from every ethnic group worshipping before God's throne, and we should all do our part in cooperating with God to work to that end. Thus all of God's people should show Christ's love to every member of every ethnic group whom they encounter. God may lead some of His servants to specifically target people of different cultures, either by sending and supporting church planters, or by going themselves. Those who are sent should make disciples, proving themselves to be disciple-making ministers!

Final Words

I am so thankful that God has enabled us to print this book in your language and make it possible for you to have a copy to read. I hope it has been a blessing to you. If it has, would you be so kind to write and tell me? I can only read English, so you'll have to write me in English or have your letter translated into English before you send it to me!

The most certain way to reach me is to send an e-mail, and my e-mail address is: tdmm@shepherdserve.org. If you don't have access to e-mail, you can also write to me at my ministry address, but depending on when you received this book, that may have changed. In any case, in the year 2006 it is: Shepherd Serve, P.O. Box 12854, Pittsburgh, PA 15241 USA.

For additional teaching, visit our website: www.ShepherdServe.org.